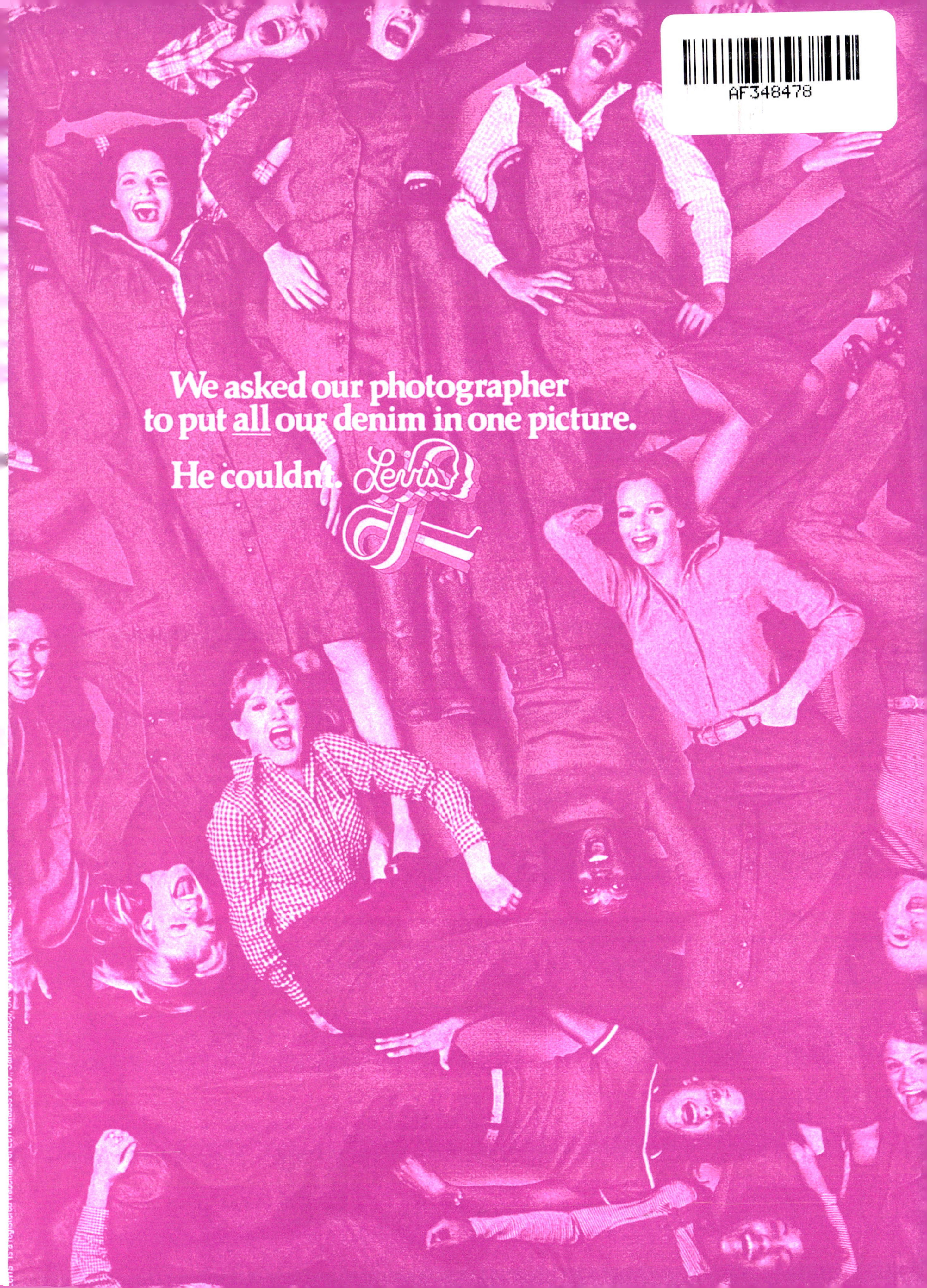

We asked our photographer
to put all our denim in one picture.
He couldn't. Levi's
AF348478

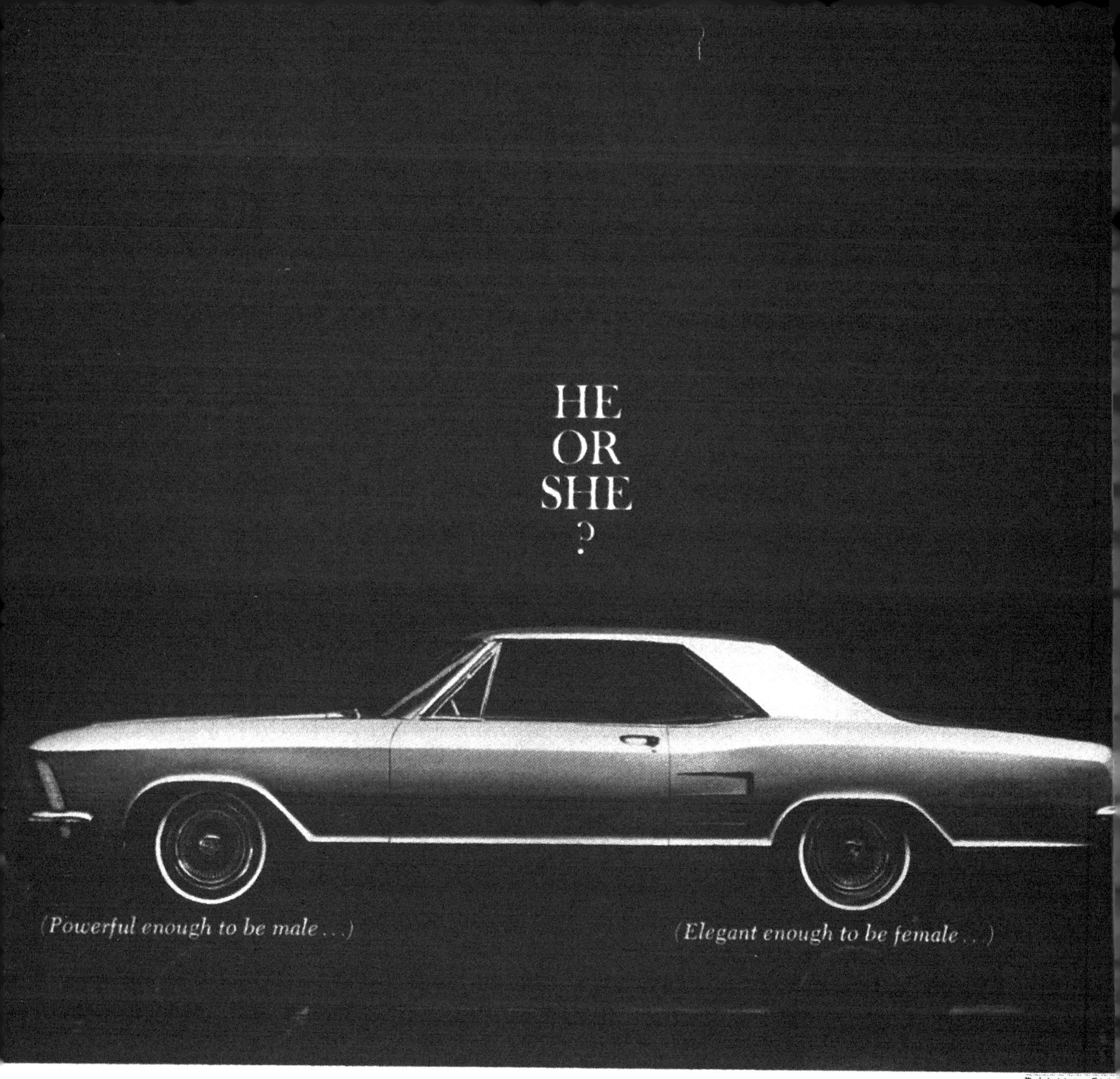

**IN LOVING MEMORY OF
ANDREW HEWITT**

The Psychedelic Chicks

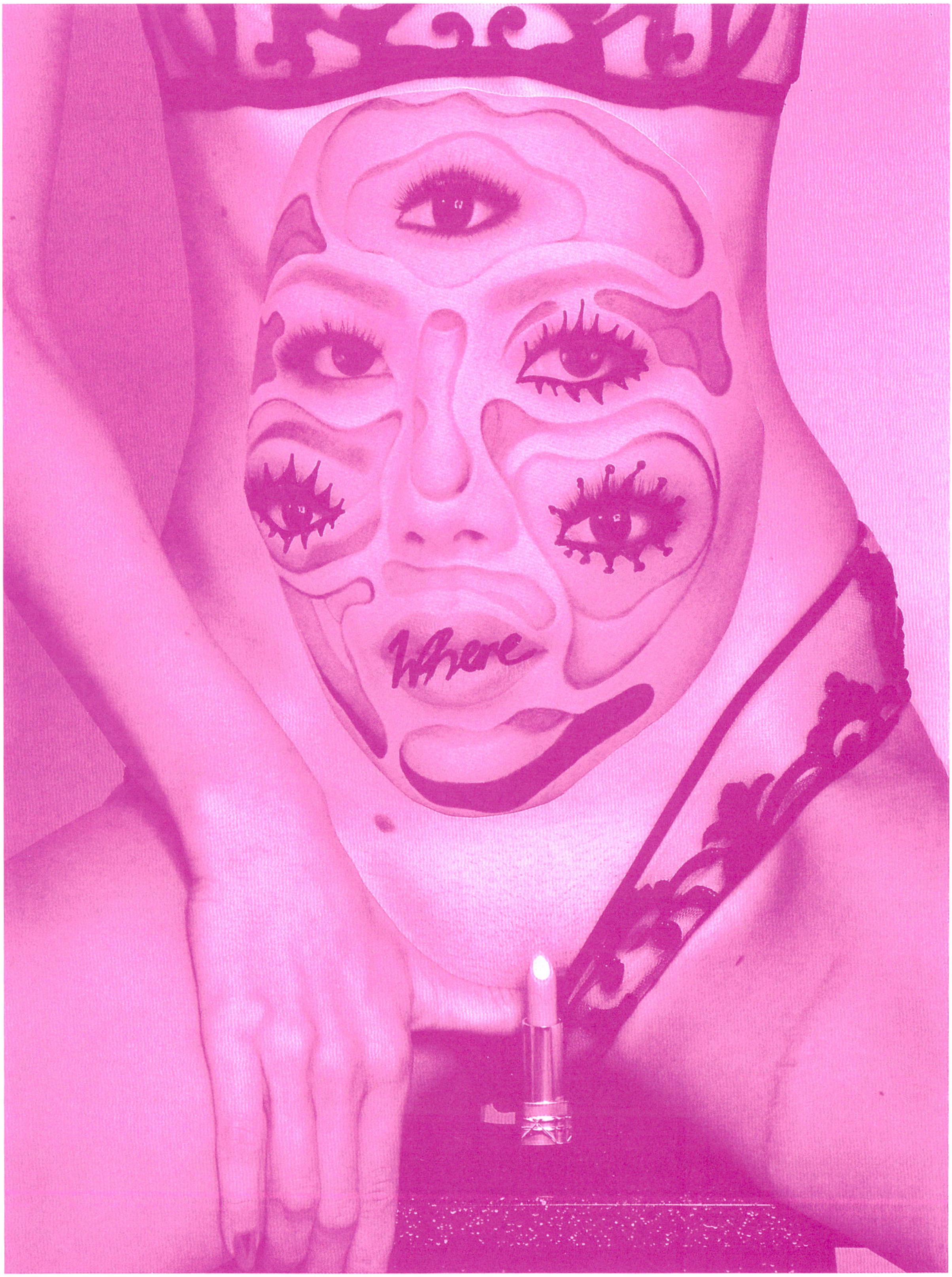

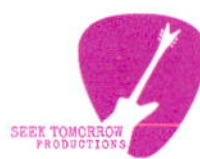

New Album Release

NOTE BY THE EDITOR

Immediately after the founding of the California Institute of the Arts (CalArts), which, alongside John Baldessari, was also decisively shaped by Allan Kaprow and Michael Asher, the first feminist art class was established in 1971 under Judy Chicago and Miriam Schapiro and run until 1975. Artists such as Faith Wilding or Suzanne Lacy, whose performance-oriented art would come to influence an entire generation, studied under Chicago and established a strong dynamic that linked art and activism. The performative and collective actions, the medium-transcending experiments, and the reflexive use of photography and film led to unmistakably new and innovative art forms. Against this background, the emancipatory dynamics developed through the school were largely sparked by individual groups or communities. The radical pedagogy that characterized CalArts's first years manifested itself partly in the formal parodying of everything academic. This corresponds to an artistic culture of knowledge that does not base research, education, and learning on a corpus of objective truths but rather contributes to their development through social and performative contexts of action.

This part of the magazine focuses on the Feminist Art Program (FAP) at CalArts by Miriam Schapiro and Judy Chicago. Experimentally conceived, the program focused on personal experience, especially that of women, and established radically feminist perspectives on both art and society. The experience of the self and the study of psychology in the context of gender relations were natural components of the teaching program, alongside experimentally conceived excursions.

The project *Womanhouse* (1972), an environment conceived by 27 female artists in an abandoned house in Hollywood, counts today as one of the early landmarks in the history of feminist art. Numerous installations throughout the house contributed to an exhibition that altogether parodied social stereotypes of femininity.

The artists often developed performances collaboratively, as was the case with *Ablutions* (1972), which provoked much controversy at the time. In this performance by Suzanne Lacy, Judy Chicago, Sandra Orgel, and Aviva Rahmani, women bathed in tubs as female voices recounted various cases of assault by men.

Suzanne Lacy's performance *Three Weeks in May* (1977), in which the artist revealed the extent of registered sexual assaults in Los Angeles with the help of maps and radio reports, can be seen as a further development of the ideas stimulated at the FAP at CalArts and is therefore of particular interest.

This is a collaboratively produced, interdisciplinary academic magazine in book form, published by international scholars and students of two master's classes at the Institute for Theater Studies at Freie Universität Berlin. This progressively developed publication provides resources for readers and scholars engaged in work that goes beyond traditional, text-centric models of research, using cross-platform and supplemental images and materials from various archives, as well as introducing and reflecting on a great variety of artworks and projects. The publication project *Tacit Knowledge* aims to create and utilize practice-based research methods of publishing as a method for disrupting and intervening in centralized, culturally specific discourses.

CONTRIBUTORS

Kim Albrecht KA
Lea Becker LB
Katharina Brandt KB
Léïla Douliba LD
Carla Gabriel CG
Jennifer Gaschler JG
Pauline Gründing PG
Verena Kittel VK
Friederike Krause FK
Vivien Lambert VL
Annette Jael Lehmann AJL
Alice Rugai AR
Jeffrey Schnapp JS
Anna Sønderup AS

"Women only drive automatic transmissions."

Some car manufacturers actually believe women buy cars for different reasons than men do.

So they build "a woman's car." Oversized, hopelessly automatic and dull.

At Honda we designed just one thing. A lean, spunky economy car with so much pizzazz it handles like a sports car.

If you're bored with cars designed only to get you from point A to point B, without responding to you the driver, maybe you ought to take the Honda Civic for a spin.

We've got a stick shift with an astonishing amount of zip. Enough to surprise you. We promise.

Or, if you prefer, Hondamatic.™ It's a semi-automatic transmission that gives you convenience, but doesn't rob you of involvement.

Neither one is a woman's car.

Honda Civic.
We don't make "a woman's car."

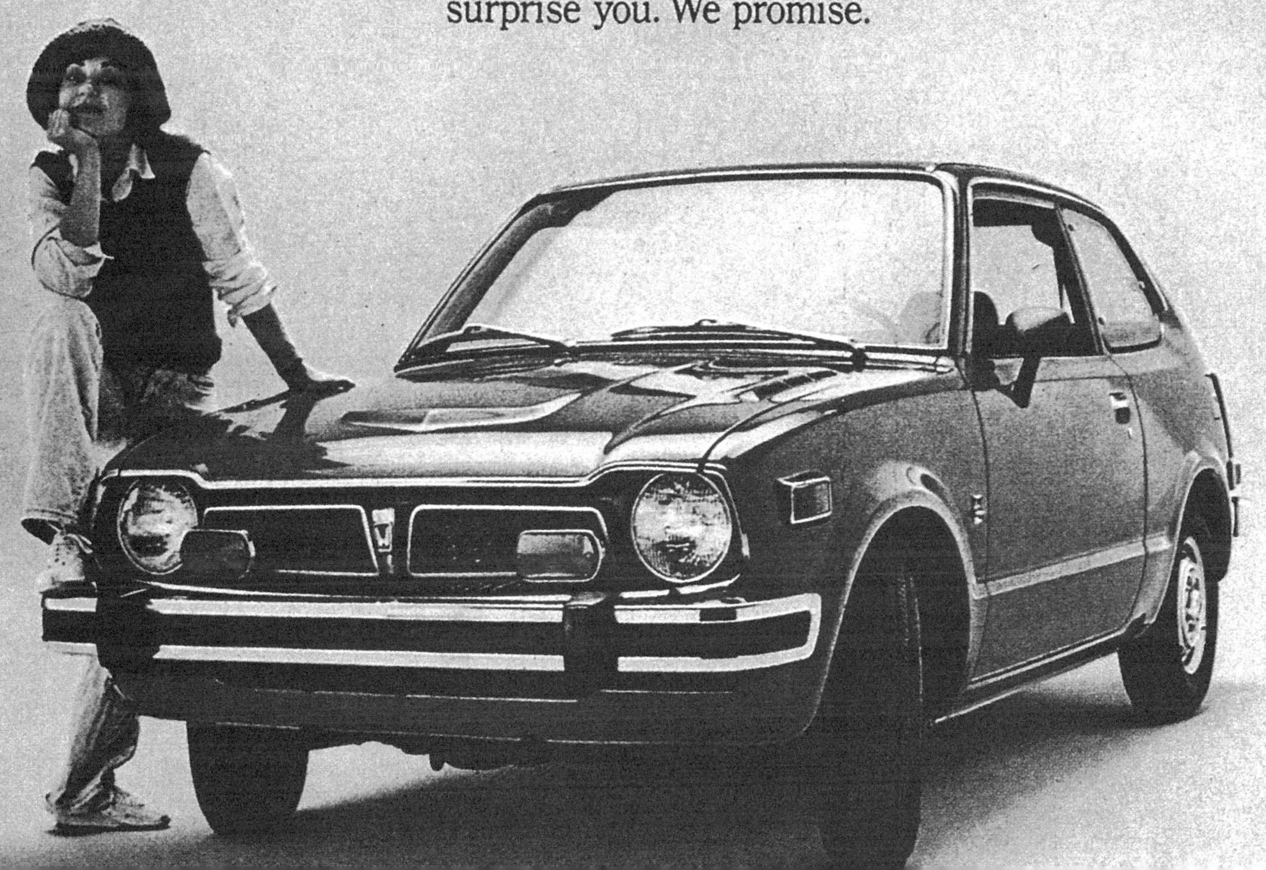

CONTENT

CONTENT

STATEMENTS

"In order to accomplish a project as demanding as *Womanhouse*, the women had to work in a manner that they were totally unaccustomed to. They had to do hard physical labor, use tools they knew nothing about, complete their projects by the opening date, work in a scale larger than most of them had ever tackled. At first they were very excited, but the excitement soon gave way to waves of resentment about having such intense demands placed upon them. They began to see us as monsters, terrible people asking impossible things of them. Many of them complained incessantly, sure that they would fail, that the House would be a failure, that we would never finish. Endurance became a dirty word."

— Judy Chicago, Miriam Schapiro

"After studying at CalArts, many of the women artists dropped out of the art world. Many students did not want to be in the Feminist Art Program with Mimi [Miriam] Schapiro and Judy Chicago because they were so dogmatic. For some, those two were really frightening. It was especially difficult for many of the female students who were neither embraced by the Feminist group nor found a home with the Post-Studio people, which was so male dominated."

— Nancy Chunn

"I didn't have any women teachers; not only that, I didn't realize that I didn't have any women teachers. That's the way it was. Unless the guys wanted to fuck you, they didn't pay attention to you."

— Nancy Chunn

"She [Miriam Schapiro] and Judy [Chicago] are developing a feminist art program for young women students which freaks all the liberals around here in exactly the same way other liberals were freaked by the black power thing, you know, the idea of black nationalism. The idea that women might want to get away from us in order to get themselves together, to come back to us on different terms, is very disturbing to a lot of people...."

— Paul Brach

"She believes that she has had the single vision of a liberated woman artist and we must trust her with our lives for the next few months and she will lead us to the Promised Land. I told her that I thought she was using [us] as tools to create *her* vision and was very upset when we tried anything on our own. She didn't like that too much."

— Mira Schor about Judy Chicago

"At this point in time (1970, I think) there was a massive amount of feminist consciousness and activity there, which CalArts has still not recovered from or else they'd admit that they had it. They've totally blocked it from their historical memory. Instead we hear a lot about David Salle et al." —Suzanne Lacy

"You know, Baldessari was one pole of the conceptual world, and Kaprow was the other, and then there was Chicago and Schapiro, which was a very strong feminist influence. It turned out that the feminists who were conceptually oriented gravitated toward Kaprow, because he was infinitely more receptive to that than Baldessari, who used to discuss such things as how rape might be considered an artform. In all fairness John didn't bring it up; it was one of his students that brought it up. Such topics were common, however." —Suzanne Lacy

"I began to learn the game. It was called Making It on the Art Scene. The players were men and women. The rules prescribed that the men were to make decisions, pick shows, support each other, bring messages about money, sales and shows to each other. The women were to wait until tapped by the men. Certain moves were allowed the women independently, i.e., the women might give themselves as sex offerings and/or take care of the men, e.g., cook, clean, etc.—then, if everything went well, the women would receive artistic support and recognition, providing that they had comported themselves well in the other departments.... If you were a woman and you played this game, you were an ass-licker. I played this game all my life." —Miriam Schapiro

"Judy Chicago is short, has short straight black hair, a big nose and wire-rim glasses, a loud voice, is didactic, and in her mind there is no grey." —Mira Schor

"... because there was so much feminism that I think the men were reacting. I wouldn't even be surprised if David Salle's early works as a student with women in semi-pornographic poses had something to do with that, because he was there when there was this very polarized energy between women and men." —Suzanne Lacy

"I think Judy, Arlene, and Sheila had actually come up against this in the very first year, because when they hired me, they said, 'One thing you have to be aware of is that the students will try to divide us. They will do all kinds of manipulative things because this is how women have learned to take power. Some of them take the mode of rage as a kind of channel to pass through. And if you're going to work with us, you have to be absolutely committed to not allowing divisiveness....' I thought at the time, 'This is crazy,' until, of course, I got into it and realized how intense an all-woman's environment, in fact, really is." —Suzanne Lacy

THE FEMINIST ART PROGRAM AT CALARTS

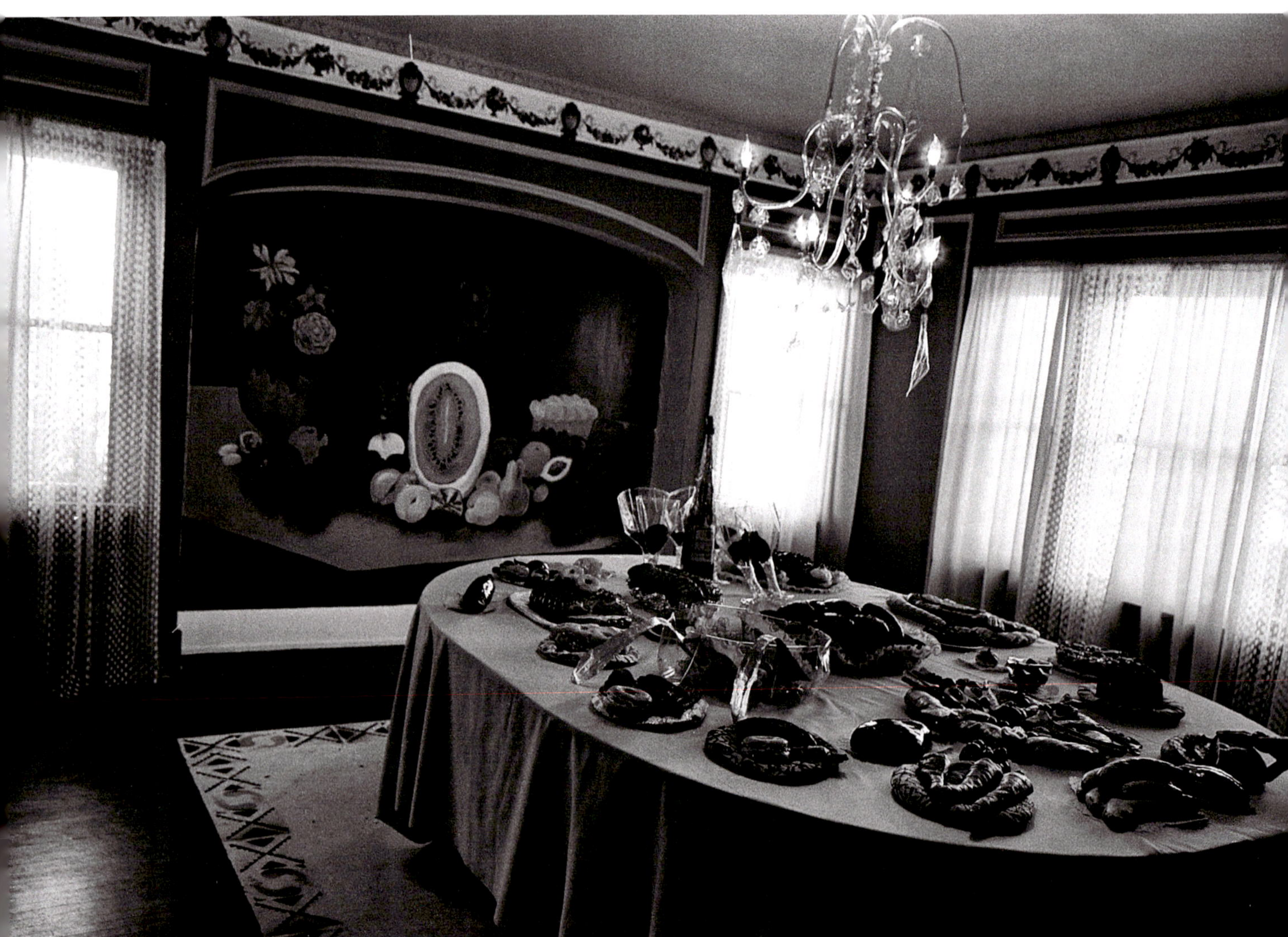

Beth Bachenheimer, Sherry Brody, Karen LeCocq,
Robin Mitchell, Miriam Schapiro, and Faith Wilding,
Womanhouse: Dining Room (1972).

The Feminist Art Program (FAP), which took place from 1971 to 1975 at the California Institute of the Arts (CalArts), was a pioneering educational art class provided by woman artists exclusively for female students who wanted to become artists. The project ended up becoming quite an experiment. The forerunner to the Feminist Art Program was developed by Judy Chicago in 1970 at Fresno State College (Fresno). In the beginning, 14 female students joined the feminist art class.[1] They rented a studio off-campus as a collective working and art space, thereby creating a specific environment to enable independence from predominately male art education. The feminist art class at Fresno was initially drafted as a one-year-long study class following an experimental project design that combined practice and theory.[2] The program mainly concentrated on concepts of participation and experience in art-making processes, as well as collaborative practice and inclusive structures for sharing thoughts and personal experiences.[3]

Judy Chicago continued working on the program by transferring and implementing it at CalArts, collaborating with faculty member and artist Miriam Schapiro. As co-founders they officially began the FAP at CalArts in 1971 with 22 students.[4] The program was based on the following principles: a non-authoritarian and inclusive pedagogy, participation-centered working processes, group consciousness-raising sessions, and a team-based teaching method. It incorporated performance and role-playing workshops, lectures on feminist literature, and women's art history. A unique component was the absolute freedom of choosing in the usage of materials and techniques in art-making.[5]

Unfortunately, the program established at CalArts had only a short run. It began to diverge in its second year before ending in the third. According to Judy Chicago, CalArts "erased" the program and its achievements out of their own institutional history for decades.[6] *Womanhouse* was the main and most successful undertaking of the FAP at CalArts.

Womanhouse started as a 17-room abandoned mansion in L.A., which was transformed into an immersive feminist art environment through collaborative practice. The project was a cooperation between the art students and the local female artists Sherry Brody, Wanda Westcoast, and Carol Edson Mitchell under the participative guidance of Schapiro and Chicago. *Womanhouse* was a synthesis of an art installation, exhibition, and working space, which evolved into a particular female environment of experimenting and creating art. In this sense, it became a safe environment for exploring female experience, imagination, and fantasies. Alongside the exhibited rooms and pieces created either in collaboration or solo, several performances were staged in the living room. The opening of *Womanhouse* for public exhibition was on January 30, 1972. The exhibition period went on until February 28. Around 4000 visitors viewed the immersive installation complex and its performances.[7] LB

The FAP was deeply rooted within the formation of a feminist art movement and played a crucial role in a socio-cultural change characterized by the foundation and organization of many further feminist programs and projects.

1971

Sheila Levrant de Bretteville formed the Women's Design Program at CalArts.

1973

The Feminist Studio Workshop (FSW) was co-founded by Judy Chicago, Sheila Levrant de Bretteville, and the art historian Arlene Raven after they left CalArts in 1973 and 1974. "The first independent school for women artists"[8] closed in 1981.

Sheila Levrant de Bretteville established the Women's Graphic Center, as part of the FSW, which she ran until 1983.

Foundation of the Woman's Building, an independent art and education center for women in L.A.. It arose out of the FSW. The Woman's Building as an art-culture center continued to exist until the closing of its exhibition and performance spaces in 1991.

1974

The Feminist Art Festival at CalArts campus took place between May 27–31.

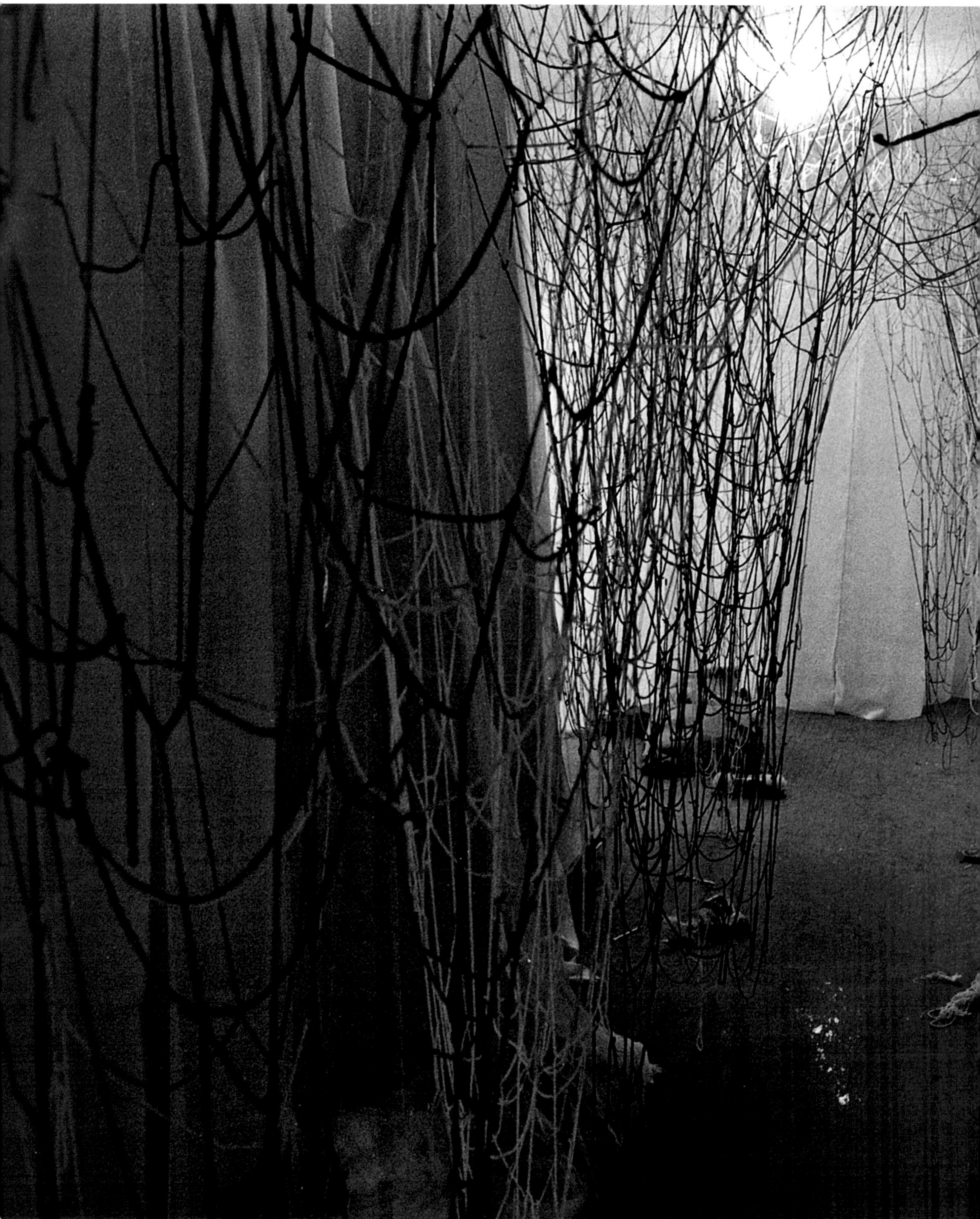

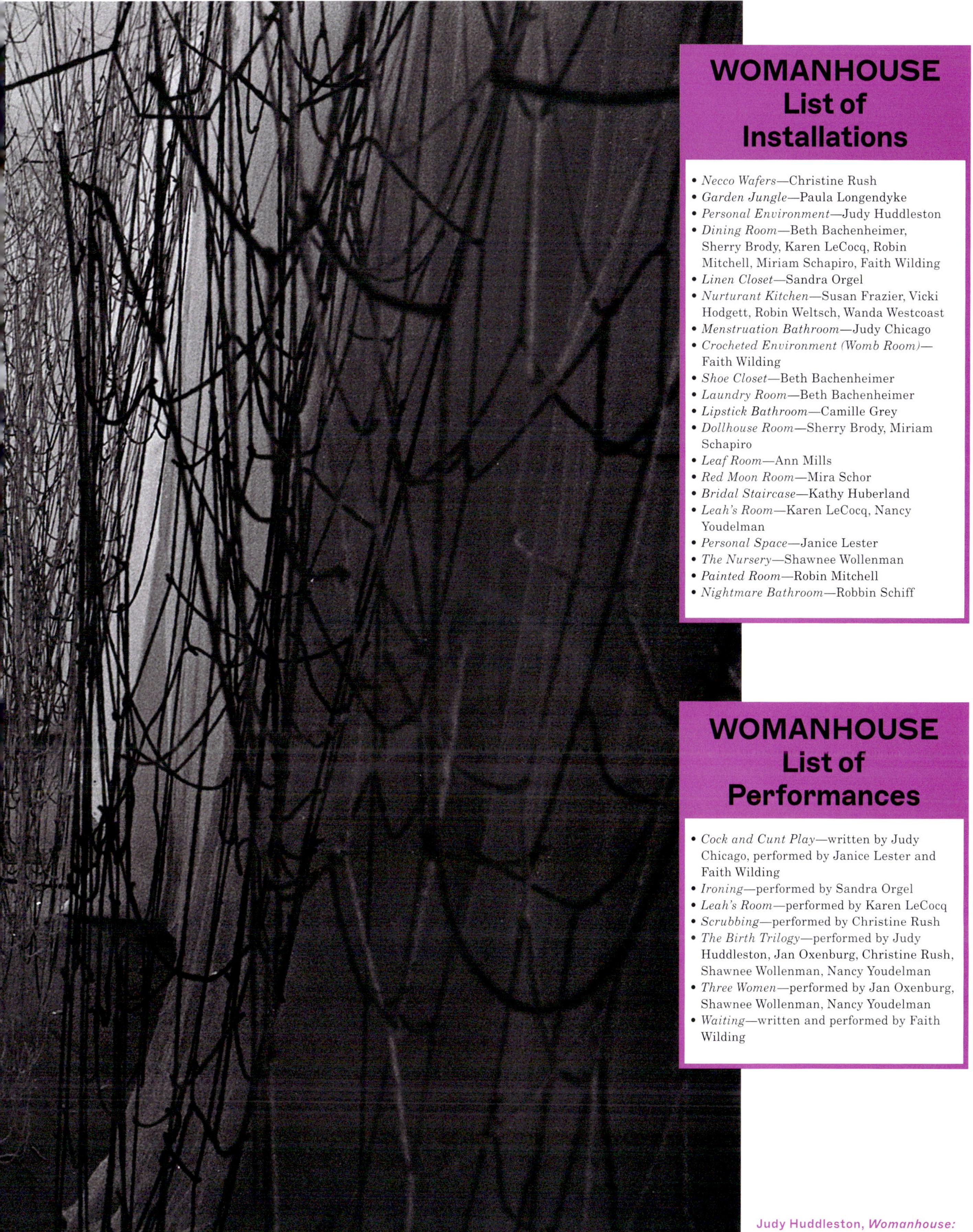

WOMANHOUSE
List of Installations

- *Necco Wafers*—Christine Rush
- *Garden Jungle*—Paula Longendyke
- *Personal Environment*—Judy Huddleston
- *Dining Room*—Beth Bachenheimer, Sherry Brody, Karen LeCocq, Robin Mitchell, Miriam Schapiro, Faith Wilding
- *Linen Closet*—Sandra Orgel
- *Nurturant Kitchen*—Susan Frazier, Vicki Hodgett, Robin Weltsch, Wanda Westcoast
- *Menstruation Bathroom*—Judy Chicago
- *Crocheted Environment (Womb Room)*—Faith Wilding
- *Shoe Closet*—Beth Bachenheimer
- *Laundry Room*—Beth Bachenheimer
- *Lipstick Bathroom*—Camille Grey
- *Dollhouse Room*—Sherry Brody, Miriam Schapiro
- *Leaf Room*—Ann Mills
- *Red Moon Room*—Mira Schor
- *Bridal Staircase*—Kathy Huberland
- *Leah's Room*—Karen LeCocq, Nancy Youdelman
- *Personal Space*—Janice Lester
- *The Nursery*—Shawnee Wollenman
- *Painted Room*—Robin Mitchell
- *Nightmare Bathroom*—Robbin Schiff

WOMANHOUSE
List of Performances

- *Cock and Cunt Play*—written by Judy Chicago, performed by Janice Lester and Faith Wilding
- *Ironing*—performed by Sandra Orgel
- *Leah's Room*—performed by Karen LeCocq
- *Scrubbing*—performed by Christine Rush
- *The Birth Trilogy*—performed by Judy Huddleston, Jan Oxenburg, Christine Rush, Shawnee Wollenman, Nancy Youdelman
- *Three Women*—performed by Jan Oxenburg, Shawnee Wollenman, Nancy Youdelman
- *Waiting*—written and performed by Faith Wilding

Judy Huddleston, *Womanhouse: Personal Environment* (1972).

THE FEMINIST ART PROGRAM AT FRESNO STATE COLLEGE, 1970–71.
List of Students

Dori Atlantis
Susan "Sue" Boud
Gail Escola
Vanalyne Green
Suzanne Lacy
Cay Lang
Karen LeCocq
Janice (Jan) Lester
Christine (Chris) Rush
Judy Schaefer
Henrietta Starkman
Faith Wilding
Shawnee Wollenman
Nancy Youdelman
Cheryl Zurilgen

THE FEMINIST ART PROGRAM AT CALIFORNIA INSTITUTE OF THE ARTS, 1971–75.
List of Artists at Womanhouse

Beth Bachenheimer
Sherry Brody
Judy Chicago
Susan Frazier
Camille Grey
Vicky Hodgett
Kathy Huberland
Judy Huddleston
Janice Johnson
Karen LeCocq
Janice (Jan) Lester
Paula Longendyke
Ann Mills
Carol Edson Mitchell
Robin Mitchell
Sandra (Sandy) Orgel
Jan Oxenburg
Christine (Chris) Rush
Marsha Salisbury
Miriam Schapiro
Robbin Schiff
Mira Schor
Robin Weltsch
Wanda Westcoast
Faith Wilding
Shawnee Wollenman
Nancy Youdelman

ART OUT OF EXPERIENCE

JUDY CHICAGO'S ASSIGNMENTS AT THE FEMINIST ART PROGRAMS AT FRESNO AND CALARTS

By Verena Kittel

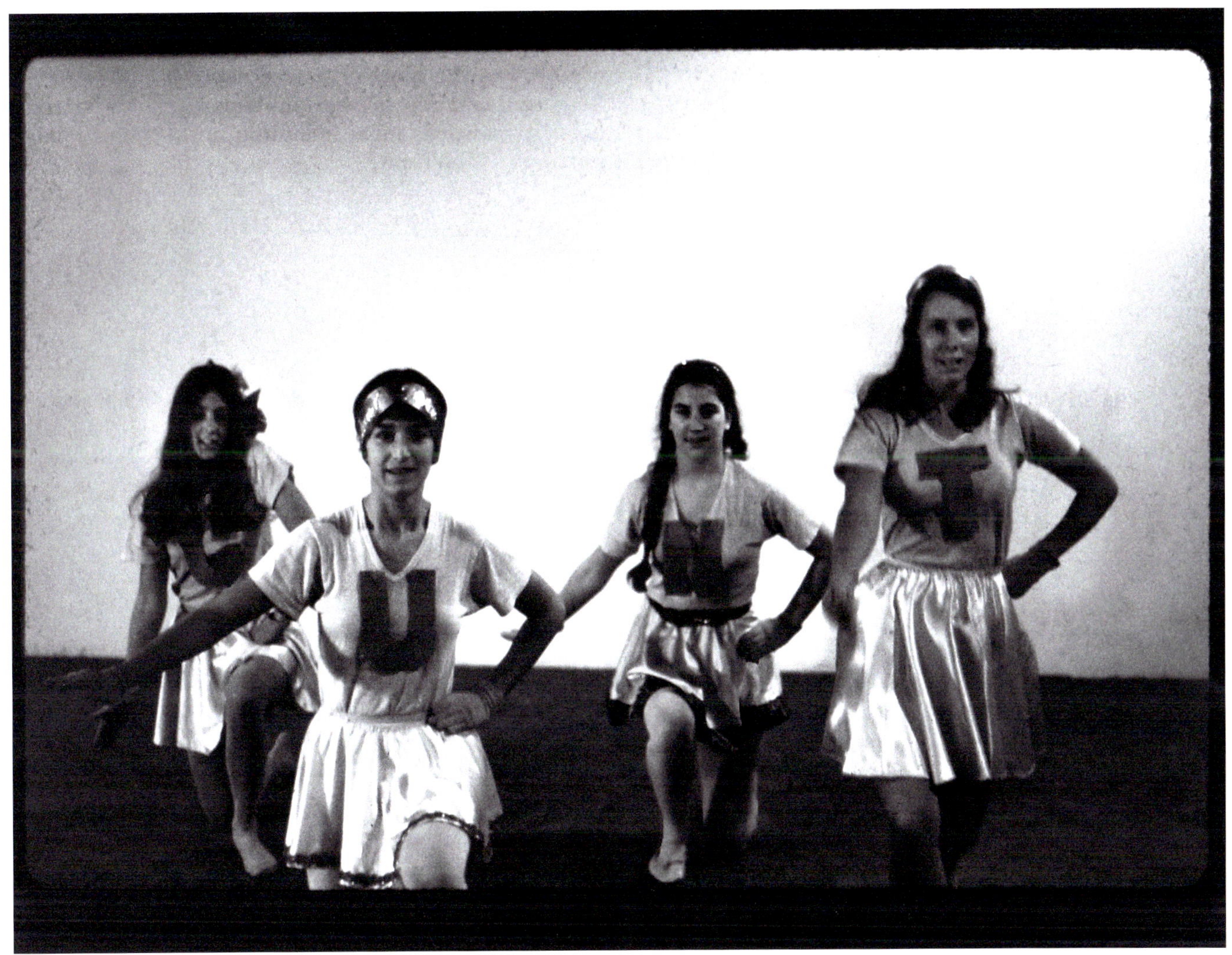

Feminist Art Program Cheerleaders (1971), left to right: Cay Lang, Vanalyne Green, Dori Atlantis, Sue Boud. Photo by Dori Atlantis.

n the founding years of the California Institute of the Arts (CalArts), a curriculum or assignments in the traditional sense did not exist. As becomes evident in the formative iconic piece *CalArts Post-Studio Art: Class Assignments (optional)* (1970), the teaching of the initiator of the first Post-Studio Art class at CalArts, John Baldessari, functions like a game his students are invited to join.[1] Baldessari's 'assignments' can thus be understood as playful, thought-provoking impulses to stimulate students to develop their own original ideas, rather than authoritative instructions. The tasks Judy Chicago, founder of the first feminist art class, employed in her teaching at both CalArts (1971–73) and Fresno State College (today California State University, Fresno) (1970–71) were also quite unconventional. Chicago's assignments, however, revolved around social conflicts or concepts and served as a means to reveal the emotions and experiences of her female students. Contrary to Baldessari, Chicago, as stated by her former student Suzanne Lacy, "intentionally steered us away from anything that was conceptual, that was removed from a direct engagement with our feelings. We made art out of experience."[2]

Together with the artist and CalArts teacher Miriam Schapiro, Chicago initiated the Feminist Art Program (FAP) at the art school in 1971, where it joined a Women's Design Program by Sheila Levrant de Bretteville and a Women in Literature and Women's Writing course by Deena Metzger. The FAP was the continuation of a similar program Chicago formed one year before at the experimental Fresno State College (Fresno)—the first university art class employing feminist pedagogical principles. Both courses allowed only women and were held off-campus to create an autonomous space, allowing their participants to develop an understanding as artists and pursue their creative practices, away from the patriarchal structures of the male-dominated institutions. The fact that two thirds of the art students were female, but less than 20% of the women succeeded as professional artists,[3] as well as Chicago's own experiences as a woman artist in the male-centered art scene in L.A., were the driving factors to organize an all-women art class.[4] Even though, in hindsight, most of its former members considered their participation in the FAPs as valuable and formative experiences, the separatism both programs generated was the most criticized aspect of the FAP by its alumnae. Many viewed this separatism as outright hostility towards men, including towards their male partners at the time.[5]

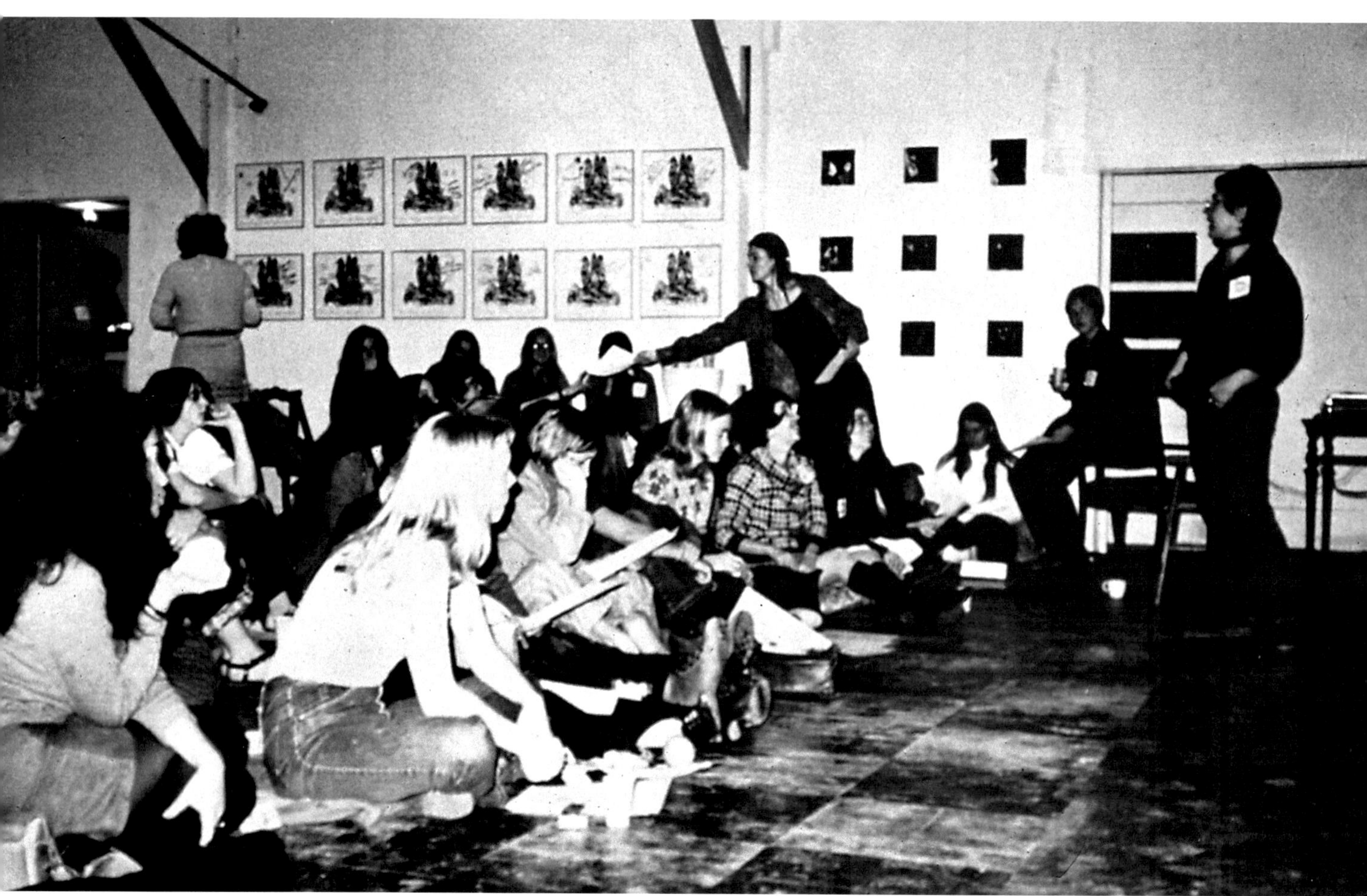

BUILDING A FEMALE ENVIRONMENT

A basic component of Chicago's pedagogical principles at both Fresno and CalArts was the creation of a 'female' context and environment. Such a safe space protected the women from male intimidation, but also helped them to develop mechanical and negotiating skills. One of the first assignments at Fresno was therefore to find a studio space in which they could hold their classes. At CalArts, the program started with the search for a building they could transform into the artistic environment *Womanhouse*. In both cases, they found abandoned edifices, which they could lease for several months (Fresno) or were slated for demolition (CalArts), and thus had to be renovated and converted according to their artistic needs. As Faith Wilding recalls about the art class in Fresno,

Building and using tools were techniques most of the participants were not used to, which often led to frustration. Dealing with such physical challenges, but also with funding issues and realtors, who often did not take them seriously, were important learning processes to foster the women's self-confidence and self-reliance. As Janice Lester remembers about the negotiation processes in Fresno,

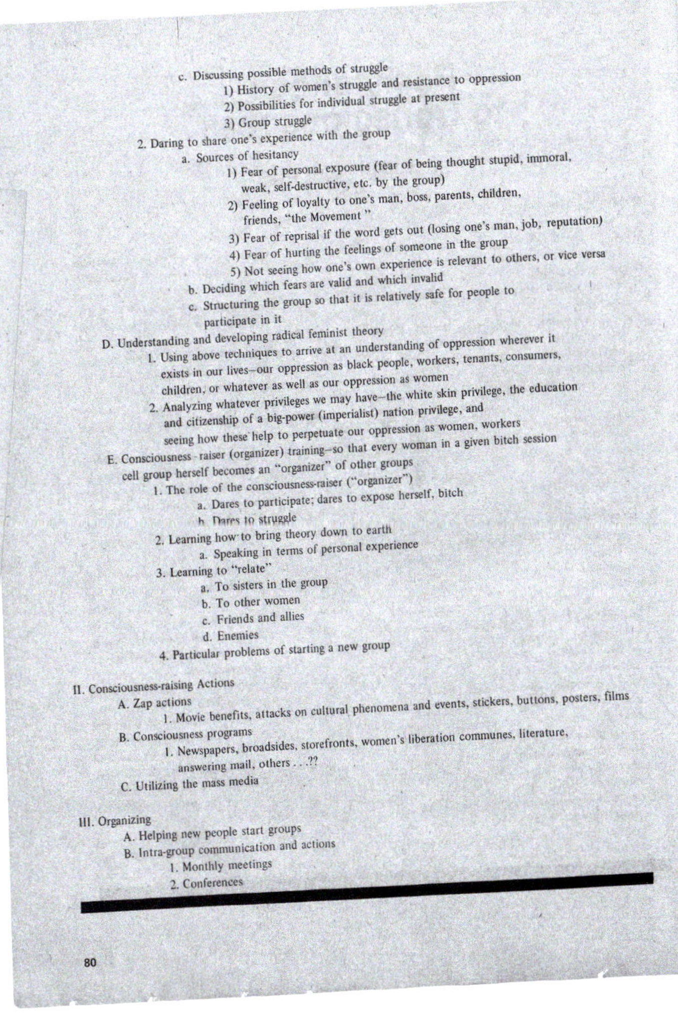

This is a consciousness-raising program for those of us who are feeling more and more that women are about the most exciting people around, at this stage of time, anyway, and that the seeds of a new and beautiful world society lie buried in the consciousness of this very class which has been abused and oppressed since the beginning of human history. It is a program planned on the assumption that a mass liberation movement will develop as more and more women begin to perceive their situation correctly and that, therefore, our primary task right now is to awaken "class" consciousness in ourselves and others on a mass scale. The following outline is just one hunch of what a theory of mass consciousness-raising would look like in skeleton form.

I. The "bitch session" cell group
  A. Ongoing consciousness expansion
    1. Personal recognition and testimony
      a. Recalling and sharing our bitter experiences
      b. Expressing our feelings about our experiences both at the time they occurred and at present
      c. Expressing our feelings about ourselves, men, other women
      d. Evaluating our feelings
    2. Personal testimony – methods of group practice
      a. Going around the room with key questions on key topics
      b. Speaking our experience – at random
      c. Cross stimulation
    3. Relating and generalizing individual testimony
      a. Finding the common root when different women have opposite feelings and experiences
      b. Examining the negative and positive aspects of each woman's feelings and her way of dealing with her situation as a woman
  B. Classic forms of resisting consciousness, or: How to avoid facing the awful truth
    1. Anti-womanism
    2. Glorification of the oppressor
    3. Excusing the oppressor (and feeling sorry for him)
    4. False identification with the oppressor and other socially privileged groups
    5. Shunning identification with one's own oppressed group and other oppressed groups
    6. Romantic fantasies, utopian thinking and other forms of confusing present reality with what one wishes reality to be
    7. Thinking one has power in the traditional role—can "get what one wants," has power behind the throne, etc.
    8. Belief that one has found an adequate personal solution or will be able to find one without large social changes
    9. Self-cultivation, rugged individualism, seclusion, and other forms of go-it-alonism
    10. Self-blame!!
    11. Ultra-militancy; and others??
  C. Recognizing the survival reasons for resisting consciousness
  D. "Starting to Stop" – overcoming repressions and delusions
    1. Daring to see, or: Taking off the rose-colored glasses
      a. Reasons for repressing one's own consciousness
        1) Fear of feeling the full weight of one's painful situation
        2) Fear of feeling one's past wasted and meaningless (plus wanting others to go through the same obstacles)
        3) Fear of despair for the future
      b. Analyzing which fears are valid and which invalid
        1) Examining the objective conditions in one's own past and in the lives of most women throughout history
        2) Examining objective conditions for the present

79

    c. Discussing possible methods of struggle
      1) History of women's struggle and resistance to oppression
      2) Possibilities for individual struggle at present
      3) Group struggle
    2. Daring to share one's experience with the group
      a. Sources of hesitancy
        1) Fear of personal exposure (fear of being thought stupid, immoral, weak, self-destructive, etc. by the group)
        2) Feeling of loyalty to one's man, boss, parents, children, friends, "the Movement "
        3) Fear of reprisal if the word gets out (losing one's man, job, reputation)
        4) Fear of hurting the feelings of someone in the group
        5) Not seeing how one's own experience is relevant to others, or vice versa
      b. Deciding which fears are valid and which invalid
      c. Structuring the group so that it is relatively safe for people to participate in it
  D. Understanding and developing radical feminist theory
    1. Using above techniques to arrive at an understanding of oppression wherever it exists in our lives—our oppression as black people, workers, tenants, consumers, children, or whatever as well as our oppression as women
    2. Analyzing whatever privileges we may have—the white skin privilege, the education and citizenship of a big-power (imperialist) nation privilege, and seeing how these help to perpetuate our oppression as women, workers
  E. Consciousness-raiser (organizer) training—so that every woman in a given bitch session cell group herself becomes an "organizer" of other groups
    1. The role of the consciousness-raiser ("organizer")
      a. Dares to participate; dares to expose herself, bitch
      b. Dares to struggle
    2. Learning how to bring theory down to earth
      a. Speaking in terms of personal experience
    3. Learning to "relate"
      a. To sisters in the group
      b. To other women
      c. Friends and allies
      d. Enemies
    4. Particular problems of starting a new group

II. Consciousness-raising Actions
  A. Zap actions
    1. Movie benefits, attacks on cultural phenomena and events, stickers, buttons, posters, films
  B. Consciousness programs
    1. Newspapers, broadsides, storefronts, women's liberation communes, literature, answering mail, others . . .??
  C. Utilizing the mass media

III. Organizing
  A. Helping new people start groups
  B. Intra-group communication and actions
    1. Monthly meetings
    2. Conferences

80

Opposite page: Rap Weekend (spring 1971), Fresno, California. Weekend of performances and exhibited work to a large group of both local and out of town visitors at the studio of the Fresno Feminist Art Program. Photo by Vaughn Rachel.
This page: Kathie Sarachild, "A Program for Feminist Consciousness-Raising," in *Notes From the Second Year: Women's Liberation. Major Writings of the Radical Feminists,* eds. Shulamith Firestone and Anne Koedt (1970).

When Chicago first met the participants of the FAP at Fresno, she described the young women she encountered as not being used to articulating opinions, establishing personal goals, or asking for their own needs and desires.[8] Cheryl Zurilgen, a student at the Fresno class, explains that women in the early 1970s were ascribed primarily two roles: the mother and the wife. Their "entire personality structure" was therefore "trained to orient itself around the needs of others, children and men, to be 'good girls.'"[9] Chicago was convinced that the difficulties women had in pursuing professional artistic careers were rooted in such socially conditioned behavior. She considered the male-centered art scene, one that rejected art related to experiences, emotions, colors, and forms categorized as female or using methods women were trained in, and the educational system believing in myths of the male genius,[10] to be further reasons. If young women wanted to succeed as artists, they thus had to make use of content and techniques that did not relate to their daily life.[11] As a result, Chicago's first endeavor was to help her students to develop self-assurance, gain strength, be ambitious, and pursue and achieve their own goals. Besides the finding and building of an exclusive artistic space, other assignments included learning to introduce oneself confidently, role-playing, for example, realtor encounters,[12] as well as the discussion of sophisticated literature, concerts, theater, and movie visits in order to encourage their own voices.[13] Even though Chicago's main concerns, on the one hand, were to foster autonomy in her students and to build up a democratic program "with an emphasis on consensus, sharing and a leveling of the traditional teacher-student relationship,"[14] on the other hand, she also expected them to accept her ultimate authority, which, as some students felt, she often asserted too strongly. Vanalyne Green and Robin Mitchell, for example, remember Chicago imposing her views and ideas on aesthetic questions like the rejection of abstraction and the presentation of artworks on them.[15] Moreover, according to several Mira Schor letters written during the FAP at CalArts, Chicago had difficulties relinquishing control, was not very open to alternative perspectives, and projected her own struggles and goals on the group.[16]

CONTENT RESEARCH

Throughout both programs in Fresno and in CalArts, Chicago employed specific assignments in order to help her students to get in touch with their feelings and needs and to find content they could use in their art. One important strategy she consistently referred to was consciousness-raising (CR). Chicago, as well as her students, built on the experiences of Wilding and Lacy, who had already organized a feminist CR group at Fresno based on instructions by the radical feminist Kathie Sarachild.[17] They "developed a critique methodology that was personal and emotionally resonant for women makers. It was an empowerment process through recognizing unconscious patterns, desires, and impediments (like suppressed experiences) in one's work." As Lacy further describes it, the practices used in Chicago's programs were not "strictly CR per se, but more like encounter groups which were popular at the time"[18] and can rather be defined as "modified consciousness-raising," which should "help the women understand the implications of … [their] experiences in order to change their behavior patterns."[19] Foregrounding the process rather than any product, the CR sessions in Chicago's classes were always related to art making and thus aimed at a specific outcome. Even though she valued the process and the experience gained through it, they were still subordinated to the goal: the production and exhibition of a content-based artwork.[20]

In such sessions, participants sat in a circle and each spoke about their experiences and their self-perception related to a key topic they had pre-selected, such as body image, sexuality, family relations, or violence.[21] In such a context, taboo issues in the 1970s, like the sexual desires of women or sexual violence, were addressed for the first time. After the CR sessions the group brainstormed artistic ways to make these subjects visible. Through such a process they created empowering, positive 'female' body images, which contributed to the formation of so-called 'cunt art.' Inspired by a "cunt alphabet" made by Judy Chicago out of cut paper, they developed vulvar or womb-like imagery[22] (as in Judy Chicago's *Through the Flower* (1973), Faith Wilding's *Peach Cunt* (1971), but also the *Cunt Cheerleaders*)[23] that act as a counterweight to the often pornographic or medicalized representation of female anatomy and the dominating phallic images of Eurocentric iconography.[24] According to Wilding, it "signified to us an awakened consciousness about our bodies and our sexual selves."[25]

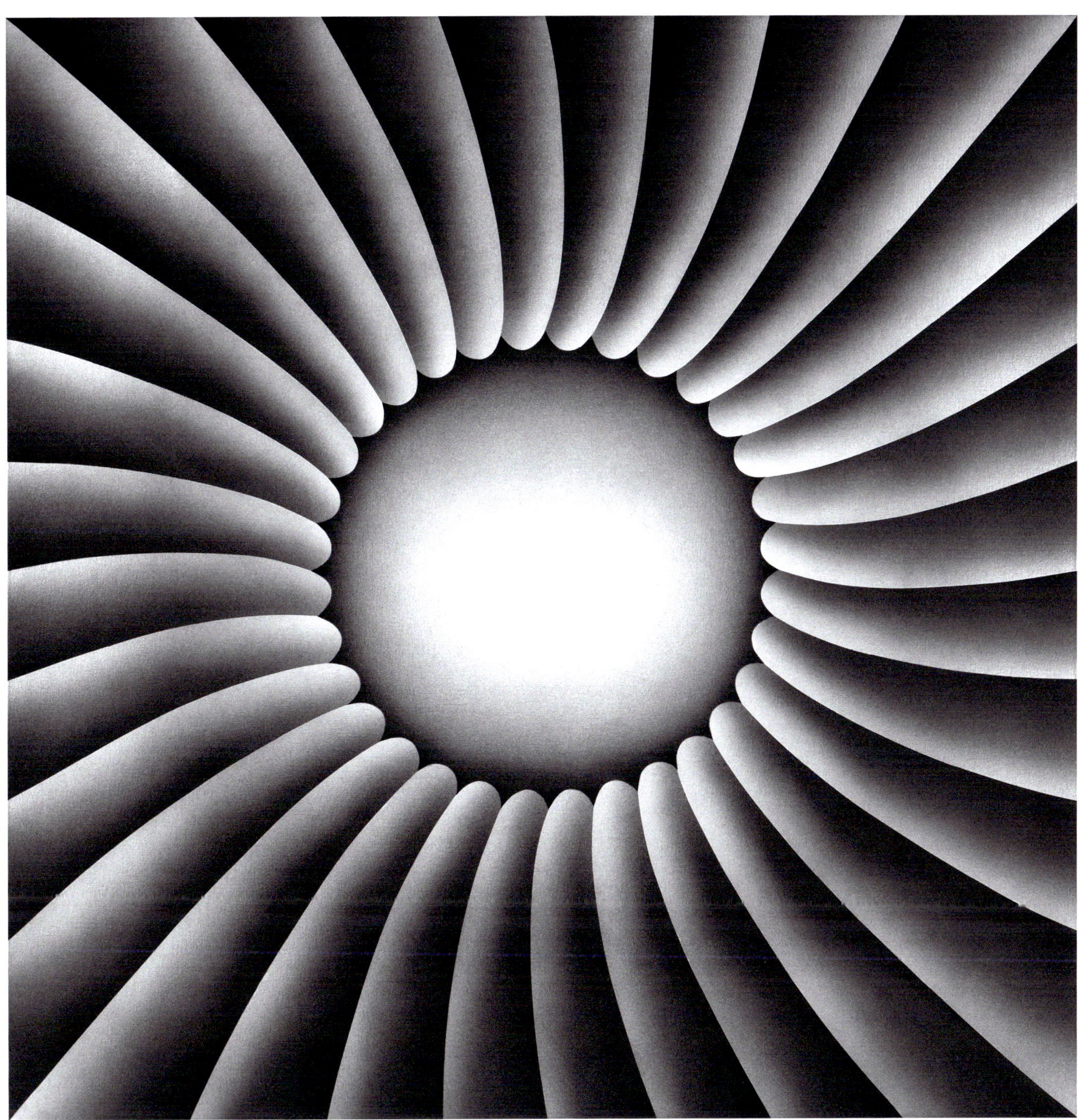

Judy Chicago, *Through the Flower* (1973).

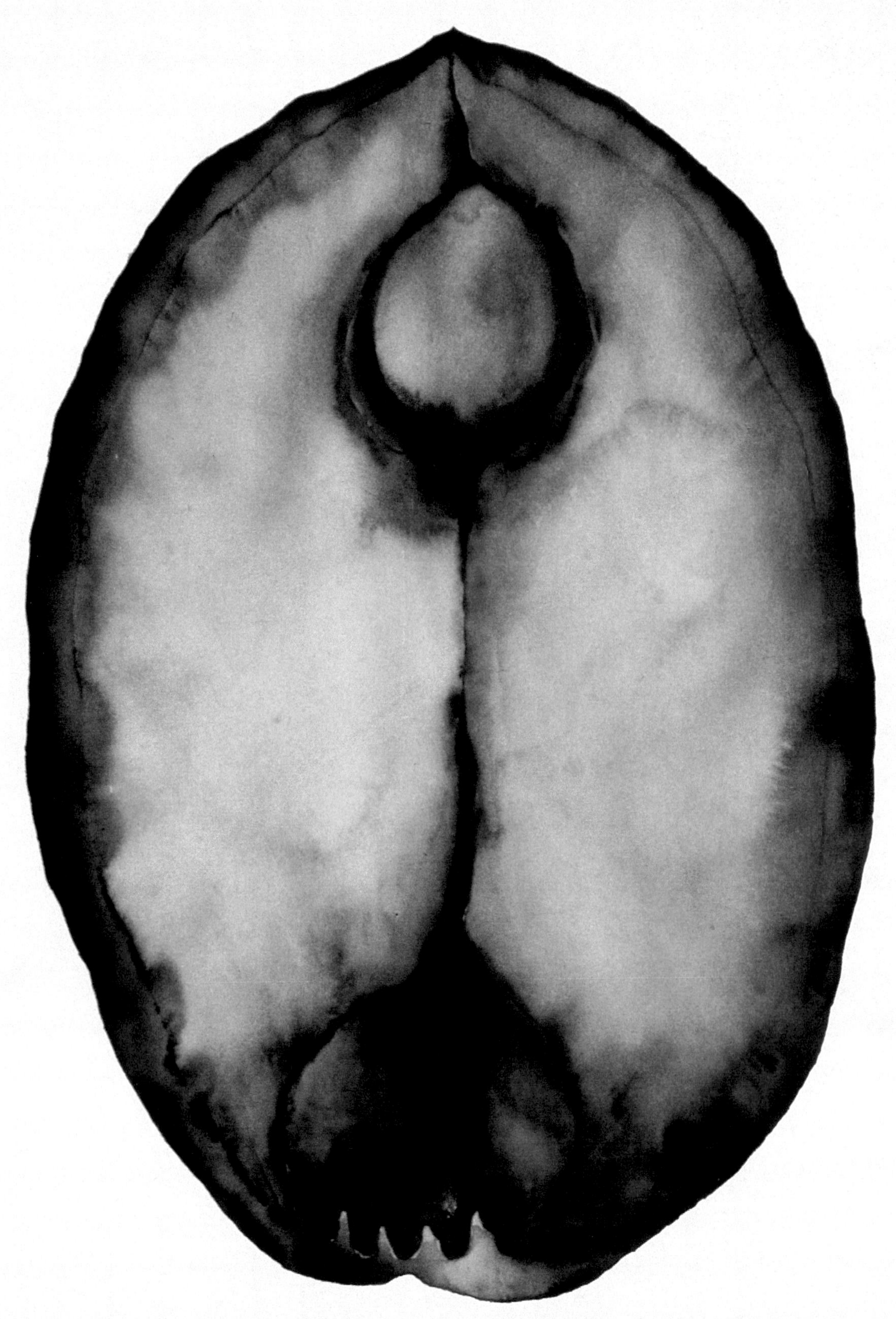

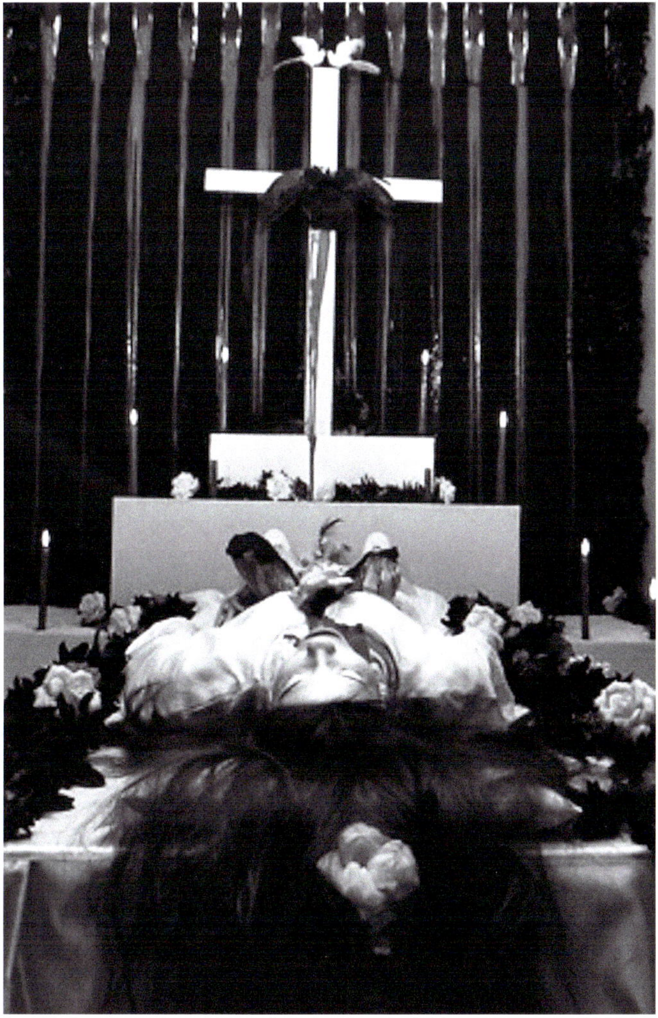

An early assignment at Fresno, Zurilgen remembers, dealt with the feeling of being psychically invaded:

> "Think about walking down the street and try to contact those feelings you get when guys start 'coming on.' Put those feelings into some form, a poem, a script, a drawing, painting, sculpture, whatever expresses most accurately those feelings, so that the rest of us can identify immediately."[26]

Resulting artworks included a poem by Chris Rush about a trip to Mexico City where she was harassed by a group of young men, a performance by another student about the dominating male presence, consuming and surrounding her even in her dreams,[27] and a womb-like room by Karen LeCocq that consisted of a polyurethane foam floor and a ceiling draped with moving plastic disks. To enter this *Soft Environment*, one had to go through a foam-covered door consisting only of a slit. Wilding created the room-size installation *Sacrifice*, which presented an effigy dressed like a bride with her torso cut open and filled with fresh cow guts in front of an altar that carried a cross with a dead pheasant nailed to it. The wall behind the installation was plastered with red sanitary pads. According to Wilding, *Sacrifice* dealt with "the feelings of entrapment and sexual repression I experienced growing up on the Bruderhof (Society of Brothers)."[28] Chicago recalls the resulting artworks showing,

> "images of feelings and experiences that none of us had ever seen portrayed before …
> all revealing the way women saw men …
> The images that day came out with an incredible force, as if they had been bottled up and suddenly released. They were so powerful that they frightened me …."[29]

Such exercises helped the students discover the commonality of their experiences as women and raised awareness about their social conditioning on the basis of their gender. Being in line with the slogan of the second-wave feminism "the personal is political,"[30] expressing that the experiences of women are rooted in their political and social situation, they thus connected their personal stories to larger cultural and social narratives and mechanisms.[31]

The class at Fresno consisted in its first weeks mainly of "extended consciousness-raising sessions" concerning the issues and difficulties of its students before they "began to do any work." The FAP at CalArts, however, with the intent to deal "with those same problems while working on a project,"[32] began the year with *Womanhouse*, a large-scale artistic collaboration involving all its participants, during which the methodologies developed at Fresno were employed. Through CR and role-playing they developed a concept and imagery for each room of the house. As Natalie Musteata describes, "Although most of the rooms are credited to a single artist, their design and conceptual underpinning were for the most part generated communally."[33] The result was an artistic environment that was frequently activated through performances during the opening hours of its exhibition (January 30–February 28, 1972), addressing gender roles and expectations in the domestic domain.

RESEARCH

Another approach in their art making was to research art created by women artists of the past, especially those that dealt with the experiences, emotions, and sensations of women. As most of the canonized artists were male, they sometimes felt "like an excavation team" when rediscovering the histories of women artists "buried so well."[34] Based on their research, they built up an archive that became the first "West Coast file on women artists' work."[35] Chicago, furthermore, often invited other women artists to classes, not only to provide her students with further female role models than herself, but also to gain inspiration from them. Among them was Miriam Schapiro, who gave a talk at Chicago's Fresno class six months after it started—an encounter that ultimately brought the FAP to CalArts.

MEDIA DIVERSITY

"We experimented tactically with media that would best embody the 'feel' of the content—groping toward a phenomenology and aesthetics of our cultural experience of 'becoming women.'*"*[36]

As Wilding suggests, the assignments Chicago employed in her art classes could be carried out in all kinds of media, evident in the diverse range of materials the students used in their artworks. These also included blood and viscera such as in Wilding's *Sacrifice*, which stemmed from visits to a nearby slaughterhouse, often resulting in ritualistic and performance work having "a cathartic effect on the group." The following account describes such a process at Fresno:

> *"… watching mesmerized as the cow is stunned, her throat slit, the blood we have come for collected in buckets. This is violent territory, a place of daily death and pain as hidden from public life as are our own lives as women. We carry the buckets of steaming blood back to the Women's Studio. We make blood paintings; blood performances; we bathe in the blood. Later we take tape-recorders and film cameras to the slaughterhouse. In a performance imitating ritual sacrifice and domination we superimpose sounds and images of the slaughterhouse on a young woman who is hanging from a meathook by her bound hands. As she 'milks' blood out of herself at the behest of a booted 'cowhand,' buckets of blood are thrown over her."*[37]

For Chicago, the performances created in the FAPs turned out to be among the "most powerful work."[38] The FAP that followed *Womanhouse* through the spring of 1973 was split up in several workshops. In this context, Judy Chicago offered a performance class, in which one of her first assignments was referred to as Route 126.[39] The only instructions included, as Lacy remembers, "to drive along this two-hour stretch of road between CalArts and the coast and at some point stop the caravan of cars and get out and do a performance that had to somehow be identifiable as done by a woman."[40]

Motivated by the desire to transfer their personal experiences as women, such as menstruation, to public space, their spontaneous actions included the attachment of sanitary pads to telephone posts (Judy Chicago and Shawnee Wollenman) and the renovation of an old, abandoned, rusted car with "pink paint, red velvet, and a big stuffed heart" (Suzanne Lacy). Nancy Youdelman, furthermore, did a performance at the beach, where she wrapped herself in flowing scarves and walked into the water until she disappeared.

Judy Chicago's assignments aimed not only at fostering her students' self-confidence and their self-belief in order to prepare them to confront the tough demands of a male-centered art world, but also at allowing them to create art from content they could relate to their daily lives. Focusing on experience-based knowledge such as building, negotiating skills, and a self-assured appearance, as well as a collaborative working process, Chicago's teaching at Fresno and CalArts differs strongly from traditional art education.[41] Whereas conventional studio instruction usually does not start with goal-setting or intensive group discussions and reflections on the content that informs the resulting artworks, equally involving all participants, Chicago's teaching puts the objective to produce and exhibit a content-based artwork at the fore. For *Womanhouse*, for example, she brought in practicing artists "to set a model for the students" and "to support the aesthetic goals of the project."[42] With its focus on art related to personal content, Chicago's pedagogy, however, could rather be associated with "connected learning." Whereas, according to Jill Tarule, "separated learning," such as the banking model by Paulo Freire, puts argument at the center of learning and thus disconnects the learning person from the information he or she delivers, "connected learning asks questions like, 'How is this experienced?' 'What does it make you think?' 'How does it make you feel?' Connected learning attempts to include the knower in that which is known."[43] Judy Chicago's assignments, especially during the CR sessions, likewise ask for the feelings and perceptions of each participant related to specific topics and situations and also, through her self-introduction and negotiating exercises, strongly involve the students personally in the learning process. Chicago's approach to art education and art making,

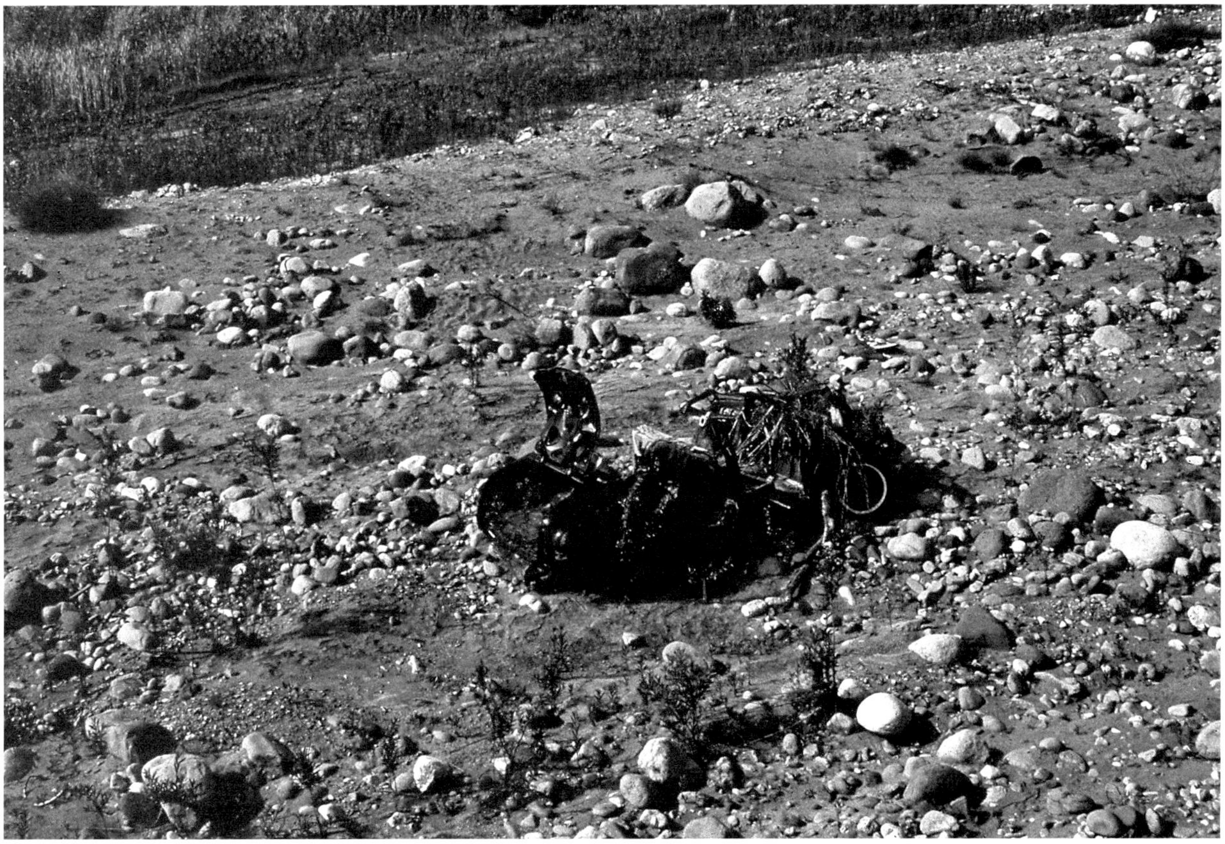

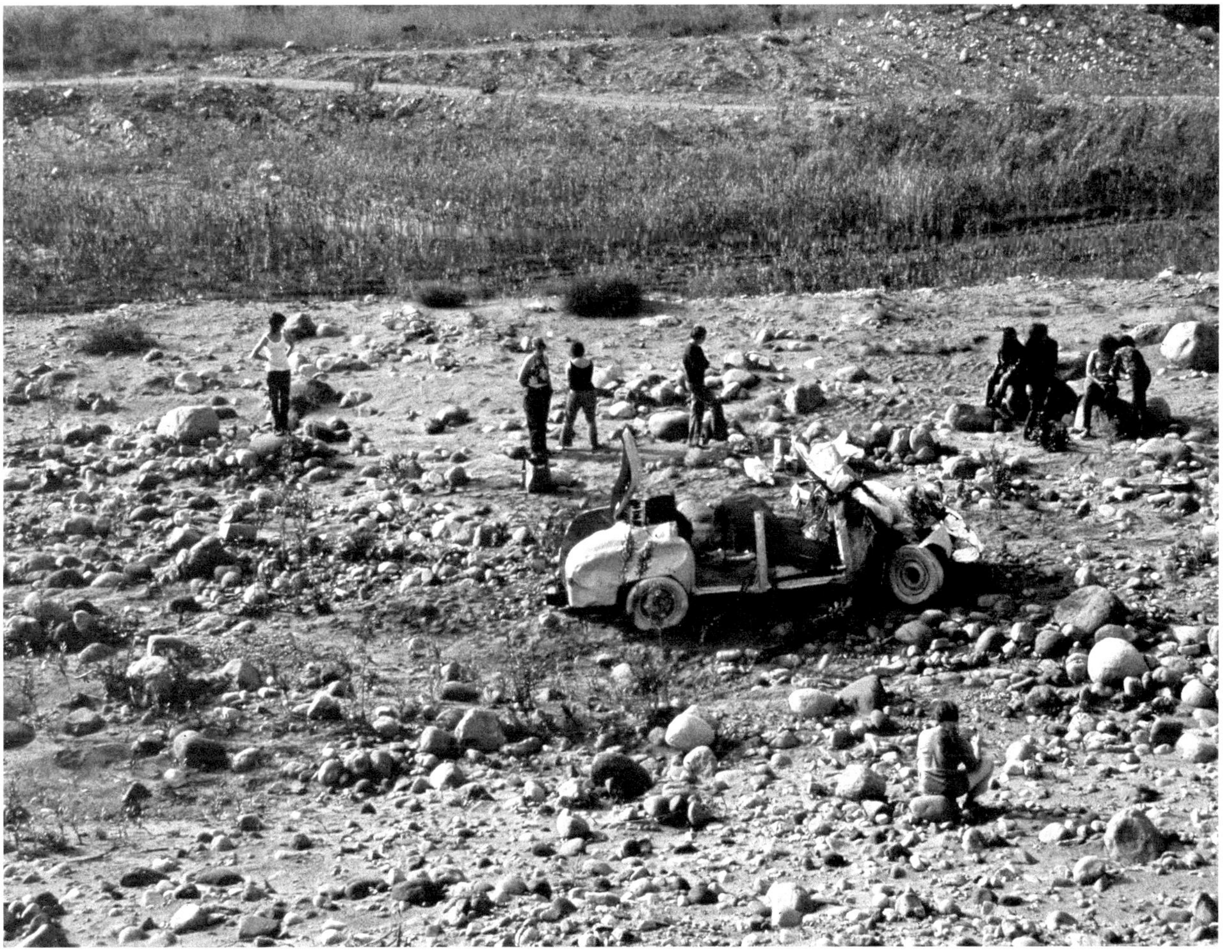

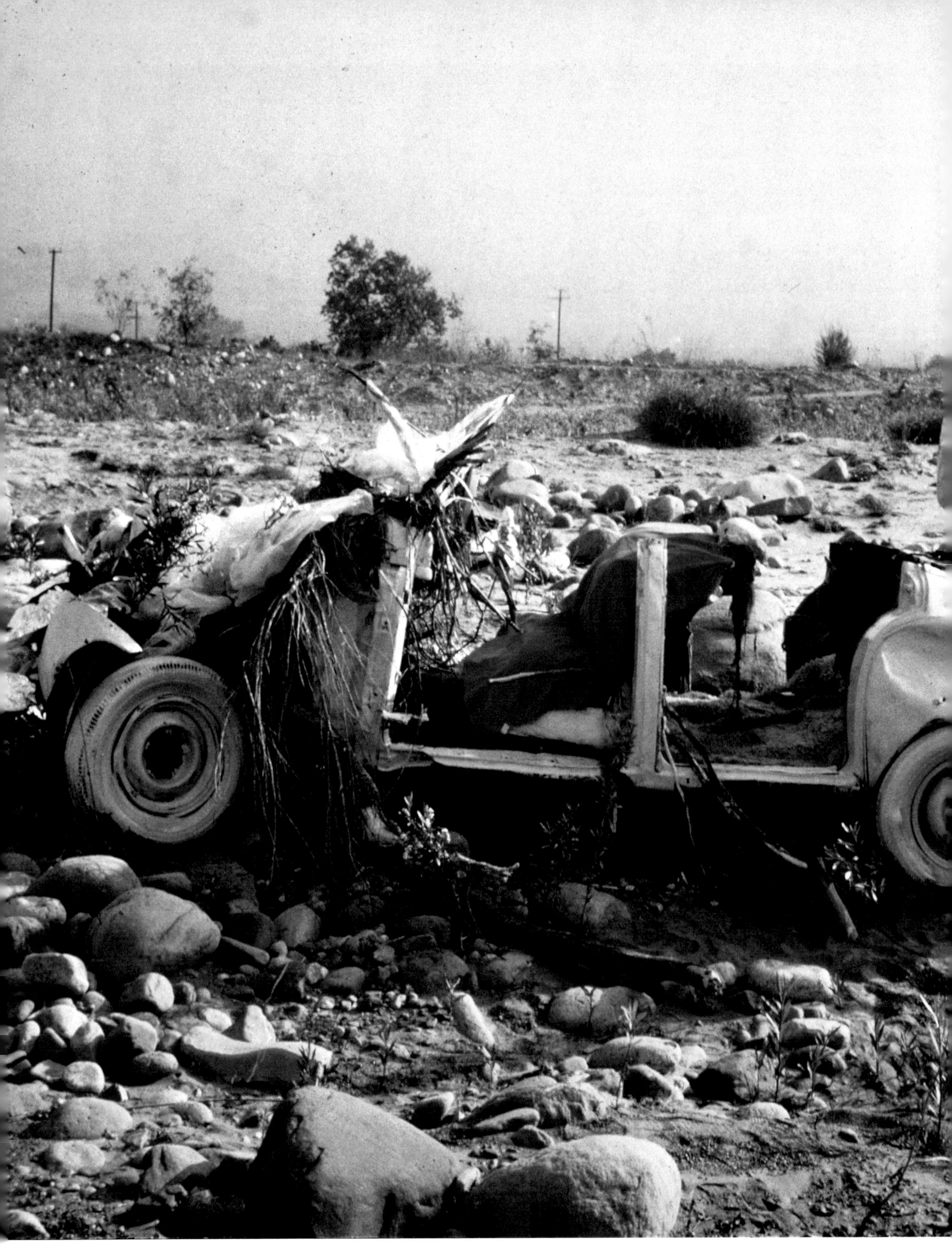

furthermore, differs not only from conventional but also from the pedagogical strategies of her colleagues such as Baldessari, whose game-like, open classroom situations investigating and challenging mechanisms of conveying semantic and aesthetic information contrast with Chicago's focus on personal experiences and feelings and her goal-oriented working method. With her primacy of subject-centered inquiries over formalist concerns, the inclusion of a wide range of unconventional media, and the collaborative approach to art production, Chicago not only occupies a special position among the faculty members at Fresno and CalArts, but also deviates strongly from the prevailing modes of art making in the post-war era in general.[44]

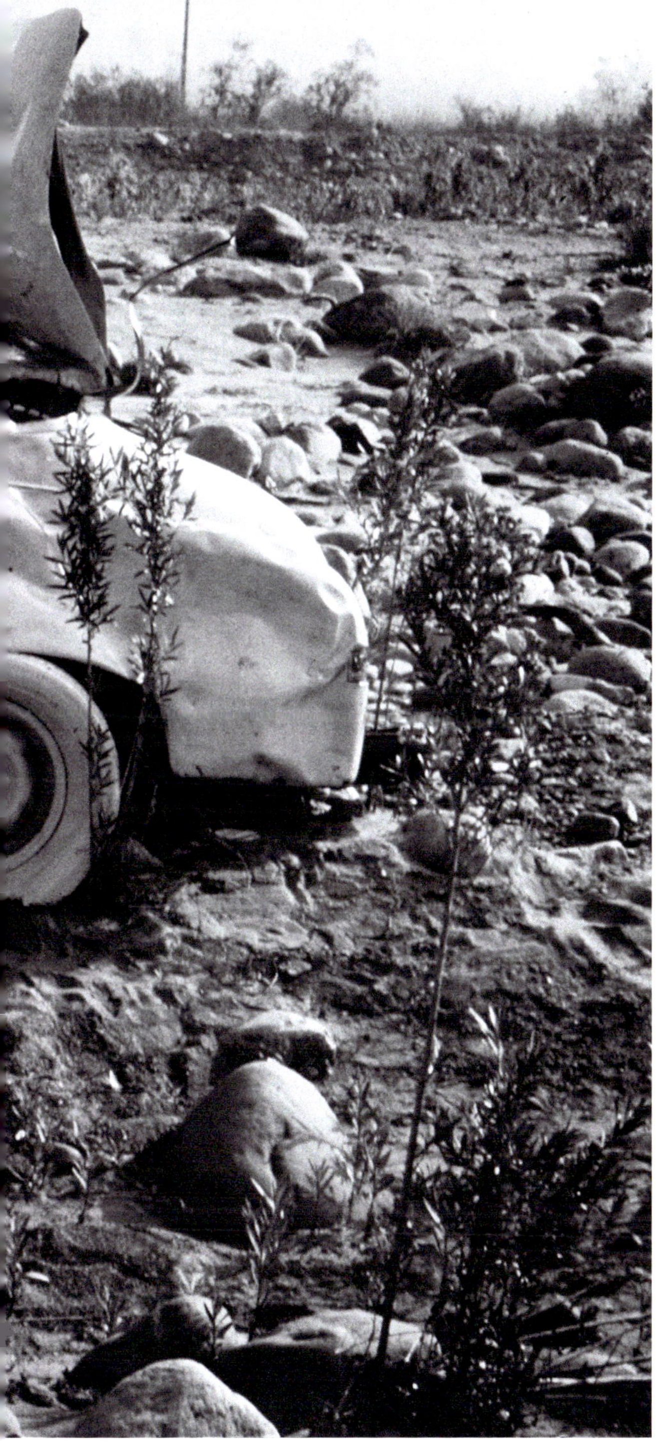

Previous and this spread: Suzanne Lacy, *Car Renovation* (1972).

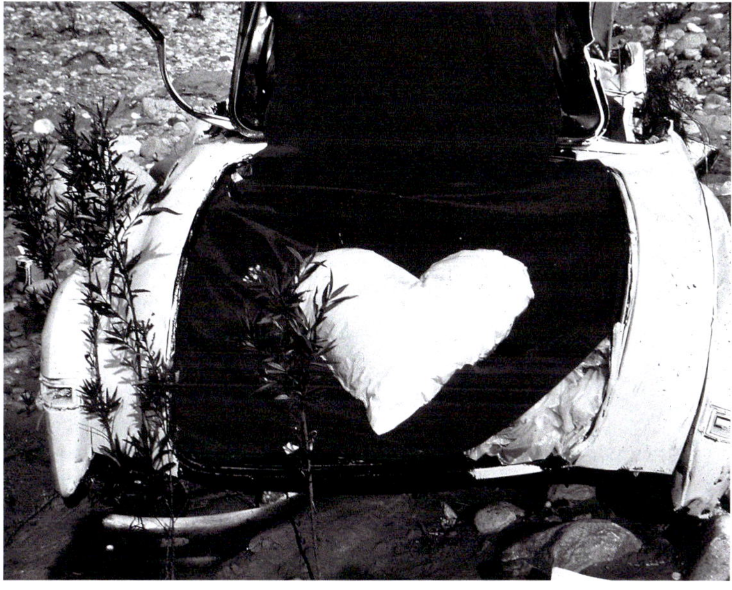

SHULAMITH FIRESTONE,
ANNE KOEDT (eds.)
Notes From the Second Year:
Women's Liberation.
Major Writings of the Radical
Feminists, 1970

I WOMEN'S EXPERIENCE:

The Bitch Manifesto

by JOREEN

Jo Freeman, organizer of the first independent women's liberation group in the nation (Chicago, 1967), editor of the first national newsletter, "Voice of the Women's Liberation Movement" (now disbanded), is currently active in the Chicago movement as well as nationally.

...man is defined as a human being and woman is defined as a female. Whenever she tries to behave as a human being she is accused of trying to emulate the male ....

—Simone de Beauvoir

BITCH is an organization which does not yet exist. The name is not an acronym.

BITCH is composed of Bitches. There are many definitions of a bitch. The most complimentary definition is a female dog. Those definitions of bitches who are also *homo sapiens* are rarely as objective. They vary from person to person and depend strongly on how much of a bitch the definer considers herself. However, everyone agrees that a bitch is always female, dog or otherwise.

It is also generally agreed that a Bitch is aggressive, and therefore unfeminine (ahem). She may be sexy, in which case she becomes a Bitch Goddess, a special case which will not concern us here. But she is never a "true woman."

Bitches have some or all of the following characteristics:

1) *Personality.* Bitches are aggressive, assertive, domineering, overbearing, strong-minded, spiteful, hostile, direct, blunt, candid, obnoxious, thick-skinned, hard-headed, vicious, dogmatic, competent, competitive, pushy, loud-mouthed, independent, stubborn, demanding, manipulative, egoistic, driven, achieving, overwhelming, threatening, scary, ambitious, tough, brassy, masculine, boisterous, and turbulent. Among other things. A Bitch occupies a lot of psychological space. You always know she is around. A Bitch takes shit from no one. You may not like her, but you cannot ignore her.

2) *Physical.* Bitches are big, tall, strong, large, loud, brash, harsh, awkward, clumsy, sprawling, strident, ugly. Bitches move their bodies freely rather than restrain, refine and confine their motions in the proper feminine manner. They clomp up stairs, stride when they walk and don't worry about where they put their legs when they sit. They have loud voices and often use them. Bitches are not pretty.

3) *Orientation.* Bitches seek their identity strictly through themselves and what they do. They are subjects, not objects. They may have a relationship with a person or organization, but they never *marry* anyone or anything; man, mansion, or movement. Thus Bitches prefer to plan their own lives rather than live from day to day, action to action, or person to person. They are independent cusses and believe they are capable of doing anything they damn well want to. If something gets in their way, well, that's why they become Bitches. If they are professionally inclined, they will seek careers and have no fear of competing with anyone. If not professionally inclined, they still seek self-expression and self-actualization. Whatever they do, they want an active role and are frequently perceived as domineering. Often they do dominate other people when roles are not available to them which more creatively sublimate their energies and utilize their capabilities. More often they are accused of domineering when doing what would be considered natural by a man.

A true Bitch is self-determined, but the term "bitch" is usually applied with less discrimination. It is a popular derogation to put down uppity women that was created by man and adopted by women. Like the term "nigger," "bitch" serves the social function of isolating and discrediting a class of people who do not conform to the socially accepted patterns of behavior.

BITCH does not use this word in the negative sense. A woman should be proud to declare she is a

5

ISSUES: CONSCIOUSNESS-RAISING

The Personal Is Political
by CAROL HANISCH

For this paper I want to stick pretty close to an aspect of the Left debate commonly talked about— namely "therapy" vs. "therapy and politics." Another name for it is "personal" vs. "political" and it has other names, I suspect, as it has developed across the country. I haven't gotten over to visit the New Orleans group yet, but I have been participating in groups in New York and Gainesville for more than a year. Both of these groups have been called "therapy" and "personal" groups by women who consider themselves "more political." So I must speak about so-called therapy groups from my own experience.

The very word "therapy" is obviously a misnomer if carried to its logical conclusion. Therapy assumes that someone is sick and that there is a cure, e.g., a personal solution. I am greatly offended that I or any other woman is thought to _need_ therapy in the first place. Women are messed over, not messed up! We need to change the objective conditions, not adjust to them. Therapy is adjusting to your bad personal alternative.

We have not done much trying to solve immediate personal problems of women in the group. We've mostly picked topics by two methods: In a small group it is possible for us to take turns bringing questions to the meeting (like, Which do/did you prefer, a girl or a boy baby or no children, and why? What happens to your relationship if your man makes more money than you? Less than you?). Then we go around the room answering the questions from our personal experiences. Everybody talks that way. At the end of the meeting we try to sum up and generalize from what's been said and make connections.

I believe at this point, and maybe for a long time to come, that these analytical sessions are a form of political action. I do not go to these sessions beccause I need or want to talk about my "personal problems." In fact, I would rather not. As a movement woman, I've been pressured to be strong, selfless, other-oriented, sacrificing, and in general pretty much in control of my own life. To admit to the problems in my life is to be deemed weak. So I want to be a strong woman, in movement terms, and not admit I have any real problems that I can't find a personal solution to (except those directly related to the capitalist system). It is at this point a political action to tell it like it is, to say what I really believe about my life instead of what I've always been told to say.

So the reason I participate in these meetings is not to solve any personal problem. One of the first things we discover in these groups is that personal problems are political problems. There are no personal solutions at this time. There is only collective action for a collective solution. I went, and I continue to go to these meetings because I have gotten a political understanding which all my reading, all my "political discussions," all my "political action," all my four-odd years in the movement never gave me. I've been forced to take off the rose-colored glasses and face the awful truth about how grim my life really is as a woman. I am getting a gut understanding of everything as opposed to the esoteric, intellectual understandings and _noblesse oblige_ feelings I had in "other people's" struggles.

This is not to deny that these sessions have at least two aspects that are therapeutic. I prefer to call even this aspect "political therapy" as opposed to personal therapy. The most important is getting rid of self-blame. Can you imagine what would happen if women, blacks, and workers (my definition of worker is anyone who _has_ to work for a living as opposed to those who don't. All women are workers) would stop blaming ourselves for our sad situations? It seems to me the whole country needs that kind of political therapy. That is what the black movement is doing in its own way. We shall do it in ours. We are only starting to stop blaming ourselves.

for everybody (else). But there is really a lot more to it than that. I can't quite articulate it yet. I think "apolitical" women are not in the movement for very good reasons, and as long as we say "you have to think like us and live like us to join the charmed circle," we will fail. What I am trying to say is that there are things in the consciousness of "apolitical" women (I find them very political) that are as valid as any political consciousness we think we have. We should figure out why many women don't want to do action. Maybe there is something wrong with the action or something wrong with why we are doing the action or maybe the analysis of why the action is necessary is not clear enough in our minds.

A Program for Feminist "Consciousness Raising"

by KATHIE SARACHILD

Kathie (Amatniek) is a founder of the women's liberation movement in New York and the originator of the concept of "consciousness-raising." She is now active in Redstockings. The following program was prepared for the First National Women's Liberation Conference outside Chicago, November 27, 1968.

We always stay in touch with our feelings.

Our feelings (emotions) revolve around our perceptions of our self-interest.

We assume that our feelings are telling us something from which we can learn ... that our feelings mean something worth analyzing ... that our feelings are saying something *political*, something reflecting fear that something bad will happen to us or hope, desire, knowledge that something good will happen to us.

Feelings aren't something we assume ahead of time that we should be on top of or underneath. Feelings are something that, at first anyway, we are *with*, that is, we examine and try to understand before we decide it's the kind of feeling to stay on top of (that is, control, stifle, stop), or the kind of feeling to be underneath (that is, let ourselves go with, let it lead us into something new and better ... at first to a new and better *idea* of where we want to go and then to action which might help us get there).

Now male culture assumes that feelings are something that people should stay on top of and puts women down for being led by their feelings (being underneath them).

We're saying that women have all along been generally *in touch* with their feelings (rather than underneath them) and that their being in touch with their feelings has been their greatest strength, historically and for the future. We have been so in touch with our feelings, as a matter of fact, that we have used our feelings as our best available weapon —hysterics, whining, bitching, etc.—given that our best form of defense against those with power to control our lives was their feelings toward us, sexual and otherwise, feelings which they always tried to fight themselves.

We're saying that for most of history sex was, in fact, both our undoing and our only possible weapon of self-defense and self-assertion (aggression).

We're saying that when we had hysterical fits, when we took things "too" personally, that we weren't underneath our feelings, but responding with our feelings correctly to a given situation of injustice. I say correctly because at that time in history (and maybe even still), by first feeling and then revealing our emotions we were acting in the best strategical manner. And this may be the reason we learned how to be so in touch with our feelings to begin with.

In our groups, let's share our feelings and pool them. Let's let ourselves go and see where our feelings lead us. Our feelings will lead us to ideas and then to actions.

Our feelings will lead us to our theory, our theory to our action, our feelings about that action to new theory and then to new action.

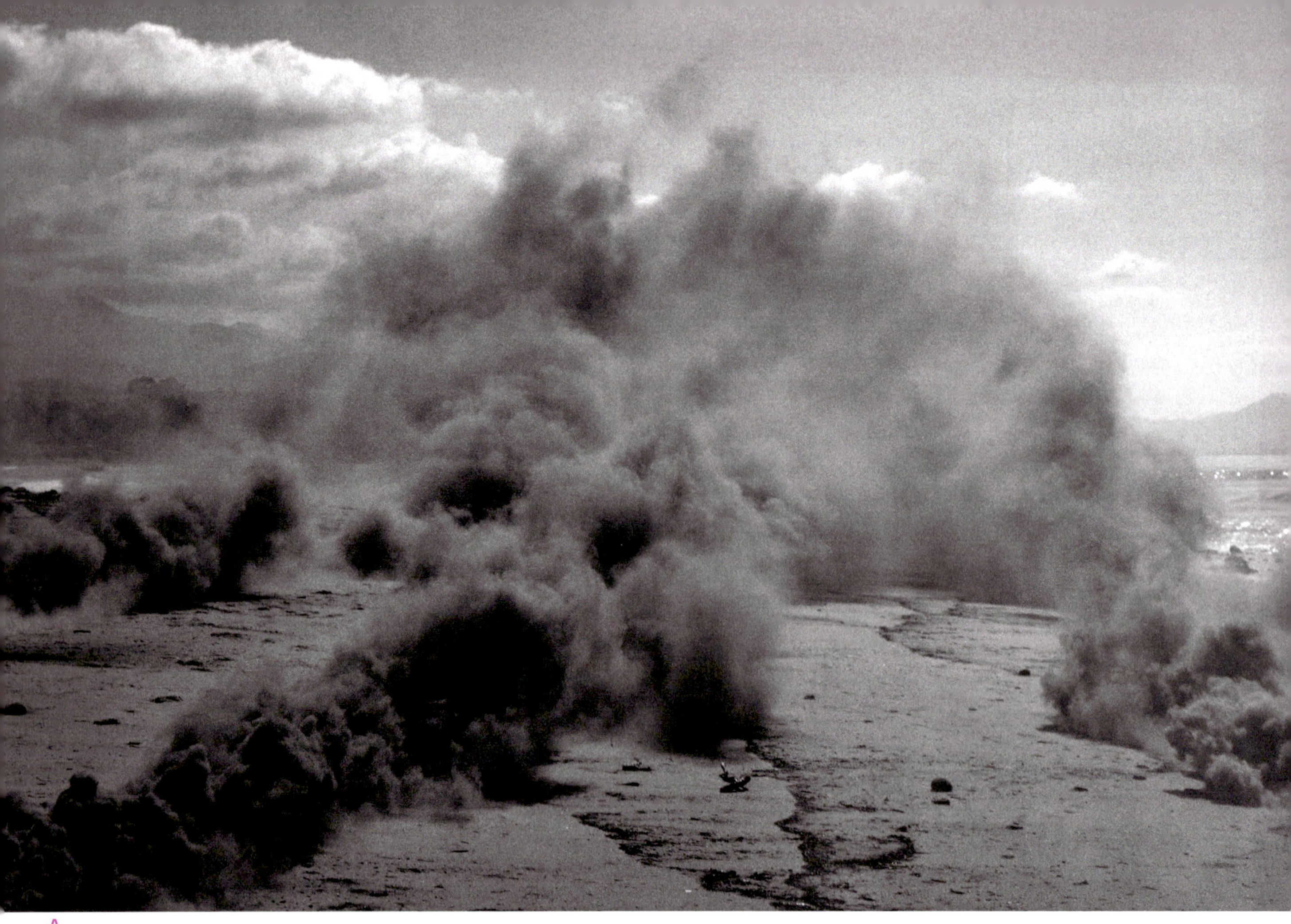

A   Judy Chicago, *Purple Atmosphere* (1969), fireworks performance, Santa Barbara Beach, Santa Barbara (CA).

B   Judy Chicago, *Immolation* from *Women and Smoke* (1972), fireworks performance, performed in the Californian Desert, featuring Faith Wilding.

JUDY CHICAGO

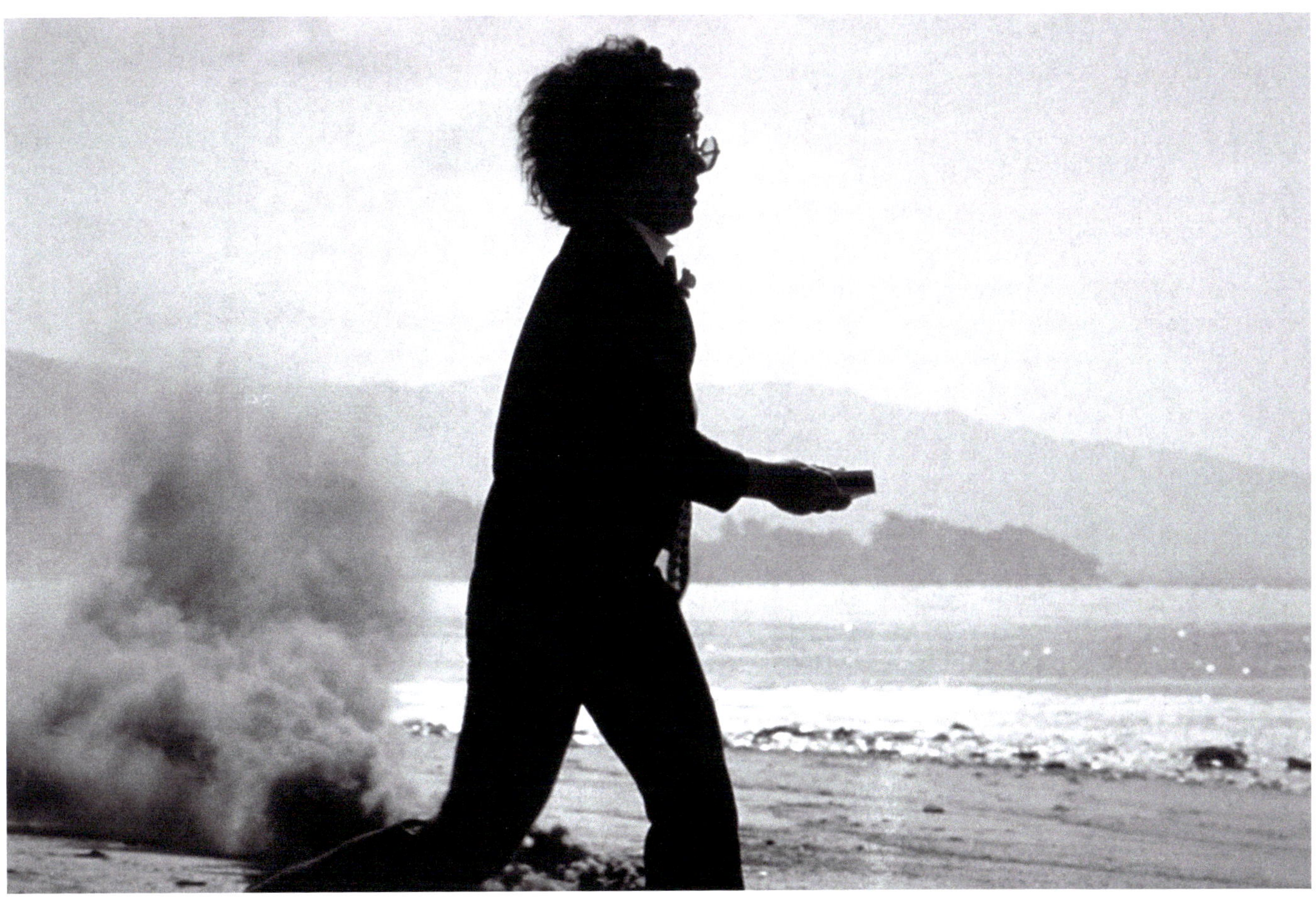

* July 20, 1939, Chicago (IL), USA

is an American feminist artist, writer, and art educator known for her paintings, installations, sculptures, performances, and the foundation of the first Feminist Art Programs (FAP) at Fresno State College (1970) and the California Institute of the Arts (CalArts) (1971), making her a pioneer within the feminist art movement of the 1970s. Especially successful was her large-scale collaborative installation *The Dinner Party* (1973–79) and the *Womanhouse* project (1972), produced in collaboration with Miriam Schapiro as part of the FAP at CalArts.[1] Foundational to the program were concepts of participation, experience, collaboration, approximation of craft, and construction skills, as well as an experimental approach and emancipation from the male-occupied realm of Fine Art.[2] In 1973, Chicago left CalArts and co-founded the Woman's Building in Los Angeles. Chicago started her career as a painter and sculptor working with predominantly geometric forms, but in the early 1970s she drastically modified her aesthetic, incorporating more female imagery and themes related to womanhood. Chicago's more recent work, *Resolutions: A Stitch in Time* (1994–2000) took six years to be completed and was, in 2000, exhibited at the Museum of Art and Design in New York.[3]

Judy Chicago's art has been shown in various international art institutions and exhibitions, such as *Inside the Dinner Party Studio,* National Museum of Women in the Arts, Washington D.C. (2017–18), *Why Not Judy Chicago?*, CAPC musée d'art contemporain de Bordeaux, France (2016), the Azkuna Zentroa, Bilbao, Spain, (2015–16), and *Pacific Standard Time* (2011–12) hosted by The Getty Trust in various L.A.-based institutions. In September 2019, the solo exhibition *The End: A Meditation on Death and Extinction* will open at the National Museum of Women in the Arts in Washington D.C.[4] **LB**

Judy Chicago, *Purple Atmosphere* (1969), fireworks performance, Santa Barbara Beach, Santa Barbara (CA).

Womanhouse
Exhibition
Announcements
1972

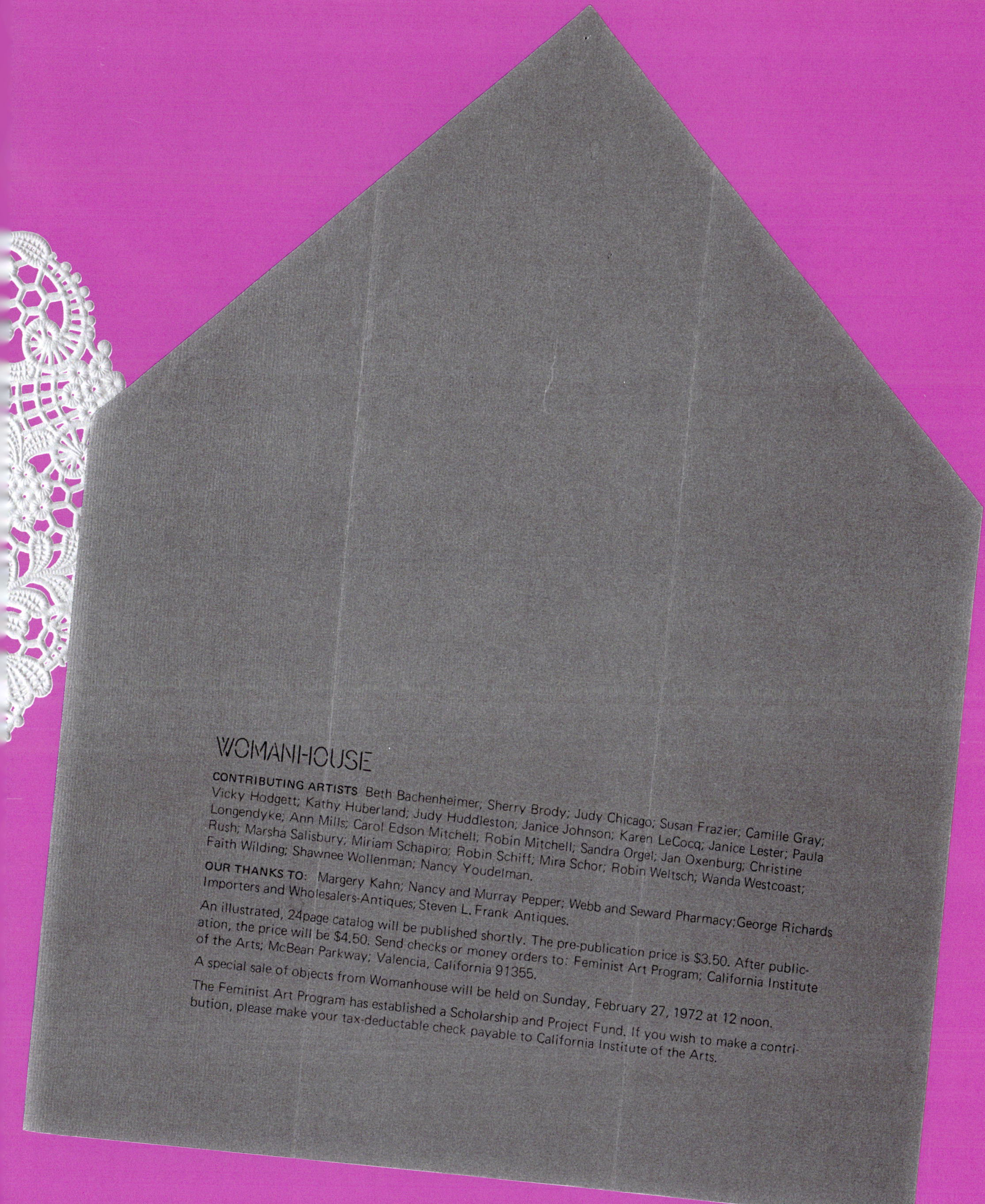

WOMANHOUSE

CONTRIBUTING ARTISTS Beth Bachenheimer; Sherry Brody; Judy Chicago; Susan Frazier; Camille Gray; Vicky Hodgett; Kathy Huberland; Judy Huddleston; Janice Johnson; Karen LeCocq; Janice Lester; Paula Longendyke; Ann Mills; Carol Edson Mitchell; Robin Mitchell; Sandra Orgel; Jan Oxenburg; Christine Rush; Marsha Salisbury; Miriam Schapiro; Robin Schiff; Mira Schor; Robin Weltsch; Wanda Westcoast; Faith Wilding; Shawnee Wollenman; Nancy Youdelman.

OUR THANKS TO: Margery Kahn; Nancy and Murray Pepper; Webb and Seward Pharmacy; George Richards Importers and Wholesalers-Antiques; Steven L. Frank Antiques.

An illustrated, 24page catalog will be published shortly. The pre-publication price is $3.50. After publication, the price will be $4.50. Send checks or money orders to: Feminist Art Program; California Institute of the Arts; McBean Parkway; Valencia, California 91355.

A special sale of objects from Womanhouse will be held on Sunday, February 27, 1972 at 12 noon.

The Feminist Art Program has established a Scholarship and Project Fund. If you wish to make a contribution, please make your tax-deductable check payable to California Institute of the Arts.

NANCY YOUDELMAN

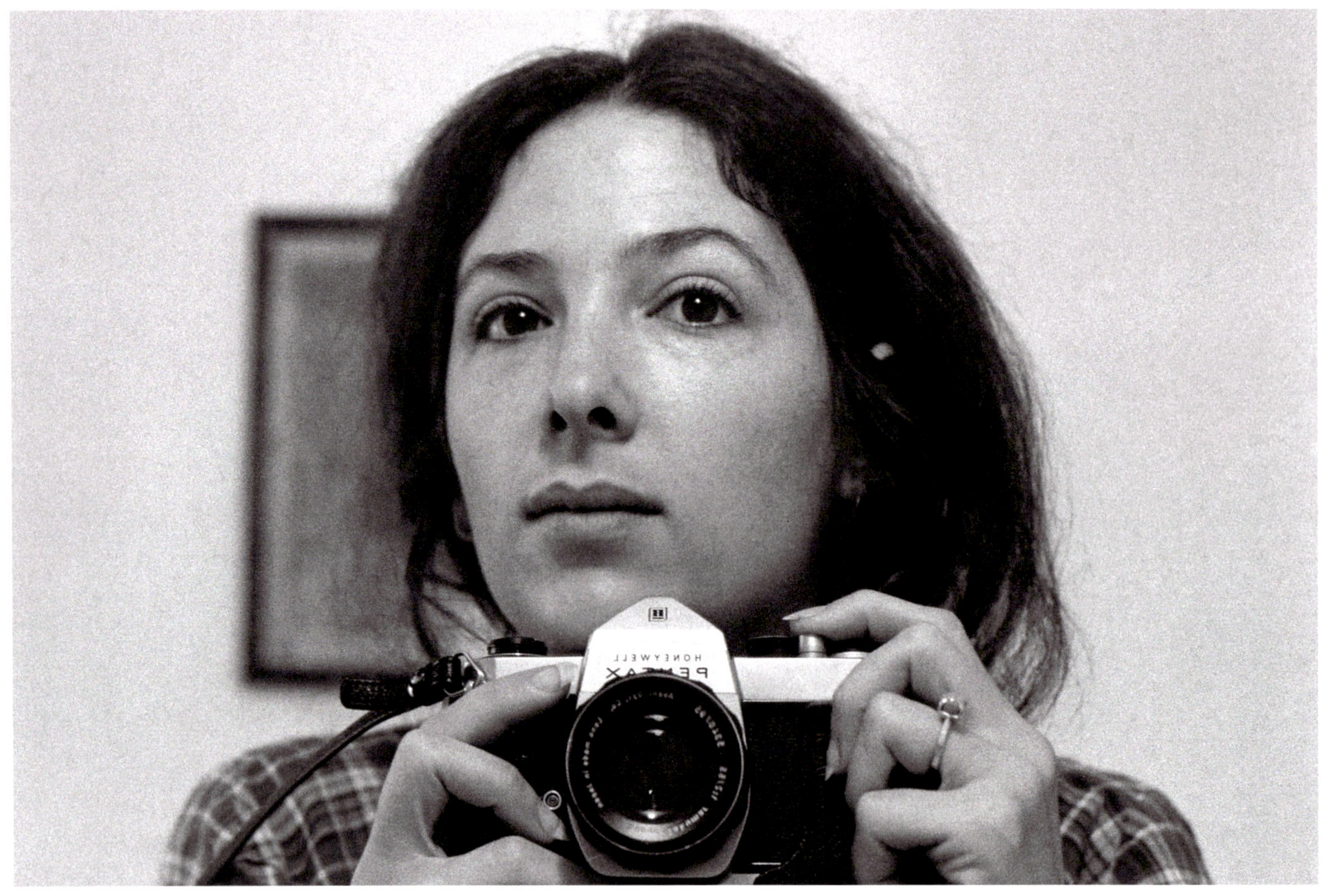

* June 10, 1948 in New York (NY), USA

is a mixed media sculptor based in California. She has also worked as a lecturer and art instructor, most recently at California State University, Fresno (Fresno) (since 2013). Youdelman was a founder of the Grandview Gallery at Woman's Building and Double X—a feminist art collective.

Nancy Youdelman studied Costume and Make-Up for the Theater and Art as well as English Literature at Fresno, before studying at the California Institute of the Arts (CalArts) from 1971–73. She joined the Feminist Art Program led by Judy Chicago at Fresno in 1970 and in 1971 the co-founded program at CalArts. Here, she participated in the art environment *Womanhouse* (1972), where she co-created the installation *Leah's Room* with Karen LeCocq.

After that influential experience, she finished her BFA and went to the University of California, L.A. She received her MFA from UCLA in 1976, with a focus on sculpture. Early works include *I Tried Everything* with Suzanne Lacy, Dori Atlantis, and Jan Lester (CalArts, 1972), and *Leaves* (1973). An early exhibition featuring her work was *Sculpture & Assemblage*, Art Rental Gallery, Los Angeles County Museum of Art (1974).

In her artistic work Youdelman uses women's clothing, feminine textiles, and fashion items, as well as household objects, which she often brings into assemblages with plant-based materials. She combines conventional women's clothes, shoes, belts, and gloves with dolls, jewelry, and organic materials like flowers or fruit peels, such as in *Vintage Eggbeater with Orange Peels*

and Jewelry (2016) and *Roller Skate* (2016). Elements of the household, like yarns or buttons, as well as photographs, print media, and letters are also integrated. Through assemblage, these objects are transformed into sculptures. Embellishing is a commonly used technique by Youdelman, along with 'femmage.'

Her most recent exhibition is *Nancy Youdelman: Fashioning a Feminist Vision 1972–2017* at California State University, Northridge, Art Galleries (2018) and at Fresno Art Museum (2017).[1] **LB**

Nancy Youdelman, *Self Portrait in Mirror* (1974).

KAREN LECOCQ

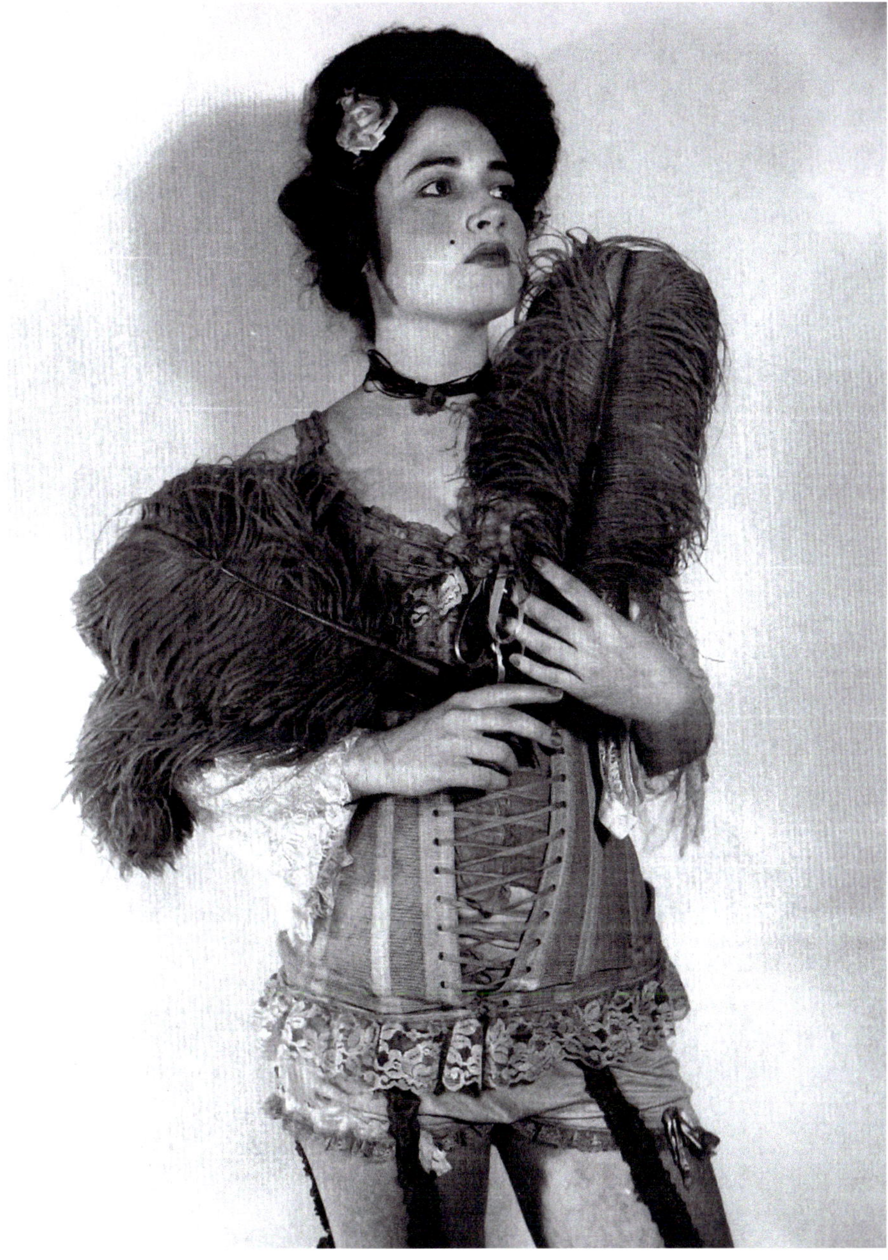

Victorian Whore (1970), Karen Le Cocq, model,
Feminist Art Program, Fresno State College.

* 1949, Santa Rose (CA), USA

is an American mixed media sculptor, author, curator, and academic teacher at the University of California, Merced. Her artistic work is characterized by the use of assemblage techniques. She creates multi-textured sculptures and installations out of a variety of organic, industrial, and art materials, as well as found items. In this sense, Karen LeCocq's work is concerned with the ecological concept of *upcyling*.[1] Some of her works, such as *Fiberworks* (1992) and *Naked Parasol* (2000), are inspired by indigenous artistic craft, the connection to nature, Zen philosophy, and Japanese culture.[2]

LeCocq was a member of the very first Feminist Art Program (FAP) at the former Fresno State College (1970–71). She finished her BFA in 1971 and then continued her studies at the California Institute of the Arts, Valencia (CalArts). When Judy Chicago transferred to CalArts to collaborate with Miriam Schapiro, LeCocq enrolled there.[3] For the collaborative project *Womanhouse* of the CalArts FAP, she worked with Nancy Youdelman on *Leah's Room*: a room installation evoking the atmosphere of a French boudoir , which was activated through a performance by LeCocq, demonstrating the struggle of an aging woman to sustain her beauty by repetitiously applying make-up.[4] For *Womanhouse* LeCocq also took part in the collaboration *The Dining Room*. She finished her MFA at Fresno in 1976.

Her works have been presented mainly on a national level in art institutions such as the Whitney Museum of American Art, N.Y., the UCLA Hammer Museum, L.A., and in several galleries and universities. The use of her work in the *Absolut Vodka Signature Artist Campaign* led to further attention on an international scale.[5]   **LB**

WOMANHOUSE: CONSTRUCTION PROCESS

By Pauline Gründing

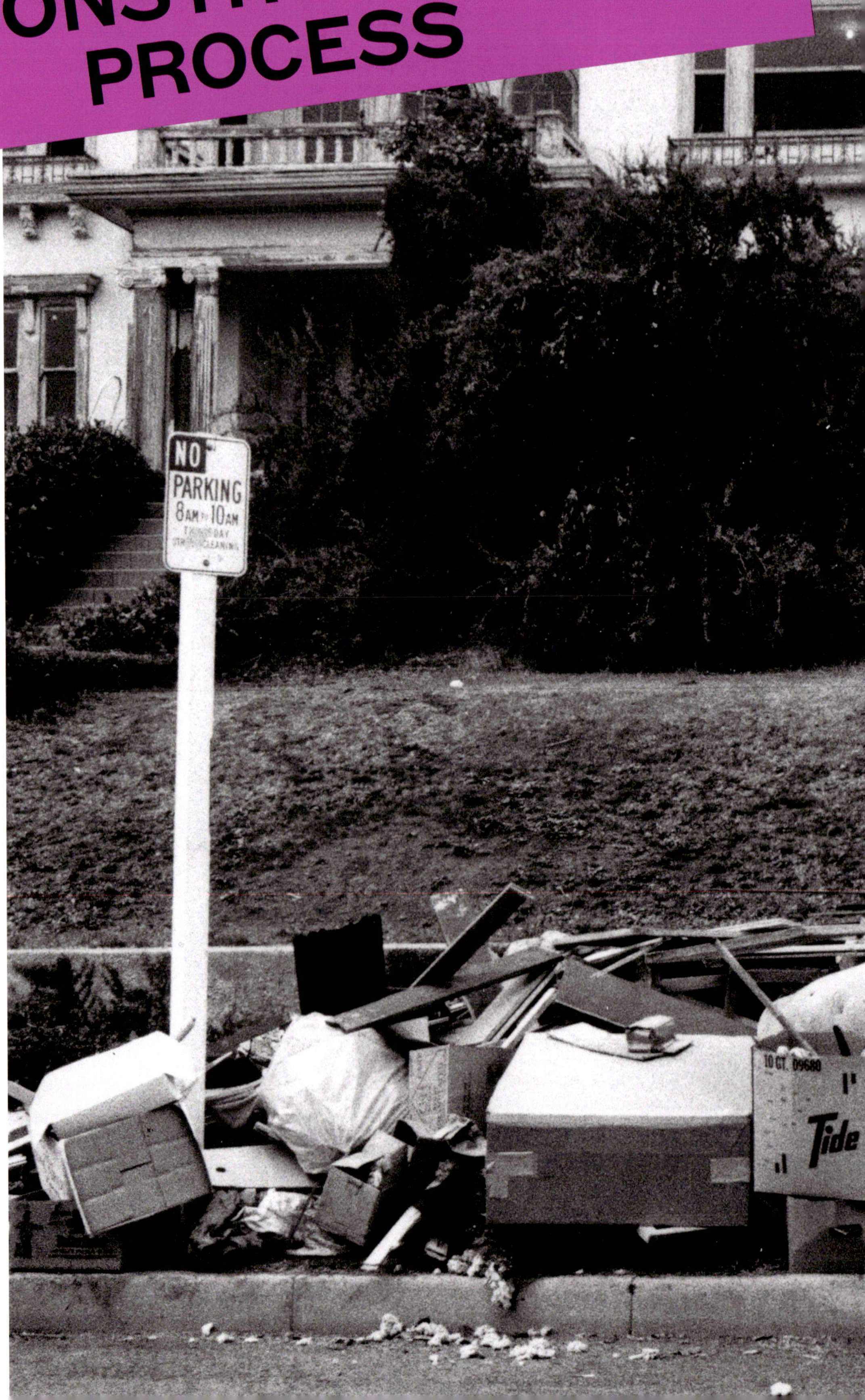

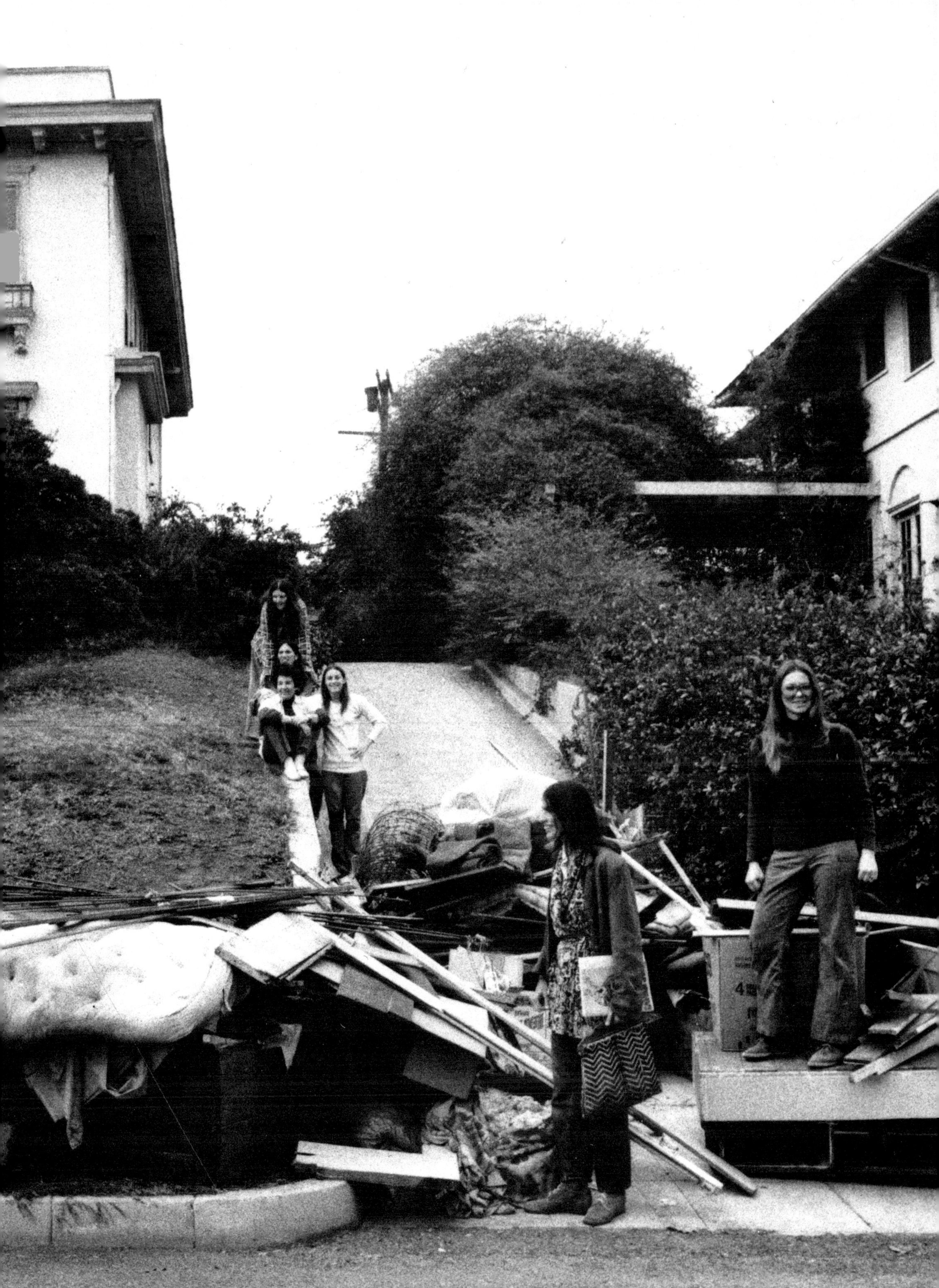

Over time, each of the 17 rooms were increasingly transformed according to their artistic needs. Additional work groups were formed; joining together in meetings, they talked about their struggles and difficulties, as well as their feelings about the project and possible expectations.[5] The construction took place from November 1971 to January 1972.[6]

For the project, a suitable detached house was needed. After extensive research the *Womanhouse* group found a 75-year-old condemned mansion at 533 N. Mariposa Street in a rundown section of Hollywood, L.A., in California. The house included 17 rooms. After asking numerous neighbors about the owner of the property and being told that the elderly lady possessing the house would never be interested in their project, they went to the Hall of Records to find the owner's name—Amanda Psalter—and wrote her a letter. The Psalter family was intrigued by their intentions and, in response, granted the group the house through a special lease agreement for the three-month duration of the project. After *Womanhouse* was finished the house would finally be pulled down.[2]

There was a lot for the 22 students to do when starting *Womanhouse*. In general, but especially for the art project, the house was in need of extensive reconstruction. "Vandals had broken windows, fixtures and furnishing required replacement. There was no hot water, heat, or plumbing."[3] As they started in November, when it was cold, they needed to fix all these problems in advance before they could reconstruct the house. The tasks the women were confronted with, such as cleaning, painting, scraping, wallpapering walls, replacing windows, sanding floors, and installing lights, had never been part of art processes at the California Institute of the Arts (CalArts) and were completely new to most of them. They furthermore had to build new walls for practical and aesthetic reasons and hire a crew to advise them on basic electrical wiring, installing locks, and helping them paint the exterior of the house. The long working hours, usually eight hours a day or more, and the intensive physical labor were challenging, which some participants even "described as grueling."[4]

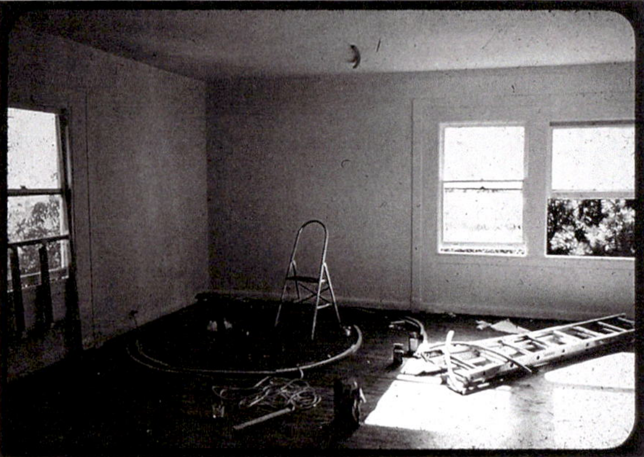

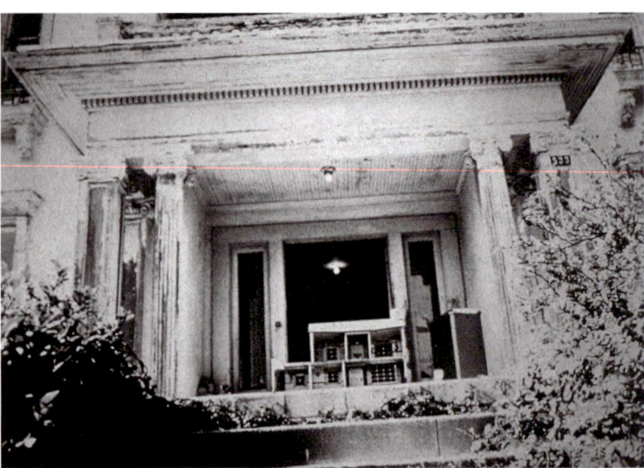

Previous spread: Exterior of *Womanhouse*. Work began on the house in the fall of 1971. Top to bottom: Janice Lester, Robin Schiff, Miriam Schapiro, Susan Frazier, standing in front: Christine Rush, unknown person on the right.
This page from top to bottom: *Womanhouse*, construction process (1971–72).
Entrance to *Womanhouse* before construction (1972).

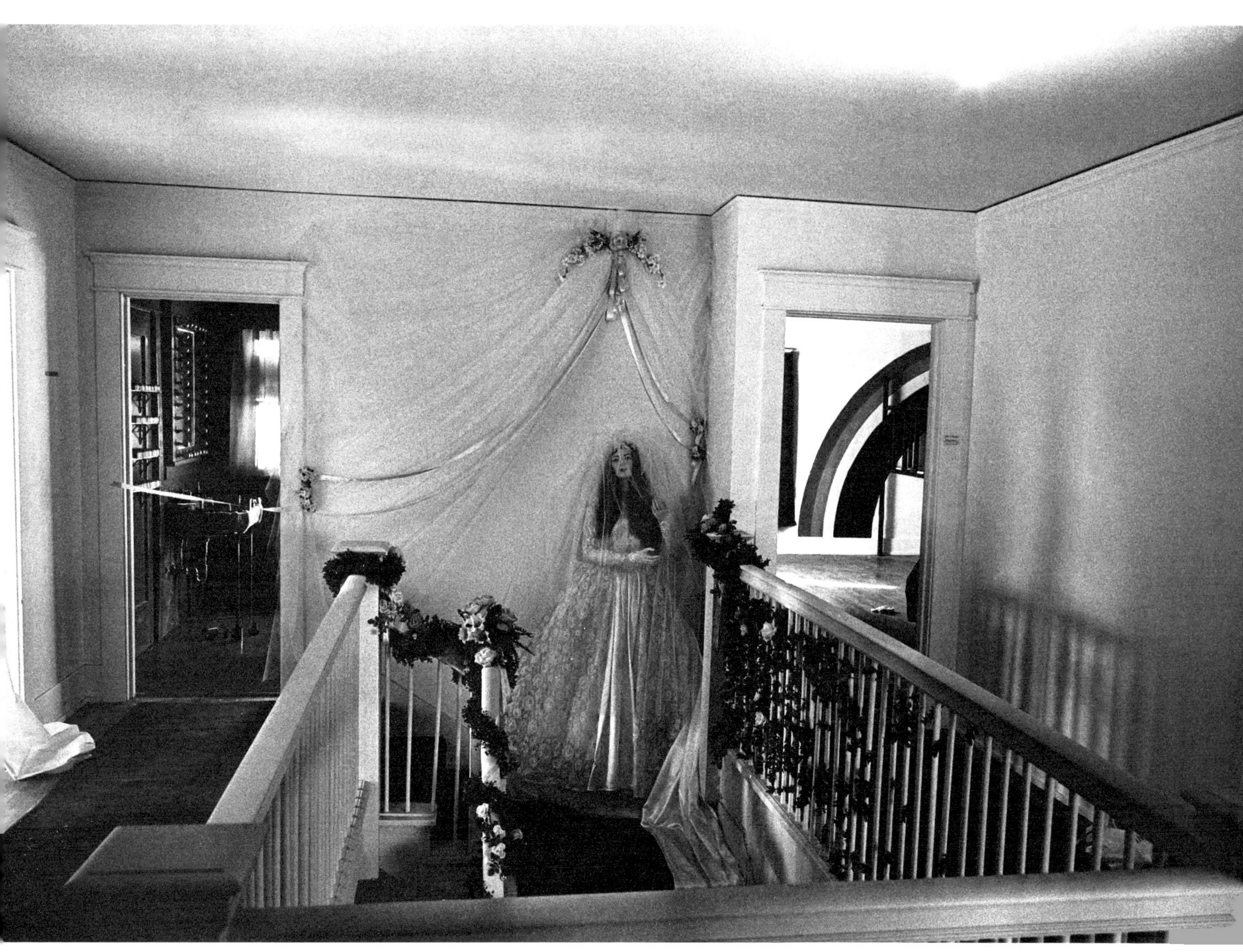

Kathy Huberland, *Womanhouse: Bridal Staircase* (1972).

PAULO FREIRE

PEDAGOGY of the OPPRESSED

• 30TH ANNIVERSARY EDITION •

Translated by Myra Bergman Ramos

With an Introduction by Donaldo Macedo

continuum
NEW YORK • LONDON

RESSED · 79

eatened by the specter

use of liberation are
climate which gener-
ceive its true signifi-
; then, they utilize
consider an effort
d as "innocents,"
ild challenge this
ple by alienating
nization—is not
raxis: the action
ld in order to
liberation can
s as an empty
f domination
on.

inking con-
and men
tent upon
osit-mak-
n beings
education, re-
ousness—intentionality—rejects
bodies communication. It epitomizes the spe-
characteristic of consciousness: being *conscious of*, not only as
intent on objects but as turned in upon itself in a Jasperian
"split"—consciousness as consciousness of consciousness.
Liberating education consists in acts of cognition, not transferrals
of information. It is a learning situation in which the cognizable
object (far from being the end of the cognitive act) intermediates
the cognitive actors—teacher on the one hand and students on the
other. Accordingly, the practice of problem-posing education entails
at the outset that the teacher-student contradiction to be resolved.
Dialogical relations—indispensable to the capacity of cognitive

actors to cooperate in perceiving the same cognizable object—are
otherwise impossible.

Indeed, problem-posing education, which breaks with the vertical
patterns characteristic of banking education, can fulfill its function
as the practice of freedom only if it can overcome the above contradiction. Through dialogue, the teacher-of-the-students and the stu-
dents-of-the-teacher cease to exist and a ... emerges: teacher-
... student with students-teachers. The t...
the-one-who-teaches, but one who is hi...
the students, who in turn while bein...
come jointly responsible for a proce...
process, arguments based on "authori...
to function, authority must be *on t*...
it. Here, no one teaches another, n...
teach each other, mediated by the...
which in banking education are "...

The banking concept (with its...
thing) distinguishes two stages in...
the first, he cognizes a cognizab...
sons in his study or his laborato...
to his students about that obje...
to know, but to memorize the...
do the students practice any...
wards which that act shoul...
teacher rather than a medi...
teacher and students. Her...
culture and knowledge" v...
true knowledge nor true...

The problem posing m...
the teacher-student: she...
tive" at another. She is a...
ect or engaging in dial...
cognizable objects as...
flection by himself an...
educator constantly ...

students. The students—no longer docile listeners—are now critical
co-investigators in dialogue with the teacher. The teacher presents
the material to the students for their consideration, and re-considers
her earlier considerations as the students express their own. The
role of the problem-posing educator is to create; together with the
students, the conditions under which knowledge at the level of the
doxa is superseded by true knowledge, at the level of the *logos*.

Whereas banking education anesthetizes and inhibits creative
power, problem-posing education involves a constant unveiling of
reality. The former attempts to maintain the *submersion* of consciousness; the latter strives for the *emergence of consciousness and
critical intervention* in reality.

Students, as they are increasingly posed with problems relating
to themselves in the world and with the world, will feel increasingly
challenged and obliged to respond to that challenge. Because they
apprehend the challenge as interrelated to other problems within a
total context, not as a theoretical question, the resulting comprehension tends to be increasingly critical and thus constantly less alien-
ated. Their response to the challenge evokes new challenges,
followed by new understandings; and gradually the students come
to regard themselves as committed.

Education as the practice of freedom—as opposed to education
as the practice of domination—denies that man is abstract, isolated,
independent, and unattached to the world; it also denies that the
world exists as a reality apart from people. Authentic reflection considers neither abstract man nor the world without people, but people in their relations with the world. In these relations consciousness
and world are simultaneous: consciousness neither precedes the
world nor follows it.

> La conscience et le monde sont donnés d'un même coup: exté-
> rieur par essence à la conscience, le monde est, par essence re-
> latif à elle.[8]

8. Sartre; *op. cit.*, p. 32.

MIRIAM SCHAPIRO

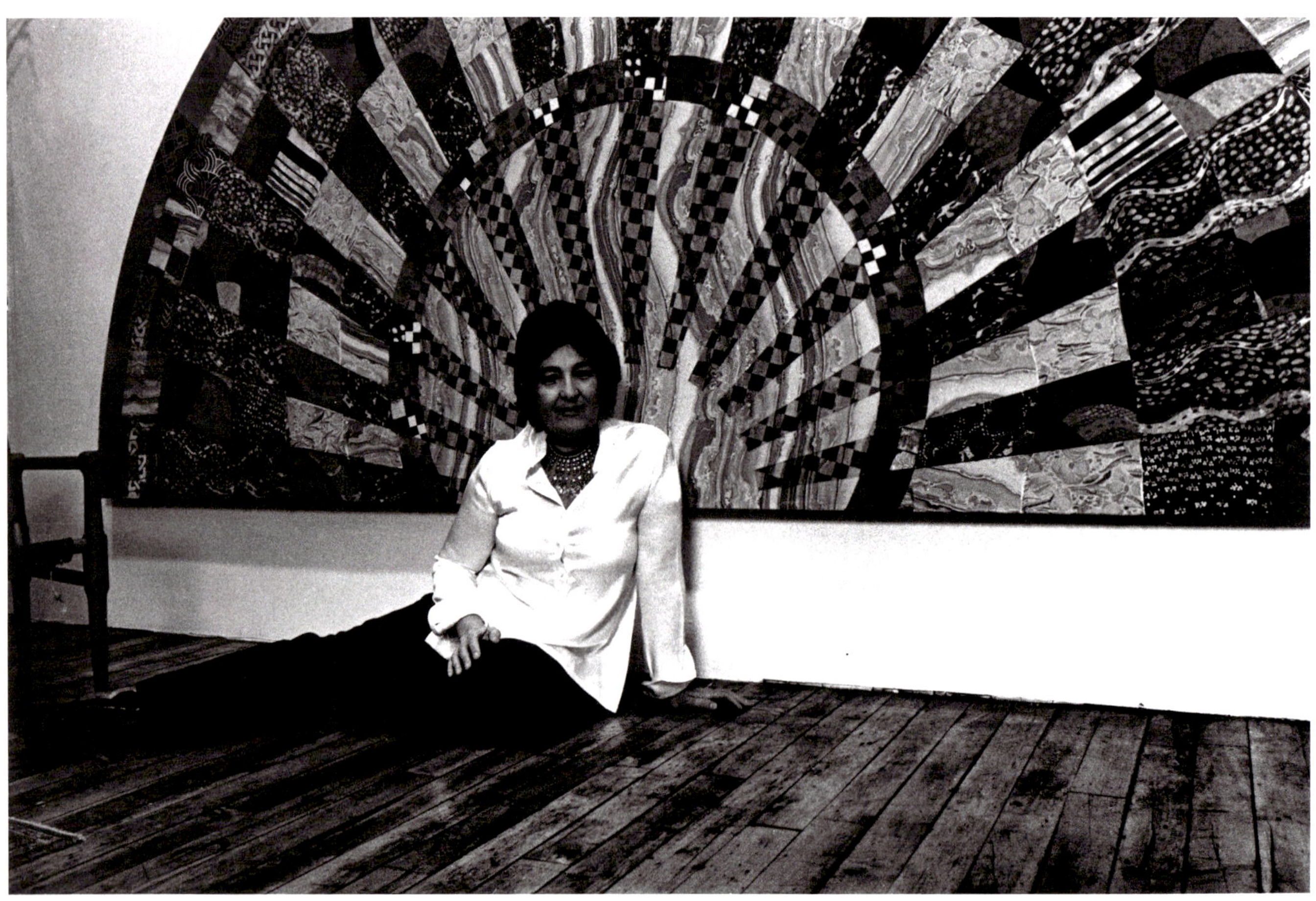

* November 15, 1923, Toronto, Canada
† June 20, 2015, Hampton Bays (NY), USA

was an American artist with Canadian roots, well-known for her paintings, sculptures, prints, and influences on the feminist art movement. Her early career as a painter started in the 1950s, as part of the second generation of abstract expressionism and hard-edge painting predominated by men. Schapiro's artistic development led to an inclusion and revitalization of methods, materials, and imagery of "woman's work"[1]—traditionally feminine crafts like sewing, quilting, or fabric and wallpaper design—to integrate them into Fine Art. She developed a singular aesthetic by combining the forms and brushwork of her earlier painting styles with "a body of work that addressed the uniqueness of female identity."[2] She had a formative influence on 'femmage,' which includes techniques like both assemblage, collage, or montage, and the usage of mixed media.[3] Schapiro was a faculty member at the California Institute of the Arts (CalArts), where she co-founded the Feminist Art Program with Judy Chicago in 1971 and co-initiated the project *Womanhouse* (1972).[4] Further important visual works are her *Shrine* series (1963), *Collaboration* series (1975–76), *Gates of Paradise* (1980), and *Agony in the Garden* (1991).[5]

She has received a lifetime achievement award from the College Art Association, among other honors. Schapiro's work has been shown in many art institutions and is held in several collections, including the National Gallery of Art and the Smithsonian American Art Museum, Washington, D.C., the Whitney Museum of Art, and the MoMA, N.Y., as well as the Australian National Gallery, Canberra.[6] In 2016, there was a retrospective solo exhibition of her work entitled *Miriam Schapiro: The California Years, 1967–1975* at Eric Firestone Gallery, N.Y. Upcoming in 2019, L.A.'s MoCA will feature her work in the *Pattern and Decoration* exhibition.[7] **LB**

Miriam Schapiro, portrait.

MEMORY THEATER

A project by Kim Albrecht and Jeffrey Schnapp, metaLAB (at) Harvard

The Feminist Art Program (FAP) at the California Institute of the Arts (CalArts) was barely three months old when, in November 1971, work commenced on the program's inaugural exhibition project. From the start, provisionality, process, teaching by example, conversation, happenings, and live performances were its touchstones. Action (not memory), provocation (not permanence) were the values that sought to hurl not centripetally at CalArts but centrifugally at the city of Los Angeles and at the world beyond.

The choice of venue was a once-patrician, now-run-down mansion slated for demolition at 533 North Mariposa Avenue in East Hollywood: some 34 miles from the CalArts's sparkling new Valencia campus. After months of student and teacher mopping, sanding, wallpapering, painting, plastering, and installing, this repurposed, imperiled domestic space opened to the public between January 30 and February 28, 1972. Rechristened, it garnered more than its share of attention from the public and press; though, after closing, it mostly faded into the collective memory as 'a precedent.' This is in part because one year later the Feminist Art Program lost one of its founders, the artist Judy Chicago, who, along with her colleagues, the graphic designer Sheila Levrant de Bretteville and the art historian Arlene Raven, departed CalArts to continue their journey downtown. There they founded a more enduring institution: the Los Angeles Woman's Building which operated continuously in diverse locations between 1973 and 1991. Other womanhouses and women's buildings were established elsewhere, from San Francisco to New York, as well as across the Atlantic. Soon enough, the mansion at 533 North Mariposa was no more. The current site is occupied by a characterless apartment complex, free from historical markers.

Enshrined in cultural memory as a pivotal event thanks, in part, to a one-hour documentary shot by Johanna Demetrakas, *Womanhouse* was never intended as a destination. Rather, it was devised as a momentary place of passage towards a new social and institutional order, where the "repository of the daydreams women have as they wash, bake, cook, sew, clean, and iron their lives away" could be "taken to fantasy proportions;"[1] a place of convening where women artists in the making could hang their work alongside that of more established artists (like Sherry Brody); and a laboratory where the feminist future could be incubated in the very space where patriarchal tenets

continued to find their firmest hold: the household. Nor was it ever intended as just a safe house. Discomfort and ephemerality were integral features of a pedagogy that sought to help "women to restructure their personalities to be more consistent with the desires to be artists and to help them build their art making out of the experiences as women."[2] This meant operating power tools, making politically pointed site-specific art, teaching and learning, and moving on.

Repositories of daydreams tend to leave only the frailest of documentary trails and *Womanhouse* is no exception. So, in compiling the layouts on the following pages, we have brought together an assortment of materials. Maps drawn from memory by two participants (Faith Wilding and Nancy Youdelman) 47 years later provide a mnemonic grid for each of the two floors at 533 North Mariposa Avenue and how they were programmed. Documentary photographs fill in the 'rooms.' Press clippings chart the reception history of the event as it unfolded and how the media understood and represented the various rooms that composed the house. It is the bare beginnings of a gossamer memory theater whose construction is still very much a work in progress.

THE FOLLOWING MAPS ARE DRAWN BY THE FAP ALUMNAE FAITH WILDING AND NANCY YOUDELMAN 47 YEARS AFTER *WOMANHOUSE*

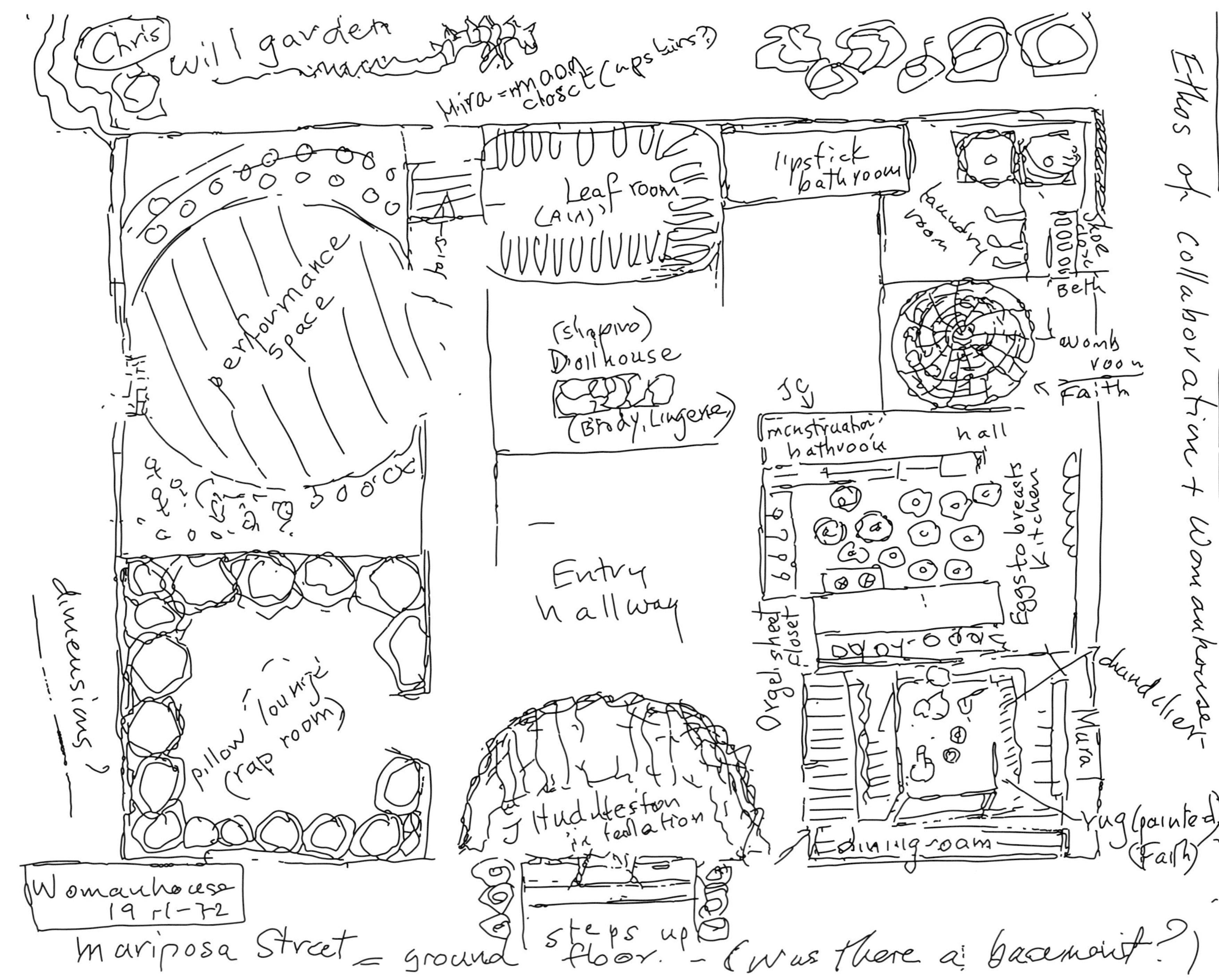

Chris
Will garden
Miriam
Mira = womxn closet (upstairs?)
Leaf room (Air)
lipstick bathroom
laundry room
Beth
Shoe closet
performance space
(Shapiro) Dollhouse (Brody, Lingerie)
JC
menstruation bathroom
hall
womb room
Faith
Eggs to breasts Kitchen
Entry hallway
Orgel sheet closet
chandelier
dimensions?
pillow lounge (rap room)
J Huddleston in installation
Mural
dining room
rug (painted) (faith)
Womanhouse 1971-72
Mariposa Street = ground floor — steps up (Was there a basement?)
Ethos of collaboration + Womanhouse

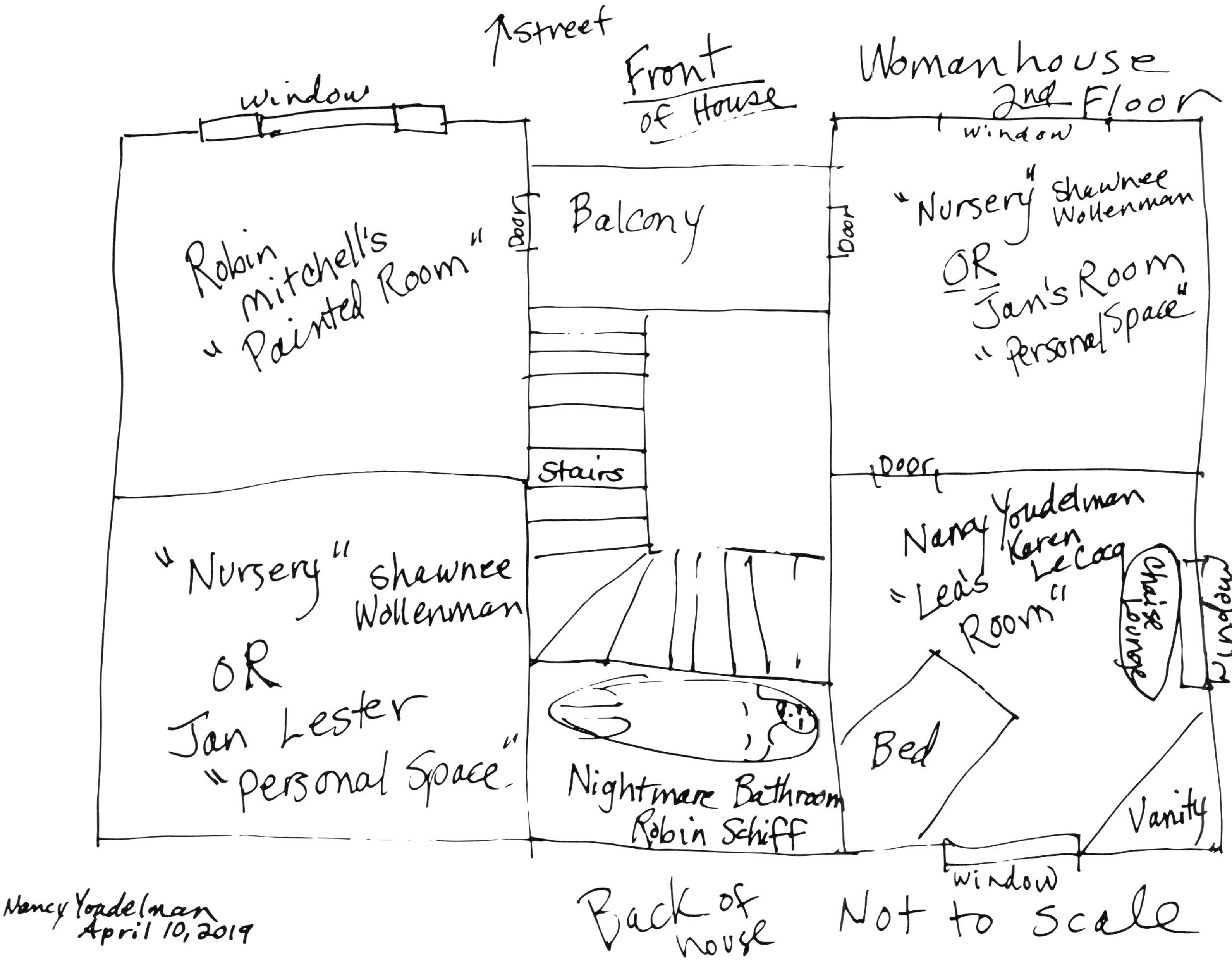

↑ Street
Front of House
Woman house 2nd Floor
window
window
Robin mitchell's "Painted Room"
Balcony
Door
Door
"Nursery" Shawnee Wollenman
OR
Jan's Room
"Personal Space"
Stairs
Door
"Nursery" Shawnee Wollenman
OR
Jan Lester
"personal Space"
Nancy Youdelman Karen LeCocq
"Lea's Room"
Chaise Lounge
window
Nightmare Bathroom Robin Schiff
Bed
Vanity
window
Back of house
Not to Scale
Nancy Youdelman
April 10, 2019

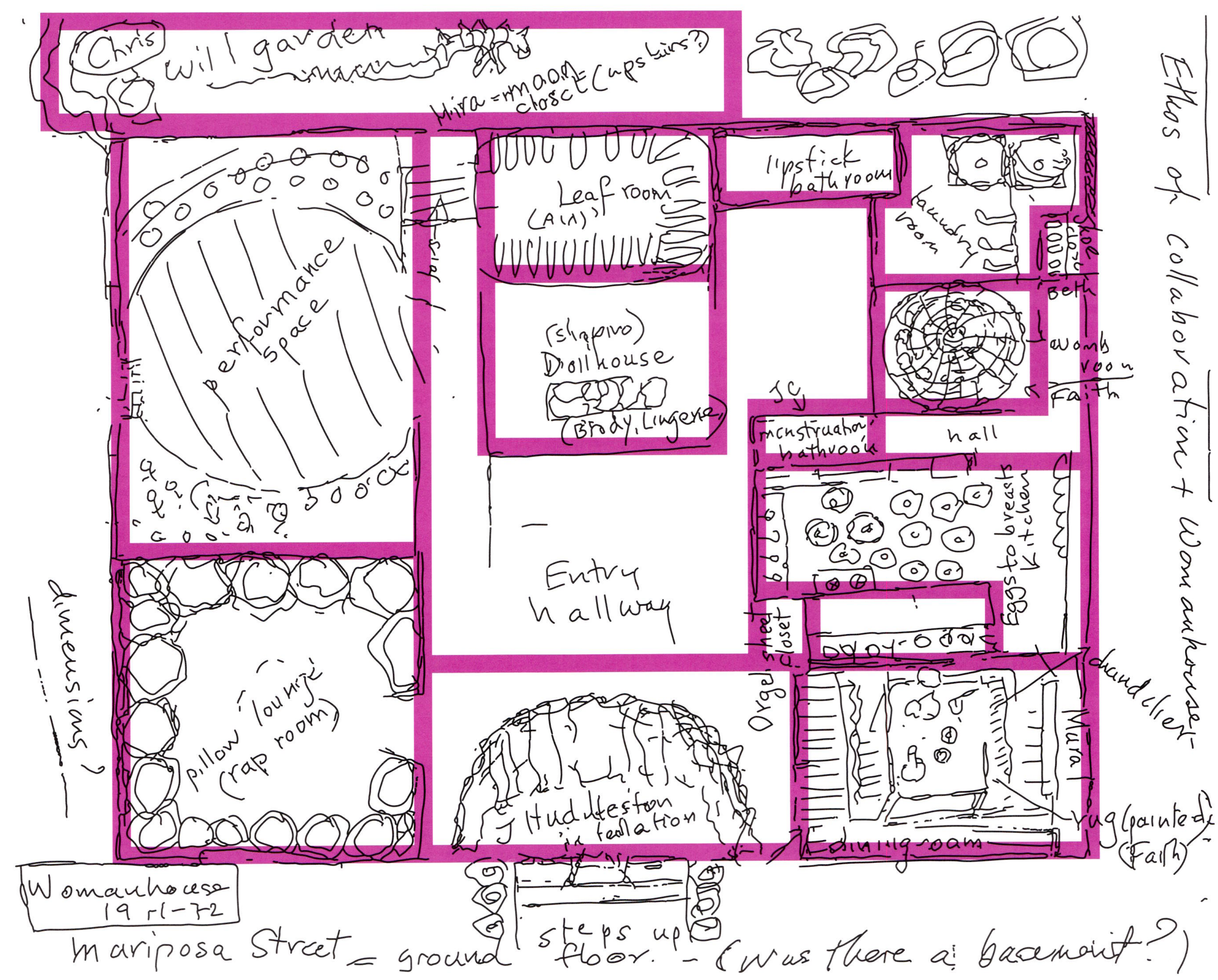

Chris will garden
Mira = moon closet (upstairs?)
Ethos of collaboration + Womanhouse
Leaf room (Cain)
lipstick bathroom
laundry room
shoe closet Beth
(Shapiro) Dollhouse (Brady Lingerie)
womb room Faith
performance space
JC
menstruation bathroom
hall
Eggs to breasts Kitchen
Entry hallway
Orgel sheet closet
chandelier
dimensions?
pillow lounge (rap room)
Huddleston installation
Mura
rug (painted) (Faith)
dining room
Womanhouse 1971-72
mariposa Street = ground floor. steps up - (was there a basement?)
48

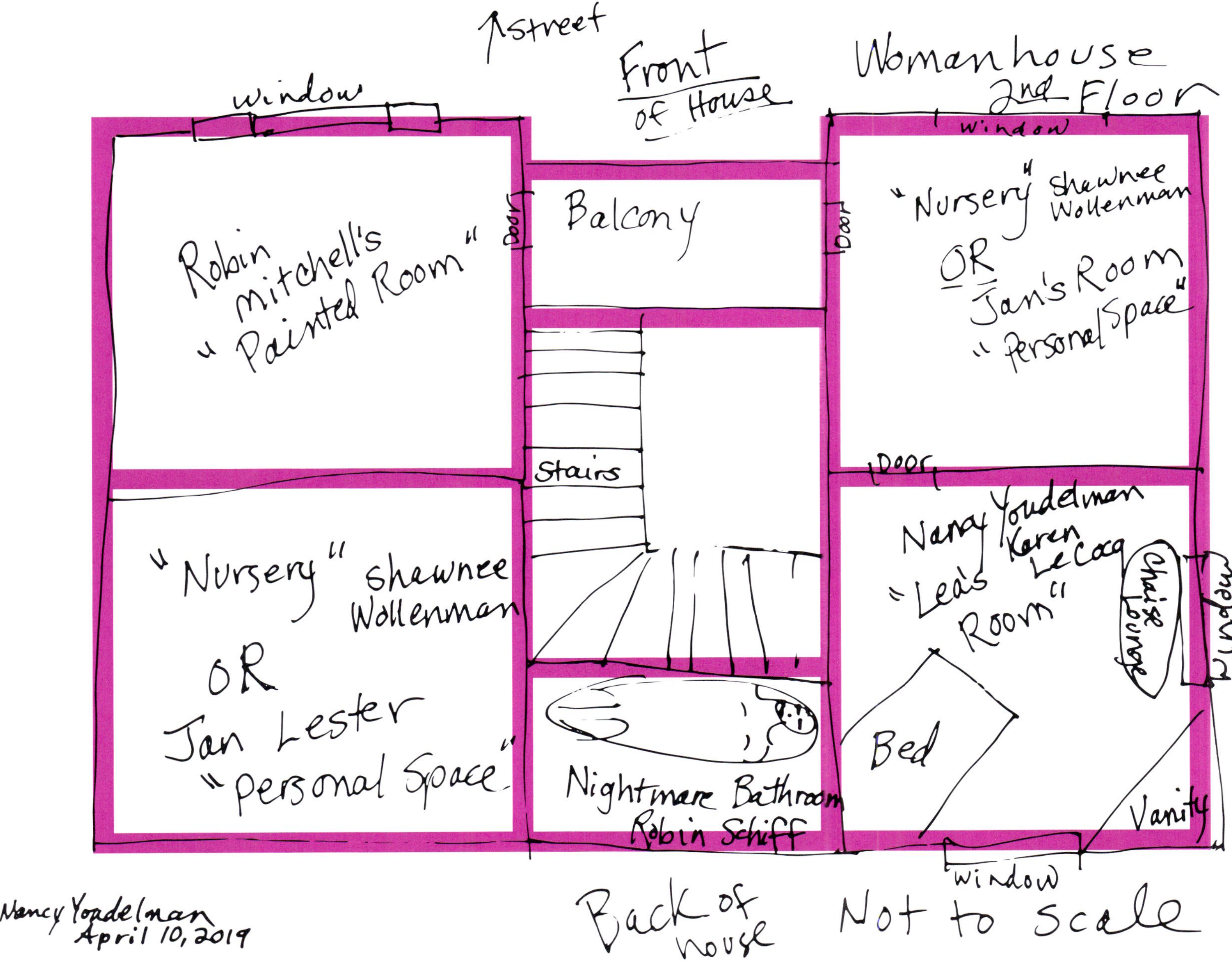

↑ Street
Front of House
Womanhouse 2nd Floor
window
window
Robin mitchell's "Painted Room"
Balcony
Door
Door
"Nursery" Shawnee Wollenman OR Jan's Room "Personal Space"
Stairs
Door
"Nursery" Shawnee Wollenman OR Jan Lester "personal Space"
Nancy Youdelman Karen LeCocq "Lea's Room"
Chaise Lounge
window
Bed
Nightmare Bathroom Robin Schiff
Vanity
window
Nancy Youdelman April 10, 2019
Back of house
Not to Scale

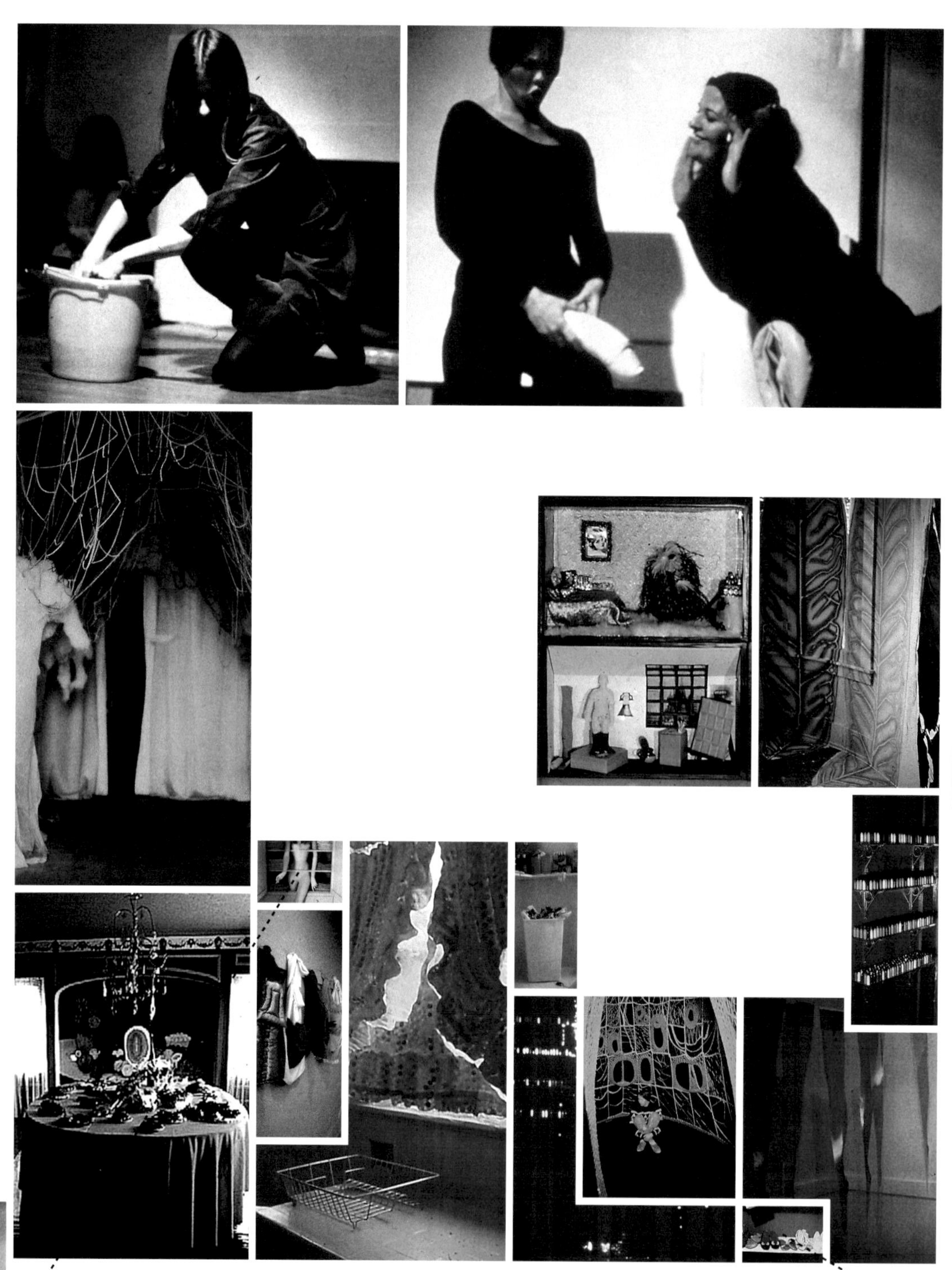

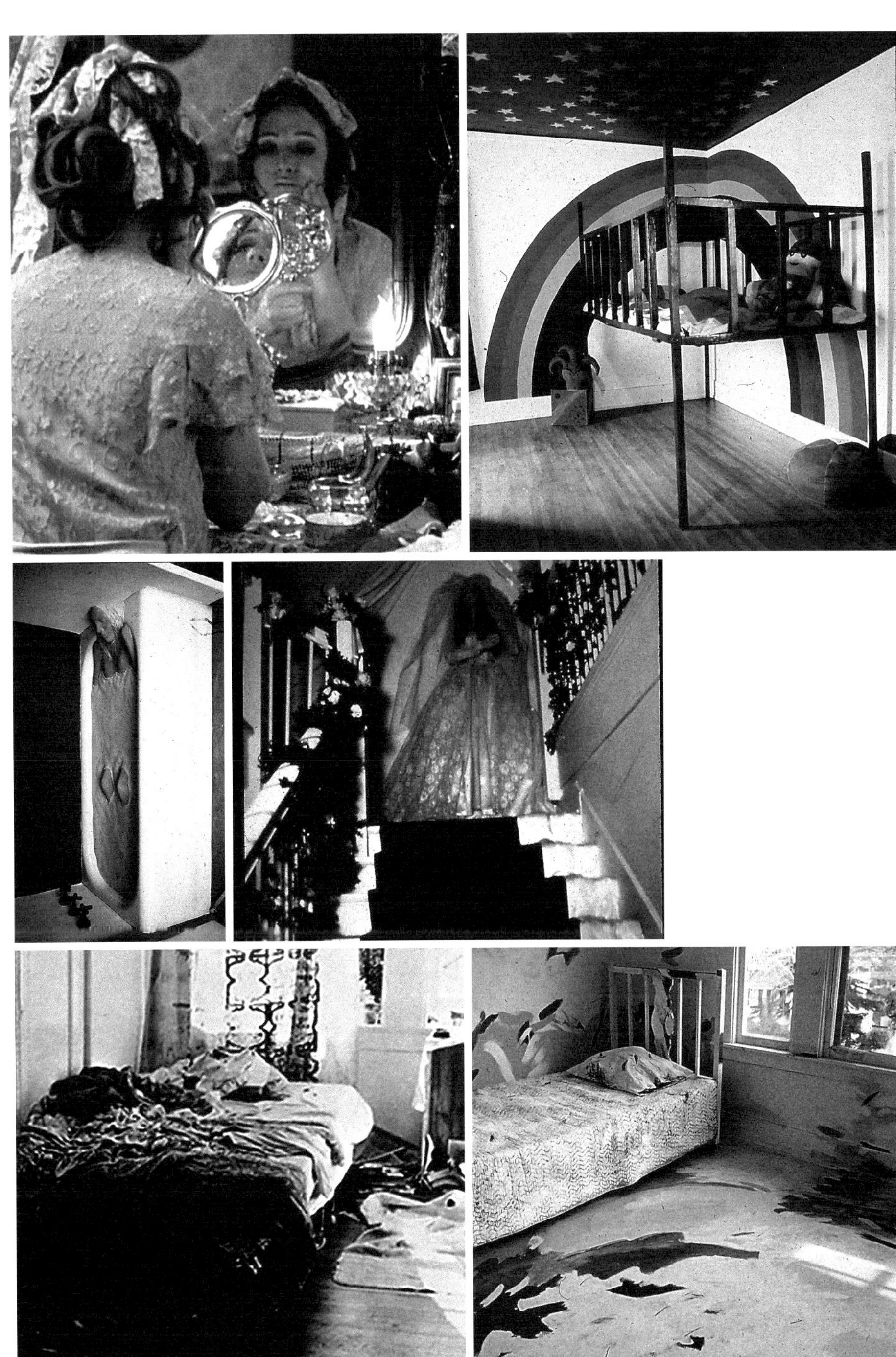

gender as a construct based on the body.

The myth that women find enjoyment and fulfillment through housework was also the subject of two "maintenance" pieces: *Scrubbing*, performed by Chris Rush, and *Ironing* (Fig. 5), performed by Sandra Orgel.[21] The stage directions were as follows: "A woman is scrubbing the floor on her hands and knees. All fours. Back and forth, over and over, her arms circle and circle the floor in continuous motion scrubbing with a brush and plenty of elbow grease. Later another woman irons a sheet, then another. Or is it the same sheet? Then another."[22] Breaking down, isolating, and performing such monotonous, banal (and dehumanizing) chores for an audience served to foreground the performative nature of the tasks and their role in the construction of gender, radically undercutting their ideological power. In the process of questioning the domestic arena, the artists involved in *Womanhouse* revealed the underlying patriarchal expectations that governed the domestic sphere during this period as a first step to reclaiming the space on their own terms, or even abandoning it altogether as a patriarchal fiction that had been outgrown—much like a dollhouse.

HE But you don't have a cock! (grasps cock and begins stroking it proudly)

SHE What's that got to do with?

HE A cock means you don't wash dishes. You have a cunt. A cunt means you wash dishes.

SHE (looking at cunt) I don't see where it says that on my cunt.

HE (pointing at her cunt) Stu-upid, your cunt/pussy/gash/hole or whatever it is, is round like a dish. Therefore it's only right for you to wash dishes. My cock is long and hard and straight and is meant to shoot like guns or missiles. Anyone can see that (strokes cock on each emphasis).[16]

Moreover, every contributor to Womanhouse was forever changed by the experience. Each felt taken apart and put back together, but altogether differently. T[…] self-image, self-esteem, and artistic i[…] uals in the group to such an extent t[…] launched on challenging personal an[…]

Abandoned and condemned, the […] nue was still architecturally imposing […] extensive reconstruction. Vandals ha[…] and furnishings required replacem[…] water, heat, or plumbing. In Nov[…] when the […] the hou[…] nount of […] Another […] CalArts Progr[…]

Marsha Salisbury and a fantasy dollhouse by Sherry Brody with its aspirations of a sultanic bedroom and touching young-woman's doubts about monsters in the nursery.

Womanhouse is pervaded with the spirit of comfort and magic that women bring to living, their endless inventiveness, bottomless energy and gentle pervasive humor.

Judy Chicago's "Men-[…] whether or n[…] "Cunt Art" […] out of rol[…]

---

vironment. Most rooms retain the guise of traditional functions but are painted in hues that would do justice to an Easter egg.

The dining room table is laid with a feast of painted plaster food. The flamingo pink of the kitchen engulfs even the cream-of-wheat boxes. Ceiling and walls are decorated with sunnyside eggs that shade into sponge-rubber breasts. A nursery by Shawnee Wollenman turns us all back into infants with its oversize crib and toys.

---

white, middle-class, housewife as happily devoted to serving the needs of others, most evident in *Nurturant Kitchen* (Fig. 4) by Susan Frazier, Vicki Hodgetts, and Robin Weltsch. Applied egg forms on the ceiling gradually become breasts moving down the wall, eventually surrounding the other sources of nutrition found on the shelves of food and in the refrigerator. These items underscore the traditional role of the female as nurturer as do the increasingly sagging breasts that reference the physiological changes attendant upon breastfeeding. The parody of the kitchen, however, reveals these expectations to be monotonous and burdensome. This was shown not only by the elision of difference between the housewife and the room itself—both have breasts—but was also reinforced in the adjoining pantry. Here the viewer saw a repetitive assembly line of dishes prepared for the

obviously addressed in the two rooms on the middle floor, dressing room and the bedroom, both of which contain b[…] In a subversive remaking of these spaces, Brody and Scha[…] expose the role of the housewife as a sex object during a per[…] when such women were expected to have few interests outs[…] the domestic arena. Nominally a woman's private space, […] dressing room is devoted to the wife's ongoing concern w[…] beauty and the effects of aging in order to satisfy her husb[…] in the adjacent bedroom. Moreover, a framed photograph […] movie star represents the impossible beauty ideals tow[…] which women strived. The woman's diminutive size and […] position at the dressing table indicate her status in the ho[…] especially in contrast to the much larger, upright male fig[…] above. The bedroom, significantly named "The Seragl[…] suggests an exotic setting where harems were kept, comp[…] with carpeted walls, brightly patterned bed coverings, pill[…]

ic protection and hope that she can d[…] order to maintain her security.

Lipstick Bathroom by Camille Grey, and *Shoe Closet* (Fig. 3) by Beth Bachenheimer reinforced the association of the female with makeup, beauty, and self-display for the pleasure of a male partner. The extravagant number of shoes in the closet (excessive in an early-1970s, pre–Carrie Bradshaw context), like the fiery lipstick-red bathroom, underscored women's sometimes-frantic attempts to meet societal expectations to be beautiful and fashionable. The parodic exaggeration in the two rooms exposed the construction

room, complete with a basket[…] r. These rooms led off fro[…] stockings preserved in plast[…] ds overflowed from the sink[…] room more museum-like than e[…] house and miniature pillow[…] animal motifs were abundant[…] ing through the window at th[…] rds pecking in the bedroom, […] leaves stretching from floo[…]

not yet finished. The tour continued up a staircase draped
with plastic flowers. A bride model posed on the landing.
The second floor included unfinished murals and baby's rooms
with a gigantic crib; a room full of shoes in horrifying and
funny colors; a linen closet with a macabre model pinned between the freshly starched piles of sheets and pillowcases;
a bedroom painted on the floors, chair and bed as well as the
walls, a blood red bathroom with lipstick displays and soft
furry sink, toilet and bath; a second bathroom with ominous
sand-filled bottles and a sand-filled bathtub with a sand
woman in it; and a bedroom based on Cheri by Colette, complete with a performer putting on layer after layer of make-
up to age herself beside the oppressive lace bed.

After the tours, women were led into the living room to
wait for performances arranged by Judy Chicago. Most of the
performances arose from consciousness-raising sessions at the
feminist programs both at Fresno and California Institute of
the Arts. Three girls exchanged their stories about the tra-
gic episodes of their lives; one woman ironed a sheet; one
woman scrubbed the performance area floor; several danced thei
births through long red tassled arms. Particularly moving was

WOMAN AS ARTIST

Bridal Staircase

Picking favorites is a bit
unfair here since every individual pleasure is part of
an ever-increasing veloci-
ty of, well, sweetness at its
best. All the same I especially liked the unexpected b r i d a l staircase by
K a t h y Huberland a n d
Marsha Salisbury and a
fantasy dollhouse by Sher-

parodied in several rooms in *Womanhouse*. The longing to look
beautiful and the concomitant fear of aging associated with the
white, middle-class housewife was movingly addressed in *Leah's
Room* (Fig. 2), created by Karen LeCoq and Nancy Youdelman.
The space was a watermelon-pink bedroom inhabited by Léa, a
character from Colette's novel, *Chéri* (1920), about an aging courtesan.[18] Though stunning in her youth, as Léa ages, her young
lover, Chéri, loses interest. In the continuous daily performances,
visitors encountered Léa sitting at a dressing table meticulously
applying makeup, then removing it in dissatisfaction, only to
begin again in her futile effort to remain youthful looking.
According to Butler, subject formation takes place specifically as
the "incorporation of norms,"[20] and it is precisely this internaliza-
tion of expectations that is being explored in this piece. The
repetitive nature of the performance in *Leah's Room* reveals the
application of makeup by white, middle-class housewives as a
performance done for men as well as for their own internalized
narratives about what constitutes the feminine and the beautiful.
The underlying suggestion, that the housewife is to be constantly
sexually available, is made overt here by the fact that Léa is a
high-priced courtesan. The housewife, not encouraged to pursue

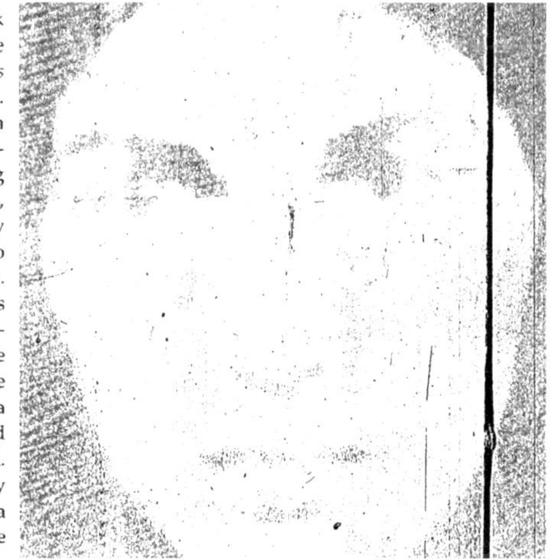

INTERVIEW WITH KIM ALBRECHT & JEFFREY SCHNAPP

Jeffrey Schnapp is a cultural historian, designer, and curator, who in 2011 founded metaLAB (at) Harvard, a coalition of experimental researchers from various fields with an interest in the digital arts, design, and humanities. The visual researcher and information designer Kim Albrecht joined the team in 2017 and since then has been an integral part of the cluster. Reflecting on historical and contemporary memory and knowledge cultures, for *Tacit Knowledge* they developed experimental formats to visualize diverse strands of narration revolving around the California Institute of the Arts (CalArts) in its past decades, its protagonists, and projects; first and foremost, the art environment *Womanhouse* collaboratively created by the members of CalArts's Feminist Art Program and almost completely destroyed after its exhibition. Based upon floorplan sketches of *Womanhouse* drawn by the former participants Nancy Youdelman and Faith Wilding from their memories 47 years later, *Memory Theater* offers alternative, very personal storylines of the feminist art project. *CalArts Data Portraiture*, moreover, compares the portrayal of the art school through the open data platform Wikidata against narrations created by art historians and researchers. In this interview, Jeffrey Schnapp and Kim Albrecht give insights into their approaches to the projects and the leading ideas behind them. They furthermore discuss possibilities and forms of knowledge production in digital open data networks and share their curatorial vision for the exhibition of ephemeral arts.

VERENA KITTEL   Jeffrey, as the founder of the 'knowledge-design lab,' could you tell us more about metaLAB, its direction, and concept?

JEFFREY SCHNAPP   metaLAB is an experimental platform founded in January 2011 committed to modeling new forms of cultural communication, creative/critical practice, and scientific knowledge production. Some of our core concerns involve reimagining libraries, archives, and museums for the 21st century; critical and creative uses of AI in the cultural field; database storytelling and critical visualization practices; forms of pedagogy that wed the hand to the mind; and experimental publishing (from print to digital). metaLAB is part of the Berkman Klein Center for Internet and Society at Harvard, where we see ourselves as a catalyst for change across faculties and disciplines. I coined the phrase 'knowledge design' to suggest a higher set of ambitions than, say, 'digital humanities' or 'civic humanities.'

VK   Kim and Jeffrey, with *Memory Theater* and *CalArts Data Portraiture* you provide and weave together alternative narratives about CalArts and its protagonists, particularly of the legendary art and exhibition project *Womanhouse*. Can you describe your approach to *Memory Theater*? Why did you choose to do a project on *Womanhouse*?

JS   *Womanhouse* has rightly become a standard point of reference in the historiography of feminist art. It crystallizes all the energies, powers, personalities, and contradictions of the community that (however briefly) assembled around CalArts during the initial years and went on to reshape both activism and art practice during subsequent decades. Its very ephemerality renders it a fascinatingly paradoxical 'founding' moment. The run-down 17 room mansion at 533 North Mariposa Avenue was chosen precisely because it was condemned for demolition. It was less a home than a ruin with a wrecking ball in its immediate future. And the one-month occupation under the *Womanhouse* banner was a constant work in progress. It involved both stable built-in components (none of which survived), a constantly shifting set of programs and events, and served as a momentary community center … all of which made it place of *process* rather than *product*. One result is that the memory trails, both contemporary and successive, that document *Womanhouse* tend to be selective, partial, and incomplete. This provided a direct inspiration for our mappings. They seek to translate into visual form this process of gathering and scattering: whether of persons, rooms, careers, reputations, bodies of belief. Our interest fell as much on meaningful gaps as well as on the most significant connective nodes.

VK   Could you tell us more about the idea behind the mappings and their reference to the memory theaters evoked in the title of the project?

JS   Memory theaters were integral features of classical mnemotechnics. They were mental constructs designed to support a live oratorical performance, in which the sequencing of an argument was spatialized and associated with imaginary 'stations' of emotional intensity (fear, pleasure, etc.). There's, of course, no direct connection between *Womanhouse* and the memory palaces of the Renaissance. But the analogy struck me as productive because of the transitory character of *Womanhouse*, the key role played by performance and site-specific artworks that were subsequently dismantled, and the selective nature of the memory trails that it left in its wake—all the more so because we were unable to obtain the actual floor plans of 533 North Mariposa Avenue. The physical architecture of the site lives on only in the memory of its surviving participants, so 47 years after the event we asked several key participants to draw up floor plans entirely from memory. Naturally, they diverge very significantly from one another. Memories are like that; they are selective, unruly, even messy.

VK   According to Temma Balducci, one of the reasons why *Womanhouse* for a long time generated little scholarly interest lies in its ephemeral nature and thus difficulties to exhibit and communicate its events and its impact.[1] What, in your opinion, should the exhibition and archiving of ephemeral arts that counteract representational logics of exhibitions look like?

JS   This is a profound question, and one that I have thought about a great deal in my curatorial work in Italy *(Trento Tunnels, BZ '18–'45)*, as well as during the Stanford Humanities Lab's collaboration with Lynn Hershman Leeson in the mid-2000s *(Dante Hotel)*. Despite decades of critique and efforts to dismantle it, the object-centric bias of exhibition culture remains solidly in place. There are some good reasons for this tenacity of objects: among them, the fact that people visit galleries and museums in pursuit of the sorts of multisensorial experiences that are associated with, and usually most readily accessible via, physical originals (like most site-specific, performance, and installation art, *Womanhouse* didn't leave behind any such originals.) This said, there are curatorial strategies that infuse legacy originals with a sense of contingency and ephemerality and, conversely, bring ephemeral or performance-based work back to life without falling into the trap of recreating them. Among these, I am particularly interested in strategies that expose research problems rather than solutions; that place objects and materials that 'didn't make the cut' alongside the ones that did within the setting of an exhibition; and that creatively and critically interbreed and extend originals with copies. I suppose that I would define such strategies as rethinking the distinction between the archive and the museum. Is that a distinction that is productive anymore? I'm unsure that it is.

VK   Kim, how did the idea for *CalArts Data Portraiture* come about? Could you tell us more about your working process?

KIM ALBRECHT   The question we asked was: how do we, in our moment in time, capture the past? How do we remember the history of an institution like CalArts? Such historical traces are stored in archives, the individual's memories, in books, and narratives. But contemporary history is also preserved in the networked structures of databases. Computers, algorithms, graphical user interfaces, communication networks, and digital storage allow for alternative, non-linear stories and preservations of the past. Organizations mostly maintain archives; historical narratives are written by one or a small number of authors. The databases storing our digital preservation and the computation that allows access are often created by a large and obscured number of authors. First and foremost, anyone can add a website to the internet, and anyone can edit any Wikipedia article. In the context of *CalArts Data Portraiture*, we were interested in the portrayal of the history of CalArts from the perspective of our contemporary networked non-linear data structures. Such a view allows investigations into what is captured and at the same time, what has been left out. For our investigation, we looked into several perspectives the World Wide Web allows and settled on using Wikidata as a starting point. The platform is an open and editable knowledge database founded by the Wikimedia Foundation. Wikidata informs Wikipedia but also many other internet platforms, like for example the Google search infoboxes. It is a powerful and influential source of information apprising how we perceive entities such as CalArts on the internet. For *CalArts Data Portraiture*, we scraped all human individuals who are listed in Wikidata and either worked at CalArts or studied there. Nearly 500 individuals were listed in the database. Besides this, we scraped a large number of dimensions that Wikidata associated with these people, from birth and death date, their occupations, their influences, their descriptions on Wikipedia, degrees, employees, and many more data dimensions. The outcome of these historical traces are not linear stories anymore but networked associations of words and categorizations. The network allows for very different preservation of the past than writing does. To capture this, we used information visualization, the mapping of points, lines, areas, and text on the computer screen's two-dimensional surfaces, to get a sense for the scope of the history captured by Wikidata. We ended up with two static, printable visualizations, one timeline, and one networked list graphic capturing the data structure.

actor Ed Harris. Our graphical representations of the Wikidata entries allow us to question who is writing history and for what a purpose. How should we decide what we are capturing from the past, and what stays unmentioned? With the help of the research by Verena Kittel, we were able to add missing and outstanding individuals back into the visualizations. We are creating a display of the gap between a scholarly perspective on CalArts and the view of the database.

VK What are the opportunities and risks of using open knowledge platforms like Wikidata? How, in your opinion, do such projects influence our modes of knowledge production and our concept of knowledge in general?

KA Every medium shines through the realizations made with it. Writing and printed books offer a particular perspective on history. Reality is aggregated in words which are chained together in a linear narrative over time—the database is on the other side, as a networked structure of relations without linearity and predefined narrations. From any point in the network, we can get to any other position within a small number of leaps. But not only that, the way these structures are created is extraordinarily different from an author's perspective, including a vast and obscured set of edits. The history captured by the database gives a very different impression of the past than an article or book would. In the case of our work on the early years of CalArts, this manifested itself strongly. The discussions in the team very much focused on the work of Judy Chicago as one of the many figures and drivers of the Feminist Art Program, as well as John Baldessari, as the head of the Post-Studio class. Wikidata connected neither Judy Chicago nor John Baldessari to CalArts. Suddenly the history of CalArts was written by individuals like David Hasselhoff, Walt Disney chief creative officer John Lasseter, or Apollo 13

FAITH WILDING

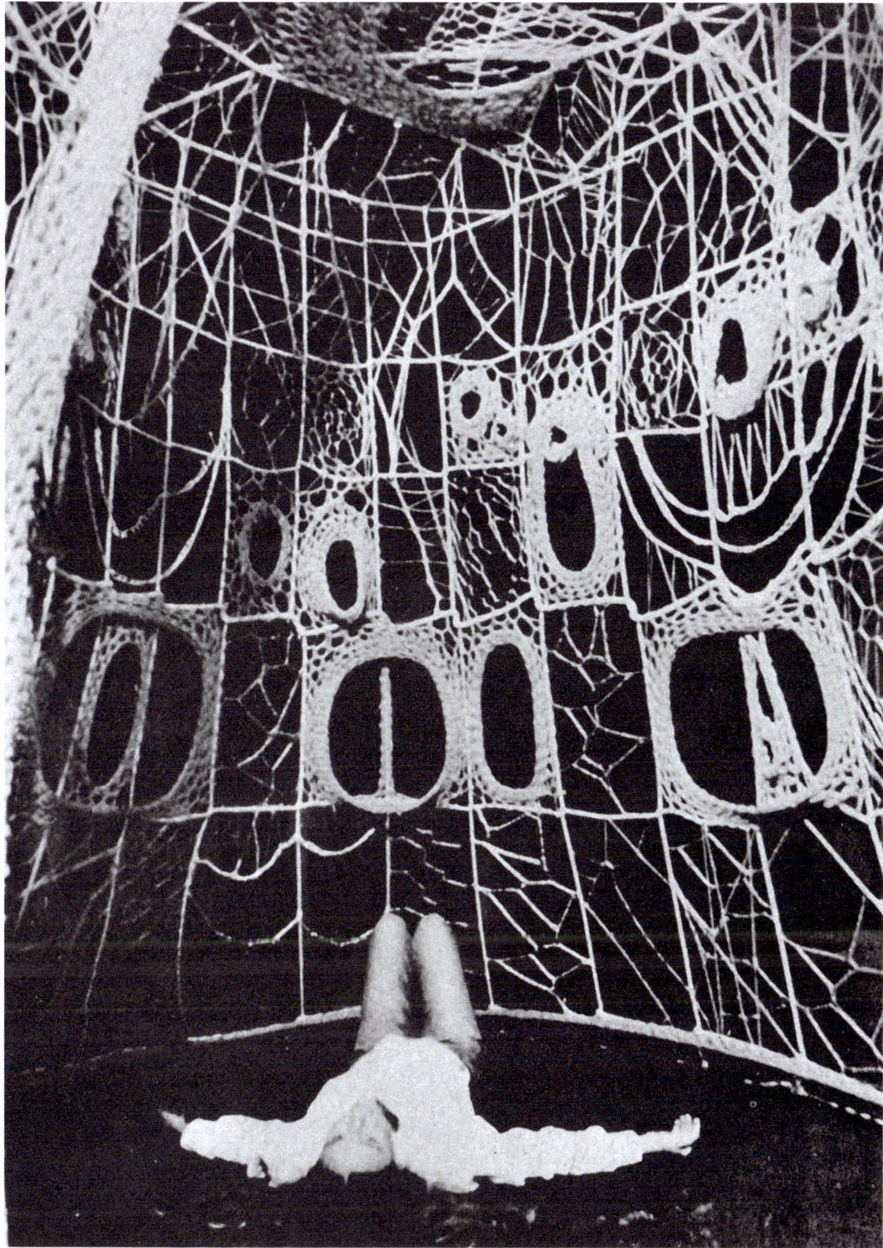

Faith Wilding, *Womanhouse: Crocheted Environment/ Womb Room* (1972).

*1943, Paraguay

is a multidisciplinary artist, writer, and activist in the field of critical pedagogy. Wilding works with performance, installation, environment, audio, painting, and drawing. She is well-known for revitalizing traditional female craft methods like crocheting and weaving for neo-avant-garde feminist art-making.[1]

After emigrating to the U.S. in 1961 from Paraguay, she studied at the University of Iowa, receiving a BFA in 1968. Studies followed in Art and Art History at Fresno State College (1969–71), where she participated in the early Feminist Art Program (FAP), an all-female class led by Judy Chicago, and then enrolled at CalArts to be a graduate student in the FAP there. In 1973, Wilding graduated with a MFA in Feminist Art, Performance, 2D Media, and Critical Studies.[2] She contributed to *Womanhouse* (1972) as a teaching assistant.[3] In this context, she also created *Crocheted Environment (Womb Room)* and collaborated on *Dining Room*.[4] Also at *Womanhouse*, she wrote and performed *Waiting* and co per-formed in *Cock and Cunt Play*, written by Chicago.[5] Well-known performances in her career include, furthermore, *Invitation to a Burning* (1980) and *Duration Performance* (1999).[6] Other visual works by Wilding that deal with feminist and body issues are the painting series *Battle Dresses* (1995–97) and *Wall of Wounds* (1996).[7]

Wildings works have been exhibited internationally, for example at the Whitney Museum of Art, N.Y., the MoCA, L.A., Kunsthaus Bremen, and the Museum of Contemporary Art, Toulouse.[8] Wilding is professor emerita of performance art at the School of the Art Institute of Chicago. She is a founding member of the cyberfeminist organization subRosa which connects art and activism.[9] **LB**

FAITH WILDING
Duration Performance:
The Economy of Feminized
Maintenance Work,
lecture performance, 1998

1

Duration Performance: The Economy of Feminized Maintenance Work
Faith Wilding

This is a story about invisible hands.
This is a story about endless work.
This is a story about women's work of maintenance and survival.
This is a story about the laboring female body in the invisible feminine economy of production and reproduction.
This is a story about repetition, boredom, exhaustion, stress, crashes.
This is a story about tedious, repetitive, straining, manual labor harnessed to the speed of electronic machines.
clean, wash, dust, wring, iron, sweep, cook, shop, phone, drive, clean, iron, enter, mix, drive, delete, clean, purge, wash, merge, edit, shop, fold, phone, file, select, copy, curse, cut, sweep, paste, insert, format, iron, program, type, assemble, cook, email, fax, cry, forward, sort, type, click, dust, clean, etc.

1. Feminist Maintenance Performance Art:
In recent decades, the mass deployment of electronic technology in offices and workplaces has profoundly changed the structure of work, and the relationship of home and work life in ways that are having particularly disturbing effects on women. In the US, women who have largely been concentrated in the lower echelons of the labor market--such as clerical work, the garment industries, manufacturing and service jobs--are increasingly being thrown out of waged labor and forced into part time privatized telework, home-based piece work, and service labor. This situation is once again confining many women to the private sphere of the home where they perform double maintenance labor: that of taking care of the family, and that of working in the global consumer economy. Made possible by automated Information Technology (IT), and controlled by mobile

tal, it is a market economy based on just-i
gies that speed up and control the pace o
The global disappearance of secure salar
e end of hard labor or tedious, repetitive
de, much of the rote maintenance work
parts assembly, and service labor is still
tly by women. But the spread of auton
d the hidden nature of homework anc
n's work and women's laboring bodie
cyberfeminists have begun to meet,
begin to strategize ways of analyzing
en's current relationship to IT, as w
ional gender structures in electronic
ggest some ways in which these co
ions worldwide. Before describing
maintenance and telework, I wan
ces from the 1970s as a way of co
t analysis of women's work, and
that could serve as a departure

ping changes in women's work
omen's liberation movement o
eated pioneering performance
laboring bodies and their dail
aid work that sustains and ma
uals, families, and institutions. This perform
by groundbreaking studies like Simone de Beauvior's The
and Betty Friedan's The Feminine Mystique, which analyzed the cult
economic, and political construction of women's gender roles, the tr

...ivision of labor, and the increasing rebellion of (mostly middle-class) women
...against their confinement to the private sphere of the home.

The landmark feminist collaborative artwork *Womanhouse* was produced by students and teachers of the California Institute of the Arts in three months from November 1971 to February 1972. *Womanhouse* was installed in a family dwelling house on a residential street in Hollywood, Los Angeles. To create the work, art students had to leave the (public) academy and enter the domestic, private space of (women's) domestic life. The artists of *Womanhouse* examined and commented on the content, forms, and history of gender roles and of women's work in the home, and delved into the complex socio/political, emotional, and psychic dynamics and relations that have constituted women's ...eparate sphere in the division of labor. This installation revealed the complex ...laborious work and pleasurable craft; of boring repetition and ...finement and loving nurturance. The different ...ife were enacted tell their own tales of ...ression. The kitchen, the dinin groom, ...ce is crammed with the evidence of ...isible to the public world. ...omanhouse also centered around domestic ...ce labor, such as scrubbing, ironing, ...ese performances introduced the duration ...al performance of a domestic task such as ...etc. that lasts as long as the real-life task--thus ...ence the real-time tedium of women's ...gical experience of women's domestic service ...'s "Waiting" performance, which condensed a ...otonous, repetitive monologue; her maintenance

2

...roduction and distribution
...nd life.
...waged jobs does not
...l maintenance work.
...arding, data entry,
...anually,
...achinery into the
...rk is contributing to
...ble again.
...e to face and
...ing, and
...ervening in the
...Later in this
...elate to women's
...ent political
...w and discuss
...g current
...crete
...r

...sonal lives
...50s, some
...stallation
...enance
...sible the
...was
...*Sex,*
...al

5

...y in women's domestic work

...conditions in the US, but
...ries, Canada, and

...oviding female reproduction and family service th...
...agency.
..., Mierle Ukeles Laderman developed her own
...er Maintenance Art Manifesto describes
...ng of Personal, General, and Earth Maintenance.
...interviewed people from more than 50 different
...r maids, sanitation men, grocery workers,
...ovie stars, and artists. She asked: "What do
...ou feel about spending whatever parts of
...ctivities? What is the relationship between
...relationship between maintenance and

...Tracks" at the Wadsworth Atheneum in
...r washing the steps and outside plaza
..., cleaning and washing the floors in
...his performance Miwon Kwon has

the ...
...requires work. It requires the kind of work that not
that continuously erases the marks of bodies and time, such as dirt, dust, and decay, but work
laborer). It's the kind of work that renders itself invisible (including the body of the
invisible, in order to make other things ("real" work?) possible." (1)
...and eternal stasis [of the museum], or
Ukeles' subsequent performances, in which she became artist-in-residence
with the New York Sanitation Department and addressed the issues of waste,
sanitation, and garbage collection, point to the intricate webs of maintenance
work that connect the private household with urban, regional, national, and
global maintenance and disposal systems.
Thus feminist maintenance and duration performances were a strategy to
make women's labor visible, and to foreground issues of working conditions, the

WOMANHOUSE: SEXUALITY

By Anna Sønderup

"Lea's room [*Leah's Room*] is a room of lush beauty and suffocating oppression."[1] — Karen LeCocq & Nancy Youdelman

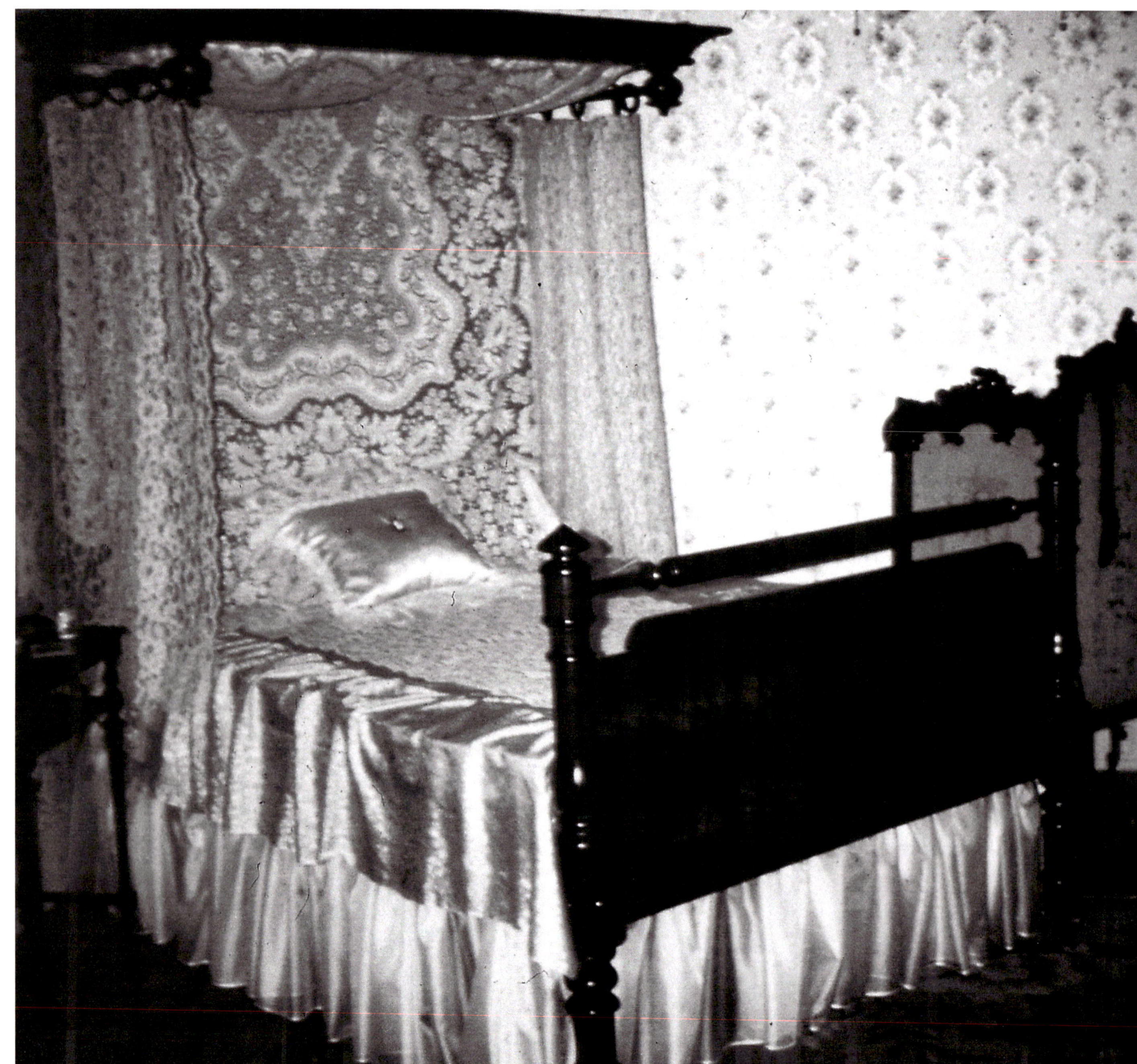

The theme of female sexuality was embedded in various performances and works throughout the *Womanhouse* project, where gender roles and the formation of sexuality especially served as focus.

In *Womanhouse*, gender roles were generally the subject matter and they were often exaggerated or otherwise made extreme as a way of highlighting the construction of gender and sexuality. This construction of female sexuality was (and maybe still is) based on the assumption that the woman is the object of male desire and therefore passive, without any desires of her own. If the woman is to be an object of male desire then she must look the part, which is why female sexuality and beauty standards of the time were inseparable. This was satirized in *Lipstick Bathroom* by Camille Grey, in which an entire bathroom was painted red with lipstick and decorated with 200 plastic lipsticks.[2] This installation showed the deep connection between beauty standards and the construction of female sexuality and identity.

Another subject related to female sexuality that was addressed, albeit more implicitly, was the dichotomy between the two archetypal portrayals of women, the whore and the Madonna, and the implications that these clichés carry. Almost all rooms somehow related to the idea of the woman as homemaker and a good wife, while at the same time other rooms highlighted the discomfort this role brings. In the performance installation *Leah's Room* by Karen LeCocq and Nancy Youdelman, Léa, a courtesan inspired by her namesake in Colette's novel *Chéri*, just like the housewife, must be sexually available to the man/husband. Both the housewife and the courtesan use sex and sexuality as a means to ascertain economic stability.[3] However, the role of the housewife and the role of the courtesan are not valued equally. *Leah's Room* is also an example of the passiveness expected of women, since she is only dressing herself up for the sake of men to meet the standards of a beautiful woman/object.

Lastly, the biological difference between men and women as a basis for the construction of gender roles was also made visible. A performance called *Cock and Cunt Play* showed the absurdities of claims such as 'women belong in the house' with a dialogue between 'He' and 'She,' who each had prop genitals made from plastic. As Temma Balducci writes on this performance: "This parody of traditional roles pointedly addresses these functions as social constructions based on the body."[4]

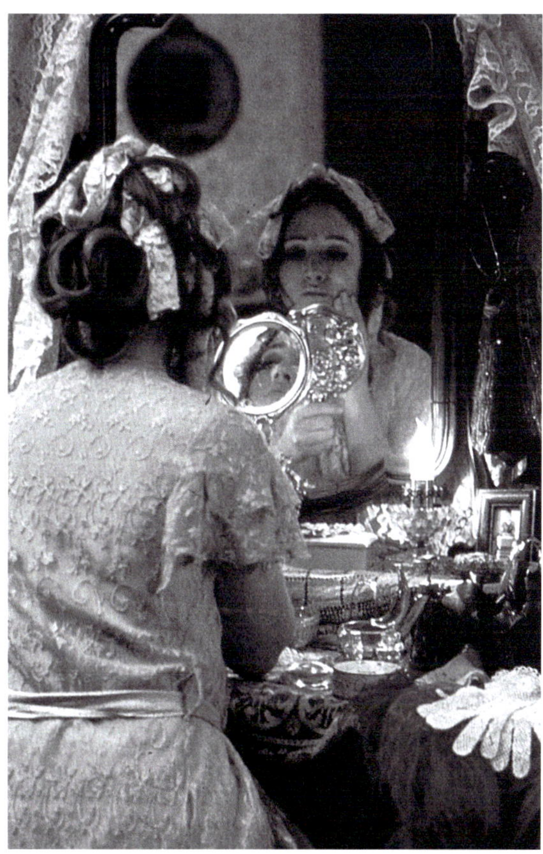

LEAH'S ROOM

Karen LeCocq and Nancy Youdelman's performance installation featured LeCocq as the courtesan Léa meticulously applying and removing her makeup as a symbol of the woman's need to maintain her youthful beauty and the interest of men.

The connection between normative beauty and femininity, as well as the pain associated with ageing and loss of beauty, were key themes of this piece, which also served as a comment on female sexuality. The idea of a woman's sexuality as passive and that sex is something she gives to men to keep them satisfied is closely bound to standards of beauty. Women should stay beautiful and youthful so that men do not lose their sexual interest.

"We wanted to deal with the way women are intimidated by the culture to constantly maintain their beauty and the feeling of desperation and helplessness once this beauty is lost."[5]
— Karen LeCocq & Nancy Youdelman

Opposite page: Karen LeCocq, Nancy Youdelman, *Womanhouse: Leah's Room* (1972).
This page: Karen LeCocq, Nancy Youdelman, *Womanhouse: Leah's Room* (1972), performance by Karen LeCocq at mixed media site installation. Photo by Lloyd Hamrol.

COCK AND CUNT

Judy Chicago wrote *Cock and Cunt Play* before the *Womanhouse* project began, but it was included because of its theme of gender roles. In this performance, Faith Wilding and Janice Lester both wore oversized genitalia props and performed the traditional roles of man and woman. 'She' asks for help with her domestic tasks, but 'He' does not want to provide this help because of his gender (and genitalia). The performance ends with 'Him' killing 'Her' because of her demands for domestic and sexual equality. This story shows the construction of gender and how certain expectations are inscribed on the female body.

Excerpt from *Cock and Cunt Play*

SHE Well they're your dishes as much as mine!

HE But you don't have a cock! (grasps cock and begins stroking it proudly)

SHE What's that got to do with?

HE A cock means you don't wash dishes. You have a cunt. A cunt means you wash dishes.

SHE (looking at cunt) I don't see where it says that on my cunt.

HE (pointing at her cunt) Stu-upid, your cunt/pussy/gash/hole or whatever it is, is round like a dish. Therefore it's only right for you to wash dishes. My cock is long and hard and straight and is meant to shoot like guns or missiles. Anyone can see that (strokes cock on each emphasis).[6]

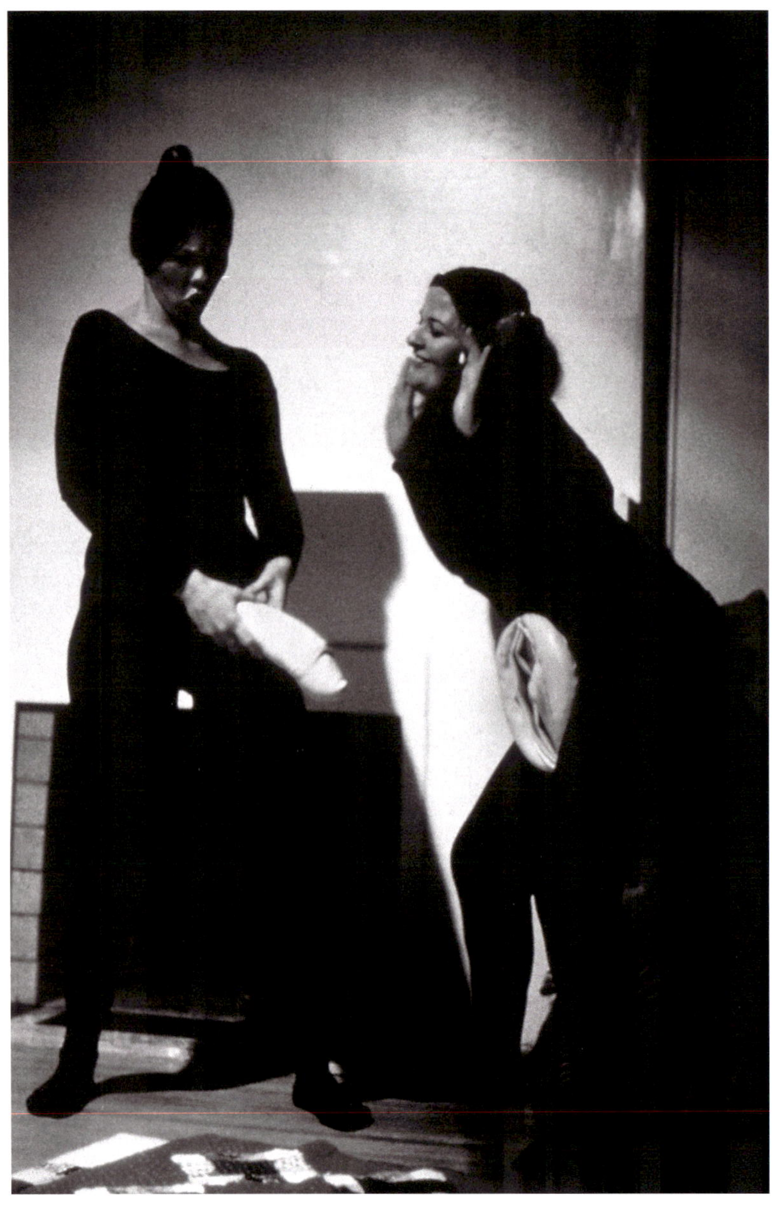

Keep her where she belongs...

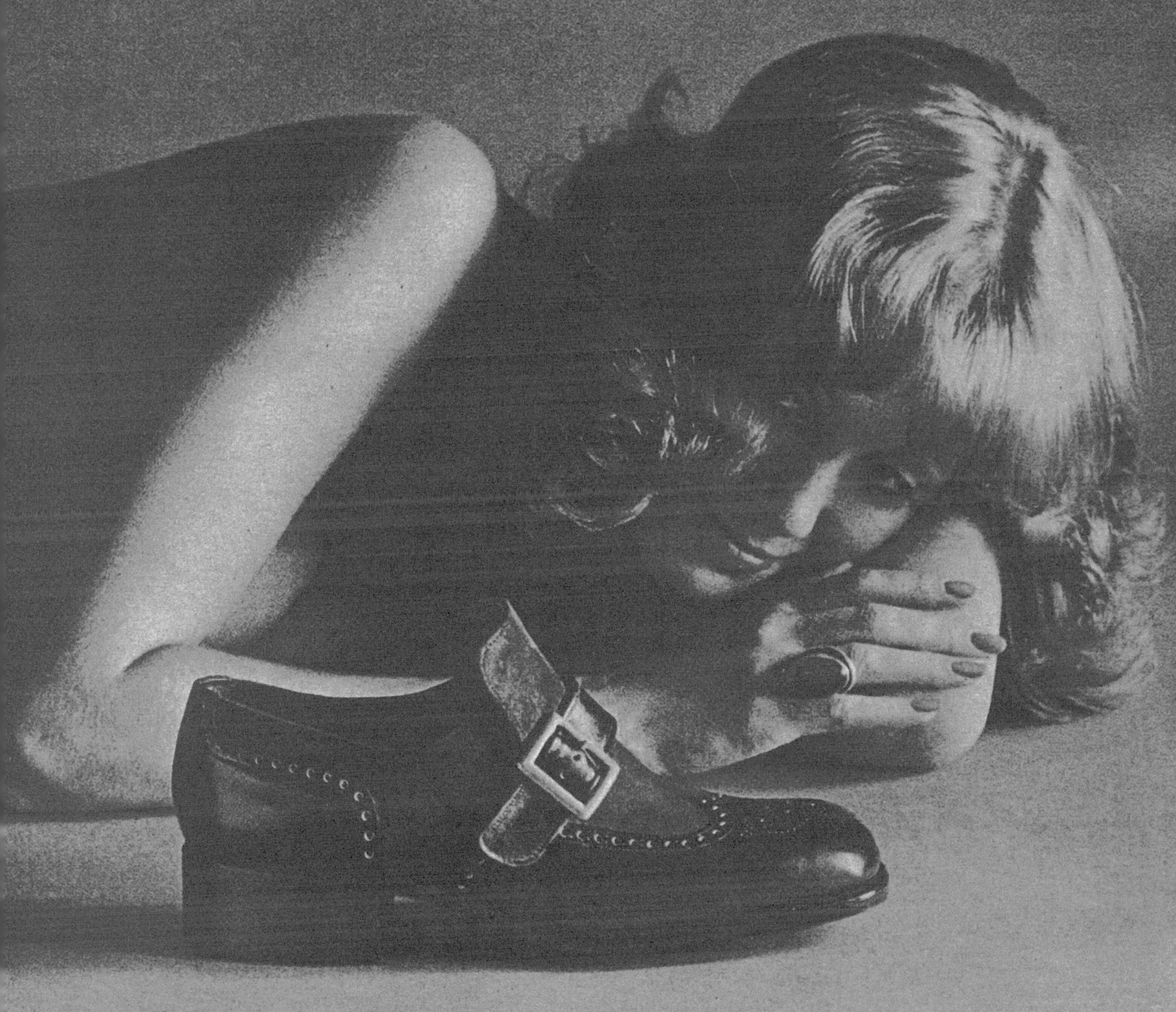

WOMANHOUSE: BIRTH AND MOTHERHOOD

By Katharina Brandt

Becoming a mother for most women is a joy. But it is also deeply connected with physical and psychological changes, and is one of the most significant identity shifts a woman will ever experience.[1] The idealized image of "the Good Enough Mother"[2] is based on the idea of putting the child's needs first, and women often feel forced to be accepted or seen in society as the perfect mother figure.

The rooms of *Womanhouse* included 'birth' and 'motherhood' as urgent themes that had to be addressed in order to revolutionize these stereotypes about women. "In the 1970s, the two biggest issues were sex and housework. Since then, more women entered the workforce and have been battling against the glass ceiling and experiencing our form of male terrorism, which is sexual harassment."[3] Issues related to sex and housework persist in many domestic spaces all over the world today.

Lots of women feel oppressed by domestic spaces and are "pigeonholed as a [typical] housewife or mother."[4] These strong female feelings are pictured in Miriam Schapiro's and Sherry Brody's *Dollhouse* (1972). Seen from the perspective of women, the room expresses at first sight a well-ordered domestic space, its harmony, and supposed safety. This domestic scene is transformed into a place of horror by some "real and imaginary invading creatures,"[5] reflecting the inner anxieties of a housewife or mother.

Another important part of being a good mother is related to the need to put her child first. From the moment of giving birth (pictured in the performance *The Birth Trilogy*), women often feel obliged to leave their own needs behind for the sake of their child. The focus is fixed completely on the child's life and the maintenance of a happy family and an intact household, thereby fulfilling the requirements of an ideal mother. The performance *Waiting* by Faith Wilding and the room installation *The Nursery* by Shawnee Wollenman at *Womanhouse* give an impression of what it might feel like to dedicate a life to birth and motherhood. The installation recaptures the childhood feeling of growing up in a nursery, while the performance shows the viewpoint of a mother taking the right decisions for her child and waiting for things to happen in a structured domestic space.

DOLLHOUSE

Dollhouse is a six-room miniature house and part of the *Dollhouse Room*, created by Miriam Schapiro and Sherry Brody. Nowadays, besides Faith Wilding's *Crocheted Environment* (also referred to as *Womb Room*) that was recreated for an exhibition at the Bronx Museum of the Arts in 1995 and is now part of the ICA Boston's collection, it is the only publicly available piece of *Womanhouse* and was acquired by the Smithsonian Institution in 1995.

"There are birds pecking at rocks in the seraglio … Outside the nursery window, a giant grizzly bear stares at the monster in the crib, while the real baby sits nearby in an alabaster egg, menaced by a scorpion, unmindful of the alligator resting on a shelf in the bookcase. Ten men stare in at the kitchen window, representing a mysterious menace from the outside."[6]

— Miriam Schapiro

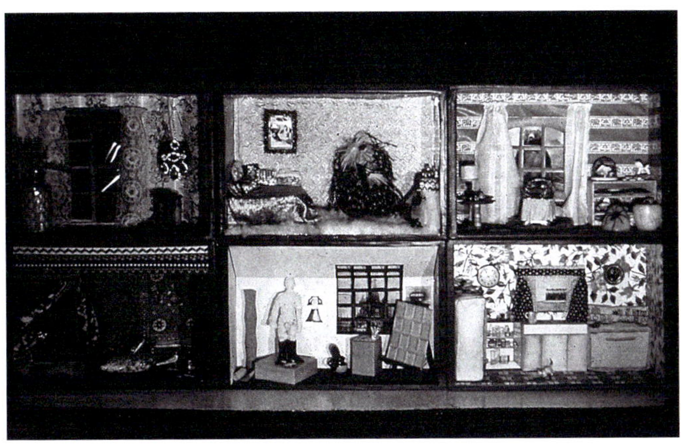

Above: Miriam Schapiro, *Womanhouse: Dollhouse* (detail) (1972).
Below: Shawnee Wollenman, *Womanhouse: The Nursery* (1972).

THE NURSERY

The room installation *The Nursery* by Shawnee Wollenman is meant to visualize the perfect living space for a small child. By creating a room with gigantic toys and furniture, she tries to simulate the effect of being a little human growing up in a comfortable domestic space for most of their early childhood.

"I created a room with giant furniture and toys in order to recapture the childhood feeling of being so small in such a big room. I also looked at the room from the viewpoint of a woman considering what the ideal living space might be for a child. I have made the room as androgynous as possible because my early memories are of having no sex and being able to do all the things that boys and girls do."[7] — Shawnee Wollenman

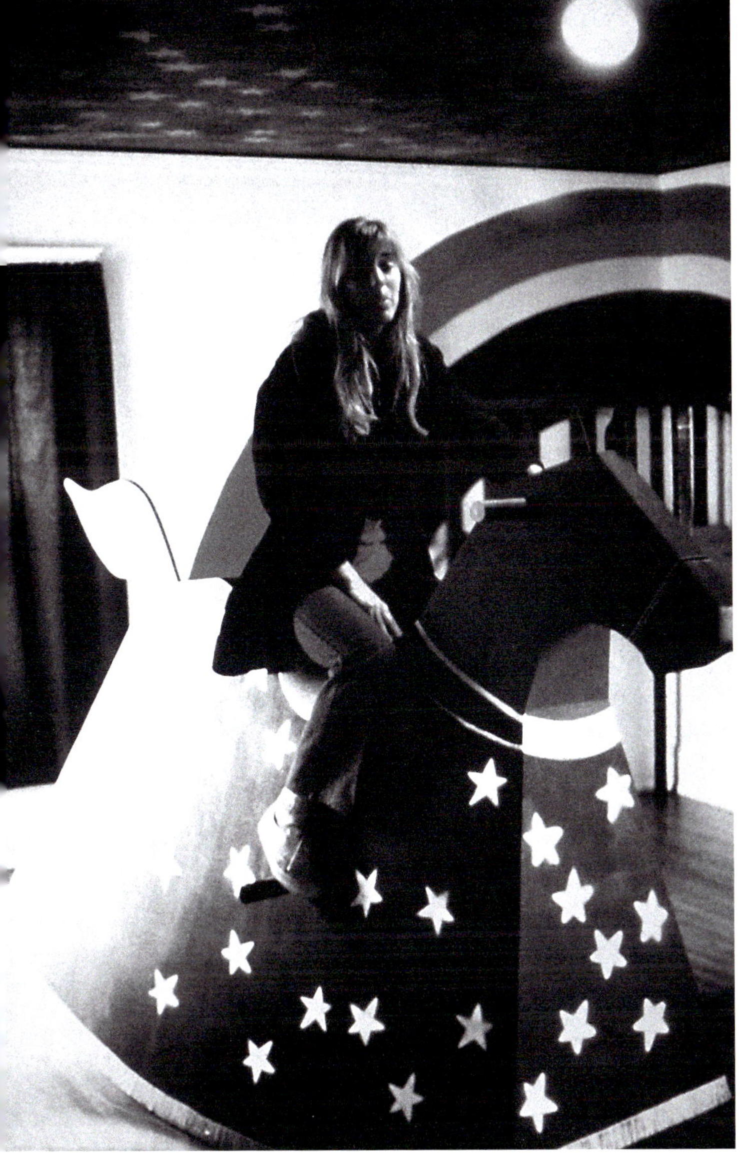

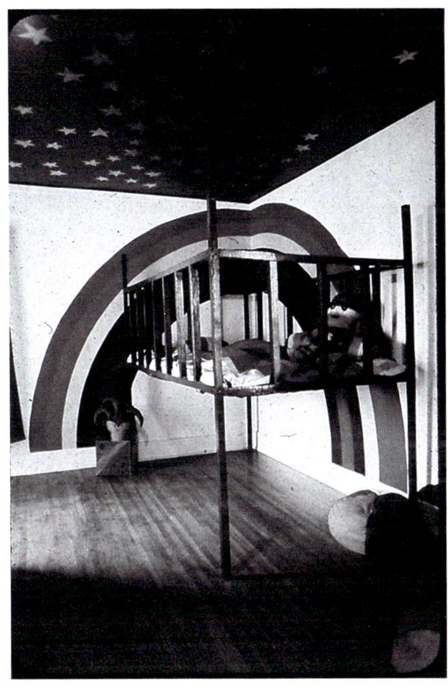

WAITING

In *Waiting*, a performance by Faith Wilding, a woman sits in a chair, reviewing the events of her life and waiting for a big happening to come. It was one of four performances taking place in the living room of *Womanhouse*.[8]

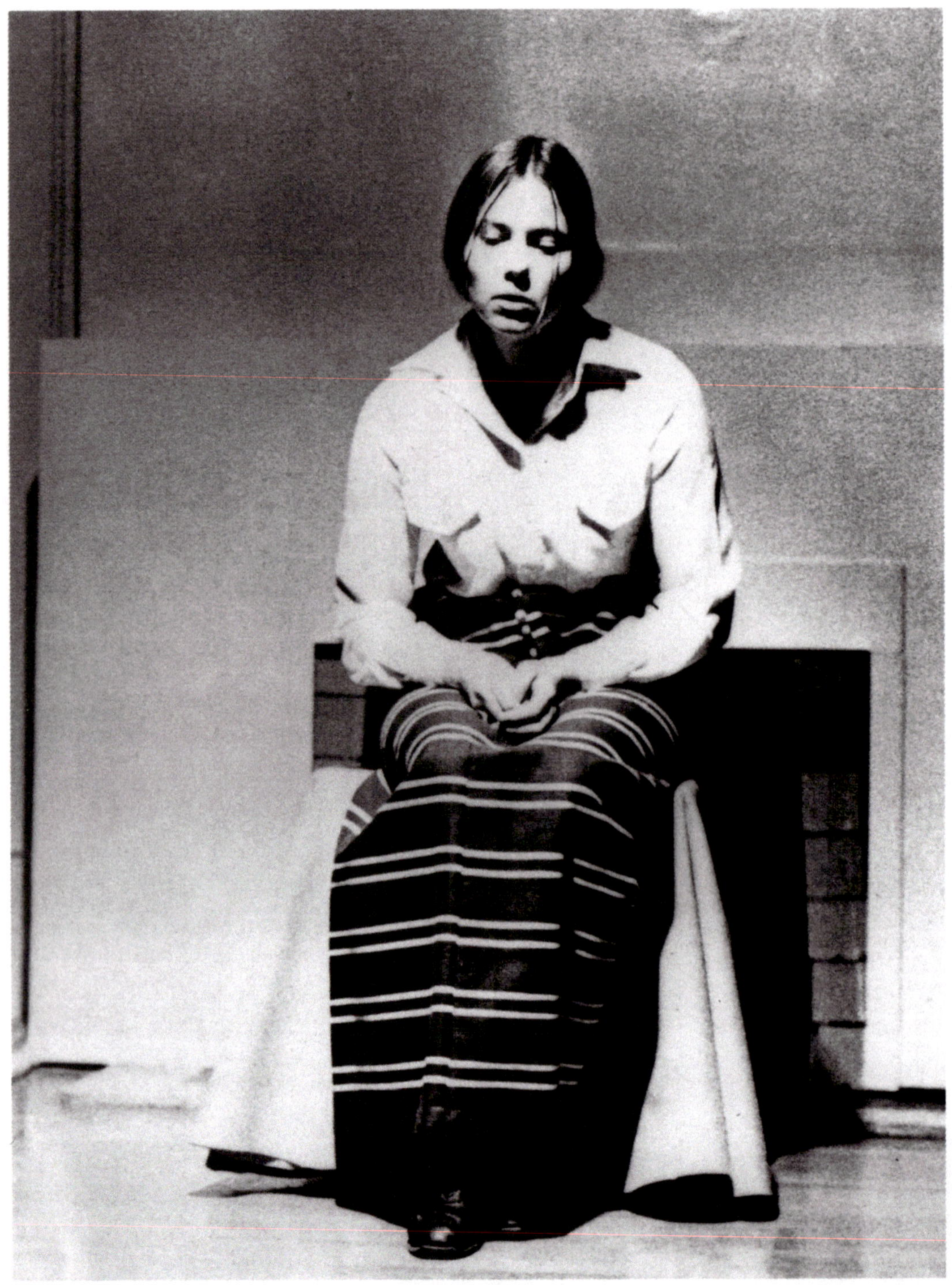

Faith Wilding, *Womanhouse: Waiting* (1972).

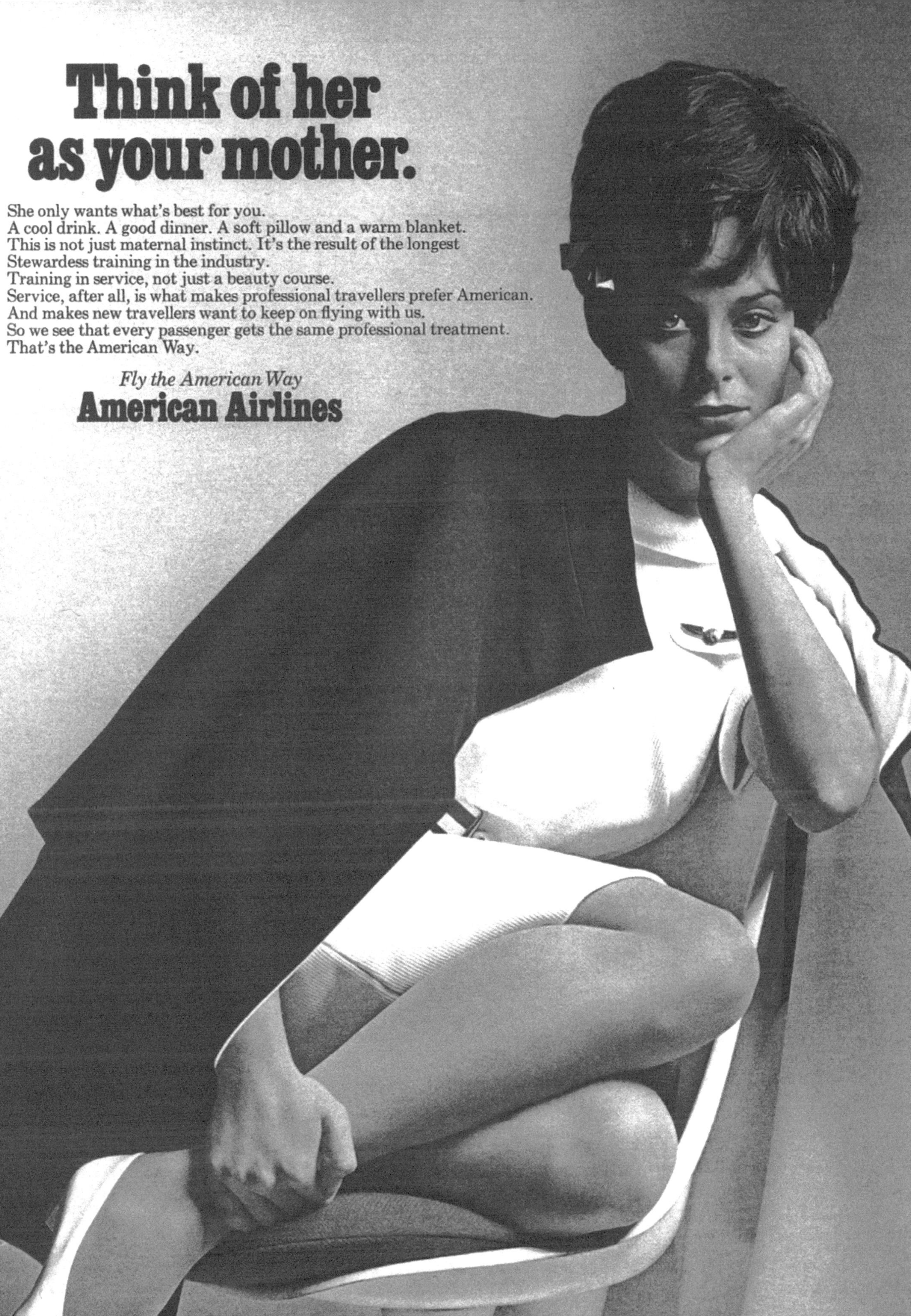

Think of her
as your mother.

She only wants what's best for you.
A cool drink. A good dinner. A soft pillow and a warm blanket.
This is not just maternal instinct. It's the result of the longest
Stewardess training in the industry.
Training in service, not just a beauty course.
Service, after all, is what makes professional travellers prefer American.
And makes new travellers want to keep on flying with us.
So we see that every passenger gets the same professional treatment.
That's the American Way.

Fly the American Way
American Airlines

WOMANHOUSE: NURTURANT KITCHEN

By Jennifer Gaschler

**"The soft skin of a kitchen pink
Is openers, strainers, blenders
Is cups, pots and hot ovens
Is boxes, cans and glass packages
Is faucets and nippled knobs
A toaster, juicer, and waffler
All pink skinned
How would you like your eggs done
this morning?"[1]**
— Robin Weltsch

Kitchens are often considered to be the 'home' and 'pride' of a woman, an assertion that was even more widespread in the 1970s. Robin Weltsch is exaggerating that common assumption by equipping the kitchen of *Womanhouse* with only pink, 'girlish' furniture, devices, and utensils. In the poetic description of her artwork she is connecting the femininity of such kitchens with the 'soft skin' of a woman—another female attribute desirable for men. With a single sentence, 'How would you like your eggs done this morning?,' she manages to initiate reflections about the public presumption of wives being mostly responsible for their husbands' well-being by providing food and coziness.

Art historian Temma Balducci explains that the artists participating in *Womanhouse* used parody and exaggeration "as tools to undermine essentialist stereotypes about women that limited them to domestic roles."[2] Art historian Matilda Felix describes *Womanhouse* as a concept where many "domestic communication and working processes became objects of artistic disputes about identity."[3] Furthermore, she argues that the most striking point of the project was the "integration of the private daily routine of reproduction into public exhibition space," which was still regarded as "non-standard" in the 1970s.[4]

The kitchen space of *Womanhouse* was collaboratively created by Weltsch, Vicki Hodgett, Wanda Westcoast, and Susan Frazier. Its ceiling and walls are covered with plastic casts of sunny-side-up eggs—referring also to Weltsch's poem about the submissive provision of food. However, as they reach the eye level of the observer they slowly turn into breasts. The eggs themselves have double entendre, drawing parallels with the female ova, while the breast, providing the mother's milk, is part of a woman's nurturing role in the household. This section of the mixed media installation was executed by Vicki Hodgett. Nevertheless, she states that it was a "collective idea" that "simply would never have existed if women had not tried to work together."[5]

Further parts of the *Nurturant Kitchen* are Wanda Westcoast's triangular flesh-colored curtains which, with their holes and cuts, provoke thoughts about the loss of virginity, possibly in an aggressive manner.

Susan Frazier was the fourth artist to collaborate on the installation, working with aprons, that had sewed on breasts, kissing lips, and soft paddings. "[E]xperience the heart of the home with me," her description says, "you are now embraced by my nurturing pink womb, giving life" while the apron strings are a continuation of the umbilical cord. But it quickly shifts to open criticism of the assumed role of the housewife:

The approximately ten thousand people who entered were confronted, as Balducci states, "with a deconstruction of the myth of the white, middle-class housewife as satisfied, fulfilled, domestic goddess."[8]

"We had a consciousness-raising session on kitchens. … I had a fleeting image of fried eggs stenciled over everything—walls, ceiling, floor—and some people saw breasts. Breasts were nurturing—kitchens were the extension of mothers' milk. I felt a little railroaded. I still wanted eggs. And then Robin said, 'Why not have a transformation from eggs to breasts,' and we were all delighted."[6]
— Vicki Hodgett

"I am not a habit! Release me, let me go, you don't know me, you don't own me. I am a human being, not just a source of cheap labor for lazy people. I want to undo these apron strings, to see what the rest of the world is doing, to see if I can help … to see myself once again. I want to travel, to see wonders I only dream of daily … to see wonders I only dream of daily, right here in the heart of the home façade."[7]
— Susan Frazier

Next spread: Susan Frazier, Vicki Hodgett, Robin Weltsch, Wanda Westcoast, *Womanhouse: Nurturant Kitchen* (1972), detail: Robin Weltsch, *The Kitchen* and Vicki Hodgett, *Eggs to Breasts*.

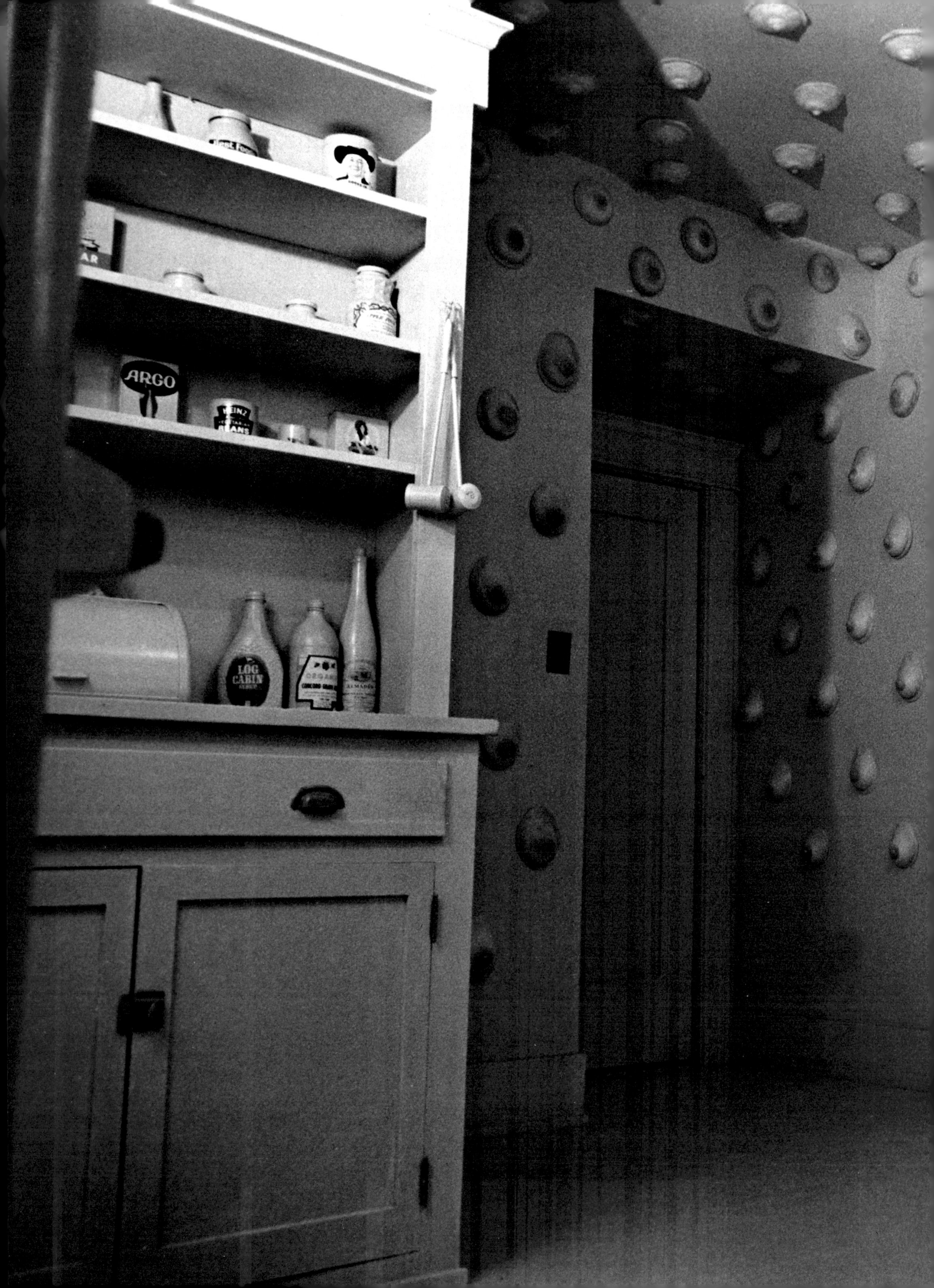
ARGO
LOG CABIN
HEINZ
BEANS

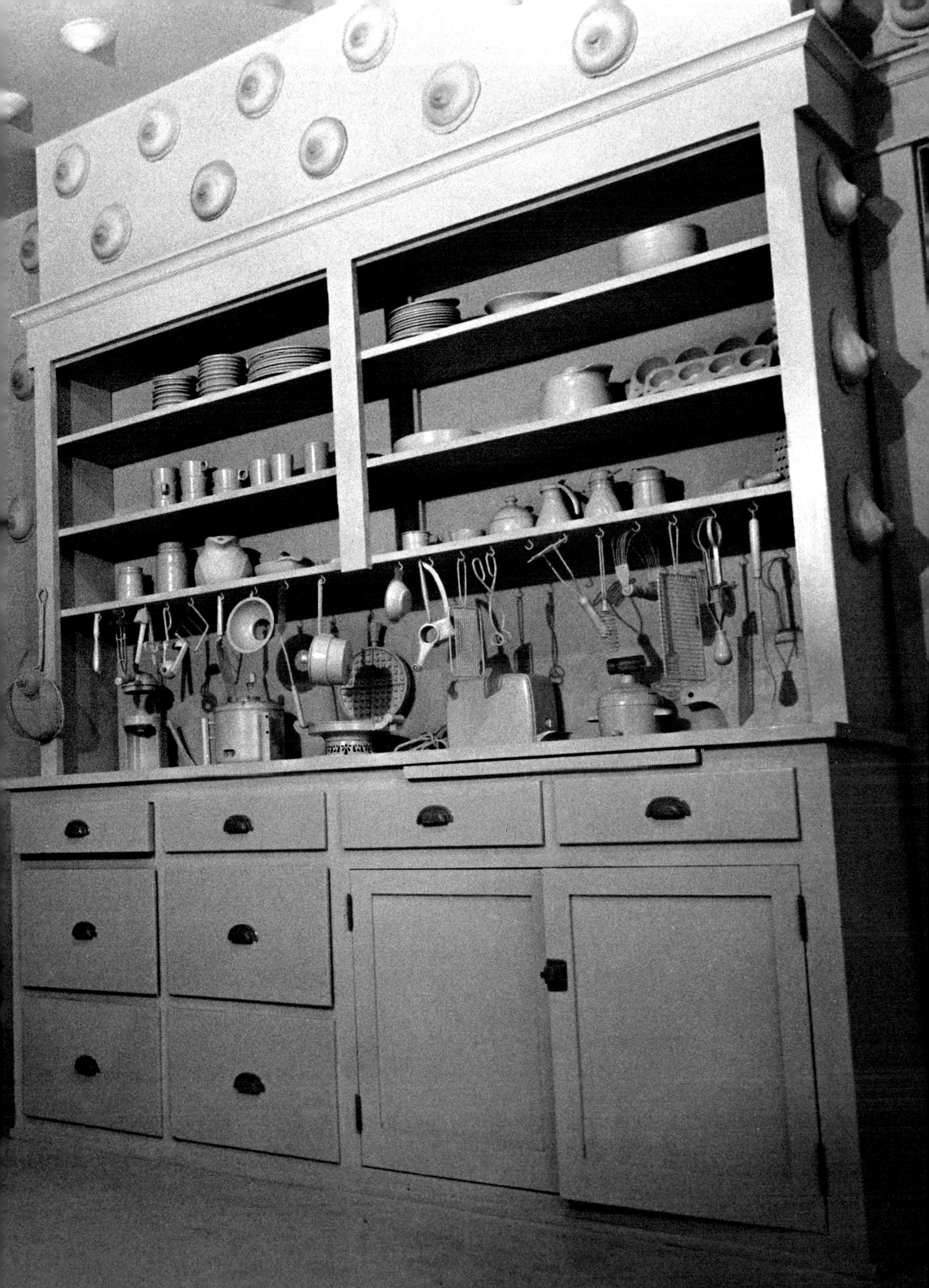

WOMANHOUSE: DOMESTICITY AND PRIVACY

By Vivien Lambert

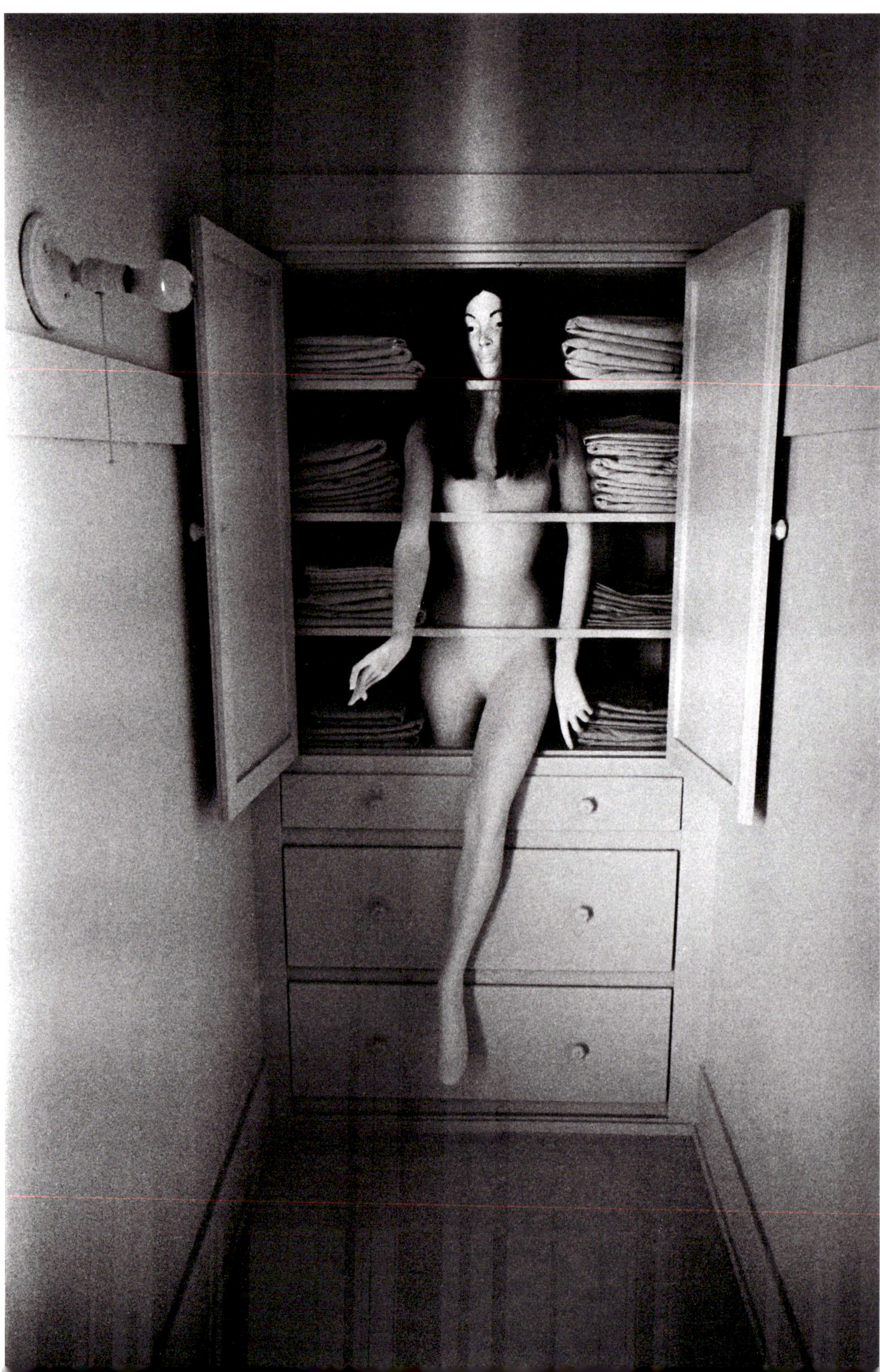

"The Cult of True Womanhood," or better known as "the Cult of Domesticity" depicts an ideal of how women should be.[1] This ideal is related to the gender roles of America's 19th-century upper and middle class. At that time, men were responsible for the public sphere, while women were supposed to occupy the private sphere. This meant that women were supposed to be at home, taking care of the household, while men were supposed to go to work to earn money.[2]

The underlying belief was that women were frail, and therefore too weak to leave the home and in need of protection by men, who provided them with shelter. Therefore, because of women's supposed fragility, physical activity was forbidden, as was obtaining an education. Instead, women were supposed to find fulfillment within the home, through being a wife and mother.[3]

The characteristics of 'True Womanhood' were spread in women's magazines, books, sermons, and religious texts.[4] According to the ideals, a 'True Woman' had to adhere to certain values: Piety, Purity, Submission, and Domesticity. Women were supposed to be devoted, untouched before marriage, and obedient to men, taking care of the private sphere and the family. Women symbolized their husband's wealth and success, giving birth to their children and ensuring their legacy, next to their role as a caregiver and moral support for the family.

At a time of rapid social and technological change, many began to fear the loss of traditional values. Responding to these anxieties, many people sought to maintain the separation between the private and the public spheres.[5]

ROOMS AND PERFORMANCES

In *Womanhouse* the work *Linen Closet* by Sandy Orgel portrays a woman 'in her place.'[6] In relation to the 'Cult of Domesticity,' this would mean being at home, doing the laundry, and taking care of the household. By showing the doll stepping out of the closet, the artist was suggesting that women should step out of their role as well and become something different.

Scrubbing by Christine Rush and *Ironing* by Sandra Orgel, in which Rush scrubs the floor and Orgel irons numerous identical sheets, were the so-called "maintenance pieces."[7] These performances play with routine, maintaining an activity in a repetitive monotonous motion to criticize gender roles.

In Faith Wilding's performance *Waiting*, she is sitting in a rocking chair, slowly moving back and forth, saying:

> "… Waiting for him to give me pleasure … Waiting for the children to grow up and leave home… Waiting to have some time to myself … Waiting for life to begin … Waiting … Waiting … Waiting …"[8]

Here the passivity of women's life is criticized. This performance plays with the fact that woman had to remain at home all the time; the only thing they could do was to wait.

Nurturant Kitchen, a collaborative project by Susan Frazier, Vicki Hodgett, Robin Weltsch, and Wanda Westcoast, is completely painted in pink.[9]

Furthermore, the ceiling and the walls are decorated by Vicki Hodgett's work *Eggs to Breasts*, which shows a transformation of eggs that hang from the ceiling into breasts that hang from the wall. Wanda Westcoast's vacu-formed *Curtains* enhance the nurturing womb-like feeling the room seems to evoke, portraying the feeling of being taken care of as associated with women. Susan Frazier's work *Aprons in the Kitchen* shows five aprons with different attachments sewn to them: for example, breasts for feeding milk, lips to give pleasure, and the womb that gives life. In general, the aprons are supposed to portray domesticity, but they also show how women are 'tied' to their gender roles, unable to escape.

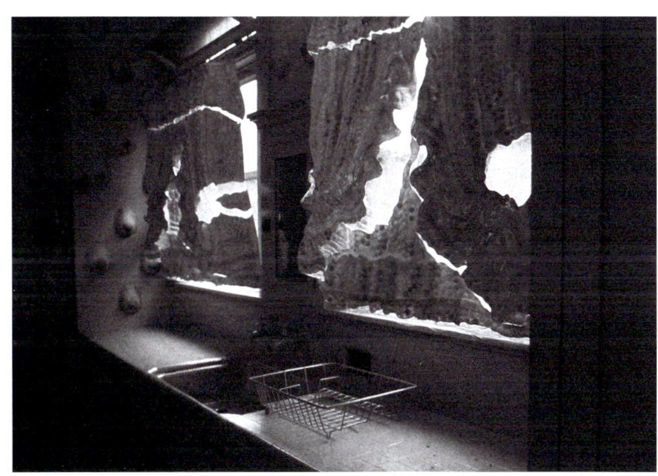

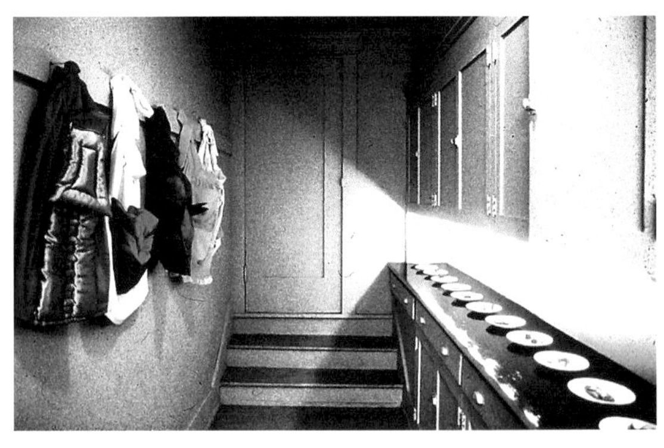

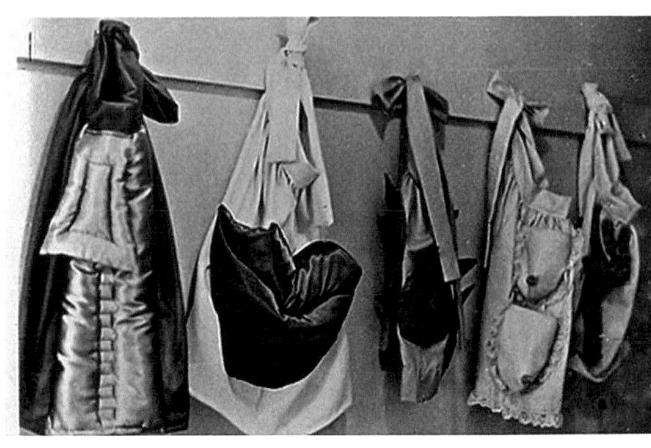

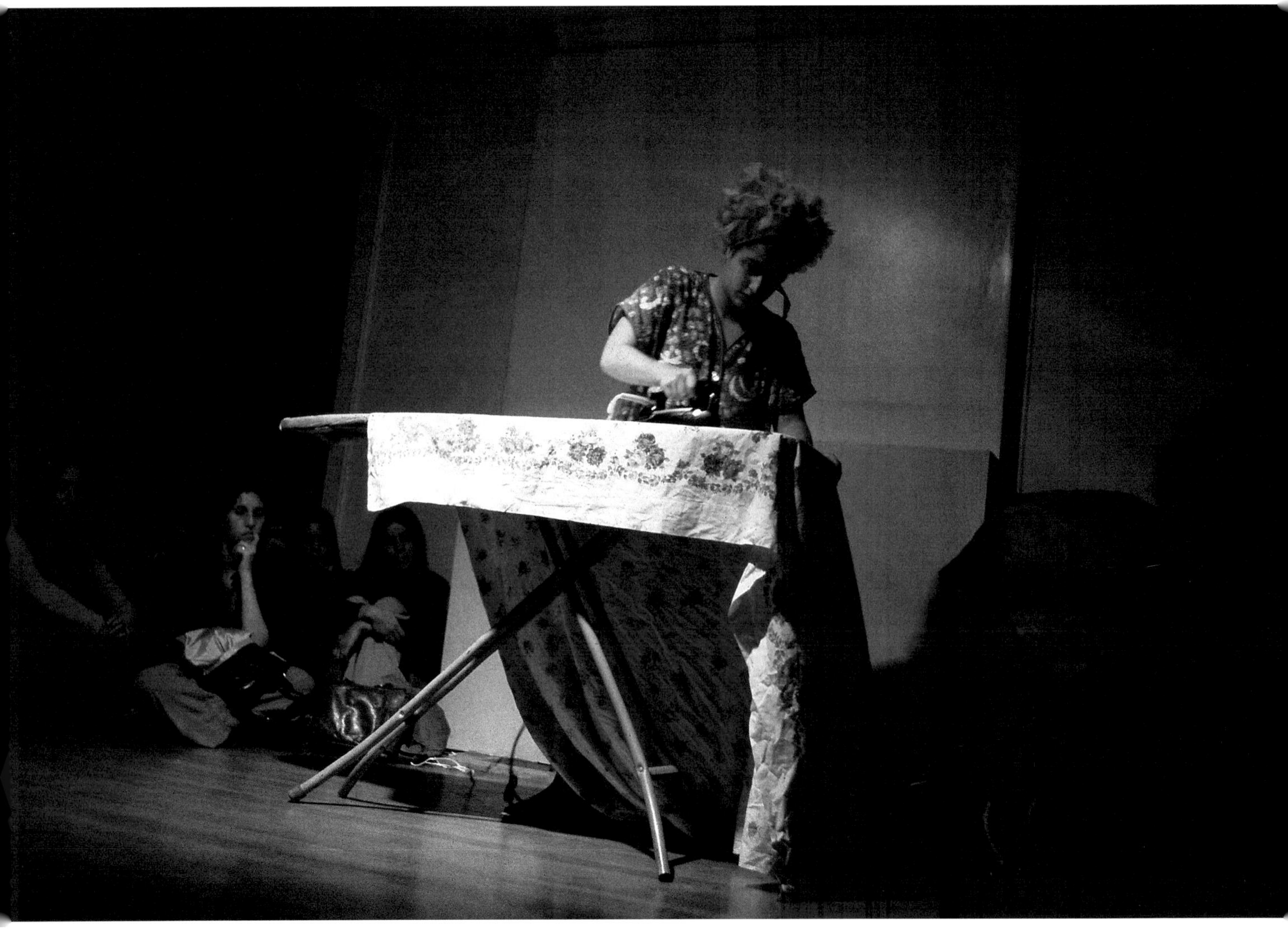

Previous spread, left: Sandra Orgel, *Womanhouse: Linen Closet* (1972).
Previous spread, right: Susan Frazier, Vicki Hodgett, Robin Weltsch, Wanda Westcoast, *Womanhouse: Nurturant Kitchen* (1972), detail: Wanda Westcoast, *Curtains*, and Vicki Hodgett, *Eggs to Breasts*.
Previous page, from top to bottom: Susan Frazier, Vicki Hodgett, Robin Weltsch, Wanda Westcoast, *Womanhouse: Nurturant Kitchen* (1972), detail: Susan Frazier, *Aprons in the Kitchen*.
Sandra Orgel, *Womanhouse: Maintenance performance, Ironing* (1972).
This page: Christine Rush, *Womanhouse: Maintenance performance, Scrubbing* (1972).

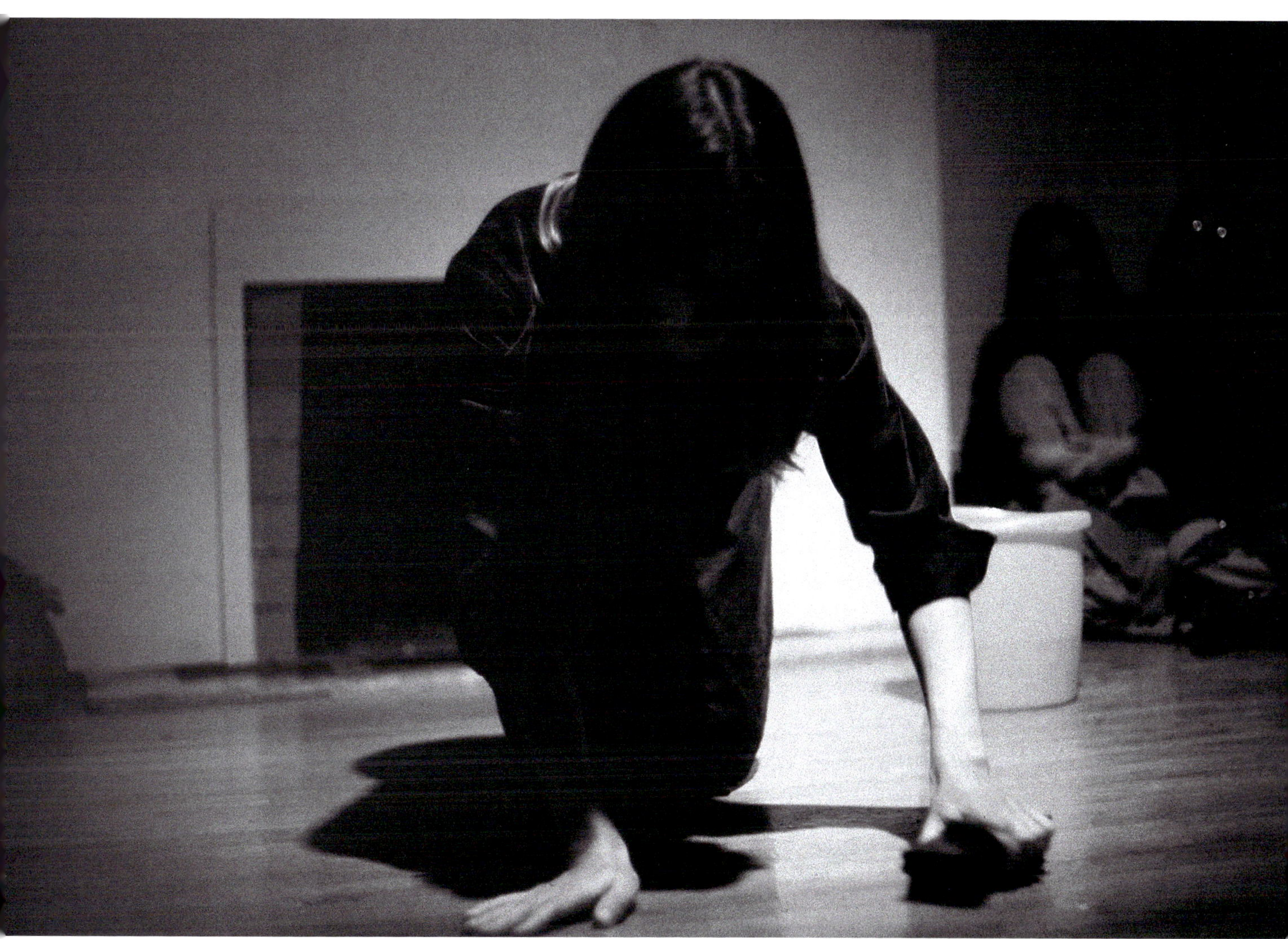

WOMANHOUSE: DOLLHOUSE

By Jennifer Gaschler

Art historian Temma Balducci argues that, at the beginning of the 17th century, "when modern gender roles first began to take shape in Europe" and the private sphere was assigned to women, "elaborate miniature houses first came into use as conversation pieces of upper-class women."[1] They reinforced gender stereotypes by "becoming an outward manifestation" of them.[2] However, Miriam Schapiro's *Dollhouse* (in collaboration with Sherry Brody) can be seen as a counter-model to those norms and playhouses, as it critically addresses "the construction of gender."[3]

Like some of the other artworks of *Womanhouse*, for instance the *Nurturant Kitchen*, the artists of *Dollhouse* are working with exaggeration and parody. The six rooms of the wooden house are all decorated opulently and in a seemingly 'feminine' manner, with flower-covered wallpapers, curtains made of lace, and "personal mementos that Schapiro and Brody had collected from women all over the country."[4]

The six rooms are: a parlor, a kitchen, a film star's bedroom, a sleeping/sitting room with a harem theme, a nursery, and an artist's studio. To some, the tiny rooms "evoke cells in which the hopes of women are often imprisoned."[5] However, there is also a darkly humorous twist to this piece: "*Dollhouse* combines the beauty, charm and supposed safety and comfort of the home with the unnameable terrors existing within its walls," Schapiro says.[6] She includes disturbing "invading creatures" such as a snake, woodpeckers, or a bear lurking inside. Numerous men stare in at the kitchen window, "representing a mysterious menace from the outside."[7]

The art historians of the Smithsonian American Art Museum argue that those "different symbols challenge the idea that the domestic lives of women prevent them from making 'serious' art."[8] But even if the imaginary resident of this house is constrained by her domesticity, in her artist studio she manages to reverse gender roles and paints a male nude model.

Dollhouse, besides Faith Wilding's *Crocheted Environment* or *Womb Room*, now part of the ICA Boston's collection, is the only piece of *Womanhouse*—that did not receive its deserved attention in the 1970s—that is still preserved and on display.

"There is also a studio, since we are both artists. Here we switch the usual roles of artist and model. The artists are women and the model is a man. Taking a cue from Linda Nochlin, the feminist art historian, we reverse the association of fruit and 'women as object,' by placing a tray of bananas at the model's feet. A further reversal is to put one of my abstract paintings on the easel and some of Sherry's costume drawings on the wall, ignoring our poor model altogether."[9] — Miriam Schapiro

Sherry Brody, Miriam Schapiro, *Womanhouse: Dollhouse* (1972).

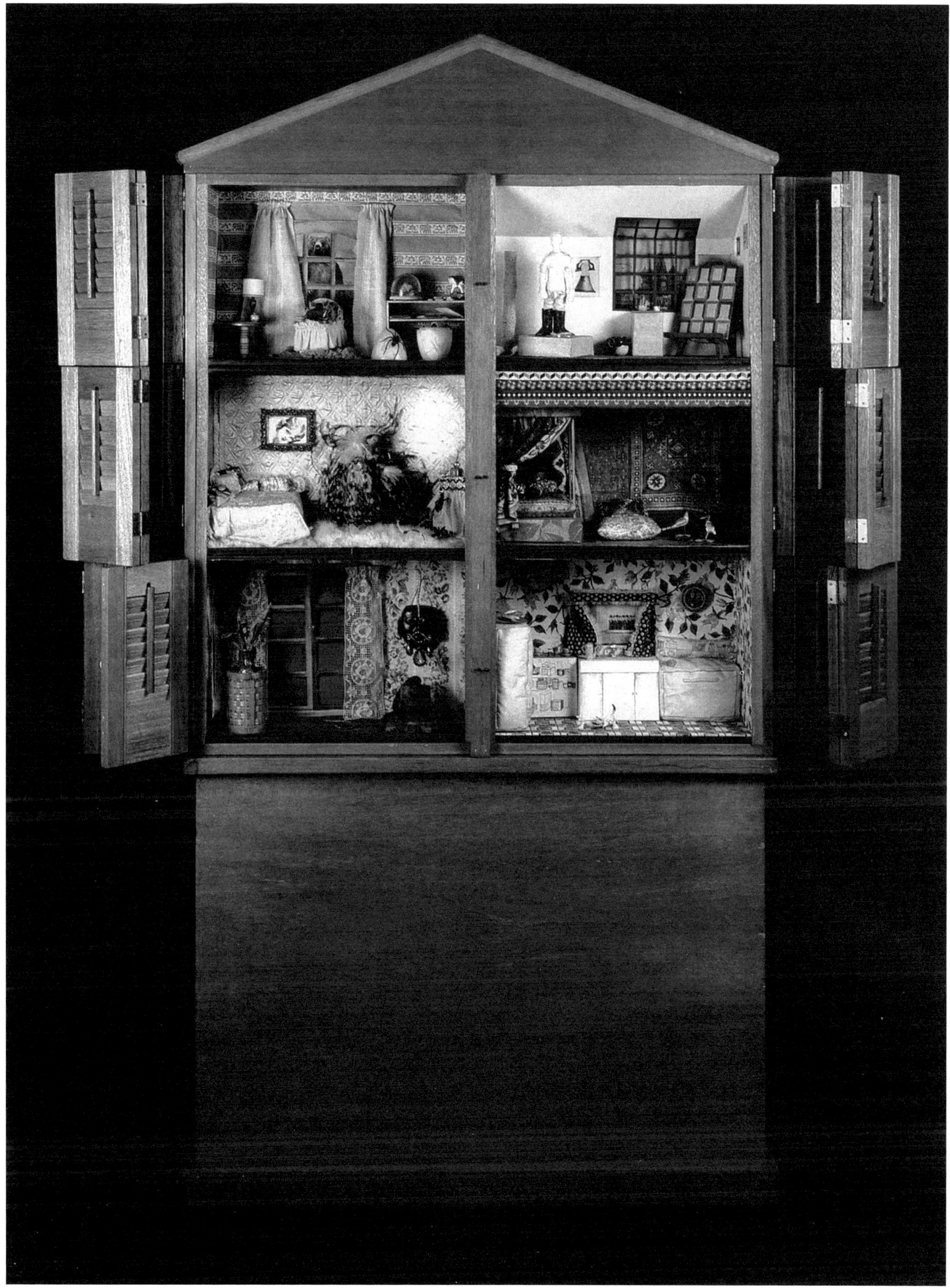

WOMANHOUSE: BODY AND BEAUTY

By Friederike Krause

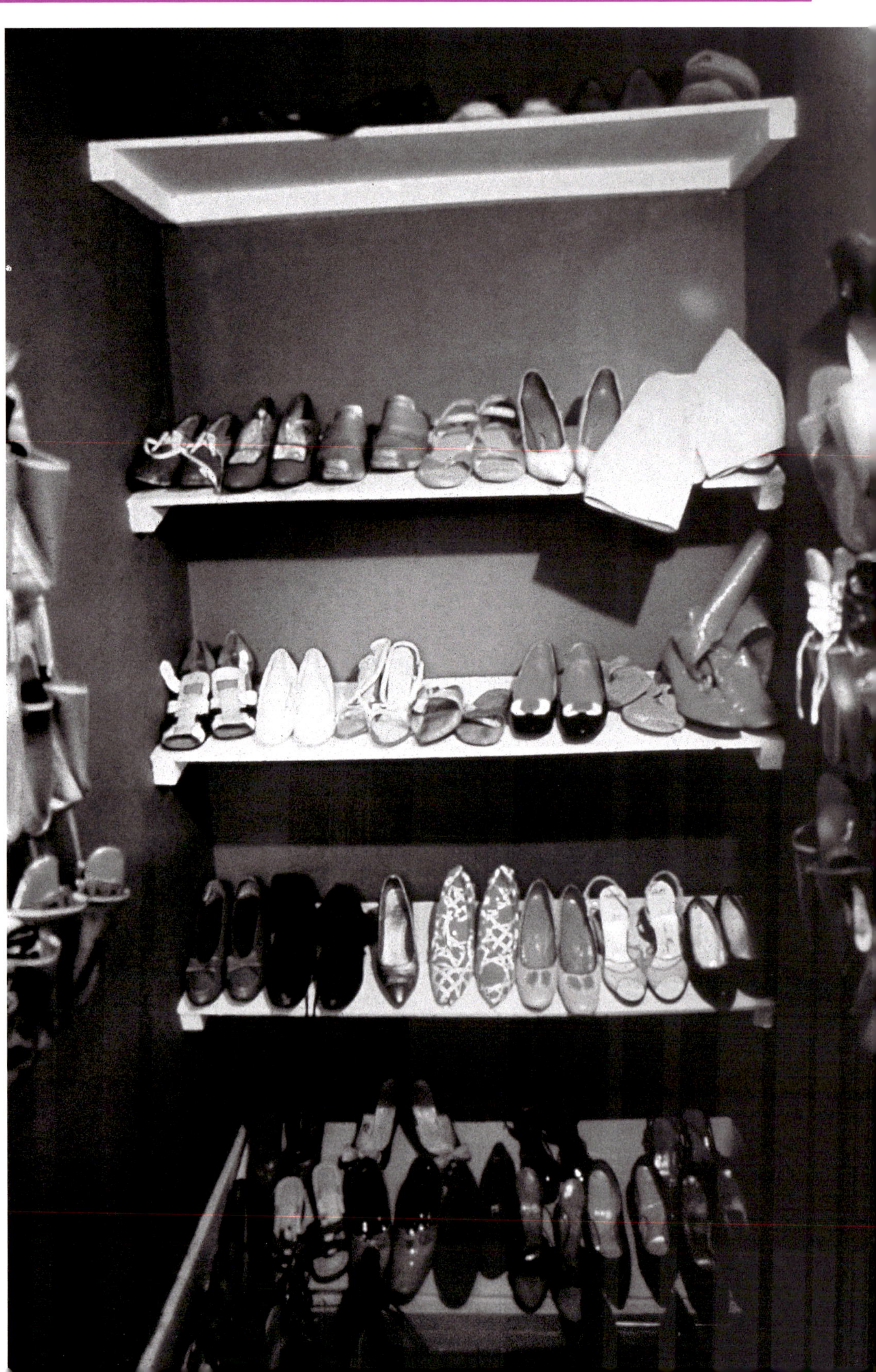

William Wilson states that there is a direct connection between "the patriarchal attitudes about women's connection to the body, nature, and the domestic."[1] The acceptance of women in society is predictated on ideals related to beauty and whether or not they are fulfilled, a phenomenon still observed today. The rooms of *Womanhouse* acted as a platform for addressing these beauty ideals and the structures women are living in.

Connected to beauty is the desire to look as youthful as possible. In the 1970s, white, middle-class women were usually housebound and economically dependent on their husbands. As a consequence, many women felt the urge to please their husbands through taking care of their body and dressing nicely, in order to be cared for and secured.[2] The fear of aging and the possible loss of attraction is captured in Karen LeCocq's and Nancy Youdelman's *Leah's Room* (1972). To achieve the standards of beauty, the use of products such as makeup, creams, and clothing play a major role. This urge to please is even "sometimes-frantic."[3] Judith Butler describes a transformational process of women, an "incorporation of norms,"[4] of the standards set by society about femininity and beauty. These attempts to fit in are further being addressed in Camille Grey's *Lipstick Room* (1972) and Beth Bachenheimer's *Shoe Closet* (1972).

Another topic related to the female body is the experience of menstruation. In order to be desirable, women must be clean and untouched, which stands in contradistinction with the natural reaction of the body to bleed every month. Menstruation is seen as a messy, nearly sinful affair, and not to be mentioned in either public or private. Although nearly every woman experiences this natural reaction of the body, women often find it hard to openly talk about the issues that come with it because of the negative associations society has created around the topic. Judy Chicago's *Menstruation Bathroom* (1972) addresses exactly this at *Womanhouse*, saying:

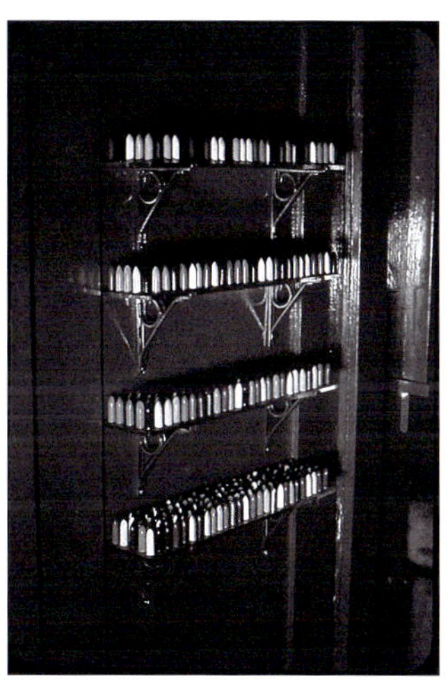

"Menstruation is something women either hide, are very matter-of-fact about, or are ashamed of. Until I was 32 years old, I never had a serious discussion with my female friends about menstruation. The bathroom is an image of women's hidden secret, covered over with a veil of gauze, very, very white and clean and deodorized—deodorized, except for the blood, the only thing that cannot be covered up. However we feel about our own menstruation is how we feel about seeing its image in front of us."[5] — Judy Chicago

In addressing issues of beauty and the body, the artists of *Womanhouse* questioned "the boundaries between essential and constructed meaning."[6] The artists wanted to unfold the consequences of stereotyping rather than aligning essentialist notions about the female body.[7] By emphasizing the performative nature of women's assigned roles, the artists exposed the performance needed to preserve the roles of the middle-class housewives in the 1970s.[8] It has to be stated, though, that these are topics which affect more than this single demographic, concerning all women, regardless of race, ethnic identity, age, class, or sexual orientation[9] existing in some form even today. The use of the woman in the rooms of *Womanhouse* have often been misinterpreted, "either as essentializing or as reiterating male paradigms for the representation of women."[10]

LEAH'S ROOM

In the performance installation *Leah's Room* by Karen LeCocq and Nancy Youdelman, both artists wanted to show the frustration of the aging woman, exemplified by the character Léa from Colette's 1920 novel, *Chéri*.

The aging courtesan Léa sits at her dressing table, in her watermelon-pink bedroom, and precisely applies makeup, only to then remove it in dissatisfaction before starting the application process again. The repetition of putting makeup on is used to show the constant, desperate struggle of many aging women, searching for anything that can make them look younger and therefore remain sexually attractive to men.[11]

"The performance ... portrays the pain: the pain of aging, of losing beauty, pain of competition with other women. We wanted to deal with the way women are intimidated by the culture to constantly maintain their beauty and the feeling of desperation and helplessness once this beauty is lost."[12] — Karen LeCoq & Nancy Youdelman

LIPSTICK BATHROOM & SHOE CLOSET

**"She cannot take a bath
The tub is lined with fur
200 plastic lipsticks
Painted repeated colors that
will not stain her lips...."[13]**
— Camille Grey

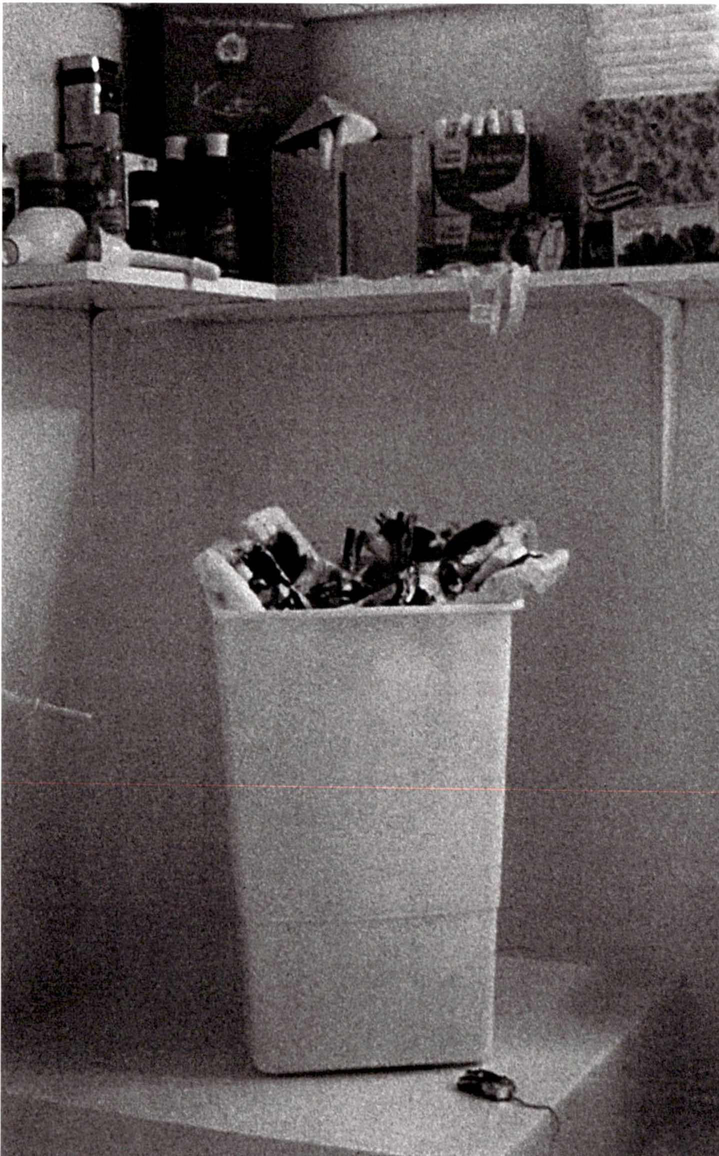

Lipstick Bathroom by Camille Grey and *Shoe Closet* by Beth Bachenheimer demonstrate the ways in which women try to "self-display"[14] in order to please their male partners. Through exaggeration, which lies in the amount of the lipsticks and shoes used, the artists want to show the doll-like character attributed to women. They are always ready to change their costume and mask (face) according to the likes of their partner.

**"The process of creating
this shoe-filled environment
was itself obsessive.
I collected hundreds of shoes
and painted or treated
each shoe individually...."[15]**
— Beth Bachenheimer

MENSTRUATION BATHROOM

Judy Chicago's *Menstruation Bathroom* was meant to visualize the struggle women face every month with the natural reactions of their body. The side effects that accompany menstruation include physical pain, depressive episodes, and premenstrual syndrome (PMS) caused by hormonal change, which can lead to social isolation, exclusion, and even disgust of one's own body. The bathroom shows all of those feelings, whereas some of them, like disgust, are often created by society. The bucket full of bloody hygiene articles visualizes Chicago's endeavor to no longer picture menstruation as a taboo, but rather a process that nearly every women goes through and gives her the chance to create life.

Previous spread, left: Beth Bachenheimer, *Womanhouse: Shoe Closet* (1972).
Previous spread, right: Camille Grey, *Womanhouse: Lipstick Bathroom* (1972).
Previous page: Judy Chicago, *Womanhouse: Menstruation Bathroom* (1972).
This page: Judy Chicago, *Womanhouse: Menstruation Bathroom* (1972).

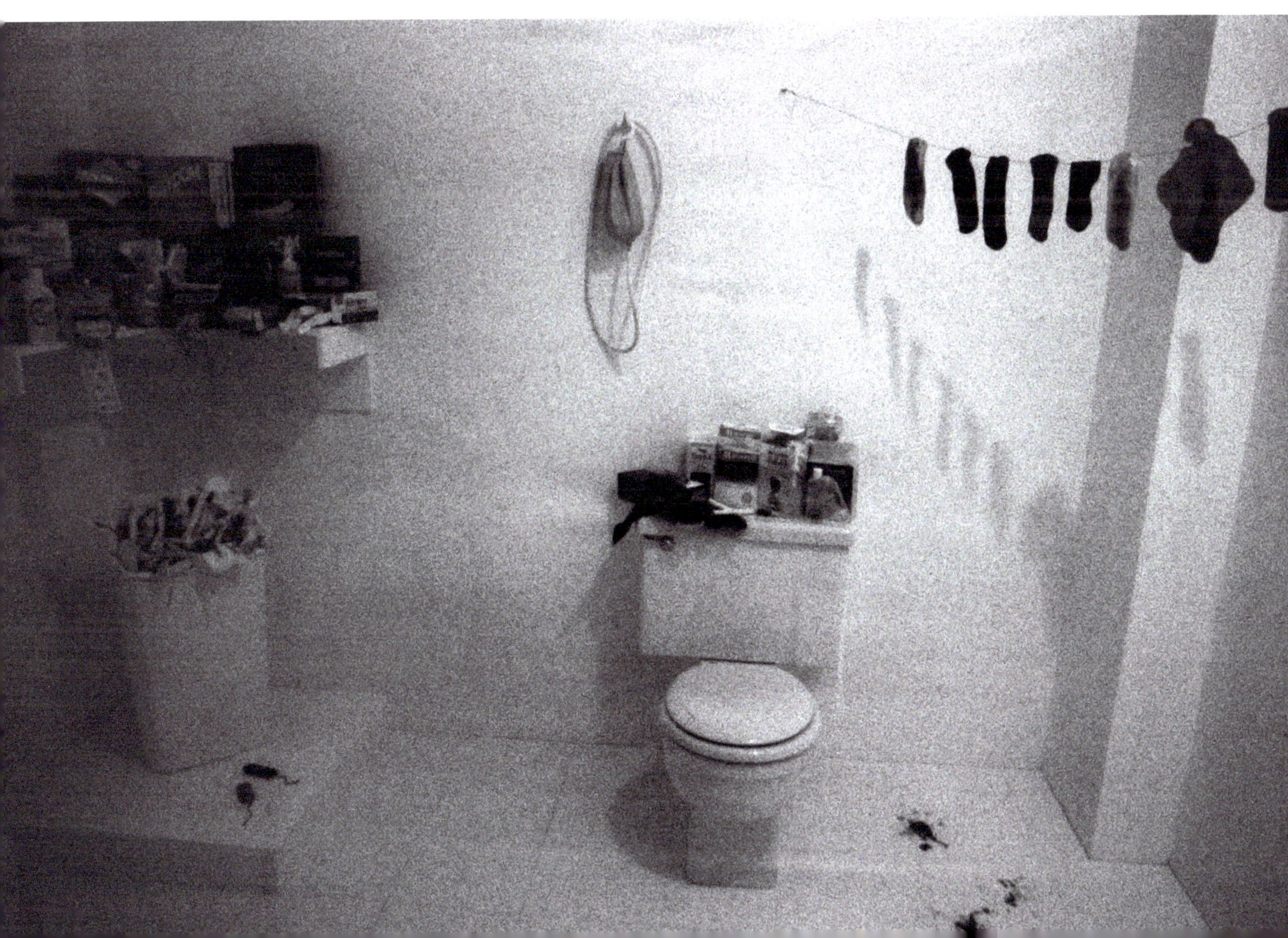

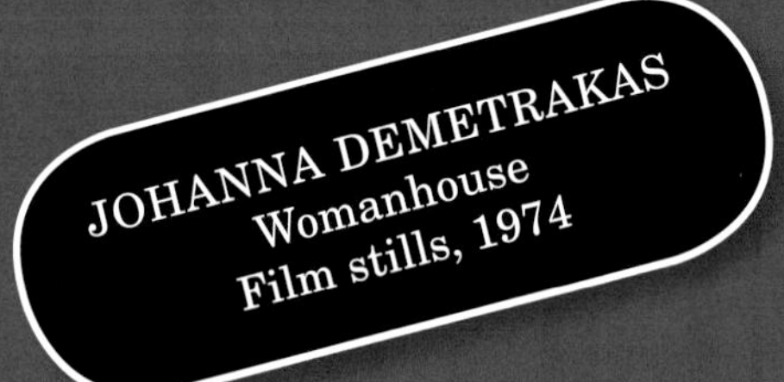

This 47-minute film, made by Johanna Demetrakas in 1974, shows the impact of *Womanhouse*. Combining interview-like situations with visitors with original footage of the performances and works, it shows the *Womanhouse* project through the means of historic documentary. With such an approach, Demetrakas not only gave a voice to the artists of *Womanhouse*, but the house itself also got a chance to speak.

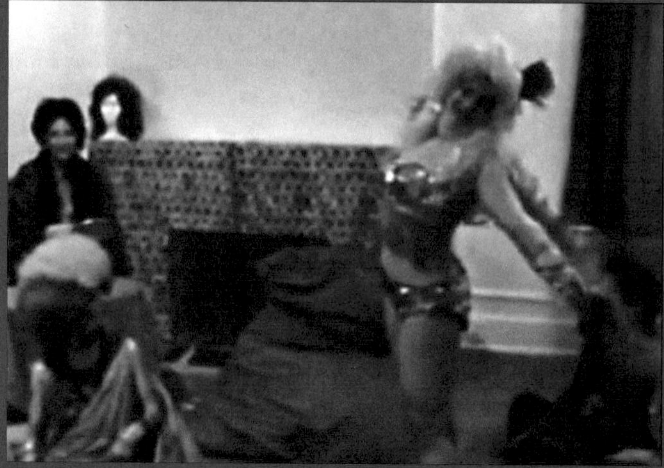

In *Three Women*, Jan Oxenburg, Shawnee Wollenman, and Nancy Youdelman represent three characters based on their own experiences: *Sparkly*, the tough hustler, *Rainbow*, the hippie chick, and *Roselyn*, the naive mother. They appear at first as stereotypes, both in the way they look and the story of the lives they are portraying. However, as they are telling their stories, their humanity and the suffering they experienced as women progressively appear.

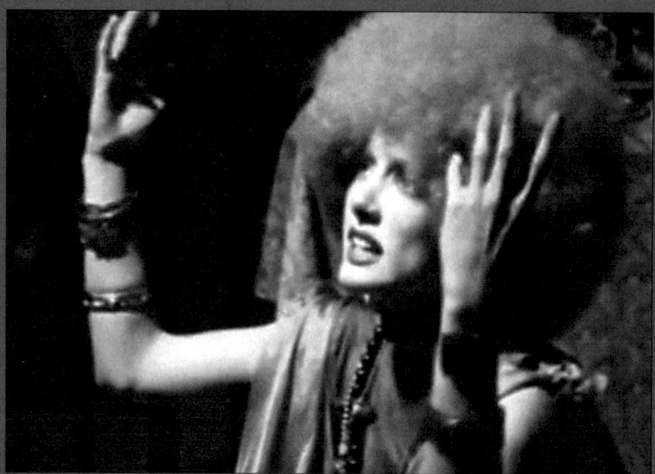

Rainbow, for instance, began her story by speaking about love and drugs in a clichéd, comical way. By the end of the story, however, she recalls a party where she was forcibly drugged and gang raped.

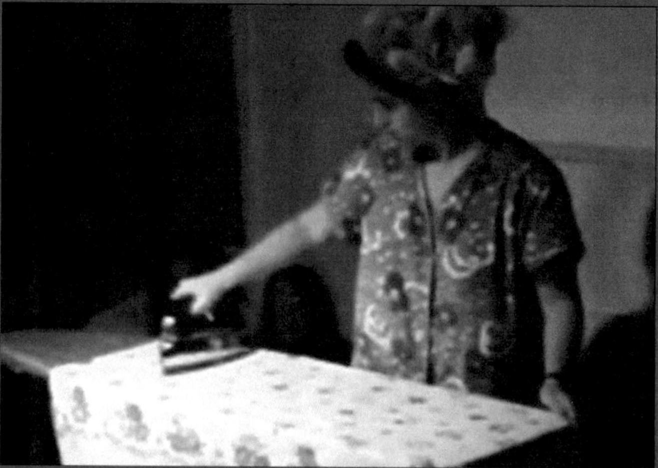

In *Ironing Piece*, Sandra Orgel carefully irons a large sheet. By highlighting the monotony of domestic tasks considered to be women's work, Orgel questions the idea of women finding fulfillment in their roles as housewives and invites women to free themselves from their socially ascribed positions.

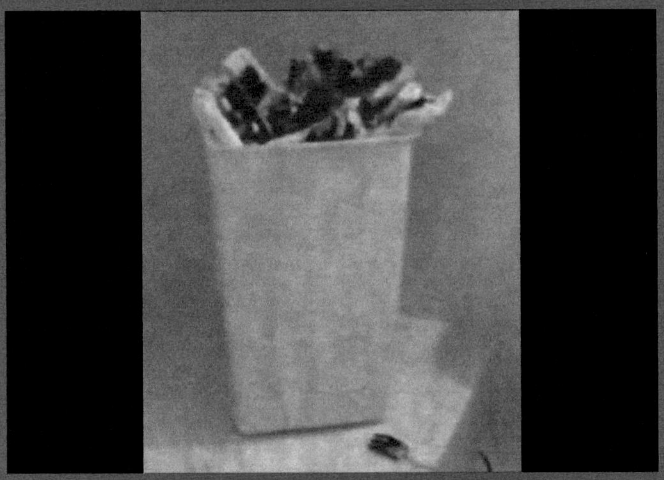

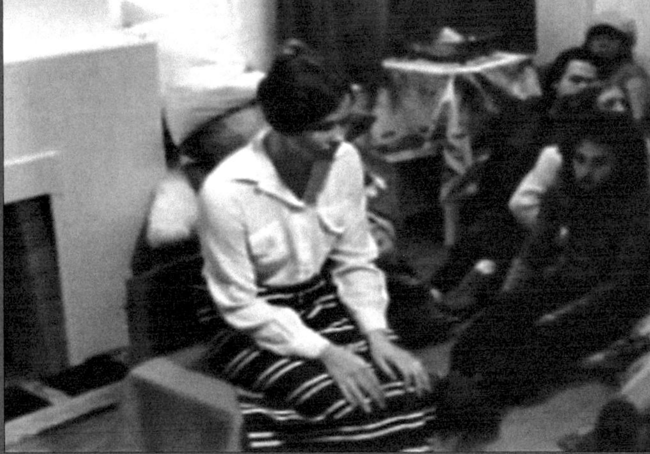

The purpose of *Menstruation Bathroom* by Judy Chicago is to bring into plain sight what is usually hidden and taboo. In the film, a female visitor describes her reaction to the installation. She said that seeing these kind of things, usually hidden behind a closed door, in public and with other people standing around her and looking at her, made her choke. As Chicago elucidates: "However we feel about our own menstruation is how we feel about seeing its image in front of us."[1]

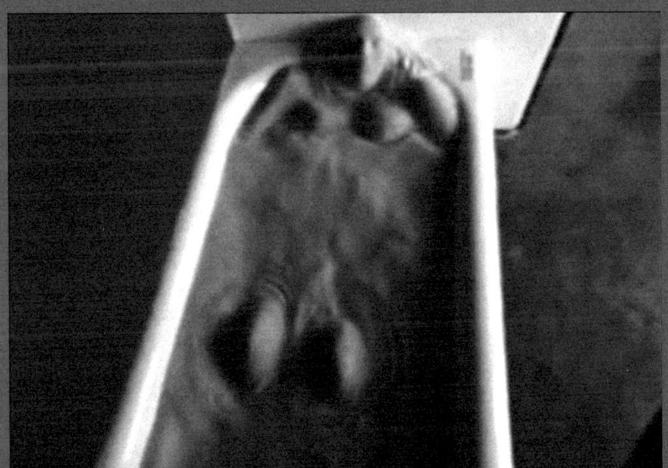

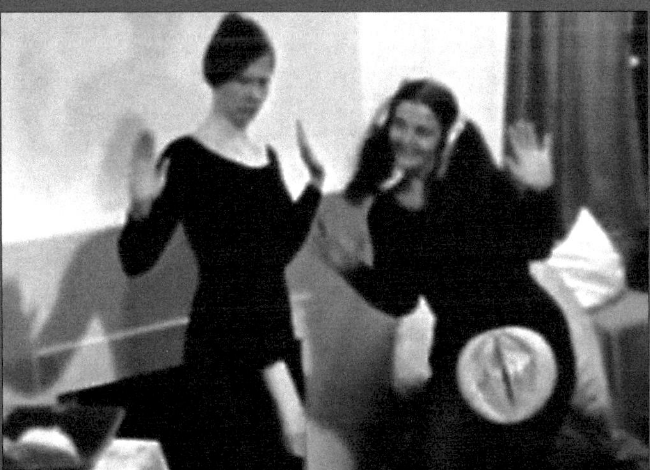

Another room installation at *Womanhouse* was Robin Schiff's *Nightmare Bathroom*. At its center is a sand sculpture of a woman lying in a bath-tub. The fragility of the sculpture conveys the vulnerability of women and, in the bathroom naked and exposed, the fear of being invaded. CG, LD

Cover of the first issue of *Womanspace Journal*, 1973

The *Womanspace Journal* was an integral part of the collaboratively-run gallery Womanspace devoted to artistic activities by women and founded in 1973. Due to lack of funding only three issues could be realized. In the second edition, Judy Chicago and Miriam Schapiro published their famous essay "The Female Imagery," in which they elaborate their concept of 'Central-Core Imagery.'

ABLUTIONS: A COLLABORATIVE PERFORMANCE

Ablutions was a collaboratively produced performance by Judy Chicago, Suzanne Lacy, Sandra Orgel, and Aviva Rahmani that took place in an art studio in Venice, California. The event was sponsored by the Feminist Art Program at the California Institute of the Arts (CalArts) and grew out of images developed during a performance class offered by Chicago after the *Womanhouse* project. The project was about rape, one of the first to deal with this issue in the modern era. It used audio recordings of women who described their experiences of rape, recorded by Lacy and Chicago, and was informed by Rahmani's earlier performance works on rape. Artists carefully selected images from each one's repertoire, including a binding image from Chicago and a construction image of animal organs and twine from Lacy. One of the most striking images was that of Sandra Orgel's bathing in eggs, to which the artists collectively added tubs of blood and clay, giving rise to the title of *Ablutions* (ritual bathing). Lacy described it this way:

"The audience entered a large open art studio, drawn by Chicago's visibility and her social network. Three body-sized galvanized metal tubs on the concrete floor were each filled with a different substance—eggs, blood, and clay. Around the tubs broken eggshells, piles of rope and chain, and animal kidneys were strewn. The soundtrack played continuously, one woman after the other telling the intimate and explicit details of their rapes—information not part of public culture at that time. A nude woman was slowly bound from feet to scalp with gauze bandages while two others bathed in the tubs, first eggs, then blood, then clay. As each one emerged from the final tub, caked with clay cracked to reveal rivulets of blood, she was wrapped in a sheet like a corpse. Throughout the performance, Lacy nailed 50 beef kidneys to the wall, encasing the room like a spinal column surrounded by its organs. The performance ended with two women— Lacy and Jan Lester, the bandager— stringing light rope over the set, until the performance stage was a spider web of entrapment. The voices on the tape droned on as if there was no escape from the brutalization, ending with the audio tape stuck on a chilling note, repeating like a broken record: 'I felt so helpless, all I could do was just lie there.'"[1]

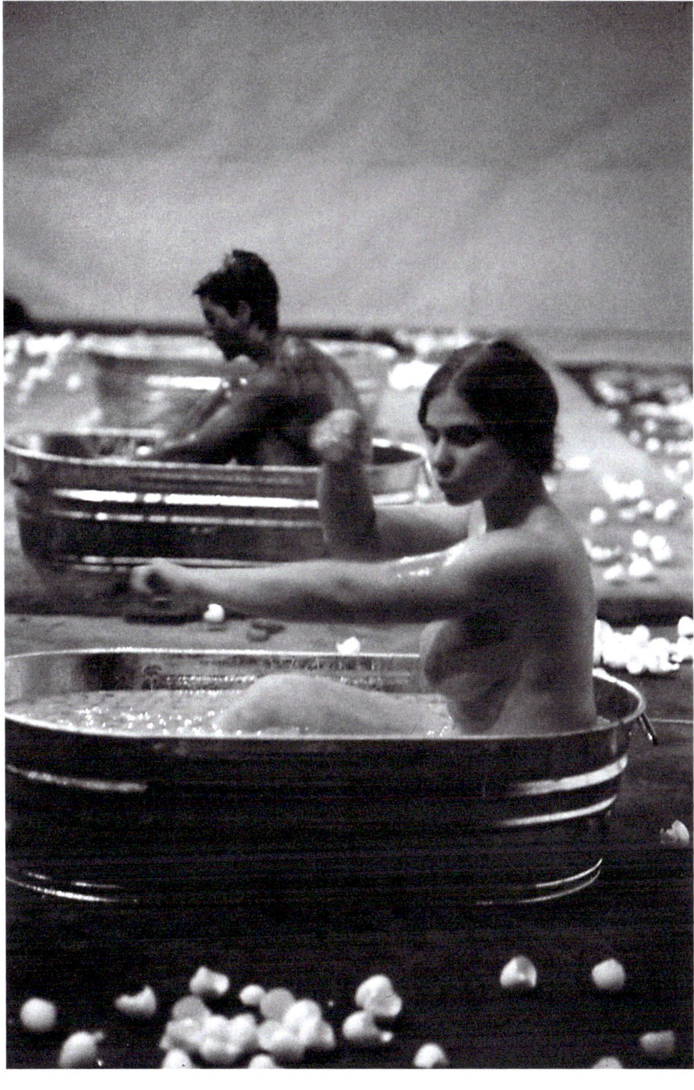

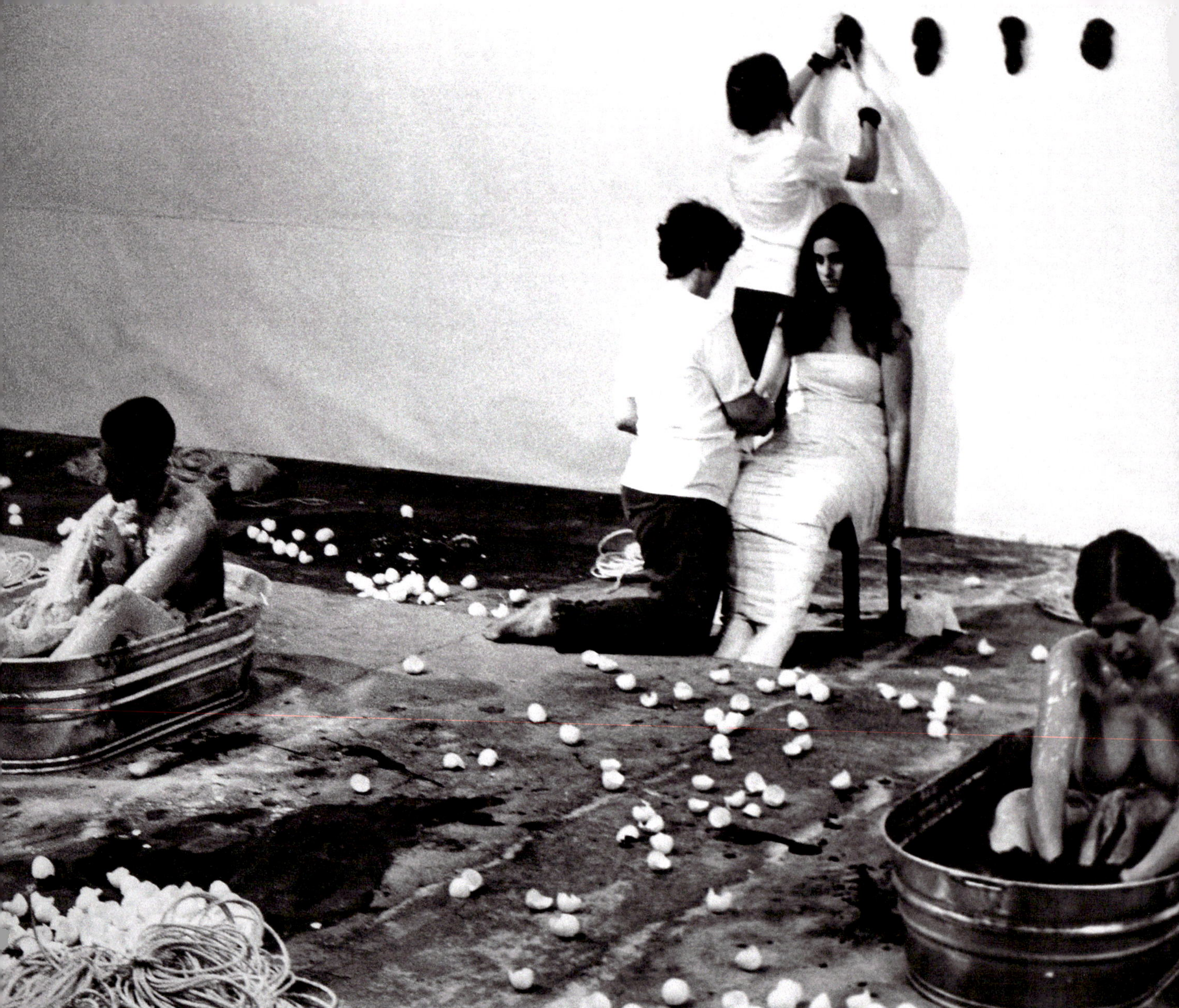

In a recent interview (September 2012), Suzanne Lacy recalls the importance of Allan Kaprow as an influence on her work in this performance:

"At CalArts (1971–73), I worked with Judy, Sheila Levrant de Bretteville and Miriam Schapiro in their feminist programmes, and I also began a life-long relationship with Allan Kaprow. It was a fertile moment when art was changing in the direction of performance, conceptual art, and installation. In 1972, I did a performance with Judy, Sandra Orgel and Aviva Rahmani called *Ablutions*. We staged a series of images around our bodies: a woman was bound with gauze; women bathed in raw eggs, earth and blood; and a tape recording of women talking about rape droned throughout."[2]

This work was, as she later stated,

"influenced by the formal stylizations of Happenings as promoted by Kaprow—a form of experimental performance that Rahmani was also fluent in. The narrative structure of the work was abstracted, less like traditional literary theater where actors assume roles in a 'plot,' and drawn instead from the narratives of reportage and an assembly of abstract visual sequences. Happenings like *Meat Joy* by Carolee Schneeman and artists like Kaprow himself thus must be seen as one part of the heritage of this work, along with the passionate advocacy and social import brought into contemporary art by artists like Chicago and other feminists of the era. This, I think, demonstrates the fertility of the CalArts experiment."[3]
AJL

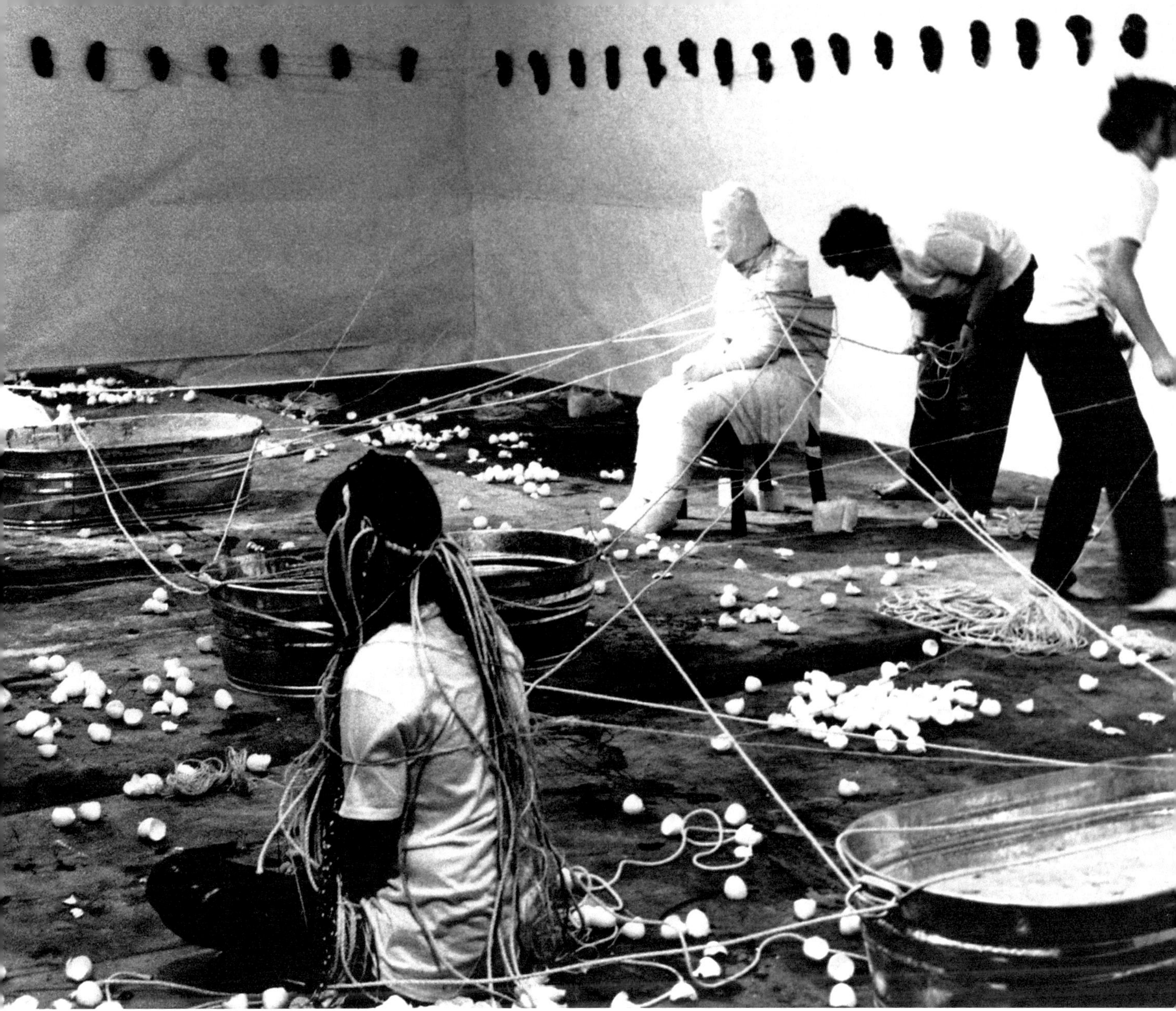

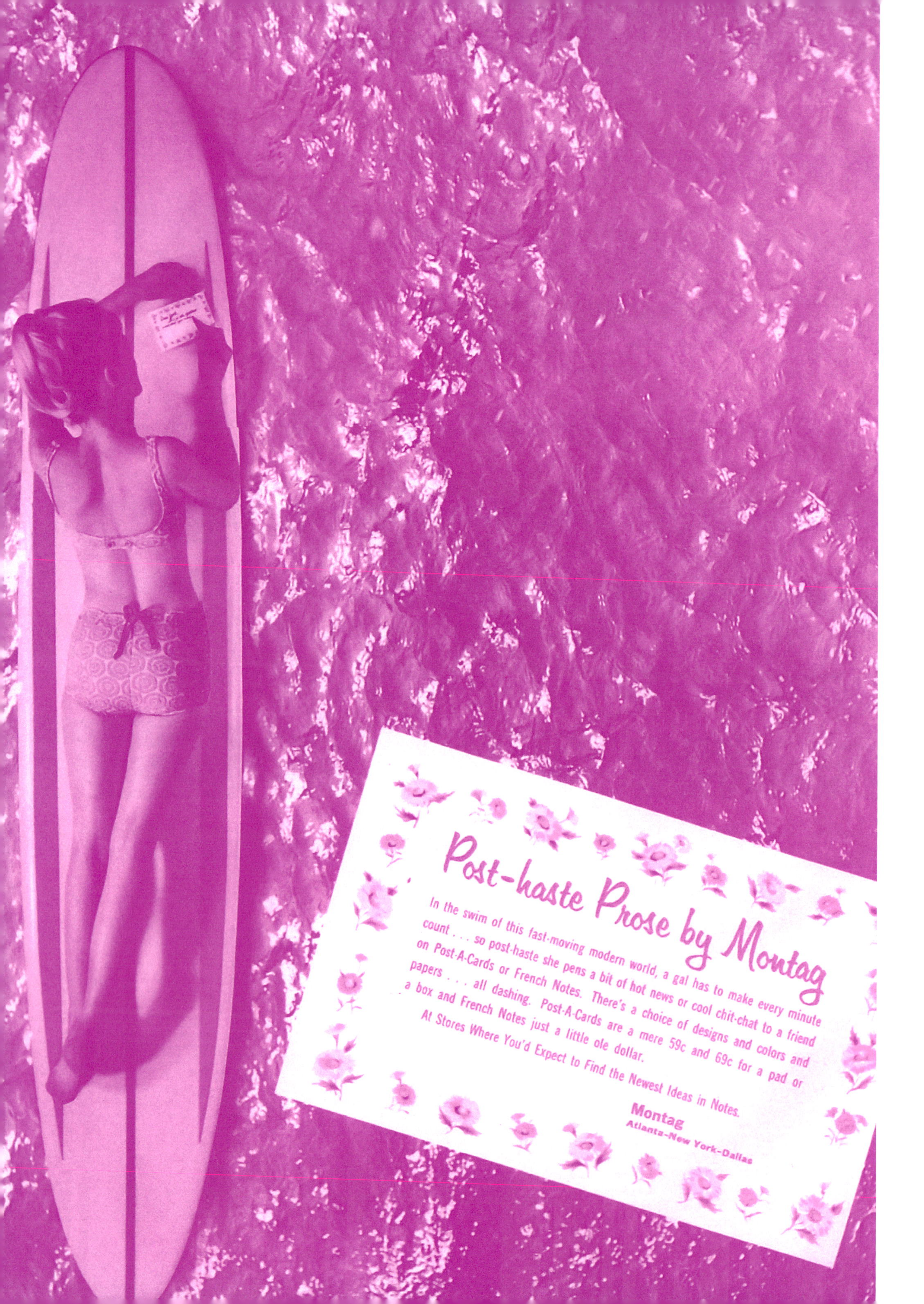
Post-haste Prose by Montag
In the swim of this fast-moving modern world, a gal has to make every minute count . . . so post-haste she pens a bit of hot news or cool chit-chat to a friend on Post-A-Cards or French Notes. There's a choice of designs and colors and papers . . . all dashing. Post-A-Cards are a mere 59c and 69c for a pad or a box and French Notes just a little ole dollar.
At Stores Where You'd Expect to Find the Newest Ideas in Notes.
Montag
Atlanta—New York—Dallas

ULRIKE ROSENBACH AND THE L.A. FEMINIST ART SCENE

By Verena Kittel

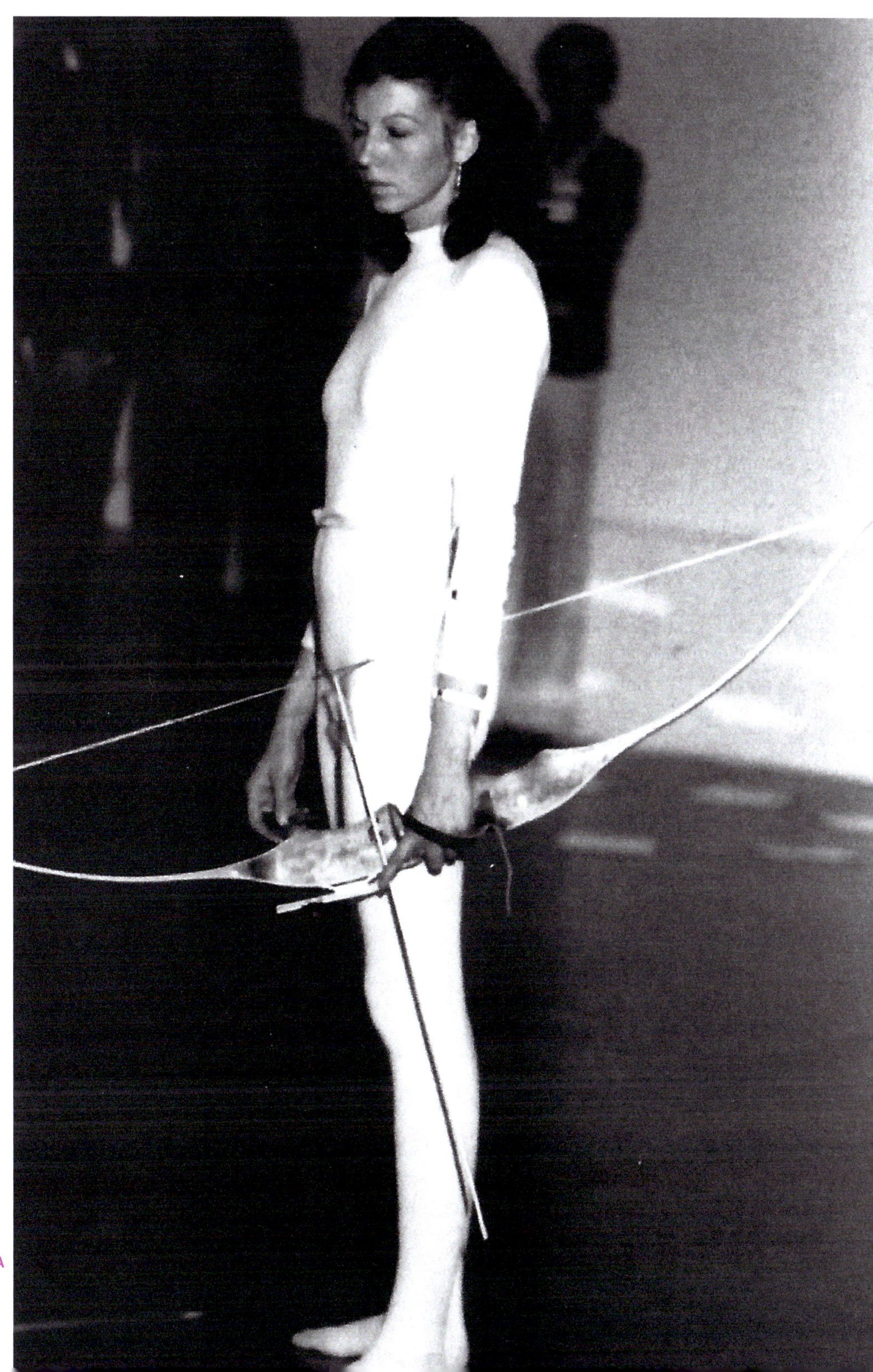

A

"And then there was Miriam Schapiro, and she was very tough…. She was so extreme with her views that she scared people. I found her extreme myself. She was so aggressive, but very nice. I didn't really want to get so close to her though, that was a bit much for me. Then the two women [Schapiro and Chicago] had to leave. And then, of course, there were all of those female students who had studied with them. These women didn't really want to give up studying with these two women, which is why the institute created the Feminist Art Board … it was something they could control. They could kick people out, like me. I didn't know any of that when I started."[1]

With these words, Ulrike Rosenbach gives her impression of Miriam Schapiro, co-founder of the Feminist Art Program (FAP) at the California Institute of the Arts (CalArts) in 1971, and the situation of feminist education at the institute when she arrived at the art school in 1975. After the first feminist art exhibition, *Womanhouse*, difficulties between its founders Schapiro and Judy Chicago and in maintaining its feminist and institutional-critical approach on a permanent basis meant that, by 1973, the FAP consisted only of several workshops and, by 1975, was reduced to one painting class per week led by Schapiro. As Rosenbach recalls, when Schapiro left, CalArts established a "Feminist Art Board," in which students could propose lecturers with a feminist focus. In this context, Rosenbach, who studied sculpture with Joseph Beuys at the Kunstakademie Düsseldorf from 1964 to 1972, was invited to teach "Practical Video Art and Feminist Art" for two terms[2] at CalArts upon the advice of John Baldessari. The German artist had had several connections to the L.A. art scene through, among others, the U.S. American art critic Lucy Lippard, who included her in her signature exhibition *c. 7000*, Willoughby Sharp, publisher of the art magazine *Avalanche*, who saw Rosenbach's first video live performance at Kölner Kunstmarkt in 1973, as well as her fellow student Leslie Labowitz-Starus. Labowitz-Starus had studied at Otis Art Institute in Los Angeles from 1969 to 1971 before coming to the Kunstakademie in Düsseldorf on a Fulbright Fellowship to study with Beuys. Rosenbach, together with Labowitz-Starus, who with *Menstruation Wait* had already experimented with feminist performance at Otis, Maria Fisahn, and Claudia Andre—the only women responding to her original call—formed a women's video group. The four women, referencing the Canadian artist Carolee Schneeman and her famous performance piece *Interior Scroll*, exhibited video and narrative photographs dealing with menstruation in the exhibition *between 7* at the Kunsthalle Düsseldorf.[3] As menstruation was still a taboo topic and, according to Labowitz-Starus, "the feminist concept 'the personal is political' was virtually unknown"[4] at the Kunstakademie, their presentation was highly controversial.[5] But, as Rosenbach recalls, the audience at Düsseldorf was already outraged after Labowitz-Starus's video-taped performance of her simply untwisting her curls in public. The artist attributed such negative reactions to these feminist forays to the domination of abstraction and minimalism and the art market's demand for an art without context.[6]

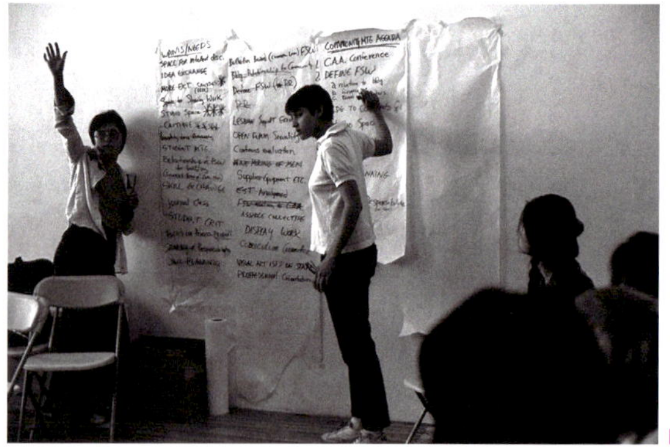

B

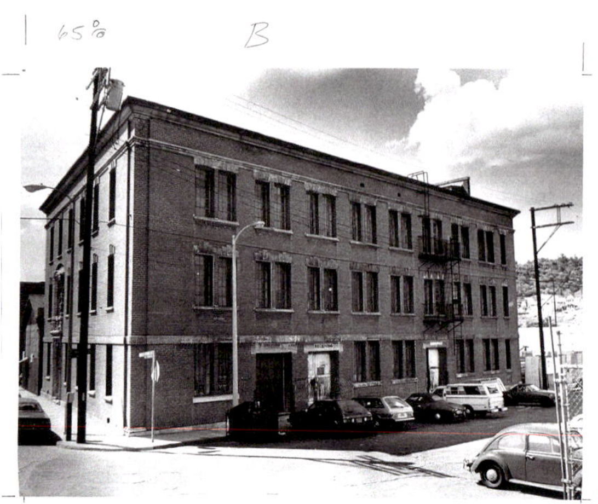

C

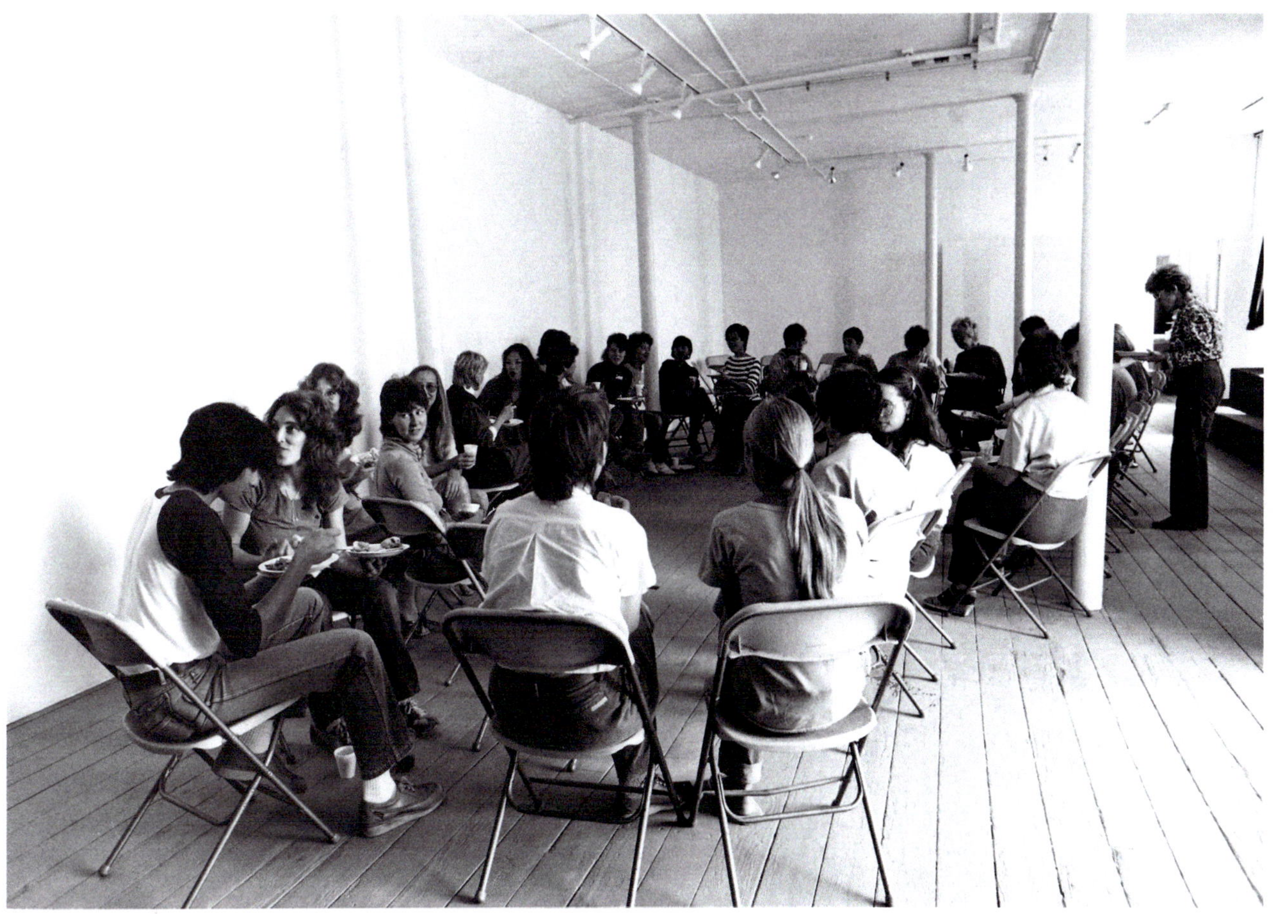

D

When Rosenbach arrived in L.A. in 1975, she encountered a much more active feminist art scene. Even though neither Chicago nor Schapiro, for whom Rosenbach originally came to CalArts,[7] were still teaching at the art school, she was in close contact with the feminist art scene in L.A., particularly with the Woman's Building. The community center for the promotion of women artists opened its doors in 1973 and included, among other things, a gallery, a women's press, a coffee shop, and the Feminist Studio Workshop[8] founded by Judy Chicago, Sheila Levrant de Bretteville, and Arlene Raven, with its focus on feminist art education following the structure of the FAPs at Fresno and CalArts. The Woman's Building, furthermore, offered several young women artists a public platform to present their work in the form of exhibitions, performances, lectures, and workshops, including Ulrike Rosenbach, who showed her performance *Reflections on the Birth of Venus* at the Woman's Building in 1976—the conclusion of her working cycle in the United States.[9]

In L.A., Rosenbach deepened her artistic investigation of female identity, which began in Europe with the video performance *Don't Believe I'm an Amazon* at the 9th Biennale de Jeunes in Paris in 1975. The exchange with the feminist art scene in L.A. inspired her to expand her visual language with explicitly female forms and symbols.[10] In the artworks that followed, Rosenbach explored women's relationship to aspects of

A/E/F	Ulrike Rosenbach, *Glauben Sie nicht, dass ich eine Amazone bin* (1975).
B	FSW community meeting (1976).
C	Side view of Woman's Building on Spring Street (undated). Side entrance and parking lot on Aurora Street.
D	Open House (undated), Woman's Building. Group photo of women sitting in folding chairs in a circle.
G	Ulrike Rosenbach, *Madonnas of the Flowers* (1975).
H	Ulrike Rosenbach, *Aphrodite TV* (1975) .
I	Ulrike Rosenbach, *Reflections on the Birth of Venus* (1976).
J	Ulrike Rosenbach, *Female Energy Exchange: Zehn Bilder zum Tarot* (1976).
K	Ulrike Rosenbach, *Female Energy Exchange: Venus* (1975/76).

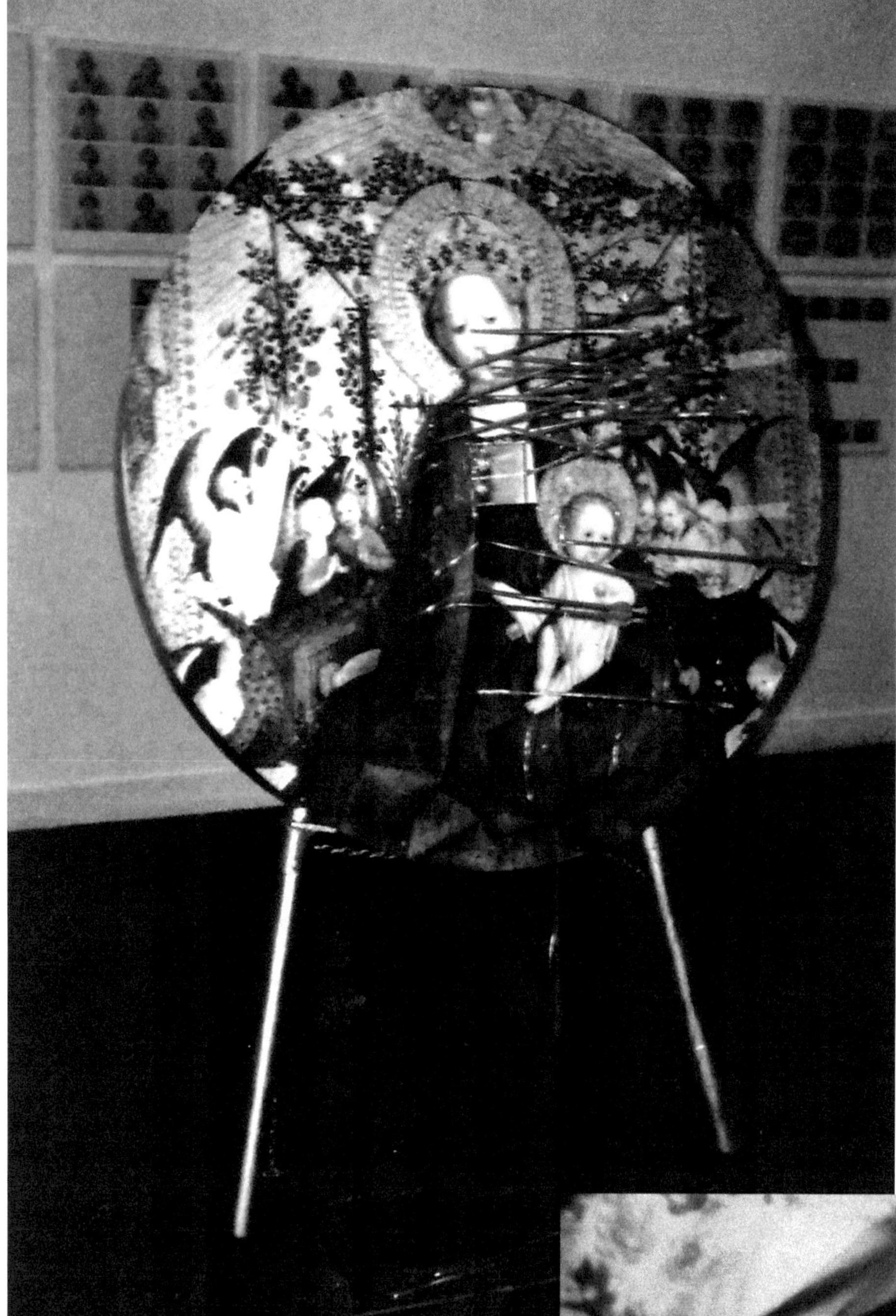

E

F

beauty and motherhood, hotly debated issues in the feminist movements of the 1970s, as visible in demonstrations against the Miss America pageant in 1968, but also in the artworks produced in the FAPs at Fresno and CalArts, most notably *Womanhouse*. Her encounter with the American entertainment industry and advertising spectacles like the Pasadena Rose Parade, both of which portrayed a sexist image of women and exploited figures like Venus to fulfill the erotic needs of a male gaze, led to an intensified examination and questioning of the expected role of women and beauty ideals in her works, particularly through the use of Venus and Madonna imagery.[11] The photograph tableau *Aphrodite TV* (1976) portrays prominent Hollywood actresses on video monitors inside small shells, accompanied by text extracts from interviews about their own self-images. These themes are also visible in the video *Madonnas of the Flowers* (1975), in which the faces of Rosenbach and her daughter appear in front of transparent coronae, veiled with gauze and abstracted through light reflexes. The work addresses the reduction of female identity to being beautiful and young. In her photo series *Female Energy Change (Venus, Minerva, Supergirl)* (1975) and *Zehn Bilder zum Tarot* (1976)), but also in the later performance *Reflection on the Birth of Venus*, Rosenbach works with superimpositions of her own image over photographs of historical paintings such as Sandro Botticelli's *The Birth of Venus* and works by William H. Hunt and Edward Burne-Jones, artists Rosenbach found in the library at CalArts.[12] By taking up strong, self-confident poses, she converted the clichéd representation of women as passive, obedient, and innocent into active, independent, and self-determined images of women. *Reflections on the Birth of Venus* was Rosenbach's first large-scale slide production. Since, in the 1970s, the projection of video was prohibitively expensive,[13] Rosenbach instead threw a life-size still image of Boticelli's original onto a wall; in front was a triangle of salt and a shell made out of styrofoam. Carrying a small video screen, she stepped into the projection and slowly turned around for 15 minutes. Wearing a tricot that was black on the rear and white on the front allowed Rosenbach to become one with the symbol of youth and beauty, but also to detach herself from the image when turning around.

Rosenbach's experiences with the feminist art scene in L. A., especially the activities at the Woman's Building, not only influenced her imagery, becoming evident in the increased use of symbols analogous to the female genitalia such as the shell or the triangle,[14] but also inspired her to lead her own activist feminist pedagogical ventures. According to Rosenbach, her attempt to organize a women's conference, with programs in performance that brought together different departments at CalArts, led to negative reactions in the art department and ultimately to the non-renewal of her contract.[15] When she ultimately returned to Germany in 1976, Rosenbach became involved in Alice Schwarzer's newly founded magazine *Emma*, co-initiated the first cultural center for women, and in 1977 founded the School of Creative Feminism in Cologne. Inspired by the educational methods and activities of the Woman's Building, Rosenbach organized a work group for interested women to express and talk about their experiences and to extend their possibilities of artistic expression.[16] Weekly sessions were dedicated to consciousness-raising practices, in which each woman related their experiences regarding a certain topic without judgement, in order to open access to new creative potential and politicize lived experience, to re-evaluate art history with regards to the role of women artists, and finally art making.[17] One of the aims of the School of Creative Feminism was to work against a definition of art that follows a male concept of creation and assigns women a reproductive role.[18] In the United States, the ground for feminist art organizations and activities had already been laid, yet the artistic environment in Europe was less open to feminist ideas.[19] Ulrike Rosenbach, with her use of media such as video, photography, large-scale slide projections, combined with performance, and her work with superimposition, not only introduced an unconventional approach to feminist art to the L. A. art scene. Her contact and experiences with the Woman's Building, moreover, gave her insights into new methods and ways of organization to support, politicize, and unite women artists that she brought to and employed in Cologne, playing an important role in the formation and development of the feminist art scene in Germany.

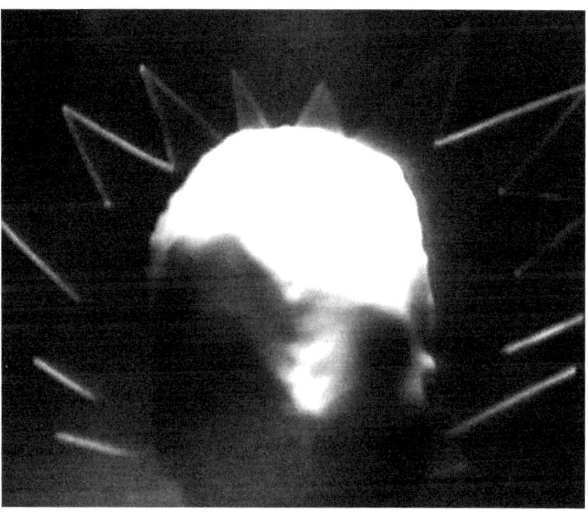

G

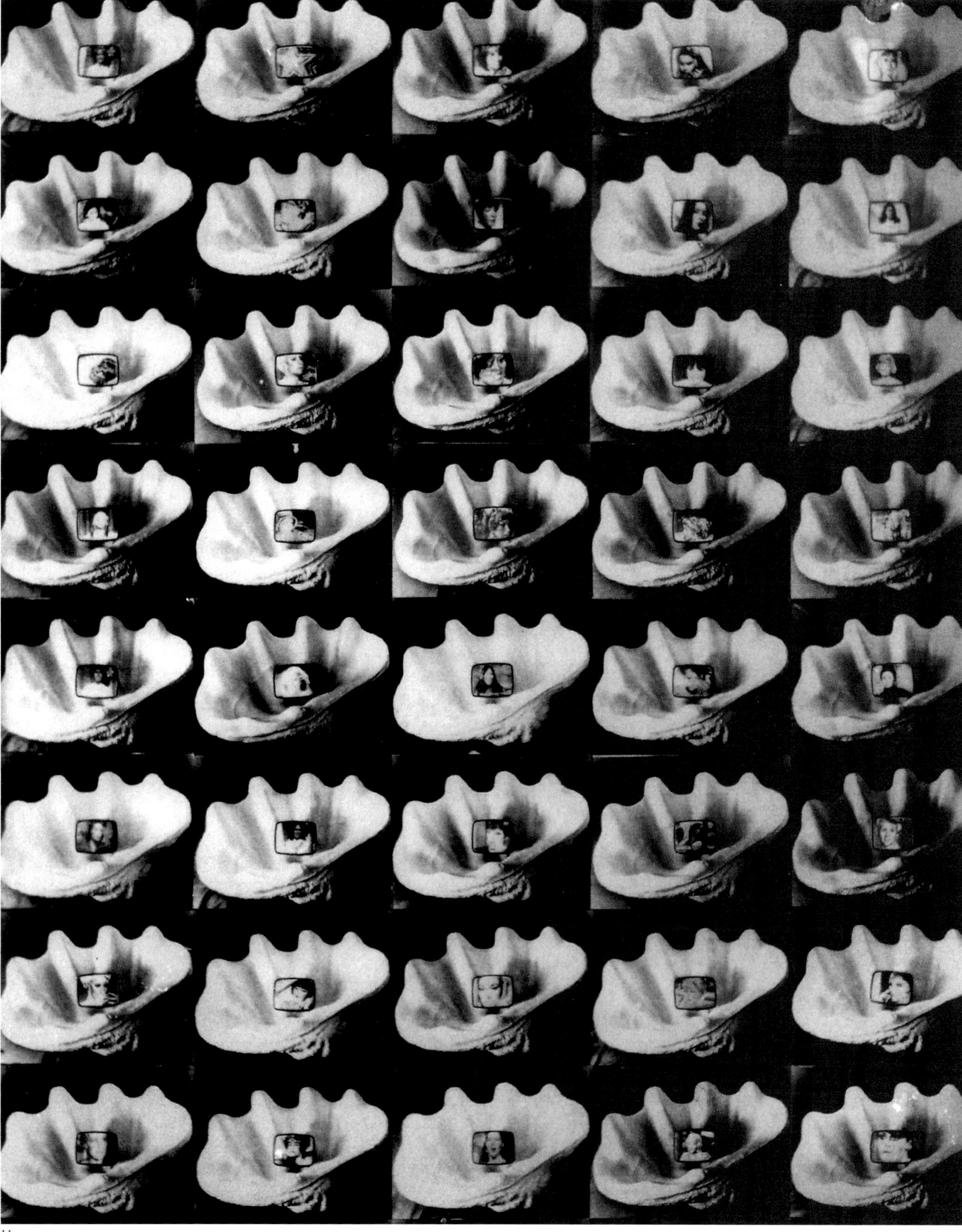

H

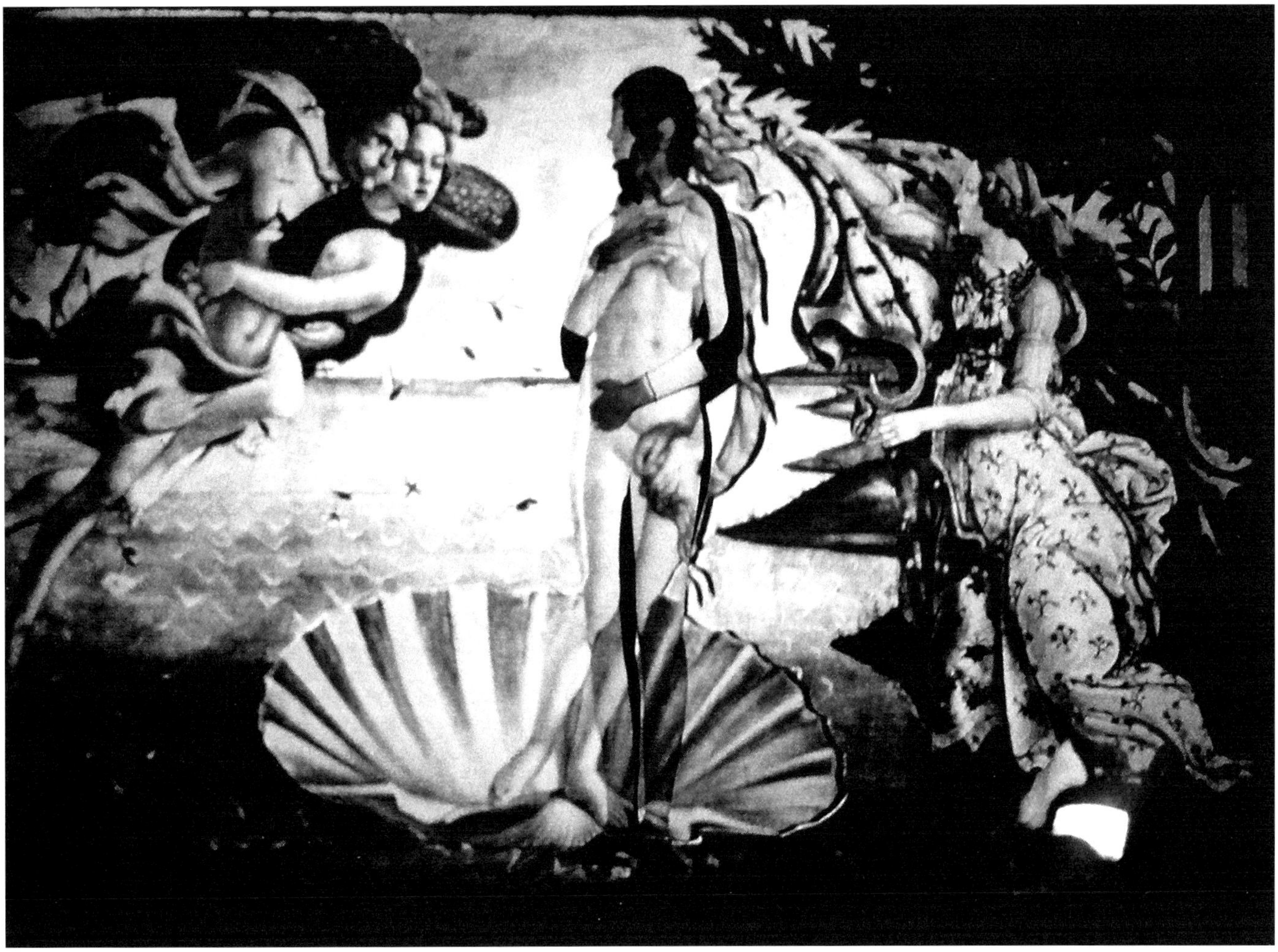

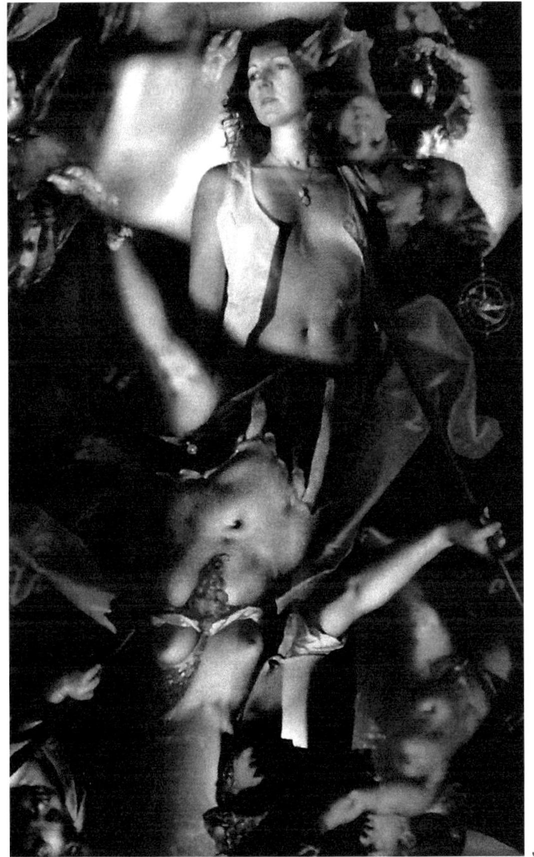

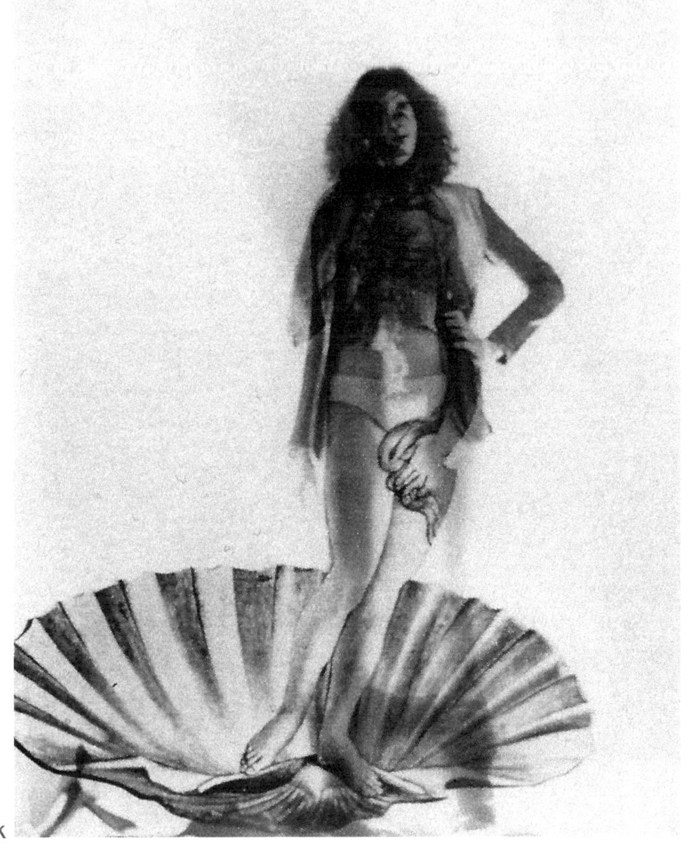

The "notice anything different about me tonight dear?" Pudding.

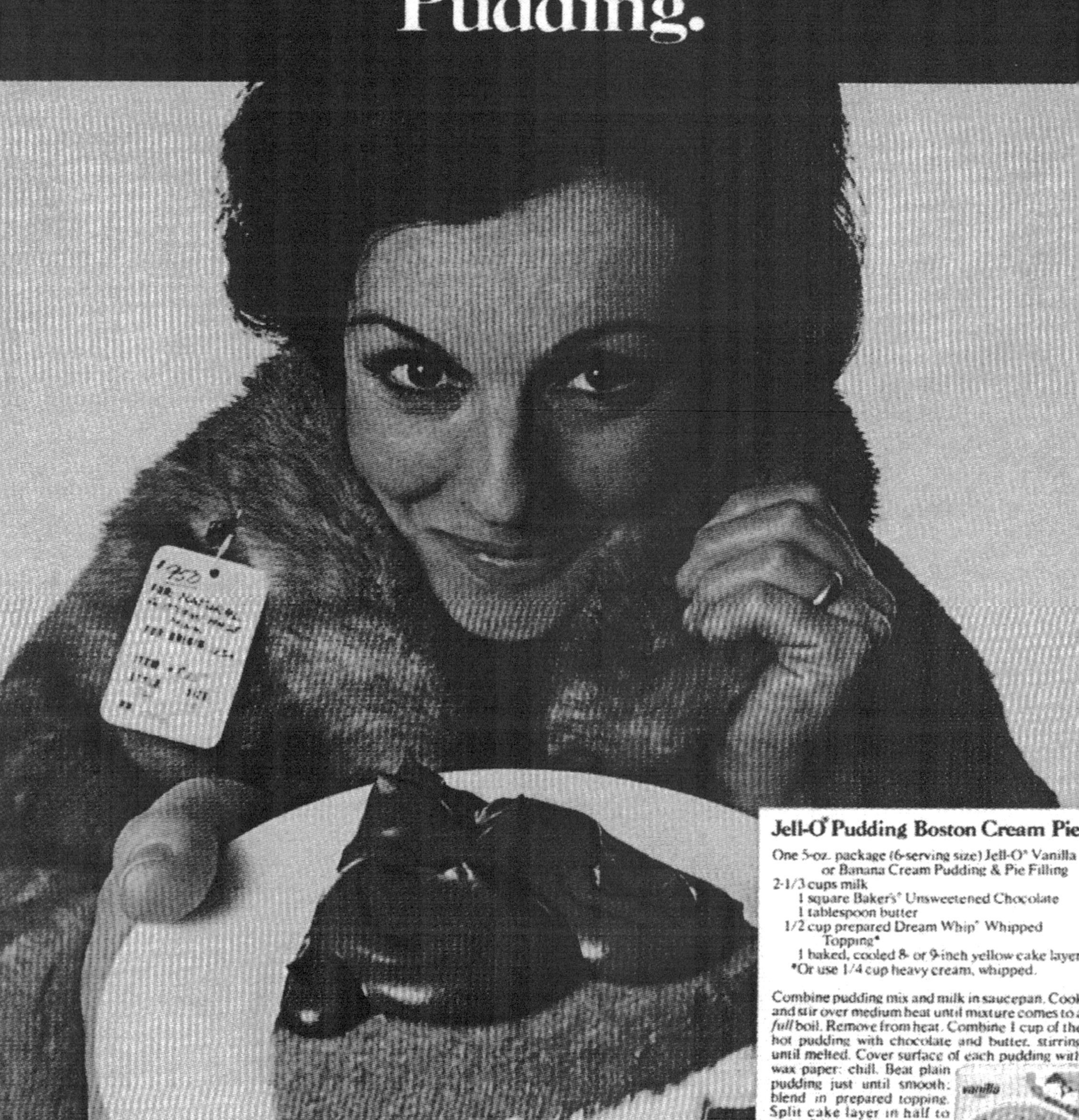

SUZANNE LACY

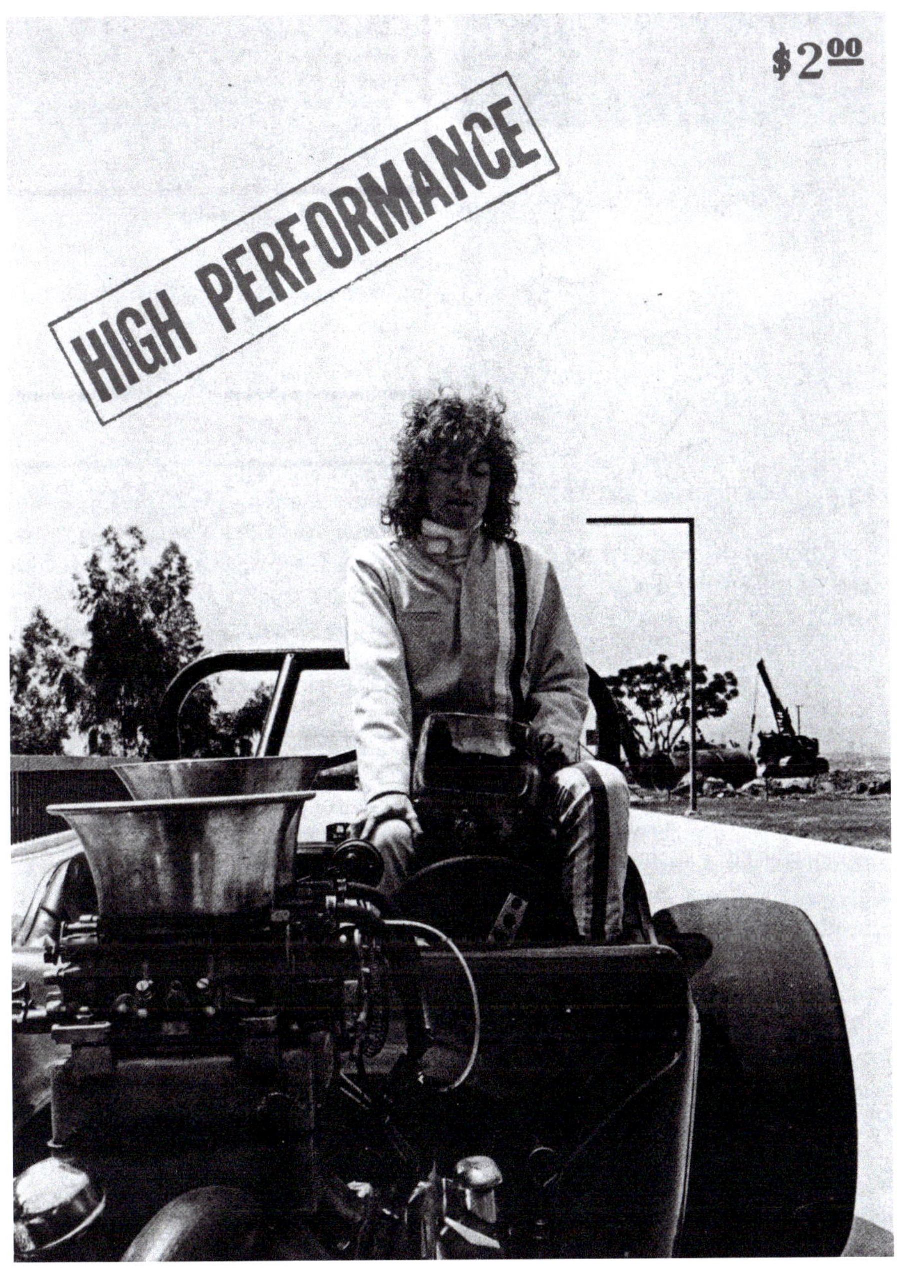

Cover of *High Performance* 1, no. 1 (1978), featuring Suzanne Lacy's traveling project *Cinderella in a Dragster* (1976). Photo by Susan Mogul.

* 1945, Wasco (CA), USA

is an artist who works in performance, video, installation, and critical writing. Her work is well-known for dealing with the intersection of art and activism and its specific mode of public and social practice in happening-like situations or installations within communities, which are often conceptualized as interventionist long-term projects.[1] Aiming to initiate public discourse and community-building, her projects implement the political idea of local networking and social exchange and contributed heavily to the formation of socially engaged art. She examines social and urban concerns such as rape, violence, racism, class, and gender.[2]

Lacy studied at the California Institute of the Arts (CalArts) and participated in the Feminist Art Program. During this time, together with Judy Chicago, Sandra Orgel, and Aviva Rahmani, she co-produced *Ablutions* (1972) by connecting different images produced by the artists and their work approaches.[3] For *Three Weeks in May* (1977), she created a performance series that combined performance, installation, and other events to address rape culture and sexual violence against women.[4] Together with Leslie Labowitz-Starus she created *In Mourning and In Rage* (1977).[5] The more recent project *Between the Door and Street* (2013) involved 360 participants—women on stoops in Brooklyn debated the intersection of activism and gender.[6] Further works include *Storying Rape* (2012), *The Oakland Projects* (1991–2001) and *The Crystal Quilt* (1985–87).

Lacy has received reviews from the *L.A. Times*, *Artforum*, and *Art in America* and is exhibited internationally, e.g. at the Tate Modern, London, the Liverpool Biennial, the MoCA, L.A., and at Museo Pecci Milano. She currently teaches at Roski School of Fine Arts at University of Southern California.[7] **LB**

A THREE-WEEK-LONG PERFORMANCE

Tues MAy 10, 1977
~~Sat, April 5, 1975~~
4:00 pm this afternoon

This incident oscurred in ~~San Pedro~~. [SAnta Mon]

~~V-F-0-22~~
~~Suspects 2M-0-30~~

S#2 and V previously engaged. S's gave V a' ride. S#1 ordered V to take off her pants. S#1 forc3d V to have sexual inter. ~~S#1 then forced V to orally cop him.~~ S#2 then forced V to have sex int.

THE PERFORMANCE

For *Three Weeks in May,* Lacy created a large map of the City of Los Angeles posted in a mall underneath City Hall. Each day for three weeks Lacy went to the Los Angeles Police Department's central office to pick up rape reports (with identities redacted) and approximate locations from the day before. She marked the locations on the map with a stamp, which left an impression of the word RAPE in capital letters. A second map was exhibited alongside showing "sites of resistance—organizations and self-help activities for injured women."[2]

Initially, Lacy wanted to show the rape reports on the white wall of a gallery, but then, as Lacy further developed the idea, her former CalArts teacher Sheila Levrant de Bretteville asked, "'Why would you put it on a wall of a gallery?' And she said, 'Do it outside, do it in public space, because public space is where it will have the most impact on women's lives.'"[3]

The performance became a social and political matter. Together with the police department and the city council, Lacy developed a network which helped her to raise awareness. It was important to her that in addition to public events, there were also private group sessions for victims, a platform for exchange in which they could talk about their experiences.

The performance *Three Weeks in May* was a three-week-long performance by Suzanne Lacy, which included several large-scale performances and in total over 30 events. Her aim was to actively draw the public's attention toward violence against women.

"I have never been free of the fear of rape. From a very early age I, like most women, have thought of rape as a part of my natural environment— something to be feared and prayed against like fire or lightning. I never asked why men raped; I simply thought it one of the many mysteries of human nature."[1]

ARTISTS

Barbara Cohen, Melissa Hoffman, Leslie Labowitz-Starus, Jill Soderholm, Barbara T. Smith, Cheri Gaulke, and many more.

SUPPORT

Three Weeks in May was supported by the Los Angeles Department of Public Works and various local organizations and government officials in Los Angeles, California. FK

"We are at a time where women are speaking out loud and clear that sexual violence must end. By breaking the silence on all forms of sexual violence and harassment, a major transition is taking place."[4]

Suzanne Lacy, Notations on police rape reports, *Three Weeks in May* (1977).

THREE WEEKS IN MAY: PERFORMANCES

By Alice Rugai

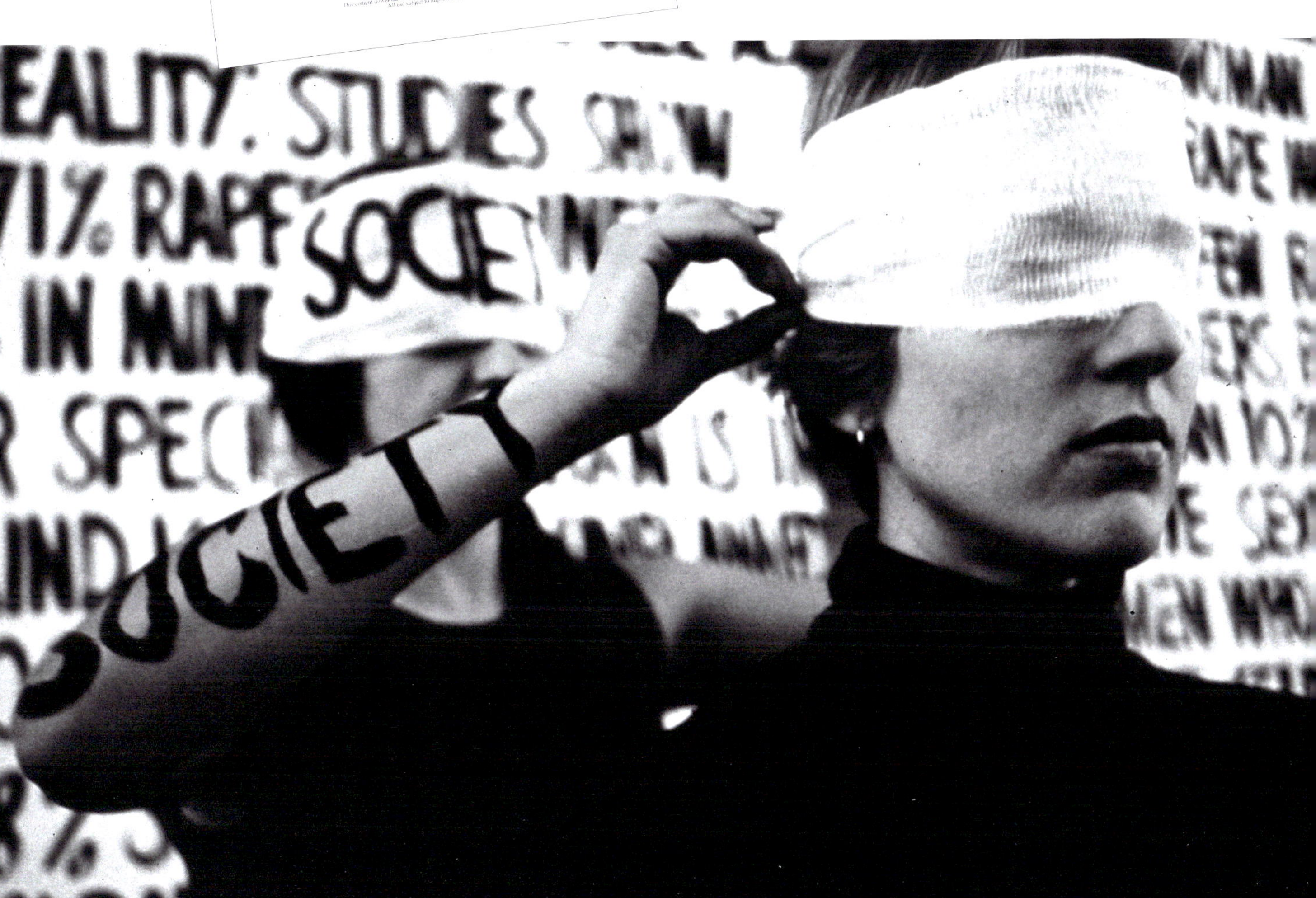

Lacy

[The wide variety of public activities in "Three Weeks in May" is shown in the schedule of events, which follows.]

"Three Weeks in May": Schedule of Events

May 9
12 noon
Installation ceremonies, with city officials, representatives from the Hotline Alliance, and sponsoring organizations. City Mall.

May 11
9:30 a.m.
Los Angeles Commission on Assaults Against Women speaks to the Southern California Committee for International Women's Decade.

May 11
1:00 p.m.
Discussion with the Artists of "Three Weeks in May." City Mall.

May 14
Coalition on Battered Women presents "Battered Women: A Time for Action." University of Southern California.

May 16
11:45 a.m.
Readings from the Map, Suzanne Lacy on CLOSE Radio.

May 18, 19
Self-Defense Demonstration, Betty Brooks. Sponsored by "Women's Pursepower Jobs." Los Angeles Trade Technical School.

May 19
12:30 p.m.
Women Against Violence Against Women speak. Los Angeles Trade Technical School.

May 20
11:00 a.m.
Self-Defense Demonstration, Mary Conroy. ARCO Plaza.

May 20
11:00 a.m.
Talks by the Sheriff's Department, the East Los Angeles Hotline, and a Self-Defense Demonstration by Yvonne Beatty. Sponsored by Women in County Government.

May 20, 21
1-5 p.m.
Art Performance and Testmonial Event, Part 1, Suzanne Lacy. A private sharing for women only.

May 21
8-10 p.m.
Art Performance, Part 2, Suzanne Lacy. Installation open to the public, one night only. Garage Gallery.

May 22
2:00 p.m.
Rape Speakout. Public testimonial, workshops, self defense, music, and readings. Sponsored by the Alliance of Rape Crisis Hotlines. For women only. The Woman's Building.

May 23
12 noon
Street Performance, "Myths," Leslie Labowitz-Starus. Self-Defense Demonstration for Senior Citizens. City Mall.

68

> **"Political and communication necessities shaped the form language of art, where a union between art, its content, and its context was possible."**[1]
> — Suzanne Lacy

Over 30 events were produced during Suzanne Lacy's *Three Weeks in May* and television and print media covered many of them. Participating artists included Barbara Cohen, Melissa Hoffman, Leslie Labowitz-Starus, and Jill Soderholm. The performance series was supported by the Los Angeles Department of Public Works and various local organizations and government officials in Los Angeles, California.[2] In this text, I will analyze some of these events and try to clarify the aim of this type of activism, as well as describe the socio-historical atmosphere of the time.

WHERE DOES SUZANNE LACY'S APPROACH COME FROM?

Suzanne Lacy's art was not only art, nor was it only activism. She developed her own artistic approach to social issues, focusing on feminism and harvesting some impulses from other artists. She learned, from Fluxus artist Allan Kaprow, the political role of art in a process of direct engagement with the audience. For Kaprow, the difference between 'inside' and 'outside' art was very important. The former was to be found in museums, galleries, and art magazines; the latter was the art of the body acting politically in streets, communities, and other spaces. As Vivien Green Fryd elucidates, "Kaprow defined his art form, developed in the 1950s, as 'events in real time' that incorporated all the 'mundane' aspects of traditional performance, including plotting, staging, acting, script development, and rehearsal."[3]

Thanks to this variety of influences, the formal diversity of *Three Weeks in May* was outstanding. The performance series included installations, speeches by politicians, interviews with hotline activists, self-defence demonstrations, speak-outs, media articles, programs, and performance art, all designed to attract media attention and create awareness of and discussion about rape in American culture.

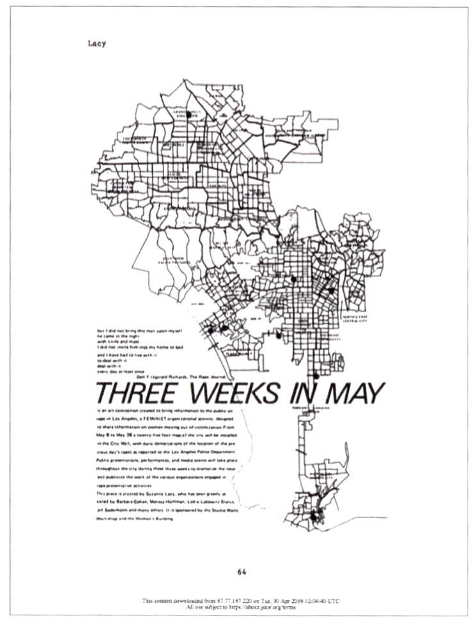

MAPS

At the center of *Three Weeks in May* was an installation featuring municipal maps showing the number of rapes in the city. Over the course of a three-week period, Lacy stamped the word 'RAPE' onto the map at every location where a woman had been raped. On the basis of data provided by the Los Angeles Police Department, she updated it every day. Alluding to the under-reporting of the crime at that time, Lacy also added fainter 'RAPE' stamp marks each time she posted a report from the police, in order to highlight the estimated nine unreported rapes for each reported. A second map, which indicated "the locations of sites of assistance and resistance: prevention centres, rape hotlines, hospital emergency rooms, and crisis and counselling centres, offered a link to the 'revelation of the problem' and to counteract any suggestion of 'continuous victimization.'"[4] In 1975, Lacy had imagined *Three Weeks in May* to be a process piece, with rape statistics to be reported daily onto a white gallery wall, but to avoid the diminishment of the work's political impact and to augment the element of surprise, as well as to reach a wider audience, she decided to situate the work within a public, non-art space.[5]

Three Weeks in May is Lacy's first art project that can be described as "'public activist art,' or what she called a 'public informational campaign.' The 'map-in-time' made rape visible as a social phenomenon because the project made possible countless empathetic connections among individuals, whether artists, police, hotline counsellors, self-defence instructors, politicians, or the women who shared their stories about rape."[6]

PUBLIC ART PERFORMANCES

When Lacy was developing her methods, she met Leslie Labowitz-Starus, who was returning from Germany where she had been influenced by Brechtian theory and practice. Bertolt Brecht, the German poet and playwright, developed 'epic theatre' to encourage audiences to think rather than just be immersed in the story.[7]

Myths of Rape was the first of four public street performances by Labowitz-Starus, created for *Three Weeks in May*. The six female performers, who all participated in the Feminist Art Program at the Woman's Building, were dressed in black and white and wore transparent white gauze blindfolds. They carried hand-painted protest signs showing myths about rape, alongside real instances of sexual violence. The blindfolds not only provided anonymity for their wearers but also stood for the many misunderstandings that surround rape in society. While the performers marched through the mall, Labowitz-Starus handed out flyers some of these myths were printed on. At the end of the march the performers froze immobile in positions of self-defence or defencelessness, next to the signs.[8]

Labowitz-Starus's second performance was performed by Women Against Rape, Men Against Rape. It represented the victim of rape, a victim of both their attacker and an institutionalized society that finds her to blame. A woman was encircled by performers wearing paper costumes, each representing a different social institution, the names of which were painted on. The cones were the symbols of patriarchy, taken from both the Ku Klux Klan and Catholic feasts like the Santa Semana, used to give the impression of censorship, silenced victims, and blame.[9]

The third performance, performed by the Los Angeles Men's Collective, addressed the fact that it is primarily men who rape. Their focus was on the poor emotional education young boys receive from childhood, particularly the subliminal messages of violence and machismo that surround them and are difficult to eliminate. Attributes associated with masculinity, such as aggression, tend to be valued over traits considered to be more 'feminine' and the performance uses toys to reexamine those sexist messages. This performance may be one of the earliest attempts to create a different emotional register for men, which could now be called 'tender masculinity.' At the very least, the performance highlighted the need of a new type of masculinity.

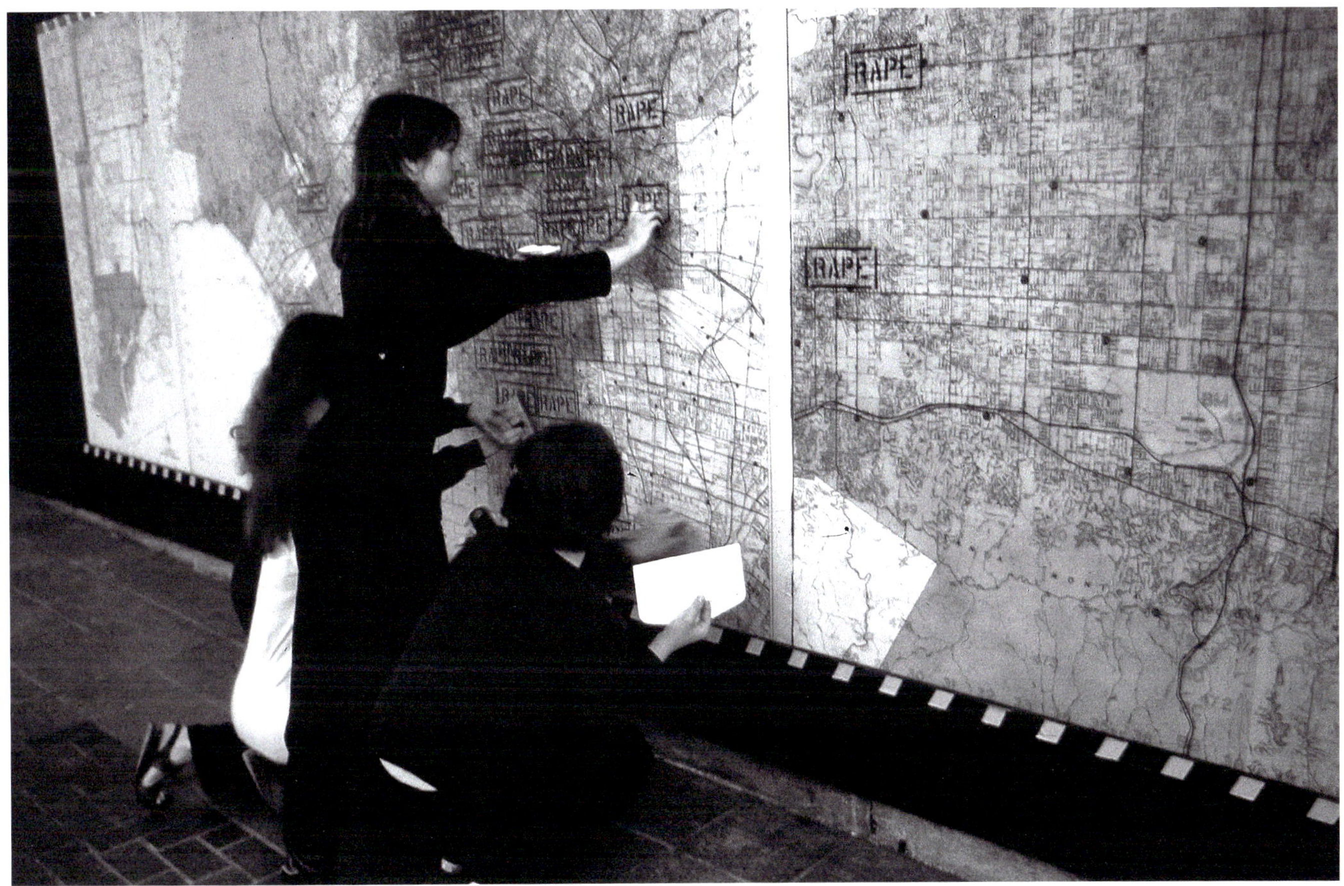

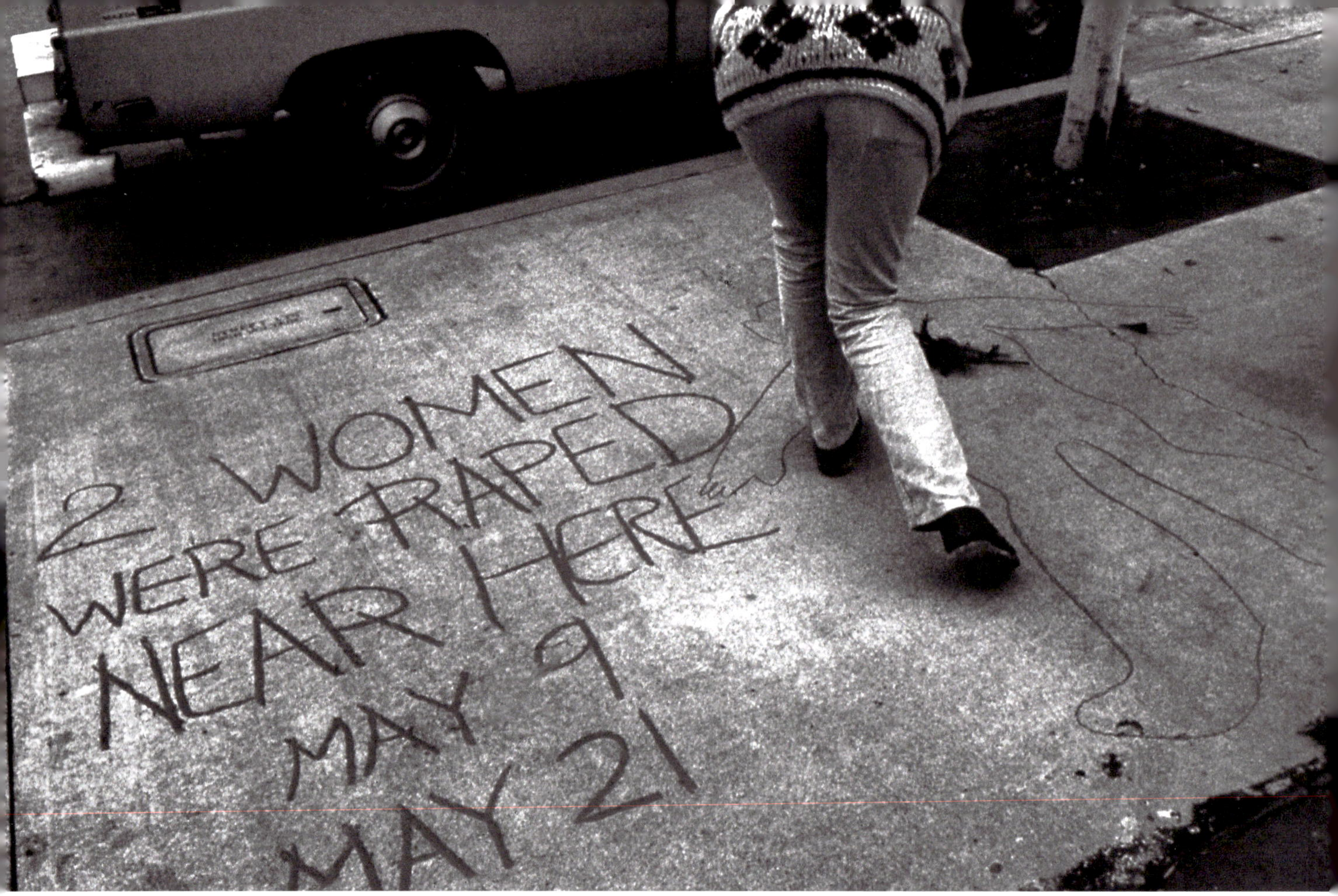

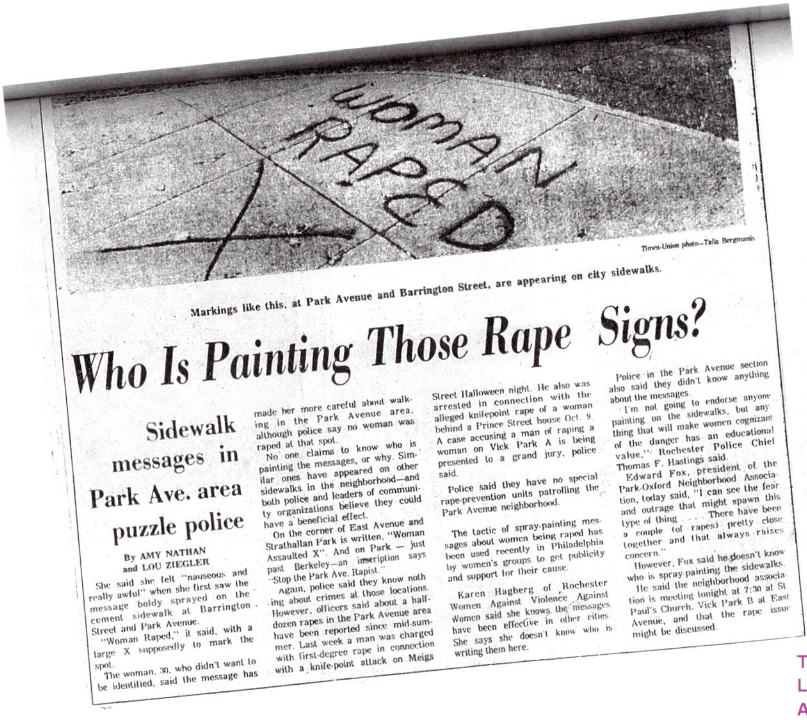

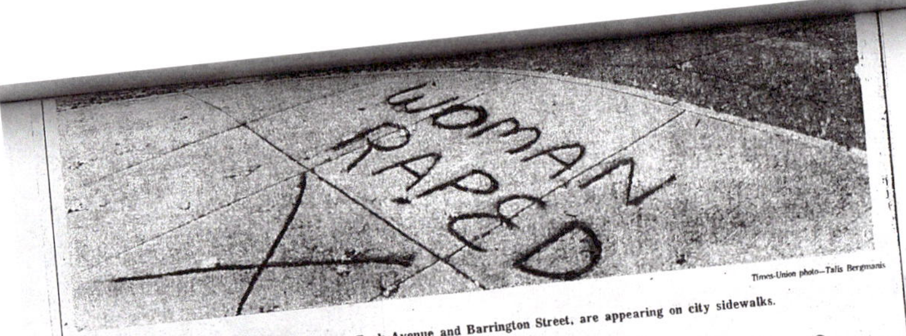

Times-Union photo—Talis Bergmanis

Markings like this, at Park Avenue and Barrington Street, are appearing on city sidewalks.

Who Is Painting Those Rape Signs?

Sidewalk messages in Park Ave. area puzzle police

By AMY NATHAN and LOU ZIEGLER

She said she felt "nauseous and really awful" when she first saw the message boldly sprayed on the cement sidewalk at Barrington Street and Park Avenue.

"Woman Raped," it said, with a large X supposedly to mark the spot.

The woman, 30, who didn't want to be identified, said the message has made her more careful about walking in the Park Avenue area, although police say no woman was raped at that spot.

No one claims to know who is painting the messages, or why. Similar ones have appeared on other sidewalks in the neighborhood—and both police and leaders of community organizations believe they could have a beneficial effect.

On the corner of East Avenue and Strathallan Park is written, "Woman Assaulted X". And on Park — just past Berkeley—an inscription says "Stop the Park Ave. Rapist."

Again, police said they know nothing about crimes at those locations. However, officers said about a half-dozen rapes in the Park Avenue area have been reported since mid-summer. Last week a man was charged with first-degree rape in connection with a knife-point attack on Meigs Street Halloween night. He also was arrested in connection with the alleged knifepoint rape of a woman behind a Prince Street house Oct. 9. A case accusing a man of raping a woman on Vick Park A is being presented to a grand jury, police said.

Police said they have no special rape-prevention units patrolling the Park Avenue neighborhood.

The tactic of spray-painting messages about women being raped has been used recently in Philadelphia by women's groups to get publicity and support for their cause.

Karen Hagberg of Rochester Women Against Violence Against Women said she knows the messages have been effective in other cities. She says she doesn't know who is writing them here.

Police in the Park Avenue section also said they didn't know anything about the messages.

"I'm not going to endorse anyone painting on the sidewalks, but anything that will make women cognizant of the danger has an educational value," Rochester Police Chief Thomas F. Hastings said.

Edward Fox, president of the Park-Oxford Neighborhood Association, today said, "I can see the fear and outrage that might spawn this type of thing . . . . There have been a couple (of rapes) pretty close together and that always raises concern."

However, Fox said he doesn't know who is spray-painting the sidewalks.

He said the neighborhood association is meeting tonight at 7:30 at St. Paul's Church, Vick Park B at East Avenue, and that the rape issue might be discussed.

The last performance ran in parallel to the closing rally of the project and consisted of large cones painted with phrases typically seen in self-defence classes, such as 'gouge eyes' and 'turn fear into anger.' Women were hiding under these cones and, during the performance, revealed themselves to symbolize liberation from their centuries-long silencing.[10]

GUERRILLA ACTION

"Early in the morning we drove to several street corners listed as close to rape sites listed on the maps. We outlined a woman's body on the sidewalk with red chalk, wrote, 'A woman was raped near here …' and gave the date. We left a flower in the woman's outline. Several months later, we began receiving reports of other women's groups doing the same thing."[11]

LIEBESTOD: PERFORMANCE AND BANQUET

Lacy organized a banquet to gather women working towards the same goals, but from different social contexts and with different perspectives and political ideas. She invited artists Barbara T. Smith and Cheri Gaulke to work with her to create an elegant dinner and a performance.

In *Liebestod*, Chinese foot binding and other actions that restrict women's freedom were enacted throughout the dinner. The dessert, Cherries Jubilee, was accompanied by simulated flames and the music of Richard Wagner's *Liebestod*.[12]

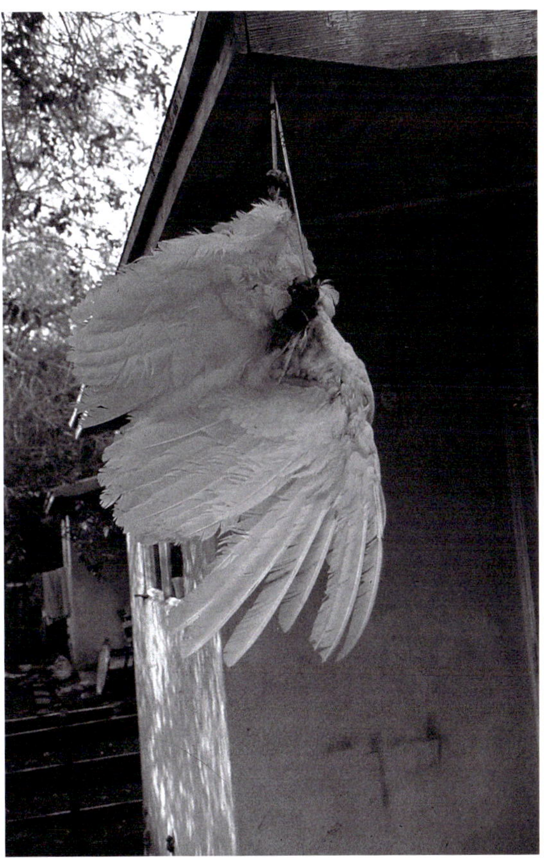

EXORCISM

The performance *Exorcism* by Laurel Klick was a private ritual, in ten steps, to exorcize a sexual assault the artist had experienced the previous May. Klick circled her old apartment three times for three days. Thinking about rape, she dripped menstrual blood onto the floor of her kitchen, buried objects, shaved all of her body hair (excluding her head), ate cold fish, and realized many other 'rituals' to protect her in her new home and break with the past.[13]

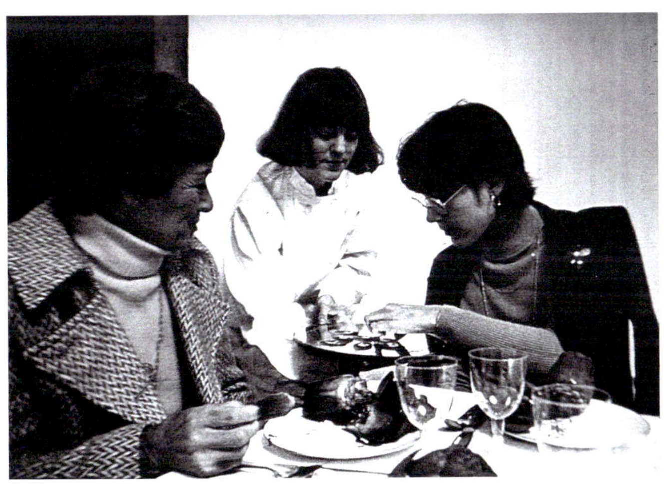

BREAKING SILENCE

The ritual performance by Anne Gauldin and Melissa Hoffman took place in a private studio in Pasadena (CA) and revealed and transcended the rape experiences of both artists. This performance was not private like Klick's; rather, a select group of women were invited to form an audience. The two protagonists were dressed in black, one with a gun, one wrapped in white gauze. At the outset of the performance, the imagery was very violent, yet as the performance reached its end there was a transition toward healing emotions.[14]

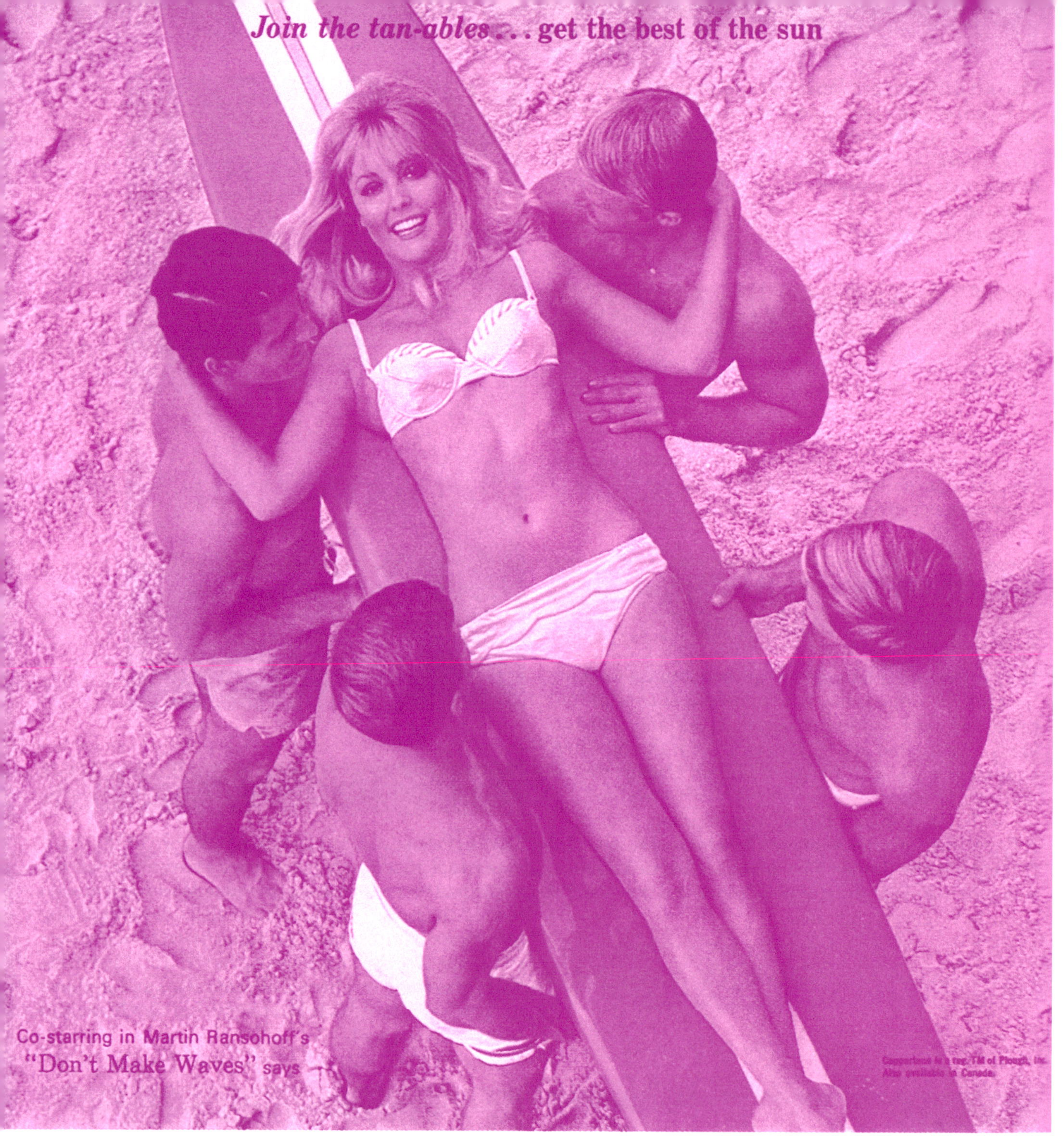

"Coppertone gives you a *better* tan"

(—it's enriched to give extra protection, too!)

You *do* get a better tan with Coppertone. The fastest tan possible with maximum sunburn protection . . . plus extra safeguards against skin dryness. Coppertone contains the most widely beach-tested sunscreen. It's also enriched with lanolin, cocoa butter and other moisturizers that make your skin more tan-able . . . keep your skin soft and satiny sleek.

So join the tan-ables. Get a better tan . . . deep, dark, superbly smooth. Coppertone outsells them all because it out-tans them all! Get the best of the sun with enriched Coppertone. Save on large size.

TAN, DON'T BURN—*with America's most popular, most complete line of suntan products: Lotion, Oil, Cream, Spray, Shade®, Noskote®, Lipkote®, Royal Blend®. Also new, Baby Tan® for young children and Royal Blend Soap.*

COMMUNITY BUILDING

HOW TO REBUILD A BROKEN COMMUNITY?

A sense of community can easily disappear when we focus on difference. This seemed to be the case in Lancashire, UK, where, upon the closure of the Brierfield Mill, two groups of former employees, one English and the other Pakistani, no longer associated with one another, despite having worked side-by-side for almost 40 years. In *The Circle and the Square*, the artist Suzanne Lacy used collective singing to create a space where cultural differences could be accepted and explored. Such community re-building acknowledged cultural distinctions, using difference as a catalyst for dialogue and relationship-building, thus bringing the two communities back together.[1]

Public art and community-building both have in common the potential to reach people outside of the usual art sphere. In museums and galleries, we often meet one type of audience. By broadening the understanding of where art can happen, as well as thinking about reaching new audiences and participants, real changes can occur within a community.

"In a sense, we operate like other activists, although our attention to form is often quite different. Visual artists have inventive ways of seeing and addressing problems. On the local level we can raise issues and engage people in creative solutions."[2] —Suzanne Lacy

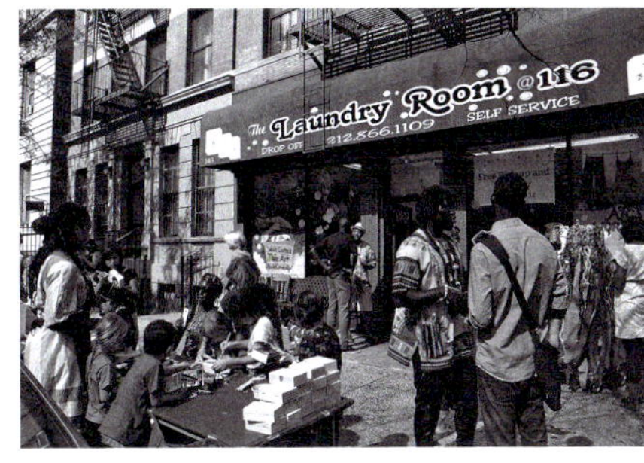

OTHER STRATEGIES— CREATING CREATIVE SPACES

Another example of how art can help build a community is *The Laundromat Project* in New York. This project supports art in local laundromats, where artists and community members create spaces for communication and collaboration. Examples vary, and might include yoga classes, creating community mixtapes, or re-naming local street names according to social or personal history.[3] The project aims to give agency to locals and artists. **AS**

"Making art and culture in a community and fostering new leadership helps shape a world in which members feel truly connected and have the ability to influence their communities in creative and effective ways."[4] —Vivien Green Fryd

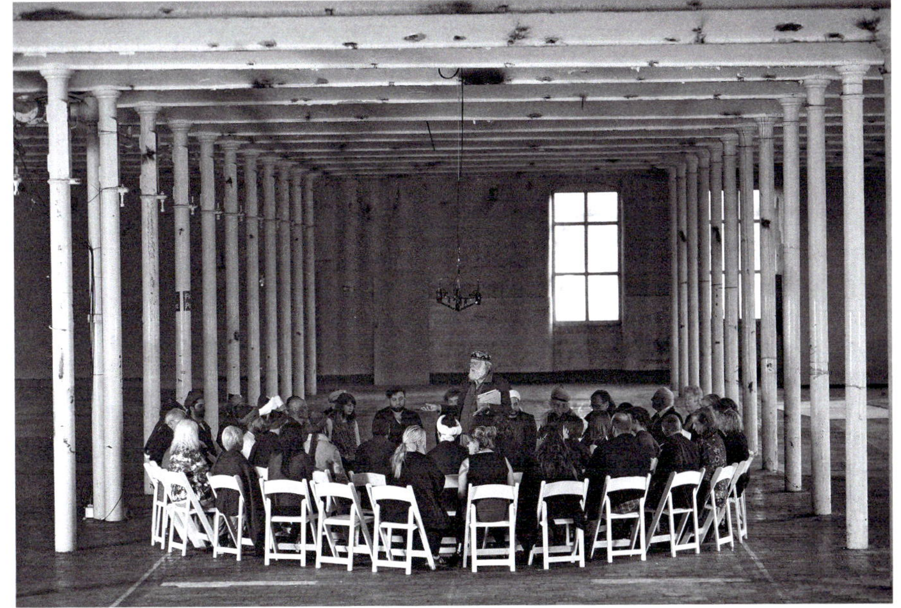

Above: *The Laundromat Project* (2015), Harlem.
Left: Suzanne Lacy, *The Circle and the Square* (2015–17). Photo by Chris Payne.

SUZANNE LACY THREE WEEKS IN MAY: SHE WHO WOULD FLY

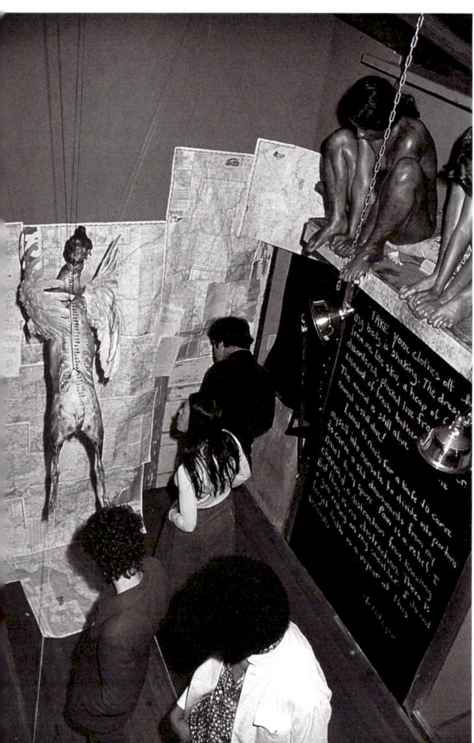

"This performance marked a concern with public persuasion and established a precedent, in later works, of distinguishing different audiences for different imaginaries, a frequent subject in Lacy's writings."[1]

One performance that took place during Suzanne Lacy's performance series *Three Weeks in May* (1977) was *She Who Would Fly*, an installation in the Studio Watts Workshop's Garage Gallery that was structured in three parts:

TALKING TO WOMEN

During this performance, women were invited to participate and share their stories about sexual abuse and rape with the artist. Later, those stories were written on paper, which they attached to maps on the walls of the gallery. The women were also free to come and leave as they pleased. It also echoed the "circle-based pedagogy practiced by feminist artists in Judy Chicago's Feminist Studio Workshop …."[2]

CEREMONIES AND CONSTRUCTION

In this performance, Suzanne Lacy and four of her friends, who were also artists—Nancy Angelo, Laurel Klick, Melissa Hoffman, and Cheryl Williams—shared their stories about sexual abuse in private (while preparing for the performance). This performance was not accessible for the public and had some similarities with a ritual. They shared food and covered each other's bodies with red paint. The artists also noted on maps hanging on the wall where these abuses and rapes happened.[3]

SHE WHO WOULD FLY

The naming part of this performance took place on May 21, 1977. In the middle of the gallery there was a skinned lamb with white feathered wings. In Christianity, the lamb represents a "symbol of gentleness, innocence, and purity"[4] because of its white color. In the performance, the mutilated lamb symbolizes how those women had their innocence and purity taken away by force. Only four visitors were allowed to stay in the room at the same time, surrounded by the maps indicating the locations of the artists' rape and sexual abuse. Nude women colored in red paint sat above the entrance, staring at the visitors. The women appeared as though vultures, looking at the people under them. CG

"The masculine spectator's gaze, scopophilic and fetishizing, thereby, was subverted. These predatory-looking, grotesque women watched over the female spectators to protect them from further violation."[5]
—Vivien Green Fryd

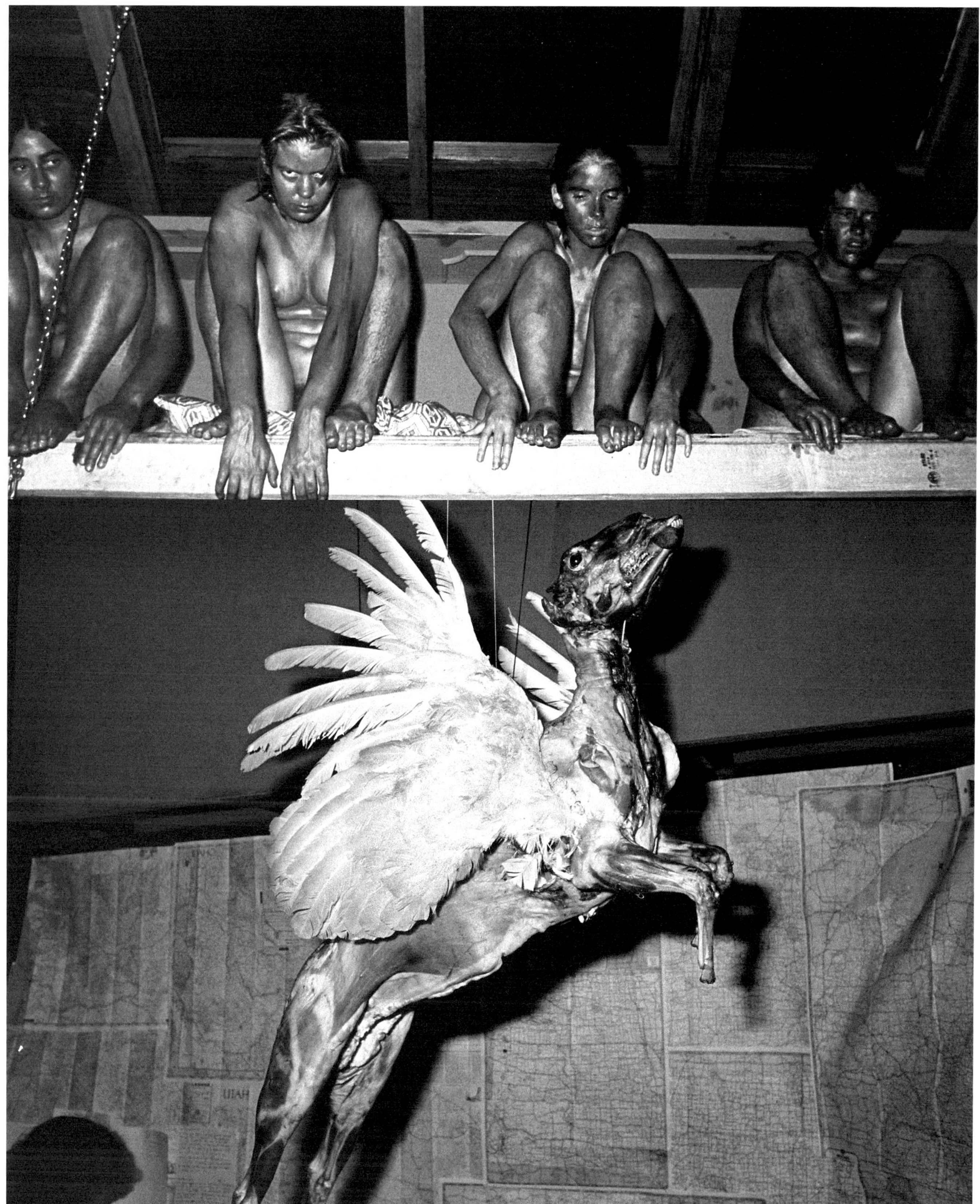

THREE WEEKS IN MAY: ART IN PUBLIC & PARTICIPATION

By Katharina Brandt

"Do it outside, do it in public space, because public space is where it will have the most impact."[1]
— Sheila Levrant de Bretteville

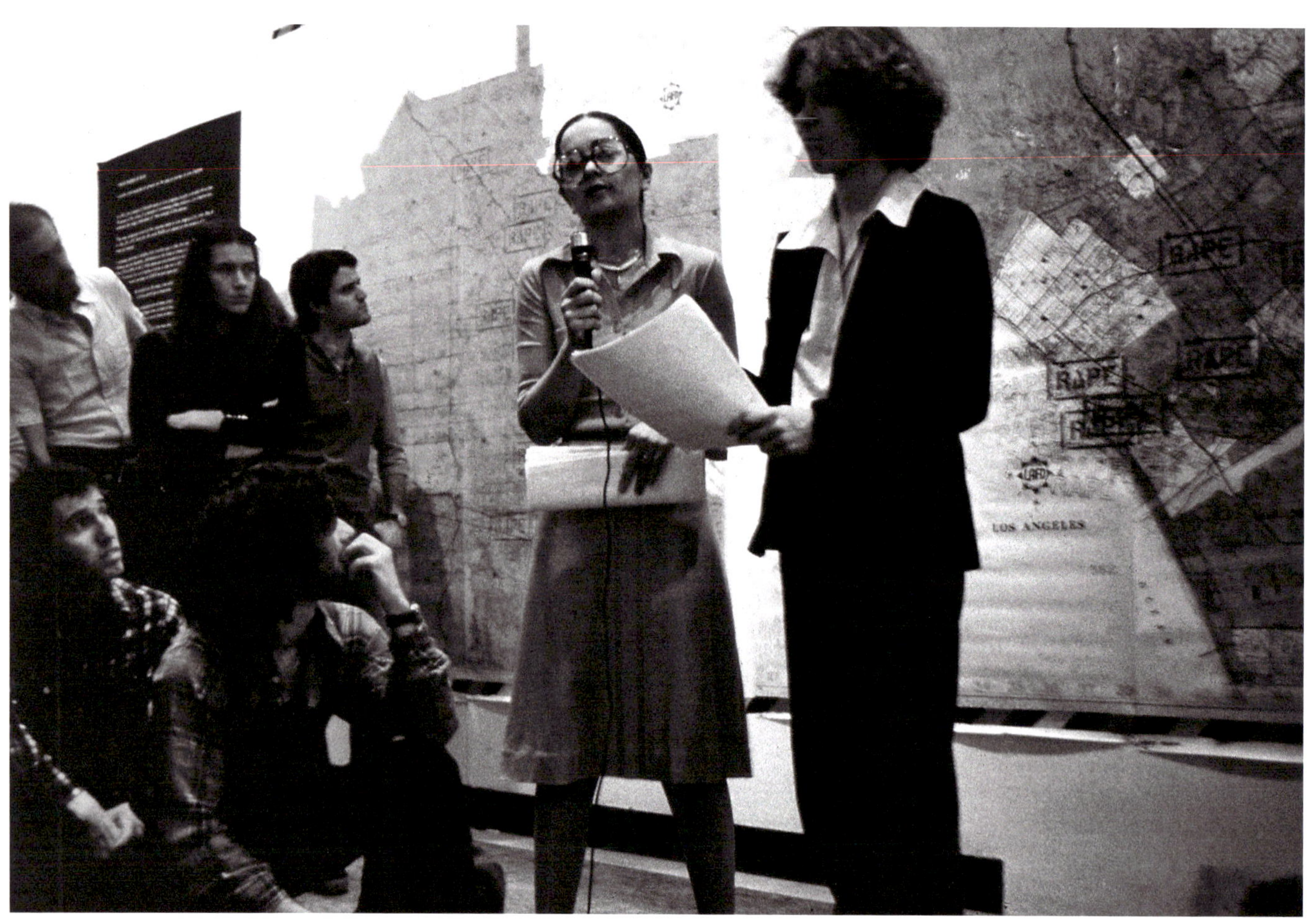

Above: Suzanne Lacy, *Three Weeks in May* (1977), at the Bologna Art Fair (1978). Opposite page: Jack Slater, "Helping to Stamp Out Rape," *Los Angeles Times*, May 23, 1977, excerpt.

The performance series *Three Weeks in May*, that took place in several locations in Los Angeles in 1977, was Suzanne Lacy's first public artwork, created to help transform the way sexual violence was seen by American society. At first sight, Lacy's approach in *Three Weeks in May* could be described as politically motivated, bringing as it does political art to public audiences. However, her strategy of "activist politics with artmaking"[2] was also designed to critique American culture and provoke social action on the myths, knowledge, and attitudes towards rape against women.

When aiming for as much publicity as possible, one should make use of mass communication. With this in mind, Lacy and her crew taught themselves the game of media, learning "the media's approach to newsworthiness,"[3] how to write press releases, and playing to the media's inexorable greed for sensationalized stories and huge ratings. They created a well-structured network to make contact with decisive people from radio, television, and press to make the biggest impact in the media.

"The strategy … was to essentially recreate the networking phenomenon of the piece within the mass media, through interviews and feature programs. As with the other events, we mixed and matched the participants from various political, professional and aesthetically diverse organizations with each other."[4] — Suzanne Lacy

Three Weeks in May could be described as experimental art. Her focus on gathering public interest among a large, mixed crowd led her to create art as public participation. *Three Weeks in May* became a public activity. Its central installation involved a map that was located on a wall near the entrance of a well-trafficked shopping area. Its location meant that passers-by would visually confront incidents of rape, marked by Lacy in big letters and bright colors. Lacy's purpose and process of creating public art aimed at demystifying such a dreadful social fact, something also represented in the three-part performance *She Who Would Fly*, which took place in the context of *Three Weeks in May*, as an opportunity for private testimonials by women.[5]

"We are discussing our personal experiences with having been molested or raped. If you have had any such experience, would you please tell us about it and write it down on this piece of paper for our map."[6] — Suzanne Lacy

In this case, the participation of women in the performance developed a mode of 'inter-performance.' Later the work was opened to the public, where audiences were free to participate, interact, and share their personal experiences to all viewers. This mixture of traditional and non-traditional forms of activism, educational theory, and performance led to a new relationship between artists and audience, who could experience direct participation in this socially and politically engaged artwork. Griselda Pollock once described the phenomenon of the "social viewer" as someone "who assumes the 'position of the [artwork's] imagined partner,'"[7] which in Lacy's art is represented as "a large and extremely varied conglomeration of audiences,"[8] stimulating them towards political empowerment.

Using key elements of performance art, in *Three Weeks in May* Suzanne Lacy reached a large audience, including the general public, politicians, and anti-violence organizations, making use of radio and television media. The opening press event draw the first media attention for the project, and interest in this curious public event grew over time, after stories appeared in several local newspapers, television and radio stations.[9]

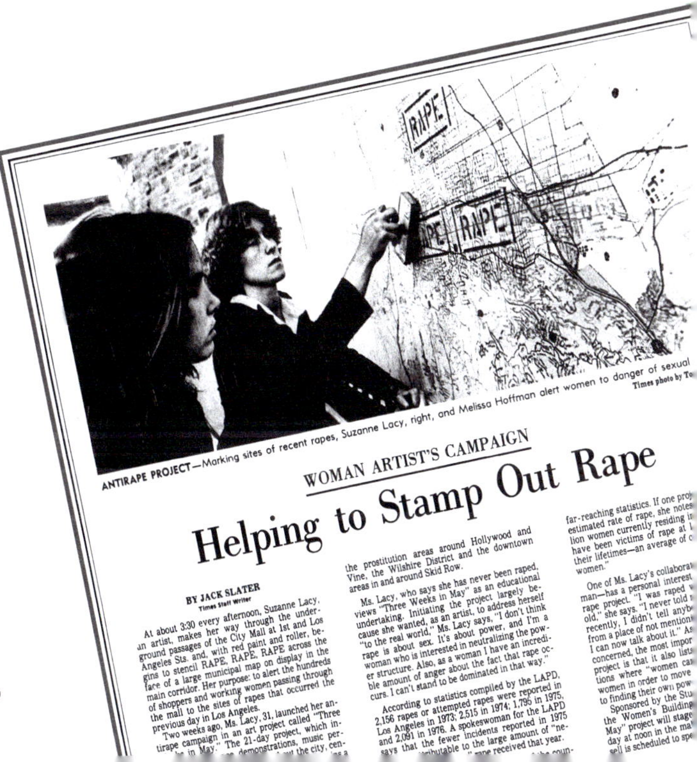

SITE SPECIFICITY IN ART

WHAT IS SITE SPECIFICITY?

Site-specific art and performances use a specific space as a conceptual frame for a project. The chosen place will often play an important role for the artwork, because of its social, temporal, or spatial context. Ideally, if the site-specific artwork were to be removed, it would either change or lose its meaning.[1]

In the project *Between the Door and the Street* (2013), the artist Suzanne Lacy drew on both community-building and site specificity. A neighborhood in Brooklyn, more precisely 60 stoops, served as the site for choreographed debates between men and women from activist organizations from the area.[2]

Site-specific art is enormously varied and can be experienced in many different sites through various media. Performance, sculpture, or, as is the case in *Between the Door and the Street*, choreographed debates, are all types of site-specific art.

Likewise is the use of 'Podwalks'— "the site specific podcast player."[3] 'Podwalk' is an app that allows the user to explore one's city or community in new ways. 'Podwalk' can also be used for audio walks in museums or other institutions.

In 2016, an audio walk through the Vesterbro neighborhood in Copenhagen called *Behind Vesterbro* took place. The stories of a community through time evolved as you walked around the city.

Like in *Between the Door and the Street*, the community surrounding the site plays a big role in the creation of the project, showing that art can happen anywhere and is for everyone. **AS**

From top to bottom: Suzanne Lacy, *Between the Door and the Street* (2013), New York City. Photo by Jonathan Dorado. Produced by Creative Time and the Elizabeth Sackler Center at the Brooklyn Museum of Art. Julie Thing, *Vesterbro bag facaden* (2016).

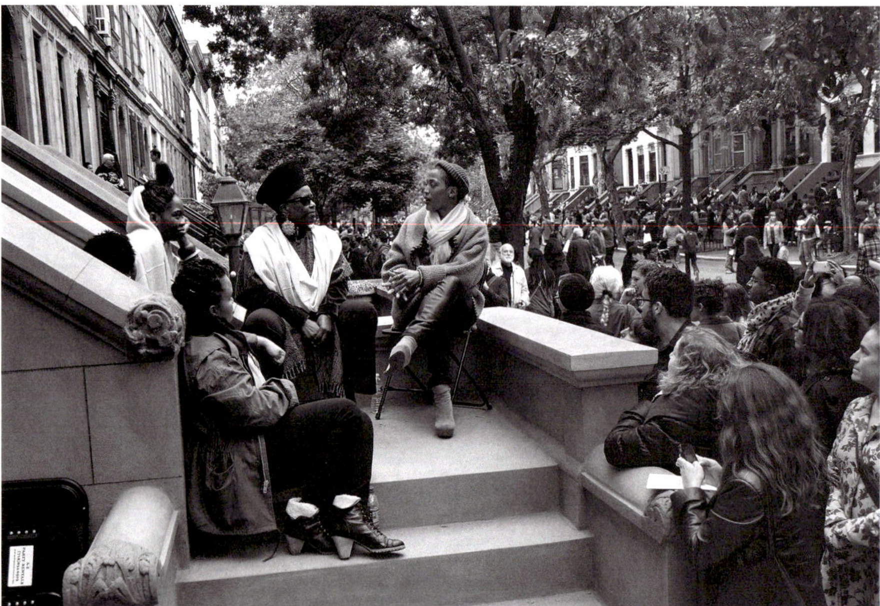

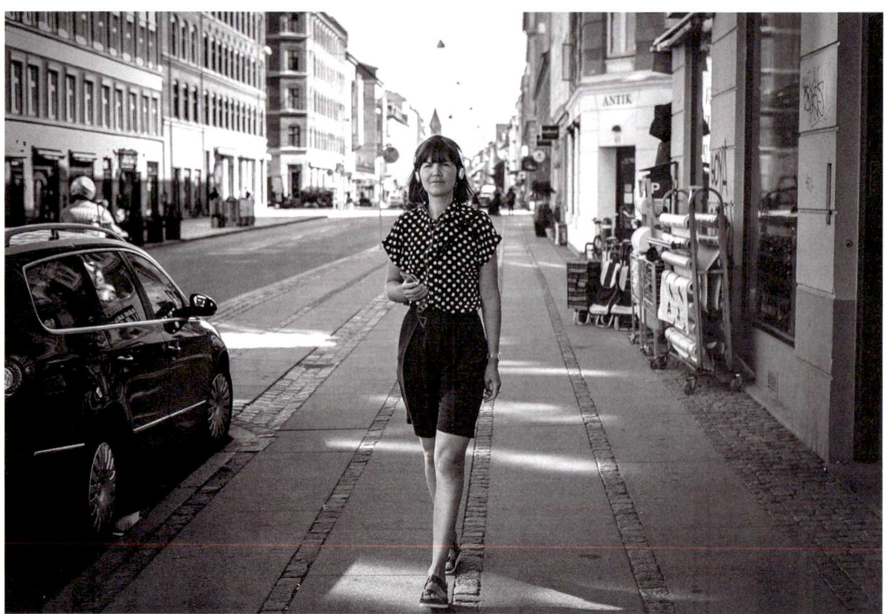

PUBLIC ART

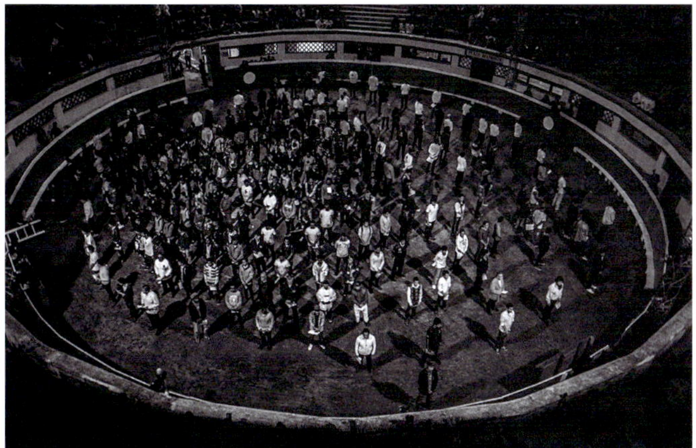

Suzanne Lacy, *de tu Puño y Letra (By Your Own Hand)* (2012), Quito, Ecuador. Photo by Raúl Peñafiel.

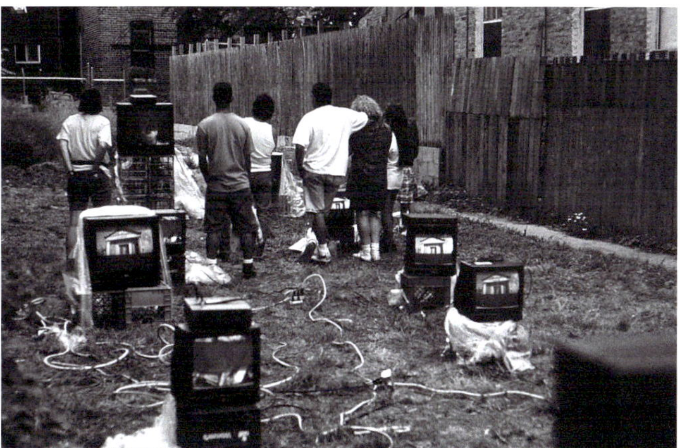

Iñigo Manglano-Ovalle's block party in West Town, part of the public art exhibition *Culture in Action*, May–September 1993, Chicago.

WHAT IS PUBLIC ART?

Public art relates closely to site specificity, as well as audience participation. The term describes any work of art within public places and communities conveyed through any type of media. Public art, as the name suggests, is accessible to the public, often found in squares, parks, or public buildings—anywhere outside of the usual art setting. In some cases, public art might be a sculpture that gives character to an otherwise impersonal space.[1] In other cases, public art focuses on specific communities or social issues related to where the art is situated.

SUZANNE LACY'S PUBLIC ART

This is also the case with many of Suzanne Lacy's recent works, where she engages communities and audiences by setting the stage somewhere new and unexpected. Her project *de tu Puño y Letra* (By Your Own Hand), for example, was set in a bullring in Quito, Ecuador, and engaged both men and women in a conversation about violence against women.[2] By using public spaces as the backdrop for her projects, Lacy stages situations for communication and understanding.

ART IN COMMUNITIES

The art exhibition *Culture in Action*, which took place in Chicago in 1993, aimed to foster communication and understanding, and gave the stage to a silenced community. The exhibition consisted of eight different projects to create artworks in underserved communities. Here, these communities were simultaneously creators and subjects.

"By fundamentally contradicting high art's aesthetic principles, its privileging of vision and the commensurate disengagement of passive viewers from static objects—i.e., the physically alienating experience of most cultural institutions—*Culture in Action* framed its artists, its communities and its viewers themselves as the structure and content of its art."[3] —Josephe Scanlan

Suzanne Lacy also participated in this exhibition, along with nine other artists and artist groups. **AS**

SUZANNE LACY: REENACTMENTS & RECEPTION

THREE WEEKS IN JANUARY: END RAPE IN LOS ANGELES

In 2012, 683 reported rapes occurred in Los Angeles. That is "one quarter of what we had in 1977, is much less than the city ever had in its recent history—but let's not forget: one rape is one too many,"[1] stated the L.A. police chief at Suzanne Lacy's 2012 performance. In *Three Weeks in January: End Rape in Los Angeles,* Lacy reenacted her groundbreaking public pedagogical performance *Three Weeks in May,* originally from 1977. The reenactment was commissioned by the Getty Pacific Standard Time performance festival which took place in January, leading to the title *Three Weeks in January: End Rape in Los Angeles.* The police chief continued his speech with: "One of the ways that we can keep women safe against sexual violence is to increase awareness. And to me, that is the core, that is the result that I wish from this project."[2]

Lacy recreated key aspects of the original work. Both instances centered around maps of L.A., which were marked daily with red stamps with the word 'RAPE' according to the prior day's rape reports. This map was visually the most persistent element from the original project and therefore the figurehead of the reenactment, but the rape reports were contemporary. In 1977, the map was installed in a shopping mall; in 2012, it featured more prominently in front of the L.A. Police Department (L.A.P.D.). As Getty curator Glenn Phillips underlines: "In 1977 there was some cooperation by City Hall and the LAPD, but this time around there is *much* more, as both now fully stand behind Lacy."[3]

As *Three Weeks in January* was simultaneously a reenactment and an updated version of *Three Weeks in May* it could also serve as a platform for more than 50 contemporary private and public events by artists and activists, educators, media makers, and politicians. In 2012, present-day issues regarding sexual violence in L.A. could be addressed, such as rape on college campuses.[4]

Art historian Vivien Green Fryd argues that Lacy's *Three Weeks in May* marked the beginning of "New Genre Public Art."[5] Like the original project, Lacy designed *Three Weeks in January* to "tak[e] place within the context of popular culture."[6] In 1977, she devised a mass media performance, press conferences, television and radio talk shows as means to enact social change. In the latter enactment, not only was the project covered by all traditional media, but Lacy's team also collaborated extensively with bloggers. In addition, 'I Know Someone, Do You? #RapeEndsHere' served as a slogan for a social media campaign on Twitter to help raise awareness for a global anti-rape movement.[7]

Key performances from the earlier work were also reenacted—for instance *Myths of Rape* (by Lacy's collaborator Leslie Labowitz-Starus), a street performance correcting false yet widely held assumptions about sexual crimes was reenacted by Audrey Chan and Elana Mann. However, the project concluded with two new performances directed by Lacy; *Storying Rape* and *Call to Action/Candlelight Vigil.* The latter was a "rally-as-performance that paired spontaneous audience participation with filmed and animated instructions, exploring a range of communication techniques used currently in organizing."[8] *Storying Rape* was a performance/debate at the top of the tower of Los Angeles City Hall. Through a headset, Lacy directed the moderator, a local TV reporter, in leading a discussion between the police chief of L.A., a professor of narrations for social change, a psychologist, an anti-male-violence activist, the deputy mayor, and a screenwriter.[9] Using ideas from literary theory—how stories are told—as a starting point, the representatives from each field in the discussion reflected on how rape narratives are presented in their field and whether reframing these narratives might improve public understanding of sexual violence.[10] Social media reporters communicated the conversation online from their own perspectives, although the debate itself was only witnessed by a small live audience.

"I can't just put a rape story on television. There's got to be a twist," stated the screenwriter in *Storying Rape,* as Lacy herself repeats in a later interview. According to her, "[a]n artist who wants to work with rape today is not digging in the unknown,"[11] so she had to take that into account during her reenactment. JG

"The point in 1977 was to reveal something—rape—that was not spoken about publicly, and blast it to the front page. That context doesn't exist today…. Both have greatly evolved. The general public is different in its awareness, too. In the 1970s there weren't social media and the internet; journalism didn't cover rape from a woman's perspective."[12]
—Suzanne Lacy

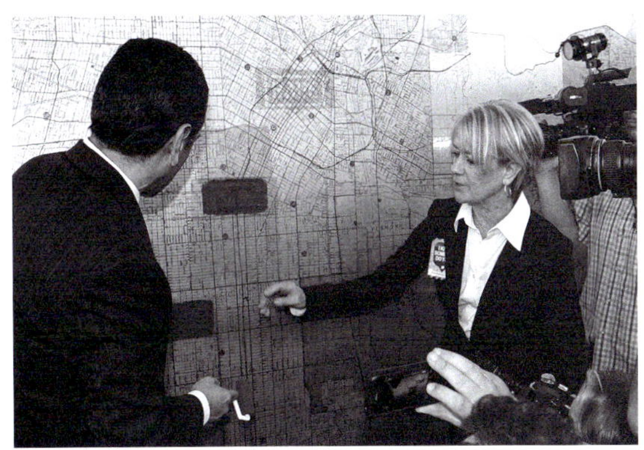

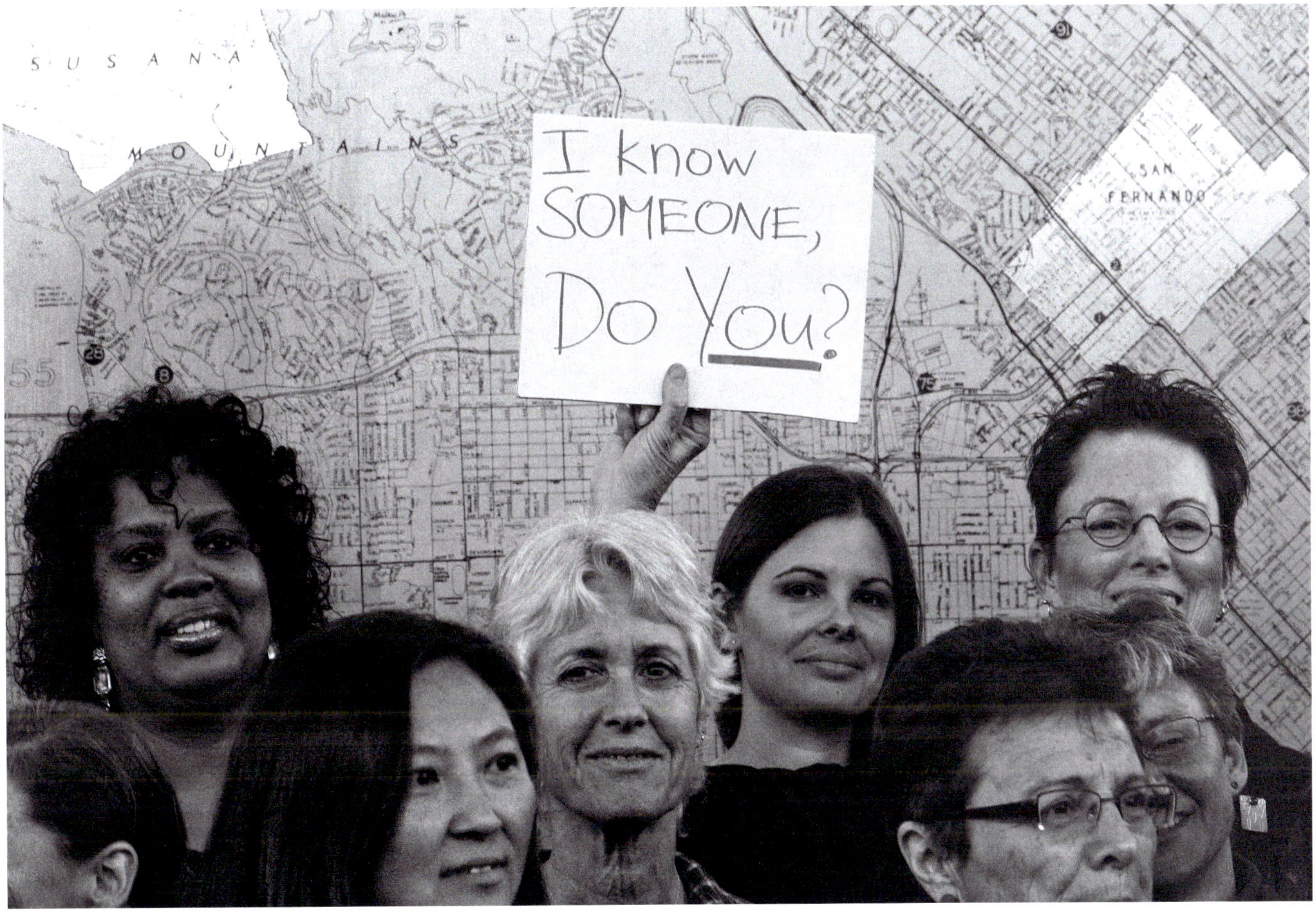

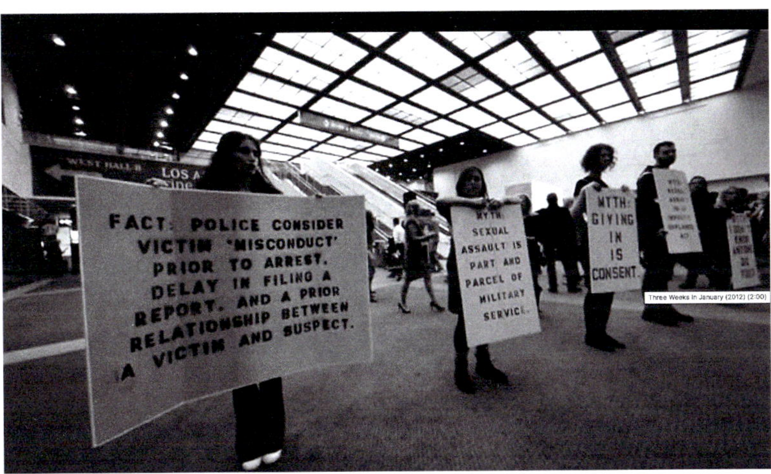

This page, top: Mayor Anthony Villaregosa with Suzanne Lacy, *Three Weeks in January* (2012). Photo by Neda Moridpour.
This page, middle: Suzanne Lacy, *Three Weeks in January* (2012). Photo by Tara Sterling.
This page, bottom and next page: Audrey Chan & Elana Mann, *Myths of Rape* (2012), a reinterpretation of Leslie Labowitz-Starus's *Myths of Rape* (1977), part of Suzanne Lacy's *Three Weeks in May* (1977), Los Angeles.

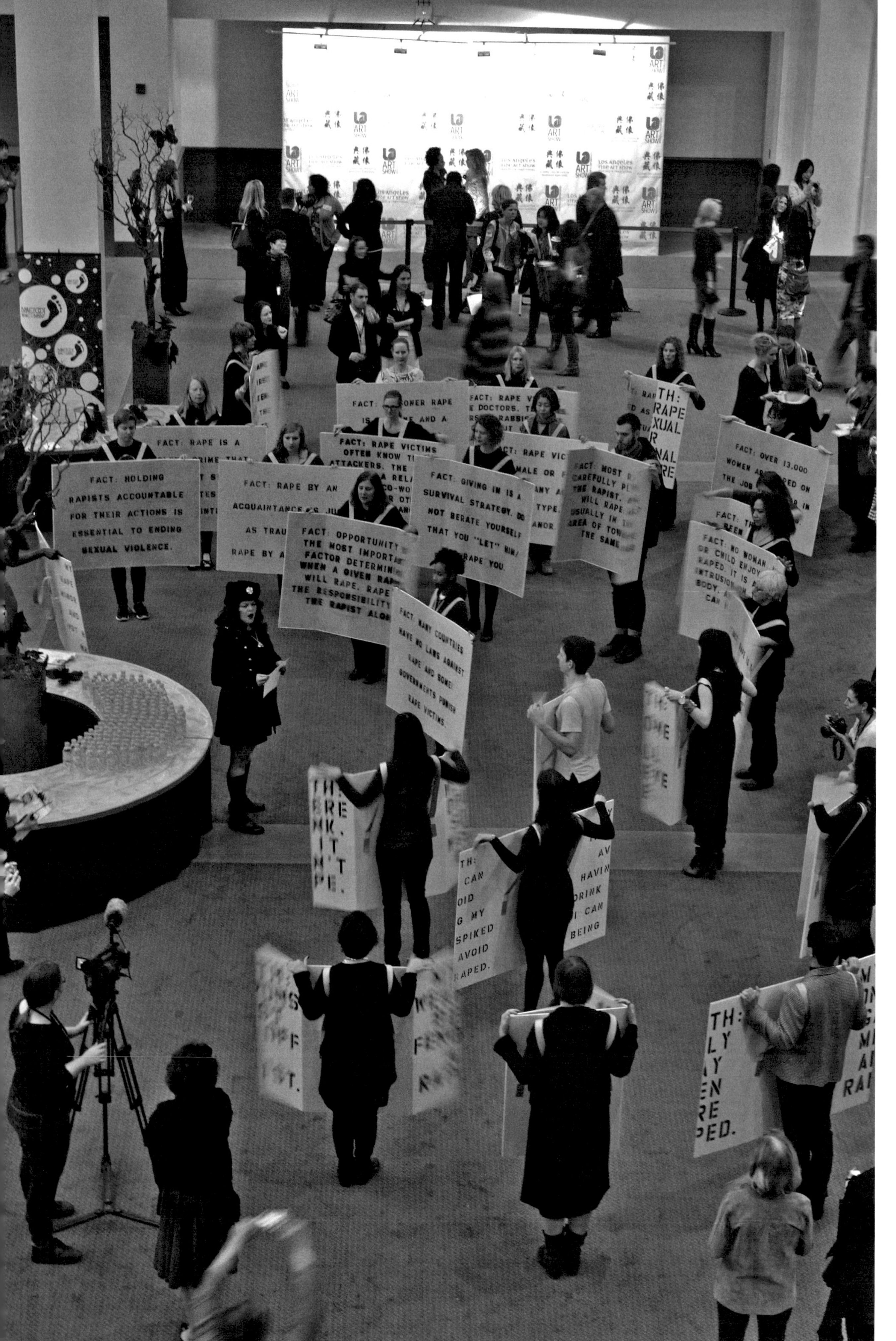

GERMAN PIZZA

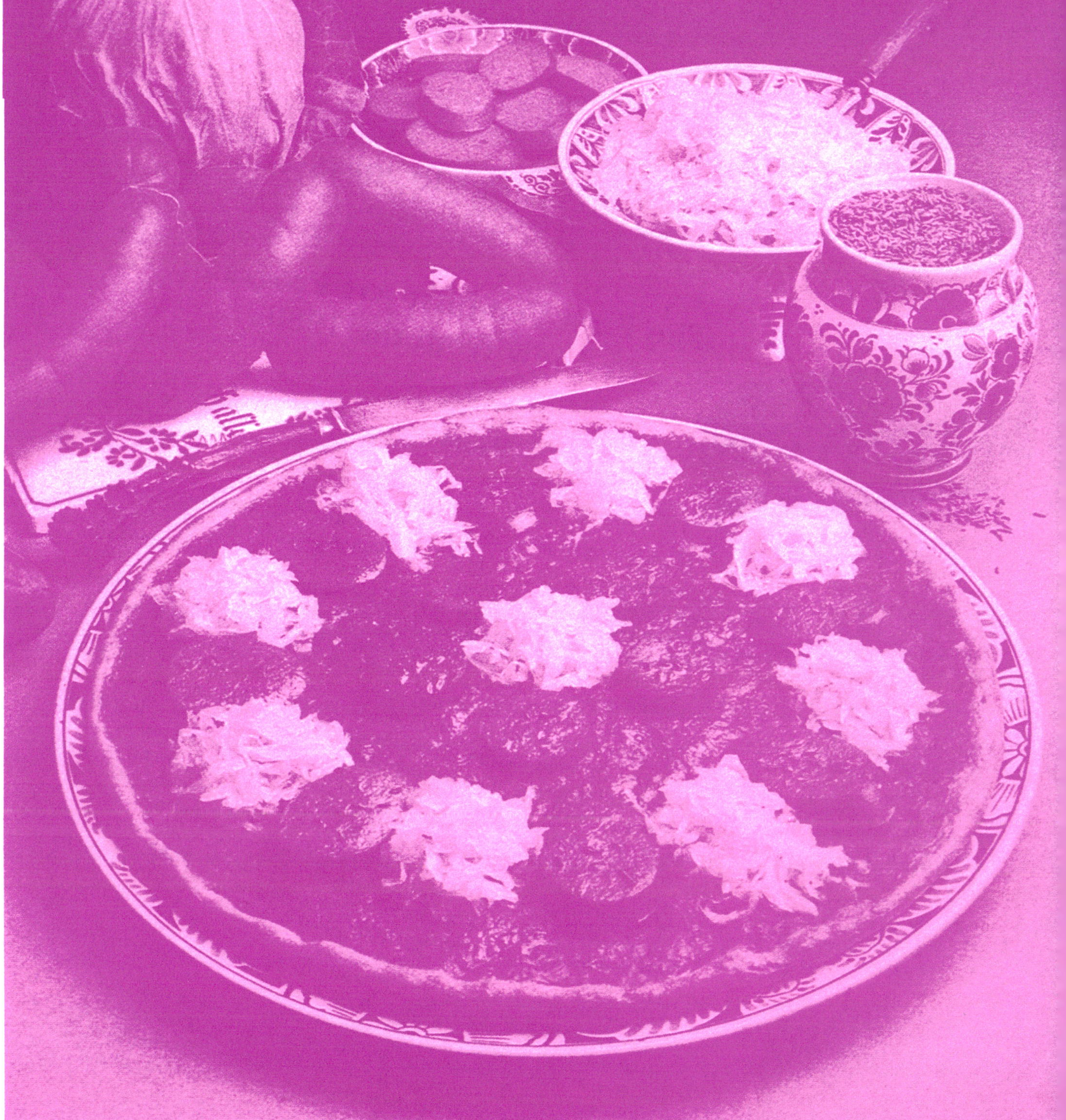

No one has to tell you how great pizza tastes. Especially when you make it with Chef Boy-ar-dee® the world's most popular pizza mix.

Just thinking about the freshly baked dough, the rich pizza sauce and tangy cheese is enough to make anyone hungry.

And you can vary Chef Boy-ar-dee Cheese Pizza Mix in so many ways.

Just make it according to directions and in the last five minutes of baking, vary the toppings.

You can make German Pizza by adding sliced knockwurst and sauerkraut (rinsed and drained). Then sprinkle generously with caraway seeds.

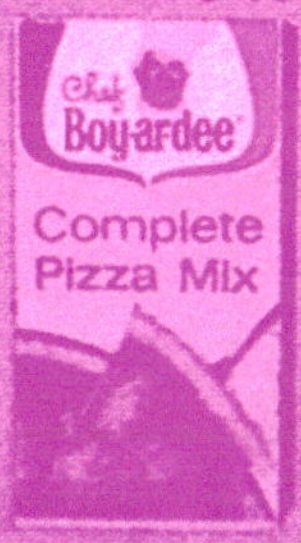

Polynesian Pizza: Top with chopped cooked ham and green pepper (browned together in a skillet) and small pineapple chunks.

Indian Pizza: Begin by adding ¼ to ½ teaspoon of curry powder (according to taste) to the pizza sauce, then top in the last five minutes of baking with chopped cooked (or canned) chicken and chopped green pepper. Sprinkle on nuts and raisins.

Chef Boy-ar-dee. The world's most popular pizza mix.

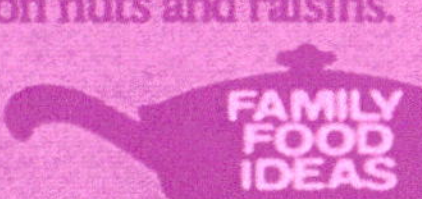

Revisions/Reports

The First Feminist Art Program: A View from the 1980s

Paula Harper

In October 1971, at the California Institute of the Arts in Valencia, California, twenty-one young women who wanted to become professional artists entered the radically new Feminist Art Program (FAP) organized as a community of women by its designers, Judy Chicago and Miriam Schapiro. While the experiment had a short life—faltering in its second year and ending in its third—this vanguard community made itself a memorable place in the history of both feminism and art.

Several values underlay its formation. Both Chicago and Schapiro held that women in our culture have not been able to express their creativity through the fine arts in the same way or to the same degree as men have: their potential has not been given the same interest or their achievements the same recognition. With the right kind of encouragement and supportive environment, Chicago and Schapiro believed, women's creativity could flower. Chicago, who had experimented with some radical educational techniques in her courses for women at Fresno State in 1970–71, was the chief architect of the program; Schapiro, impressed by what Chicago had done with the Fresno group, committed her considerable experience, energy, and professional skills to the collaboration.

Looking back on her own education, Chicago felt a growing conviction that she had been thwarted by her male teachers, who had not understood the images she had tried to make and had imposed their own forms, artistic language, and subject matter on her. One of her motivations was to "redo" her own education while providing other women with the extra support they needed to develop the strong sense of self necessary for an artist.

[Signs: Journal of Women in Culture and Society 1985, vol. 10, no. 4]
© 1985 by The University of Chicago. All rights reserved. 0097-9740/85/1004-0004$01.00

762

Signs

Summer 1985   763

Building strong egos in the young women took a high priority in the educational program because a firm sense of self is indispensable to an artist, the center and source from which personal and therefore original expression flows. Since women are conditioned to please and defer to men, the presence of men would interfere with women students' self-development and expressiveness. Chicago decided that men would have to be excluded. She wanted the young women to compare themselves only with each other and establish their identities in this nonthreatening ambience.

Schapiro was farther away from her own formal education (she was forty-eight years old to Chicago's thirty-two) and had enjoyed considerably more success as an artist. To her the most important condition of the community was not the exclusion of men, but she agreed that the women needed to work together as a separate group. As she has said, looking back on the experience, "We knew we had to take a hard look at who we were—and when we're in the society of men, we're generally prohibited from doing that. We're permitted to see ourselves as men want us to see ourselves but not as we really are." And practically speaking, "Men are not interested in encouraging any challenge to the patriarchy. They just want to keep order, according to their habits."[1]

Schapiro knew that it was very difficult to break habits—especially in art making. To her, the basic drama of the FAP was in "making something happen against the grain. We felt we were just as important to ourselves and to the world—now this is going to sound very pretentious—as all the scientists gathered together at Los Alamos felt when they were making the atom bomb. We felt that way. We saw ourselves as instruments of history."[2]

Both Schapiro and Chicago, and many of the former students of the FAP, have a keen sense of its historical mission. They see it in the context of the late 1960s in California—a time of social and psychological experimentation, of the self-development movements in which women participated, and of the burgeoning of feminism. California Institute of the Arts, or Cal Arts, is a professional art school that prides itself on commitment to the avant-garde and that sought out and encouraged innovators and visionaries. And the head of the School of Visual Arts at Cal Arts happened to be Schapiro's husband, Paul Brach. So a combination of circumstances, both general and specific, created a favorable historical moment for the program.

At Cal Arts, the students of the FAP were separated from the institution both physically and psychologically. They had their own communal space, the large "Feminist Studio." During group meetings and con-

1. Miriam Schapiro, interview with author, New York City, June 1982.
2. Ibid.

First Feminist Art Program

780   *Harper*

opened up the possibility of a wider range of subject matter for artists in general and, after decades of formalist abstraction, seems to have stimulated an interest in content. But since the kind of imagery and attitudes that were engendered, recognized, and described in the early 1970s have been, to some extent, subsumed into the mainstream, women's art seems less visible now than it did ten years ago.

In the climate of feminist thought in 1985, a separatist experiment such as the FAP would probably not have much appeal. Now the challenge, as articulated by several former students, is to return with feminist goals to a social dialogue that includes men. Yet the problematic nature of the relationship between a community of women and the prevailing male culture remains. Some students felt that the FAP had failed to prepare them for the shock of the world of men in which they would have to compete; others said the experience of being in a women's community "strengthened" them. Clear answers have not yet emerged on the most effective ways to strengthen women's consciousness of their own constellation of interests, activities, and powers; effectively communicate this to the general culture; and achieve and maintain public recognition of the equal value of women's contribution. Recent events suggest that some degree of separatism is desirable, even if only to maintain a position from which a visibly female contribution can be made.

The differing directions taken by Chicago and Schapiro serve as illustration of the dilemma. While Chicago feels that an experiment such as the FAP could not be carried out now in a period of reaction and retrenchment, with institutions alert to potential disruption, she is still devoted to the idea of women's community—although not one tied to a specific place. The women whose needlework completes her designs for her *Birth Project* live all over the country. They consult with her by mail and telephone; she visits them in their homes, and they assemble periodically at her studio in Benicia, California. A regular newsletter documents progress. The sense of community necessary to women artists, she feels, comes from working together toward a shared goal, not from being together in the same place.

The *Birth Project* is a decentralized community. It's about building a sense of community in people who are separated geographically. . . . It's still very frustrating for me to watch women refuse to accept the evidence of history—which is that women do not achieve in isolation. They achieve in a context of support, and it's what's required and it's what's usually not there and that's why women go mad. The old communities of women huddled together for a sense of identification and survival. At some stage in their development women need to go through this. But huddling together is hardly a strategy for the

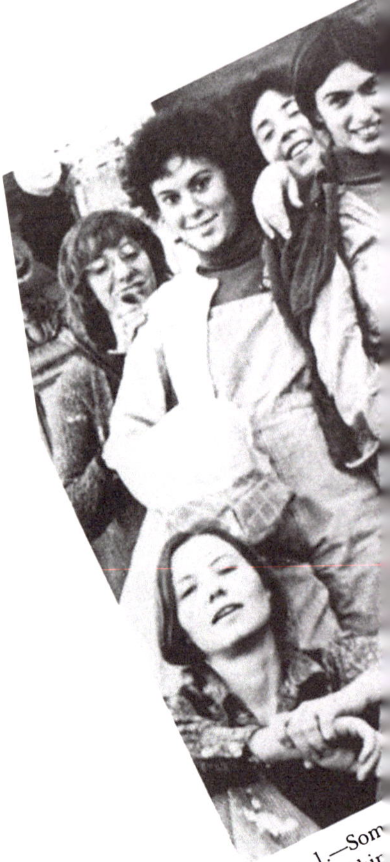

Fig. 1.—Som[...] Chicago, Robbin[...] Huddleston. ([...]

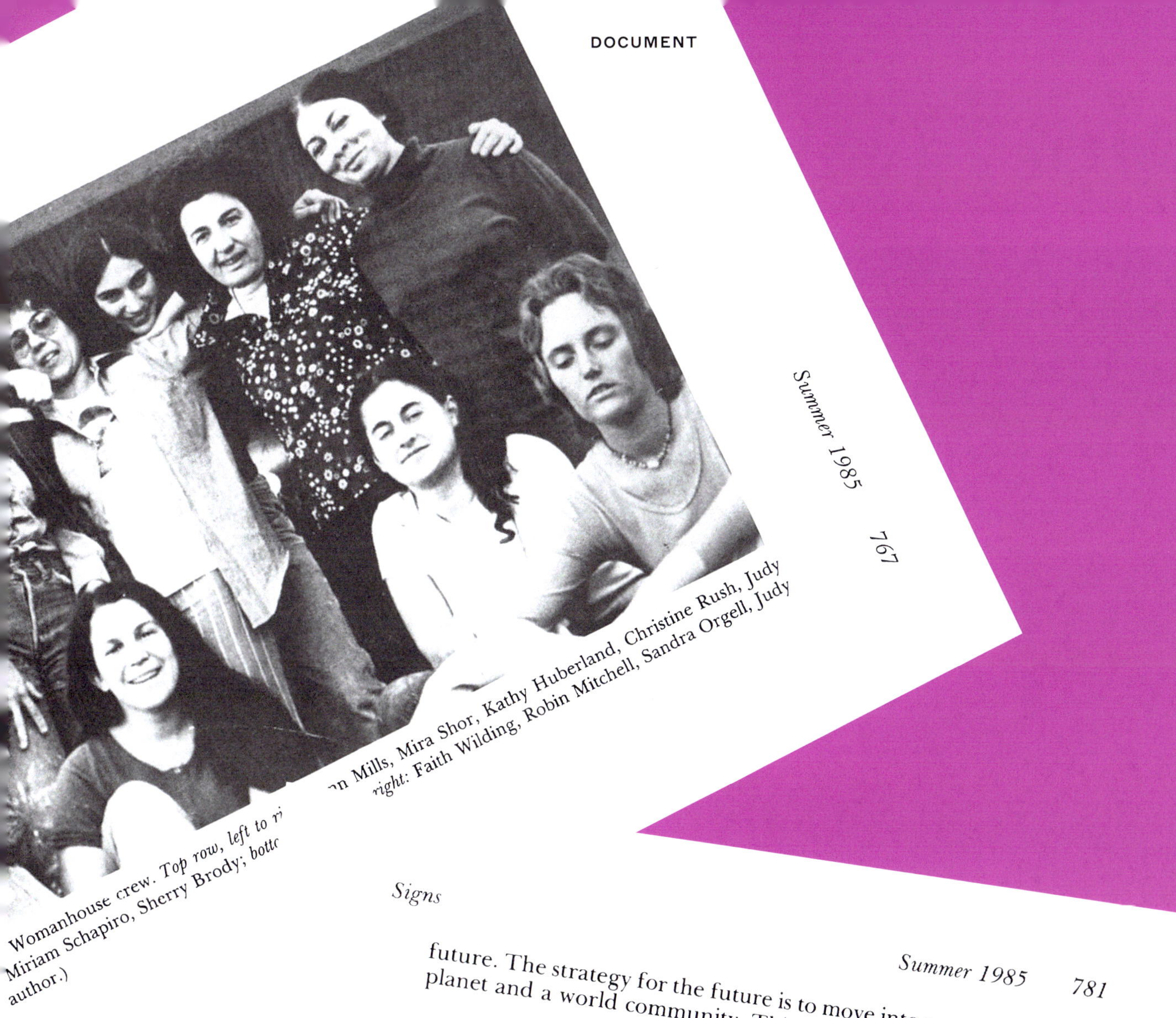

Womanhouse crew. *Top row, left to ri...* ...n Mills, Mira Shor, Kathy Huberland, Christine Rush, Judy ... *right:* Faith Wilding, Robin Mitchell, Sandra Orgell, Judy ... Miriam Schapiro, Sherry Brody; *bottc...* author.)

future. The strategy for the future is to move into a new sense of the planet and a world community. This is where I feel I'm working.[26]

Schapiro has returned to the world she successfully inhabited before the FAP. Her combinations of collage and painting are formally excellent and can be situated in an aesthetic continuity with other twentieth-century developments. But to gain acceptance, she has had to compromise her feminist challenge to some extent. She is working within the system, and her art has necessarily been assimilated to it. Since she believes that "all feminist revolutions are doomed in a patriarchy," it would be foolish for her to take a revolutionary stance. From her current position she can make gains and offer younger women a solid model of a successful woman artist whose work has been nurtured by feminist ideas.

Women in the academic community face a similar situation. We exist within institutions that are dominated by male interests, preferences, and traditions. We are accustomed to working within the system, making the necessary compromises, "hopping on one foot and then the other," as Schapiro put it. This is a practical path, one resigned to small gains. While requiring tenacity and endurance over the long haul, it lacks the purity, drama, and possibility of creative leaps that a women's community can provide.

Department of Art and Art History
University of Miami

26. Interview with Chicago.

VANALYNE GREEN

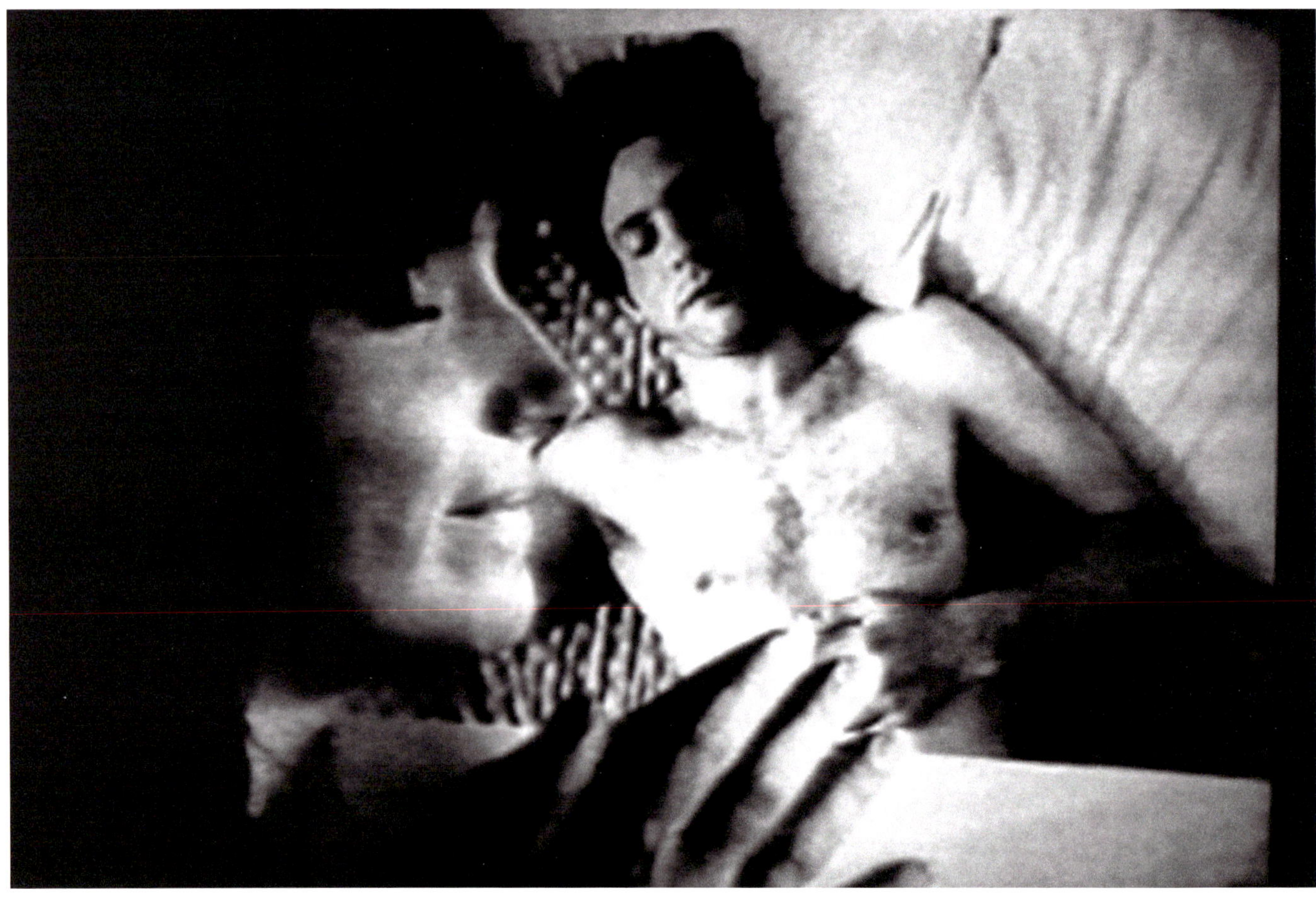

* 1948, Ft. Knox (KY), USA

is an American video artist, activist, and lecturer. Her videos often analyze and reveal power structures of meaning at the intersection of sex and privilege.[1] She "appropriates the conventions of various genres" in order to investigate those hierarchies.[2] Her video work includes *Trick or Drink* (1984), *A Spy in the House that Ruth Built* (1990), *Saddle Sores* and *I'm Still a Feminist* (2015).[3] *A Spy in the House that Ruth Built* was listed one of the 1,000 best films ever made by film critic Jonathan Rosenbaum.[4] Green is an activist within the feminist movement and was a member of *Feminist Art Workers* (L.A.) and *Double X* (L.A.), as well as a co-founder of collaborative artist groups, such as *No More Nice Girls* (N.Y.) and *Feel Tank Chicago*.[5]

Green studied art in Judy Chicago's Feminist Art Program at Fresno State College (CA) and worked with Sheila Levrant de Bretteville in the Feminist Design Studio and at California Institute of the Arts, Valencia (CA). She graduated with a BFA from Cal-Arts in 1974.[6] Green taught at Temple University in Philadelphia, the École Nationale Supérieure des Beaux-Arts in Paris, France (where she initiated its first video program), and the University of Leeds (UK).[7] She was Chair of the Undergraduate Fine Art Department at ArtCenter College of Design in Pasadena and of the Video Department at the School of the Art Institute of Chicago.

Green's video work has been shown nationally and internationally at festivals, universities, and art institutions, including the Whitney Biennial, the Whitney Museum of American Art, the Rotterdam International Film Festival, the Guggenheim Museum, the Museum of Modern Art, the American Film Institute, and the Robert Flaherty Film Seminar.[8]   **LB**

Vanalyne Green, *Trick or Drink* (1984), video still.

The Museum of Modern Art

For Immediate Release
December 1989

Video and Myth
exhibition at MoMA
January 4–February 27, 1990

<u>VIDEO AND MYTH</u>

January 4 - February 27, 1990

A video exhibition exploring the role of women in society is on view at The Museum of Modern Art through February 27, 1990. VIDEO AND MYTH, featuring nineteen works produced over the last seven years, explores aspects of femaleness shaped by contemporary culture, family life, history, politics, memory, and reflection. The artists represented in this exhibition examine myths created through cultural stereotypes and seek new, more personally relevant truths.

In <u>A Spy in the House That Ruth Built</u>, Vanalyne Green appropriates the all-male arena of professional baseball to create a visual essay about family, loss, and sexuality. In the seriocomic <u>Womb with a View</u>, Sherry Millner compares the bliss of an ideal pregnancy with the discomfort, confusion, and delight of her actual one. In <u>Consider Anything Only Don't Cry</u>, Helen DeMichiel begins with a quote from <u>Alice in Wonderland</u> to explore ways in which we learn and remember. (Complete program list attached.)

MYTH was organized by Barbara London, assistant curator, Video, Department of Film, The Museum of Modern Art. The Museum's video programs are made possible by grants from the New York State Council on the Arts and the National Endowment for the Arts.

*   *   *

No. 120
For further information, contact Sarah Eaton, film press representative, Department of Public Information, 212/708-9750.

11 West 53 Street, New York, N.Y. 10019-5498 Tel. 212-708-9400 Cable MODERNART Telex 62370 MODART

"MYTH"
January 4 - February 27, 1990

<u>Programs</u>

I

Ida Applebroog and Beth B, <u>Belladonna</u>. 1989. 12 min.
Martha Rosler and Paper Tiger Television, <u>Born to be Sold: Martha Rosler Reads the Strange Case of Baby $M</u>. 1988. 35 min.
Ayoka Chenzira, <u>Secret Sounds Screaming: The Sexual Abuse of Children</u>. 1986. 30 min.

II

Marina Abramovic and Charles Atlas, <u>SSS</u>. 1989. 5 min.
Vanalyne Green, <u>A Spy in the House that Ruth Built</u>. 1989. 29 min.
Helen De Michiel, <u>Consider Anything, Only Don't Cry</u>. 1987. 23 min.
Sherry Millner, <u>Womb with a View</u>. 1986. 40 min.

III

Kathy High, <u>I Need Your Full Cooperation</u>. 1989. 28 min.
Susan Rynard, <u>1932</u>. 1988. 9 min.
Branda Miller, <u>That's It, Forget It</u>. 1985. 4 min.
Dara Birnbaum, <u>Damnation of Faust: Evocation</u>. 1983. 10 min.
Mako Idemitsu, <u>Kyoko's Situation</u>. 1989. 25 min.

IV

Lisa Steele, <u>Some Call It Bad Luck</u>. 1982. 50 min.
Mona Hatoum, <u>Measures of Distance</u>. 1987. 15 min.
Pratibha Parmar, <u>Sari Red</u>. 1988. 50 min.
Sara Diamond, <u>Ten Dollars or Nothing</u>. 1989. 12 min.

V

Laura Kipnis, <u>A Man's Woman</u>. 1988. 52 min.
Eleanor Antin, <u>From the Archives of Modern Art</u>. 1988. 24 min.
Rhonda Abrams, <u>Billy of Meek Cove</u>. 1988. 25 min.

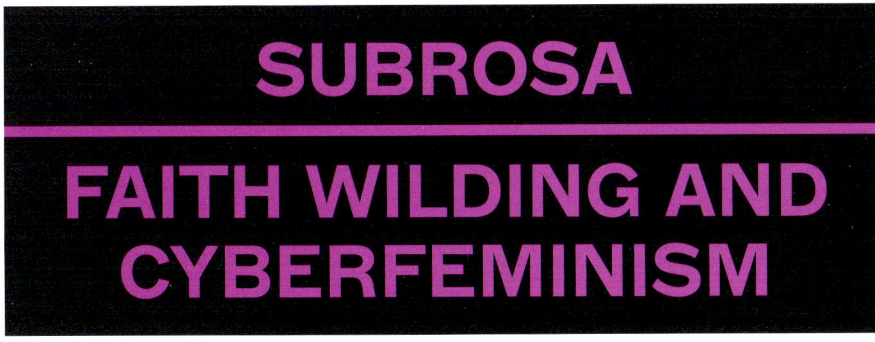

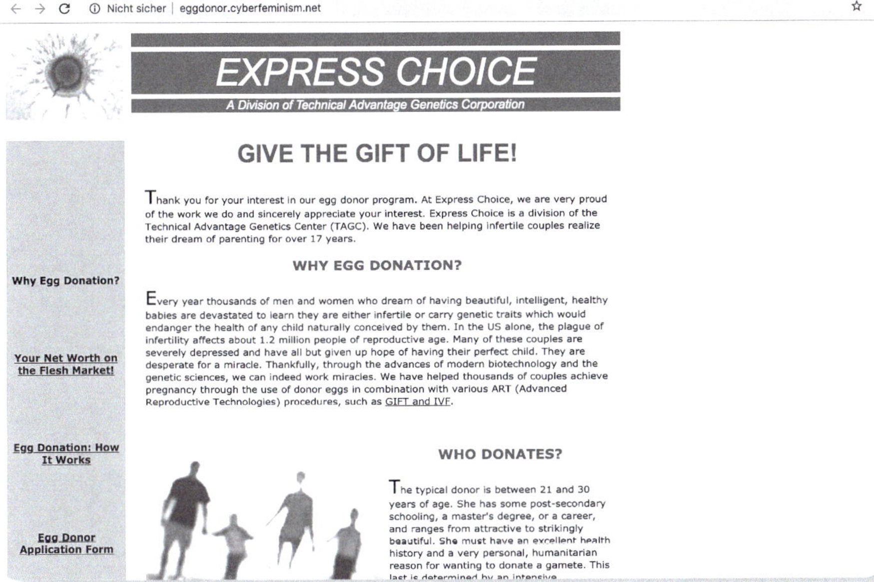

What is cyberfeminism? Cyberfeminism is, by definition, not determined. The history of feminist art and cyberfeminism is rarely taught as part of academic curricula and it is often up to artists on the margins to spread such discourses. Faith Wilding's artistic career started long before the beginnings of the internet, in the 1970s in the context of *Womanhouse*. For at least two decades, Wilding authored a significant number of essays about feminist issues and remains widely cited in feminist literature and academia today. Her exhibition record is impressive: Wilding's work has been shown at the Whitney Museum of Art, the Museum of Contemporary Art, and the UCLA Hammer Museum in Los Angeles, the Museo Reina Sofía in Madrid, among many others.

Less known about Wilding is that she identified with the cyberfeminists in the 1990s, as, for instance, illustrated in her *Recombinants* works. Though these are not digital or web-based projects, they unfold on the intersection of plant, animal, human, and technological bodies, an important aspect of cyberfeminist ideas. Wilding's series of drawings, collages, and paintings depict hybrid, cyborgian bodies. Donna Haraway's 1985 essay "A Cyborg Manifesto" was a strong influence for Wilding, as it was for most participants of the cyberfeminist movement, including a younger generation of artists such as Cornelia Sollfrank, Linda Dement, Melinda Packham, or Shu Lea Cheang.

In 1998, Wilding founded the cyberfeminist organization subRosa with the artist Hyla Willis. Their manifesto states:

"subRosa is a reproducible cyberfeminist cell of cultural researchers committed to combining art, activism, and politics to explore and critique the effects of the intersections of the new information and biotechnologies on women's bodies, lives, and work … Let a million subRosas bloom!"[1]

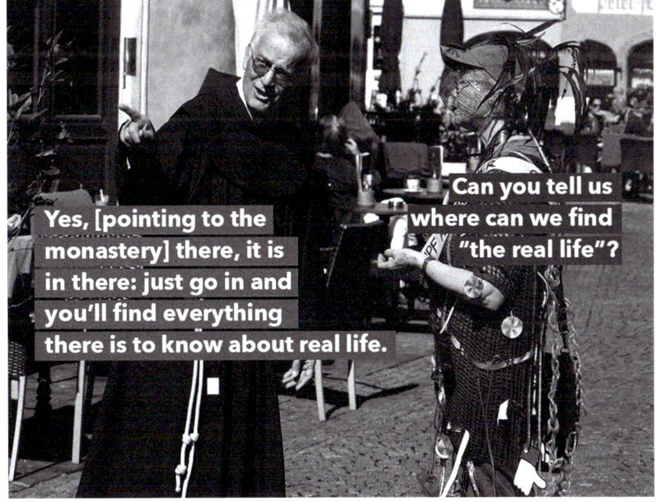

From top to bottom: subRosa, *Express Choice. A Division of Technical Advantage Genetics Corporation* (2002), website screenshot.
subRosa, *Cyberswamp Escapees*, as part of *Down with Self-Management* (September 2014), Steirischer Herbst Festival, Graz.

Most of subRosa's works were either performances or texts, and as an 'anti-copyright' collective, they make their materials freely available online and downloadable as PDFs. For a 2002 performance, they created a website on which the user can participate in a parody quiz that analyzes "your net worth on the flesh market."[2] Checkboxes include "I have blonde hair, fair skin, and blue eyes"[3] and "I like shopping more than most activities";[4] if checked, the website increases the participant's 'value' as a potential egg donor, calling attention to how reproduction has become not only customizable, but that it also problematically replicates oppressive societal values.   AJL

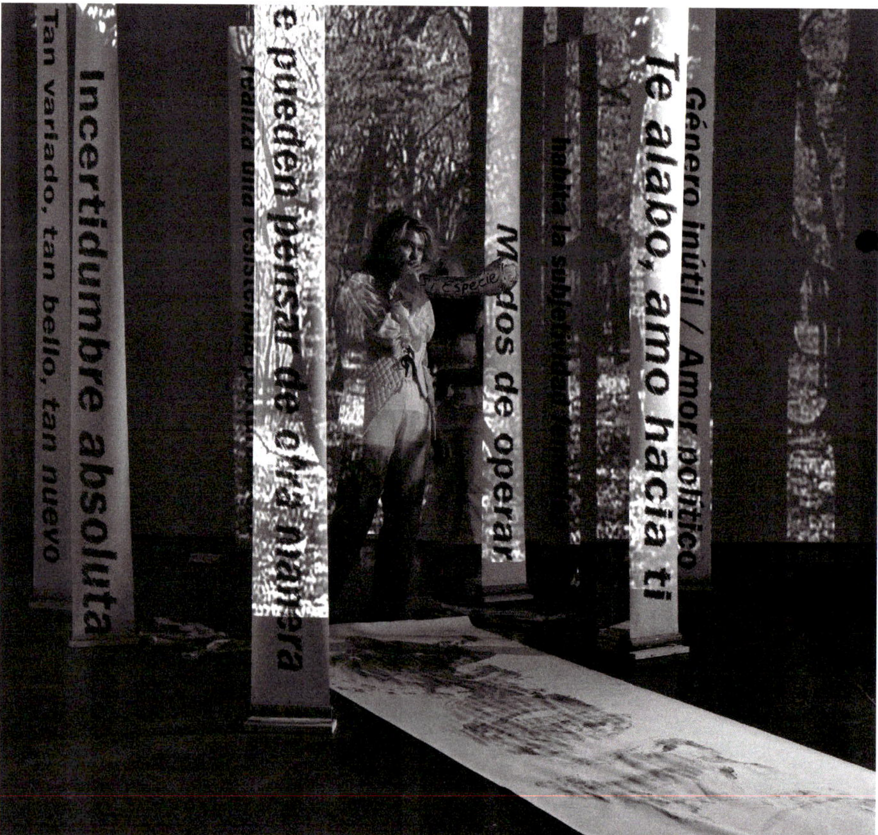

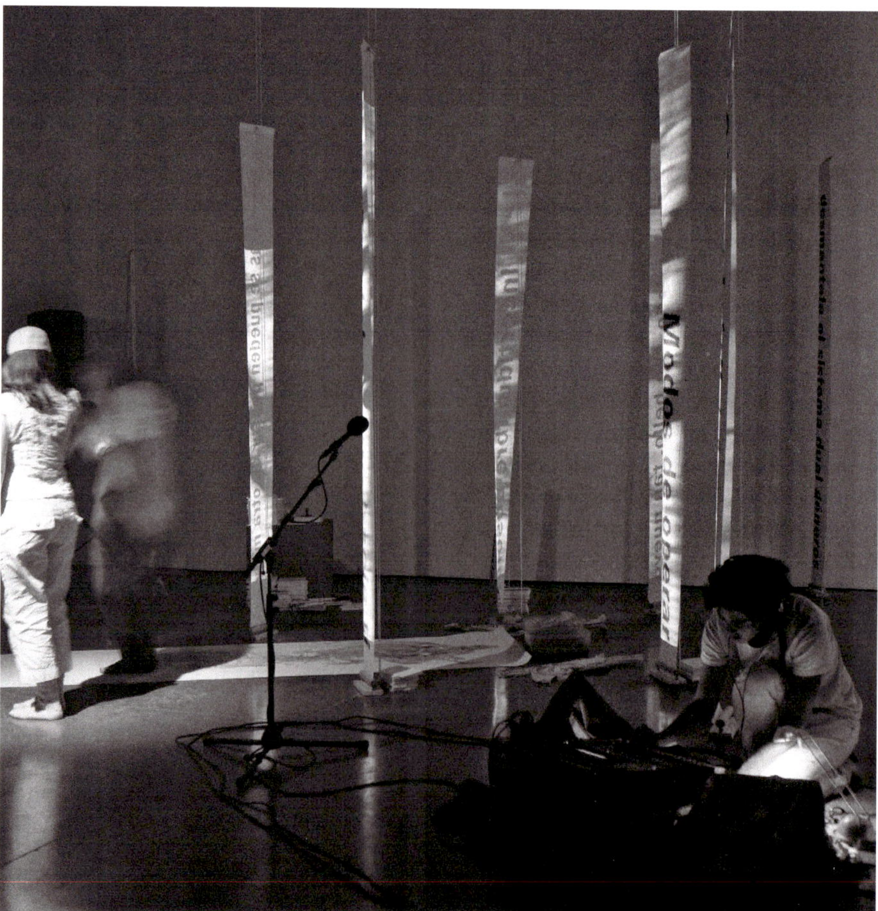

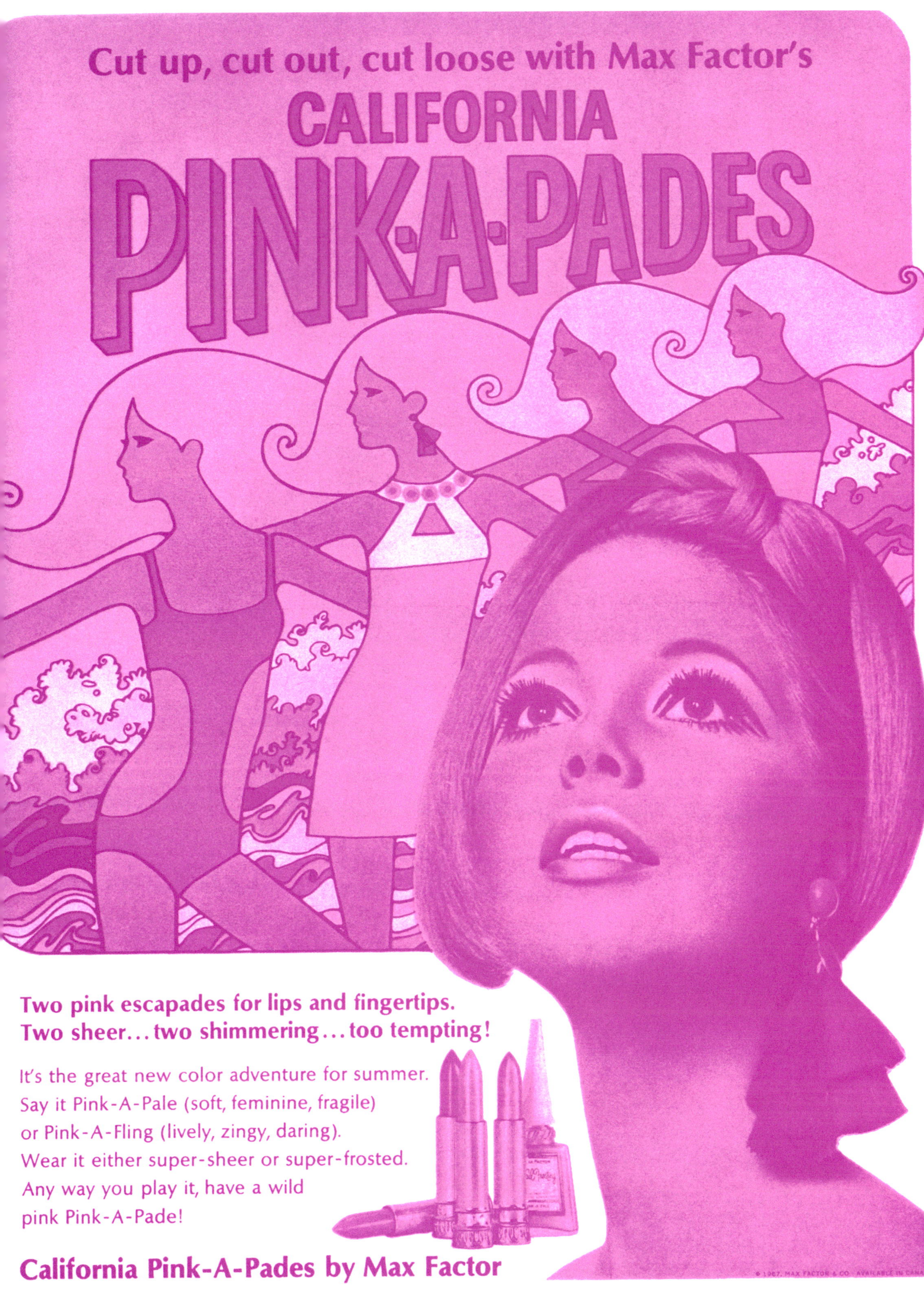

Cut up, cut out, cut loose with Max Factor's
CALIFORNIA
PINK·A·PADES

Two pink escapades for lips and fingertips.
Two sheer...two shimmering...too tempting!

It's the great new color adventure for summer.
Say it Pink-A-Pale (soft, feminine, fragile)
or Pink-A-Fling (lively, zingy, daring).
Wear it either super-sheer or super-frosted.
Any way you play it, have a wild
pink Pink-A-Pade!

California Pink-A-Pades by Max Factor

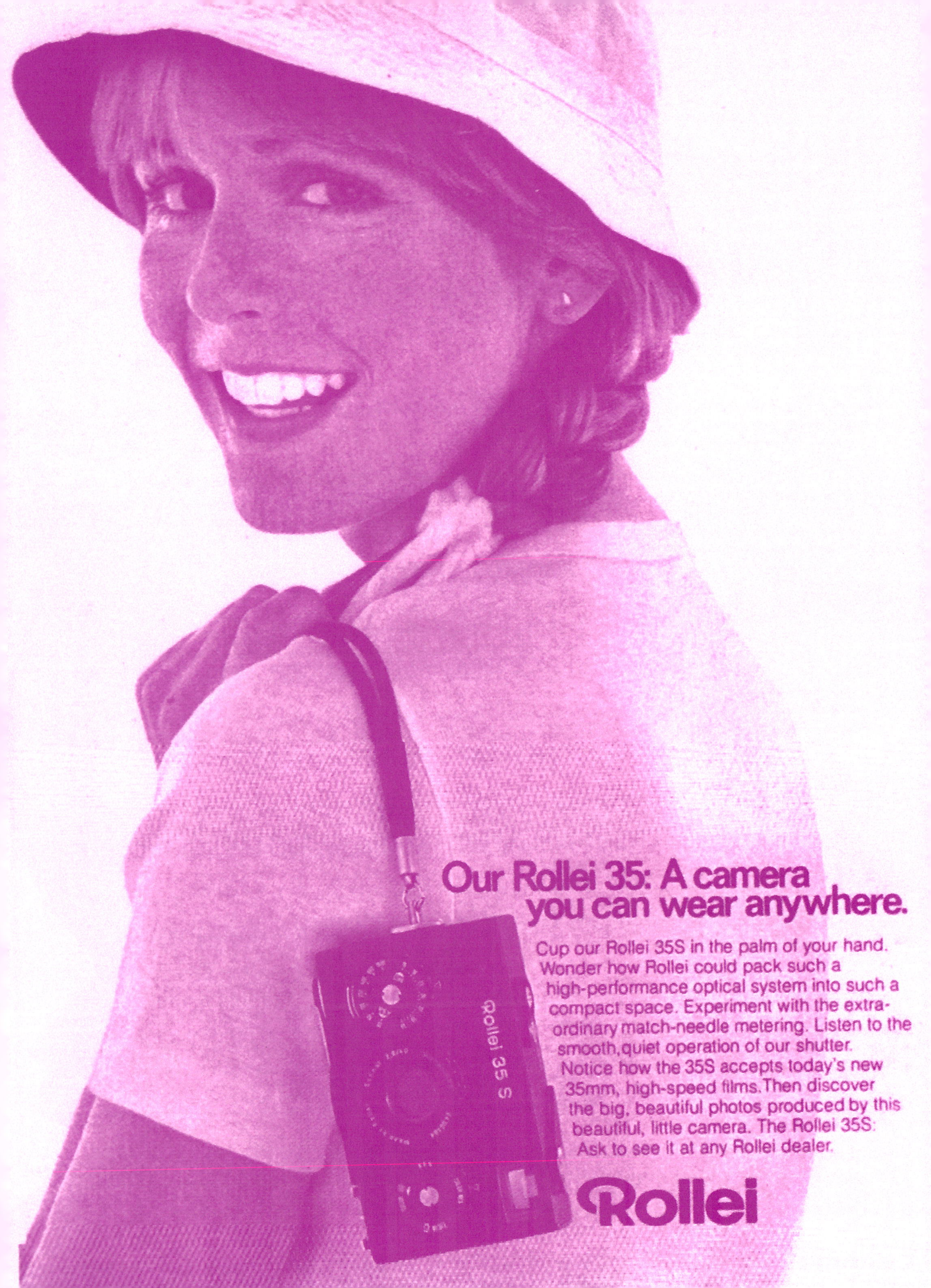

Our Rollei 35: A camera
you can wear anywhere.

Cup our Rollei 35S in the palm of your hand.
Wonder how Rollei could pack such a
high-performance optical system into such a
compact space. Experiment with the extraordinary match-needle metering. Listen to the
smooth, quiet operation of our shutter.
Notice how the 35S accepts today's new
35mm, high-speed films. Then discover
the big, beautiful photos produced by this
beautiful, little camera. The Rollei 35S:
Ask to see it at any Rollei dealer.

Rollei 35 S

Rollei

THE ART WORLD IS PART OF THE REAL WORLD

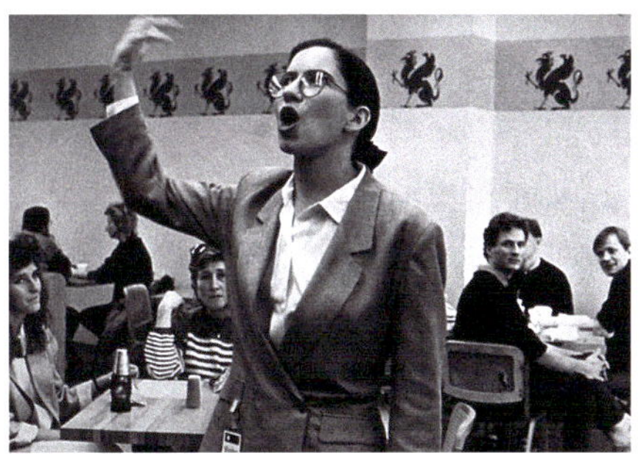

In her 2005 essay "From the Critique of Institutions to an Institution of Critique," Andrea Fraser points out the basis for her institutional critique.[1] To explain her position, she refers to the artist Hans Haacke. His conceptual artworks were not only seen as an attempt to tear down the museum, but also aimed to defend art from instrumentalization by political or economic interests.

Fraser underlines the fact that the art world is still part of the real world, reproducing the same economic disparities that exist in wider society. Representations of the art world maintain and reproduce the myth of voluntarist freedom and creative omnipotence into the avant-garde. Even though many artistic works promise to reevaluate society, they exist within a system the whole society is working in.

Art is simultaneously a means of reflecting on society and an encapsulation of societal conditions. Such conditions are maintained by institutions and the wider public. Fraser declares this a 'misalignment' between the social conditions of art and its symbolic systems.[2] There is a huge difference between what art is and the discourse surrounding it. The fundamental question, Fraser claims, is: how can art reflect on society, if art itself contains that same societal issue?

In her critique, Fraser refers to Pierre Bourdieu and his position on social drafts and systems. She looks at art in terms of its social dimensions. **PG**

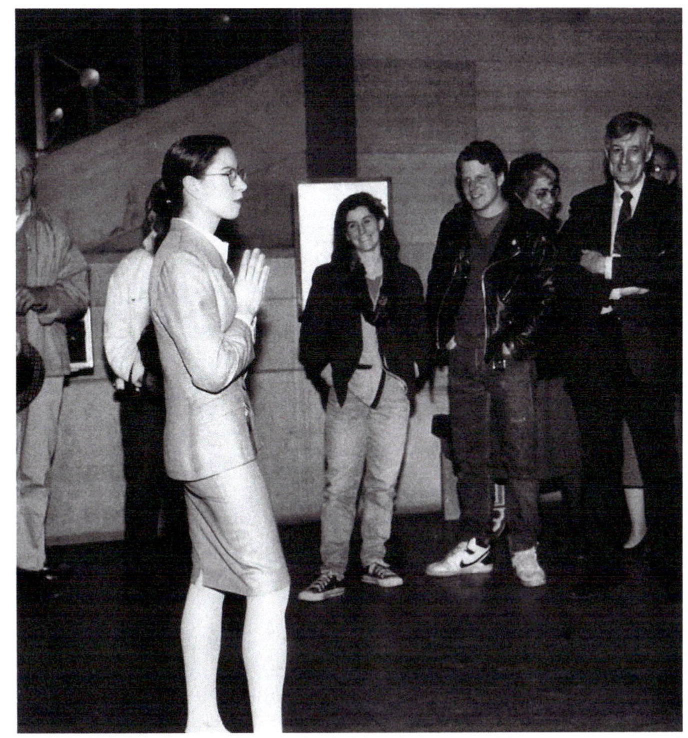

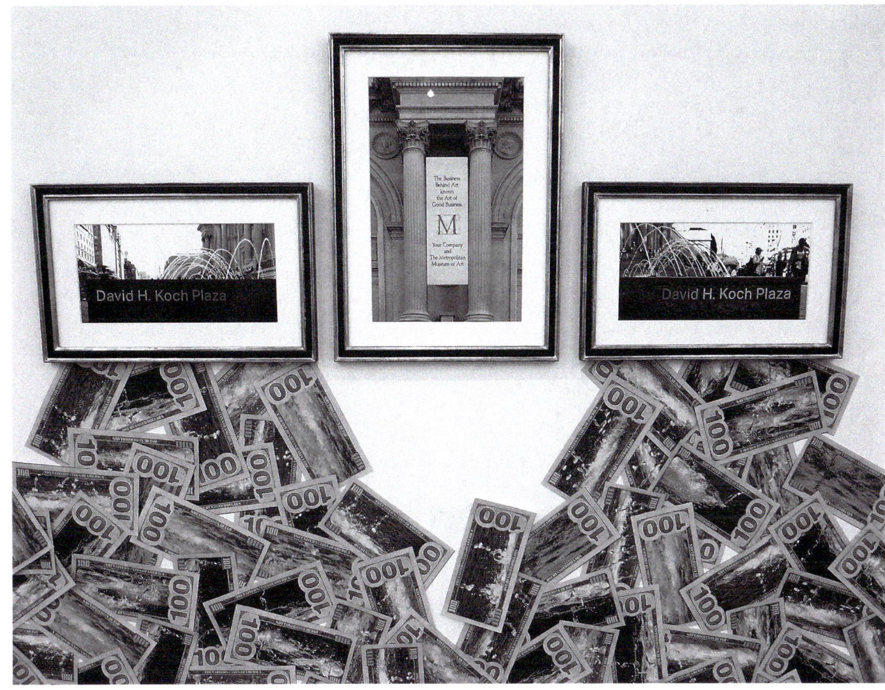

From top to bottom: Andrea Fraser, *Museum Highlights: A Gallery Talk* (1989), performance at the Philadelphia Museum of Art (PA). Hans Haacke, *The Business Behind Art Knows the Art of the Koch Brothers* (2014), Paula Cooper Gallery, New York.

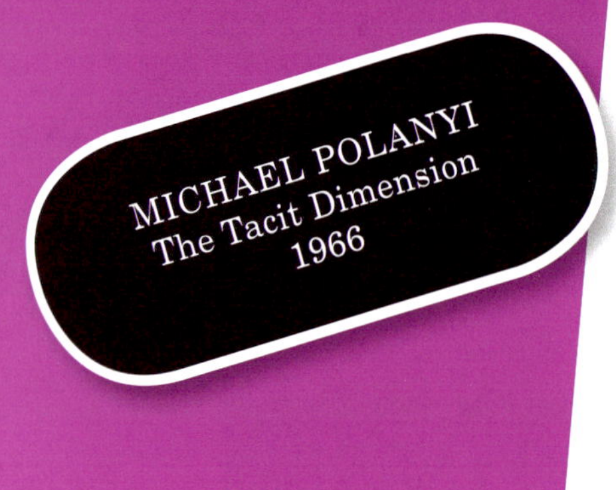

THE TACIT DIMENSION

———

MICHAEL POLANYI

DOUBLEDAY & COMPANY, INC.

GARDEN CITY, NEW YORK

1966

CONTENTS

Introduction

page ix

— 1 —

TACIT KNOWING

page 1

— 2 —

EMERGENCE

page 27

— 3 —

SOCIETY OF
EXPLORERS

page 53

Notes

page 93

Bibliography

101

from these internal
things outside. Thes
al processes *mean* t
y experiences into t
le may now appe
of the transposition
ich we have found to
all tacit knowing.
the feelings transpose
hose transposed by th
being hardly noticea
their transposition.
st part of an answer t
riments extending sub
i. Hefferline and colla
t when spontaneous
the subject—but obse
ion-fold amplification o
re followed by the cessa
, the subject responded
ing the frequency of the twitches and th
the noise much of the time.[3] Tacit kno
to operate here on an internal action
quite incapable of controlling or even
self. We become aware of our opera
in the silencing of a noise. This expe
seems closely analogous to the proce
become aware of subliminal proce
body in the perception of objects
This view of perception, that it
the transposition of feelings which
use of probes and in the process
borne out by the fact that the
ternal objects must be acquire

14

TACIT KNOWING

probes and the feats of subception, by a process of
learning which can be laborious.

Modern philosophers have argued that perception does not involve projection, since we are not
previously aware of the internal processes which we
are supposed to have projected into the qualities of
things perceived. But we have now established that
projection of this very kind is present in various instances of tacit knowing. Moreover, the fact that we
do not originally sense the internal processes in
themselves now appears irrelevant. We may venture,
therefore, to extend the scope of tacit knowing to
include neural traces in the cortex of the nervous
system. This would place events going on inside our
brain on the same footing as the subliminal twitches
operated by Hefferline's subjects.*

This brings us to the point at which I hinted
when I first mentioned perception as an instance of
tacit knowing. I said that by elucidating the way our
bodily processes participate in our perception[s we]
will throw light on the bodily roots of all th[ought]
including man's highest creative powers. L[et me]
show this now.

Our body is the ultimate instrument of a[ll our]
external knowledge, whether intellectual or [practi-]
cal. In all our waking moments we are *relyi[ng]*

* Such a hypothesis does not explain how per[ceptions,]
sights, or any other state of consciousness, arise i[n con-]
junction with neural processes. It merely appli[es the]
principle that wherever some process in our body [gives]
rise to consciousness in us, our tacit knowing [of the]
process will make sense of it in terms of an expe[rience]
[t]o which we are attending.

15

[left-edge fragment]

n
rs
ar
ex-
ac-
f an
[i]ncreas-
ncing
s seen
we are
g in it-
it only
[ic]al result
which we
nside our

[e.]
instance of
[f]ound in the
[su]bception, is
[ili]ty to see ex-
[e] the use of

[right fragment]

KNOWING

[his] mind on his music, the
[...]my and the details of a pat-
[...] [m]ore from a distance: they all
[...] [reco]ver their meaning and their
[...]ship.

[...] to note that this recovery
[...] original meaning. It may im-
[...] [st]udies, which tend to paralyze
[...] it when followed by practice.
[...] [rem]embering of a text, which can
[...] can also supply material for a
[...] [unders]tanding of it. In these cases,
[...] [part]iculars, which by itself would
[...] [ser]ves as a guide to their subse-
[...] [an]d thus establishes a more

[lower-right fragment]

TACIT KNOWING

and Lipps represented aesthetic appreciation as an
entering into a work of art and thus dwelling in the
mind of its creator. I think that Dilthey and Lipps
described here a striking form of tacit knowing as
applied to the understanding of man and of works
of art, and that they were right in saying that this
could be achieved only by indwelling. But my analysis of tacit knowing shows that they were mistaken
in asserting that this sharply distinguished the humanities from the natural sciences. Indwelling, as
derived from the structure of tacit knowing, is a far
more precisely defined act than is empathy, and it
underlies all observations, including all those described previously as indwelling.

We meet with another indication of the wide
functions of indwelling when we find acceptance to
moral teachings described as their *interiorization.*
To interiorize is to identify ourselves with the teachings in question, by making them function as the
proximal term of a tacit moral knowledge, as applied
in practice. This establishes the tacit framework for
our moral acts and judgments. And we can trace this
kind of indwelling to logically similar acts in the
practice of science. To rely on a theory for understanding nature is to interiorize it. For we are attending from the theory to things seen in its light, and
are aware of the theory, while thus using it, in terms
of the spectacle that it serves to explain. This is why
mathematical theory can be learned only by practicing its application: its true knowledge lies in our
ability to use it.

WOMEN HOUSE

AN EXHIBITION 46 YEARS AFTER WOMANHOUSE

"Women's place is still a hot topic, and the domestic realm remains a gendered space still associated with women and femininity."[1]
— The NMWA chief curator Kathryn Wat

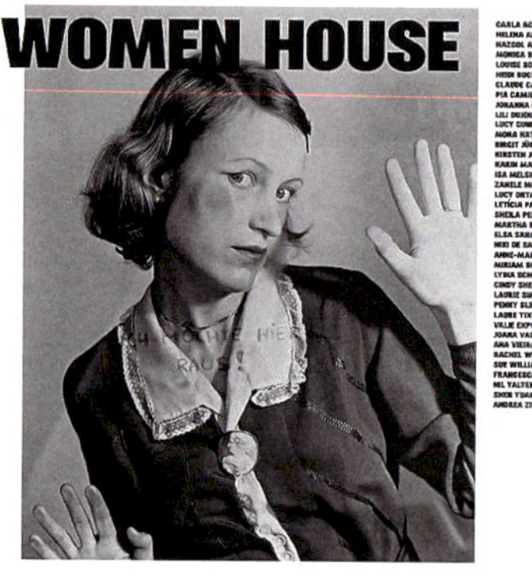

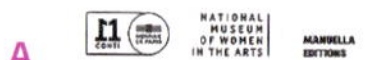

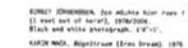

A

46 years after *Womanhouse*, a new exhibition called *Women House* featured the work of 36 contemporary artists inspired by Miriam Schapiro, Judy Chicago, and their students. The exhibition was organized by Camille Morineau and Lucia Pesapane at La monnaie de Paris between October 20, 2017, and January 28, 2018, and took place at the National Museum of Women in the Arts (NMWA) in Washington D. C. from March 9 to May 28, 2018. The featured artworks challenged gender stereotypes and the concept of domesticity.

There were eight main sections:
- "Desperate Housewives" focusing on the depiction of the domestic world as a world of male dominancy
- "Home is Where It Hurts" revolving around images of domestic drudgery and enforced gender roles
- "Femmes-Maisons" dealing with the portrayal of the female body as the representation of the home
- "A Room of One's Own" featuring videos and photographs that show women merging with their environment and using their body as architecture
- "Marks" showing artists' maps of spaces they inhabited
- "A Doll's House" portraying the idealization of the domestic space from childhood
- "Construction as Self-Construction"
- "Mobile Homes" exploring ideas related to nomadism and exile[3]   **AR**

"All these women said they didn't want to be called that. Now I get emails from young women all over the world who say, 'I'm a feminist artist.' That's what I set out to do…. I'd been told in the 1960s that I couldn't be both a woman and an artist…. That has completely changed. Young women, artists of color, artists of the range of sexual orientation can now be themselves openly in their work. That's a fabulous change."[2] — Judy Chicago

A   Cover of the catalog of the exhibition *Women House* at the 11 Conti Museum, Paris, October 20, 2017–January 28, 2018, and at the National Museum of Women in the Arts, Washington D. C., March 9–May 28, 2018.
B   Miriam Schapiro, *Lost and Found* (1998).
C   Laurie Simmons, *Walking House* (1989).
D   Cindy Sherman, *Untitled Film* Still #84 (1978).

"*Women House* shows the enormous contributions of women artists to a topic that has received surprisingly little scholarly attention since 1972. It is about traditional gender roles in our society and demonstrates how women artists have challenged and revised our ideas about women, home, and hearth."[4] — The NMWA Director Susan Fisher Sterling

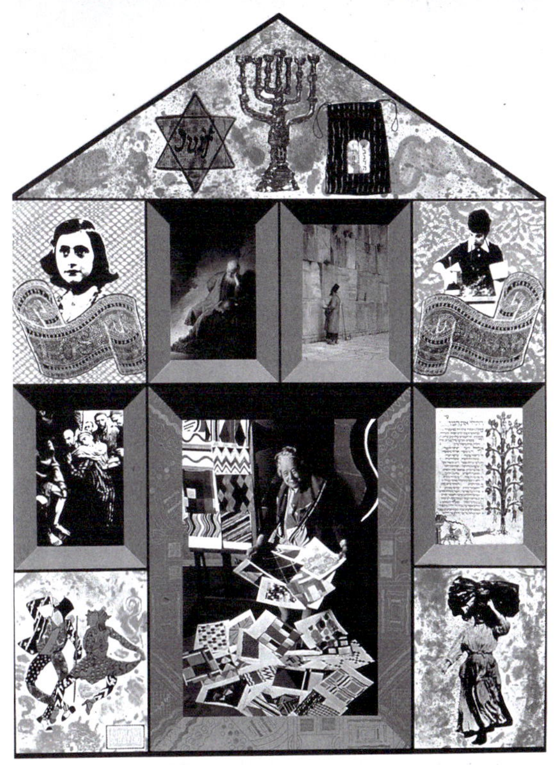

B

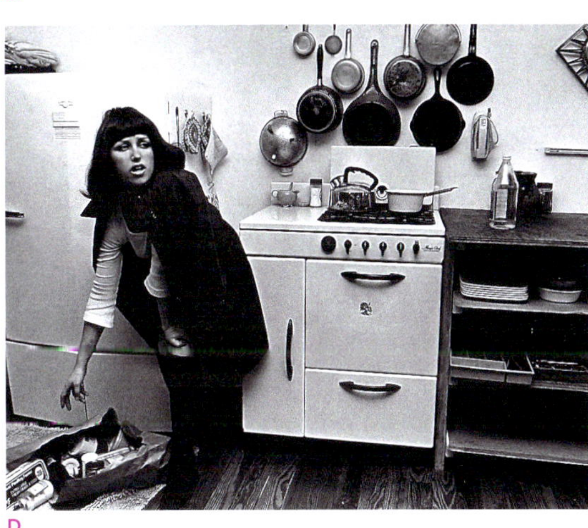

D

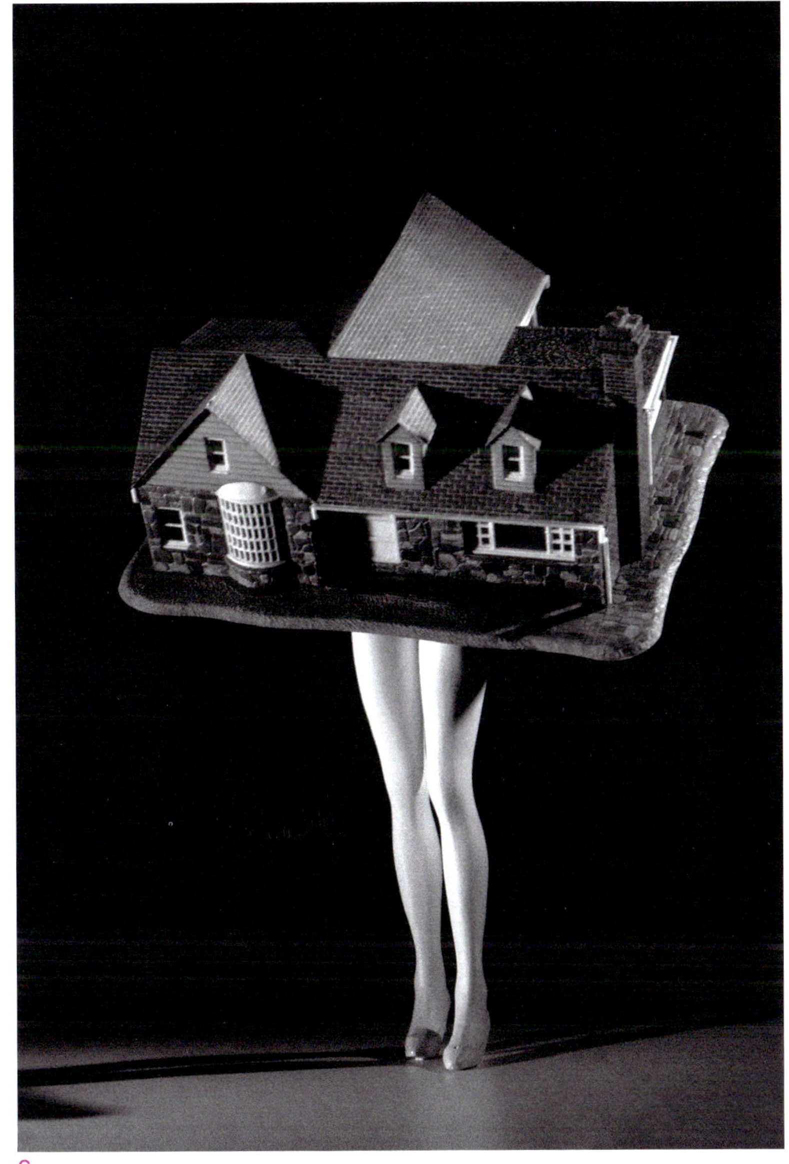

C

"We really didn't have any literature telling us it was a good thing to be a woman artist. When I was trained, there were no precedents, and that was something to get really angry about."[5] — Miriam Schapiro

JUDITH ADLER
Artists in Offices:
An Ethnography of an
Academic Art Scene
1976

ARTISTS IN OFFICES: AN ETHNOGRAPHY
OF AN ACADEMIC ART SCENE

A Dissertation

Presented to

The Faculty of the Graduate School of Arts and

Brandeis University

Department of Sociology

In Partial Fulfillment
of the Requirements of the Degree
Doctor of Philosophy

by

Judith Elena Adler

December 1976

community. Once the seed money had been spent on a facility, it was inevitable that (1) in the absence of a windfall, the Institute would remain unmitigatedly dependent upon the Disneys to underwrite its deficit from one year to the next; (2) the school's uncertain future would create an atmosphere of chronic crisis and collective insecurity, and (3) that all school policies and activities would soon have to be regarded in the light of their effects upon the institution's economy. In the absence of a substantial endowment, any activities or "manners" which could be construed as making fund-raising difficult were thus likely to become the subject of major controversy, until eventually the imperatives of institutional survival defined "reality" for artists who had come to the school in order to affirm the reality of their dreams. Later, as the artists moved painfully from one shared reality to the other, each in his own way would age, weigh his shifting occupational altern-atives, measure his integrity and that of his fellows, and try to make sense of that portion of his life which was bound to the institution's fate. Perhaps, after all, the combined styles in which they did so formed the grand collective work - played primarily before the eyes of colleagues and breaching the boundaries between art and life - which many of them came to the Institute hoping to do and when they left believed they had never accomplished. This thesis is an attempt to document that "piece."

was characterized by an emphasis upon the openness with
which resources of any kind should be dispensed and the
ease with which gratification could be taken. To this
period belong naked swimming parties, memos from one
administrator to another ending with the words, "I
embrace you," sexual orgies in the music practice rooms,
a hippie "free store," a student-operated "free restaurant
in which payment was discretionary, and a fairly un-
guarded attitude toward expensive equipment with one
faculty member, for example, expressing an anarchist
desire to "give away the tools to anybody who needs
them." This list may seem to include quite disparate
items, but members of Cal Arts would have understood
the grouping. When the school finally had to recognize
the precariousness of its financial situation and budgets
had to be slashed, people stated sadly that things were
"tightening up," that it would be more difficult to get

to equipment and that there would be "no more
nd no more sex." In this subsequent period, the
estaurant ceased operating and the title of a
t publication, "No More Free Lunches," symbolized
w tone. What, in short, I would like to suggest
t the easy spending of the early period was, at
ry least, in tune with a wider sense of expansive-
nd a utopian expectation of release from scarcity
nstraint of many kinds.
he financial decisions of the administration - for
e, the decision to open with an extremely costly

l structure.

n which would

ntly developed

Dean of

"The Center of the Revolution"

If the deans regarded the Insti
personal "works" reflecting the qua
imaginations, the aesthetic by whic
administrative art was an avant-ga
one. While, in assembling their
took pride in the range and repr
llections," claiming that the
ssional w

Cal Arts' students and staff saw themselves as
subjects of a utopian experiment in the reorganization
of their education, work and life. This was the common
understanding which underlay all the talk about whether
"it" ever could have worked, about who had betrayed "it"
and where "it" had gone wrong - conversations which
accompanied the life of the institution almost from the
time it opened and which formed a major collective pastime.
Competent participation in institutional gossip, appre-
ciative observation of the unfolding institutional drama,
comprehension of the community's various hierarchies of
moral credibility - in short, membership - required an
awareness of this shared understanding that Cal Arts
(like all utopian communities) was a "promise" to be
fulfilled, a "difference" to be maintained, a "refuge
and a hope."

The school recruited its members and worked on
shaping its public image and its mandate during a period
(1967-1970) of unusual millenarian fervor in the Western
world. Student revolts, ghetto riots, the events of
May-June 1968 in France, the increasing visibility of a
distinct youth culture organized around values opposing
those of the dominant culture, were widely taken as signs
of "The Beginning of the End" - signs which at once pro-
claimed a millenarian presence and served as supportive
evidence for a millenarian orientation. Since the social

In 1976, Judith Adler, a former teacher of CalArts's Criticial Studies department, completed her dissertation with the title *Artists in Offices: An Ethnography of an Academic Art Scene.* Choosing CalArts as its focus of study, this very early ethnography based on fieldwork and interviews examines critically the utopian aspirations of the art school's early years and their clash with its bureaucratic and financial reality.

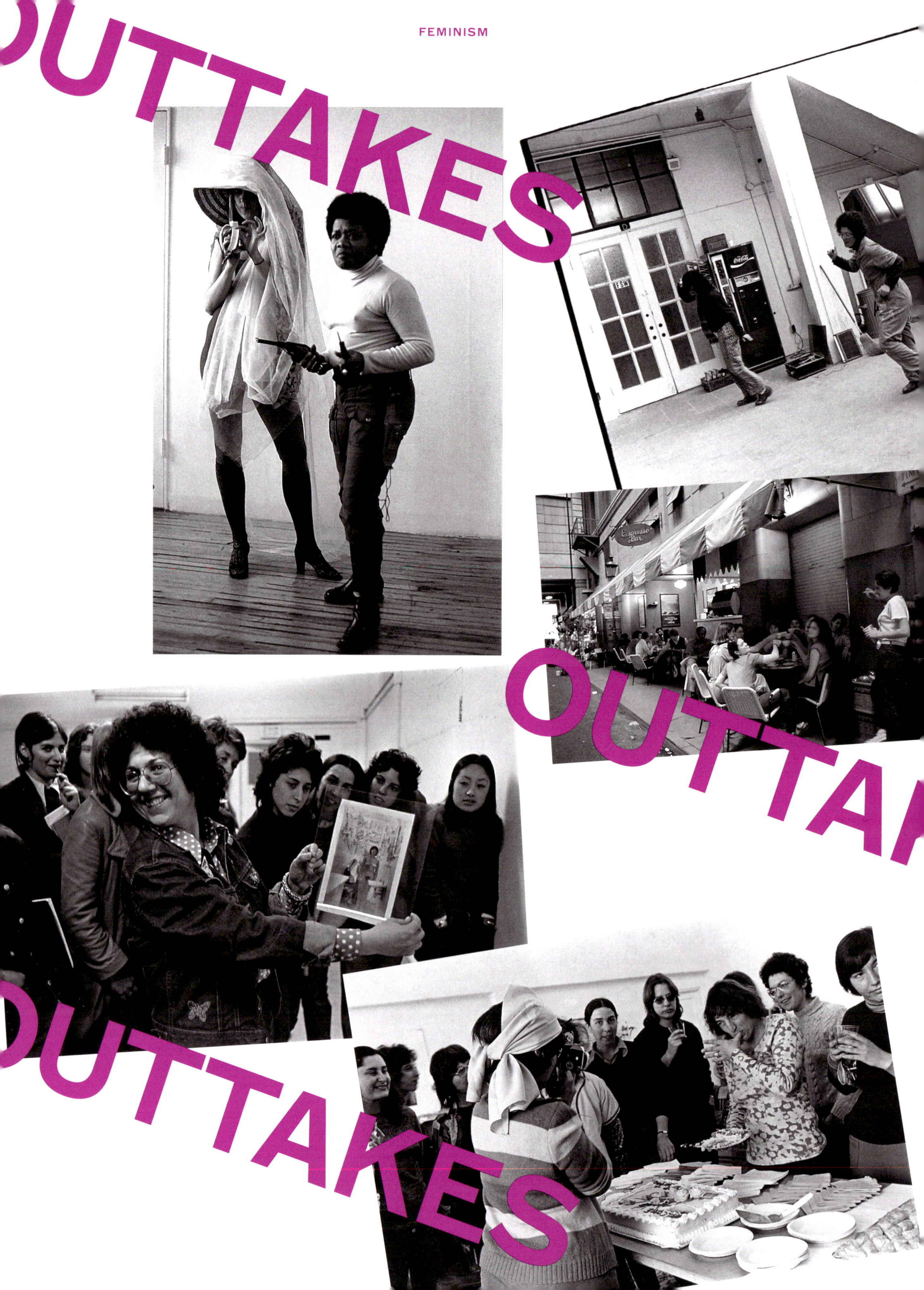

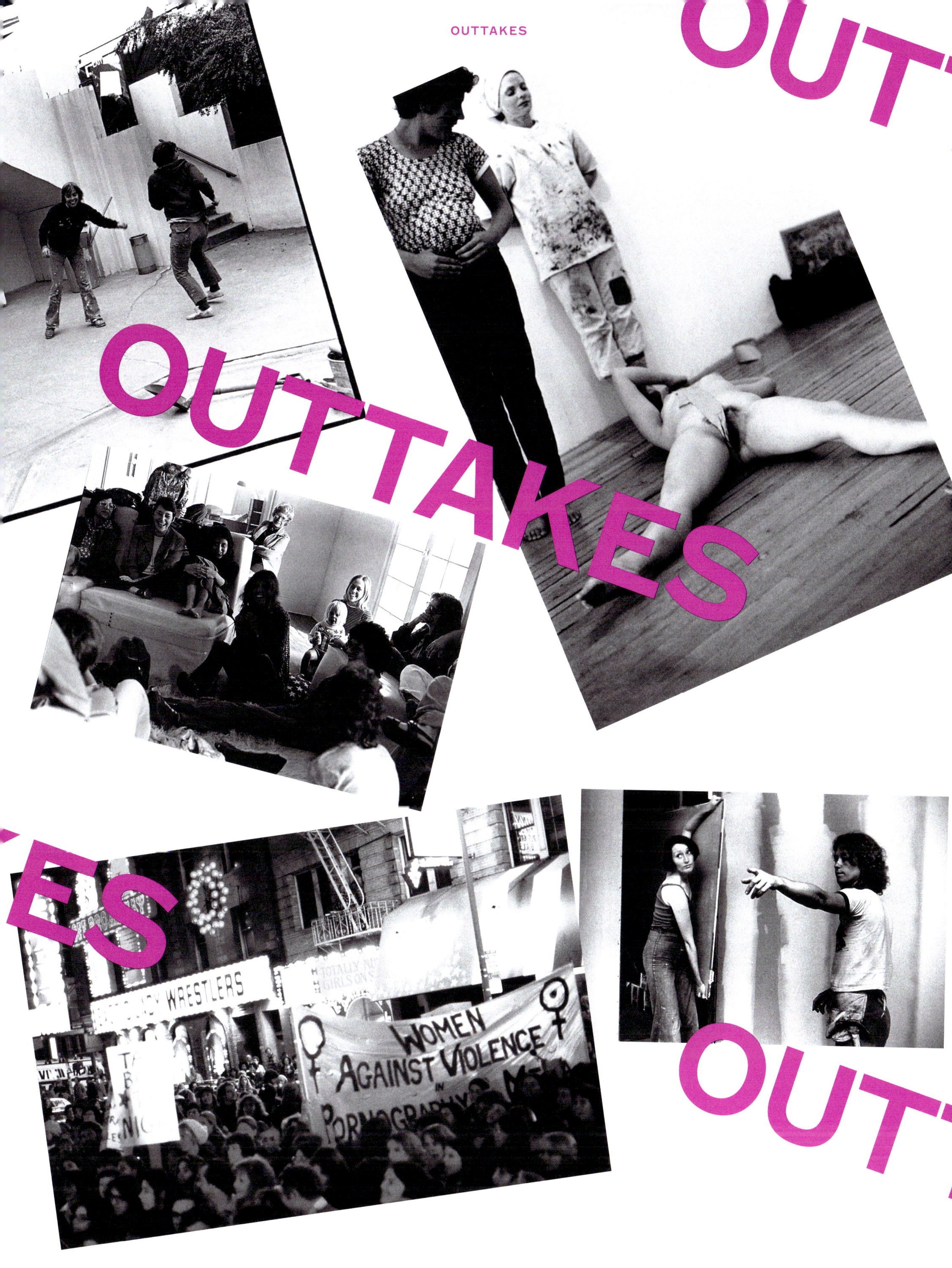
OUTTAKES
OUTTAKES
OUT
ES
OUTT
WRESTLERS
TOTALLY N
GIRLS ON
WOMEN
AGAINST VIOLENCE
IN
PORNOGRAPHY

NOTES

STATEMENTS

1 Judy Chicago and Miriam Schapiro, "Introduction," *Womanhouse*, eds. ibid. (Valencia: California Institute of the Arts, 1972), catalog of an exhibition by the Feminist Art Program, Los Angeles (CA), January 30–February 28, 1972.
2 Nancy Chunn, "Reflections by Nancy Chunn," in *Jack Goldstein and the CalArts Mafia*, ed. Richard Hertz (Ojai: Minneola Press, 2003), 80.
3 Ibid., 70.
4 Paul Brach, "Oral History Interview with Paul Henry Brach," interview by Barry Schwartz, Smithsonian Institution Archives, Archives of American Art, 'Art World in Turmoil' Oral History Project, ca. 1971, transcript, accessed June 13, 2019, https://www.aaa.si.edu/collections/interviews/oral-history-interview-paul-henry-brach-11865#transcript.
5 Mira Schor in a letter to her sister, November 7, 1971, quoted in Mira Schor, *A Decade of Negative Thinking. Essays on Art, Politics, and Daily Life* (Durham/London: Duke University Press, 2009), 77.
6 Suzanne Lacy, "Interview with Suzanne Lacy," interview by Moira Roth, Women in the Arts in Southern California Oral History Project, March 16–September 27, 1990, transcript, accessed June 13, 2019, https://www.aaa.si.edu/collections/interviews/oral-history-interview-suzanne-lacy-12940#transcript%205D.
7 Ibid.
8 Miriam Schapiro, "Out of Isolation," *Everywoman* 2, no. 7, issue 18 (May 1971): 22.
9 Mira Schor in a letter to her sister, October 23, 1971, quoted in Schor, *A Decade*, 76.
10 Lacy, interview.
11 Ibid.

THE FEMINIST ART PROGRAM AT CALARTS | LB

1 See Laura Meyer and Faith Wilding, "Collaboration and Conflict in the Fresno Feminist Art Program. An Experiment in Feminist Pedagogy," *n-paradoxa* 26 (July 2010): 42.
2 See Judy Chicago, "On Womanhouse," filmed at Dupont Studios, Washington D.C., video, 35:53, accessed June 3, 2019, https://www.youtube.com/watch?v=Z9muNnozFGY.
3 See Faith Wilding, "The Feminist Art Programs at Fresno and CalArts (1970–75)," in *The Power of Feminist Art. The American Movement of the 1970s, History and Impact*, eds. Norma Broude and Mary D. Garrard (New York: Harry N. Abrams, 1994), 34 ff.
4 See Miriam Schapiro, "The Education of Women as Artists: Project Womanhouse," *Art Journal* 31, no. 3 (Spring 1972): 270, accessed June 18, 2019, https://www.queercsuf.com/visuality.org%201/feministtheories/schapiro_womanhouse.pdf.
5 See Arlene Raven, "Womanhouse," in *The Power of Feminist Art: The American Movement of the 1970s, History and Impact*, eds. Norma Broude and Mary D. Garrad (New York: Harry N. Abrams, 1994), 48 f.; Wilding, "The Feminist Art Programs," 39.
6 Judy Chicago, "Feminist Art Education: Made in California," in *Entering the Picture. Judy Chicago, the Fresno Feminist Art Program and the Collective Visions of Women Artists*, ed. Jill Fields (New York/London: Routledge, 2012), 107.
7 See Raven, "Womanhouse," 48.
8 "A Brief History," The Women's Building, accessed June 3, 2019, https://thewomansbuilding.org/history.html.

ART OUT OF EXPERIENCE JUDY CHICAGO'S ASSIGNMENTS AT THE FEMINIST ART PROGRAMS AT FRESNO AND CALARTS | VK

1 See Kit Hammond, "Learning to Read with John Baldessari," in *Learning to Read with John Baldessari*, ed. ibid. (Zürich: JRP Ringier, 2017), catalog of an exhibition at Museo Jumex, Mexico City, November 11, 2017–August 04, 2018, 46.
2 Suzanne Lacy, "Interview with Suzanne Lacy," interview by Moira Roth, Women in the Arts in Southern California Oral History Project, March 16–September 27, 1990, transcript, accessed June 4, 2019, https://www.aaa.si.edu/collections/interviews/oral-history-interview-suzanne-lacy-12940#transcript%205D. (Lacy, interview)
3 See Natalie Musteata, "Judy Chicago, Miriam Schapiro, and the CalArts Feminist Art Program: *Womanhouse* (1972)," *Mousse Magazine* 10, no. 51 (December 2015): 1.
4 Also Chicago's students describe intimidating and sexist situations with male teachers during their art education, in which their professors told them that they preferred teaching "guys," as "girls … just grow up and get married" or considered "art schools the hunting ground for mistresses and second wives." Robin Mitchell, in Betty Ann Brown, "Feminist Art Education at the Los Angeles Woman's Building," in *Fromsite Tovision. The Woman's Building in Contemporary Culture*, eds. Sondra Hale and Terry Wolverton (Los Angeles: Otis College of Art and Design, 2011), 144.
5 See Paula Harper, "The First Feminist Art Program. A View from the 1980s," *Signs* 10, no. 4 (Summer 1985): 777.; Ulrike Müller, "Re:Tracing the Feminist Art Program," accessed June 4, 2019, http://www.encore.at/retracing/index2.html.
6 Faith Wilding, "The Feminist Art Programs at Fresno and CalArts (1970–75)," in *The Power of Feminist Art. The American Movement of the 1970s, History and Impact*, eds. Norma Broude and Mary D. Garrard (New York: Harry N. Abrams, 1994), 34.
7 Janice Lester, "Building the Studio," *Everywoman* 2, no. 7, issue 18 (May 1971): 12.
8 See Judith Dancoff, "Interview with Judy Chicago," in ibid., 4.
9 Cheryl Zurilgen, "Becoming Conscious," in ibid., 8.
10 Cf. Wilding, "The Feminist Art Programs," 35; Linda Nochlin, "Why Have There Been No Great Women Artists?," *ArtNews* 69, no. 9 (January 1971): 22–39.
11 See Judy Chicago, *Through the Flower. My Struggle as a Woman Artist* (New York: Doubleday & Company, Inc., 1975), 34, 79.
12 See ibid., 78.
13 See ibid.
14 Harper, "A View," 774.
15 See Laura Meyer and Faith Wilding, "Collaboration and Conflict in the Fresno Feminist Art Program. An Experiment in Feminist Pedagogy," *n-paradoxa* 26 (July 2010), 41; Robin Mitchell in Harper, "A View," 777.
16 See Mira Schor, *A Decade of Negative Thinking. Essays on Art, Politics, and Daily Life* (Durham/London: Duke University Press, 2009), 75–87.
17 See Meyer, "Collaboration," 42; Kathie Sarachild, "A Program for Feminist 'Consciousness-Raising,'" in *Notes From the Second Year: Women's Liberation. Major Writings of the Radical Feminists*, eds. Shulamith Firestone and Anne Koedt (New York: N.N., 1970), 78, accessed June 4, 2019, https://repository.duke.edu/dc/wlmpc/wlmms01039.
18 Suzanne Lacy quoted in Elana Mann, "Between Radical and Critical Pedagogy. Interview with Suzanne Lacy and Leslie Labowitz-Starus," in *In the Canyon. Revise the Canon*, ed. Géraldine Gourbe (Lescheraines: Shelter Press ESAAA Editions, 2015), 31.
19 Chicago, *Through the Flower*, 75.
20 See Karen Keifer-Boyd, "From Content to Form. Judy Chicago's Pedagogy with Reflections by Judy Chicago," *Studies in Art Education* 48, no. 2 (2007), 144.
21 See Musteata, "*Womanhouse*," 7.
22 See Wilding, "The Feminist Art Programs," 35.
23 Members of the art class in Fresno used to greet visitors of the program, such as Ti-Grace Atkinson, with C-U-N-T cheers. Cf. Wilding, "The Feminist Art Programs," 39; Judith Dancoff, "Ti-Grace Atkinson speaks at Fresno State College, 1971," filmed 1971 at Fresno Airport (CA), excerpt from the film *Judy Chicago & the California Girls*, edited, directed, and produced by Judith Dancoff, Fresno (CA) 1971, 1:55, accessed June 5, 2019, https://www.youtube.com/watch?v=0EcyQLQLvCo.
24 See Meyer, "Collaboration," 44.
25 Wilding, "The Feminist Art Programs," 35.
26 Zurilgen, "Becoming Conscious," 9.
27 See Chicago, *Through the Flower*, 80.
28 Faith Wilding quoted in Meyer, "Collaboration," 45.
29 Chicago, *Through the Flower*, 80.
30 Carol Hanisch, "The Personal is Political," in *Notes From the Second Year: Women's Liberation. Major Writings of the Radical Feminists*, eds. Shulamith Firestone and Anne Koedt (New York: N.N., 1970), 76–77, accessed June 4, 2019, https://repository.duke.edu/dc/wlmpc/wlmms01039.
31 See Wilding, "The Feminist Art Programs," 35.
32 Judy Chicago and Miriam Schapiro, "Introduction," in *Womanhouse*, eds. ibid. (Valencia: California Institute of the Arts, 1972), catalog of an exhibition by the Feminist Art Program, Angeles (CA), January 30–February 28, 1972.
33 Musteata, "*Womanhouse*," 7.
34 Faith Wilding, "Women Artists and Female Imagery," *Everywoman* 2, no. 7, issue 18 (May 1971): 18.
35 Chicago, *Through the Flower*, 86.
36 Faith Wilding quoted in Meyer, "Collaboration," 44.
37 A journal entry by Faith Wilding, 1970, reprinted in Wilding, "The Feminist Art Programs," 38.
38 Chicago, *Through the Flower*, 87.
39 See Wilding, "The Feminist Art Programs," 41.
40 Lacy, interview.
41 See Keifer-Boyd, "From Content to Form," 140.
42 Judy Chicago quoted in ibid., 146. It was art historian Paula Harper, who came up with the idea to locate the project inside a home and outside an institutional framework. See Musteata, "*Womanhouse*," 6.
43 Brown, *Fromsite Tovision*, 153.
44 See Musteata, "*Womanhouse*," 1.

SHULAMITH FIRESTONE, ANNE KOEDT NOTES FROM THE SECOND YEAR: WOMEN'S LIBERATION. MAJOR WRITINGS OF THE RADICAL FEMINISTS

Shulamith Firestone and Anne Koedt, eds., *Notes From the Second Year: Women's Liberation. Major Writings of the Radical Feminists* (New York: N. N., 1970), accessed June 4, 2019, https://repository.duke.edu/dc/wlmpc/wlmms01039.

JUDY CHICAGO | LB

1 See "Biography," Judy Chicago website, accessed June 18, 2019, http://www.judychicago.com/about/biography/.
2 See Arlene Raven, "Womanhouse," in *The Power of Feminist Art. The American Movement of the 1970s, History and Impact,* eds. Norma Broude and Mary D. Garrad (New York: Harry N. Abrams, 1994), 48 ff.
3 See *Resolutions: A Stitch in Time* (1994–2000)," Judy Chicago website, accessed July 18, 2019, http://www.judychicago.com/gallery/resolutions-a-stitch-in-time/rs-artwork/.
4 See "Judy Chicago—The End," National Museum of Women in the Arts, accessed June 18, 2019, https://nmwa.org/exhibitions/judy-chicago-the-end.

NANCY YOUDELMAN | LB

1 All information used for this article is obtained from the Nancy Youdelman website, accessed June 15, 2019, https://www.nancyyoudelman.com/.

KAREN LECOCQ | LB

1 See Karen LeCocq, "UC-AFT Member Spotlight–Karen LeCocq: Artist, Author, Zen Practitioner, Mountain Woman and Local President at UC Merced," interview by University Council-AFT, accessed June 14, 2019, https://ucaft.org/content/uc-aft-member-spotlight-karen-lecocq-artist-author-zen-practitioner-mountain-woman-and-local.
2 See "Artist Statement," Karen LeCocq website, accessed June 14, 2019, http://karenlecocq.com/pages/statement.html.
3 See LeCocq, interview; "Biography," Karen LeCocq website, accessed on June 14, 2019, http://karenlecocq.com/pages/bio.html.
4 See "Lea's Room," The Womanhouse Online Archive, accessed June 14, 2019, http://www.womanhouse.net/works.
5 See "Biography," website; "Resume," Karen LeCocq website, accessed June 14, 2019, http://karenlecocq.com/pages/resume.html.

WOMANHOUSE: CONSTRUCTION PROCESS | PG

1 Judy Chicago, *Through the Flower. My Struggle as a Woman Artist* (New York: Doubleday & Company, Inc., 1975), 114.
2 See Judy Chicago and Miriam Schapiro, "Introduction," in *Womanhouse*, eds. ibid. (Valencia: California Institute of the Arts, 1972), catalog of an exhibition by the Feminist Art Program, Los Angeles (CA), January 30–February 28, 1972; "Construction," The Womanhouse Online Archive, accessed June 5, 2019, http://www.womanhouse.net/the-location/.

3 Arlene Raven, "*Womanhouse*," in *The Power of Feminist Art. The American Movement of the 1970s, History and Impact,* eds. Norma Broude and Mary D. Garrad (New York: Harry N. Abrams, 1994), 50.
4 "Construction," The Womanhouse Online Archive.
5 See Raven, "*Womanhouse*," 51.
6 See "Construction," The Womanhouse Online Archive.

PAULO FREIRE PEDAGOGY OF THE OPPRESSED

Paulo Freire, *Pedagogy of the Oppressed,* trans. Myra Bergman Ramos, with an introduction by Donaldo Macedo (New York: The Continuum International Publishing Group Ltd, 2005), accessed June 12, 2019, https://commons.princeton.edu/inclusivepedagogy/wp-content/uploads/sites/17/2016/07/freire_pedagogy_of_the_oppresed_ch2-3.pdf.

MIRIAM SCHAPIRO | LB

1 "Miriam Schapiro. American Painter, Sculptor, and Printmaker," Artists, The Art Story, accessed June 17, 2019, https://www.theartstory.org/artist-schapiro-miriam.htm.
2 "Miriam Schapiro," !Women Art Revolution. Voices of A Movement, Stanford Libraries, accessed June 16, 2019, https://exhibits.stanford.edu/women-art-revolution/feature/miriam-schapiro.
3 See "Miriam Schapiro", Artworks, artnet, accessed June 17, 2019, http://www.artnet.com/artists/miriam-schapiro/.
4 See "Miriam Schapiro," !Women Art Revolution.
5 See Milja Ficpatrik, "Miriam Schapiro," Widewalls, May 16, 2015, accessed June 18, 2019, https://www.widewalls.ch/artist/miriam-schapiro/.
6 See "Miriam Schapiro," artnet.
7 See " Miriam Schapiro," CV, artsy, accessed June 17, 2019, https://www.artsy.net/artist/miriam-schapiro/cv.

MEMORY THEATER | KA & JS

1 Judy Chicago and Miriam Schapiro, "Introduction," in *Womanhouse*, eds. ibid. (Valencia: California Institute of the Arts, 1972), catalog of an exhibition by the Feminist Art Program, Los Angeles (CA), January 30–February 28, 1972.
2 Ibid.

INTERVIEW WITH KIM ALBRECHT & JEFFREY SCHNAPP

1 See Temma Balducci, "Revisiting *Womanhouse*: Welcome to the (Deconstructed) Dollhouse," *Woman's Art Journal* 27, no. 2 (Winter–Fall 2006): 17.

FAITH WILDING | LB

1 See Faith Wilding website, accessed June 16, 2019, http://faithwilding.refugia.net/.
2 See Lauren DeLand, "Reviews: Faith Wilding," *Art in America*, February 1, 2018, accessed June 16, 2019, https://www.artinamericamagazine.com/reviews/faith-wilding/.
3 See Stephanie Crawford, "A Re (Re) (Re)-Telling of the Narrative of *Womanhouse*, or in the Beginning There Was a Woman With a Hammer," The Womanhouse Online Archive,

February 16, 2019, accessed June 16, 2019, http://www.womanhouse.net/related-content/2016/2/16/a-re-re-retelling-of-the-narrative-of-womanhouse-or-in-the-beginning-there-was-a-woman-with-a-hammer.
4 See Arlene Raven, "*Womanhouse*," in *The Power of Feminist Art. The American Movement of the 1970s, History and Impact*, eds. Judith K. Brodsky, Norma Broude, and Mary D. Garrad (New York: Harry N. Abrams, 1994), 52.
5 See ibid., 58.
6 See "Curriculum Vitae," Faith Wilding website, accessed June 16, 2019, http://faithwilding.refugia.net/cv.pdf.
7 See "Selected Works," Faith Wilding website, accessed June 16, 2019, http://faithwilding.refugia.net/.
8 See "Curriculum Vitae," website.
9 See "Faith Wilding," !Women Art Revolution, Voices of a Movement, Stanford Libraries, accessed June 16, 2019, https://exhibits.stanford.edu/women-art-revolution/feature/faith-wilding; Faith Wilding, "Faith Wilding," interview by Jason Foumberg, February 3, 2014, *Artforum,* accessed July 4, 2019, https://www.artforum.com/interviews/faith-wilding-on-her-life-and-work-45141.

FAITH WILDING, DURATION PERFORMANCE: THE ECONOMY OF FEMINIZED MAINTENANCE WORK

Faith Wilding, *Duration Performance: The Economy of Feminized Maintenance Work*, script of the lecture performance, May 19, 1998, Ars Electronica Center, Linz, Austria, accessed June 6, 2019, http://faithwilding.refugia.net/durationperformance.pdf.

WOMANHOUSE: SEXUALITY | AS

1 Karen LeCocq and Nancy Youdelman, "*Lea's Room*," accessed June 5, 2019, http://www.womanhouse.net/works/3mdvx9wcrhllxdiw737dz9es89dk4q.
2 See Temma Balducci, "Revisiting *Womanhouse*: Welcome to the (Deconstructed) Dollhouse," *Woman's Art Journal* 27, no. 2 (Winter–Fall 2006), 19.
3 See ibid.
4 Ibid., 20.
5 LeCocq, Youdelman, "*Lea's Room*."
6 Quoted in "Balducci," "Revisiting *Womanhouse*," 18.

WOMANHOUSE: BIRTH AND MOTHERHOOD | KB

1 See Alexandra Sacks, "The Birth of a Mother," *The New York Times*, May 8, 2017, accessed June 5, 2019, https://www.nytimes.com/2017/05/08/well/family/the-birth-of-a-mother.html.
2 Ibid.
3 Judy Chicago quoted in Sarah Cascone, "Judy Chicago and Miriam Schapiro's Epoch-Making Feminist Installation *Womanhouse* Gets a Tribute in Washington, D.C.," accessed June 5, 2019, https://news.artnet.com/exhibitions/women-house-judy-chicago-national-museum-women-arts-1234649.
4 Orin Zahra quoted in ibid.
5 Miriam Schapiro, "*Dollhouse*," The Womanhouse Online Archive, accessed June 5, 2019, http://www.womanhouse.net/works/8xlqtp3tyiq2jzccvn8z98hmm5heyu.

6   Ibid.
7   Shawnee Wollenman, "*The Nursery*," The Womanhouse Online Archive, accessed June 5, 2019, http://www.womanhouse.net/works/5sgxbdpswhkns79269n7yvd2t5wrc5.
8   See Faith Wilding, "*Waiting*," The Womanhouse Online Archive, accessed June 5, 2019, http://www.womanhouse.net/performances-1/2016/1/23/faith-wilding-waiting.

WOMANHOUSE: NURTURANT KITCHEN | JG

1   Robin Weltsch, "*The Kitchen*," The Womanhouse Online Archive, accessed June 5, 2019, http://www.womanhouse.net/works/9bs3fogisrc9fgnii10her36m2al3q.
2   Temma Balducci, "Revisiting *Womanhouse*: Welcome to the (Deconstructed) *Dollhouse*," *Woman's Art Journal* 27, no. 2 (Winter–Fall 2006), 17.
3   Matilda Felix, *Nadelstiche. Sticken in der Kunst der Gegenwart* (Bielefeld: transcript Verlag 2010), 33.
4   Ibid.
5   Vicky Hodgett quoted in Jane F. Gerhardt, *The Dinner Party. Judy Chicago and the Power of Popular Feminism, 1970–2007* (Athens (GA): University of Georgia Press, 2013), 51.
6   Vicky Hodgett, "*Eggs to Breasts*," The Womanhouse Online Archive, accessed June 5, 2019, http://www.womanhouse.net/works/l8ms9e17wdm5vwjvrvqhjt088hgswx.
7   Susan Frazier, "*Aprons in the Kitchen*," The Womanhouse Online Archive, accessed June 5, 2019, http://www.womanhouse.net/works/qu3yog9expsjc2avx945zw3sul12d1.
8   Balducci, "Revisiting *Womanhouse*," 17.

WOMANHOUSE: DOMESTICITY AND PRIVACY | VL

1   Erica Cummings, "Cult of Domesticity: Definition & Significance," Study.com, accessed June 5, 2019, https://study.com/academy/lesson/cult-of-domesticity-definition-significance.html.
2   See ibid.
3   See ibid.
4   See ibid.
5   See ibid.
6   See Sandra Orgel, "*Linen Closet*," The Womanhouse Online Archive, accessed June 6, 2019, http://www.womanhouse.net/works/99f1dt8x7fmm2rwtltjtiznx9iccax.
7   Judy Chicago, *Through the Flower. My Struggle as a Woman Artist* (New York: Doubleday & Company, Inc., 1975), 122.
8   Faith Wilding, "*Waiting*," The Womanhouse Online Archive, accessed June 6, 2019, http://www.womanhouse.net/performances-1/2016/1/23/faith-wilding-waiting.
9   See Robin Weltsch, "*The Kitchen*," The Womanhouse Online Archive, accessed June 6, 2019, http://www.womanhouse.net/works/9bs3fogisrc9fgnii10her36m2al3q.

WOMANHOUSE: DOLLHOUSE | JG

1   Temma Balducci, "Revisiting *Womanhouse*: Welcome to the (Deconstructed) *Dollhouse*," *Woman's Art Journal* 27, no. 2 (Winter–Fall 2006): 20; cf. Halina Pasierbska, *Dolls's Houses* (Haverfordwest: Shire Publishers, 1997), 3–9.

2   Balducci, "Revisiting *Womanhouse*," 20.
3   Ibid.
4   "*Dollhouse*," Smithsonian American Art Museum, accessed June 6, 2019, https://americanart.si.edu/artwork/dollhouse-35885.
5   Ibid.
6   Miriam Schapiro, "*Dollhouse*," The Womanhouse Online Archive, accessed June 6, 2019, http://www.womanhouse.net/works/8xlqtp3tyiq2jzccvn8z98hmm5heyu.
7   Ibid.
8   "*Dollhouse*," Smithsonian.
9   Schapiro, "*Dollhouse*."

WOMANHOUSE: BODY & BEAUTY | FK

1   William Wilson in Temma Balducci, "Revisiting *Womanhouse*: Welcome to the (Deconstructed) *Dollhouse*," *Woman's Art Journal* 27, no. 2 (Winter–Fall 2006): 18.
2   See ibid., 19.
3   Ibid.
4   Judith Butler, *The Psychic Life of Power: Theories in Subjection* (Stanford: Stanford University Press, 1997), 18–19.
5   Judy Chicago, "*Menstruation Bathroom*," The Womanhouse Online Archive, accessed June 6, 2019, http://www.womanhouse.net/works/5qwpw0phhr0jf7zuf62ov07j6hqnzg.
6   Balducci, "Revisiting *Womanhouse*," 17.
7   See ibid., 19.
8   See ibid., 18.
9   See ibid.
10   Ibid., 22.
11   See ibid., 19.
12   Karen LeCocq and Nancy Youdelman, "*Lea's Room*," The Womanhouse Online Archive, accessed June 6, 2019, http://www.womanhouse.net/works/3mdvx9wcrhllxdiw737dz9es89dk4q.
13   Camille Grey, "*Lipstick Bathroom*," The Womanhouse Online Archive, accessed June 6, 2019, http://www.womanhouse.net/works/bb47w8u3p02is1b9ihk9zuoubc735j.
14   Balducci, "Revisiting *Womanhouse*," 19.
15   Beth Bachenheimer, "*Shoe Closet*," The Womanhouse Online Archive, accessed June 6, 2019, http://www.womanhouse.net/works/jng60yeiv6z99wcj1xpb4hslwdwk0t.

JOHANNA DEMETRAKAS WOMANHOUSE | CG & LD

1   Judy Chicago, "*Menstruation Bathroom*," The Womanhouse Online Archive, accessed June 6, 2019, http://www.womanhouse.net/works/5qwpw0phhr0jf7zuf62ov07j6hqnzg.

ABLUTIONS: A COLLABORATIVE PERFORMANCE | AJL

1   "*Ablutions* (1972)," Suzanne Lacy website, accessed June 16, 2019, http://www.suzannelacy.com/ablutions.
2   Suzanne Lacy, "Questions & Answers," interview by Jennifer Higgie, *frieze*, September 1, 2012, accessed June 16, 2019, https://frieze.com/article/questions-answers.
3   Suzanne Lacy, email conversation with the artist, July 29, 2019.

ULRIKE ROSENBACH AND THE L. A. FEMINIST ART SCENE | VK

1   Ulrike Rosenbach quoted in Meike Rotermund, *Metamorphosen in inneren Räumen.*

Video- und Performancearbeiten der Künstlerin Ulrike Rosenbach (Göttingen: Universitätsverlag, 2012), 421. English translation. Original quote: "Und dann war da noch Miriam Shapiro, und die war sehr tough.… Sie war so extrem auch mit ihren Ansichten, die hat den Leuten Angst gemacht. Die fand ich selbst auch extrem. Sie war so aggressiv, aber sehr nett. Aber ich wollte ihr auch nicht so nahe kommen, das war mir ein bisschen viel. Die beiden Frauen mussten dann gehen. Und dann gab es natürlich noch diese vielen Studentinnen, die bei denen studiert hatten. Diese Frauen, die eigentlich gar nicht darauf verzichten wollten, bei diesen zwei Frauen zu studieren, und deswegen hat das Institute dann das Feminist Art Board geschaffen … Also es war etwas, worüber man die Kontrolle hatte. Die man raussetzen konnte, wie mich. Ich wusste das alles nicht, als ich da anfing."
2   See ibid., 422.
3   See Ulrike Rosenbach, "Ulrike Rosenbach," interview by Franziska Leuthäußer, Oral History Project Café Deutschland, Städel Museum, Frankfurt, January 28, 2016, last accessed June 7, 2019, https://cafedeutschland.staedelmuseum.de/gespraeche/ulrike-rosenbach.
4   Leslie Labowitz-Starus quoted in Elana Mann, "Between Radical and Critical Pedagogy. Interview with Suzanne Lacy and Leslie Labowitz-Starus," in *In the Canyon. Revise the Canon*, ed. Géraldine Gourbe (Lescheraines: Shelter Press ESAAA Editions, 2015), 40.
5   See Rotermund, *Metamorphosen,* 52.
6   See Rosenbach, interview.
7   See Rosenbach, interview; Rotermund, *Metamorphosen*, 84; Ulrike Rosenbach, "Feministische Kunst—und dann?," in *Das Verhältnis der Geschlechter*, eds. Annette Kuhn and Valentine Rothe (Pfaffenweiler: Centaurus Verlag, 1989), 141.
8   See Faith Wilding, *By Our Own Hands. The Women Artist's Movement, Southern California 1970–76* (Santa Monica: Double X, 1977), 62.
9   See Rotermund, *Metamorphosen*, 423.
10   See ibid., 101.
11   See ibid., 96 f.
12   See Klaus Honnef, ed., *Ulrike Rosenbach: Weiblicher Energie-Austausch, 1972–2013, Werkblock Frauenbilder* (Heidelberg: Kehrer Verlag, 2014), catalog of an exhibition at LVR-LandesMuseum Bonn, Bonn, May 15–October 5, 2014, 68.
13   See Rosenbach quoted in Rotermund, *Metamorphosen,* 100.
14   See ibid., 101.
15   See ibid., 422; Rosenbach, interview.
16   See Rotermund, *Metamorphosen*, 103.
17   See ibid., 104.
18   See Ulrike Rosenbach, "Kreativer Feminismus," *EMMA* 12 (1980), 56.
19   See Rotermund, *Metamorphosen*, 103.

SUZANNE LACY | LB

1   See "Who is Suzanne Lacy?," Tate, accessed June 16, 2019, https://www.tate.org.uk/art/artists/suzanne-lacy-13736/who-is-suzanne-lacy.
2   See ibid.; "About," Suzanne Lacy website, accessed June 16, 2019, http://www.suzannelacy.com/about; "Suzanne Lacy," A Blade of Grass, accessed June 16, 2016, http://www.abladeofgrass.org/fellows/suzanne-lacy/;

Interview with Suzanne Lacy by Paksy Plackis-Cheng, impactmania, accessed June 16, 2019, http://www.impactmania.com/article/suzanne-lacy/.

3   See "*Ablutions* (1972)," Suzanne Lacy website, accessed June 16, 2019, http://www.suzannelacy.com/ablutions.

4   See "*Three Weeks in May* (1977)," Suzanne Lacy website, accessed June 16, 2019, http://www.suzannelacy.com/three-weeks-in-may.

5   See "*In Mourning and in Rage* (1977)," Suzanne Lacy website, accessed June 16, 2019, http://www.suzannelacy.com/early-works#/in-mourning-and-in-rage-1977/.

6   See "Suzanne Lacy," A Blade of Grass.

7   See "About," website.

A THREE-WEEK-LONG PERFORMANCE | FK

1   Susan Griffith quoted in "Documenting *Three Weeks in May,* Suzanne Lacy 1977," Suzanne Lacy website, video, 8:41, accessed June 8, 2019, http://www.suzannelacy.com/three-weeks-in-may/.

2   "*Three Weeks in May* (1977)," Suzanne Lacy website, accessed June 8, 2019, http://www.suzannelacy.com/three-weeks-in-may/

3   Suzanne Lacy quoted in "Documenting *Three Weeks in May*," website.

4   Leslie Labowitz-Starus, "Introduction," ARIADNE: A Social Art Network, accessed June 8, 2019, https://www.againstviolence.art/ariadne-intro.

THREE WEEKS IN MAY: PERFORMANCES | AR

1   Suzanne Lacy quoted in Vivien Green Fryd, "Suzanne Lacy's *Three Weeks in May*: Feminist Activist Performance Art as 'Expanded Public Pedagogy,'" *NWSA Journal* 19, no. 1 (Spring 2007), 29.

2   See "*Three Weeks in May* (1977)," Suzanne Lacy website, accessed June 8, 2019, http://www.suzannelacy.com/three-weeks-in-may/.

3   Green Fryd, "Suzanne Lacy's *Three Weeks in May*," 24.

4   Ibid., 29.

5   See ibid.

6   Ibid., 31.

7   See ibid., 26.

8   See Leslie Labowitz-Starus, "Public Art Performances," ARIADNE: A Social Art Network, accessed June 8, 2019, https://www.againstviolence.art/twim-public-art-performances.

9   See ibid.

10 See ibid.

11 "Suzanne Lacy, Melissa Hoffman, Phranc, Judith Loischild: Guerilla Action," ARIADNE: A Social Art Network, accessed June 8, 2019, https://www.againstviolence.art/twim-performances.

12 See "Cheri Gaulke, Barbara T. Smith: *Liebestod*: Performance & Banquet," ARIADNE: A Social Art Network, accessed June 8, 2019, https://www.againstviolence.art/twim-performances.

13 See "Laurel Klick: *Exorcism*," ARIADNE: A Social Art Network, accessed June 8, 2019, https://www.againstviolence.art/twim-performances.

14 See "Anne Gauldin, Melissa Hoffman: *Breaking Silence*," ARIADNE: A Social Art Network, accessed June 8, 2019, https://www.againstviolence.art/twim-performances.

COMMUNITY BUILDING | AS

1   See "Shapes of Water, Sounds of Hope," Suzanne Lacy website, accessed June 8, 2019, http://www.suzannelacy.com/recent-works/#/sounds-of-hope/; Laura Robertson, "Shapes of Water—Sounds of Hope," *frieze*, October 5, 2016, accessed June 8, 2019, https://frieze.com/article/shapes-water-sounds-hope.

2   Suzanne Lacy, "5 Questions for Contemporary Practice with Suzanne Lacy," interview by Thom Donovan, *Art21 Magazine*, November 13, 2012, accessed June 8, 2019, http://magazine.art21.org/2012/11/13/5-questions-for-contemporary-practice-with-suzanne-lacy/#.XFl4KaB7nIU.

3   See Laura Zabel, "Six Creative Ways Artists Can Improve Communities," *The Guardian,* February 12, 2015, accessed June 8, 2019, https://www.theguardian.com/culture-professionals-network/2015/feb/12/creative-ways-artists-improve-communities.

4   "About," The Laundromat Project, accessed June 8, 2019, https://laundromatproject.org/about-2/.

SUZANNE LACY, THREE WEEKS IN MAY: SHE WHO WOULD FLY | CG

1   "*Three Weeks in May* (1977)," Suzanne Lacy website, accessed June 10, 2019, http://www.suzannelacy.com/three-weeks-in-may/.

2   Vivien Green Fryd, "Suzanne Lacy's *Three Weeks in May*: Feminist Activist Performance Art as 'Expanded Public Pedagogy,'" *NWSA Journal* 19, no. 1 (Spring 2007), 30.

3   See ibid.

4   Helmut Hark, "Lamm," Symbol Online, accessed June 10, 2019, https://symbolonline.de/index.php?title=Lamm.

5   Green Fryd, "*Three Weeks in May*," 31.

THREE WEEKS IN MAY: ART IN PUBLIC & PARTICIPATION | KB

1   Sheila Levrant de Bretteville quoted in "Documenting *Three Weeks in May*, Suzanne Lacy 1977," Suzanne Lacy website, video, 8:41, accessed June 10, 2019, http://www.suzannelacy.com/three-weeks-in-may/.

2   Vivien Green Fryd, "Suzanne Lacy's *Three Weeks in May*: Feminist Activist Performance Art as 'Expanded Public Pedagogy,'" *NWSA Journal* 19, no. 1 (Spring 2007), 33.

3   Suzanne Lacy, "Working with Media," 40, accessed June 10, 2019, https://static1.squarespace.com/static/59d735cff9a61e180f59e912/t/5ad102c0f950b77bff2cec39/1523647185912/WorkingWithMedia.pdf, 40.

4   Ibid., 41.

5   See Linda Rosengarten, "On the Subject of Rape," *LAICA Journal* 15, no. 4 (1977), 50, accessed June 10, 2019, https://static1.squarespace.com/static/59d735cff9a61e180f59e912/t/5acfd73688251b631623de71/1523570508802/OnTheSubjectOfRape_148-150.pdf.

6   Suzanne Lacy quoted in Rosengarten, "On the Subject of Rape," 50.

7   Griselda Pollock quoted in Green Fryd, "*Three Weeks in May*," 27.

8   Ibid.

9   See Emily Louise Krause, "Suzanne Lacy: *Three Weeks in May*" (PhD diss., California State University, 2010), 71–72, accessed

June 10, 2019, http://scholarworks.calstate.edu/bitstream/handle/10211.3/118918/EmilyKRAUSE.pdf?sequence=1.

SITE SPECIFICITY IN ART | AS

1   See "Site-Specific," Tate, accessed June 11, 2019, https://www.tate.org.uk/art/art-terms/s/site-specific.

2   See "*Between the Door and the Street,*" Suzanne Lacy website, acccessed June 10, 2019, http://www.suzannelacy.com/between-the-door-and-the-street/.

3   "Podwalk," accessed June 11, 2019, http://podwalk.org/.

PUBLIC ART | AS

1   Cf. Jack Becker, "Public Art: An Essential Component of Creating Communities," *Monograph* (March 2004), accessed June 11, 2019, https://www.americansforthearts.org/by-program/reports-and-data/legislation-policy/naappd/monograph-public-art-an-essential-component-of-creating-communities.

2   See "*de tu puno y letra,*" Suzanne Lacy website, accessed June 11, 2019, http://www.suzannelacy.com/recent-works/#/de-tu-puno-y-letra-2/.

3   Josephe Scanlan, "Culture in Action. Sculpture Chicago," *frieze*, November 5, 1993, accessed June 11, 2019, https://frieze.com/article/culture-action.

SUZANNE LACY: REENACTMENTS & RECEPTION. THREE WEEKS IN JANUARY: END RAPE IN LOS ANGELES | JG

1   L.A. police chief quoted in "*Three Weeks in January*. Getty Pacific Standard Time. Los Angeles City Hall, 2012", Suzanne Lacy website, video, 01:34, accessed June 11, 2019, http://www.suzannelacy.com/early-works/#/three-weeks-in-january/.

2   Ibid.

3   Glenn Phillips, "Join Suzanne Lacy to Demand that #RapeEndsHere," *The Iris,* January 8, 2012, accessed June 11, 2019, http://blogs.getty.edu/iris/join-suzanne-lacy-to-demand-that-rape-ends-here/.

4   See "*Three Weeks in January,*" website.

5   Vivien Green Fryd, "Suzanne Lacy's *Three Weeks in May*: Feminist Activist Performance Art as 'Expanded Public Pedagogy,'" *NWSA Journal* 19, no. 1 (Spring 2007), 23–38.

6   Sharon Irish quoted in Wikipedia contributors, "*Three Weeks in May*," *Wikipedia, The Free Encyclopedia,* accessed June 11, 2019, https://en.wikipedia.org/w/index.php?title=Three_Weeks_in_May&oldid=895650230.

7   See Phillips, "Join Suzanne Lacy."

8   "*Three Weeks in January,*" website.

9   See Suzanne Lacy, "The Suzanne Lacy Network," interview by Paul David Young, *Art in America,* May 31, 2012, accessed June 11, 2019, https://www.artinamericamagazine.com/news-features/magazines/the-suzanne-lacy-network/.

10 "*Storying Rape* (2012). Suzanne Lacy with Corey Madden," website, accessed June 11, 2019, http://www.suzannelacy.com/storying-rape.

11 Suzanne Lacy quoted in Lacy, interview.

12 Ibid.

PAULA HARPER, THE FIRST FEMINIST ART PROGRAM. A VIEW FROM THE 1980s

Paula Harper, "The First Feminist Art Program. A View from the 1980s," *Signs* 10, no. 4 (Summer 1985), 762–781, accessed June 11, 2019, https://www.jstor.org/stable/3174313?seq=1#metadata_info_tab_contents.

VANALYNE GREEN | LB

1   See "Vanalyne Green," Video Data Bank, accessed June 13, 2019, http://www.vdb.org/artists/vanalyne-green.
2   Ibid.
3   See ibid.
4   See "Vanalyne Green," LUX, accessed June 13, 2019, https://lux.org.uk/artist/vanalyne-green.
5   See ibid.
6   See ibid.
7   See "Vanalyne Green," Video Data Bank.
8   See "Vanalyne Green," LUX.

VIDEO AND MYTH, EXHIBITION AT MOMA

Video and Myth, The Museum of Modern Art, January 4–February 27, 1990, press release, December 1989, MoMA, accessed June 11, 2019, https://www.moma.org/calendar/exhibitions/2117.

SUBROSA. FAITH WILDING AND CYBERFEMINISM | AJL

1   "subRosa Manifestations," in *Domain Errors: Cyberfeminist Practices!*, eds. Maria Fernandez, Faith Wilding, Michelle M. Wright (New York: Autonomedia 2002), 217.
2   "Give the Gift of Life," Express Choice, subRosa, accessed June 16, 2019, http://eggdonor.cyberfeminism.net/.
3   "Calculate Your Net Worth on the Flesh Market!," Express Choice, subRosa, accessed June 16, 2019, http://eggdonor.cyberfeminism.net/ed_fleshmarket.html.
4   Ibid.

THE ART WORLD IS PART OF THE REAL WORLD | PG

1   See Andrea Fraser, "From the Critique of Institutions to an Institution of Critique," *Artforum* 44, no. 1 (September 2005), 278–286, accessed June 11, 2019, http://www.marginalutility.org/wp-content/uploads/2010/07/Andrea-Fraser_From-the-Critique-of-Institutions-to-an-Institution-of-Critique.pdf.
2   Cf. Andrea Fraser, "Über die soziale Welt sprechen," trans. Karl Hoffmann, *Texte zur Kunst*, no. 81 (March 2011), 83–94, accessed June 11, 2019, https://www.textezurkunst.de/81/uber-die-soziale-welt-sprechen/.

MICHAEL POLANYI THE TACIT DIMENSION

Michael Polanyi, *The Tacit Dimension* (Garden City, NY: Doubleday & Company, 1966), accessed June 25, 2019, https://monoskop.org/images/1/11/Polanyi_Michael_The_Tacit_Dimension.pdf.

WOMEN HOUSE. AN EXHIBITION 46 YEARS AFTER WOMANHOUSE | AR

1   Kathryn Wat quoted in Alix Strauss, "Women, Art and the Houses They Built," *The New York Times*, March 12, 2018, accessed June 11, 2019, https://www.nytimes.com/2018/03/12/arts/design/women-house-judy-chicago.html.
2   Judy Chicago quoted in ibid.
3   Angie Kordic, "Inspired by *Womanhouse*, Women Artists Deconstruct Domesticity at the NMWA," March 7, 2018, accessed June 11, 2019, https://www.widewalls.ch/women-house-exhibition-nmwa/.
4   Susan Fisher Sterling quoted in ibid.
5   Miriam Schapiro quoted in Steve Chawkins, "Miriam Schapiro Dies at 91; Pioneer of Feminist Art Movement," *Los Angeles Times*, July 2, 2015, accessed June 11, 2019, https://www.latimes.com/local/obituaries/la-me-miriam-schapiro-20150703-story.html.

JUDITH ADLER ARTISTS IN OFFICES. AN ETHNOGRAPHY OF AN ACADEMIC ART SCENE

Judith Adler, *Artists in Offices: An Ethnography of an Academic Art Scene* (PhD diss., Brandeis University, 1976), accessed June 25, 2019, https://www.taylorfrancis.com/books/9781351318969.

IMAGE RIGHTS

All image references are listed in order of appearance and from left to right per page beginning from top left.

Cover: Judy Chicago, *Red Flag* (1971), photolithograph, 20 × 24 in. © Judy Chicago/Artists Rights, Society (ARS), New York/VG Bild-Kunst, Bonn 2019, Photo © Donald Woodman/ARS, New York. Courtesy of the artist; Salon 94, New York; and Jessica Silverman Gallery, San Francisco.

4   Madeleine Schwinge, *The Psychedelic Chicks. New Album Release* (2019).

12–16 THE FEMINIST ART PROGRAM AT CALARTS

12   Beth Bachenheimer, Sherry Brody, Karen LeCocq, Robin Mitchell, Miriam Schapiro, and Faith Wilding, *Womanhouse: Dining Room* (1972). California Institute of the Arts, Photographic Materials Collection. Courtesy of California Institute of the Arts Archives © VG Bild-Kunst, Bonn 2019.

14–15 Judy Huddleston, *Womanhouse: Personal Environment* (1972). California Institute of the Arts, Feminist Art Materials Collection. Courtesy of California Institute of the Arts Archives.

17–27 ART OUT OF EXPERIENCE. JUDY CHICAGO'S ASSISGNMENTS AT THE FEMINIST ART PROGRAMS AT FRESNO AND CALARTS

17   Feminist Art Program Cheerleaders (1971). Left to right: Cay Lang, Vanalyne Green, Dori Atlantis, Sue Boud. Photo by Dori Atlantis.

18   Rap Weekend (spring 1971), Fresno, California. Weekend of performances and exhibited work to a large group of both local and out of town visitors at the studio of the Fresno Feminist Art Program. Photo by Vaughn Rachel.

19   Kathie Sarachild, "A Program for Feminist Consciousness-Raising," in *Notes from the Second Year: Women's Liberation. Major Writings of the Radical Feminists*, eds. Shulamith Firestone and Anne Koedt (New York: n. wp., 1970), 79, 80, accessed June 17, 2019, https://repository.duke.edu/dc/wlmpc/wlmms01039.

21   Judy Chicago, *Through the Flower* (1973), sprayed acrylic on canvas, 60 × 60 in. Collection of Elizabeth A. Sackler © Judy Chicago/Artists Rights Society (ARS), New York/Donald Woodman/ARS, New York/VG Bild-Kunst, Bonn, 2019.

22   Faith Wilding, *Peach Cunt* (1971). Courtesy of the Artist.

23   Faith Wilding, *Sacrifice* (1971). Room-size installation at the Feminist Art Program studio in Fresno, CA. Cast of life-size figure, cow guts and blood, dead bird, kotex, plastic flowers, candles. Participants were invited to light candles on the altar. By permission of Faith Wilding.

25–27 Suzanne Lacy, *Car Renovation* (1972). Photo courtesy Suzanne Lacy Studio.

82–83 JOHANNA DEMETRAKAS WOMANHOUSE

All images are screenshots from Johanna Demetrakas, *Womanhouse* (1974), film, 47 min, color, Schlesinger Library, accessed June 6, 2019, https://vimeo.com/89507624?fbclid= IwAR27YB2ZLcibFzkc7fxxrcNnxH7MZs3pwm-VP4ivC-HYNtB4DCYnv9WaxRPw.

84 COVER OF THE FIRST ISSUE OF WOMANSPACE

Womanspace Journal 1, no. 1 (cover) (1973), offset printing. Getty Research Institute, Los Angeles (2009.M.5).

85–87 ABLUTIONS: A COLLABORATIVE PERFORMANCE

85 *Ablutions* (1972), performance by Judy Chicago, Suzanne Lacy, Sandra Orgel, and Aviva Rahmani, sponsored by the Feminist Art Program at CalArts. Photo courtesy Suzanne Lacy Studio.

86–87 *Ablutions* (1972), performance by Judy Chicago, Suzanne Lacy, Sandra Orgel, and Aviva Rahmani, sponsored by the Feminist Art Program at CalArts © Judy Chicago/ Artists Rights Society (ARS), New York/ VG Bild-Kunst, Bonn, 2019. Photo courtesy of Through the Flower Archives.

89–95 ULRIKE ROSENBACH AND THE L. A. FEMINIST ART SCENE

89 Ulrike Rosenbach, *Glauben Sie nicht, dass ich eine Amazone bin* (1975) © Klaus vom Bruch, Berlin / Ulrike Rosenbach / VG Bild-Kunst, Bonn, 2019, in Klaus Honnef, ed., *Ulrike Rosenbach: Weiblicher Energie-Austausch, 1972–2013, Werkblock Frauenbilder* (Heidelberg: Kehrer Verlag, 2014), catalog of an exhibition at LVR-Landes-Museum Bonn, Bonn, May 15–October 5, 2014, 61.

90 FSW community meeting (1976). Courtesy of the Woman's Building Image Archive, Otis College of Art and Design Library.

– Side view of Woman's Building on Spring Street (undated), side entrance and parking lot on Aurora Street, b/w photo, 8 × 10 in. Courtesy of the Woman's Building Image Archive, Otis College of Art and Design Library.

91 Open House (undated), Woman's Building, group photo of women sitting in folding chairs in a circle, b/w photo, 5 × 7 in. Photo by Joyce Dallal. Otis College of Art and Design Library, Woman's Building Ephemera. Courtesy of the Woman's Building Image Archive, Otis College of Art and Design Library.

92 Ulrike Rosenbach, *Glauben Sie nicht, dass ich eine Amazone bin* (1975) © Klaus vom Bruch, Berlin / Ulrike Rosenbach / VG Bild-Kunst, Bonn, 2019, in Klaus Honnef, ed., *Ulrike Rosenbach: Weiblicher Energie-Austausch, 1972–2013, Werkblock Frauen-bilder* (Heidelberg: Kehrer Verlag, 2014), catalog of an exhibition at LVR-Landes-Museum Bonn, Bonn, May 15–October 5, 2014, 61.

93 Ulrike Rosenbach, *Madonnas of the Flowers* (1975) © Ulrike Rosenbach / VG Bild-Kunst, Bonn, 2019, in ibid., 77.

94 Ulrike Rosenbach, *Aphrodite TV* (1975) © Ulrike Rosebach / VG Bild-Kunst, Bonn 2019, in ibid., 75.

95 Ulrike Rosenbach, *Reflections on the Birth of Venus* (1976) © Klaus vom Bruch, Berlin / Ulrike Rosenbach / VG Bild-Kunst, Bonn, 2019, in ibid., 73.

– Ulrike Rosenbach, *Female Energy Exchange: Zehn Bilder zum Tarot* (1976) © Ulrike Rosen-bach / VG Bild-Kunst, Bonn, 2019, in ibid., 69.

– Ulrike Rosenbach, *Female Energy Exchange: Venus* (1975/76) © Ulrike Rosenbach / VG Bild-Kunst, Bonn, 2019, in ibid.

97 SUZANNE LACY

Cover of *High Performance* 1, no. 1 (1978), featuring Suzanne Lacy's traveling project *Cinderella in a Dragster* (1976). Photo by Susan Mogul. Courtesy Susan Mogul and Jancar Gallery. Cover reproduced by permission of Art in the Public Interest, in Rebecca Peabody, ed., *Pacific Standard Time. Los Angeles Art, 1945–1980,* (Los Angeles: Getty Research Institute, 2011), catalog of an exhibition at J. Paul Getty Museum, Los Angeles, October 1, 2011– February 5, 2012, and Martin-Gropius-Bau, Berlin, March 15–June 10, 2012, 277.

98 A THREE-WEEK-LONG PERFORMANCE

Suzanne Lacy, Notations on police rape reports, *Three Weeks in May* (1977).

99–103 THREE WEEKS IN MAY: PERFORMANCES

99 Suzanne Lacy, *Three Weeks in May* (1977), Los Angeles, map showing the locations of the performances taking place over the course of the three weeks, in Suzanne Lacy, "*Three Weeks in May*: Speaking Out on Rape. A Political Art Piece," in *Frontiers: A Journal of Women Studies* 2, no. 1 (Spring 1977): 64, accessed June 17, 2019, https://www.jstor.org/ stable/3346109?seq=1#metadata_info_tab_ contents.

– Leslie Labowitz-Starus, *Myths of Rape* (1977), one of four performances that took place during *Three Weeks in May* by Suzanne Lacy, Los Angeles. Photo by Suzanne Lacy.

100 Suzanne Lacy, *Three Weeks in May* (1977), Los Angeles, map showing the locations of the performances taking place over the course of the three weeks, in Suzanne Lacy, "*Three Weeks in May:* Speaking Out on Rape. A Political Art Piece," in *Frontiers: A Journal of Women Studies* 2, no. 1 (Spring 1977), 64, accessed June 17, 2019, https://www.jstor.org/stable/3346109?seq= 1#metadata_info_tab_contents.

101 Suzanne Lacy, *Three Weeks in May* (1977), Los Angeles. Photo courtesy Suzanne Lacy Studio.

102 Suzanne Lacy, *Three Weeks in May* (1977), Los Angeles. Photo courtesy Suzanne Lacy Studio.

– Amy Nathan, Lou Ziegler, "Who Is Painting These Rape Signs?," *Times Union,* excerpt, accessed June 17, 2019, https://www. againstviolence.art/twim-performances.

103 Laurel Klick, *Exorcism* (1977), part of Suzanne Lacy's *Three Weeks in May*, Los Angeles, in "Laurel Klick, Exorcism," ARIADNE: A Social Art Network, accessed June 17, 2019, https://www.againstviolence. art/exorcism.

– Cheri Gaulke, Barbara T. Smith, *Liebestod* (1977), performance and banquet, part of Suzanne Lacy's *Three Weeks in May*, in "Cheri Gaulke, Barbara T. Smith, *Liebestod*: Performance & Banquet," ARIADNE: A Social Art Network, accessed July 22, 2019, https://www.againstviolence.art/ liebestod.

105 COMMUNITY BUILDING

– *The Laundromat Project* (2015), Harlem, ac-cessed June 19, 2019, https://laundromatproject. org/report-from-lpfieldday2015-harlem/.

– Suzanne Lacy, *The Circle and the Square*, (2015–17). Photo by Chris Payne.

106–107 SUZANNE LACY, THREE WEEKS IN MAY: SHE WHO WOULD FLY

Suzanne Lacy, *She Who Would Fly* (1977), produced for Garage Gallery as part of *Three Weeks in May*, Los Angeles. Photo by Raul Vega.

108–09 THREE WEEKS IN MAY: ART IN PUBLIC & PARTICIPATION

108 Suzanne Lacy, *Three Weeks in May* (1977), Los Angeles. Photo courtesy Suzanne Lacy Studio.

109 Jack Slater, "Helping to Stamp Out Rape," *Los Angeles Times,* May 23, 1977, excerpt, in "Suzanne Lacy, Three Weeks in May," ARIADNE: A Social Art Network, accessed June 17, 2019, https://www.againstviolence. art/three-weeks-in-may/.

110 SITE SPECIFICITY IN ART

110 Suzanne Lacy, *Between the Door and the Street* (2013), New York City. Photo by Jonathan Dorado.

– Julie Thing, *Vesterbro bag facaden* (2016).

111 PUBLIC ART

– Suzanne Lacy, *de tu Puño y Letra (By Your Own Hand)* (2012), Quito, Ecuador. Photo by Raúl Peñafiel, in Bethany Martin-Breen, "Can Artist Help Us Find 21st Century Solutions to 21st Century Problems?," The Rockefeller Foundation Website, April 9, 2019, accessed June 17, 2019, https://www.rockefellerfoundation.org/ blog/can-artists-help-us-find-21st-century-solutions-21st-century-problems/.

– Iñigo Manglano-Ovalle's block party in West Town, as part of the public art exhibition *Culture in Action,* May–September, 1993, Chicago, in: "culture in action 2," Corner-house Publications, accessed June 17, 2019, https://www.cornerhousepublications.org/ publications/exhibition-as-social-intervention-% CA%BBculture-in-action%CA%BC-1993/ culture-in-action-3/.

112–114 SUZANNE LACY: REENACTMENTS AND RECEPTION. THREE WEEKS IN JANUARY: END RAPE IN LOS ANGELES

113 Mayor Anthony Villaregosa with Suzanne Lacy, *Three Weeks in January* (2012). Photo by Neda Moridpour.

– Suzanne Lacy, *Three Weeks in January* (2012). Photo by Tara Sterling.

– *Myths of Rape* (2012), Audrey Chan & Elana Mann, a reinterpretation of Leslie Labowitz-Starus's *Myths of Rape* (1977), part of Suzanne Lacy's *Three Weeks in May* (1977), in "Three Weeks in January: End Rape in Los Angeles (2012)," Suzanne Lacy website, video still, accessed June 17, 2019, http://www.suzannelacy.com/early-works#/three-weeks-in-january/.

114 *Myths of Rape* (2012), Audrey Chan & Elana Mann, a reinterpretation of Leslie Labowitz-Starus's *Myths of Rape* (1977), part of Suzanne Lacy's *Three Weeks in May* (1977). Photo courtesy Suzanne Lacy Studio. [Presented by Los Angeles Contemporary Exhibitions (LACE) for Suzanne Lacy's *Three Weeks in January* (2012) as part of the Getty Pacific Standard Time Performance Festival.]

---

120 VANALYNE GREEN

Vanalyne Green, *Trick or Drink* (1984), video still. Courtesy of Vanalyne Green and LUX, London.

123–124 SUBROSA.FAITH WILDING AND CYBERFEMINISM

123 subRosa, *Express Choice. A Division of Technical Advantage Genetics Corporation* (2002), website screenshot, accessed June 18, 2019, http://eggdonor.cyberfeminism.net/.

– subRosa, *Cyberswamp Escapees*, as part of *Down with Self-Management* (September 2014), Steirischer Herbst Festival, Graz, accesses June 30, 2019, https://cyberfeminism.net/category/work/performances/.

124 subRosa and James Pei-Mun Tsang, *Yes Species,* performance/installation, "Cyberfem: Feminisms on the Electronic Landscape" (October 2006), Espai d'Art Contemporani de Castello, Spain, in subRosa, "Common Knowledge and Political Love," 237, accessed June 17, 2019, https://3ts.lesoiseaux.io/library/subRosa%20-%20Common%20Knowledge%20and%20Political%20Love%20(in%20Tactical%20Politics).pdf.

– subRosa and James Pei-Mun Tsang, *Yes Species,* performance/installation, "Cyberfem: Feminisms on the Electronic Landscape" (October 2006), Espai d'Art Contemporani de Castello, Spain, in: subRosa, "Common Knowledge and Political Love," 236, accessed June 17, 2019, https://3ts.lesoiseaux.io/library/subRosa%20-%20Common%20Knowledge%20and%20Political%20Love%20(in%20Tactical%20Politics).pdf.

---

127 THE ART WORLD IS PART OF THE REAL WORLD

– Andrea Fraser, *Museum Highlights: A Gallery Talk* (1989) © Andrea Fraser; courtesy Galerie Nagel Draxler, Berlin, in "Andrea Fraser, Museum Highlights: A Gallery Talk, 1989," Tate, accessed July 12, 2019, https://www.tate.org.uk/art/artworks/fraser-museum-highlights-a-gallery-talk-t13715.

– Andrea Fraser, *Museum Highlights: A Gallery Talk* (1989), performance at the Philadelphia Museum of Art (PA) © Kelly and Massa Photography, in Andrea Fraser, "Museum Highlights: A Gallery Talk," *October* 57 (summer 1991), 105 accessed June 17, 2019, https://www.jstor.org/stable/778874?seq=1#metadata_info_tab_contents.

– Hans Haacke, *The Business Behind Art Knows the Art of the Koch Brothers* (2014), Paula Cooper Gallery, New York, UV matt laminated color inkjet photo mounted on aluminum, photo-collaged hundred dollar bills, in Merrily Kerr, "Hans Haacke at Paula Cooper Gallery, November 11, 2014, New York Art Tours, accessed June 17, 2019, https://newyorkarttours.com/blog/?p=3535.

130–131 WOMEN HOUSE. AN EXHIBITION 46 YEARS AFTER WOMANHOUSE

130 Cover of the catalog of the exhibition *Women House* at 11 Conti Museum, Paris, October 20, 2017–January 28, 2018, and the National Museum of Women in the Arts, Washington D.C., March 9–May 28, 2018, in "Women House," Audrey Templier, accessed June 17, 2019, http://www.audreytemplier.com/Women-House.

131 Miriam Schapiro, *Lost and Found* (1998), lithograph, chine collé, 32 ¼ × 24 in., printed in an edition of 30 © VG Bild-Kunst, Bonn, 2019, in "Miriam Schapiro, 'Lost and Found,'" Online Store of the Pennsylvania Academy of the Fine Arts, accessed June 17, 2019, https://store.pafa.org/products/miriam-schapiro-lost-found.

– Laurie Simmons, *Walking House* (1989). Courtesy of Simmons and Salon 94, New York, in Alix Strauss, Women, Art, and the Houses They Built, *New York Times,* March 12, 2018, accessed June 17, 2019, https://www.nytimes.com/2018/03/12/arts/design/women-house-judy-chicago.html.

– Cindy Sherman, *Untitled Film Still #84* (1978), gelatin silver print, 13 ½ × 16 ⅛ in. Courtesy of the artist and Metro Pictures, New York, in Anna Feintuck, "Domestic Spaces: Critical Responses," *Aesthetica,* February 1, 2018, accessed June 17, 2019, http://www.aestheticamagazine.com/domestic-spaces-critical-responses/.

134–135 OUTTAKES

134 Katja Biesanz and Syl Booth. Deformity/Perfection Performance Workshop facilitated by Suzanne Lacy (Fall 1976), 35 mm slide. Woman's Building Slide Archive. Courtesy of the Woman's Building Image Archive, Otis College of Art and Design Library.

– Women dancing or playing in the courtyard (L to R) Arlene Raven, Meg Harlam, Travis ? During the Grand Opening? (undated). Photo by Lilla Gilbrech Weinberger, b/w photo. Private Collection. Courtesy of the Woman's Building Image Archive, Otis College of Art and Design Library.

– Judy Chicago discussing her work (at FSW?) (undated). Photo by Lilla Gilbreth Weinberger, b/w photo. Private Collection. Courtesy of the Woman's Building Image Archive, Otis College of Art and Design Library.

– Performance Class at an Espresso Bar (1976), 35 mm slide. Woman's Building Slide Archive. Courtesy of the Woman's Building Image Archive, Otis College of Art and Design Library.

– Lucy Lippard eating cake while Maria Karras photographs her. During Lucy Lippard's first visit to the WB? (undated). Photo by Lilla Gilbrech Weinberger, b/w photo. Private Collection. Courtesy of the Woman's Building Image Archive, Otis College of Art and Design Library.

135 First Day of the FSW (1973), at Sheila Levrant de Bretteville's house in Silver Lake? Photo by Lilla Gilbrech Weinberger, b/w photo. Private Collection. Courtesy of the Woman's Building Image Archive, Otis College of Art and Design Library.

– Deformity/Perfection Performance Workshop facilitated by Suzanne Lacy (Fall 1976), 35 mm slide. Woman's Building Slide Archive. Courtesy of the Woman's Building Image Archive, Otis College of Art and Design Library.

– Take Back the Night March in San Francisco attended by members of the FSW who created a float with Suzanne Lacy and Leslie Labowitz-Starus (1978). Photo by Rob Blalack, 35 mm slide. Woman's Building Slide Archive. Courtesy of the Woman's Building Image Archive, Otis College of Art and Design Library.

– Sheila de Bretteville and Suzanne Lacy moving sheet rock, November 1975. Construction of the new space on Spring Street. Photo by Maria Karras, 35 mm slide. Woman's Building Slide Archive. Courtesy of the Woman's Building Image Archive, Otis College of Art and Design Library.

ADVERTISEMENTS

inside cover Warner Brothers Company, Fibber Bra, in *All-American Ads 60s,* ed. Jim Heimann (Köln: TASCHEN, 2002), 692.

1 Levi Strauss & Co, Jeans, in: *All-American Ads 70s,* ed. Jim Heimann (Köln: TASCHEN, 2004), 515.

2 Buick Car Division, Riviera (1963), in *All-American Ads 60s,* ed. Jim Heimann (Köln: TASCHEN, 2002), 197.

7 Honda, Civic (1974), in *All-American Ads 70s,* ed. Jim Heimann (Köln: TASCHEN, 2004), 163.

63 Weyenberg Massagic shoes (1974), in *All-American Ads 70s,* ed. Jim Heimann (Köln: TASCHEN, 2004), 499.

67 American Airlines (1968), in *The Golden Age of Advertising: The 60s,* ed. Jim Heimann (Köln: TASCHEN, 2006), 333.

88 Montag, Post-haste Prose (1966), in *All-American Ads 60s,* ed. Jim Heimann (Köln: TASCHEN, 2002), 729.

96 Jell-O Gelatin (1970), in *All-American Ads 70s,* ed. Jim Heimann (Köln: TASCHEN, 2004), 582.

104 Coppertone, Suntan Products (1967), in *All-American Ads 60s,* ed. Jim Heimann (Köln: TASCHEN, 2002), 731.

115 Chef Boy-ar-Dee, Complete Pizza Mix (1973), in *All-American Ads 70s,* ed. Jim Heimann (Köln: TASCHEN, 2004), 601.

125 Max Factor, California Pink-A-Pades (1967), in *The Golden Age of Advertising – the 60s,* ed. Jim Heimann (Köln: TASCHEN, 2006), 221.

126 Rollei Cameras (1977), in *All-American Ads 70s,* ed. Jim Heimann (Köln: TASCHEN, 2004), 224.

Tacit Knowledge. Feminism—CalArts (1970–77) is published on the occasion of a research project of the same name between the Institute for Theater Studies, Freie Universität Berlin, the Kestner Gesellschaft, Hanover, and metaLAB (at) Harvard. It also coincides with the exhibition *Where Art Might Happen—The Early Years of CalArts*, running from August 30–November 10, 2019, at the Kestner Gesellschaft, Hanover, and curated by Christina Végh and Philipp Kaiser. This part of the magazine-book deals with the feminist practices evolving at Judy Chicago's and Miriam Schapiro's Feminist Art Program at the California Institute of the Arts (1971–75) and beyond.

Institut für Theaterwissenschaft
Freie Universität Berlin
Grunewaldstr. 35
12165 Berlin
Germany

Editor-in-Chief	Annette Jael Lehmann
Editor	Verena Kittel
Copy Editing	Verena Kittel, Siobhan Leddy, Marius Legowski
Authors	Kim Albrecht (KA), Lea Becker (LB), Katharina Brandt (KB), Léïla Douliba (LD), Carla Gabriel (CG), Jennifer Gaschler (JG), Pauline Gründing (PG), Verena Kittel (VK), Friederike Krause (FK), Vivien Lambert (VL), Annette Jael Lehmann (AJL), Alice Rugai (AR), Jeffrey Schnapp (JS), Anna Sønderup (AS)
Translation	Siobhan Leddy
Design	Studio Pandan – Ann Richter & Pia Christmann
Image Editing	Norbert Dietsche Perfektbild
Printing	Druckhaus Köthen GmbH & Co. KG
Fonts	New Century Schoolbook by Linotype, Gothic by Dinamo

Published by	Spector Books, Harkortstraße 10, 04107 Leipzig, www.spectorbooks.com

Distribution: Germany, Austria: GVA, gemeinsame Verlagsauslieferung Göttingen gmbH & Co.Kg, www.gva-verlage.de; Switzerland: AVA Verlagsauslieferung AG, www.ava.ch; France, Belgium: Interart Paris, www.interart.fr; UK: Central Books Ltd., www.centralbooks.com; USA, Canada, Central and South America, Africa, Asia: ARTBOOK | D.A.P., www.artbook.com; Australia, New Zealand: Perimeter Distribution, www.perimeterdistribution.com

First edition in 2019, printed in Germany
ISBN: 978-3-95905-341-9

All rights reserved, including the right of reproduction in whole or in part in any form.

With support by: Volkswagen Foundation, German Federal Cultural Foundation

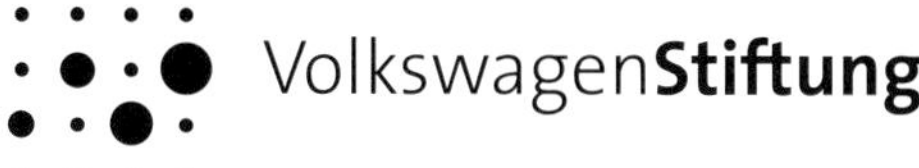

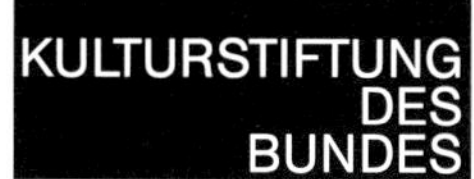

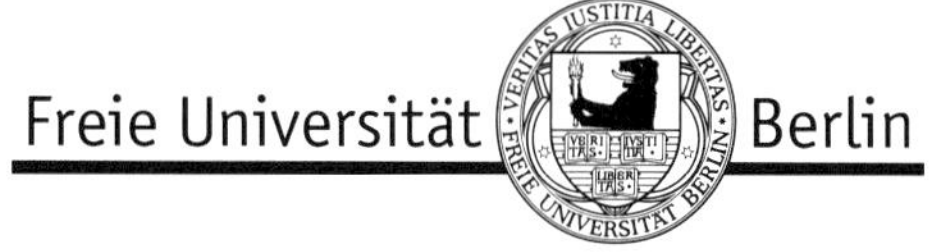

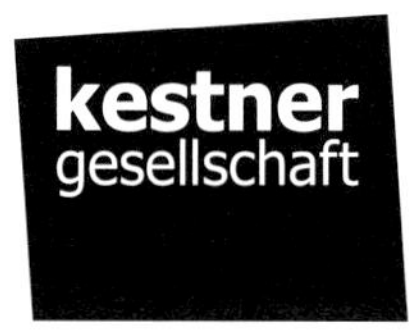

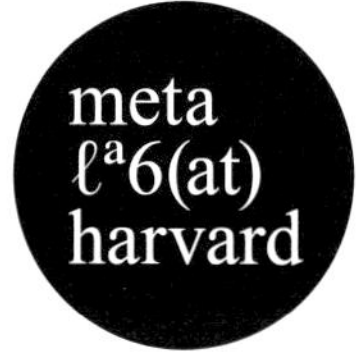

Student

Student and Employee

Employee

NOT LISTED
ON WIKIDATA
IN CONJUNCTION
WITH CALARTS

Time at CalArts: From   Until

Influences

Teachers

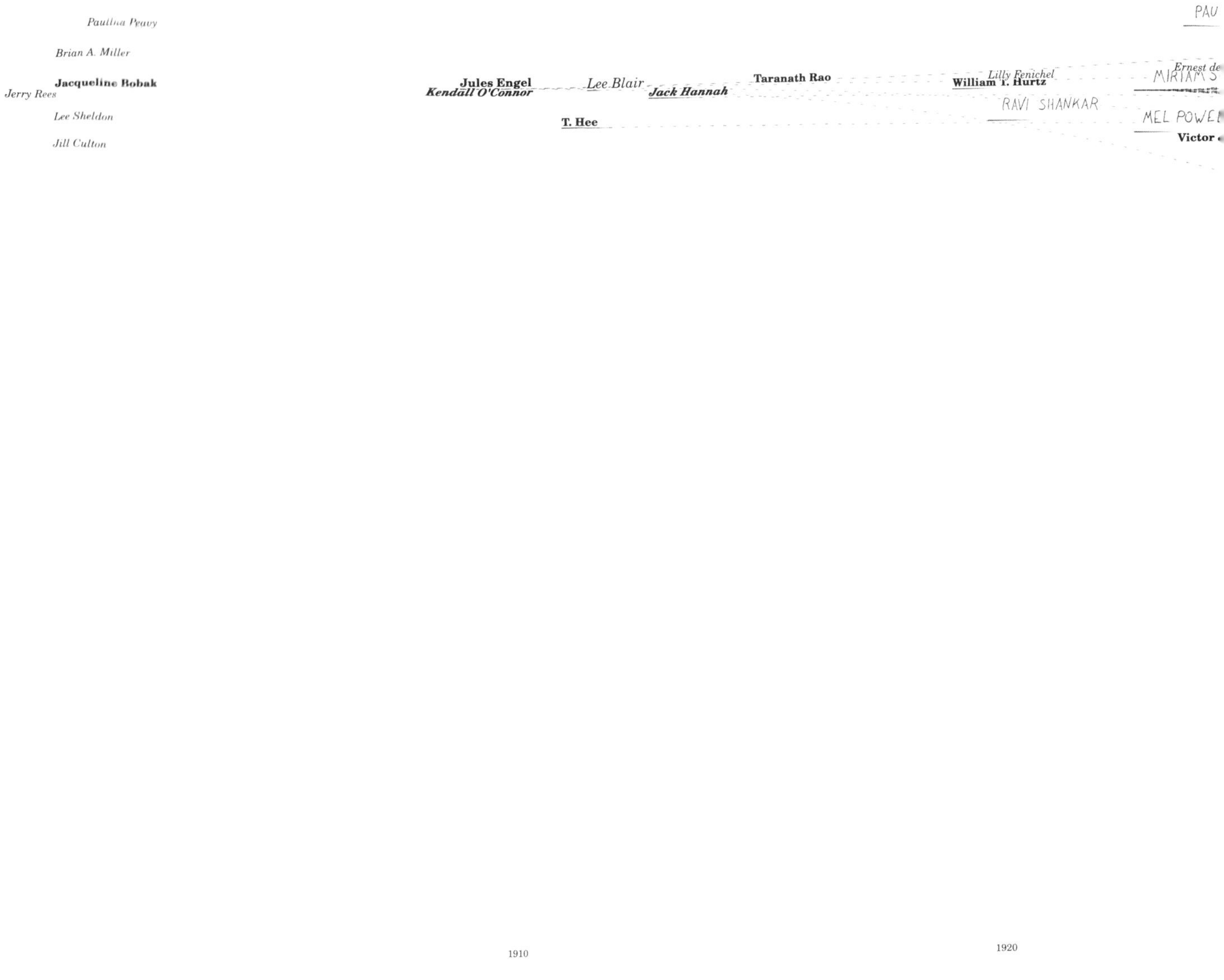

Paulina Peavy

Brian A. Miller

Jacqueline Bobak

Jerry Rees

Lee Sheldon

Jill Culton

Jules Engel
Kendall O'Connor

Lee Blair

Jack Hannah

T. Hee

Taranath Rao

Lilly Fenichel
William T. Hurtz

RAVI SHANKAR

Ernest de
MIRIAMS

MEL POWEL

Victor

PAU

VISUALIZATION
BY KIM ALBRECHT

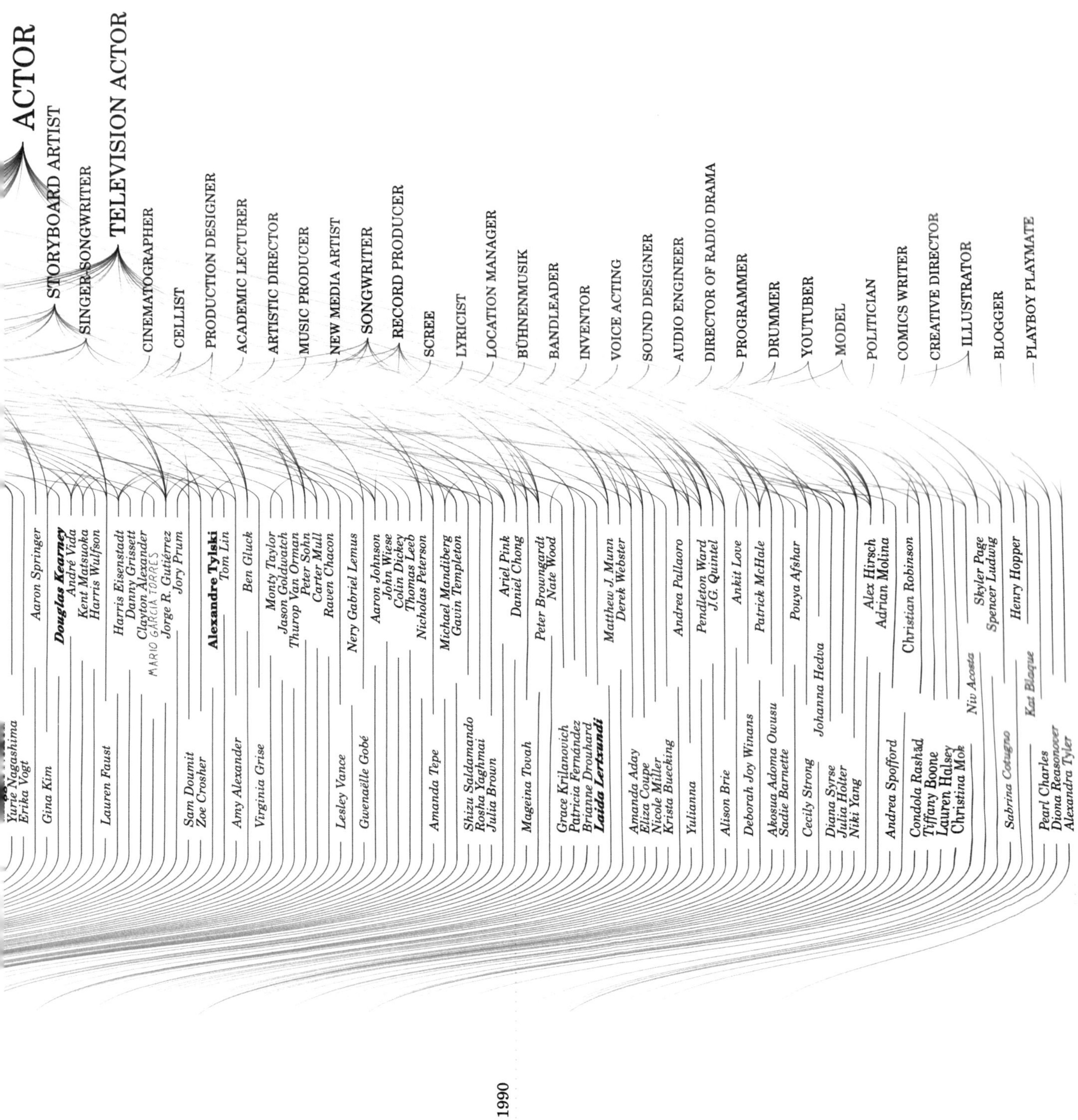

ACTOR

STORYBOARD ARTIST

SINGER-SONGWRITER

TELEVISION ACTOR

CINEMATOGRAPHER

CELLIST

PRODUCTION DESIGNER

ACADEMIC LECTURER

ARTISTIC DIRECTOR

MUSIC PRODUCER

NEW MEDIA ARTIST

SONGWRITER

RECORD PRODUCER

SCREE

LYRICIST

LOCATION MANAGER

BÜHNENMUSIK

BANDLEADER

INVENTOR

VOICE ACTING

SOUND DESIGNER

AUDIO ENGINEER

DIRECTOR OF RADIO DRAMA

PROGRAMMER

DRUMMER

YOUTUBER

MODEL

POLITICIAN

COMICS WRITER

CREATIVE DIRECTOR

ILLUSTRATOR

BLOGGER

PLAYBOY PLAYMATE

Yune Nagashima
Erika Vogt
Gina Kim
Aaron Springer
Douglas Kearney
André Vida
Kent Matsuoka
Harris Wulfson
Lauren Faust
Harris Eisenstadt
Danny Grissett
Clayton Alexander
MARIO GARCIA TORRES
Jorge R. Gutiérrez
Jory Prum
Sam Doumit
Zoe Crosher
Alexandre Tylski
Tom Lin
Amy Alexander
Ben Gluck
Virginia Grise
Monty Taylor
Jason Goldwatch
Thurop Van Orman
Peter Sohn
Carter Mull
Raven Chacon
Lesley Vance
Nery Gabriel Lemus
Guenaëlle Gobé
Aaron Johnson
John Wiese
Colin Dickey
Thomas Leeb
Nicholas Peterson
Amanda Tepe
Michael Mandiberg
Gavin Templeton
Shizu Saldamando
Rosha Yaghmai
Julia Brown
Ariel Pink
Daniel Chong
Mageina Tovah
Peter Broungardt
Nate Wood
Grace Krilanovich
Patricia Fernández
Brianne Drouhard
Laida Lertxundi
Matthew J. Munn
Derek Webster
Amanda Aday
Eliza Coupe
Nicole Miller
Krista Buecking
Andrea Pallaoro
Yulianna
Pendleton Ward
J.G. Quintel
Alison Brie
Ankit Love
Deborah Joy Winans
Patrick McHale
Akosua Adoma Owusu
Sadie Barnette
Pouya Afshar
Cecily Strong
Johanna Hedva
Diana Syrse
Julia Holter
Niki Yang
Andrea Spofford
Alex Hirsch
Adrian Molina
Condola Rashad
Tiffany Boone
Lauren Halsey
Christina Mok
Christian Robinson
Niv Acosta
Skyler Page
Spencer Ludwig
Sabrina Cotugno
Kat Blaque
Henry Hopper
Pearl Charles
Diona Reasonover
Alexandra Tyler

1990

FILM DIRECTOR

SCREENWRITER

ANIMATOR

VOICE ACTOR

CONTEMPORARY ARTIST · MUSIC DIRECTOR · MUSICIAN · SINGER · CLASSICAL GUITARIST · DIRECTOR · STAGE ACTOR · TRUMPETER · CLEAN-UP ARTIST · PRINTMAKER · CHARACTER DESIGNER · COMEDIAN · TELEVISION PRODUCER · INSTALLATION ARTIST · EXECUTIVE PRODUCER · DUB ACTOR · SCENOGRAPHER · BACKING VOCALIST · FILMMAKER · PHOTOJOURNALIST · VIDEO GAME DEVELOPER · SAXOPHONIST · FILM ACTOR · CHOREOGRAPHER · POKER PLAYER · LAYOUT STYLIST · ART DIRECTOR · CARTOONIST · GUITARIST · FACULTY MEMBER · COMICS ARTIST

Rusty Mills
Miles Coolidge
Farhad Moshiri

Steve F. Anderson
Ralph Alessi
Rich Moore
Alan Smart
James Mangold

Tony Fucile

Ray Navarro
Teddy Newton
Lorne Lanning
Tom McGrath
Kerry Conran
Don Cheadle
Michael Cudlitz
Jim Reardon
Robert Stromberg
Geefwee Boedoe
Rasoul Azadani

Butch Hartman
Lyle Ashton Harris
Jeff Pidgeon

Ravi Coltrane
Ralph Eggleston
Andrew Stanton
Nassos Vakalis
Nicholas Frances Chase

Steve Hanft
Tony Bancroft
Tranquility Bass
Tom Bancroft
Peter Epstein
Tony Leondis

Cameron Bancroft
Stephen J. Anderson
Eric Stefani
Rob Renzetti

Eduardo Abaroa
Scott Benzel
Chris Miller
Donovan Cook
Paul Tibbitt

Conrad Vernon
Mark O'Hare
Paul Rudish
Pete Docter
Rodney McMillian
Hugh Livingston
Jay Lender
Ash Brannon
Ashley Hunt
Mark Andrews

Genndy Tartakovsky

Steven Fonti
Michael Fitzpatrick
Mark Osborne
Mike Mitchell
Walt Dohrn

Art Hirahara
Rodney Evans

Zac Moncrief
Adam Samuel Goldman
Kyle Balda
Craig McCracken

Adam Burke
Jeremy Blake

Q. Allan Brocka
Gilbert Castellanos
Edgar Arceneaux
Michael "Ffish" Hemschoot
Eddo Stern

Lou Romano
Thor Freudenthal

Kira Lynn Harris

Josephine Meckseper

Kali Nikitas

Andrea Bowers

April March

Jennifer L. Hughes
Chris Innis
Melissa Hui

Kolleen Park

Mirjana Joković
Neith Hunter

Derya Arbaş

Laura Owens
Alice Könitz

Helen Hill

Jen Hofer

Kate Weare

Sofia Coppola

Tanya Haden

Kaari Upson
Julie Becker

1970

1980

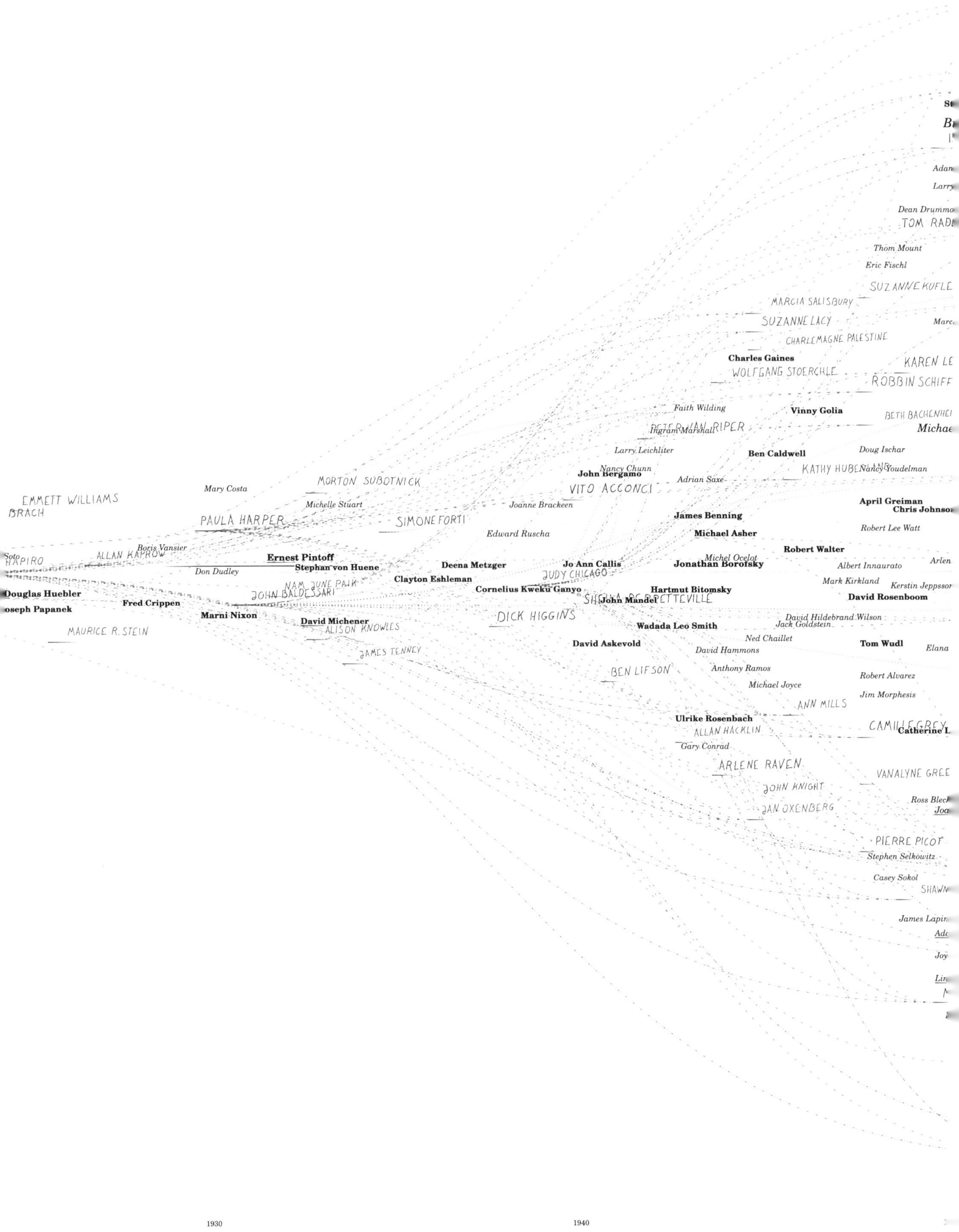

St
B
Adam
Larry
Dean Drummo
TOM RAD
Thom Mount
Eric Fischl
SUZANNE KUFLE
MARCIA SALISBURY
SUZANNE LACY
Marc
CHARLEMAGNE PALESTINE
Charles Gaines
KAREN LE
WOLFGANG STOERCHLE
ROBBIN SCHIFF
Faith Wilding
Vinny Golia
BETH BACHENHEI
PETER VAN RIPER
Michae
Ingram Marshall
Larry Leichliter
Ben Caldwell
Doug Ischar
Nancy Chunn
KATHY HUBE
Nancy Youdelman
MORTON SUBOTNICK
John Bergamo
Adrian Saxe
Mary Costa
VITO ACCONCI
Michelle Stuart
Joanne Brackeen
April Greiman
EMMETT WILLIAMS
Chris Johnso
BRACH
PAULA HARPER
SIMONE FORTI
James Benning
Robert Lee Watt
Edward Ruscha
Michael Asher
Boris Vansier
Robert Walter
Soto
ALLAN KAPROW
Michel Ocelot
HAPIRO
Ernest Pintoff
Deena Metzger
Jo Ann Callis
Jonathan Borofsky
Albert Innaurato
Arlen
Don Dudley
Stephan von Huene
Clayton Eshleman
JUDY CHICAGO
Mark Kirkland
Kerstin Jeppsso
NAM JUNE PAIK
Hartmut Bitomsky
Douglas Huebler
JOHN BALDESSARI
Cornelius Kweku Ganyo
David Rosenboom
oseph Papanek
Fred Crippen
SHEILA DE BRETTEVILLE
David Hildebrand Wilson
Marni Nixon
John Mandel
Jack Goldstein
MAURICE R. STEIN
David Michener
DICK HIGGINS
Wadada Leo Smith
ALISON KNOWLES
Ned Chaillet
Tom Wudl
Elana
David Askevold
David Hammons
JAMES TENNEY
Anthony Ramos
Robert Alvarez
BEN LIFSON
Michael Joyce
Jim Morphesis
ANN MILLS
Ulrike Rosenbach
CAMILLE GREY
ALLAN HACKLIN
Catherine L
Gary Conrad
ARLENE RAVEN
VANALYNE GREE
JOHN KNIGHT
Ross Blec
JAN OXENBERG
Joa
PIERRE PICOT
Stephen Selkowitz
Casey Sokol
SHAWN
James Lapir
Ad
Joy
Lir
N

Nery Gabriel Lemus
Raven Chacon

Jason Goldwatch

rrez

Peter Sohn
der

Virginia Grise

Amy Alexander

tadt
xandre Tylski
tt

Thurop Van Orman

er

Ben Gluck

Monty Taylor
t

GARCIA TORRES

Carter Mull
Lesley Vance

Gwenaëlle Gobé

VISUALIZATION
BY KIM ALBRECHT

UNIVERSITY TEACHER

PAINTER

LITERARY CRITIC
FEMINIST PERFORMANCE ARTIST
CLUB MANAGER
EDITOR
OBOIST
MUSIC CRITIC
CURATOR
MUSICOLOGIST
PEDAGOGUE
HORNIST
ENGINEER
LECTURER
VIDEO ARTIST
PLAYWRIGHT
STORY ARTIST
ACTIVIST
MIXED MEDIA SCULPTOR
AUTHOR
LIBRETTIST
THEATRE DIRECTOR
CONCEPT ARTIST
STAND-UP COMEDIAN
MUSICAL INSTRUMENT MAKER
JAZZ MUSICIAN
LIBRARIAN
COLLAGIST
MIME ARTIST
CLOWN
FILM EDITOR
CHARACTER ACTOR
RETIRED NURSE
HARPIST
CHOIR DIRECTOR

Mark Kirkland
TOM RADLOFF
Albert Innaurato
David Rosenboom
Tom Wudl
Robert Alvarez
Doug Ischar
Jim Morphesis
Robert Lee Watt
Stephen Selkowitz
Eric Fischl
Casey Sokol
Thom Mount
Chris Johnson
James Lapine
Dean Drummond
Ross Bleckner
Michael Richards
Adam Benjamin
Larry Cuba
Adam Beckett
Bill Irwin
Larry Huber
Steve Erickson
Randy Fullmer
Michael Pressman
Ed Harris
Arturo Márquez
Thomas Lawson
Roy Dowell
James Welling
Andre Miripolsky
MATT MULLICAN
Allan Sekula
Mark Edward
Benjamín Juárez Echenique
Sean Daniel
Lari Pittman
Jim Shaw
David Carlson
Joaquin "Kino" Gil
Anthony Christopher
David Hasselhoff
Paul Reubens
David Salle
Henry Selick
Tom Sleigh
Dustin Boyer
Scott Morse
Andrew Ahn
Michael Marcantel
MITCHELL SYROP
PIERRE PICOT
John Duncan

KATHY HUBERLAND
April Greiman
Nancy Youdelman
BETH BACHENHEIMER
ROBIN MITCHELL
VANALYNE GREEN
Kerstin Jeppsson
Catherine Lord
SUSAN FRAZIER
JUDY HUDDLESTON
KAREN LECOQ
ROBIN WELTSCH
Elana Dykewomon
Arlene Klasky
Joanna Priestley
Marcia Resnick
Joyce Borenstein
Linda Burnham
ILENE SEGALOVE
MIRA SCHOR
SUZANNE KUFLER
ERIKA BECKMAN
CHRIS RUSH
ROBBIN SCHIFF
SHAWNEE WOLLENMAN
DEDE BAZYK
Susan Allen
Barbara Bloom
VICKY HODGETTS
JANICE LESTER
SANDRA ORGEL
MARCIA SALISBURY
Jacqueline Humbert
Andrea Star Reese
Julie Taymor
Sharon Robinson
Elaine Kao
Stevie Wermers
SUSAN DAVIS
Liz Holzman
Carrie Mae Weems

1920

1930

1940

1950

Column labels (rotated):

CONCEPTUAL ARTIST · COSTUME DESIGNER · BUSINESSPERSON · OPERA DIRECTOR · SCHOOL TEACHER · TRANSLATOR · PERFORMANCE ARTIST · FILM CRITIC · INBETWEENER · CONDUCTOR · TEACHER · ANIMATION DIRECTOR · SCULPTOR · VIOLIST · ESSAYIST · GRAPHIC DESIGNER · DIGITAL IMAGING TECHNICIAN · PROFESSOR · PHOTOGRAPHER · CIRCUS PERFORMER · VISUAL ARTIST · MAGICIAN · ARCHITECT · CHARACTER ANIMATOR · PIANIST · POET · COMPOSER · ARTIST · CHILDREN'S WRITER · NOVELIST · EFFECTS ANIMATOR · WRITER · FILM PRODUCER · TELEVISION DIRECTOR · DESIGNER

Names:

Leo Kiduyjen, F. X. Feeney, John Musker

Troy Braur-tuch, John Miller, Todd Gray, Gregory Orr, STEPHEN PRINA

Leslie Dick

CAMILLE GREY, ANN MILLS

Katey Sagal

Igor Kovalyov

Glen Keane, Chris Lennon, Mike Kelley

Louise Sandhaus

Volker Hartung, Guillermo Gómez-Peña

Randall Edwards

Mark Trayle

Jill Ciment

Joel Rubin, Michael Mehaffy, Mitch Schauer

Megan Williams

CHRISTOPHER WILLIAMS

Art Jarvinen

Lisa Popeil, Fostina Dixon

Dor. Lake, Jeffery Keedy, Tony Oursler, John Lesseter, David Praksma, Rand Steiger, Brad Bird, Jeff DeGrandis

Rea Tajiri

Henry Taylor, Young Kakit

Margo Chase

Mark Henn, Tim Burton, Kirk Wise, Hendel Butoy, Miroslav Tadić, Ashley Bickerton, Anthony DeRosa, Bret Hualand

Cindy Bernard

Brian Sheesley

Sue DiCicco

Andrew Tsao, Scott MacDonald, Perry Anzilotti

Shirley Tse

Savage Steve Holland

Rita McBride

Nayland Blake

Liz Larner

Kelly Asbury, Martin Kersels, Tony Anselmo, Joe Ranft, Eric Darnell, Mark Dindal, Gary Trousdale

Meg Cranston

Ann Telnaes, Jennifer Miller

Chris Buck

Catherine Opie

Sam Durant

Mark Bradford

Jody Zellen, Judie Bamber

Mark Allen Shepherd, Douglas Pushkoff

Dana Reeve, Karen Tanaka

Peter Chung, Stephen Hillenburg, Bruce W. Smith, Wes Archer

Monique Prieto

Chris Sanders, Chris Bailey, Eill Kopp, Kevin Lima, Rob Minkoff, Shane Guffogg

Brenda Chapman, Naomi Uman

Steve Moore

MITCHELL SYROP

Michael Marcantel

Andrew Ahn

DEDE BAZYK

MATT MULLICAN

eve Erickson

ll Irwin   Dustin Boyer   CHRIS RUSH

ENE SEGALOVE

Beckett   Tom Sleigh   Peter Chung

David Hasselhoff

Cuba

Julie Taymor   Dana Reeve

ad   SANDRA ORGEL

OFF   ROBIN MITCHELL   Jody Zellen

Art Jarvinen

Andre Miripolsky   Catherine Opie   Andrea Bowers   Lou Romano

Geefwee Boedoe   Kaari Upson

Kelly Asbury   Kira Lynn Harris   Chris Miller   Michael "Ffish" Hemschoot

David Salle   VICKY HODGETTS   Adam Samuel Goldman

Sean Daniel   Randall Edwards   Nayland Blake   Gail Ann Dorsey   Cameron Bancroft

Resnick   Gregory Orr   Savage Steve Holland   Naomi Uman

Joaquin "Kino" Gil   Monique Prieto   Jim Reardon   Eric Stefani   Rodney McMillian   Kate Weare

F. X. Feeney   Bret Haaland   Bruce W. Smith

OQ   John Duncan   Ashley Bickerton   Chris Bailey   Don Cheadle   Melissa Hui   Gilbert Castellanos

Roy Dowell   Eduardo Abaroa   Tanya Haden

Hendel Butoy   Art Hirahara

Tony Leondis

David Carlson   Jill Ciment   Gary Trousdale   Kali Nikitas   Jorge R. Gut

CR   Shane Guffogg   Jennifer L. Hughes   Steven Fonti

Richards   Volker Hartung   Margo Chase   Chris Buck   Tom Bancroft

Megan Williams   Teddy Newton   Clayton Alexe

ichael Pressman   Igor Kovalyov   Henry Taylor   Josephine Meckseper   Paul Tibbitt   Laura Owens   Erika Vogt

Lyle Ashton Harris   Tony Bancroft

Barbara Bloom   John Miller   John Lasseter   Tim Burton   Alan Smart   Walt Dohrn   André Vida

Jim Shaw

Liz Holzman   Brian Sheesley   Kevin Lima   Mark Osborne   Maggie Nelson

Michael Mehaffy   Jeff DeGrandis   Mark Allen Shepherd   April March   Ashley-Hunt

Mike Kelley   Nassos Vakalis   Conrad Vernon   Harris Wulfson

Rand Steiger   Tony Anselmo   Ralph Alessi   Mirjana Joković

Susan Allen   Leslie Dick   Andrew Tsao   Craig McCracken   Harris Eisen

Fostine Dixon   Jeffery Keedy   Per Eric Darnell   Miles Coolidge   Ralph Eggleston   Jay Lender   Adam Burke   Gina Kim   Ale

Arturo Márquez   Glen Keane   Don Lake   Kirk Wise   Jennifer Miller   Tom McGrath   Kolleen Park   Paul Rudish   Genndy Tartakovsky   Sam Dou

Henry Selick   Joel Rubin   Rea Tajiri   Chris Innis   Kyle Balda   Aaron Springer

Anthony Christopher   Rich Moore   Jeff Pidgeon

Allan Sekula   John Musker   Tony Oursler   Chris Sanders   Andrew Stanton   Ash-Brannon   Q-Allan Brocka   Zoe Cros

Troy Brauntuch   Scott MacDonald   Steve Moore   Ravi Coltrane   Jeremy Blake

Mark Edward   Brad Bird   Mark Dindal   Rusty Mills   Thor Freudenthal

Lari Pittman   Chris Lemmon   Neith Hunter   Douglas Kearney

Ed Harris   Kerry Conran   Rob Renzetti   Helen Hill

kewomon   Nicholas Frances Chase   Mark Andrews   Yurie Nagashima   To

Benjamín Juárez Echenique   Louise Sandhaus   James Mangold

David Pruiksma   Joe Ranft   Karen Tanaka   Rob Minkoff   Sofia Coppola   Danny Grisse

Thomas Lawson   Todd Gray   Meg Cranston   Michael Filzpatrick

Sue DiCicco   Wes Archer   Tranquility Bass   Kent Matsuoka

Guillermo Gómez-Peña   Tony Fucile   Alice Könitz   Lauren Faust

Young Kakit   Shirley Tse   Peter Epstein   Mike Mitchell   MAR

Paul Reubens   Mark Henn   Ann Telnaes   Ray Navarro   Jen Hofer

Sharon Robinson   Stephen Hillenburg   Derya Arbaş   Jory Prum

Carrie Mae Weems   Mitch Schauer   Miroslav Tadić   Brenda Chapman   Pete Docter

Leo Rubinfien   Anthony DeRosa   Bill Kopp   Michael Cudlitz   Mark O'Hare   Rodney Evans

Cindy Bernard

Steve Hanft   Hugh Livingston

Priestley   STEPHEN PRINA   Rita McBride   Robert Stromberg   Zac Moncrief

Farhad Moshiri   Stephen J. Anderson   Edgar Arceneaux

CHRISTOPHER WILLIAMS   Liz Larner   Lorne Lanning   Scott Benzel

SUSAN FRAZIER   Donovan Cook   Eddo Stern

James Welling   PAULA LONGENDYKE   Sam Durant   Rasoul Azadani

ERIKA BECKMAN   JANICE LESTER   Martin Kersels   Julie Becker

VOLLENMAN   Mark Bradford   Butch Hartman

Judie Bamber

enjamin   Jacqueline Humbert   Lisa Popeil   Douglas Rushkoff

renstein   ROBIN WELTSCH

urnham   Elaine Kao   Steve F. Anderson

SCHOR

Huber   Katey Sagal

ly Fullmer   Mark Trayle

SUSAN DAVIS

Andrea Star Reese
Scott Morse

Stevie Wermers

BRANCA MILUTINOVIC

JUDY HUDDLESTON

1960   1970

Student NOT LISTED
Employee ON WIKIDATA
Student and Employee IN CONJUNCTION WITH CALARTS

Birth Date

Female   Non-Binary   Male

Occupations

1900

1910

INSERT

Jerry Rees
Jacqueline Bobak
Lee Sheldon
Brian A. Miller
Jill Culton
Paulina Peavy
Kendall O'Connor
Jules Engel
T. Hee
Lee Blair
Jack Hannah
Taranath Rao
William T. Hurtz
Lilly Fenichel
RAVI SHANKAR
MIRIAM SCHAPIRO
MEL POWELL
Ernest de Soto
Victor Joseph Papanek
PAUL BRACH
Douglas Huebler
EMMETT WILLIAMS
MAURICE R. STEIN
ALLAN KAPROW
Fred Crippen
Boris Vansier
Don Dudley
PAULA HARPER
Marni Nixon
Mary Costa
JOHN BALDESSARI
Ernest Pintoff
NAM JUNE PAIK
Stephan von Huene
David Michener
Michelle Stuart
ALISON KNOWLES
MORTON SUBOTNICK
JAMES TENNEY
SIMONE FORTI
Clayton Eshleman
Deena Metzger
Cornelius Kweku Ganyo
Edward Ruscha
DICK HIGGINS
Joanne Brackeen
JUDY CHICAGO
Jo Ann Callis
SHEILA DE BRETTEVILLE
VITO ACCONCI
David Askevold
John Bergamo
John Mandel
Nancy Chunn
BEN LIFSON
Larry Leichliter
Wadada Leo Smith
PETER VAN RIPER
Hartmut Bitomsky
Ingram Marshall
Jonathan Borofsky
James Benning
Ulrike Rosenbach
Faith Wilding
ALLAN HACKLIN
Adrian Saxe
Gary Conrad
Michael Asher
David Hammons
Michel Ocelot
Anthony Ramos
WOLFGANG STOERCHLE
ARLENE RAVEN
Charles Gaines
Ned Chaillet
Ben Caldwell
Michael Joyce
CHARLEMAGNE PALESTINE
JOHN KNIGHT
SUZANNE LACY
BRANCA MILUTINOVIC

WATERCOLOURIST
LITHOGRAPHER
AMERICAN POET
VISUAL ARTIST
SOCIOLOGIST
THEORETICIAN
OPERA SINGER
FEMINIST ART HISTORIAN
ART EDUCATOR
VIDEO AND MEDA ARTIST
EDUCATOR
LAND ARTIST
FLUXUS ARTIST
COMPOSER IN ELECTRONIC MUSIC
PERFORMANCE ARTIST
MUSIC THEORIST
FEMINIST ARTIST
LAYOUT ARTIST
PRINT-MAKER
FEMINIST ARTIST AND EDUCATOR
FEMINIST GRAPHIC DESIGNER
EDUACTOR
PERFORMANCE
INSTALLATION
CRITIC
MUSIC PEDAGOGUE
DANCER
CERAMIST
PERCUSSIONIST
EDUCATOR
VIDEO AND PERFORMANCE ARTIST

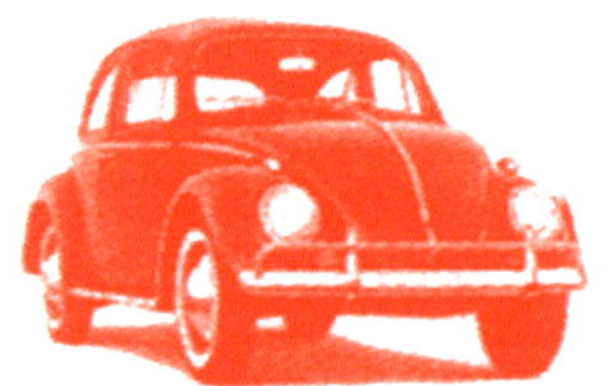

Think small.

Our little car isn't so much of a novelty any more.

A couple of dozen college kids don't try to squeeze inside it.

The guy at the gas station doesn't ask where the gas goes.

Nobody even stares at our shape.

In fact, some people who drive our little flivver don't even think 32 miles to the gallon is going any great guns.

Or using five pints of oil instead of five quarts.

Or never needing anti-freeze.

Or racking up 40,000 miles on a set of tires.

That's because once you get used to some of our economies, you don't even think about them any more.

Except when you squeeze into a small parking spot. Or renew your small insurance. Or pay a small repair bill. Or trade in your old VW for a new one.

Think it over.

Western Electric is crossing a telephone with a TV set.

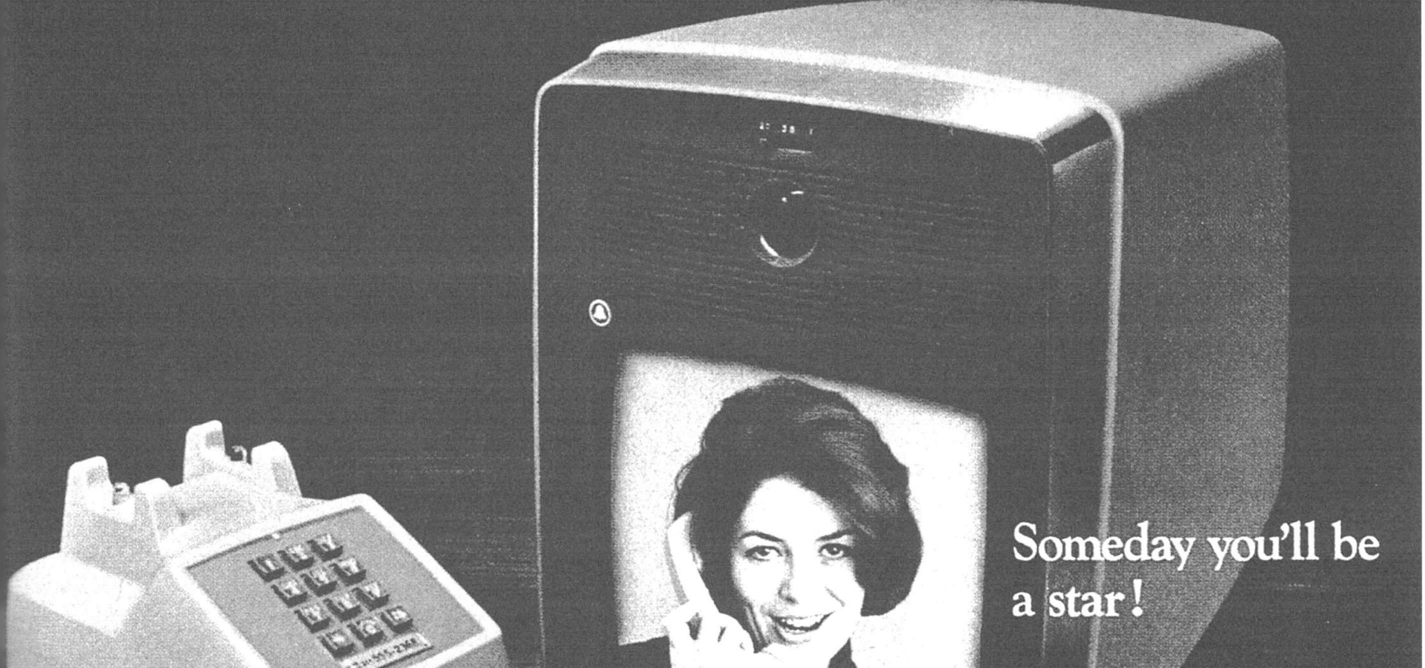

What you'll use is called, simply enough, a Picturephone® set. Someday it will let you see who you are talking to, and let them see you.

The Picturephone set is just one of the communications of the future Western Electric is working on with Bell Telephone Laboratories.

Western Electric builds regular phones and equipment for your Bell telephone company. But we also build for the future.

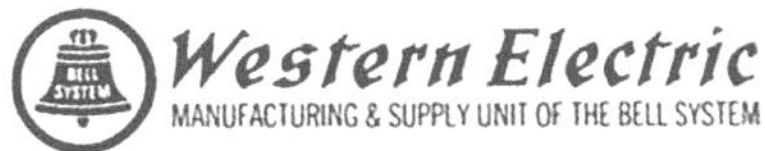

Andy Warhol's unfinished symphony.

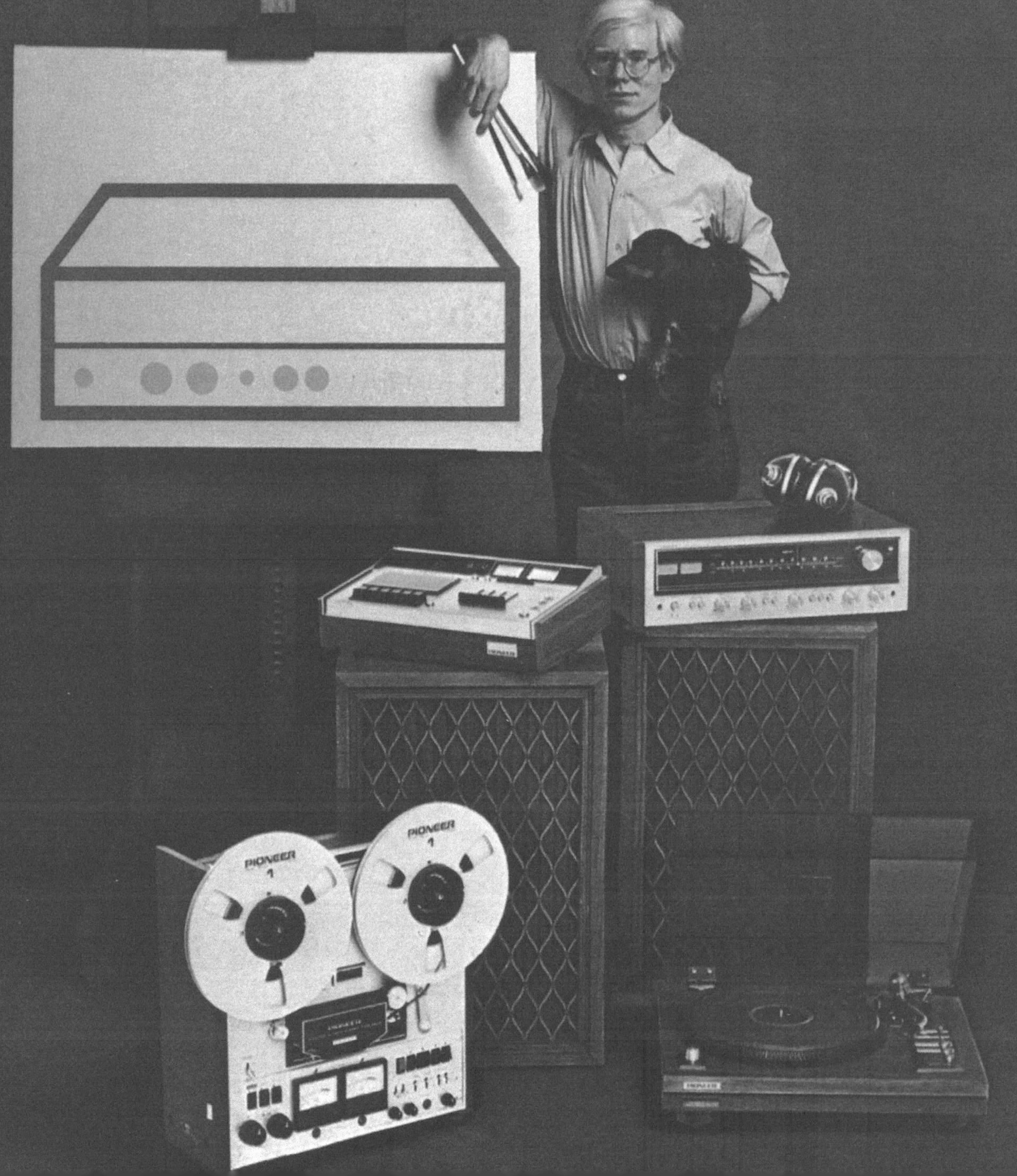

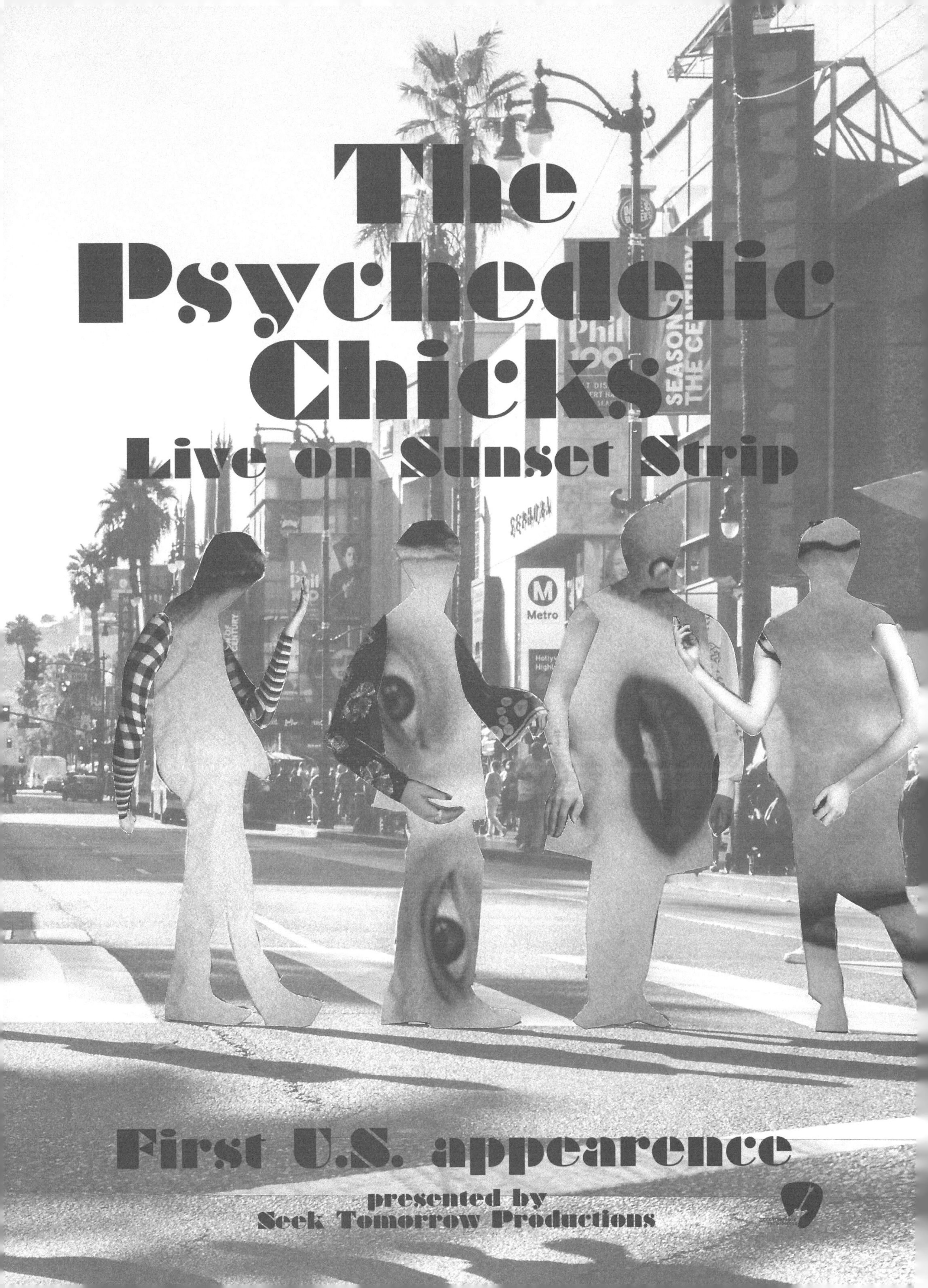

The
Psychedelic
Chicks
Live on Sunset Strip
First U.S. appearence
presented by
Seek Tomorrow Productions

NOTE BY THE EDITOR

The notion of art that takes place independently of its location, instead of developing in a studio, has obviously had a spasmodic development throughout modernity. With the initiation of Post-Studio—the now legendary chair initiated by John Baldessari in 1970 at the then newly founded California Institute of the Arts, otherwise known as CalArts—we witness the institutionalization of a paradigm shift in the field of art, one which remains operative and influential to this day. Both the emancipatory and progressive pedagogical concepts at CalArts, as well as forms of artistic practice that made claim to entirely new ideals, enabled conceptual and feminist practices to assert and differentiate themselves. This was because this paradigm shift entailed a work-immanent reflection on authorship, as it related both to art and its institutions.

Alongside this multiperspectival account of the establishment of the Post-Studio, which focuses not only on the works from that milieu but also tries to visualize and compile the new teaching methods practiced at the time, there is also a question surrounding the extent to which those methods developed can be linked to a present in which the Post-Studio seems to pervade all aspects of life. If one considers the boundary-dissolving and category-transcending tendencies that were espoused in the first years of teaching at CalArts, one also arrives at perspectives on phenomena outside of art proper, especially the teaching process and the demand for a connection between art and the realities of life. The art school CalArts was founded on a passion for art and the community that grew from a like-minded obsession. Our goal with this publication is to inspire you to do the same: follow your own path, build a community, and maybe enjoy practice-based research along the way.

This is a collaboratively produced, interdisciplinary academic magazine in book form, which is published by international scholars and students of two master's classes at the Institute for Theater Studies at Freie Universität Berlin. This progressively developed publication provides resources for readers and scholars engaged in work that goes beyond traditional, text-centric models of research, using cross-platform and supplemental images and materials from various archives, as well as introducing and reflecting on a great variety of artworks and projects. The publication project *Tacit Knowledge* aims to create and utilize practice-based research methods of publishing as a method for disrupting and intervening in centralized, culturally specific discourses.

CONTRIBUTORS

Kim Albrecht KA
Lea Becker LB
Katharina Brandt KB
Christoph Buchegger CB
Antonija Cvitic AC
Teresa Depenau TD
Léïla Douliba LD
Jacqueline Azarmi Eskandani JAE
Carla Gabriel CG
Jennifer Gaschler JG
Pauline Gründing PG
Leonie Hahn LH
Philipp Kaiser PK
Verena Kittel VK
Friederike Krause FK
Vivien Lambert VL
Annette Jael Lehmann AJL
Nazanin Namdarfard NN
Alice Rugai AR
Jeffrey Schnapp JS
Anna Sønderup AS
Christina Végh CV
Carla Weingarten CW

INTRODUCING A REVOLUTIONARY BIG PICTURE COLOR TELEVISION.

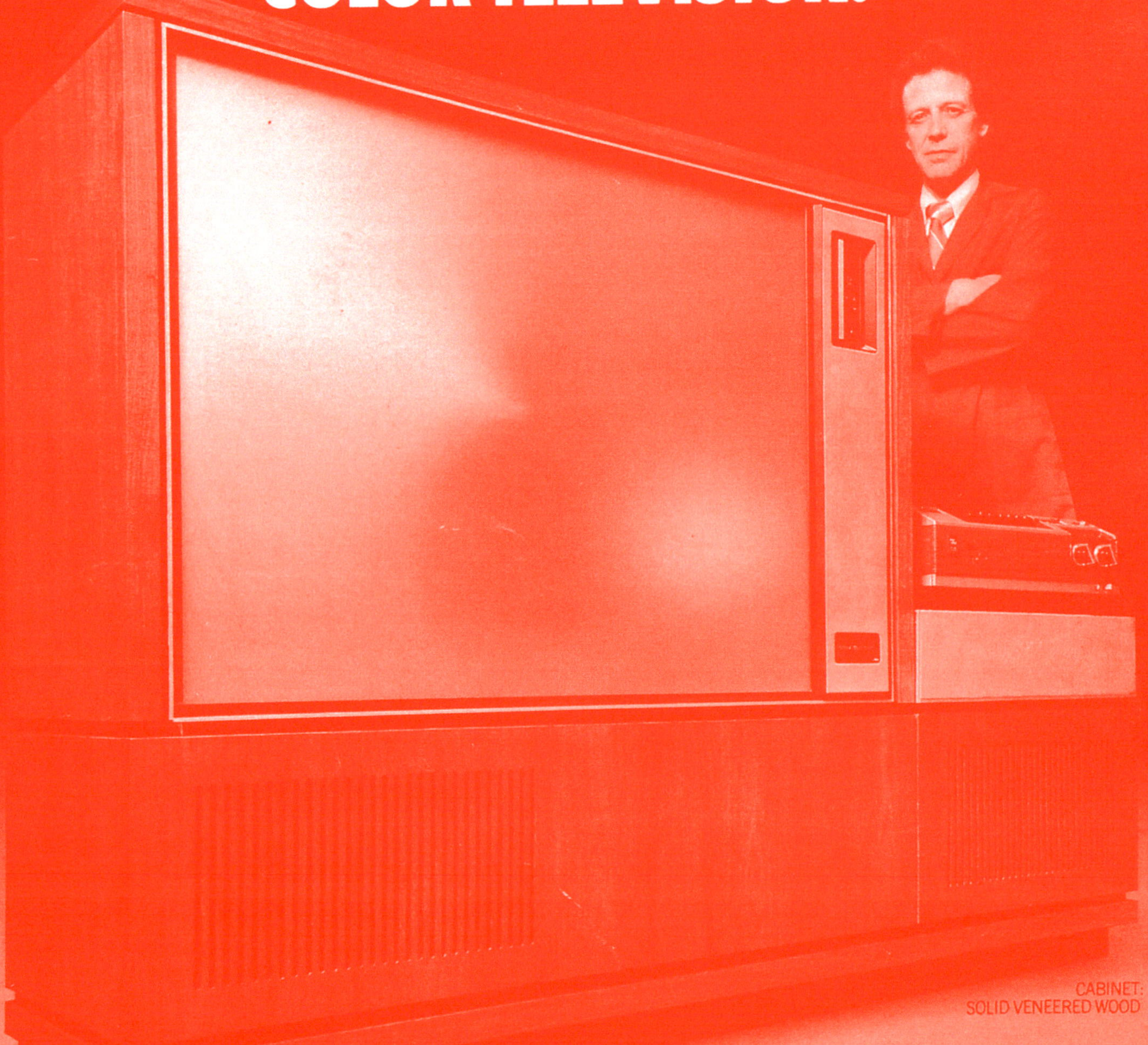

You're looking at the new General Electric Widescreen 1000. A super size color TV with a picture three times the size of a 25" diagonal console. A picture that makes you feel like you're at the movies. A set with the advanced performance features you expect from General Electric.

Like VIR. The Emmy award-winning color system that gives you realistic flesh tones, blue skies, green grass. Automatically adjusted by the broadcaster's signal on many programs. GE won the Emmy in 1977 for being the first to use VIR. And electronic tuning. With the chairside convenience of random access remote control. So you can go from channel 2 to 83 instantly. See this and other examples of General Electric leadership in television at your GE TV dealer.

THIS IS GE PERFORMANCE TELEVISION.

GENERAL 🛞 ELECTRIC

CONTENTS

CONTENTS

STATEMENTS

" … we had one guy teaching the equivalent of critical studies, and class was in session whenever you met him on campus, which I thought was really very good." — John Baldessari

"This was the same split that took place at CalArts, between those students who worked with Allan Hacklin and those who worked with John Baldessari. There were the painterly beauty artists and there were the conceptual artists. The two sides didn't cross over. Some people like Tom Wudl straddled both worlds, only to be dropped by both. It was like Viet Nam—there were the long hairs and the short hairs. It was a cultural and social dynamic that we may never see again." — Hiro Kosaka

"What really blew it … was the playful decision by a faculty member to stage a bit of radical theater by taking off his clothes during a board meeting [to discuss closing the swimming pool]. He really didn't have to go that far to mau-mau the Disney contingent. Just putting his bare feet on the table would have done it with people who, in earlier times, had spent hours arguing over whether to put skirts around the udder of cartoon cows." — James Real

"During those early years at CalArts, there was the feeling that everything was possible, not only at CalArts but in art; it was a great moment." — John Baldessari

"I remember that a class at CalArts baked as giant a meatball as could fit in an oven, had a party, and ate it. I tried to track down that giant meatball. I thought this might have happened in a class given by Emmett Williams, a Fluxus artist and poet …." — Mira Schor

"An attempt by Stein to add Marxist philosopher Herbert Marcuse to the faculty of the School of Critical Studies, coupled with rumors about goings-on at the interim campus that included 'drugs on campus, erotic posters using D. Duck and M. Mouse characters, nude swimming in the Villa Cabrini pool' had brought home to the Disneys just how countercultural the institute was shaping up to be." — Janet Sarbanes

"At CalArts I had so little money, I hardly made anything except video— videotape was free in Baldessari's class." — James Welling

"John's class soon became a cadre, almost a kind of revolutionary cell, and John was unusually accessible to his students—it seemed as though he never went home. At school, John had a ready audience, a willing workforce, and an entourage of young people who (at least in their minds) got up in the morning and moved in a new way."
— David Salle

" … I did *learn* about my own work, but very little was *taught* in anything resembling a linear transmission of information. It would be truer to say that I lived at CalArts for two years, than that I studied there. "
— Mira Schor

"The school was founded by the Disneys and for those white Republicans from Orange County, we were all raving lunatics."
— Jack Goldstein

"Only the painters were alerted about having a show. Paintings *look good*. This is what comes out of trying to make this place a show case for the public rather than a learning institution. There's the idea that the work in the gallery is what visitors are most likely to see, so let's keep the showy stuff there. This makes the students in conceptual art feel like second class citizens. The school could almost have as its motto 'Don't offend!'"
— Conceptual Artist

"CalArts hired a lot of good faculty, which attracted a lot of good students; at that point the students taught each other through sheer competitiveness. Where they came from, they were all the best; but when they got to CalArts, they were at the bottom of the heap. So they had to fight and claw their way to the top again. It was like gladiators; when you came in, you were no longer the best, you were just an artist."
— John Baldessari

"The difference between Bas Jan and me is that I wouldn't have to take that boat trip; a flyer would have been enough. He came out of a time when the artist had to be involved in making a piece; he physically had to make the journey, while I would have treated it as pure theater, so a publication would have been enough."
— Jack Goldstein

"In the early days of CalArts, it seemed like complete chaos. Now, looking back, I can see a lot of order to it."
— John Baldessari

"I started out as a public school teacher, and slowly, as I went on, I thought, if I'm not going to have to commit suicide, I'm going to have to make teaching like art. Or somehow a form of art."
— John Baldessari

It was
only
fitting
that
this
camera
be bound
in fine
leather.

By all criteria, the SX-70®
Alpha 1 is the unique
single-lens reflex camera.
Such a camera should
also look distinctive.
So we bound it in fine
leather, as one binds a
classic book, and set it off
with a velvety chrome

finish. It folds to about
1"x 4"x 7" so you can
carry it gracefully from
your shoulder or easily
in your pocket. Inside,
its sophisticated optics
let you focus through
the picture-taking lens
to as close as 10.4".

You can take instant
portraits, sequential
pictures as fast as every
1½ seconds, daylight
flash pictures, even
automatic time ex-
posures to 14 seconds.
The Polaroid® SX-70
Alpha 1 Land Camera.

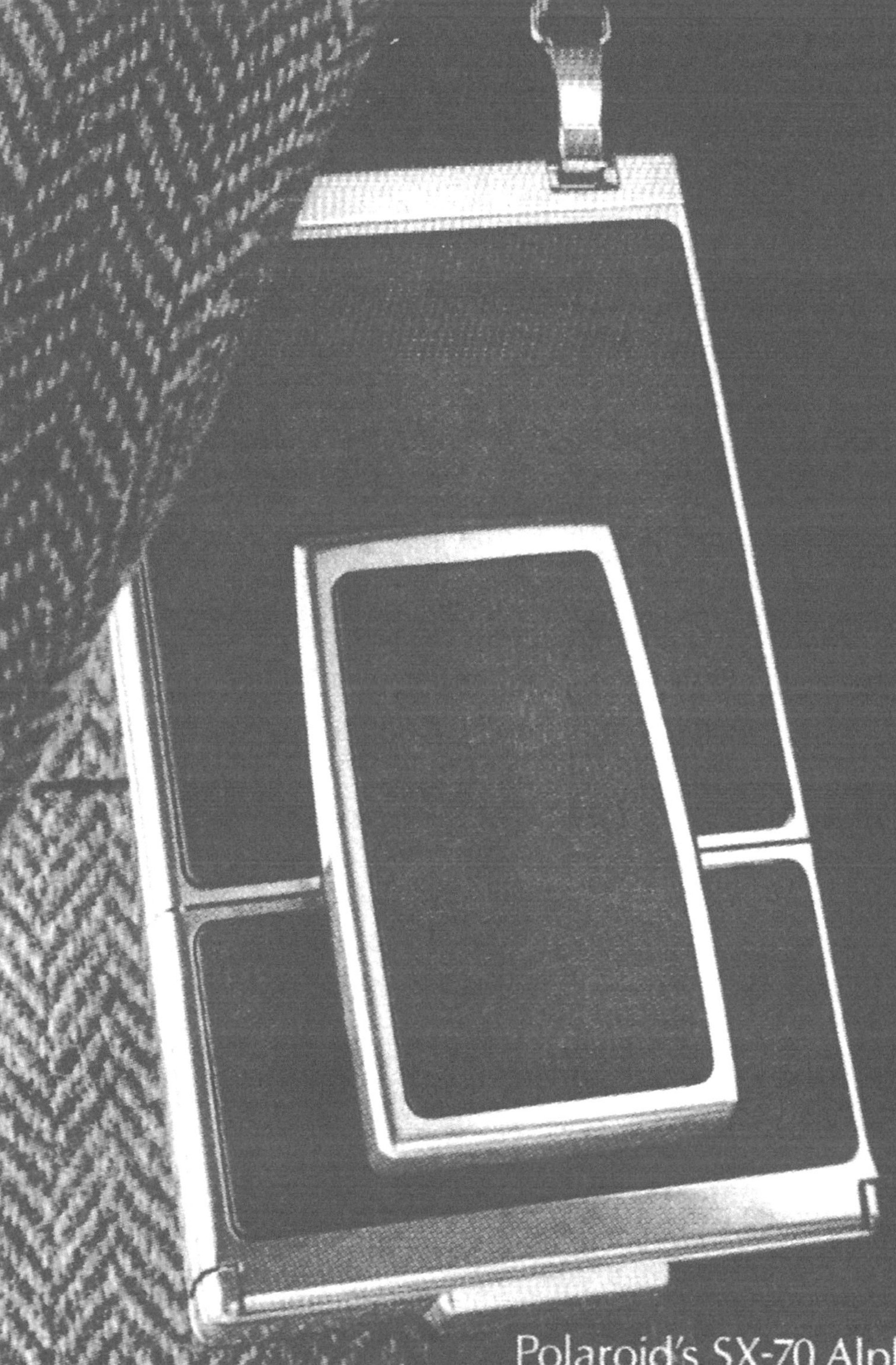

INTERVIEW WITH VERENA KITTEL & ANNETTE JAEL LEHMANN

Annette Jael Lehmann is Professor for Contemporary Art, Visual Culture, and Theater at the Freie Universität Berlin (FU). Together with Christina Végh she initiated the three-year collaborative research project *Tacit Knowledge. Post Studio/Feminism—CalArts (1970–77)* between the Kestner Gesellschaft, Hanover, the FU, and metaLAB (at) Harvard, and is chief-editor of this publication. Since its beginnings Verena Kittel, a PhD candidate at the FU, has been an integral part of the team and supports the project as editor of this book and research associate. They have already collaborated in similar cooperative research projects between university and exhibition institutions, most notably *Black Mountain Research* with the Hamburger Bahnhof—Museum für Gegenwart—Berlin, where they employed and tested a model of 'performative research'—an approach crucial to *Tacit Knowledge* In this interview, they give insights into the difficulties and 'aha moments' during their research, the idea behind this publication, and the role of practice-based research in the project.

influential in the early years of the art school. We considered the idea of tacit knowledge as an overarching principle linking all the artistic practices at CalArts, which are often characterized by a specific entanglement of cognitive and (habitual) bodily forms of knowledge. In our publication, but also in the symposium of the same name, taking place in organization with the Kestner Gesellschaft on October 26, 2019, we therefore tried to focus on the experience-based aspect of the artistic and pedagogic practices evolving around early CalArts protagonists in conceptual and feminist art, but also Fluxus and performance. Another focus was set by students from Annette Jael Lehmann's master's class "Post Studio/Feminism—CalArts the Early Years," who produced most of the book's content. As we understood the book as an open, lively, and democratic, non-hierarchichal platform to document and communicate diverse strands of research and approaches, Annette Jael Lehmann left it open to her students to decide what topics they would like to research and write on.

In your project, you are focusing on the first ten years of CalArts. How did you deal with the great amount of material?

VERENA KITTEL In order to avoid getting lost in profusion, it was indispensable to set a strong focus right from the start. We therefore put great effort into bringing the different strands dominating the artistic debates at CalArts during its founding years together. We focused mainly on conceptual and feminist approaches which, through the seminal Post-Studio class by John Baldessari and Judy Chicago's and Miriam Schapiro's legendary Feminist Art Program (FAP), became highly

VK Even though, still in 2019, we are far from being gender-equal, reading the accounts of female students at CalArts I was really shocked about how marginalized women in art education in the 1970s were, by the difficulties they encountered to be taken seriously as artists and as women, and how readily they were reduced to their roles as mother or as wife, and their sexuality. Robin Mitchell, for example, former student of the FAP at CalArts, remembered a professor telling her that he preferred teaching male students, as women

"only grow up and get married," while another considered "art schools the hunting ground for mistresses and second wives."[1] As Judy Chicago describes vividly in her book *Through the Flower*, as do her students in the special edition of the *Everywoman* magazine produced by her Fresno art class, women were frequently ignored, intimidated, or sexually approached in class by their mostly male teachers and fellow students. Keeping this in mind, but also the fact that rape and sexual assault were taboo topics— the rape of one's wife still not a crime!—explains the importance of Chicago's and, later, Miriam Schapiro's feminist art programs.

At first sight, there appear to be significant differences between the different artistic groupings at CalArts. The focus on content-based art relating to experiences of women in the FAP seems in opposition to the more distanced approach of the conceptual practices developed in the Post-Studio class, which instead revolved around mechanisms of conveying aesthetic and semantic information and thus rather abstract ideas. Yet I was surprised to find out that their basic principles of teaching were very similar. There are indeed numerous connections between the different educational approaches that cannot all be laid out here, so just to mention a few: both Judy Chicago and John Baldessari, similar to Rancière's *The Ignorant Schoolmaster*, considered their teaching role as facilitators instead of constructors, creating environments and situations to stimulate independent learning processes and dialogues instead of simply imparting their skills and knowledge. In accordance with the general pedagogical principle at CalArts, which considered the school an equal, non-hierarchical community of artists instead of dividing it into teachers and students, Baldessari, Chicago, Miriam Schapiro, and Allan Kaprow considered themselves to be on an equal footing with their students, learning with and from them. Baldessari, for example, blurred the boundaries between art and teaching and converted his classroom repeatedly into his studio, involving his students in his art production and seeking their advice concerning new ideas and work. And also Kaprow's Activities, which he undertook with his students at CalArts, involved the equal engagement of all participants in collective tasks and immediate reflection of their actions as part of the Activities, and therefore can't be clearly separated into art and teaching. Furthermore, most of the teachers, evident in Alison Knowles *House of Dust*, Kaprows Activities in the Californian desert, Baldessari's field trips to

various locations in L.A., and Chicago's and Schapiro's creation of their own studio space in downtown L.A., shared an interest in leaving the traditional classroom environment and using the public space as location and material for their artistic research and practice.

What is your definition of Post-Studio in the context of Baldessari's class at CalArts and beyond?

VK   I understand Post-Studio as a condition or a notion of art that emerged in the 1960s/1970s— most prominently connected with land artist Robert Smithson, Daniel Buren, and John Baldessari. It stood against the modernist studio paradigm, which defined the artist's studio as ivory-tower-like and as a private, isolated, and mythical space for the—usually white and male—artist-genius creating authentic and original art, mostly sculptures or paintings. Land art pieces that are created on-site or minimal art practices that separate the conception and the execution of their work, but also conceptual art with its focus on the idea and thus dematerialization, being unbound to any specific location, can be considered Post-Studio. Post-Studio practices as, for example, is the case with the artistic pedagogical activities at CalArts in its early years, moving from the seclusion of the studio into public space, these practices also often critically intervene in society and work in a wide array of media. This doesn't mean that they completely abandon the studio space altogether— as suggested by Daniel Buren in his essay "The Function of the Studio"—they rather redefine the idea of the studio and its confines, so that the studio is not necessarily bound to four walls, but can also exist in a classroom, a car, a laptop, or a hotel room. The feminist art practices at CalArts could in this respect also be considered Post-Studio, as they created and built their own studio in an abandoned mansion, which also served as an exhibition and performance space, using the surrounding stores and flea markets as resources and research spaces.

How can the artistic practices developed at CalArts during its early years be related to tacit knowledge, the title of the book? What, in your opinion, is the significance of tacit knowledge for today's education processes?

ANNETTE JAEL LEHMANN CalArts in the early years (1970–1977) was a place for experimentation and an incubator for new models of art production in society. They developed numerous new forms of artistic knowledge production—a real transformation, connected with a performative turn in the arts in general. This performative turn in the boundary-pushing art practices of the 20th century shifted the concept of knowledge, moving away from text and instead focusing on the processes of bringing forth, making, and doing. In 1949, the American philosopher Gilbert Ryle distinguished between two forms of knowledge: knowing *how* and knowing *that*. While the first refers to an everyday knowledge of how to do things that people apply without having to have any necessary familiarity with the rules governing their actions, the second primarily refers to a theoretical form of knowledge that can be described as such and expressed by rules. Ryle does not construct a hierarchy between both forms of knowledge and juxtaposes them as equals. Art's peculiar potential lies in its being a site where both forms of knowledge meet and overlap. In this context, we reflect on the particular performativity of knowledge, not as a standardized form of knowledge but rather in terms of its specific dynamics, relationality, and subjectivity. Michael Polanyi described just such a conception of knowledge that is bound up with dynamic structures and actions as 'tacit knowledge,' which, as a knowledge of rules and experiences, is also bound in a special way to (bodily) actions.[2]

This kind of knowledge production requires a stronger collaborative connection with the professional practices of curating in an expanded field of exhibition-making and disseminating cultural knowledge. Our collaboration builds upon the recognition that contemporary practice-based research and curatorial practice are resolutely challenged by profound changes in the production and the experience of knowledge and contemporary culture. This requires a profound shift in new models and methods of telling histories of art, as well as developing more experiential knowledge and learning practices in inter-institutional collaborations. So generally, our project is dedicated to research-driven and even experimental collection presentations as collaborations between universities and exhibition institutions in the public realm. I wish to continue to experiment in the field of practice-based research with dialogic and interdisciplinary modeling of new knowledge by bringing together artists, scholars, theorists, and exhibition-makers, and everything in between, who are interconnected through specific fields and scopes of interest and by collaborative institutional practices and partnerships. In compliance with a notion of a knowledge that is liquid and temporary, instead of presenting fixed solutions we thereby prefer to pose questions, carry out best-practice examples, and try to sound out possibilities of cooperation in order to develop new approaches.

What role does practice-based research play in your collaboration with the Kestner Gesellschaft and the metaLAB (at) Harvard?

AJL Since 2018, I have been collaborating on this project with a multidisciplinary team from metaLAB (at) Harvard, a knowledge-design lab. They are conducting practice-based research, grounded in social science, humanities, art, and design, to create critical interventions and prototypes in forms of tacit knowledge and new models of knowledge design. Recognizing that no individual science or humanist discipline can deal with the social and cultural changes brought about by, for instance, knowledge platforms such as Wikipedia or Wikidata, the overarching goals of metaLAB (at) Harvard are hybrid design prototypes, which embody knowledges that draw upon science, technology, and humanistic inquiry, and create spaces for interdisciplinary and transdisciplinary encounters. Our research project on CalArts touches upon a range of alignments, conflicts, and synergies in digital knowledge production. The inserts produced by Kim and Jeffrey may call for an emergent necessity for a switch in the standardized encounters of knowledge-based systems such as Wikidata. In other words, we wanted to show in our case study that we need to explore further methods of tacit knowledge production and practice-based research that can counter the quantification and standardization of dominant knowledge platforms, involving transdisciplinary collaborative experimentation.

EDUCATION: IN AND OUT OF THE CLASSROOM

By Teresa Depenau

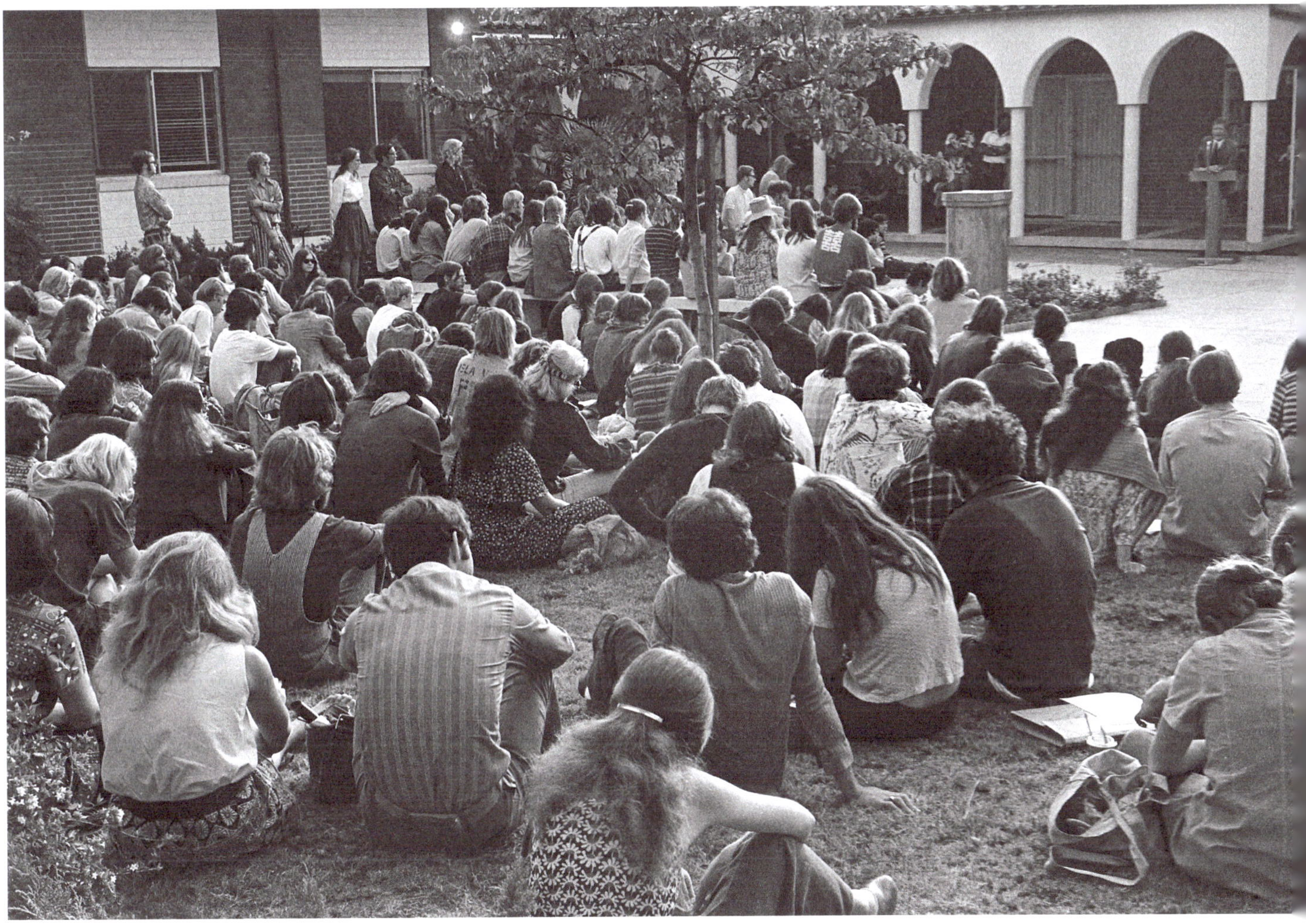

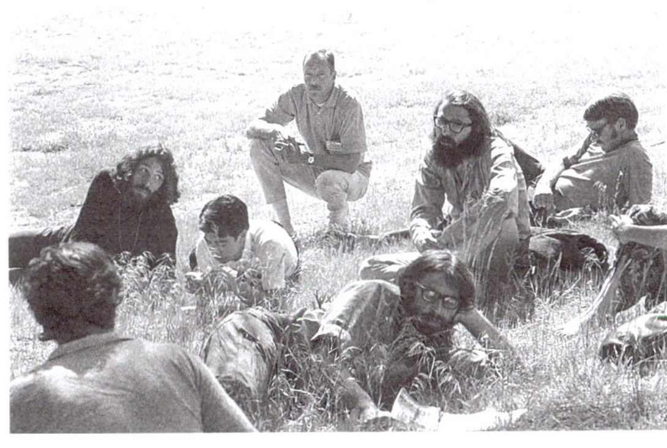

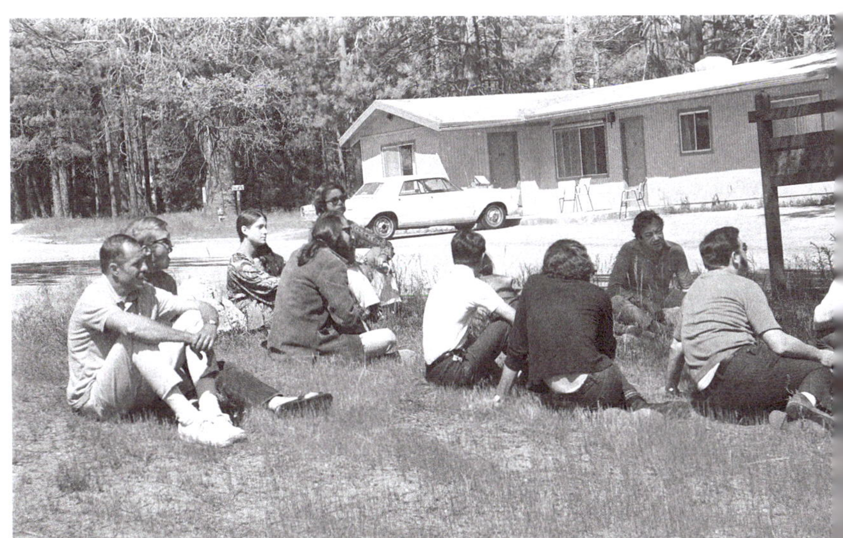

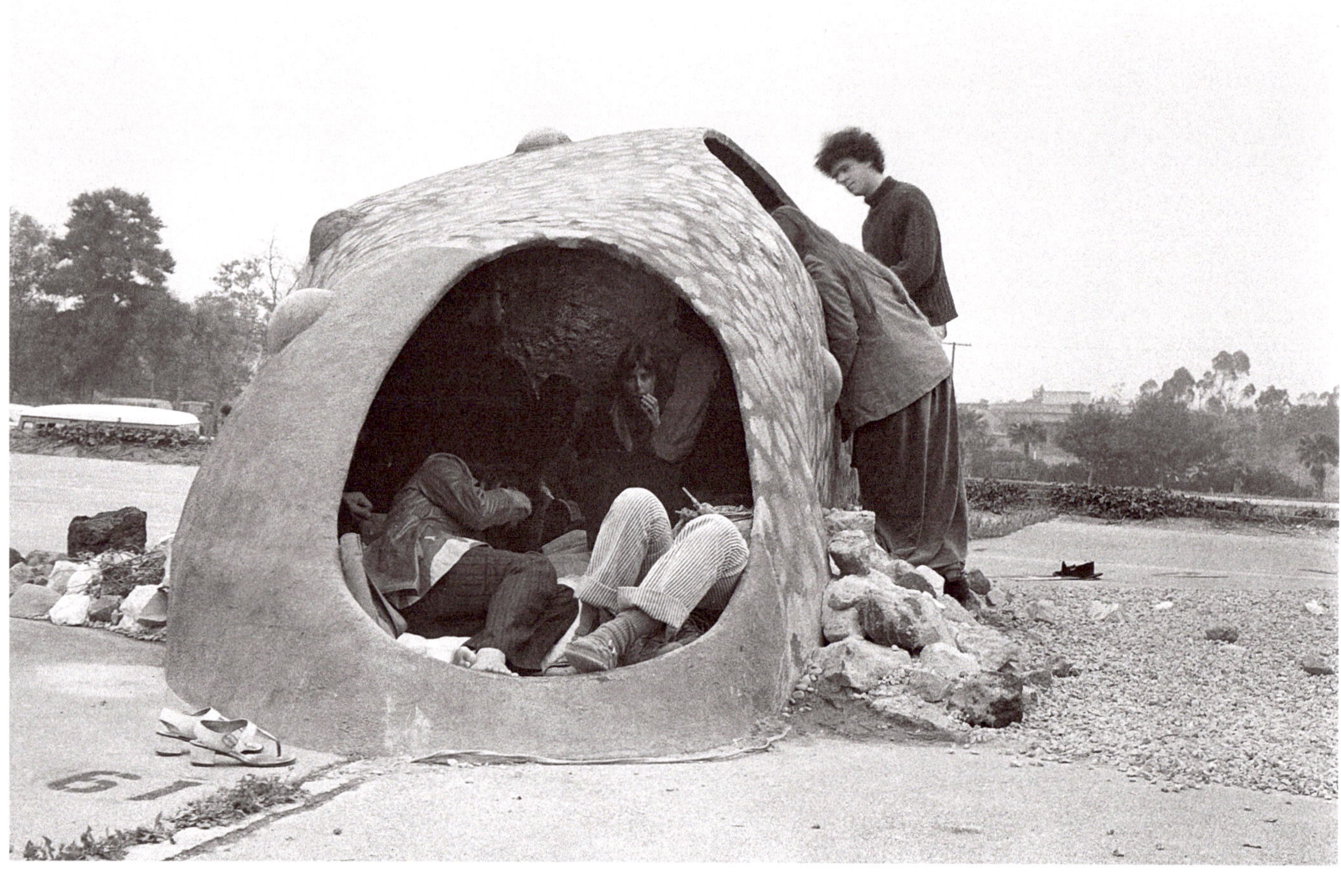

I n a climate of political and social upheaval, in which the educational system was also increasingly under criticism, CalArts took on a programmatic and content-related form. Cut off from the rest of society, an educational institution was established that was conceived as an independent entity, seeing the university as an independent institution. With the structuring of a 'free' faculty that brought together all the arts—film, theater, dance, visual arts, music, design—a learning and teaching approach was developed aiming "in some peculiar way to put the whole cracked world together again."[1] This approach resulted from the students' desire to see learning as a preparation for life. According to this, learning must be designed as an ongoing process that is directly related to life.[2]

The academic program, launched in the first two years after the opening of the institute in 1970, responded directly to the students' demands for a critique of education and at the same time exposed the romanticized notion of an art from which a liberating force emanates.[3] As Judith Adler states in her ethnography of CalArts published in 1979, the art school saw itself as a "new organization, as an institute (with its connotations of scientific and scholarly prestige) and as a community … where artists

teach students."[4] In the CalArts design concept it is expressly stated: "students [were] accepted as artists … and encouraged in the independence this implies,"[5] while other faculties regarded their students as "collaborators"[6] of the given teaching methodology.

This independence was reflected in the fact that there were no fixed curricula at CalArts. The CalArts vision of critically interfering through study and art required an anarchic and personality-oriented course system. Mel Powells, who taught at CalArts from 1969, explains:

"We must know by now that curricula, or especially descriptions of curricula, are almost always humbug. What counts is the people involved. Expansion of musical sensibility, adroitness, knowledge, experience—that has to be operative, not catalog blather."[7]

The courses and schedules at CalArts were intentionally non-binding and there was no obligation to attend. Everything was voluntary. In addition, there were no grades for the first two years and no requirements or schedules for graduation. The evaluation took the form of regular 'experience reports' written by students and validated by their mentors.[8] The

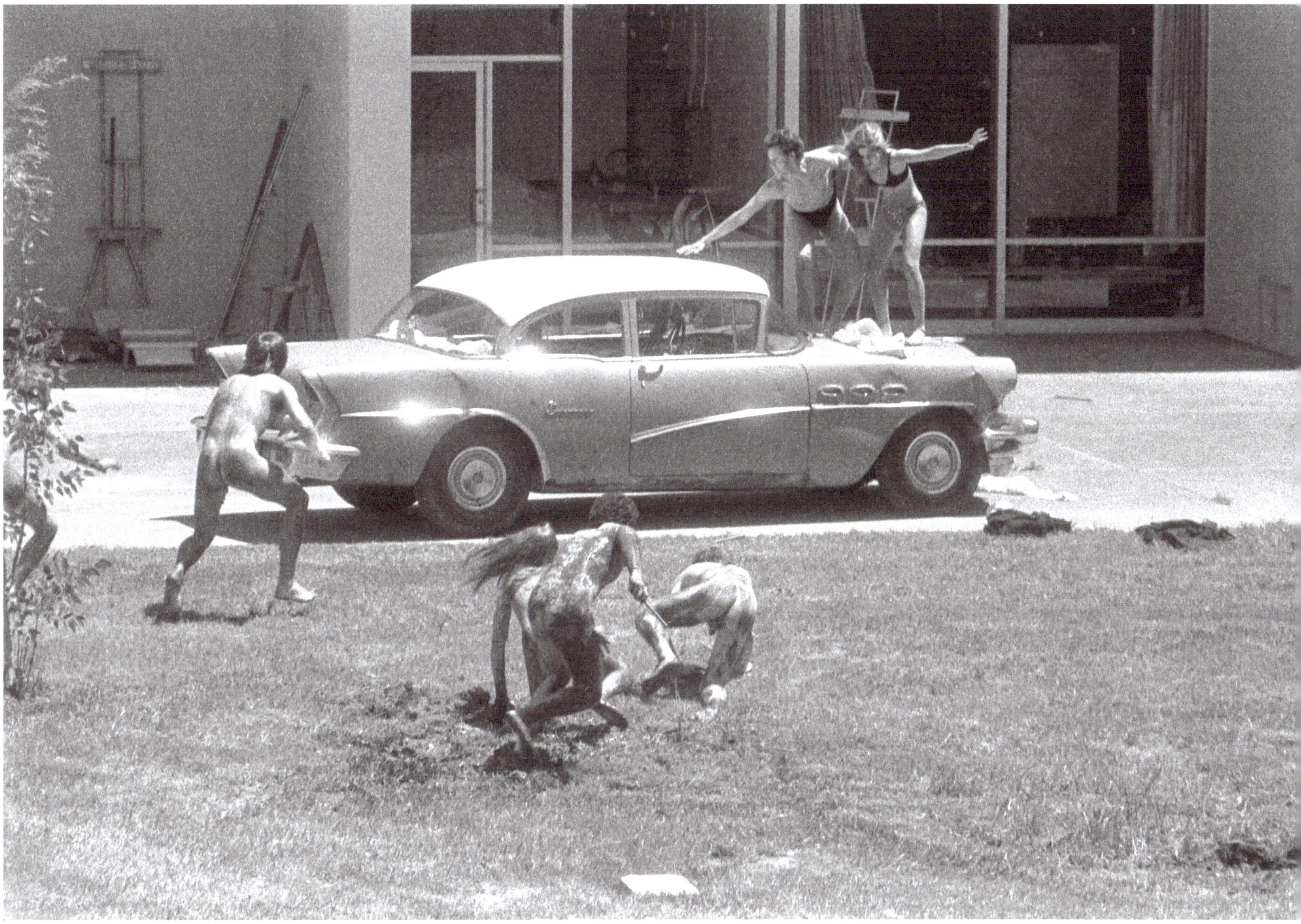

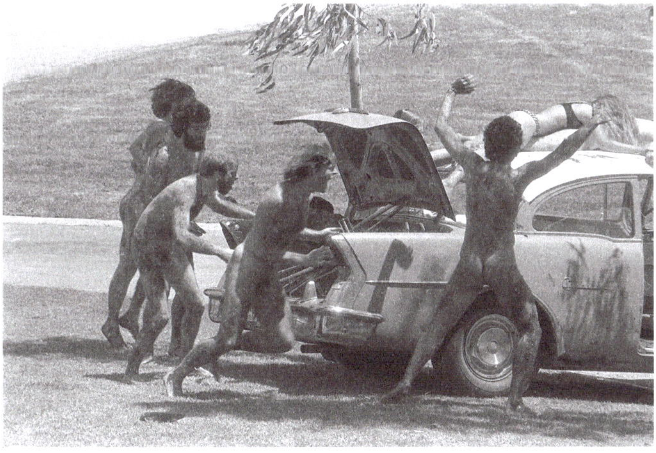

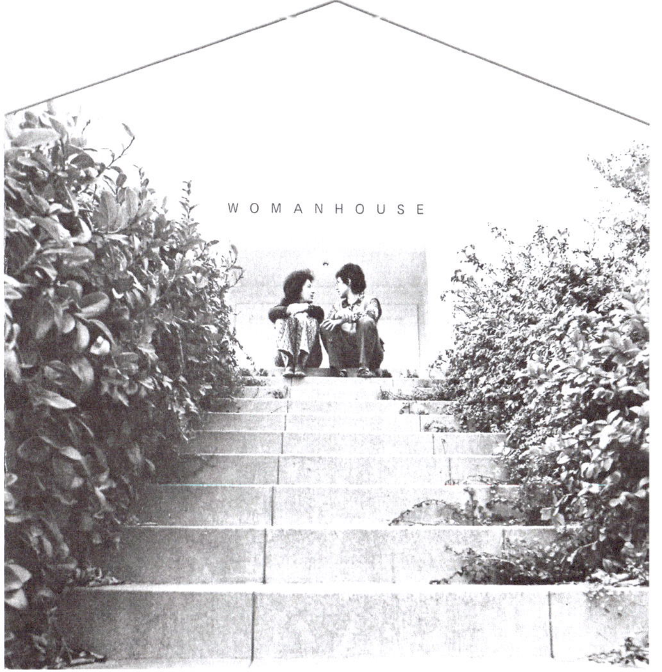

Previous spread, from top left to bottom right:
Opening Day at Burbank (1970).
Alison Knowles, *House of Dust* (1971).
CalArts Idyllwild Retreat, Faculty Conference (1971).
Idyllwild Retreat (1971).
This page, from top left to bottom right:
Grasstains Environmental Dance Concert (1981).
Cover of the *Womanhouse* exhibition catalog
(1972), edited by Judy Chicago and Miriam Schapiro
and designed by Sheila Levrant de Bretteville.

course plans were drawn up weekly and distributed on campus. For example, a lecture on "Epistemology of Design" was held at the instructor's home in 1970, while Peter Van Riper gave a lecture on "Art History or Whatever He's Into."[9] A meeting with the dean of the art school was open to all students as well as to all persons interested in "discussing and working on untraditional ways of providing psychological services (counseling, group therapy, encounter groups, etc.)."[10]

The pressure to formulate a radical pedagogical vision for the institute was great. Even though the teachers at CalArts rejected rigid structural and learning guidelines and searched for new forms of teaching and art mediation, a certain 'professionalism' was demanded of the students—despite deviations from contemporary teaching methods. This professionalism was measured by, among other things, their ability to organize themselves and their commitment to acquiring knowledge independently. Among the students, there was a duty to fulfil which, while not publicly communicated, nevertheless existed: overtime and all-day teaching units. The demand on students to be committed and willing to learn breaches the CalArts guiding principle, which is based on experimentation, non-commitment, and voluntarism.[11]

A burgeoning artistic practice of the late 1960s, the Fluxus movement, was particularly suitable for the teaching conditions at CalArts, which is why some members of Fluxus received a teaching assignment, including Alison Knowles, Peter Van Riper, and Allan Kaprow from the School of Art; Dick Higgins from the School of Design; Emmett Williams from the School of Critical Studies; James Tenney from School of Music; and Nam June Paik from the School of Film.[12]

Owen Smith comments on this: "The [Fluxus] worldview posits a view of the world and its operations which celebrates the absence of a higher meaning or a unified conceptual framework— as a manifestation of the desire to participate without fixed goals or definitive characteristics, to play, to associate, to create without a sought-after or predetermined end."[13]

The Fluxus artists' interest in a more open, experience-based pedagogy and experimentation with temporality and spatial alternatives is well-matched by the administration's desire to defy bureaucratic school conventions.[14] As dean of the art school, Allan Kaprow in particular had a strong influence on the direction of the institute in the first years after the opening of CalArts. "Kaprow was the thinking behind the school as far as I'm concerned"[15] says the artist Alison Knowles. "He had the vision of a school based on what artists wanted to do rather than what the school wanted them to do."[16]

Another node of radical experimental pedagogy at the early institute is the Feminist Art Program founded by Miriam Schapiro and Judy Chicago. The Chicago and Schapiro program, which combined awareness-raising sessions with research into women's issues and the history of women artists, broke with the formalist focus of much art and art education of the time, instead encouraging students to focus on their personal relationships and experiences as well as on their own questions and observations. The program was made famous by the work *Womanhouse*: a Hollywood villa that was transformed by students and lecturers into a huge installation that exhibited women's privacy (e.g., a collection of used tampons in the bathroom), combined with the goal of questioning class and gender boundaries.[17]

Another educational experiment was the art school's Post-Studio, founded by John Baldessari. Baldessari expressed in advance the wish to work with "students who don't paint or do sculpture or any other activity by hand."[18] The Post-Studio was a class that—equipped with all kinds of technical equipment such as Super 8 cameras, video cameras, and still cameras—visited various locations on the West Coast, dealing with the surroundings and artistically working on them. During these field trips the students were encouraged to learn from each other, teach each other, and inspire each other.[19]

Concepts such as the Post-Studio not only attempted to bridge the gap between art and life, but also sought to realize the idea that art under the right conditions could become a productive force in society and even lead to cultural transformation. With the open, improvisatory, and non-hierarchical structuring of the institute, an attempt was also made to reflect "the structure of the arts themselves,"[20] the time being ripe for "a place to exist which draws its principles of behavior from the work."[21]

Therefore, the term 'Gesamtkunstwerk,' as a description of artistic synthesis, is often used for the design and formulation of CalArts's objectives:

"The institute is close to total theater ... The vision of totality being a spirit which dominates the sensibility of the arts, the task is to restore a unitary vision to the arts and to reality itself."[22]
— Herbert Blau

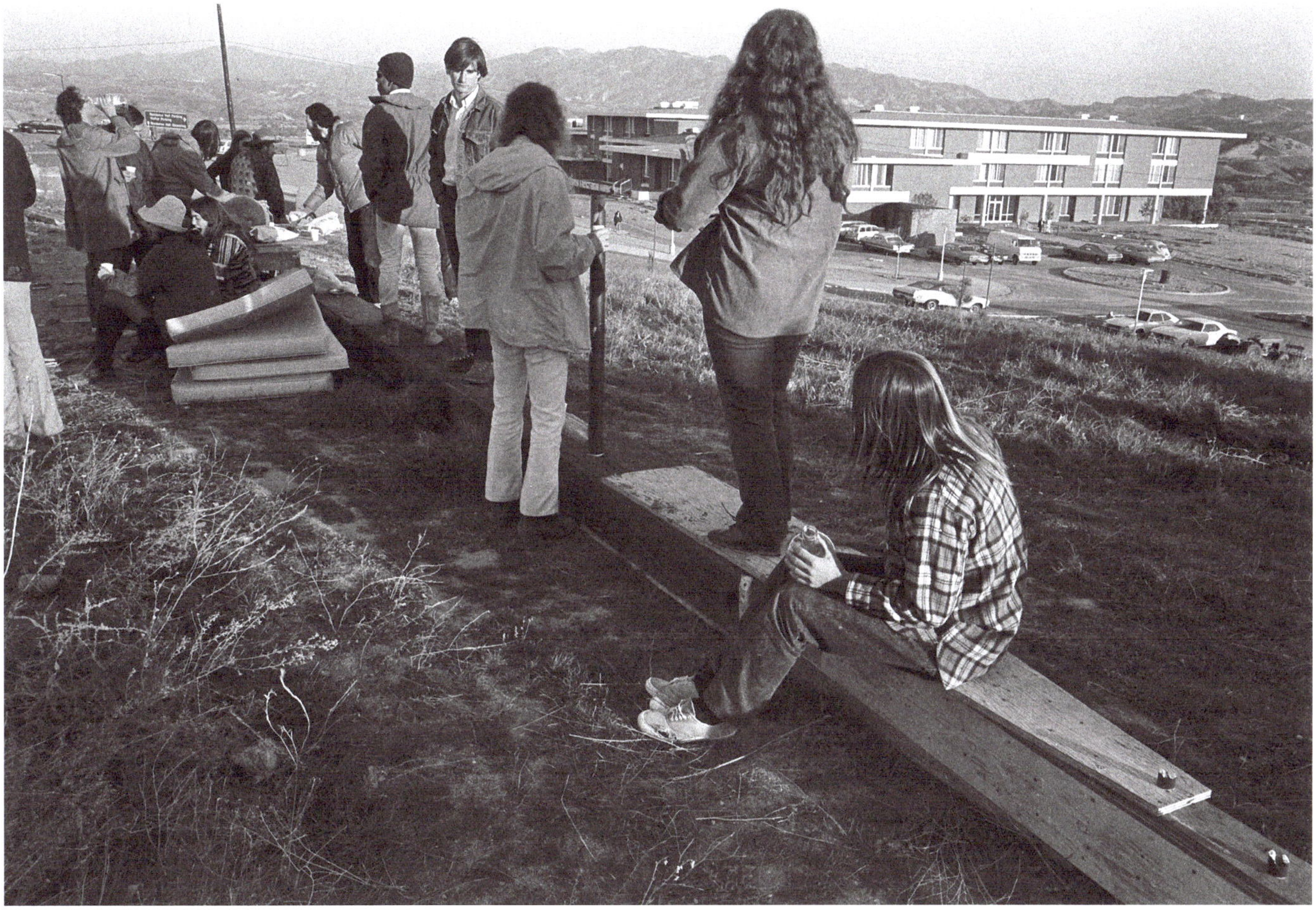

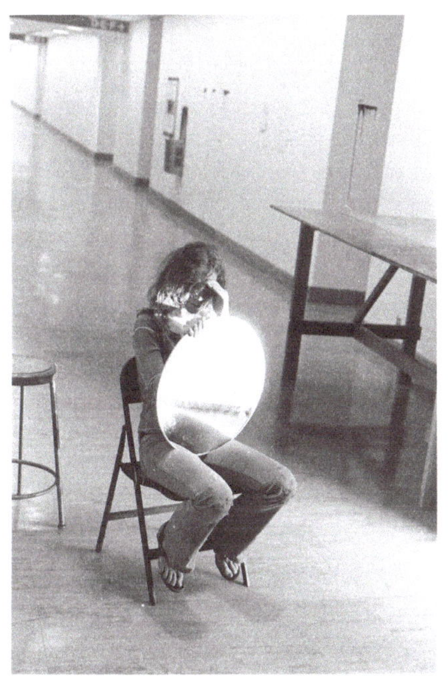

In this context, the 'Gesamtkunstwerk' is seen not only as a model for a new form of artistic education, but also as a new form of society.[23]

A light installation by Matt Mullican, a student of John Baldessari, is an example of the connection between learning and living, between art and everyday life.[24] During the lesson he reflected a ray of sunlight into a windowless classroom where a dried leaf caught fire. Four mirrors, a magnifying glass and his artist friends Suzanne Kuffler, Jill Ciment, Pierre Picot, and Tom Radloff supported him. The installation is exemplary for the structure and learning method of the early Post-Studio class, according to which art mediation is understood as a connection between everyday life and teaching and refers to the principle of randomness, spontaneity, and the joint development of ideas.

Above: Alison Knowles, *House of Dust—Orientation Bonfire* (1971).
Right: Matt Mullican, *Bringing the Light into a Windowless Room and Burning a Leaf* (1972), performance views, CalArts, Valencia (CA).

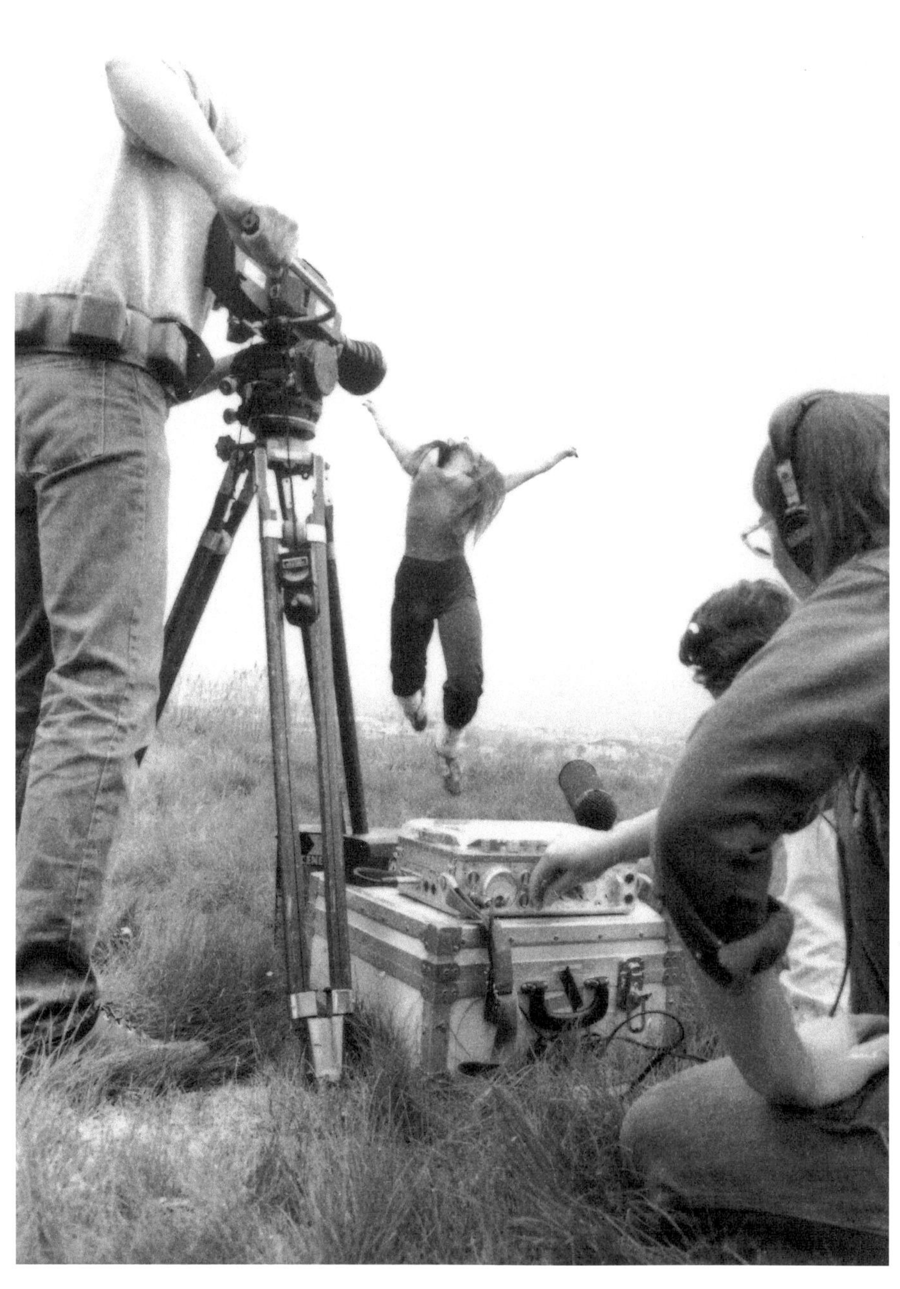

CalArts unknown (ca. 1971–72).

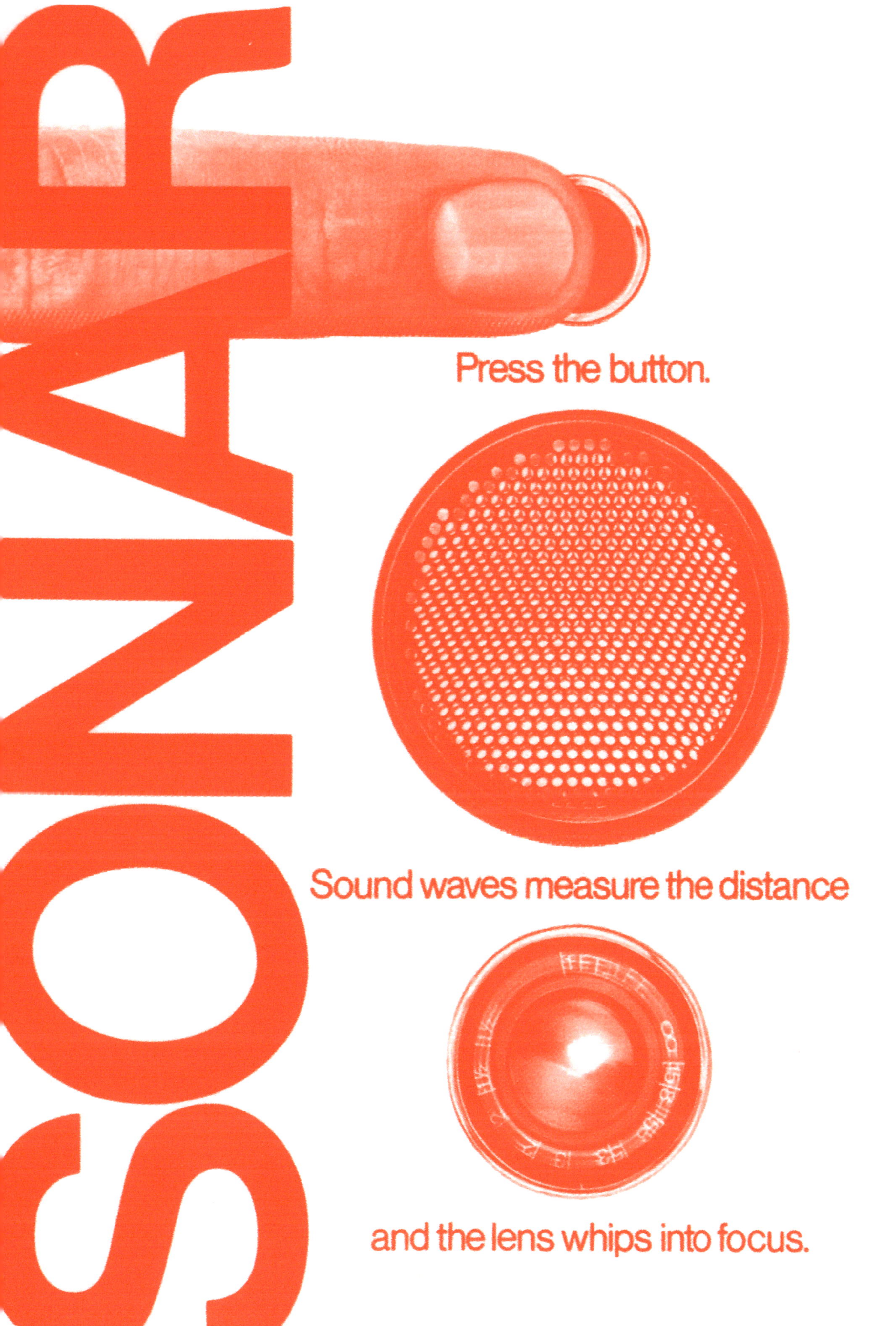

SONAR
Press the button.
Sound waves measure the distance
and the lens whips into focus.

PAULO FREIRE

PEDAGOGY of the OPPRES

• 30TH ANNIVERSAR

Translated by Myra

With an Introduction

CO
NEW

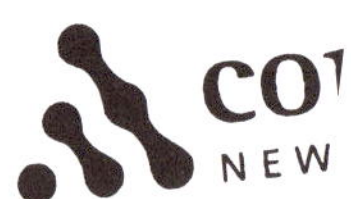

To the oppressed, and to those who suffer with them and fight at their side

the critical faculties and is not content with a partial view of reality but always seeks out the ties which link one point to another and one problem to another.

Indeed, the interests of the oppressors lie in "changing the consciousness of the oppressed, not the situation which oppresses them";[1] for the more the oppressed can be led to adapt to that situation, the more easily they can be dominated. To achieve this end, the oppressors use the banking concept of education in conjunction with a paternalistic social action apparatus, within which the oppressed receive the euphemistic title of "welfare recipients." They are treated as individual cases, as marginal persons who deviate from the general configuration of a "good, organized, and just" society. The oppressed are regarded as the pathology of the healthy society, which must therefore adjust these "incompetent and lazy" folk to its own patterns by changing their mentality. These marginals need to be "integrated," "incorporated" into the healthy society that they have "forsaken."

The truth is, however, that the oppressed are not "marginals," are not people living "outside" society. They have always been "inside"—inside the structure which made them "beings for others." The solution is not to "integrate" them into the structure of oppression, but to transform that structure so that they can become "beings for themselves." Such transformation, of course, would undermine the oppressors' purposes; hence their utilization of the banking concept of education to avoid the threat of student *conscientização*.

The banking approach to adult education, for example, will never propose to students that they critically consider reality. It will deal instead with such vital questions as whether Roger gave green grass to the goat, and insist upon the importance of learning that, on the contrary, Roger gave green grass to the rabbit. The "humanism" of the banking approach masks the effort to turn women and men into automatons—the very negation of their ontological vocation to be more fully human.

1. Simone de Beauvoir, *La Pensée de Droite, Aujord'hui* (Paris); ST, *El Pensamiento político de la Derecha* (Buenos Aires, 1963), p. 34.

mechanically the narrated content. Worse yet, it turns
to "containers," into "receptacles" to be "filled" by the
The more completely she fills the receptacles, the better a
he is. The more meekly the receptacles permit themsel
d, the better students they are.
on thus becomes an act of depositing, in whic
he depositories and the teacher is the deposito
icating, the teacher issues communiqués and n
h the students patiently receive, memorize, and
"banking" concept of education, in which the
d to the students extends only as far as receiving
he deposits. They do, it is true, have the oppo
llectors or cataloguers of the things they store.
sis, it is the people themselves who are filed
ck of creativity, transformation, and knowledge i
ided system. For apart from inquiry, apart from
als cannot be truly human. Knowledge emerges
on and re-invention, through the restless, impatie
eful inquiry human beings pursue in the world, w
ith each other.
concept of education, knowledge is a gift bestowe
sider themselves knowledgeable upon those whon
know nothing. Projecting an absolute ignorance
racteristic of the ideology of oppression, negates
wledge as processes of inquiry. The teacher pre-
students as their necessary opposite; by consid-
e absolute, he justifies his own existence. The
ike the slave in the Hegelian dialectic, accept
tifying the teacher's existence—but, unlike the
over that they educate the teacher.
libertarian education, on the other hand, lies
conciliation. Education must begin with the
r-student contradiction, by reconciling the
on so that both are simultaneously teachers

This sol…
On the contrary, ban…
the contradiction through th…
which mirror oppressive society as a

(a) the teacher teaches and the s

(b) the teacher knows everything

(c) the teacher thinks and the s

(d) the teacher talks and the stu

(e) the teacher disciplines and the students are …

(f) the teacher chooses and enforces his choice, and the students
comply;

(g) the teacher acts and the students have the illusion of acting
through the action of the teacher;

(h) the teacher chooses the program content, and the students
(who were not consulted) adapt to it;

(i) the teacher confuses the authority of knowledge with his or
her own professional authority, which she and he sets in oppo-
…the freedom of the students;
…learning process, while the

---

mistrusting of people. In either event, it is threatened by the specter of reaction.

Unfortunately, those who espouse the cause of liberation are themselves surrounded and influenced by the climate which generates the banking concept, and often do not perceive its true significance or its dehumanizing power. Paradoxically, then, they utilize this same instrument of alienation in what they consider an effort to liberate. Indeed, some "revolutionaries" brand as "innocents," "dreamers," or even "reactionaries" those who would challenge this educational practice. But one does not liberate people by alienating them. Authentic liberation—the process of humanization—is not another deposit to be made in men. Liberation is a praxis: the action and reflection of men and women upon their world in order to transform it. Those truly committed to the cause of liberation can accept neither the mechanistic concept of consciousness as an empty vessel to be filled, nor the use of banking methods of domination (propaganda, slogans—deposits) in the name of liberation.

Those truly committed to liberation must reject the banking concept in its entirety, adopting instead a concept of women and men as conscious beings, and consciousness as consciousness intent upon the world. They must abandon the educational goal of deposit-making and replace it with the posing of the problems of human beings in their relations with the world. "Problem-posing" education, responding to the essence of consciousness—*intentionality*—rejects communiqués and embodies communication. It epitomizes the special characteristic of consciousness: being *conscious of*, not only as intent on objects but as turned in upon itself in a Jasperian "split"—consciousness as consciousness *of* consciousness.

Liberating education consists in acts of cognition, not transferrals of information. It is a learning situation in which the cognizable object (far from being the end of the cognitive act) intermediates the cognitive actors—teacher on the one hand and students on the other. Accordingly, the practice of problem-posing education entails at the outset that the teacher-student contradiction to be resolved. Dialogical relations—indispensable to the capacity of cognitive

actors to cooperate in perceiving the sa[me]... otherwise impossible.

Indeed, problem-posing education, whi[ch]... patterns characteristic of banking educati[on]... as the practice of freedom only if it can ov[ercome]... diction. Through dialogue, the teacher-of-t[he]... dents-of-the-teacher cease to exist and a new... student with students-teachers. The teach[er]... the-one-who-teaches, but one who is himself... the students, who in turn while being taug[ht]... come jointly responsible for a process in w[hich]... process, arguments based on "authority" are n[o]... to function, authority must be *on the side of*... it. Here, no one teaches another, nor is anyon[e]... teach each other, mediated by the world, by th[e]... which in banking education are "owned" by the...

The banking concept (with its tendency to... thing) distinguishes two stages in the action of th[e]... the first, he cognizes a cognizable object while h[e]... sons in his study or his laboratory; during the se[cond]... to his students about that object. The students ar[e]... to know, but to memorize the contents narrated by... do the students practice any act of cognition, sin[ce]... wards which that act should be directed is the... teacher rather than a medium evoking the critical r[e]... eacher and students. Hence in the name of the '[c]... ulture and knowledge" we have a system which a[c]... rue knowledge nor true culture.

The problem-posing method does not dichotomize... [th]e teacher-student: she is not "cognitive" at one point and "narra-... [ti]ve" at another. She is always "cognitive," whether preparing a proj-... t or engaging in dialogue with the students. He does not regard... gnizable objects as his private property, but as the object of re-... nection by himself and the students. In this way, the problem-posing... educator constantly re-forms his reflections in the reflection of the...

students. The students—no longer docile listeners—are now critical... co-investigators in dialogue with the teacher. The teacher presents... the material to the students for their consideration, and re-considers... her earlier considerations as the students express their own. The... role of the problem-posing educator is to create; together with the... students, the conditions under which knowledge at the level of the... *doxa* is superseded by true knowledge, at the level of the *logos*.

Whereas banking education anesthetizes and inhibits creative... power, problem-posing education involves a constant unveiling of... reality. The former attempts to maintain the *submersion* of con-... sciousness; the latter strives for the *emergence* of consciousness and... *critical intervention* in reality.

Students, as they are increasingly posed with problems relating... to themselves in the world and with the world, will feel increasingly... challenged and obliged to respond to that challenge. Because they... apprehend the challenge as interrelated to other problems within a... total context, not as a theoretical question, the resulting comprehen-... sion tends to be increasingly critical and thus constantly less alien-... ated. Their response to the challenge evokes new challenges,... followed by new understandings; and gradually the students come... to regard themselves as committed.

Education as the practice of freedom—as opposed to education... as the practice of domination—denies that man is abstract, isolated... independent, and unattached to the world; it also denies that th[e]... world exists as a reality apart from people. Authentic reflection con-... siders neither abstract man nor the world without people, but peo-... ple in their relations with the world. In these relations consciousne[ss]... and world are simultaneous: consciousness neither precedes th[e]... world nor follows it.

La conscience et le monde sont donnés d'un même coup: exté-... rieur par essence à la conscience, le monde est, par essence re-... latif à elle.[8]

8. Sartre; *op. cit.*, p. 32.

... beg[in]... [consciou]ness" and to reflect upon them. These... [su]bjects of their consideration, and, as such, obj[ects]... and cognition.

[In problem-p]osing education, people develop their power to pe[rceive]... *the way they exist* in the world *with which* and... themselves; they come to see the world not as... as a reality in process, in transformation. Althoug[h]... [re]lations of women and men with the world exist... how these relations are perceived (or whether or... [perc]eived at all), it is also true that the form of action... [a l]arge extent a function of how they perceive them-... [in] the world. Hence, the teacher-student and the students-... teachers reflect simultaneously on themselves and the world without... dichotomizing this reflection from action, and thus establish an au-... thentic form of thought and action.

Once again, the two educational... analysis come into co[nflict]... atten...

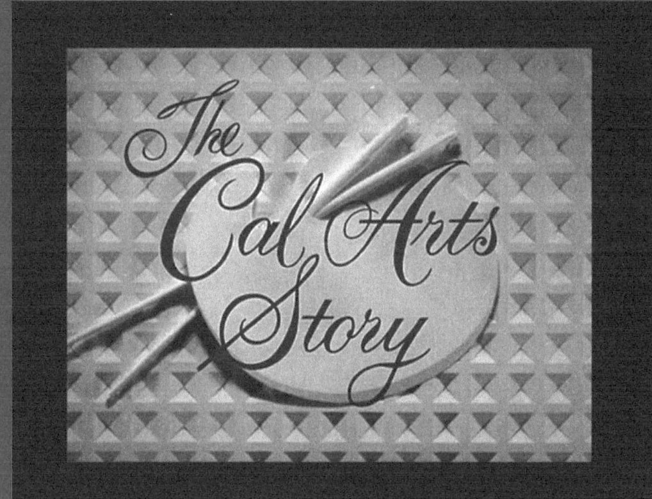

THE CALARTS STORY
Walt Disney Productions
Film stills, 1964

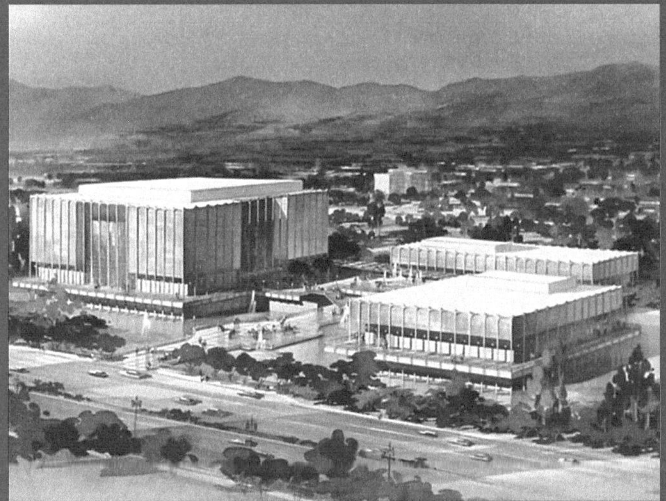

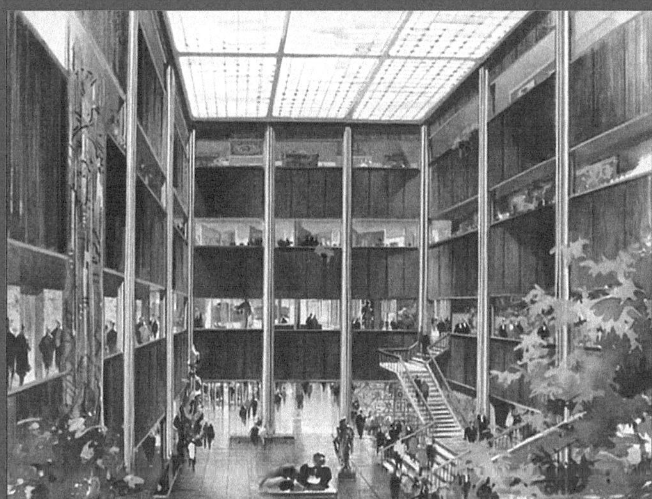

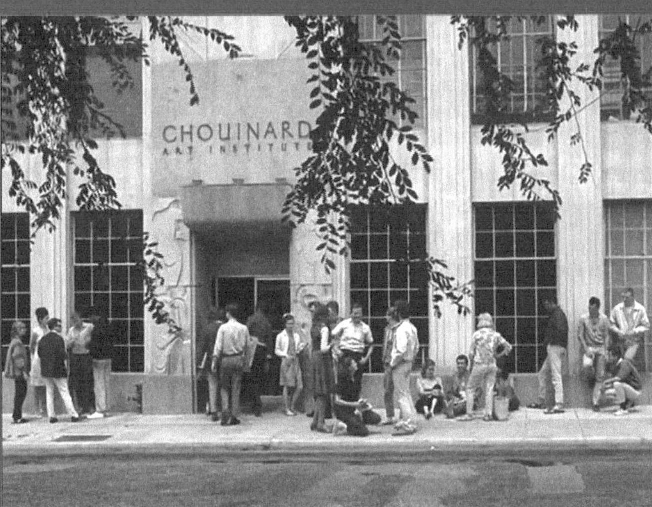

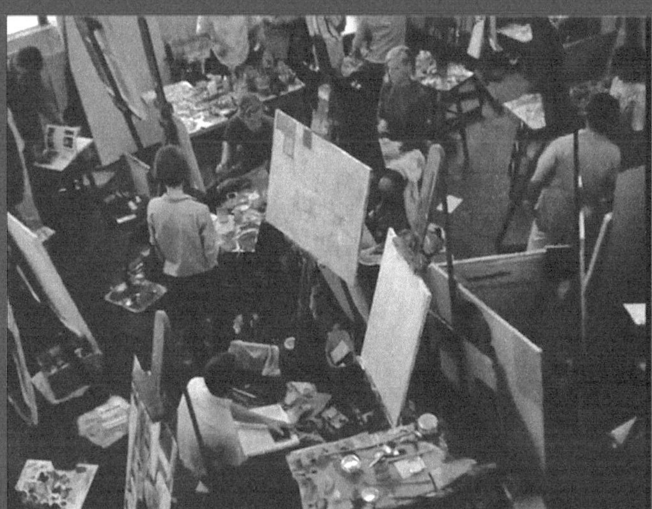

"Art and design are everywhere in our lives, filling needs, adding satisfactions to our daily existence. In fact, the well-trained artist is a decidedly useful member of society. And nowadays every industry uses him, each in his own way."

CalArts founder Walt Disney produces the promotional short film *The CalArts Story* to attract students and donators for the still-to-be-built art school. He presented the film during the world premiere of the Hollywood film *Mary Poppins* in 1964 when introducing his idea for CalArts to the public.

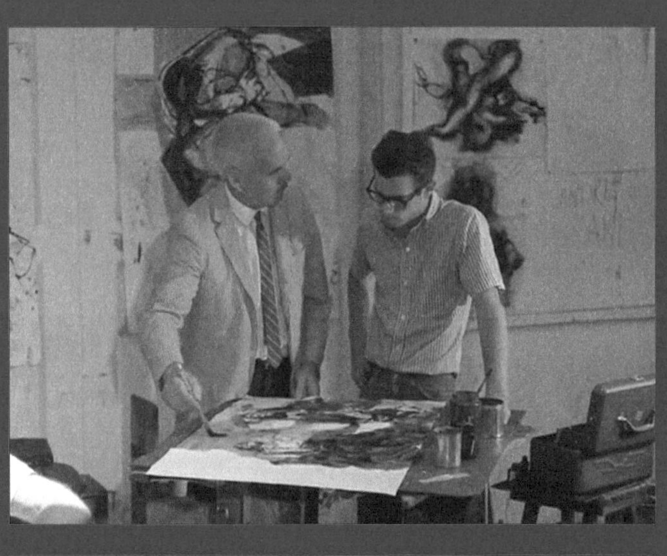

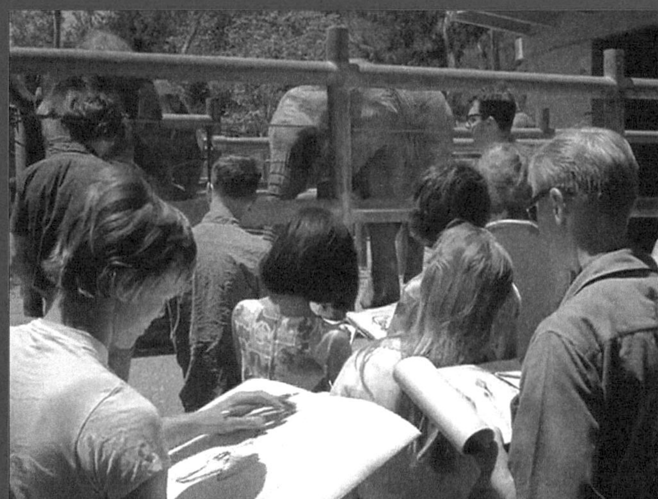

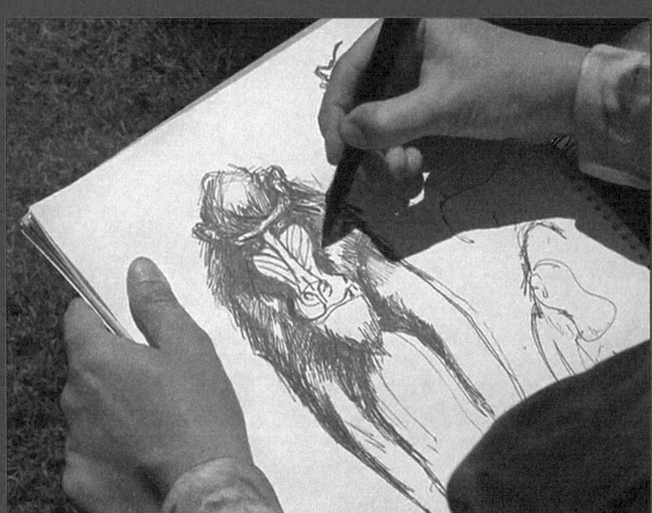

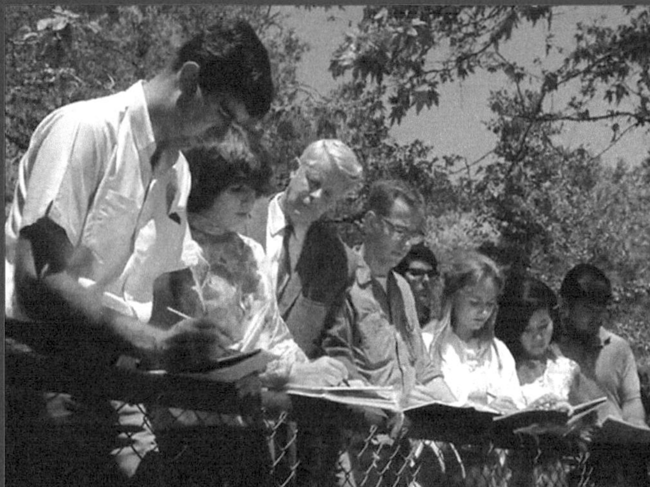

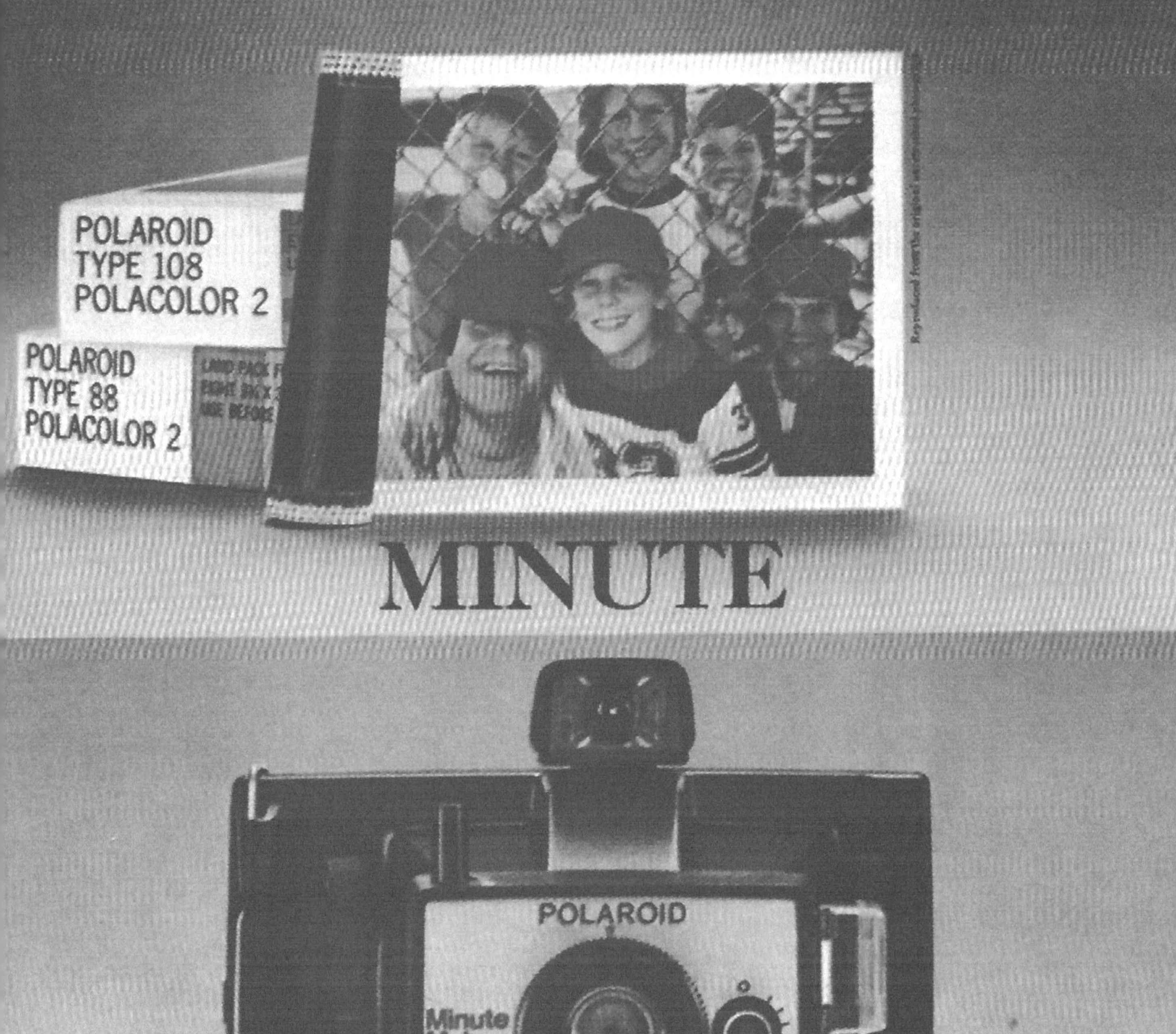

You can pass these finished pictures around for everyone to look at and share in just 60 seconds. And Polaroid's deep brilliant colors will last. They're made with our exclusive SX-70 dyes which are among the most fade-resistant ever known to photography.

Our new MinuteMaker gives you the excitement in 2 sizes, our big 3¼″ x 4¼″ or our economical square film. (The least expensive instant color there is.) This easy automatic sets all exposures for you. You can shoot 'n share in 60 seconds.

Polaroid's new MinuteMaker under $25.*

MOVEMENTS OF THE L.A. ART SCENE IN THE 1960s

By Teresa Depenau

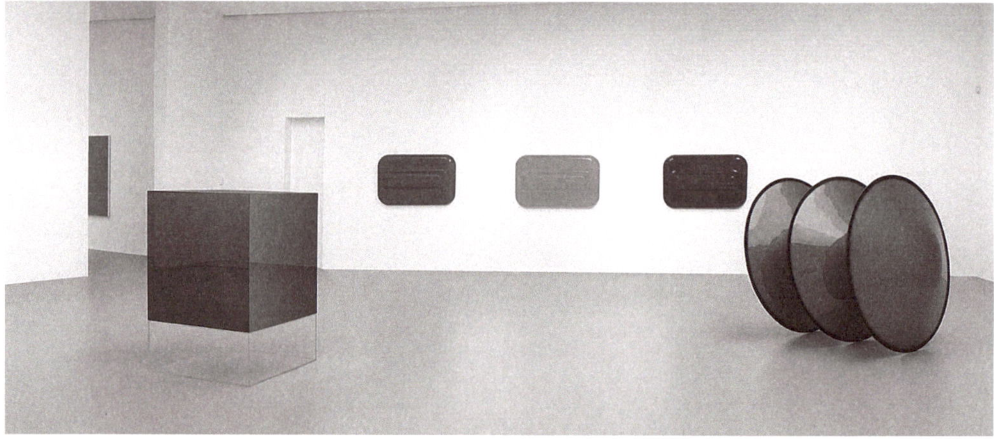

A   *Primary Atmospheres: Works from California 1960–1970*, installation view, January 8–February 6, 2010, David Zwirner, New York.

1

The L.A. art scene of the 1960s was shaped by two major currents: Finish Fetish and Light and Space. Inspired by the smoothly polished surfaces of surfboard, as well as the West Coast's car fetish, was the 1960s art movement Finish Fetish.[1] The Finish Fetish minimalists (such as Larry Bell and John McCracken) used materials including sheet metal and carbon and, much like car tuners, gave their works of art a final polish with color varnish.[2] The Light and Space artists (like Robert Irwin and Helen Pashgian), meanwhile, worked with materials such as glass, neon, fluorescent tubes, and cast acrylic. Just as the sun plays a major role in California, so did light in the Light and Space group's installations; these highly reflective materials could control the direction of natural sunlight. At the same time, these objects were supplemented by artificial light and are embedded within it. Most of the Finish Fetish and Light and Space artists were represented by the Ferus

Gallery, which was founded by curator Walter Hopps in 1957 and closed in 1966, and one of the first art galleries that promoted young Southern Californian artists. Further artists represented by the gallery were Ed Kienholz, Wallace Berman, and Edward "Ed" Ruscha.[3]

2

"Let the mind unshackle; set it free. Let it stroll, run, leap, laugh in gardens of crystal motion and sun and reality. Weave and paint with the hand of your imagination, with the fingers of your body, brush of fiberglass."[4]

— Bob McTavish, surfboard shaper and inventor of the 'shortboard'

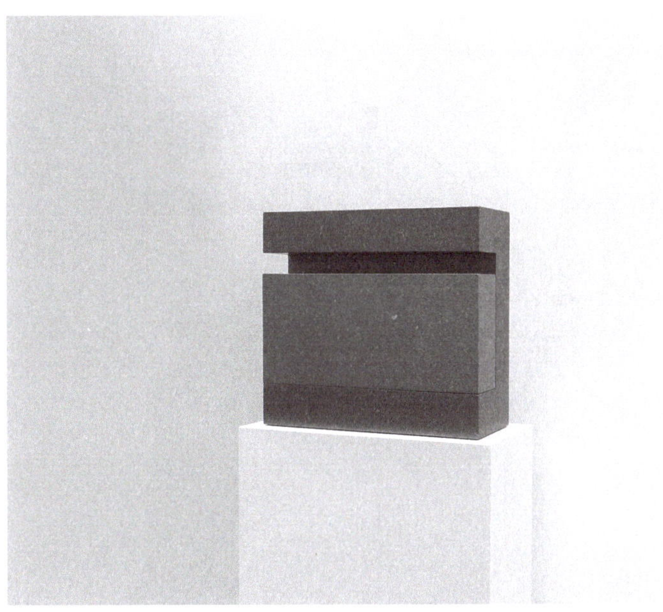

B

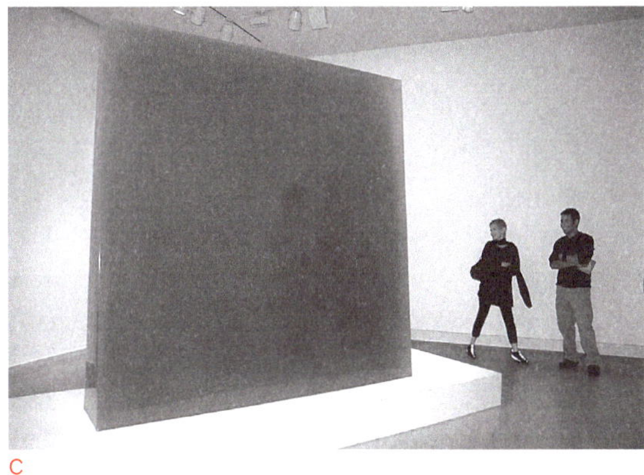

C

B   John McCracken, *Mykonos* (1965).
C   De Wain Valentine, *Large Wall* (1968).
D   Larry Bell in his studio, Venice Beach,
        California (1969). Photo by Malcolm Lubliner.
E   Helen Pashgian, *Untitled* (1968–69).
        Photo by Brian Forrest.

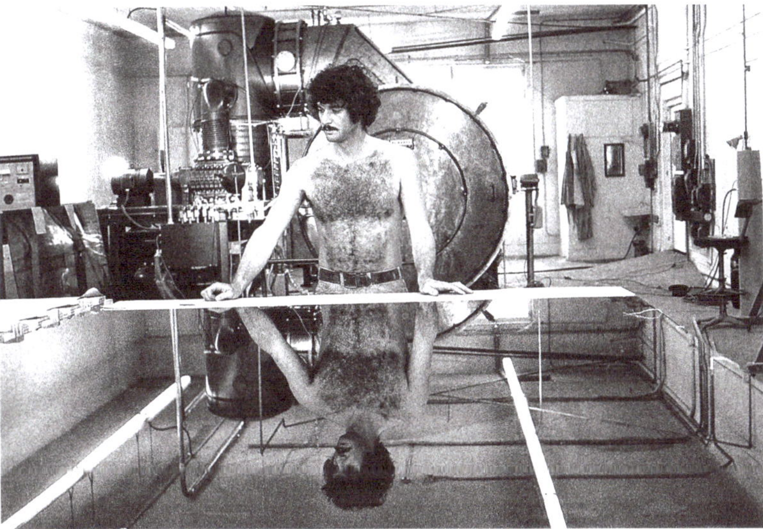

D

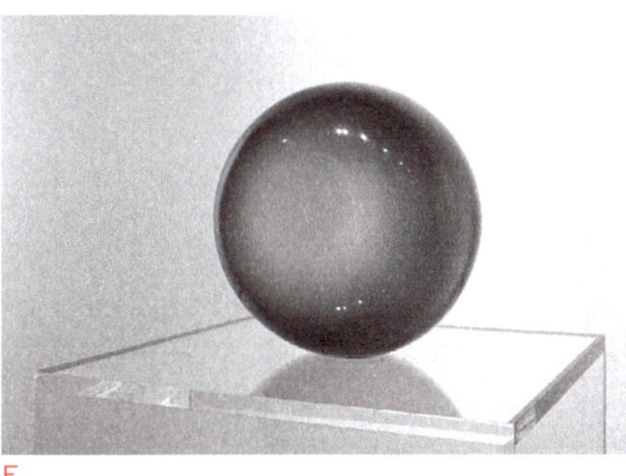

E

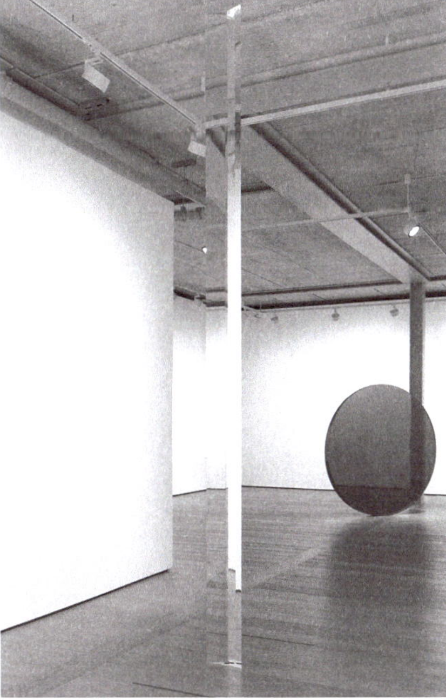

H

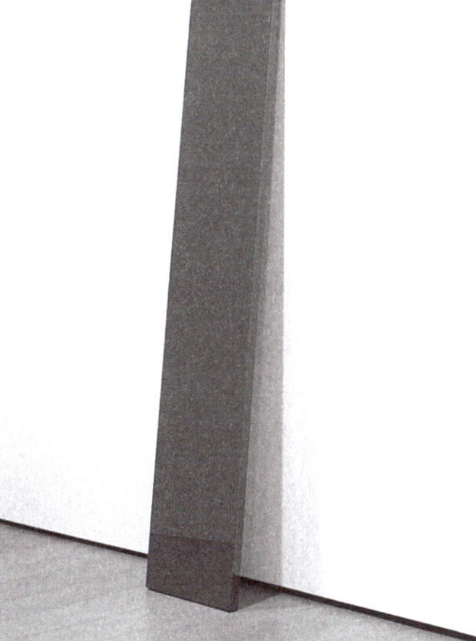

F

G

F   Robert Irwin, *Untitled* (1969).
G   John McCracken, *Untitled* (1972).
H   Robert Irwin, *Prism* (1971), installation
        view, *Plastic Show*, curated by De
        Wain Valentine, February 09—March 25,
        2017, London, Grosvenor Hill.

I   Artists outside the Ferrus Gallery in
        Los Angeles (1959). Clockwise from
        top: Billy Al Bengston, Irving Blum,
        Ed Moses, and John Altoon. Photo by
        William Claxton.
J   Wallace Berman at Stone Brothers
        (1957). Photo by Charles Brittin.

3

"You always hear the same clichés about the L.A. arts scene,"[5] complained John Baldessari. "Finish Fetish. Light and Space. Ferus—there's so much more to it."[6] Baldessari rejected self-image or aesthetics in his work, instead preferring to do 'his own thing.' "'It's weird,' said Baldessari, 'but for some reason, I need to be a little angry so I can work. And L.A. makes me a little angry. The city is really not beautiful. And I don't think people are very smart. So for me there is little distraction in Los Angeles. The weather is good. I can work really well here.'"[7]

Baldessari regarded Los Angeles as an un-European city without history. He assumed, however, that painting needs something civilized in order to grow, and that canvases must be able to lean on something.[8] While artists in New York worked in thematic reference to art history, in the 1960s artists in L.A. had an unusual approach to historiography, above all "because nobody had a clue about it [art history]."[9] as Baldessari said. This is one reason, among others, why painting never gained a foothold in L.A.—because, according to Baldessari, there is, so to speak, no cultural ground there.

Even though Baldessari encouraged his students to move to New York after graduating from CalArts, many remained in California after their studies. Through the self-organization of local artists, a functioning artistic structure was gradually built in a city that, in the early 1960s, still stood in the shadow of the East Coast metropolis of New York.[11] The students became artists, and these artists, in turn, attracted gallery owners. Over time, important museum curators also began to move to the West Coast.[12] Since the majority of the students from Baldessari's later Post-Studio classes did not leave the West Coast, some even holding professorships at established art schools, Baldessari's teachings have been passed on from CalArts students to future generations.

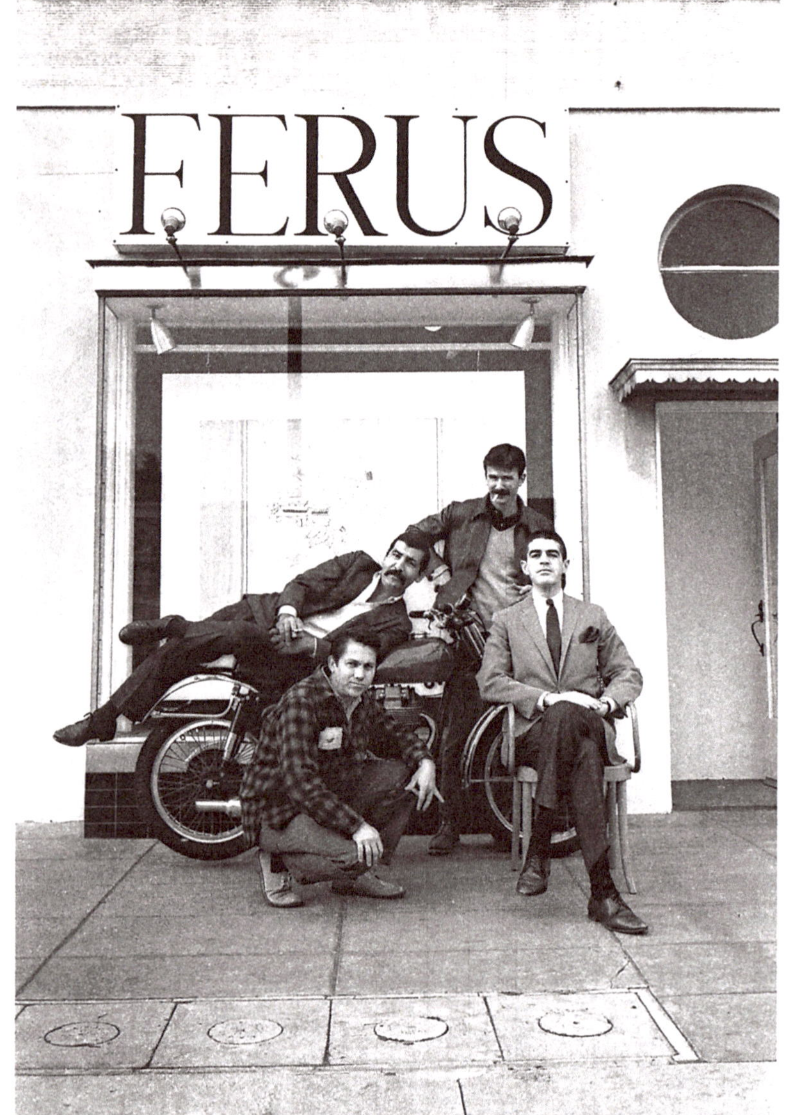

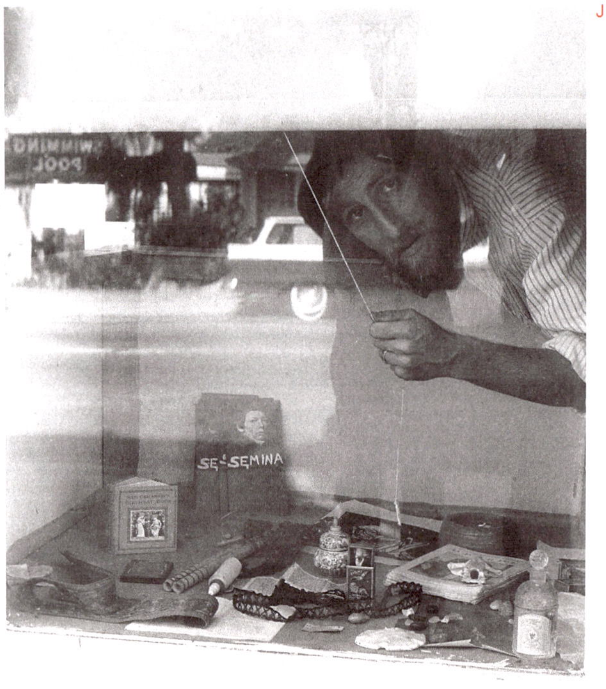

PETER PLAGENS
Reviews of West Coast Art
Exhibitions, 1970s

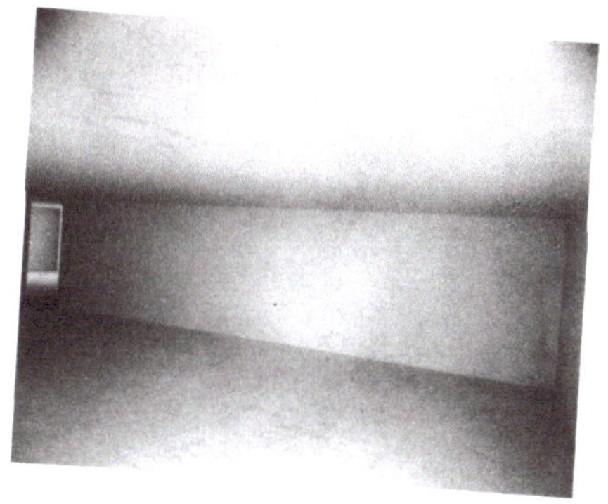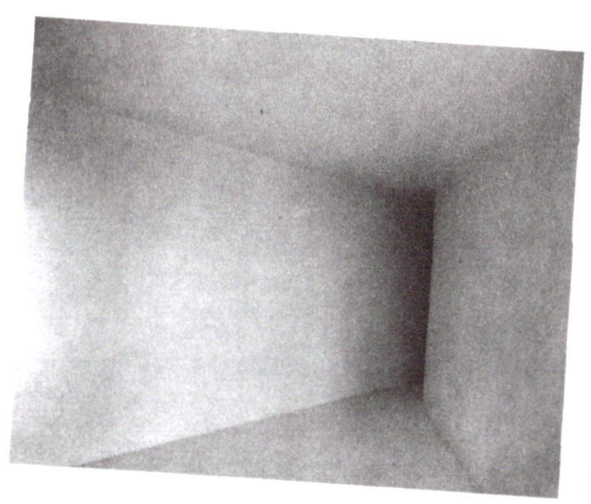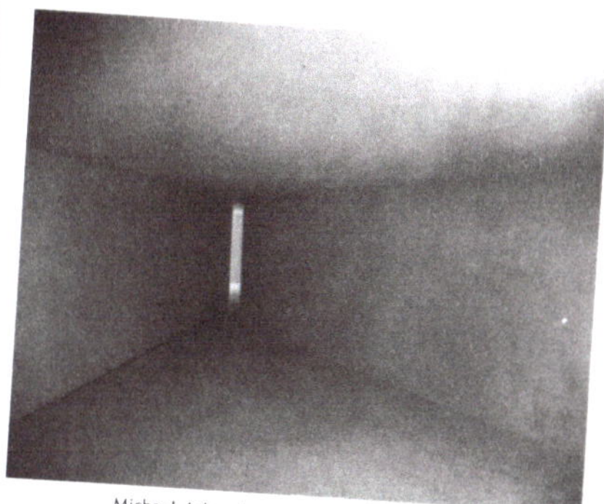

Michael Asher, installation views, Pomona College. 1970.

Michael Asher: The Thing of It Is…

LOS ANGELES

PETER PLAGENS

If the history of modern art is not itself a straight line, certainly straight lines inhabit it — unerring connections from one group of artists to another, a year, five years, or several decades apart. Until the recent proliferation of personal, neo-Romantic, magical styles, by far the deepest groove was that traced by reductive formalism; art objects (or, in painting, the surface of an object) became steadily simpler, e.g., Gabo and Gonzalez to Smith and Judd, de Kooning and Hofmann to Reinhardt and Noland. Although a still fashionable Greenbergian axiom — a work is modern to the degree it consists *only* of those means peculiar to its own medium — channeled many recent oeuvres, perhaps reductive formalism is just an aspect of industrialism's general, "If it doesn't really *do* anything, throw it out." So, along with spats, the running board, leaded glass windows, bow ties and surrey fringe, out went figuration, fancy brushwork, welding seams, patina, impasto, funny shapes, relational composition, etc. Finally, with a logic inevitable since Manet, out went the *objet d'art* itself. After all, in a technological society, static objects are deb-

its, and what do art objects *do*, save hang or sit and await the implosion of the sun?

The decline of the art object is not accompanied, however, by a paucity of artists' objects per se; only the Conceptualists, for all their puffed-up virtues and very real faults, operate with a minimum of hardware. The rest — earthworkers, big painters, foundry sculptors, et al — simply replace the bulk of finished objects with the bulk of tools. But art without "specific objects" (an early alternative title to Minimal) cannot be perfunctorily dismissed with the casual observations that: a) physical mass is now plugged in *behind* the walls; or b) Conceptualism is only Rochefoucauld come to West Broadway. Michael Asher, for instance, is, as far as I know, the best non-object formalist artist in Los Angeles, and he eloquently demonstrates the possibilities of the mode, as well as its drawbacks.

Asher, 28, agrees that the constant, abundant, early presence of certified art objects in his home may have satiated him with "things" requiring "a great deal of visual and material attention." After a student career in New Mexico, "producing more art objects faster than I thought anyone could" in order to redeem some bad anthropology grades with better ones in art, the New York Studio School ("what was important was not the post-Cubist Abstract Expressionism they wanted the students to do, but just being in New York . . . I saw Flavin's white tube show while I was there"), and U. C. Irvine, from which he escaped with a degree, Asher says the "jumping off point" came during 1967-69. The results were "air works," constructed in a garage-studio; these comprised a clean room with air blown in through small nozzles a) from the upper corners toward the center, b) downward, in a line across the room, and c) singly, straight down from the center of the ceiling, denoting, respec-

tively, the linear, planar, and ambient. A similar air work was exhibited at the Newport Harbor Art Museum, and a "curtain-of-air" became Asher's entry in the watershed 1969 Whitney "Anti-Illusion" show. (The Whitney work was ill-received: a little ahead of its time — going whole hog where the others went half — it was out of step with the floppy, proletarian New York heaviness.) The "empty room" in MOMA's later "Spaces" fared similarly; *Artforum* said it was a "mystery" why he was given a slot following the Whitney "disaster." Asher's work might be underestimated since it isn't shown often, not at all in commercial galleries because there's nothing to sell, unlike the photo-documentation of "non-object" Smithson, or the showmanship of Christo's Cardiff Giants. Each work *is* an exhibition (and vice versa, an inherent disadvantage of purist, non-object art). Then followed a proposed exhibition at the Pasadena Art Museum (a ceiling tilting to the floor in one of the cupolas — cancelled due to costs), another demiarchitectural room in bent-hourglass floor plan at Pomona, and his last shown work, a series of parallel walls in the County Museum's "24 Young Artists" of last year (*Artforum*, October, 1971).

Asher's focal difficulty as an accessible artist is his insistence-by-default on Art; he has no repertory of art history dialectics, like the post-Minimalists, no RANDy researcher's points to prove, like Irwin, no neo-Duchampian head fakes, like Nauman, and no supradecorative *tours de force*, like Bell. Asher's art is like a gentler, more expansive Reinhardt, without the withering reinforcing dogma; but he shares the attitude of art-as-art and refuses to dress his pieces up with theory. The work is the work, alluding to nothing but itself. "What is it you're after?" is the question I reinserted, in slight variations, during two lengthy conversations, hoping for a convenient quote from *Scientific American* on optic

LOS ANGELES: THE ECOLOGY OF EVIL

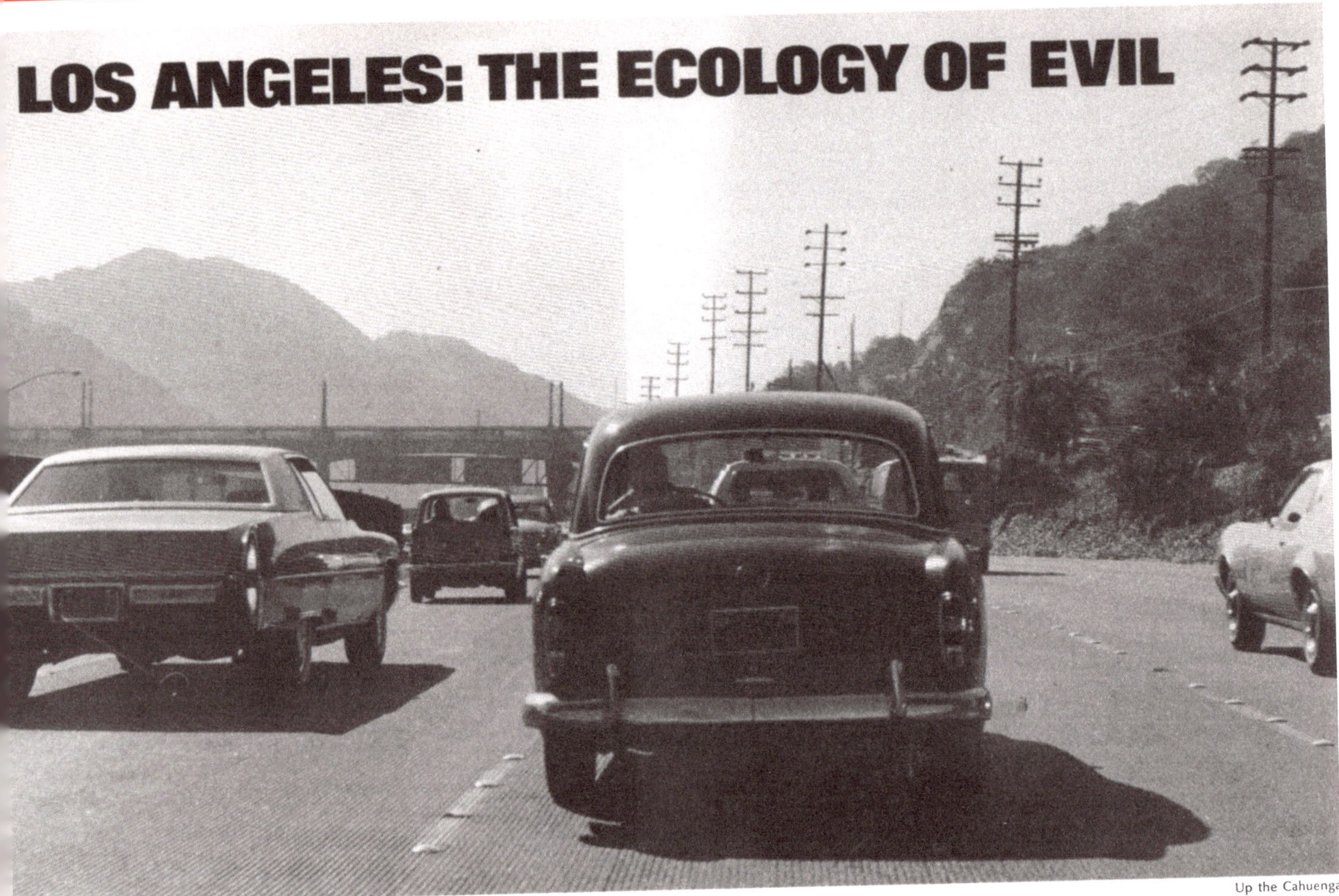

Up the Cahuenga.

All photos by Peter Plagens

PETER PLAGENS

The city of L.A.,
it ain't the way
the posters say that it'll be.
Behind the palm trees and chrome
I find a stucco home,
and another factory.
 —from "The San Diego Freeway,"
 an unpublished song by Dave Hickey

Los Angeles once had to defend itself against snotty Eastern culture critics, English novelists, and middlebrow gossip columnists like Herb Caen who, from Provincetown-on-the-Thyroid, condescendingly refers to "that flat city down south." The implication was always that Los Angeles, the world's most spacious city, was in a Culture-and-Sophistication League with Dubuque, Rochester, and Provo, that it was basically "bush" and that

Los Angeles, The Architecture of Four Ecologies, Reyner Banham, New York: Harper and Row, 1971, 256 pages, 123 black-and-white illustrations, $6.95.

by luck or by golly it possessed none of the brittle, knowing sophistication derived from real big city problems. In the '60s Los Angeles moved past Philadelphia in population into third behind New York and Chicago, held the Democratic convention, acquired a spate of major league teams, built several culture palaces and 1000 miles of freeway, suffered a racial upheaval, and generally enlarged/intensified itself into the malignant tumor of a Great American City. In fact L.A. succeeded so extraordinarily that now it finds itself plagued by a different observer: the chic debunker of current anti-L.A. mythology ("God, you don't wanna move there now. It's so crowded now, and the smog . . . you wouldn't *believe* . . . ") who finds that L.A. is really a groovy place in spite of its evils and often because of them, if you know how to look at it right. Ray Bradbury, with his noxious futuro-mystical treacle in "Los Angeles Is the Best Place in America," *Esquire*, October, 1972, is essentially harmless, but Reyner Banham, the English architect/pop scholar, has written a heavyweight "serious" book, *Los Angeles: The Architecture of Four Ecologies* (London, 1971) which is quite dangerous because it will have a trickle-down

effect (i.e., the hacks who do shopping centers, Hawaiian restaurants, and savings-and-loans, the dried-up civil servants in the division of highways, and the legions of show-biz fringies will sleep a little easier and work a little harder now that their enterprises have been authenticated). In a more humane society where Banham's doctrines would be measured against the subdividers' rape of the land and the lead particles in little kids' lungs, the author might be stood up against a wall and shot; as it is we must try to laugh through our tears at . . . *Four Ecologies'* nearly comic ineptness.

What I have aimed to do is to present the architecture (in a fairly conventional sense of the word) within the topographical and historical context of the total artefact that constitutes Greater Los Angeles, because it is this double context that binds the polymorphous architecture into a comprehensible unity that cannot often be discerned by comparing monument with monument out of context (p. 23).

This airy frappe of light architectural history, generalized architectural description, and fly-by-night sociology is halfway excused because it's intended for a general, not professional, audi-

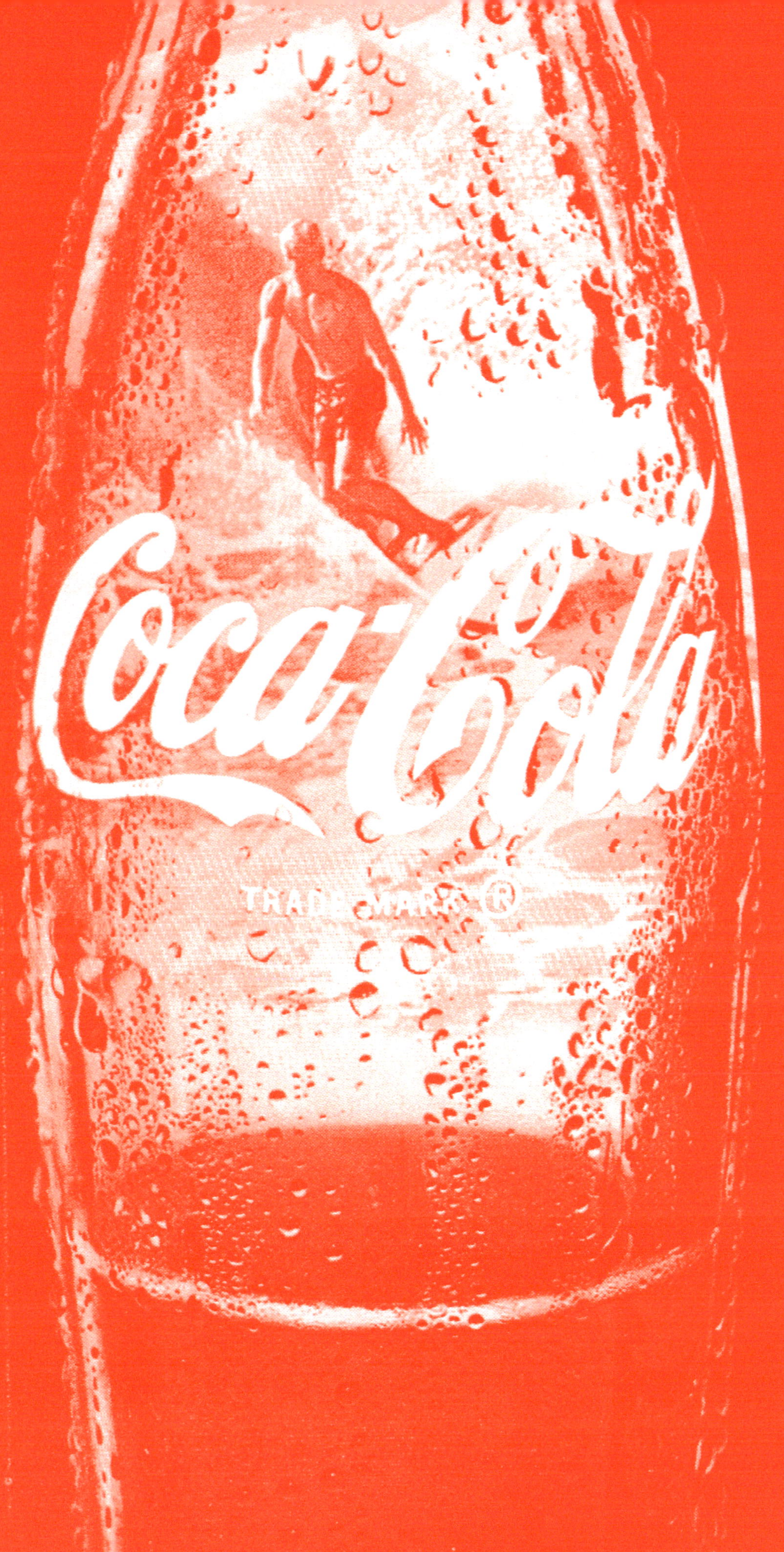
Coca-Cola
TRADE MARK ®

Wave After Wave.
Drink After Drink.

You ride the big one
all the way in.
Then: Coca-Cola, splashing
over your thirst.
Cold. Fresh. With that
one-of-a-kind taste.
Coke has the taste
you never get tired of.
It makes the best things
in life go even better.
Like the perfect wave.
Like anything.
Things
go better
with Coke

I WILL NOT MAKE ANY MORE BORING ART: PREHISTORY

By Pauline Gründing

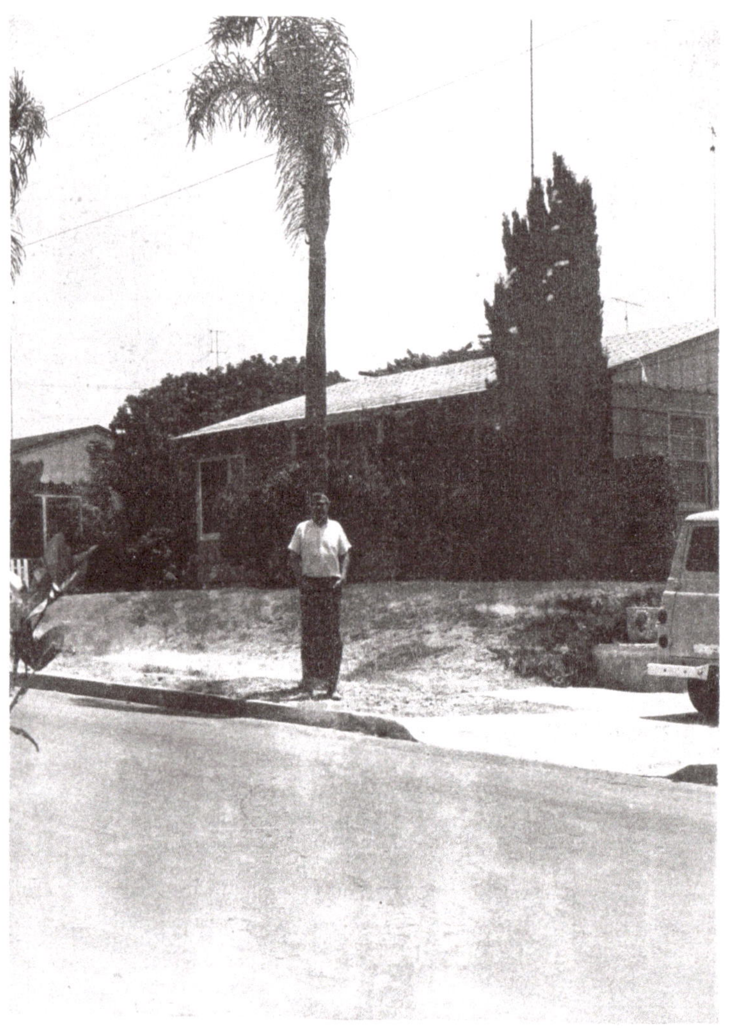

John Baldessari, *Wrong*
(1966–68).

T he 1971 work *I Will Not Make Any More Boring Art* was preceded by a major change in John Baldessari's artistic output. The sentence was initially written by him and then, based on minimal instructions, realized by students at an exhibition, which, written again and again as a series of repeated lines, thus resembles a school punishment. After its initial conceptualization in his notebook, Baldessari asks students to produce the commissioned work for an exhibition in Nova Scotia, which he did not personally attend due to excessive travel costs.

The term 'boring' is particularly unusual in art; Baldessari, therefore, wanted to make art 'interesting' again using humor and irony.[1] To get to this point, John Baldessari went through an artistic process that will be presented below. This article deals with the prehistory of *I Will Not Make Any More Boring Art*; in other words, it traces John Baldessari's artistic career up to the creation of this work, in order to understand more precisely how the artist was able to take his innovative conceptual path. The focus is on the years before 1971, when the most radical changes occurred.

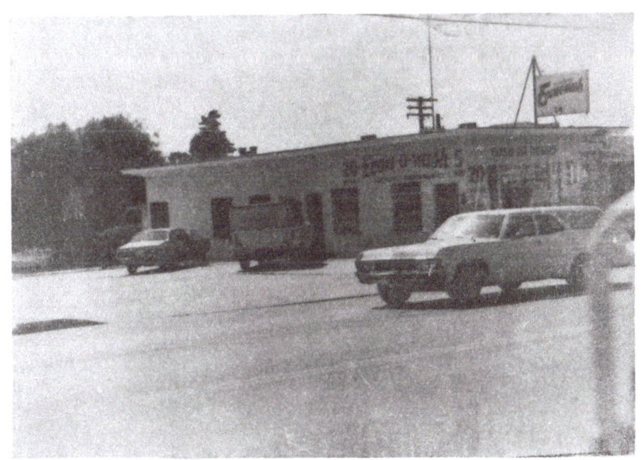

CHANGE IN STYLE

Until the mid-1960s, John Baldessari produced numerous paintings, primarily landscapes and abstractions, which over time gave way to an interest in photography. However, the traditional use of both media quickly bored the artist. At the end of the 1960s, he therefore began to break with the accepted rules of painting and professional photography, often through parody and irony.

One example of this approach is *Wrong*, from 1966–68. The photograph stages Baldessari in front of a suburban house, standing directly in front of a palm tree, as if it were growing out of his head. Underneath the photograph is the word 'WRONG.' Through its unconventional arrangement and lack of aesthetic parameters, he renounces the rules of professional photography, alluding to this further with the additional caption.

The National City series, created between 1966 and 1968, is also unusually staged. *Econ-O-Wash* is a photograph from the series that shows a building typical of the Californian region, which—as the inscription indicates—contains a launderette. The photograph is not of high quality, and the relatively large caption again refers to the intention.

Baldessari explains his choice of motifs for the entire series as follows:

> "Probably I was never going to get out of National City, so I was going to show people what it's like to make art out of where I lived without glamorizing it, and with the idea that truth is beautiful, no matter how ugly it is…. I just wanted it the way it is—it isn't really a rural sprawl."[2]

Here the close connection between Baldessari's work and the environment in which it was created becomes clear. His art and his CalArts Post-Studio class, are phenomena of the state of California that are shaped by its landscape and cultural conditions. Baldessari sought to integrate everyday life into his artworks, and the National City series in particular focuses on Californian life and its aesthetics. The viewer gets a feeling for what it meant to live in California at the end of the 1960s. Art that at that time came primarily from New York or Europe was clashing with a new aesthetic, which saw the Californian lifestyle implanted in works of art. This impression is supported by the unusual arrangement in, for example, *Econ-O-Wash*.

All photographs in this series were created in this random way. In order to take these photographs, Baldessari drove a car through the area and shot his camera out of the window, without seeing exactly

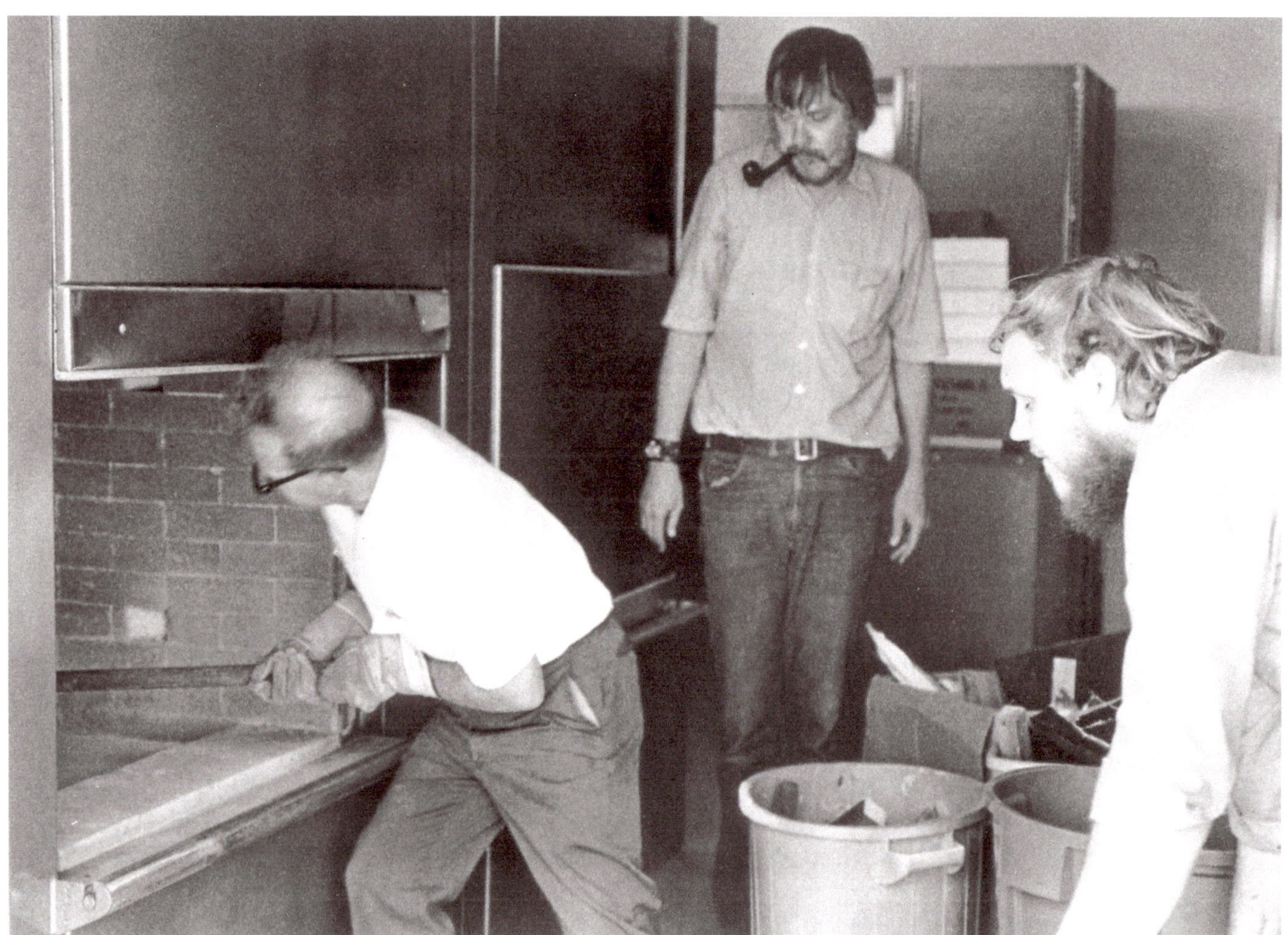

what he was photographing. Only afterwards did he add the locations as captions. Using chance and inattention, he wanted to show things as they were.[3]

At the same time, the relationship between Baldessari's artistic work and his teaching became increasingly close. At the end of the 1960s, he accepted a teaching position at CalArts—initially because he needed money, as he later confirmed in interviews.[4] However, his pedagogy came to be a decisive influence on his artistic output.

INTENTION

At CalArts, Baldessari began by teaching contemporary art, gradually introducing students to the work he had seen in exhibitions in New York and Europe. His teaching became accordingly idiosyncratic. He did not use textbooks, but brought artists as visitors to the seminars. Ultimately, his teaching approach came from a fundamental belief that art cannot be taught.[5] His advice to young artists was that they should know three things: "Talent is cheap, you have to be possessed which you can't will, and being at the right place at the right time."[6]

His classes also formed a central part of his own artistic practice. However, the focus was not on implementing the ideas or concepts that he developed. Their implementation was often carried out with others or was simply absent.

Opposite page: John Baldessari, *Econ-O-Wash, 14th and Highland, National City Calif.* (1966–68).
This page: Documentation of *Cremation Project* (1970).

CONCEPTUAL ART

John Baldessari is primarily associated with conceptual art and is often understood as its co-originator. Conceptual art was a radical reappraisal of what art could be, in which the decisive factor for the production of a work of art is not the result, but the path or process that led to it. According to a conceptual understanding, art begins with the first idea for its implementation and is further developed during the working process. The concept of dematerialization is central to conceptual art, and Baldessari's work with his students was instrumental in this. Art thus becomes an object in flux, with completion subordinate to contemplation.

    This also redefines the role of the artist. By focusing on the process of art making, the material development or the role of the artist is pushed into the background. The amateurization of art, in which works are produced without any need for talent, also demystifies the artist and destabilizes the public perception of the artist as a creative genius. This is particularly evident from the fact that Baldessari did not realize many of his pieces alone, but included and delegated to outsiders—beyond even his students. Thus he rather takes on the role of a planner who develops a concept that then shapes itself.

For example, the text-on-canvas series and the phototext series from 1966–68 were not made by Baldessari himself, but by a professional sign painter.

    According to Baldessari, the reason for this was a mixture of practical and theoretical considerations:

"I actually did teach myself to do brush lettering … So I could have done it, but one of the other things I wanted to do was not to physically do these works by myself. A lot of it was practical … there was a lack of time."[7]

For the *Commissioned Paintings* of 1969, consisting of 14 parts, he also commissioned hobby painters, who could choose one of twelve slides to paint onto a uniformly primed canvas. Then the caption with the name of the respective painter was added. This series is Baldessari's last ever use of painting. The work is about everyday, randomly chosen objects, without any special logic.

    His conceptual approach is also evident in works such as the *California Map Project* of 1969. Photographs included a written explanation of what could be seen. Baldessari visited each location according to where the letters of the word 'California' were on a map. He then arranged objects in

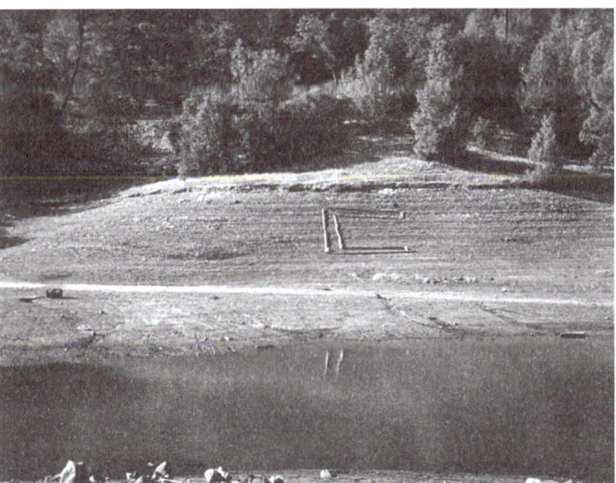

CALIFORNIA MAP PROJECT

PART I: CALIFORNIA

The following are photographs of letters that spell CALIFORNIA and of the map used for locating the site for each letter. The letters vary in scale from 1" to approximately 100'; and in materials used. The letters are located as nearly as possible within the area occupied by the letters on the map.

C. Off Jones Valley Road. 9 miles from Hiway 299 leading from Redding. On bank of finger of Shasta Lake.
Materials: Found logs.

A. On road to Paradise. 7 miles from intersection of Paradise Road and Hiway 99 (near Chico).
Materials: paint on rock.

L. 3.6 miles from Newcastle on California 193.
Materials: telephone pole and faked shadow.

I. 5 miles from San Andreas on Hiway 49. Near Angel's Camp.
Materials: Non-toxic color in creek.

F. Ben Hur Road. South of Mariposa. 3.4 miles from California 49.
Materials: scattered bits of red cloth.

O. 3.4 miles on Reed Road from junction 180. Near Minkler.
Materials: red yarn.

R. 14 miles north of Kernville in Sequoia National Forrest. In Kern River.
Materials: Found rocks.

N. 4.10 miles from Hiway 395 on Death Valley Road. .6 miles on south side of road.
Materials: rocks and dry color.

I. Outside Lucerne. 11.8 miles from Lucerne fire station. 2 miles off Old Womans Spring Road. Turn at sign reading Partin Limestone Products.
Materials: white dry color. (The letter is nearly invisible).

A. In Joshua Tree National Monument. 15 miles from Twenty nine Palms Visitor Center on road to Cottonwood.
Materials: dry color, rocks, dessert wildflower seed.

John Baldessari
George Nicolaidis
September, 1969

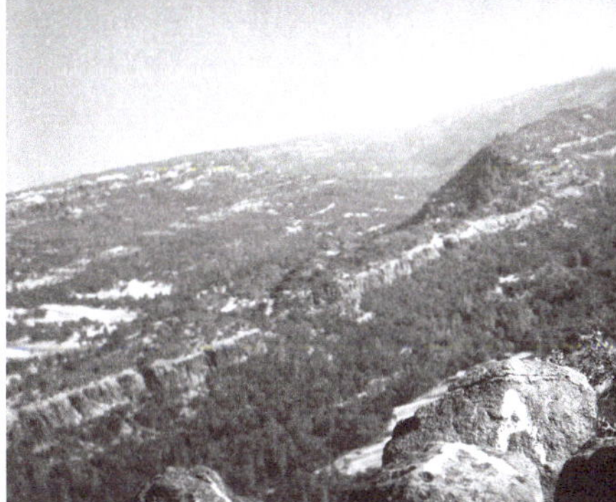

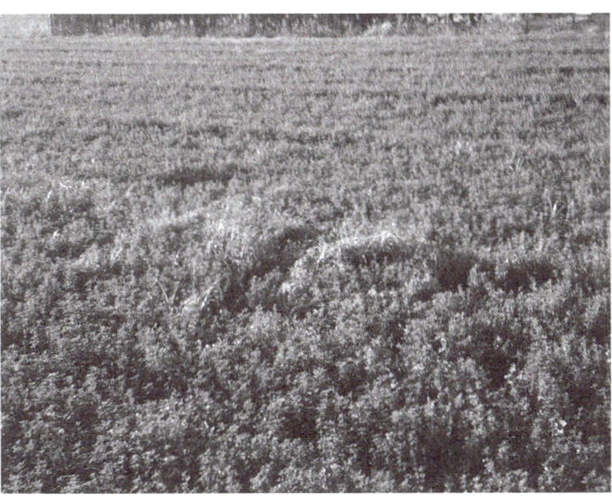

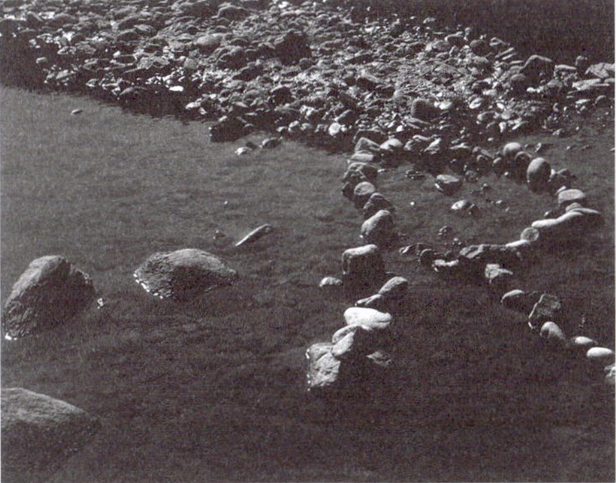

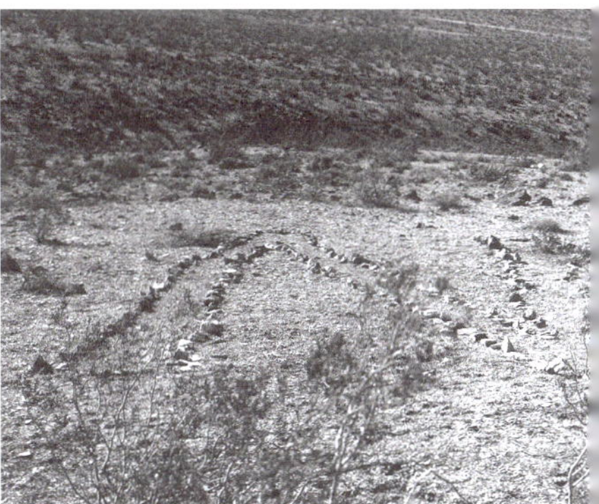

WHAT IS PAINTING

DO YOU SENSE HOW ALL THE PARTS OF A GOOD PICTURE ARE INVOLVED WITH EACH OTHER, NOT JUST PLACED SIDE BY SIDE ? ART IS A CREATION FOR THE EYE AND CAN ONLY BE HINTED AT WITH WORDS.

COMPOSING ON A CANVAS.

STUDY THE COMPOSITION OF PAINTINGS. ASK YOURSELF QUESTIONS WHEN STANDING IN FRONT OF A WELL COMPOSED PICTURE. WHAT FORMAT IS USED ? WHAT IS THE PROPORTION OF HEIGHT TO WIDTH ? WHAT IS THE CENTRAL OBJECT ? WHERE IS IT SITUATED ? HOW IS IT RELATED TO THE FORMAT ? WHAT ARE THE MAIN DIRECTIONAL FORCES ? THE MINOR ONES ? HOW ARE THE SHADES OF DARK AND LIGHT DISTRIBUTED ? WHERE ARE THE DARK SPOTS CONCENTRATED ? THE LIGHT SPOTS ? HOW ARE THE EDGES OF THE PICTURE DRAWN INTO THE PICTURE ITSELF ? ANSWER THESE QUESTIONS FOR YOURSELF WHILE LOOKING AT A FAIRLY UNCOM - PLICATED PICTURE.

PAINTING AND DRAWING

THIS PAINTING CONTAINS ALL THE INFORMATION NEEDED BY THE ART STUDENT. TOLD SIMPLY AND EXPERTLY BY A SUCCESSFUL, PRACTICING PAINTER AND TEACHER, EVERY PHASE OF DRAWING AND PAINTING IS FULLY COVERED.

the shape of those letters back into their respective physical locations, before photographing them. In playfully colliding two different sign systems, we see Baldessari's evident tendency towards conceptual art. We see the privileging of the idea behind the project over the final execution or result.

The development of ideas behind his previous works, however, finally led to the *Cremation Project*, which marks the culmination of the prehistory of *I Will Not Make Any More Boring Art*.

This spread, from top left to bottom right:
John Baldessari, *What is Painting* (1966–68).
John Baldessari, *Composing on a Canvas* (1966–68).
John Baldessari, *Painting and Drawing* (1966–68).
John Baldessari, *California Map Project, Part 1: California* (1969).
Next page, from top left to bottom right:
John Baldessari, *Commissioned Painting: A Painting by Anita Storck* (1969).
John Baldessari, *Commissioned Painting: A Painting by Pat Perdue* (1969).
John Baldessari, *Commissioned Painting: A Painting by Jane Moore* (1969).
John Baldessari, *Commissioned Painting: A Painting by George Walker* (1969)
John Baldessari, *Commissioned Painting: A Painting by Elmire Bourke* (1969).
John Baldessari, *Commissioned Painting: A Painting by Dante Guido* (1969).

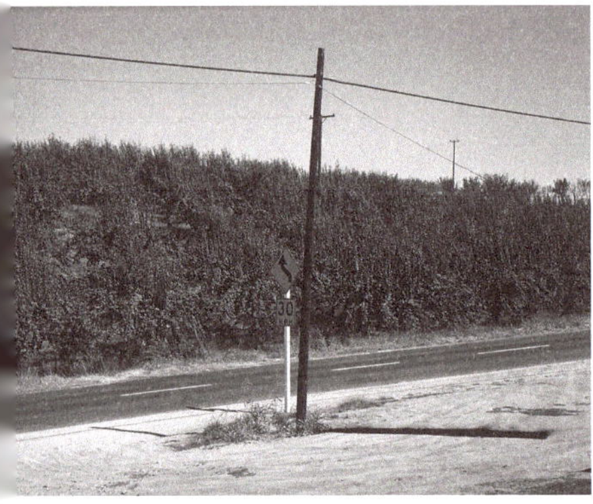
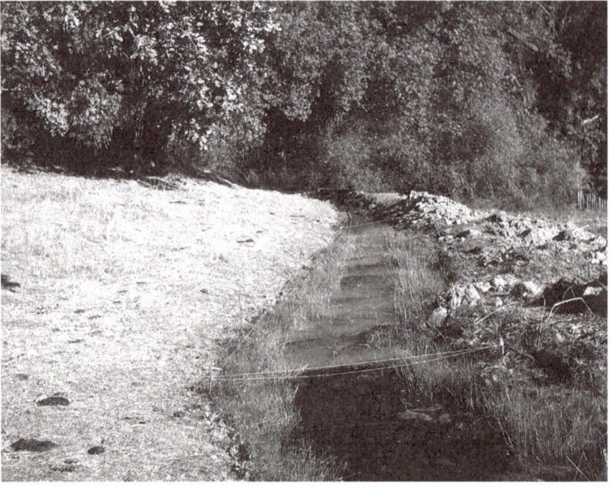
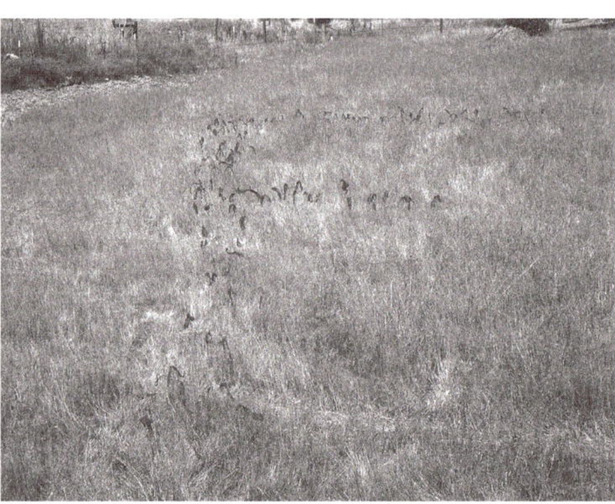
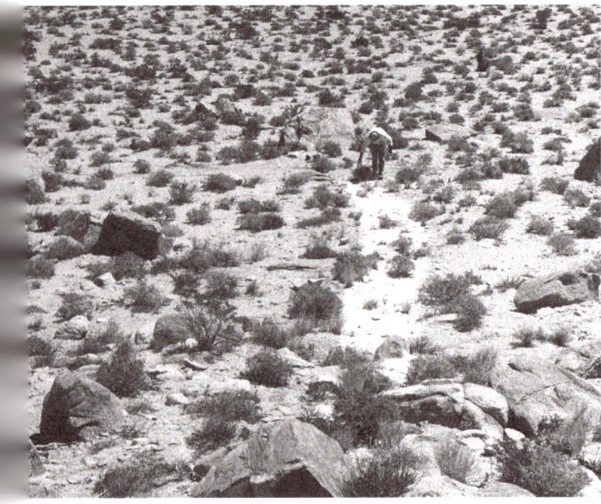
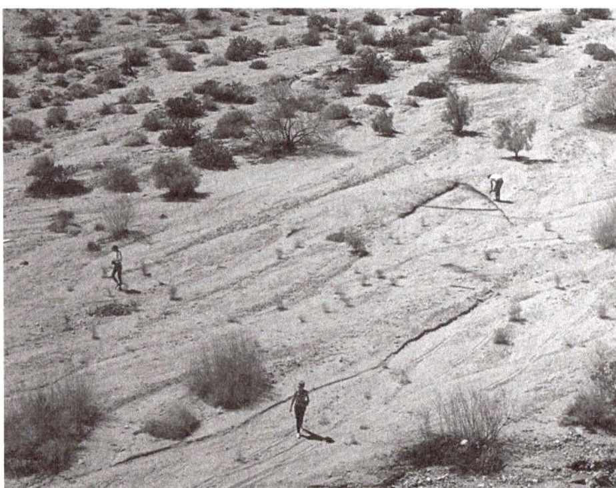
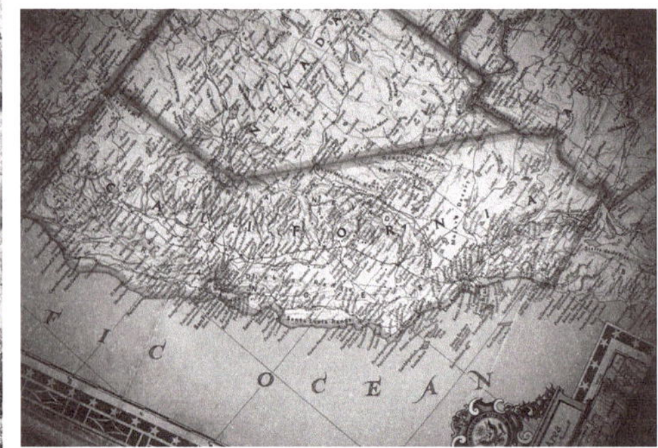

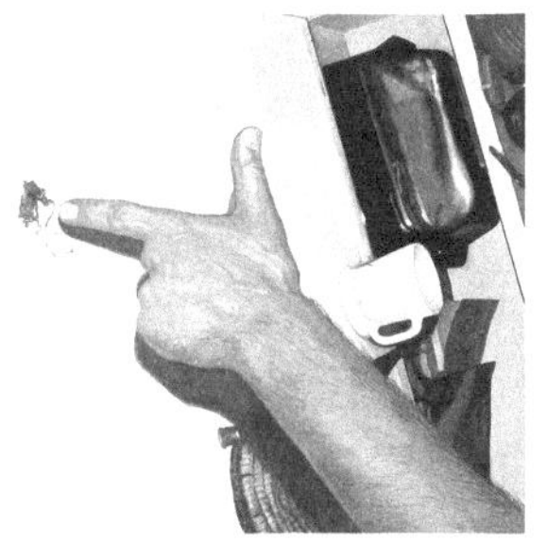

A PAINTING BY ANITA STORCK

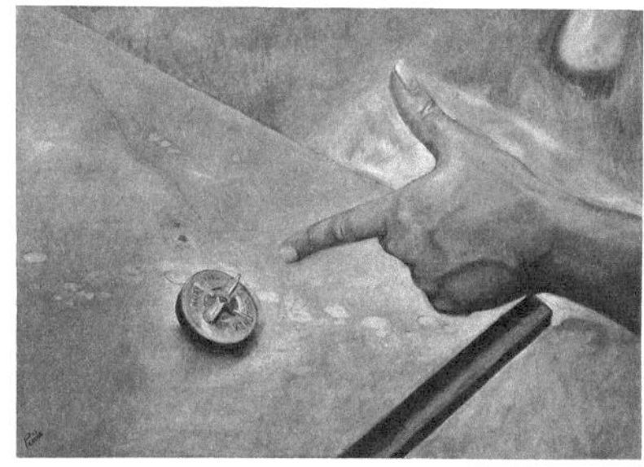

A PAINTING BY PAT PERDUE

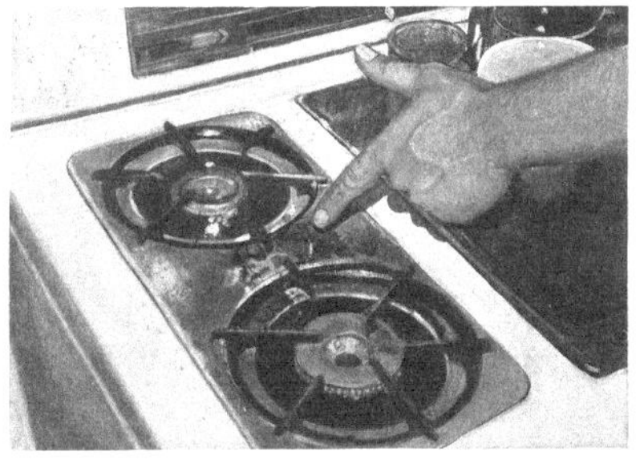

A PAINTING BY JANE MOORE

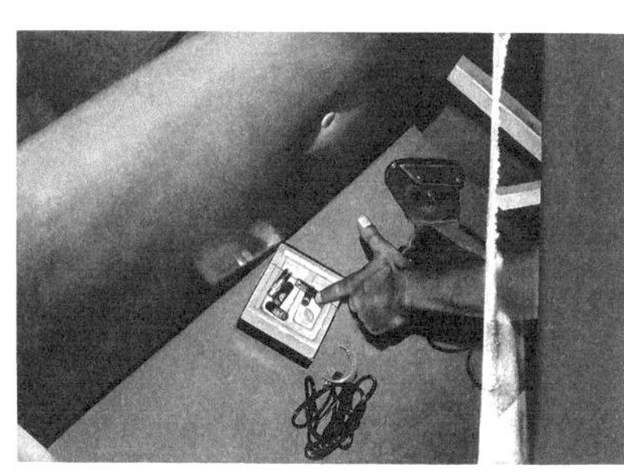

A PAINTING BY GEORGE WALKER

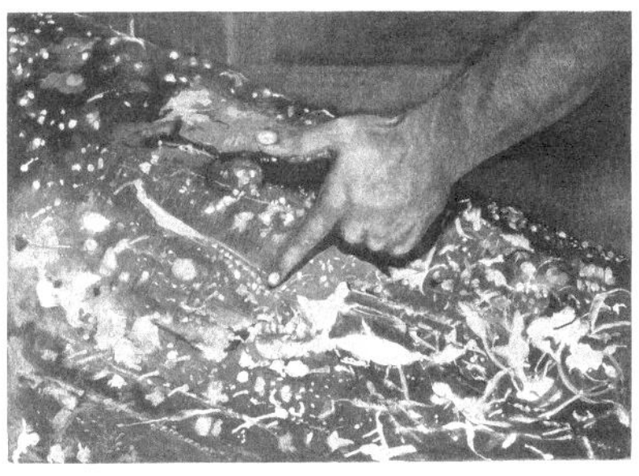

A PAINTING BY ELMIRE BOURKE

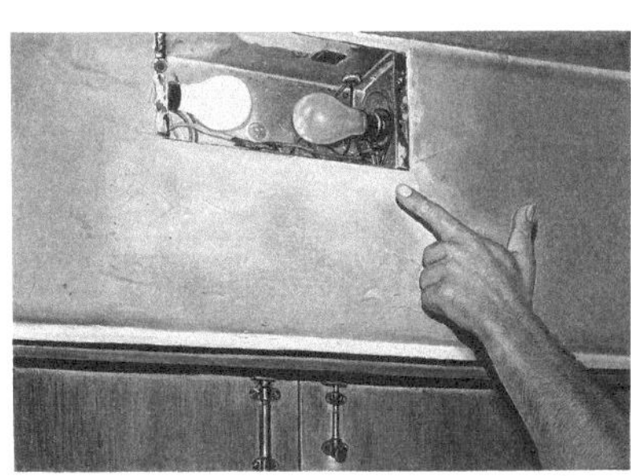

A PAINTING BY DANTE GUIDO

CREMATION PROJECT

In 1970, Baldessari caused quite a stir with the *Cremation Project*. He staged a public burning of all his previous work, as long as they were still in his possession. These were primarily landscape paintings and abstractions. The ashes of the paintings were then baked into biscuits and placed into an urn, which became part of the art installation, as well as a bronze sign inscribed with the life data of the destroyed paintings and the biscuit recipe.

This is where, through the act of destruction, Baldessari most clearly and decisively breaks with his previous approach to art making.

INTERIM CONCLUSION

The aforementioned works, as well as his teaching and intention, are united by the attempt to approach art in a new and radical way. Through Baldessari's non-compliance with previously valid formal rules, as well as through his often-ironic approach and use of banal, everyday moments, he begins to create a new concept of art. Until *Cremation Project*, Baldessari remained somewhat faithful to the canvas or flat image, which retained its direct relation to the visual arts. It was not until after *Cremation Project* that Baldessari devoted himself entirely to conceptual art, which for the most part also declared the materiality of the canvas superfluous.

California Institute of the Arts
7500 Glenoaks Boulevard
Burbank, California
91504

Bulletin 1971-1972

CALARTS BULLETIN
1971–72

4.

CONCEPT

California Institute of the Arts initiated its innovative program in October 1970. We now prepare for our second year and the inauguration of our new campus in Valencia, California.

More than a professional school, California Institute of the Arts is a community with a new concept. Our students are accepted as artists. We assume they have come to develop the talents they bring. They are treated accordingly and are encouraged in the independence that this implies.

The Institute consists of six schools: Art, Design, Music, Theater and Dance, Film and Critical Studies. About 300 new enrollments will be added in 1971-72 to the current year's registration of 630, including first-year as well as transfer and graduate students. By 1973, the maximum enrollment will be 1,500.

Instruction proceeds according to preparation and need. There is no fixed curriculum which is why this bulletin does not list courses in a conventional way. The emphasis is on projects or individual work under faculty guidance. Naturally, some programs, like theater or orchestral ensembles require collective scheduling; and so methodology varies with purpose. The work itself guides what is studied. Classes and lectures revolve around workshops and playing spaces so that craft informs knowledge and knowledge works its way into craft. The training program is thought of as a context of experience in which solutions to real problems can be discovered. The Institute is a laboratory and a performance center. Students and faculty perform as collaborators.

There are no grades. Progress is measured as it is in the arts themselves: by what's done as it's done, with evaluation an organic aspect of the process. Continuance in the programs depends on demonstrated ability. Whatever the work is, it will be rigorous. Interaction among the members of the schools is fundamental to the Institute which is a complex of workshops, galleries, studios and performing areas of extraordinary versatility. Faculty resources of all schools are available to all schools. Physical facilities are accessible as respective school priorities and accumulation of projects permit. In addition to the interdisciplinary nature of the programs, there are also special environments to be explored and activated by the students: a multi-media, an audio-visual library and data bank, and an inter-media book store and coffee shop where films will be shown, music played, art exhibited, theater events staged, political strategies planned, poetry written, magazines designed and published. These are conceived not as peripheral areas of student activity but as vital extensions of the programs.

As a community of the arts, the Institute has no intention of being hermetic. Its immediate concerns extend to the environment of the new city in which it is being built and to the surrounding megalopolis. Research and performance move into the wider community and beyond it, for the most basic commitment of the Institute, in a radically changing time, is to the development of artists with singular gifts, willing to risk private vision in the urgencies of our common life.

- - -

SCHOOL OF ART

A basic assumption of the School of Art is that from the day he enters, the student is an artist. How he proceeds depends on where he is: that means emotionally and technically, and includes the quality of his visual ideas.

This promotional document introduces the art school's basic educational principles, the concepts of each department, as well as the application and evaluation processes for the upcoming academic year (1971–72) at CalArts's new campus in Valencia.

5.

Instruction bears upon his capacity for image-making and opens up resources he requires or of which he is unaware, including his own.

If his need is to represent an object on canvas or to project one in space, he will investigate systems of seeing for an anchoring line. If, like Marcel Duchamp or some of the newest work, he is already questioning the validity of the retina and the entire visual basis of art, he will have defined for himself another field of inquiry. The same is true of technology or the most minimal art. Never mind that the form is unnameable. What is there that was never there before? And what are we to make of it, if anything at all? The questions will not be turned aside, nor what comes of them dismissed.

Thus, study begins with a period in which the student confronts himself with what he wants to do; at the end there will be an inventory of needs. Disciplines follow according to need. The student is assigned working space in well-equipped shops. He is not merely floating from class to class. His responsibility is to himself and his work, and to the acquisition of skills to sustain this responsibility. He works under the supervision of professional artists in painting, sculpture, graphics, structural principles, stage design, technology projects, environments, happenings and techniques yet to be named. Faculty and assistants are available for consultation. In the shops are craftsmen who can teach him what he requires for a specific project, whether to wire a circuit for a photoelectric cell or to enlist the properties of styrofoam. What the student sees around him may bring him back to his own work with his problem better defined or with another motive entirely.

The same is true of art history and theory in which the study of past and present develops critical awareness with which to measure progress. Where materials come in, or drawing or anatomical study or geometry, they are played off the student's intuition and may surprisingly arouse them. A material or a method is not an imposition but an experiential risk.

In that uncatalogued no-man's land between the collage and the Happening, divisions between painting and sculpture are dissolving into history. Some artists, defying the pressures of the modern, will want to reclaim the distinctions from the vanishing point. They will need every skill and insight that history can offer. Others, absolutely committed to the present, may want to work with 254 pieces of grey felt, or with fiberglass and epoxy, or with resin dye in acrylic lacquer on a plexiglass cylinder of distilled water. Well and good. If there is already a <u>tradition</u> of the New, what we will be after is a <u>discipline</u> of the New, open to the unpredictable and taking energy from doubt.

- - -

SCHOOL OF DESIGN

A character in a Russian play said, "If trees were planted all over Russia, more graceful people would walk under them." Since it's not very likely that will happen immediately in either Russia or America, a program in design must begin by asking questions about reasonable alternatives. The omnipresence of technology is not reversible; the problem is one of consciousness. If objects are not events of nature, how can they be human objects? If man-made things

STUDENT EXPERIENCE REPORTS

California Institute of the Arts does not "grade" its students. It asks them to appraise their own work, and helps them to do so.

During his stay at the Institute, the student develops an Experience File, making entries at least once each term, though he is free to file reports, observations or examples of his work at any time. At least once each term his file is "validated" by his mentor. The dean of the student's school, fellow students and teachers may also contribute their opinions, observations and judgments to a student's file.

At the end of his stay at the Institute, a student examines his file, and with the assistance of his mentor and an Institute "exit officer", creates a record of his experience at the Institute. This record, or "curriculum vita", is certified by the Institute. The student may use it to present himself and to verify his professional abilities.

The student primarily is responsible for creating his own file by recording each significant learning experience or project. He can do so in whatever form he likes, or use a Student Experience Report Form available from the Registrar's office. Appropriate for inclusion in his file are examples of his works (or slides, photographs, tapes, or films).

Each student is assigned to a mentor whose responsibility is to keep track of his work and activities. This assignment is made by the dean of the student's school. During his stay at the Institute the student is likely to be assigned to a number of mentors, but only one mentor is responsible for the student at a particular time. A request for a change of mentor may be made at the beginning of each term; the final decision is the dean's.

Whenever he completes an experience report, the student shows it to the mentor, who may simply acknowledge it, comment, or appraise the project and the student's work.

The student deposits the validated report in the registrar's office. The registrar will make a copy for the office of the student's dean and retain the master Experience File. The student or his dean may have access to the file without permission, and the dean may designate another person to examine the file (usually a mentor). Others who wish to see the file must obtain the student's or his dean's permission.

The registrar will remind the student to file at least one Experience Report each term. Candidates for a degree will not be enrolled for the following term if an Experience Report has not been filed for the previous term. This requirement arises from obligations the Institute has as an accredited college. The Experience Report of a degree candidate must describe his work in the School of Critical Studies and his projects and achievements in his own School. If he is enrolled in the School of Critical Studies, his report must cover his work in other schools.

THE SHIFT FROM RADICAL PEDAGOGY: CONCEPTUAL AND STRUCTURAL UPHEAVALS

DISSATISFACTION

The radical pedagogy of the California Institute of the Arts (CalArts) diametrically opposed the idea of Walt Disney, whose productions were oriented towards illusion, illusory worlds, and dream worlds. Some CalArts members and teachers therefore regarded the intervention in reality as a threat to fundraising efforts. In 1971 Herbert Blau, the Dean of Theater, argued that "the faculty must be better structured to reflect more of a distinction between student and faculty," and that "a better definition of competence, eligibility, and progress must be established."[1] He further proposed that "separate programs … be introduced for students who are capable of directing themselves and those students who need more specific guidance."[2] Other faculty members name "great dissatisfaction with the chaotic situation of the past year" and advocate for more pragmatism and "programs and degrees—their content and what they represent."[3]

DISNEY'S INFLUENCE

Although Disney donated more than 30 million dollars to the school shortly after the founding of CalArts, the art school soon found itself in financial

difficulties. Much of the subsidy was used to finance the building, which was more expensive than originally planned due to the workshops, workrooms, and extensive technical equipment. Robert W. Corrigan, President of CalArts, and Herbert Blau, Dean of Theater, fought against their own dismissal shortly after the opening of the art school, insisting that the contracts could not be extended or terminated by Disney Corporation alone, but only after the board of trustees had voted. As the board refused to support this, Corrigan was immediately suspended by Roy Disney. At the end of 1972, Blau was also ousted from the school's management—two years after the opening of CalArts. The faculty was then reduced in size and numerous contracts were cancelled or terminated.[4]

THE TROUBLE WITH UTOPIA

After a short episode with Walt Disney's son-in-law Bill Lund at the helm, CalArts got a new president in 1975: Robert Fitzpatrick's task was to ensure the financial solvency of the art school and to "make 'all the divisions separate.'"[5] In the strategic (re)orientation of CalArts, he showed little respect for its founding vision. In an interview in 1983 he says: "The

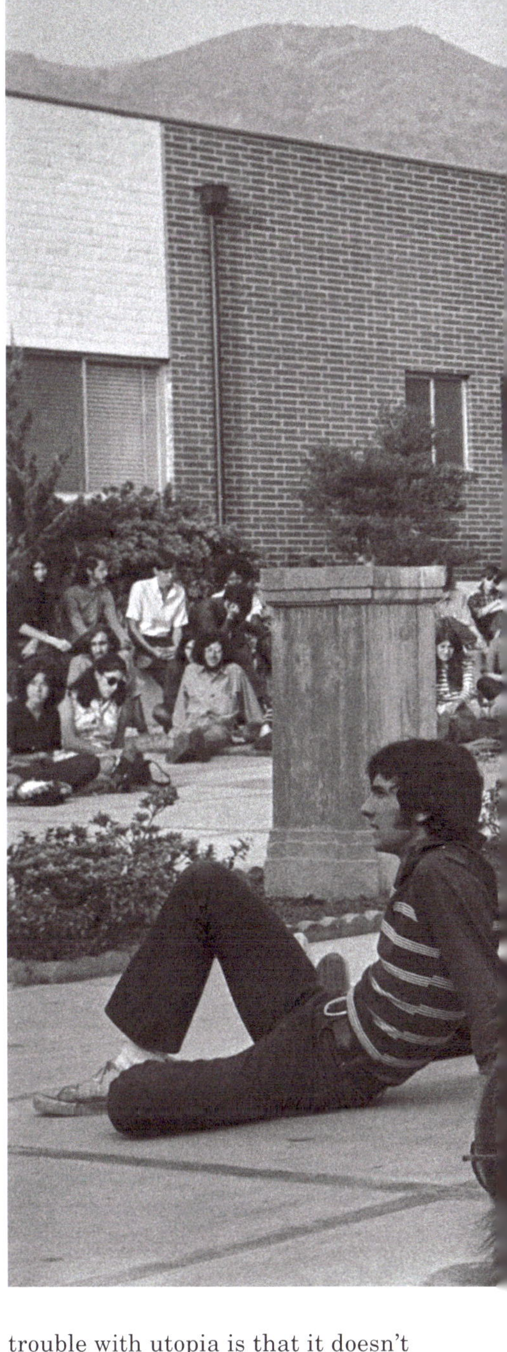

trouble with utopia is that it doesn't exist." In his statements it becomes clear how much his ideas deviated from the original idea of CalArts: "And then there was this dream of the perfect place for the arts, with all the disciplines beautifully mingling, every filmmaker composing symphonies, every actor a perfect graphic artist. Sure, it's a great idea as far as it goes. But nobody noticed that each of the arts has its own pace, its own rhythm, and its own demands."[6]

What is missing from Fitzpatrick's vision is a reference to CalArts's original conception that the school is

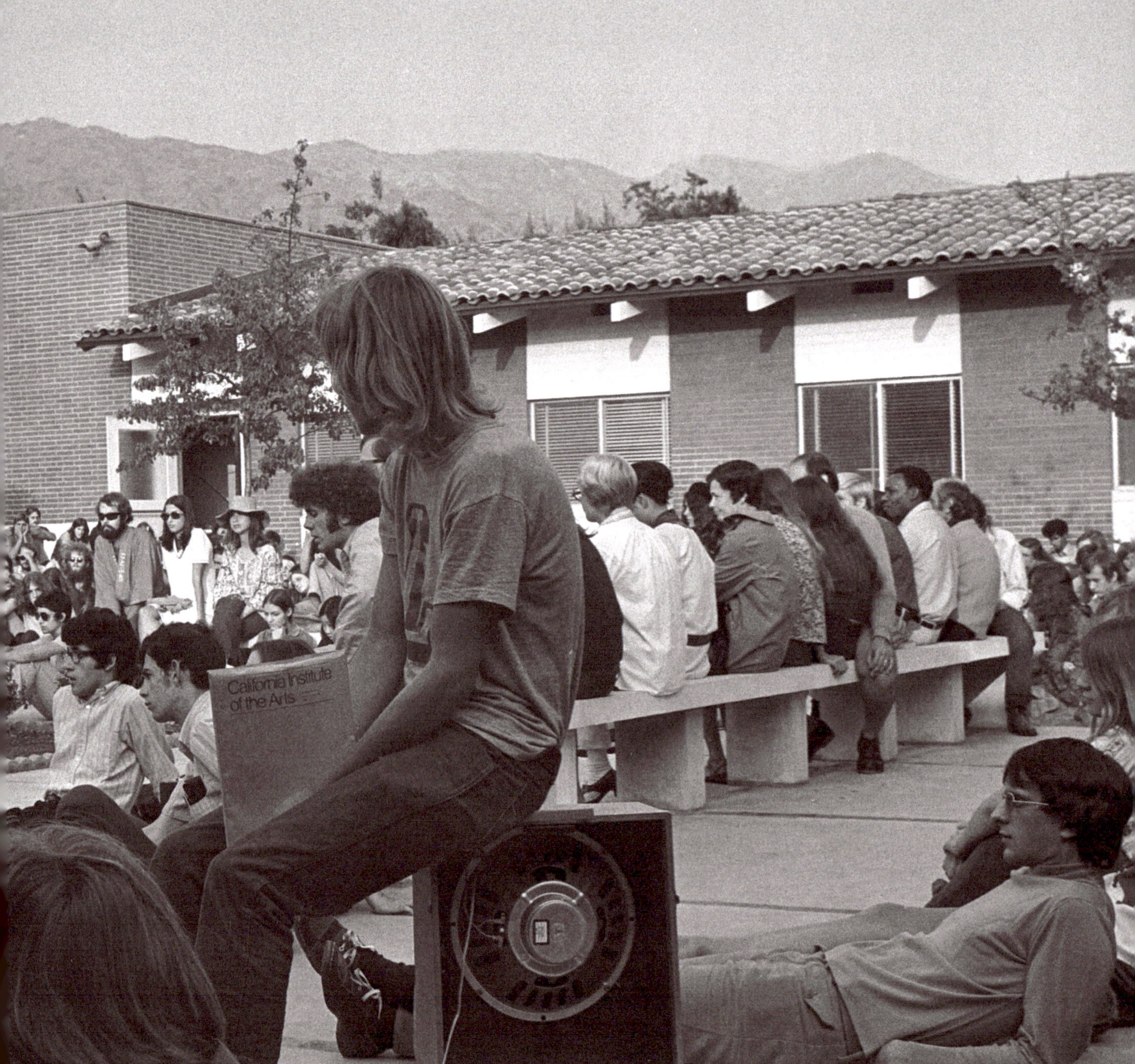

not just a place for the arts, but an ideal community shaped by the arts. In the first years after its founding, CalArts was not just a school, but a community in which students and teachers worked together and created artistic processes, explored environments together, and created new art spaces.[7] At the same time, there was no strict separation between disciplines and art movements. All the arts, experiences, observations, and personalities were interconnected and cumulated to form a 'Gesamtkunstwerk,' a self-organizing art process. This approach came to an abrupt end with the change of university management. CalArts developed into a school with grades, a structured timetable, and specific teaching requirements for each class. Nevertheless, by focusing on excursions and project-based learning, the initial investment in a new, radical pedagogy remained.   TD

Opening Day at Burbank (1970).

JOHN BALDESSARI AND THE DISSOLUTION OF THE TEACHER-STUDENT RELATIONSHIP

By Leonie Hahn

"I don't teach art.
I'm an art doctor."[1]
—John Baldessari

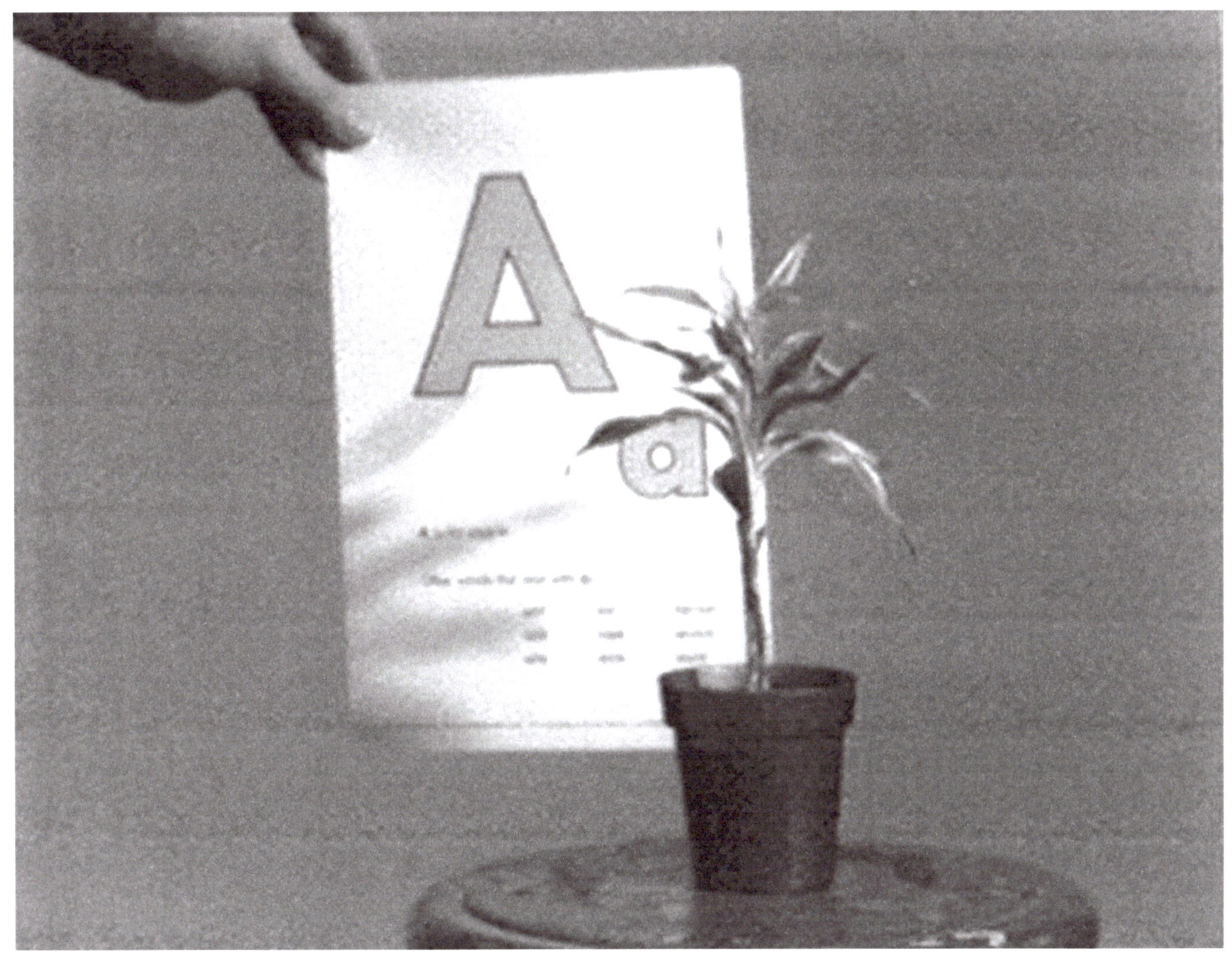

A round stool, a houseplant, a grey background. A hand holds cards behind the plant. They each show a letter of the alphabet, in lower- and upper-case. John Baldessari's voice reads the letter on the card out loud and repeats it mechanically. *Teaching a Plant the Alphabet* is the title of this analog video work from 1972.[2] The plant is supposed to learn the alphabet, much like Beuys's dead hare, to whom an exhibition was explained. Baldessari repeats every single letter at least 20 times with a monotonous voice and is consistent in his execution. The plant shows no reaction, it remains motionless on the stool. In his 18-minute clip, Baldessari visualizes the absurdity of the stereotypical teaching method of frontal teaching, which does not correspond to his own at all, in a dry and humorous manner.

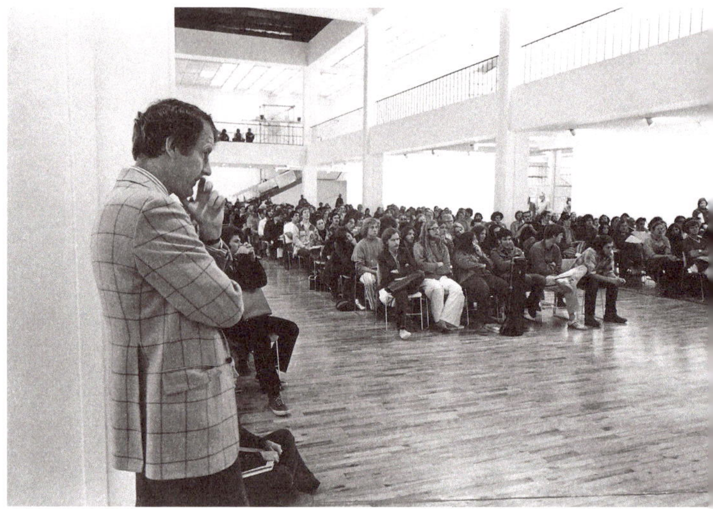

THE CALARTS METHOD

Two years earlier, in 1970, John Baldessari was appointed to teach painting at the California Institute of the Arts (CalArts). Robert W. Corrigan, co-founder of the renowned Tisch Institute at New York University, had been the first president of the new CalArts location in Valencia (CA) since 1968 (until 1972), with the vision of establishing a free art academy. This claim collided with that of the founding Disney family, who envisioned a school that was more conducive to the entertainment market. Corrigan, however, imagined the faculty more as a community of artists than as a school structure: "We're a community of artists here, some of us called faculty and some called students."[3]

John Baldessari accepted this teaching position, partly in order to be able to finance himself. He quickly understood that the professorship would not merely be another ordinary teaching job, but that teaching at CalArts would not disturb his own art production and that it could even benefit from it: "It was the closest thing to making art, I mean teaching art."[4]

A new approach would be created. As Baldessari states, "I really did think that CalArts was going to be the new Black Mountain College. I thought it was complete chaos at the time, but looking back, there was a great amount of order to it. Somehow something happened that was right."[5]

In the year of his appointment, Baldessari burned all his paintings as part of his *Cremation Project*, making a break with the past. As a result, he felt out of place in his new position as a teacher of painting classes. He constructed a new concept for his seminar. Carl André, a sculptor friend of his, brought him to the term 'Post-Studio:' "[I]t seemed to be more broadly inclusive, that it would just sort of indicate people not daubing away at canvases or chipping away at stone, that there might be some other kind of class situation. And so I elected to use that."[6]

In his class, John Baldessari did not attempt to frame students, artists, or the 'art' itself and thus constantly infiltrated or parodied the classical concept of an art academy as a university institution, which could also be seen in his works created during his time at CalArts. There was no linear transfer of knowledge by the teaching staff. Baldessari instructed his students to venture into darkness on their own, to report what they see or experience, what they think about what they want to produce. "An attitude I tried to develop, was that you were an artist when you walked in the door."[7]

More than 25 years later, the French philosopher Jacques Rancière, in his book *The Ignorant Schoolmaster*, describes this method as essential to presuppose and establish an equality of intelligences and to abolish the teacher's knowledge advantage. Nevertheless, how does one create this equality within a university institution that actually institutionally secures the superiority of the teacher?

Opposite page: John Baldessari, *Teaching a Plant the Alphabet* (1972).
This page: Robert Corrigan and students (ca. 1971–72).

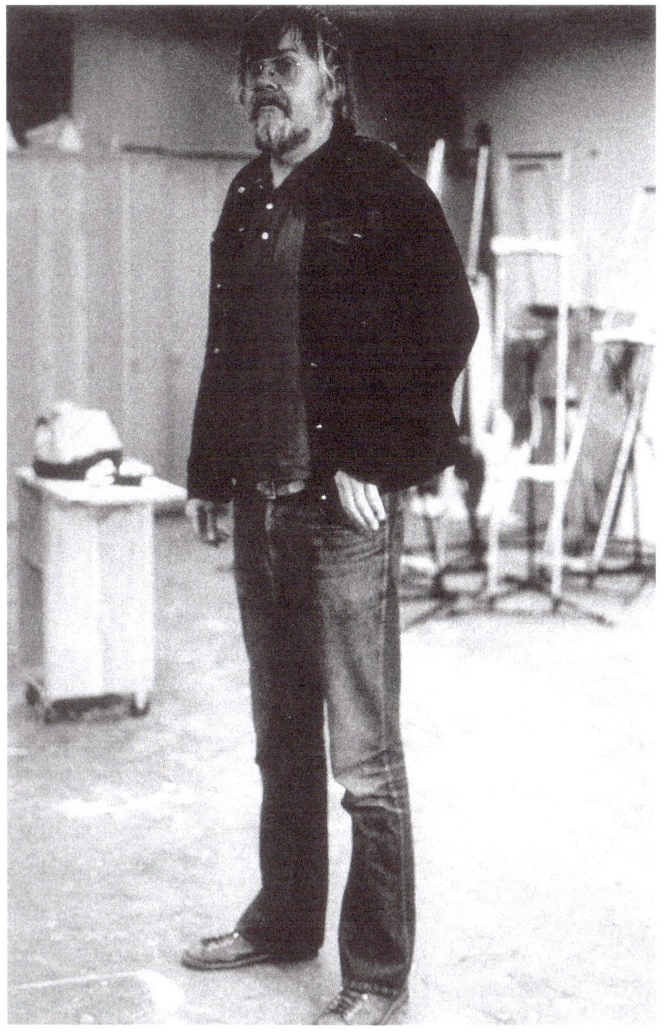

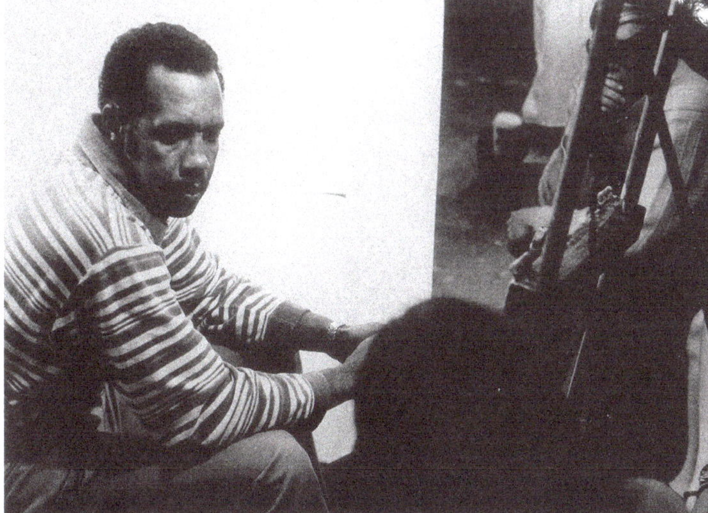

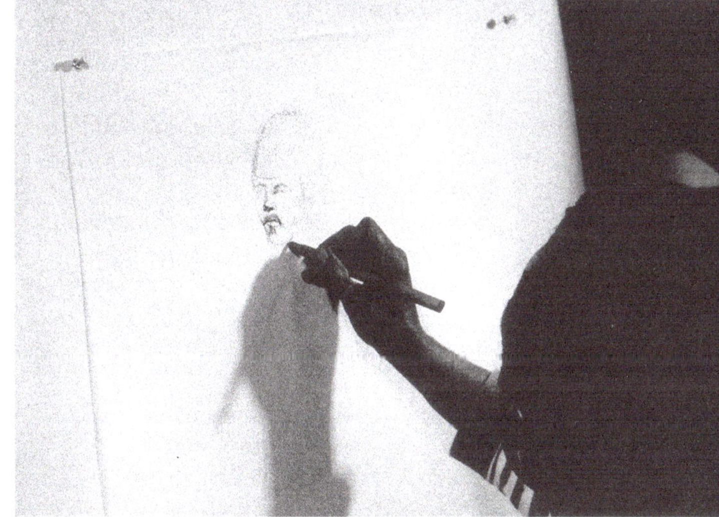

This page and opposite page: John Baldessari, *Police Drawing* (1971).

THE IGNORANT SCHOOLMASTER

In his 2007 book *The Ignorant Schoolmaster*, Jacques Rancière, after the 19th-century French educator Joseph Jacotot, sketches a pedagogical concept that not only questions the figure of the teacher, who tries to reduce the distance of knowledge between him and the student through the mediation of his knowledge, but also states that this is the only way to construct a radical abyss between the two. Rancière, rather, argues that each of these distances is a coincidental distance and that knowledge is not a quantity of knowledge but a position. Joseph Jacotot thus proposed that the 'teacher' should teach what he does not know. Therefore, in short, the teacher must not impart his knowledge, but rather encourage his students to reflect on, discuss, and interpret paintings, poems, or other prompts given by their teacher, and thus teach and emancipate themselves.

OUT OF THE STUDIO

John Baldessari's 'teaching' was no different from his art practice, which was never limited to one medium. Rather, he saw himself as an "art doctor" and the art of his students as patients: "Students come to me and say 'my art's sick,' and we help them make it well."[8]

It was also crucial that he wanted to learn as much from his teaching assignments as his students. He used the materials offered by the university and established his video practice. He gave the students situational prompts, which he then used again for his own works. This is how his famous *CalArts Post-Studio Art: Class Assignments (optional)* (1970) were created. His tasks included ideas for a project, drawing attention to triviality, reproduction, differences, change, etc. They contain instructions yet remain vague, asking a question or consisting of only two words: "36. Record all sensations, thoughts, for 1/2 hour on tape recorder," or "41. Photograph landscape in color. Make 8 × 10 color print. Make some color changes. Color landscape to match retouched photo. Color landscape to match photo. Rephoto," or "16. Given: $1. What art can you do for that amount?"

In 1971, John Baldessari entered an art class that did not know him. He set up a camera without comment, positioned it, and left the room. Then a police draughtsman entered the room and asked the students about the person they have just seen. He made a drawing that looked similar to Baldessari. The video work *Police Drawing* (1971) documents this performance. The idea for the piece was already formulated in his *CalArts Post-Studio Art: Class Assignments (optional)* from 1970: "8. Give police artist verbal description of Baldessari and have him do drawing. Perhaps everyone in class do verbal description."

Artistic as well as intellectual equality were foundational in the Post-Studio classroom, which also did not exist in a conventional form and was regularly abandoned. In practice, this meant, for example, inviting established artists to CalArts as guest lecturers or to the local pub, like Sol LeWitt, who didn't want to speak at an art school. Someone came by once or twice a week. "As students, we met absolutely everyone, from those who had just one eyeball above the dirt, basically, to some of the great masters,"[9] reports David Salle, artist and former student of Baldessari until 1975. Baldessari enabled his students further access to the international art scene by bringing catalogs from his and other exhibitions in Europe and New York City, long before they were reviewed in magazines, so that his "students had probably the quickest access to information of any art school in the US."[10]

Baldessari organized excursions to places that, at first glance, seemed to have no relation to art. They were chosen by the students throwing a dart arrow on a map of Los Angeles.

Wherever the arrow landed, they went and explored the place with photo and video cameras in an attempt to make art wherever one is: "Going into the things that introduced them to culture in the broadest sense, like going to Forest Lawn, or the Hollywood Wax Museum, or what have you. And a lot of times just anything to get out of the studio."[11]

The impact of Baldessari's teaching practice, which (almost entirely) dissolves the teacher-student relationship, has been so significant that it has been recently acknowledged by CalArts with the inauguration of the John Baldessari Studios. The building named after the famous artist pays tribute to his innovative pedagogical program initiated at the art school in 1970 that has produced some of the most famous contemporary artists. Even David Salle still stresses: "I have a kind of sideline career as a Baldessari scholar by now."[12]

"The teaching didn't stop when the day was over, class was over, or what have you."[13] —John Baldessari

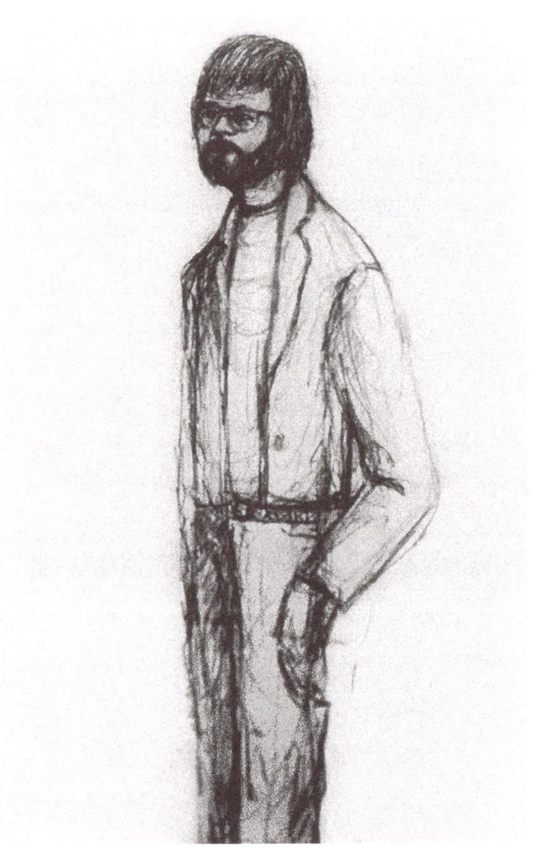

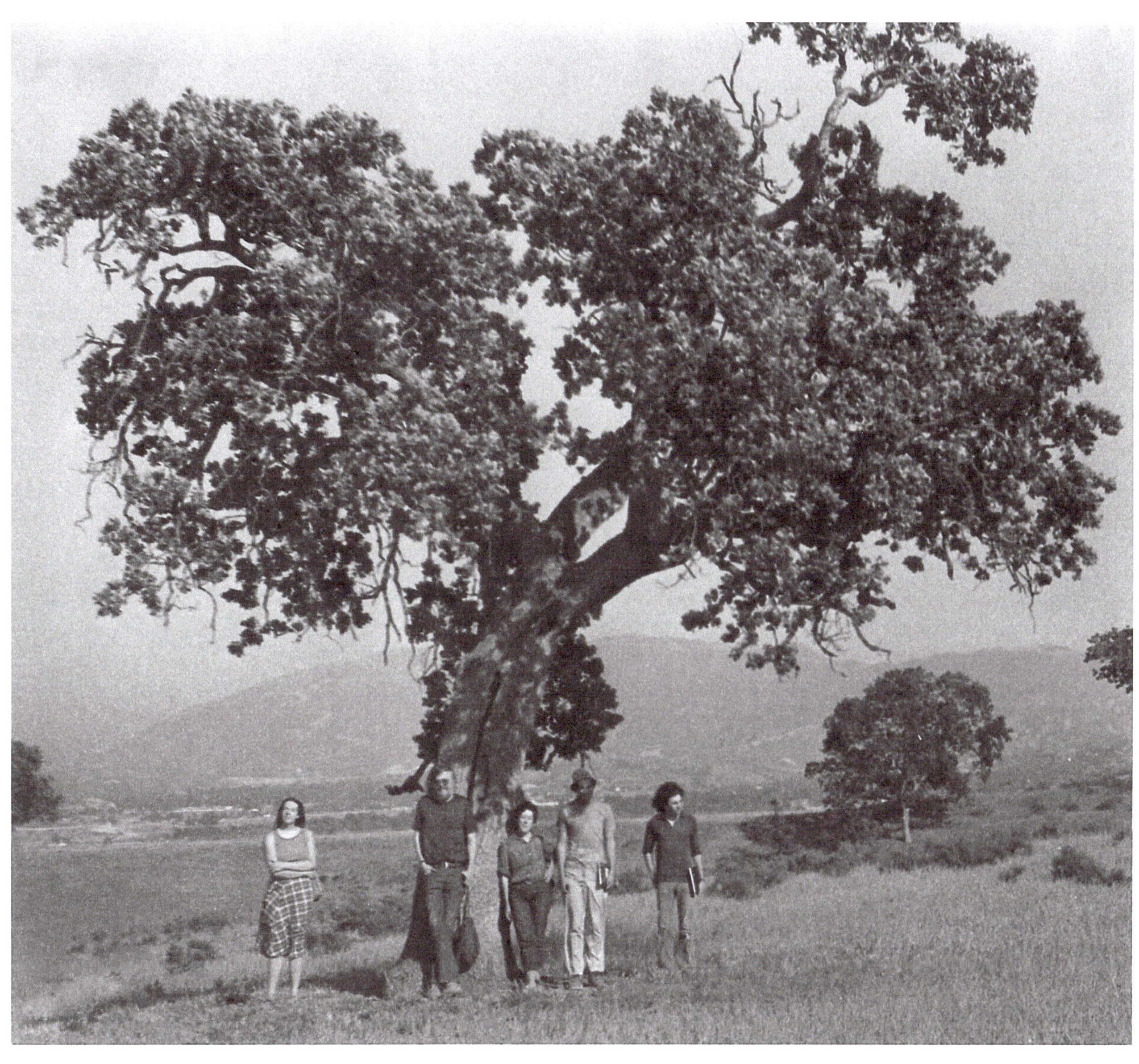

This page: John Baldessari and students (1974). Photo by James Welling.
Opposite page: John Baldessari, *Rolling: Tire* (1972).

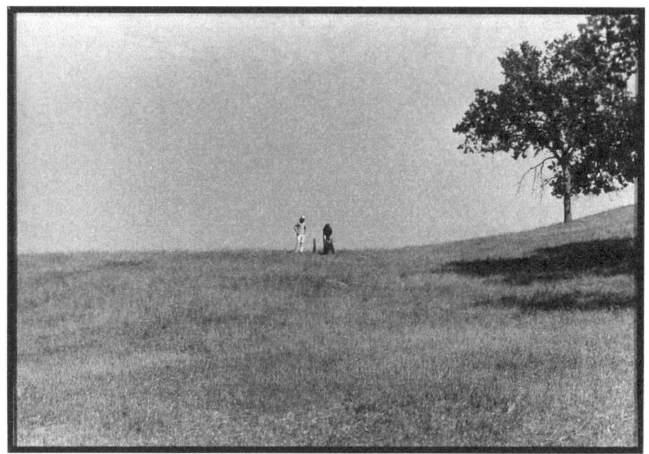

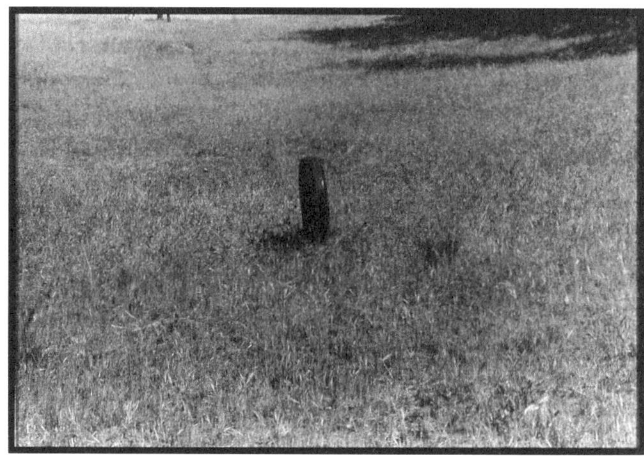

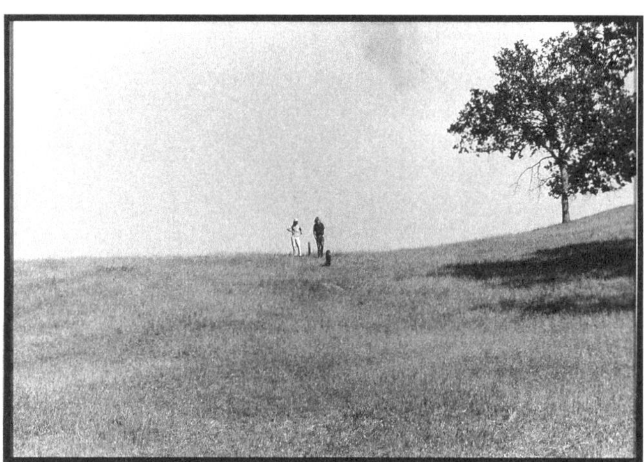

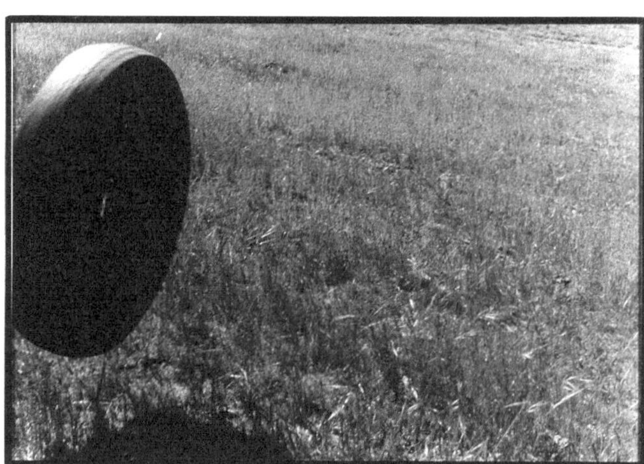

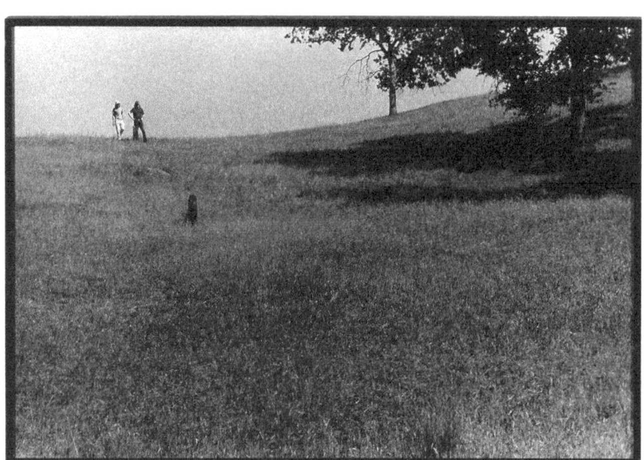

A free-rolling truck tire struck and killed a pedestrian in Delano, according to the California Highway Patrol. As Francisco Ramirez, 30, drove north on California 99, a tire came off his truck, crossed the north and southbound lanes, and hit Don Edwin Yarbrough, 21, of Denton, Tex., the CHP said. Yarbrough was reported dead at the scene.

1. Imitate Baldessari in actions and speech. Video.

2. Make up an art game. Structure a set of rules with which to play.
A physical game is not necessary; more important are the rules and
their structure. Do we in life operate by rules? Does all art?
OR ART RULES, LIKE TENANT RULES. OR ART VIOLATIONS

3. How can we prevent art boredom?

4. Write a list of art lies, un-truths that might be truthful if
we really thought about them. However consider this: Art truths
that we have often are boring in their correctness.

5. How can plants be used in art. Problem becomes how can we really
get people to look freshly at plants as if they've never noticed
them before. A few possibilities: 1. Arrange them alphabetically
like books on a shelf; 2. Plant them like popsicle trees (as in
child art) perpendicular to line of hill; 3. Include object among
plants that is camouflaged. *4 COLOR A PALM TREE PINK.*
5 PHOTO FOUND GROWING ARRANGEMENTS 6 OR A MOVIE ON HOW R *PLANT A PLANT*

6. How can gallery use be subverted, as in land art? Exchange locations
with another business? Photo gallery sq. ft. for sq. ft. and paste
up in another space? One way glass in front of gallery?

8. Give police artist verbal description of Baldessari and have him
do drawing. Perhaps everyone in class do verbal description.

9. Describe a neutral object completely with film and tape or video.
Do it until you have fully transferred all its qualities to the
medium. Perhaps better a class project in that more insights
would be available. *STEAL ITS QUALITIES.*

10. Create art from our procedures of learning. How does an infant
learn? How do we continue to learn. How do we learn speech?
To count? To know danger? Investigate Montessori methods, books
on learning and perception.

11. Do a tape recording of raw sounds and edit into a composition.

12. Make up a list of sound as art projects. (see sample).

13. How can a gallery space be used rather than put art objects into
it?

14. Two man film project. Each shoots up an amount of film. Ea.
edits the others fim. A film collage problem. Important that
the footage be "found".

15. Given: The availability of an airplane or helicopter for a
short time use, i.e., an hour. What would you do?

16. Given: $1. What art can you do for that amount?

17. Cooking art. Invent recipes. They are organizations of parts,
aren't they?

18. Subvert real systems. I.e., dial a number that records messages while the person is out and dial another number that gives recored messages. Put the two phones togehter. Put a sigh that says <u>slow</u> in the middle of a street. Get it?

19. What art can arise from magic and myth. Or just a magic trick on vidleo.

20. A sensory deprivation piece. A sensory overload piece.

21. Ecological guerilla art.

22. Disguise yourself as another object--a tree maybe. Or becoming a tree. A big bird? OR ANOTHER PERSON. BUY MAKE-UP,

23. What are the minute differences in things that are supposed to be the same? And vice versa. If you took 36 photos of a lawn, would they all be the same? Or of 36 sections of the same lawn? Or of a wall? Or 36 identical? nails (either, figner or kind you hammer).

24. Film loops or slides of all the objects one stares at in a given interval when in an arbitrarily chosen room. Or recorded on a tape recorder as one's eyes locks on them.

25. 36 slides from start to finish of simple motion like picking your nose, scatching your ass, and so on.

26. Slides of #24-projected in correct places in another (bare) room.

27. Wet and dry. I.e., how does wet gravel in a parking lot look next to another dry area. Perhaps as actual situation, where something would be constantly wetted.

28. Recreate sculpturally with other materials in a magic realist approach any 12" sq. area of earth land,. Perhaps better yet to keep your own aesth. out of it, would be to have another choose it for you.

29. Have some take a photo portrait of you just before you go into a store to steal something. Have your portrait taken immediately aafter the act. Photo the object stolen.

30. Design and have printed your calling card.

31. Steal the trash from Pres. Corrigan's wastebasket and make a collage of it.

32. Have yourself photographed in act of insulting a person. Do Repeat, each time insulting a new person.

33. Pay homage to a movie star, rock musician, etc. in form of a pilgrimage visit.. Photograph is required of the two of you with a personalized signed greeting by the culture hero. Or it could be to a famous person's grave. In this case a photo of you at the grave. Person's name on the gravestone should be visible. No signature necessary.

34. Defenestrate objects. Photo them in mid-air.

35. What kind of art can be done with real animals?

36. Record all sesations, thoughts, for ½ hr. on tape recorder.

37. What kind of works can be done literally under the earth.

38. Liquid works.

39. Chemical works.

40.. Biological works.

41. Photograph landscape in color. Make 8x10 color print. Make some color changes. Color landscape to match retouched photo. Color landscape to match photo. Rephoto.

42. Class make up list for scavenger hunt. Exhibit works at end of day.

43. Forgeries. Ea. in class tries to forge my signature on a check by looking at an orgginal. Or forgeries of forgeries of forgeries, etc.

44. Take any sentence of text to 6 signpainters to be lettered in letters of same style ad height. Study differences.

45. Punishment. Write "I will not make any more art"
"I will not make any more boring art"
" I will make good art"
(or something similar)

1000 times
om wall.

46. One, copies or make-up random captions, Another person takes photos. Match photos to captions.

47. Serial TV works. 25 ways to fold a hat, to comb your hair, 25 different people spitting.

48. Develop a visual code. Give it to another student to crack.

49. Disguize an object tp look like another object.

50. Do a film or TV script or scenario. Use TV layout paper.

51. A video tape that is a result of reading a book.. You give a book report in front of camera. *MAYBE E.T. HALL, THE HIDDEN DIMENSION.*

52. Smell pieces.

53. Touch pieces.

54. Art that you see by looking up↑or down↓.

55. How do we get eyes off the visual and into experience. Rent a service rather than an object from Yellow Pages.

56. Take a canvas stretcher, size of your choice, to an upolsterer and have it upolstered with fabric of your choice.

57. A piece that deals with measurement--up, down,right, left,etc. and where spectator is located.

58. Make up list of distractions that often occur to you. Recreate on video tape.

59. Make up art parables.

60. Edmund Scientific Catalog project. What art can you make by ordering from this catalog. Maybe grow plants chemically.

61. Hypnosis. Can art ideas be iplanted and removed in a mind?

62. A wall drawing based on numerous persons height--ea. marks his height on wall with line, signs name and date.

63. What art can arise from such phrases as; 1. Entasis, 2. Gestalt with some left over information, 3. Simple shape, simple experience, 4. Unitary form with reduced relationships, 5. Unitary form with line of fracture. Or, can pure informantion be art?

64. The structural movement of cameras as subject matter.

65. Performance pieces. I.E. Speak thru your hand to your thigh but not with your head. Or talk with your knees to something knee-high. Or what are your dog-like traits without imitating a dog. Or the delivery of a speech to an imaginary person in differente spaces in a room. Do a series of artificial voices. Can the various positions of the hand change the rsonance of the voice? Say "good morning" every morning into a tape recorder for the length of the tape. See Growtowski, Towadra Poor Theater.

66. A smapshot album of things to see in Los Angeles with exact locations so that others could locate sights (sites).

67. Document change, decay, metamorphosis, changes occuring in time. Photograph same thing at various times during day.

67. Do good and bad compositions (by photo) of same scene, objects. Frame a photo in viewfinder and move camera a foot to side before shooting.

68. Make up a list by looking at art books, talking to artists on things to avoid in making art. Do them. Ask yourself if results are good or bad art.

69. What art can come from the use of a set of walkie-talkie radios?

70. By using movie camera to follow actions and by your observations into cassete recorder, document the movements of someone secretly for an entire day. Or have someone follow you.

71. Photos are flat. Photograph flat surfaces. Maybe excange them.

72. Change, control, alter, arrange light in room environment.

73. Arte Povera. How much and what kind of art can you make from kleenex and masking tape, for instance.

74. A film, video tape, etc. that deals openly with a physical flaw of yours (in your estimation). A film called PIMPLE?

75. Information exchange. You wite letters to someone and they to you and so on. Framed letters of Refusal(I am sorry, but...), for instance. Or Thanks(Thank you for your ...blah, blah, etc.).

76. Random photos. End of, beginning of, roll photos. Camera sent up with pidgeon, balloon, given to another persons with shooting instructions, shooting from hip, etc. How do we avoid our good taste?

77. Using of time devices. Time clock(that prints time in and out), random time devices (red dot on cash register tape), a fuse, a candle.

78. Large scale art that can be seen in its entirety. For instance, if you dyed sheets ea. a separate color and arranged them checker board like, say a hundred or more, they could only be experienced by walking thru them, but they could be seen (also photoed) by helicopter or airplane.

79. Photograph backs of things, underneaths of things, extreme foreshortenings, uncharacteristic views. Or trace them.

80. Put labels on things that list their contents.

81. Design an art test.

82. Can one give and take away aesthetic content?

83. Street works, art determined by location. What would you do on top of a 30 story bldg.? What would you do under water?

84. Given $50. could you increase the sum in a period of time?

85. Describe the visual verbally and the verbal visually.

86. Film of, or video of, children's play activities--walking on a ledge, drawing a line in the dirt, etc.

87. Do a work of art by telephone. Or use TBA (John Collins).

88. An all word TV tape. Or a single word.

89. A real time movie or video tape. A steaming cup of coffee.

90. If photos come from reality, what kind of reality comes from photos? Reconstruct a photo three-dimensionally.

* INTERMISSION *

(We had just left #90.)

91. Scenarios. Do a movie form an existing, stock scenario. Or 1 person write scenario, another shoot movie. Or GRABBAG scenario-- everyone write 2-3 scenes, drop in box, someone pull out maybe 10 and they are shot in the order drawn out. Or everyone do their version of the grabag scenario.

92. Video tape of making sound effects.

93. Design a secret handshake (for our class members?).

94. Verbally describe a landscape instead of painting one.

95. A disjunctive work that is based on parts and not a whole, that is one see the parts and never the whole.

96. Prove a point as in a science fair diorama, display, tableau, such as, "How quickly does bread mould under certain conditions?", or "Is plant growth hampered by use of conditioned water?", "The effect of colored lights on plants", "Is untreated seaweed useful as fertilizer", "What effect does ultra Sonic vibrations have on plants?", "The effect of asperin on potato plants", "Why is a rainbow round?", "Do race, color, texture affect the strength of hair?", and etc.

97. Take the titles of any amateur art exhibit and illustrate them. For instance such titles as, Ah, Toro!, Autumn Leaves, Mexican Patterns, Xenogenisis #2, Xanadu, Wharf Enchantments, French Restaurant, Boat Patterns, blah, blah.

98. Repaired or patched art. Recyled. Find something broken and discarded. Perhaps in a thrift store. Mend it.

99. Art that requires the rental of a Service rather than an Object.

100. How does one react to a minor stress problem. Perhaps compare what he is thinking to his outward behavior.

101. Put new canvas over old paintings.

102. Composition based on the duration of say, one gal. of paint.

103. A 30 day continuous line on adding machine tape.

104. The shapes of shadows of well known people (or well known artists for a specific example).

105. Reversals. Be black, say things backwards, all while standing upside down. *THINK BACKWARD.*

106. Put make-up on dogs and other animals. On Trees and plants.

107. "If each of us were to confess his most secret desire, the one
that inspires all his plans, all his actions, he would say:
'I want to be praised.'" (E.M. Cioran). Do a piece that deals
with Praise as a theme. *BE PRAISED OFF CAMERA*

108. Photograph of umbrella and sewing machine on an operating
table. That's Surrealism isn't it?

109. Blow powdered color thru staw on drawing made with fat on
wall underground. That's cave art isn't it?

I THINK THAT'S THE CLOSEST YOU GET

JOHN BALDESSARI'S ASSIGNMENTS

John Baldessari states that "art can't be taught."[1] He illustrates this point in his video artwork *Teaching a Plant the Alphabet* (1972), in which he seemingly tries to teach a potted plant the alphabet with charts and monotonous repetition of each letter. Through parody, Baldessari critiques non-imaginative pedagogues with oppressive methods, especially regarding the education of future artists through a repetitive sequence of famous artists and their style.[2]

"Well, can art be taught at all? And, you know, I prefer to say, no, it can't. It can't be taught. You can set up a situation where art might happen, but I think that's the closest you get."[3] — John Baldessari

So, what was Baldessari's approach to teaching? In short, it is to set up situations "where art might happen."[4] He used so-called 'assignments' in his lessons. The Oxford Dictionary lists "duty," "task", or "errand" as synonyms,[5] consequently his choice of word in this instance can be associated with hierarchical and traditional work tasks—the 'assignment' is ironic.

His creative tasks or mental exercises refer to acting classes and self-help books, but show humorous twists such as "[w]rite a list of art lies, un-truths that might be truthful if we really thought about them" or "[g]ive police artist verbal description of Baldessari." Additionally, the assignments are multi- and cross-media which include photography, videography, creative writing, performance, and visual arts.

"… there was no curriculum. One didn't assign, let's say, class problems … and there was no reason for a student to stay in your class if he or she didn't want to," says Baldessari of the teaching conditions at CalArts.[6] The college pursued a democratic, interdisciplinary philosophy in the 1970s. Therefore, Baldessari—who was first employed as a teacher for painting, but had not painted for five years—was welcome to suggest a new lesson format, where students were not taught but "indicate[d]." He called it "Post-Studio," a term he attributed to the minimalist artist Carl André.[7]

After a short multimedia introduction to contemporary art, Baldessari organized artists' visits and "field trips"—"just anything to get out of the studio." Those were visits to "culture in the broadest sense" like the Hollywood Wax Museum or, more often, locations chosen at random by throwing a dart at a map.[8] The students took photo and video cameras and conducted spontaneous projects. For instance, one participant took

close-up shots of people's hair, since this "was the closest you could get to photographing their brain."[9]

In 2013, at the age of 83, Baldessari underlined once more that he never regarded the participants of his classes as students, but as "young artists,"[10] whose abilities could easily exceed his own later on.

"Well, if art can't be taught, maybe it would be a good idea to have people that call themselves artists around. And something, some chemistry, might happen. And then the third thing would be that to be as non-tradition-bound as possible, and just be very pragmatic, whatever works. You know, and if one thing doesn't work, try another thing."[11] — John Baldessari

I Will Not Make Any More Boring Art is an assignment by Baldessari from 1970 that became one of his most famous works. The Nova Scotia College of Art and Design (NSCAD) asked him to contribute an artwork to their exhibition, but could not offer sufficient compensation. Alternatively, he suggested a 'punishment piece,' in which the students from NSCAD had to write their plight to reform hundreds of times—just like students had to do back in the day on a blackboard. Over the course of the exhibition, the college students had to write 'I will not make any more boring art' on the gallery walls.

Through this act he is drawing parallels to Christian absolution. He adds, that if no scapegoat could be found, somebody should be paid with his wage.[12] In a humorous manner, he is once more criticizing the classical art teacher with his superior status that allows him to give orders even from a distance.[13]

In a later interview, Baldessari expressed surprise that, at the end of the exhibition, all of the gallery walls were covered according to his wishes. This seems to suggest that he succeeded in setting up—in his playful, ironic manner—a situation where art might happen.[14] JG

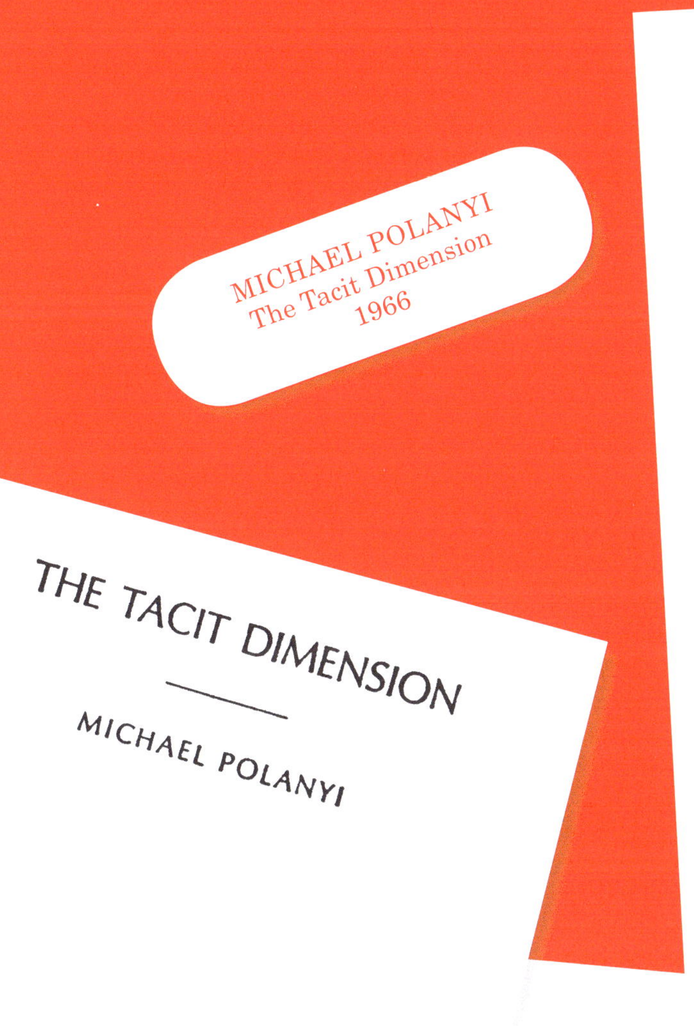

THE TACIT DIMENSION

power to thought and thus denied also any grounds for claiming freedom of thought.

I saw also that this self-immolation of the mind was actuated by powerful moral motives. The mechanical course of history was to bring universal justice. Scientific skepticism would trust only material necessity for achieving universal brotherhood. Skepticism and utopianism had thus fused into a new skeptical fanaticism.

It seemed to me then that our whole civilization was pervaded by the dissonance of an extreme critical lucidity and an intense moral conscience, and that this combination had generated both our tight-lipped modern revolutions and the tormented self-doubt of modern man outside revolutionary movements. So I resolved to inquire into the roots of this condition.

My search has led me to a novel idea of human knowledge from which a harmonious view of thought and existence, rooted in the universe, seems to emerge.

I shall reconsider human knowledge by starting from the fact that *we can know more than we can tell*. This fact seems obvious enough; but it is not easy to say exactly what it means. Take an example. We know a person's face, and can recognize it among a thousand, indeed among a million. Yet we usually cannot tell how we recognize a face we know. So most of this knowledge cannot be put into words. But the police have recently introduced a method by which we can communicate much of this knowledge. They have made a large collection of pictures showing a variety of noses, mouths, and other features. From these the witness selects the

4

definition"; and this philosophic expression conceals a gap to be bridged by an intelligent effort on the part of the person to whom we want to tell what the word means. Our message had left something behind that we could not tell, and its reception must rely on it that the person addressed will discover that which we have not been able to communicate.

Gestalt psychology has demonstrated that we may know a physiognomy by integrating our awareness of its particulars without being able to identify these particulars, and my analysis of knowledge is closely linked to this discovery of Gestalt psychology. But I shall attend to aspects of Gestalt which have been hitherto neglected. Gestalt psychology has assumed that perception of a physiognomy takes place through the spontaneous equilibration of its particulars impressed on the retina or on the brain. [...] looking at Gestalt, on the contrary, [...] shaping of experience [...] This shap[...]

particulars of the face he knows, and the pieces can then be put together to form a reasonably good likeness of the face. This may suggest that we can communicate, after all, our knowledge of a physiognomy, provided we are given adequate means for expressing ourselves. But the application of the police method does not change the fact that previous to it we did know more than we could tell at the time. Moreover, we can use the police method only by knowing how to match the features we remember with those in the collection, and we cannot tell how we do this. This very act of communication displays a knowledge that we cannot tell.

There are many other instances of the recognition of a characteristic physiognomy—some commonplace, others more technical—which have the same structure as the identification of a person. We recognize the moods of the human face, without being able to tell, except quite vaguely, by what signs we know it. At the universities great efforts are spent in practical classes to teach students to identify cases of diseases and specimens of rocks, of plants and animals. All descriptive sciences study physiognomies that cannot be fully described in words, nor even by pictures.

But can it not be argued, once more, that the possibility of teaching these appearances by practical exercises proves that we can tell our knowledge of them? The answer is that we can do so only by relying on the pupil's intelligent co-operation for catching the meaning of the demonstration. Indeed, the definition of a word denoting an external thing must ultimately rely on pointing at such a thing. This naming-cum-pointing is called "an ostensive

of a more intellectual and more practical kind; both the "*wissen*" and "*können*" of the Germans, or the "knowing what" and the "knowing how" of Gilbert Ryle. These two aspects of knowing have a similar structure and neither is ever present without the other. This is particularly clear in the art of diagnosing, which intimately combines skillful testing with expert observation. I shall always speak of "knowing," therefore, to cover both practical and theoretical knowledge. We can, accordingly, interpret the use of tools, of probes, and of pointers as further instances of the art of knowing, and may add to our list also the denotative use of language, as a kind of verbal pointing.

Perception, on which Gestalt psychology centered its attention, now appears as the most impoverished form of tacit knowing. As such it will be shown to form the bridge between the higher creative powers of man and the bodily processes which are prominent in the operations of perception.

Some recent psychological experiments have shown in isolation the principal mechanism by which knowledge is tacitly acquired. Many of you have heard of these experiments as revealing the diabolical machinery of hidden persuasion. Actually, they are but elementary demonstrations of the faculty by which we apprehend the relation between two events, both of which we know, but only one of which we can tell.

Following the example set by Lazarus and McCleary in 1949, psychologists call the exercise of this faculty a process of "subception."[1] These authors presented a person with a large number of nonsense syllables, and after showing certain of the syllables,

the[...] elec[...] [...] knowledge of them remains *tacit*. This is how we come to know these particulars, without becoming able to identify them. Such is the *functional relation* between the two terms of tacit knowing: *we know the first term only by relying on our awareness of it for attending to the second.*

In his book on freedom of the will, Austin Farrar has spoken at one point of *disattending from* certain things for attending *to* others. I shall adopt a variant of this usage by saying that in an act of tacit knowing we *attend from* something for attending *to* something else; namely, *from* the first term *to* the second term of the tacit relation. In many ways the first term of this relation will prove to be nearer to

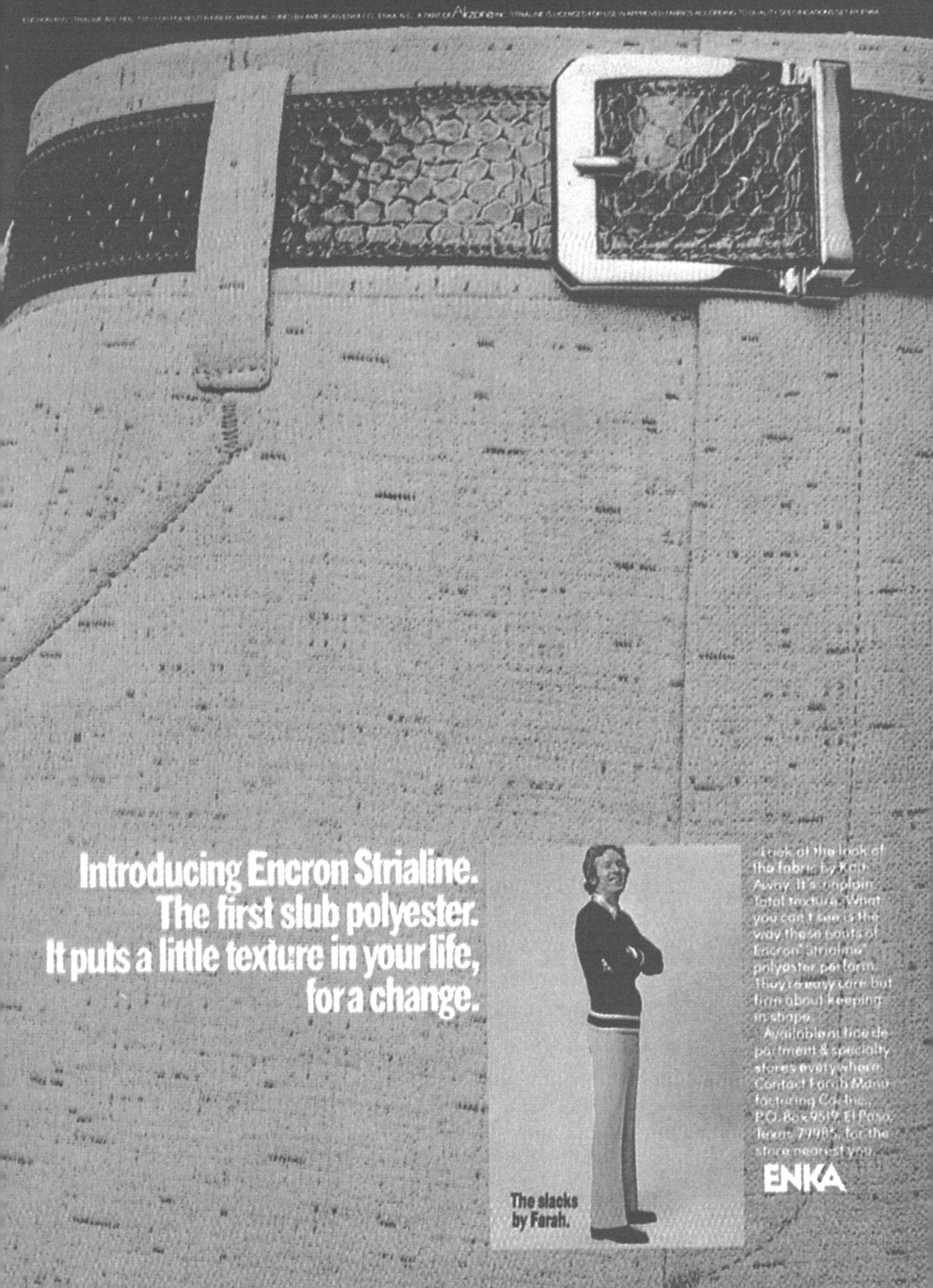

Introducing Encron Strialine.
The first slub polyester.
It puts a little texture in your life,
for a change.
The slacks
by Farah.
Look at the look of the fabric by Kati Away. It's no plain total texture. What you can't see is the way these pants of Encron Strialine polyester perform. They're easy care but firm about keeping in shape. Available at fine department & specialty stores everywhere. Contact Farah Manufacturing Co. Inc., P.O. Box 9519, El Paso, Texas 79985, for the store nearest you.
ENKA

JOHN BALDESSARI THROWING THREE BALLS IN THE AIR TO GET A STRAIGHT LINE AND OTHER WORKS FROM THE 1970s

By Friederike Krause

The 1973 photo-series *Throwing Three Balls in the Air to Get a Straight Line (Best of Thirty-Six Attempts)*, consisting of 14 lithographs, documents the artist's goal of throwing three balls into the air in such a way that they appear as one line in the photograph. The balls become abstract objects whose three-dimensionality is not immediately recognizable.

The photographs are characterized by their experimental character, since the artist, as noted in the title of the work, has made 36 attempts to come as close as possible to his goal. The photographs selected were those in which the balls were most like a horizontal or vertical line. This playful approach, and the structured specification of having a fixed goal, is typical of this creative period of Baldessari's, in which he used repetition in connection with language and image.[1]

Baldessari takes up the motif of the colored circle and the colored design again in later photographic works *Heaven and Hell* (1988), something he still uses to this day. Photomontages, the process of combining several images into a composite, were commonly used by magazines for advertisements, and are characterized by colored circles and large-area coloring. The faces and/or body parts of the persons depicted in *Heaven and Hell* (1988) are made so unrecognizable that their identity(s) remain hidden.[2]

Baldessari uses the work of other artists—painting, photography, as well as his own work—transforming them to become the author of any newly created piece. Through montage, he creates entirely new contexts.

His goal is not to create analytical or conceptual art, but rather to focus on ironic thinking in order to question art and its systems.

"Irony is integral to the artist's conceptual approach because it allowed him to mark out a necessary and meaningful displacement between what is read, what is seen, and what is understood."[3] — Marie-Josée Jean

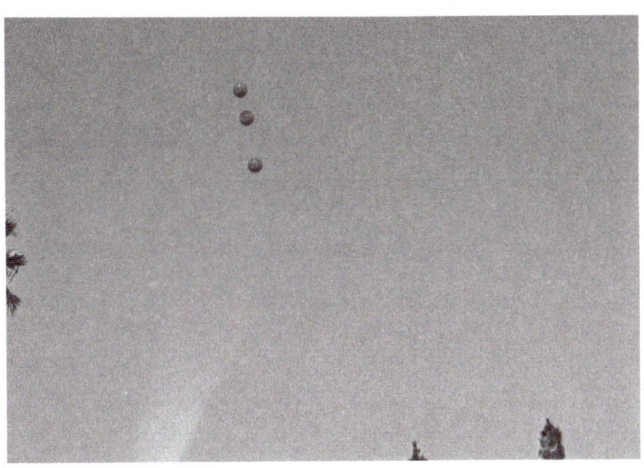
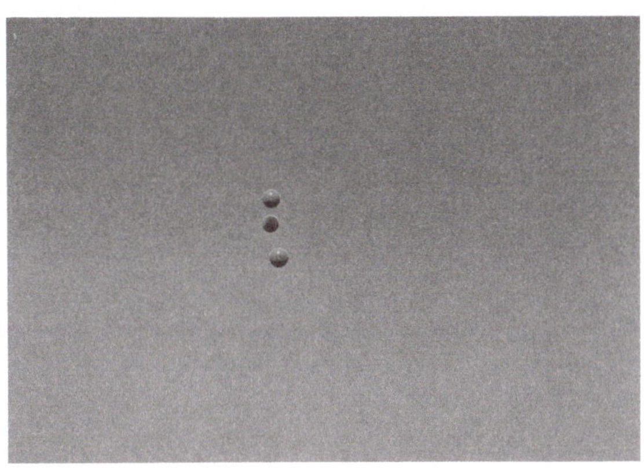

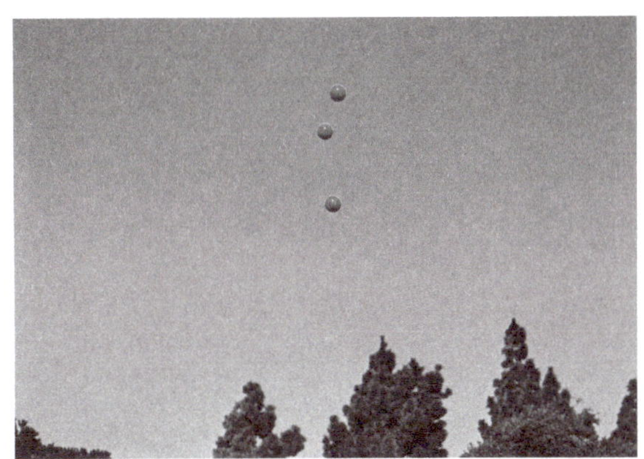
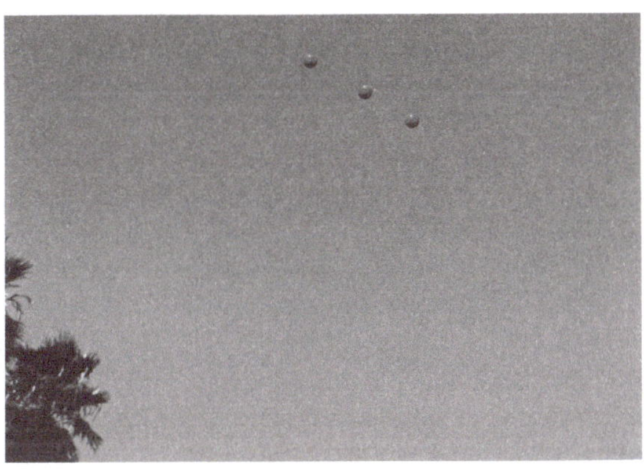

John Baldessari, *Throwing Three Balls in the Air to Get a Straight Line
(Best of Thirty-Six Attempts)* (1973).

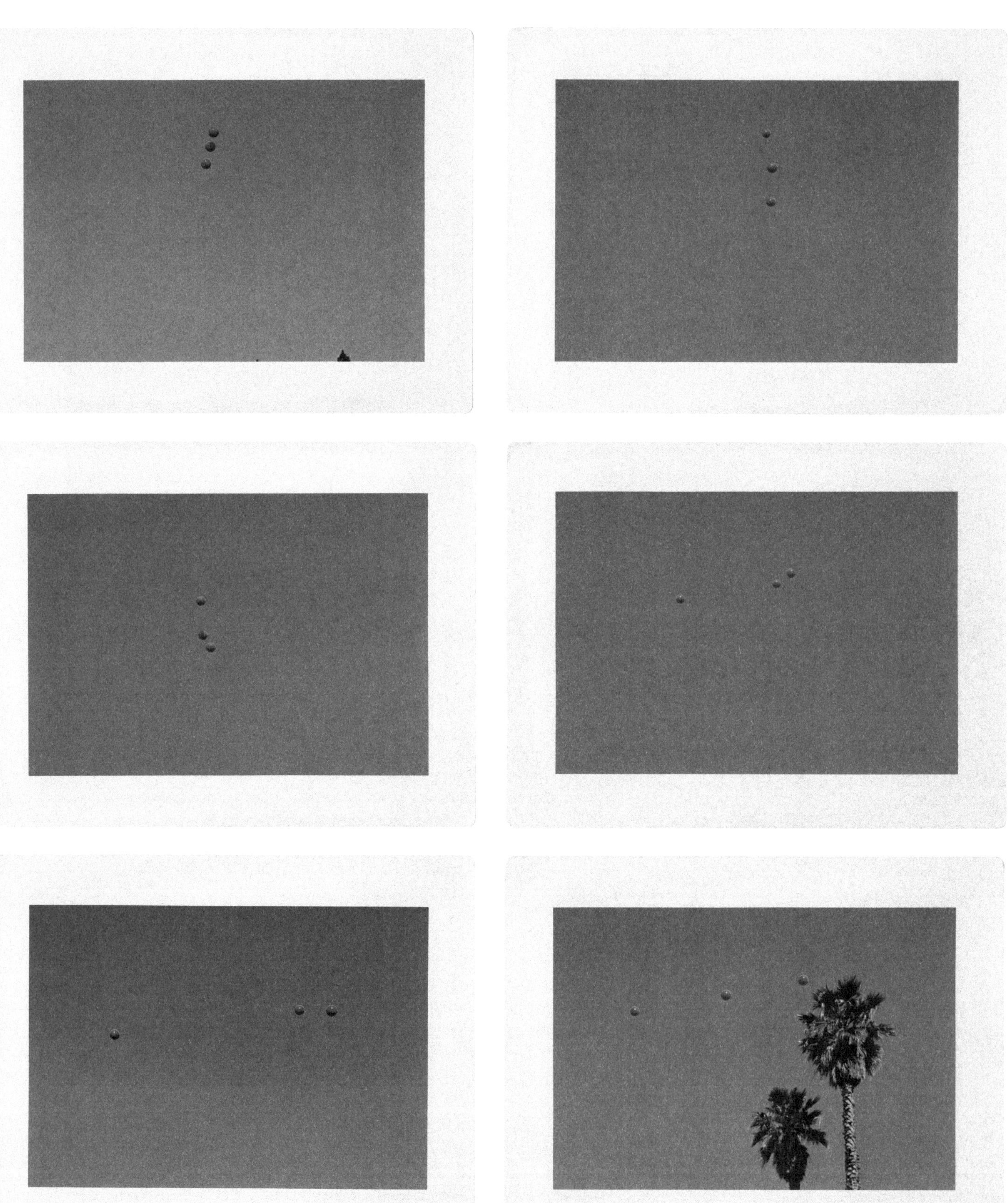

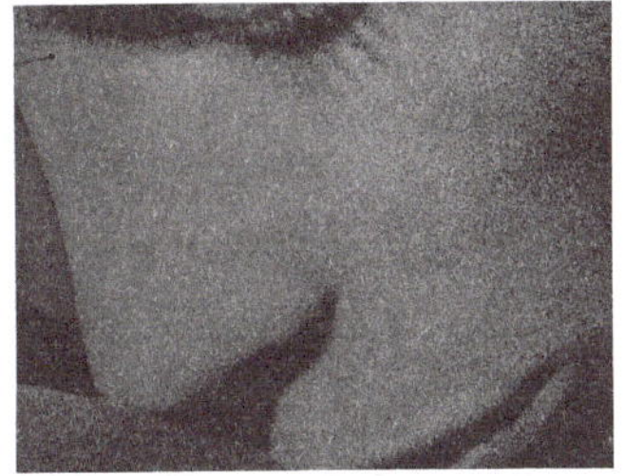

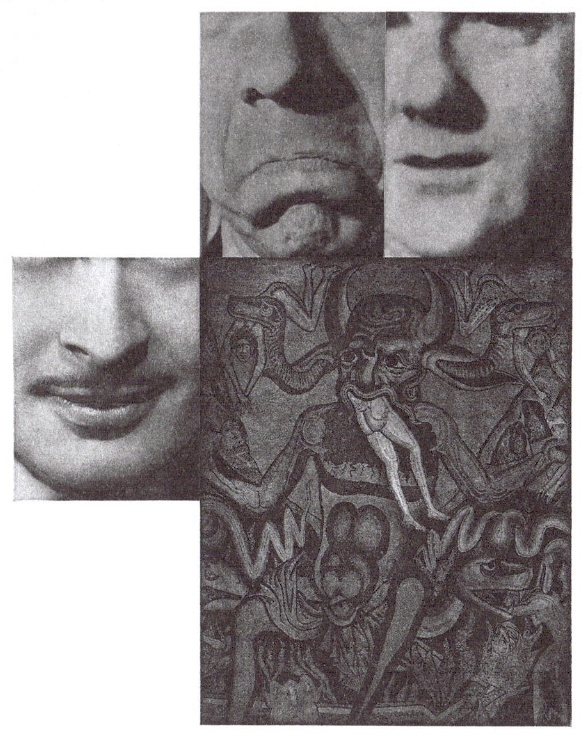

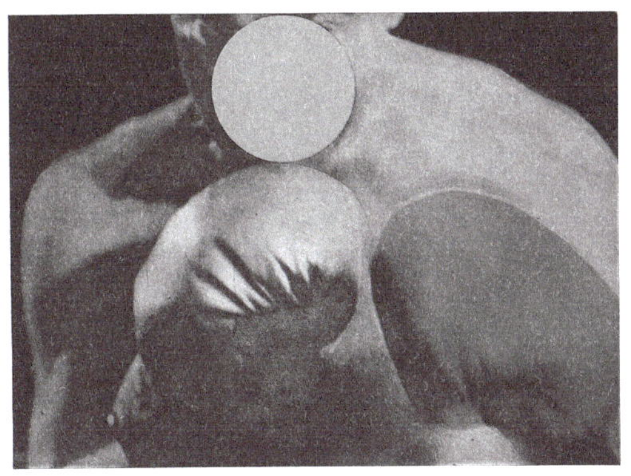

JOHN BALDESSARI
HASTE MAKES WASTE

The video work *Haste Makes Waste* from 1973 uses a repetitive phrase, much like in *I Will Not Make Any More Boring Art* (1971). With the aim of working as efficiently as possible, the artist repeatedly wrote down the sentence 'haste makes waste' onto paper, in exactly the same way and with the same formatting. This phrase is a rhyming proverb that means overhasty action can lead to mistakes, which ultimately slows down the process of creation and leads to a waste of both effort and materials.[4]

In terms of art production, this sentence could be read as a call to decelerate the pace of art-making—loosely based on the motto 'good things take time.' The rapid technical progress of the late 1960s (in 1967, for instance, Sony launched the Portapak to the US-market: a battery-powered portable half-inch video camera which, through its mobility, enabled artists to make their own films instead of artistically redesigning existing material)[5] meant that artists were able to produce more video art in considerably less time; whether this automatically resulted in higher quality work was debated.

Baldessari thus joined the Anti-Television Movement in the USA, along with Richard Serra and Chris Burden, and began to use video to convey ironic messages to enlighten viewers.[6]

"I think when I'm doing art, I'm questioning how to do it."[7]
—John Baldessari

Haste Makes Waste raises interesting questions. To what extent does he criticize the institution and value of art? What is the relevance of artistic work? The fact that the artist does not see himself as a genius, often criticizing and questioning his own work, was evident in *Cremation Project* (1970), the ceremonial burning of all work produced between 1953 and 1966. From then on, his works were characterized by combining the visual and textual, and he applied strategies from Pop Art, Surrealism, Dadaism, and Conceptual Art to his work. Text and images have the same value for him; there is no hierarchy between one category and another.

"Words and imagery are both magical conveyors of meaning. Sometimes I think a word can deal with an emotion better, and sometimes I believe an image can say it better. I'm ambivalent about prioritizing an image over a word. I build meaning in my art like a writer builds meaning from putting the right two words together. When you get it just right, it ignites meaning."[8]
—John Baldessari

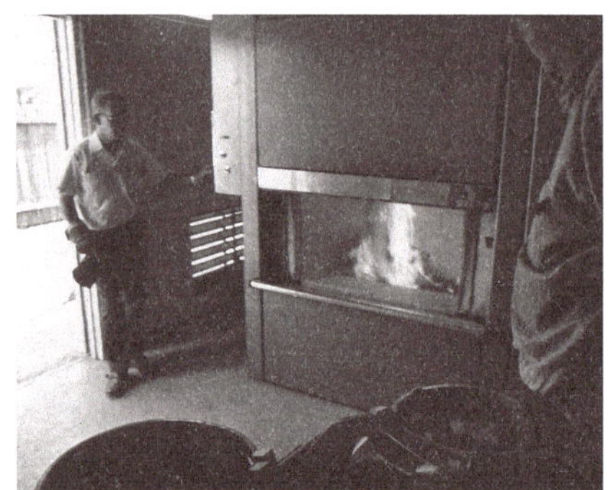
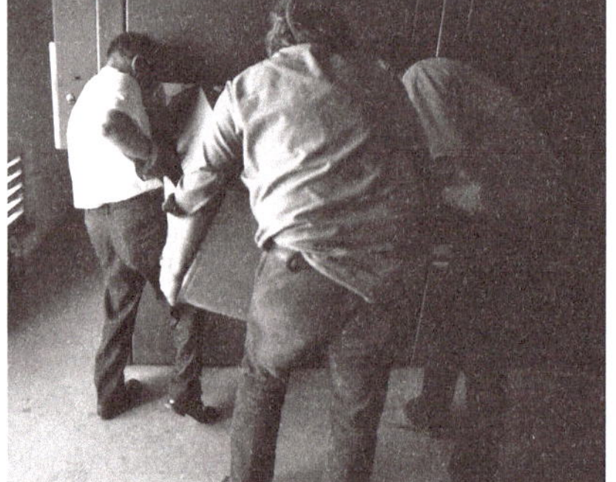
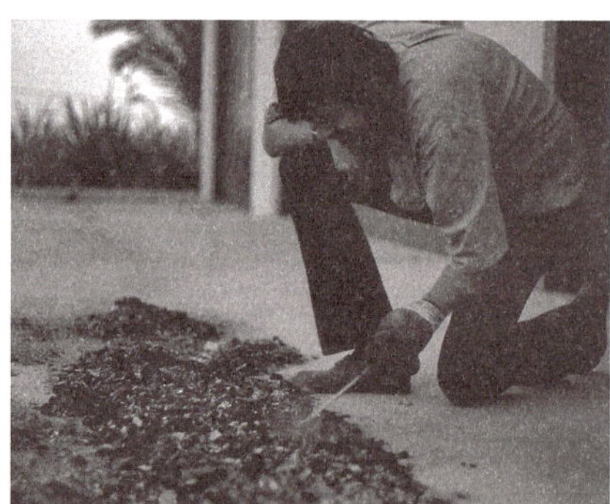
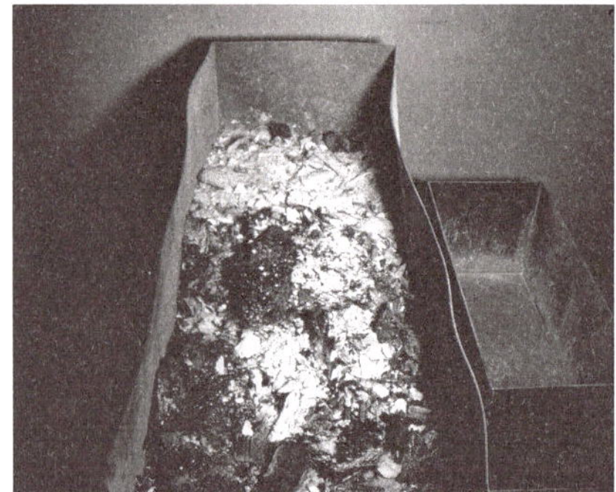
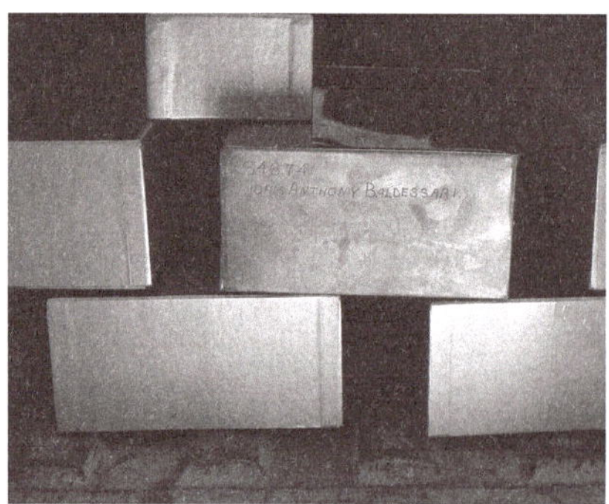
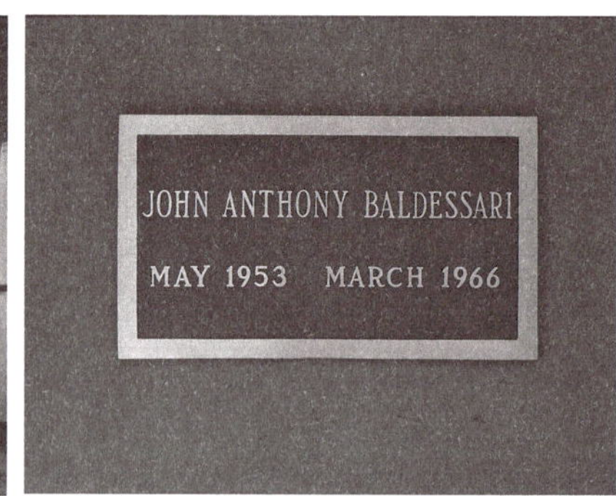

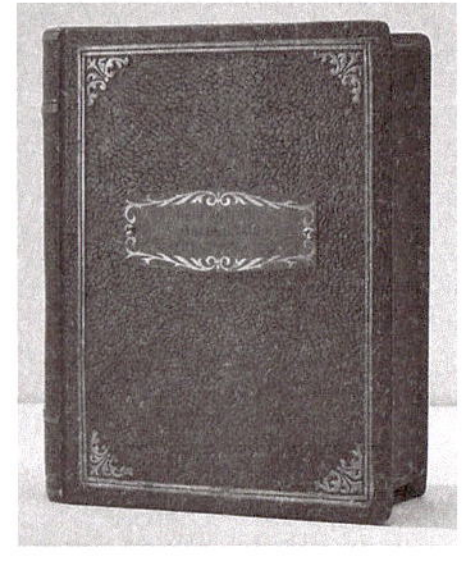
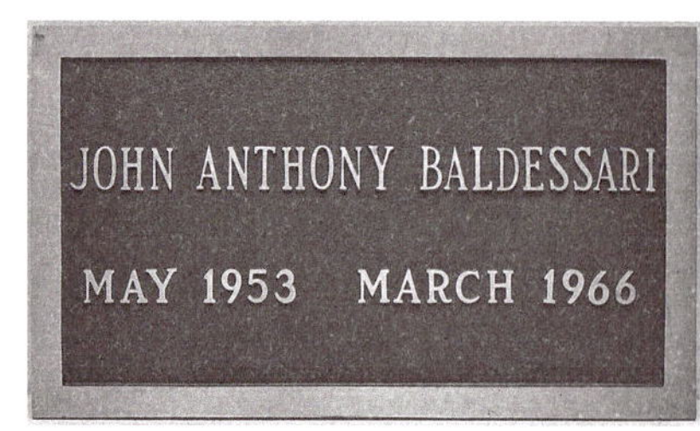

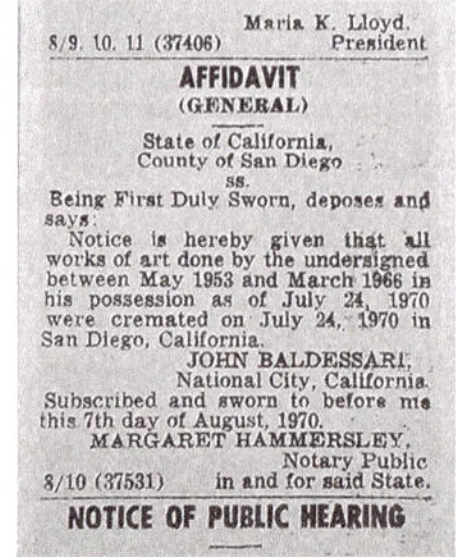

8/9. 10. 11 (37406)   Maria. K. Lloyd.
President

AFFIDAVIT
(GENERAL)

State of California,
County of San Diego
ss.
Being First Duly Sworn, deposes and says:
Notice is hereby given that all works of art done by the undersigned between May 1953 and March 1966 in his possession as of July 24, 1970 were cremated on July 24, 1970 in San Diego, California.
JOHN BALDESSARI,
National City, California.
Subscribed and sworn to before me this 7th day of August, 1970.
MARGARET HAMMERSLEY,
Notary Public
8/10 (37531)   in and for said State.

NOTICE OF PUBLIC HEARING

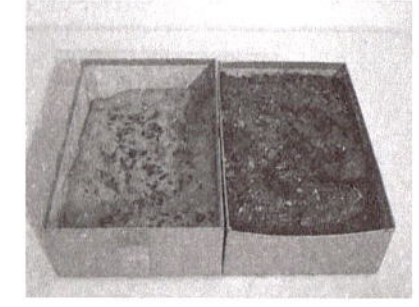

JOHN BALDESSARI
THE MEANING OF
VARIOUS PHOTOGRAPHS
TO ED HENDERSON

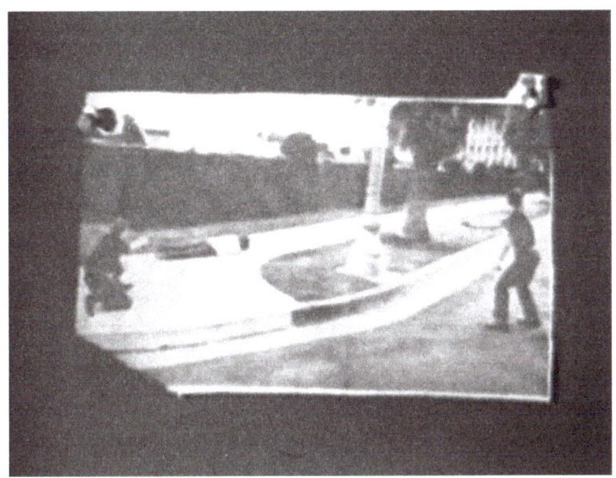

The video work *The Meaning of Various Photographs to Ed Henderson*, produced in 1973, is a 15-minute-long black and white video. In the video work Baldessari shows eight news photos to his student Ed Henderson, ranging in subject matter from zoo scenes to an accidental electrocution. The images were taken from newspapers or agency archives and are presented without any information related to what, who, when, where, and how. Henderson didn't see the articles beforehand, and only visual information was available to him.

He uses the photograph's landscapes to determine the place where each photograph was likely to have been taken. In the photograph shown in the video still above, Henderson infers that Los Angeles is most likely, due to the presence of palm trees, and that the situation was most likely an arrest because of two police-uniformed men, aiming a gun at another person lying on the asphalt.[9]

The authenticity of the photograph is questioned—is this a real situation or staged? Baldessari's intention in this work is to detach the images from their contexts and deconstruct the process of interpretation. The objectivity of interpretation is therefore questioned.[10] Viewers of the video also participate in Henderson's attempt to infer meaning from the photograph.

Baldessari describes his fascination with the moment of decontextualization as follows:

> "For most of us, photography stands for the truth. But a good artist can make a harder truth by manipulating forms. It fascinates me how I can manipulate the truth so easily by the way I juxtapose opposites or crop the image or take it out of context."[11]

Contrary to Joseph Beuys's action *How to Explain Pictures to a Dead Hare* (1965), Baldessari did not pursue a pedagogical lesson about the art object, but instead strove for confusion and the removal of context as his friend engaged with the image.

The project fascinated Baldessari to such an extent that another video, with the title *Ed Henderson Reconstructs Movie Scenarios*, was created in the same year. This time, Henderson developed film scenarios from film stills. In the following year, Baldessari asked Henderson to select background music to images that he could not see, but were described to him.[12]

In Baldessari's works, the narrative has equal weight to the image. It comes to the forefront when the meaning of the picture is not fully understood by the viewer. Craig Owens says the following about Baldessari's painting: "[it] can only be represented, never resolved."[13] Owens describes Baldessari's narratives as a search for abstruse meaning. In the end, one always comes back to the beginning, led by the unspoken question(s) that Baldessari asks. An important feature of these video works is that Baldessari does not use an analytical approach, but instead focuses on the stimulation of the imagination.[14]

In terms of the concept of authorship, Baldessari helped to shape a new approach that emerged in the 1970s, which became most evident in performance art. The works were no longer created by the artists alone, but instead required the activation of spectators and participants. Henderson and the viewers of the video therefore have an important function in completing the work. Only through them does the work emerge in its entirety.

UNREALIZED PROJECTS

By Pauline Gründing

John Baldessari's numerous unrealized works illustrate his relationship between objective, execution, realization, and end product in art. Many of Baldessari's works are merely ideas or suggestions which are not fully realized. Nevertheless, they are exhibited in some exhibitions as a concept, foregrounding process over product.

Baldessari's unrealized project *Unrealized Proposal for Cadaver Piece* from 1970 is intended to show how death is dealt with in art and society. The concept calls for a body draped like Jesus in pietá, staged within an exhibition box. By means of light and design, the focus will not be on the dead body itself, but on the representation and staging of it.

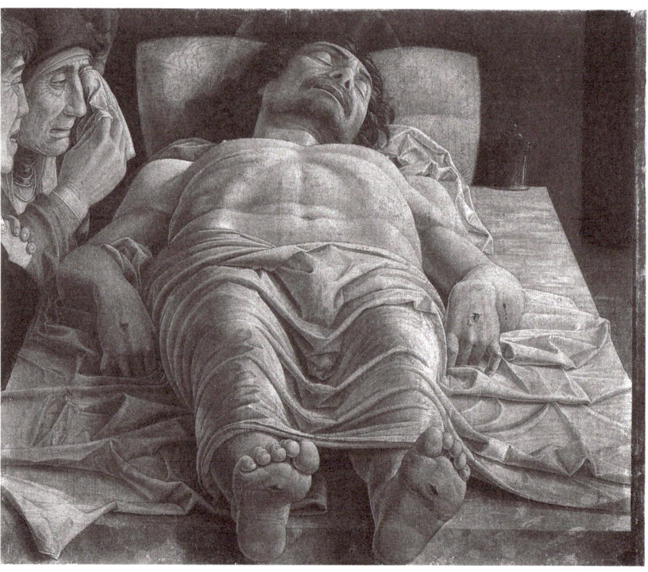

Another unfinished work suggested the exhibition of a corpse modeled on Andrea Mantegna's painting *The Lamentation of Christ* (c. 1480), which would be made accessible to visitors through a peephole. The observation, which, as in Mantegna's work, was to take place from the feet, was anticipated to bring the visitors into perspective proximity, leading to a reaction that would have rekindled the discourse between art, death, and taboo.

Since there is still no institution that has agreed to the exhibition of a corpse, *Unrealized Proposal for Cadaver Piece* has been only presented through email printouts, as for example in the exhibition *11 Rooms* at the Manchester Art Gallery in 2011. In the emails, the curators discuss the realization of the project with the respective participants. This incomplete work thus includes a moment of documentary. Here, materiality and immateriality find themselves in an ambivalent state.

In addition to this, there are numerous other unfinished works by Baldessari that exist only in their idea but not in their implementation.[1]

WORKS AFTER I WILL NOT MAKE ANY MORE BORING ART

After *I Will Not Make Any More Boring Art* from 1970, more and more works were created following this new approach, which today is classified as conceptual art, as already alluded to in I Will Not Make Any More Boring Art: Prehistory (p. 35–40 in this publication). Below, only a selection of his following works will be presented in order to get an impression of this renewed artistic concept.

In 1971, he made the video *John Baldessari Sings Sol LeWitt*. A short description on the website of the Museum Moderner Kunst Stiftung Ludwig Wien portrays it as follows: "In an ironic intersection of two systems—arcane theoretical discourse and popular music—Baldessari sings a famous tract by Minimalist artist Sol LeWitt. Introducing this performance by noting that 'these sentences have been hidden too long in exhibition catalogues,' Baldessari sings LeWitt's forty-five-point tract on Conceptual Art to the tunes of 'The Star-Spangled Banner' and 'Heaven,' among other songs. Baldessari's witty 'art aria' functions as a meta-conceptual exercise."[2]

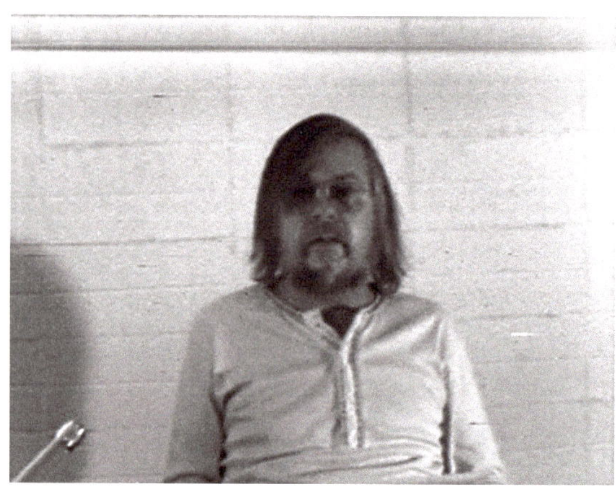

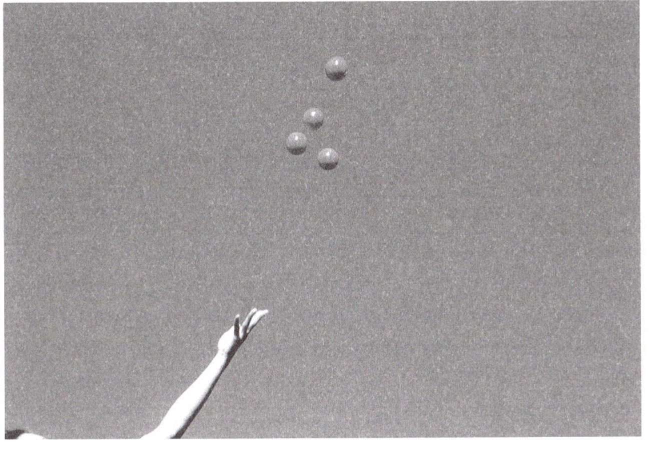
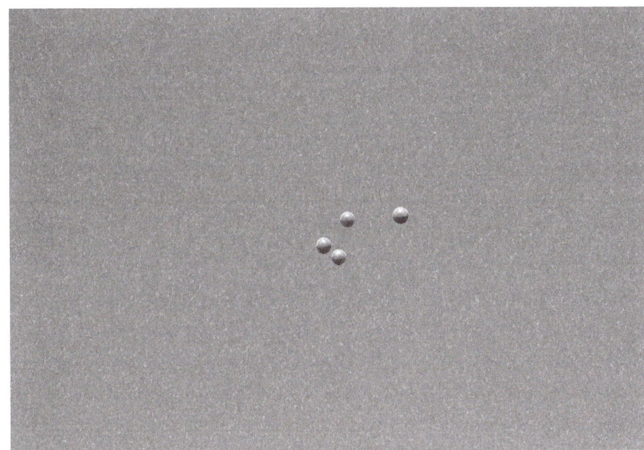
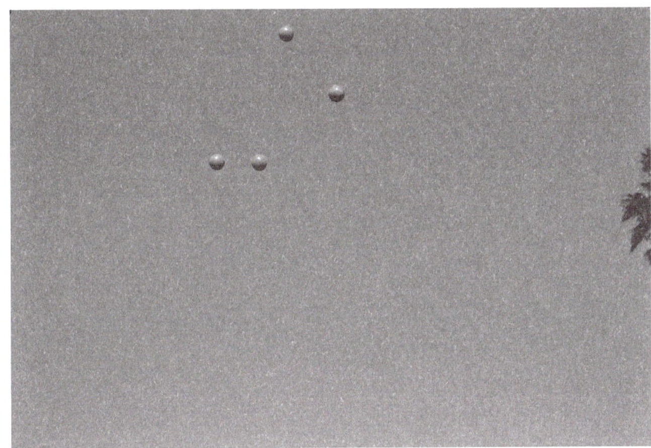
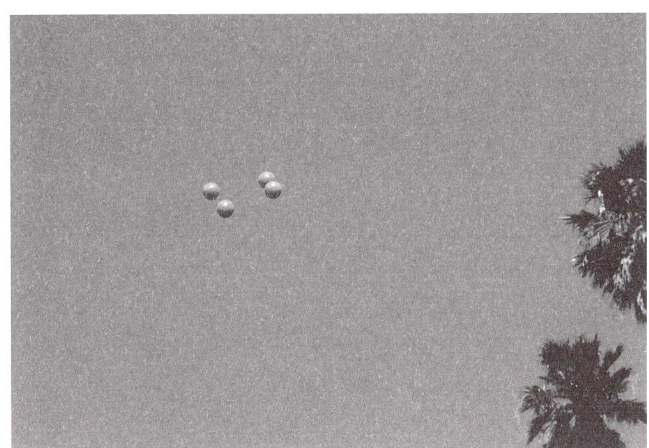

One year later, Baldessari completes another video: *Teaching a Plant the Alphabet.* The scene shows just a small pot plant on a chair. Baldessari, speaking in the style of a teacher with only his hand visible, presents the cards printed with different letters of the alphabet, one after the other. He reads out every single letter until he has finished the alphabet. The mechanical announcements and the ineducable pupil—the plant—lend the situation a dry, ironic tone. As a piece further developed from work notes (in which Baldessari noted "Does it make sense to teach a plant the alphabet?"), the video work is one of his best known. Different levels are superimposed; something logical turns into something illogical.[3]

Baldessari, however, uses his art in various ways to break up set norms. The processuality in his works, already mentioned for the *Unrealized Project of a Cadaver Piece*, is again addressed in *Throwing Four Balls in the Air to Get a Square (Best of Thirty-Six Tries)* from 1972–73.[4] This time, not so much on the level of the working process, but rather on the level of the concrete representation of a process.

In the eight-part sequence of pictures, a hand in front of a blue sky is first seen throwing four balls into the air. In the following photographs, only the balls—each falling differently—can be observed, and different formations develop during the fall. Baldessari thus represents a random sequence of actions. Due to the large number of photographs, even the smallest changes in the sequence of the balls can be observed. The process of the action becomes clear to the viewer.

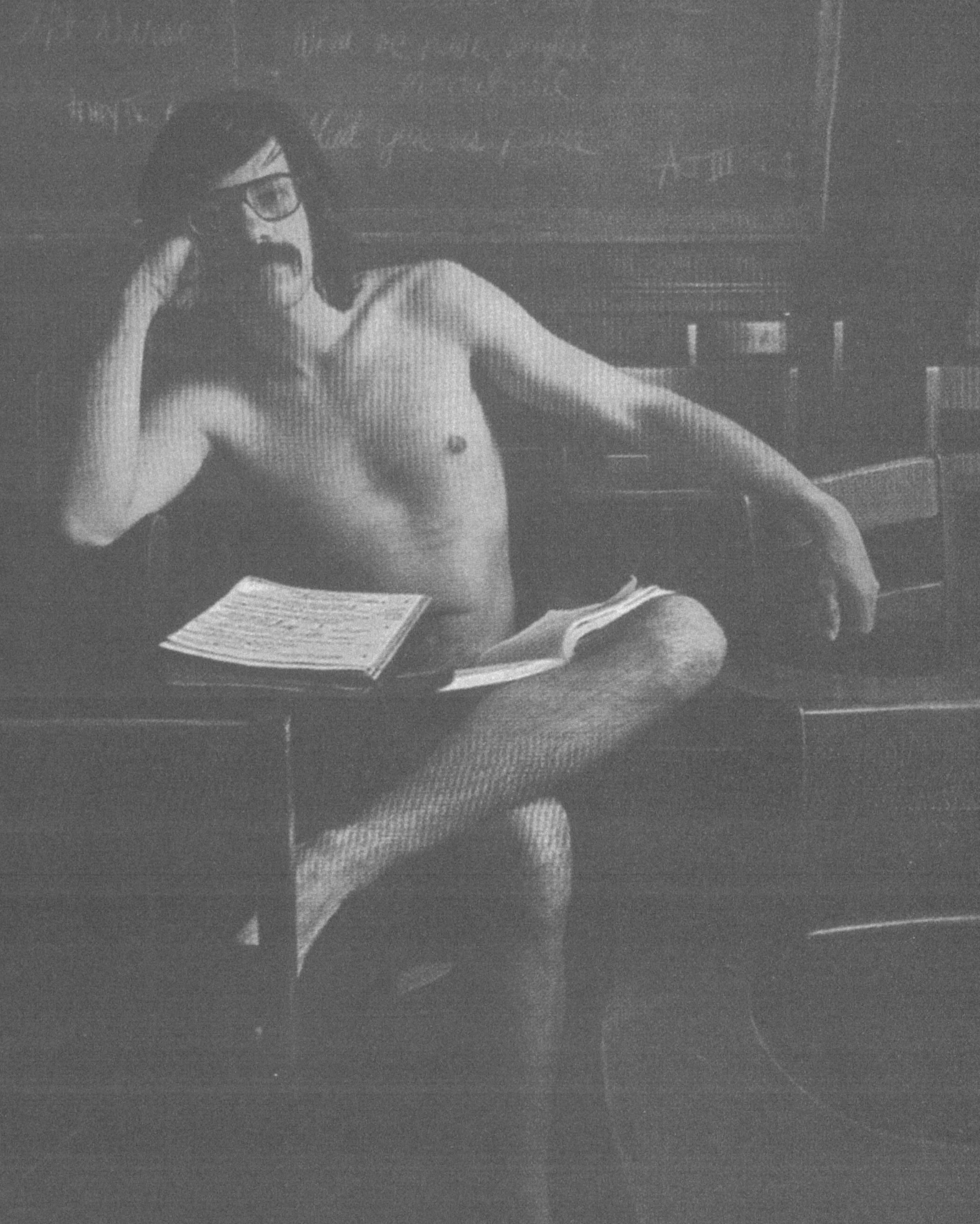

Nothing is better than Landlubber clothes.

ALISON KNOWLES

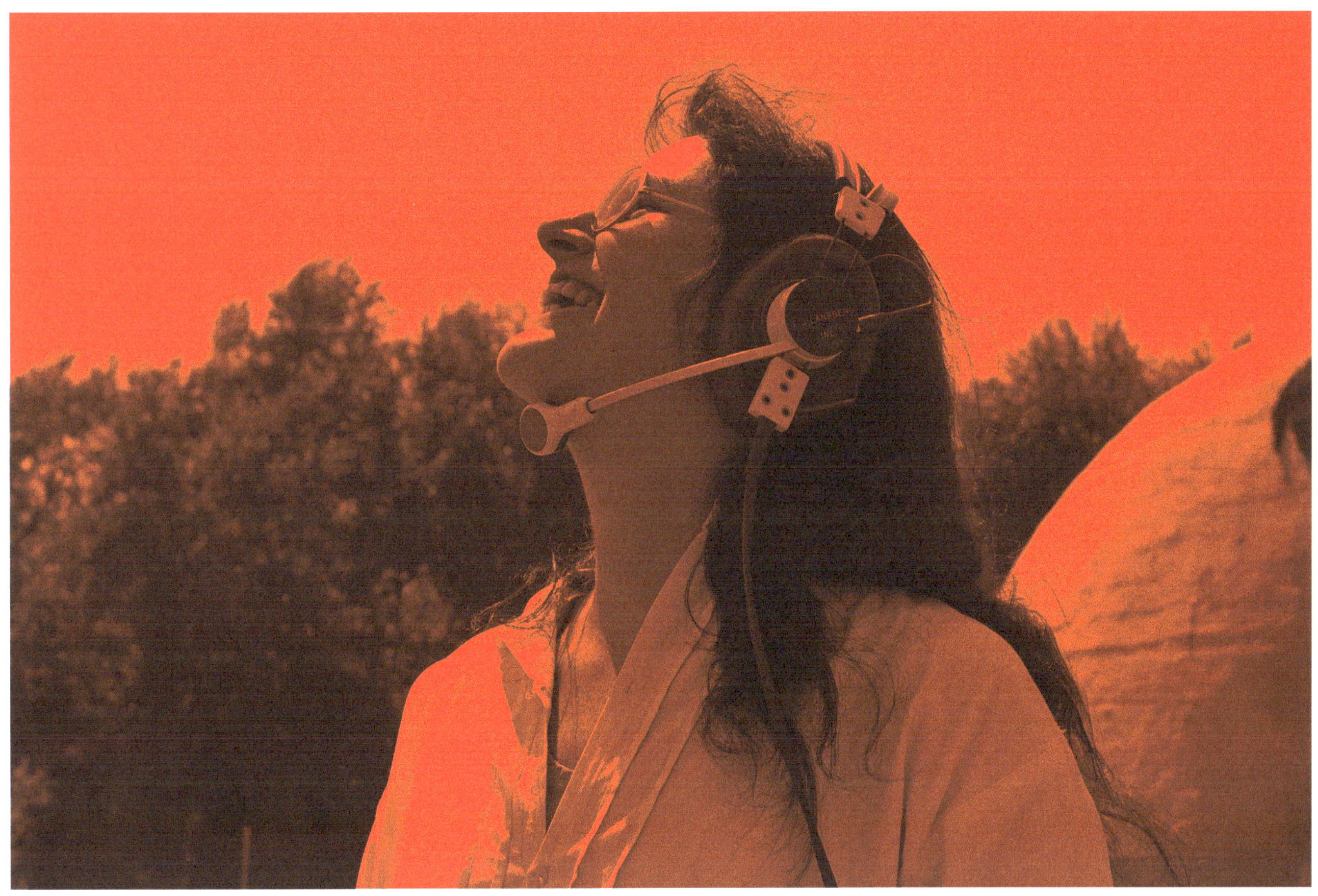

Knowles in front of *House of Dust* (1968).

*April 29, 1933, New York (NY), USA

In 1970, Allan Kaprow brought the artist Alison Knowles to California Institute of the Arts (CalArts), where she agreed to a teaching position on the condition that her architectural sculpture *House of Dust* (1968), at that time installed in New York, would be placed on the CalArts campus:

"I remember saying to Allan that I could come to CalArts only if they brought the *House of Dust*, too, and then there was sort of a long pause of a week because they had to fund the truck to bring it out from New York. But, as I said, it functioned very well not only next to the Villa Cabrini, where CalArts was temporarily, but also at CalArts itself. The small house was transported there from Villa Cabrini by helicopter."[1]

"I think each person did pretty much with that idea whatever they wanted to. I was putting up something called the *House of Dust* so I had these huge sculptures coming in on a flatbed truck and they had to be activated. I mean, I wasn't going to have them just sit on the land. They were weird-looking things, but they were important because the building itself was so unfortunate—the CalArts building—I felt you might as well put an apartment house there. So I would have my classes and my meetings out at the *House of Dust*, and we had a rail to run sound lines out there so we could do readings, and we had quite a number of food events out there. I had a piece called *Gift Event II*, where people would bring things to eat and things to present."[2] JAE

BARBARA BLOOM

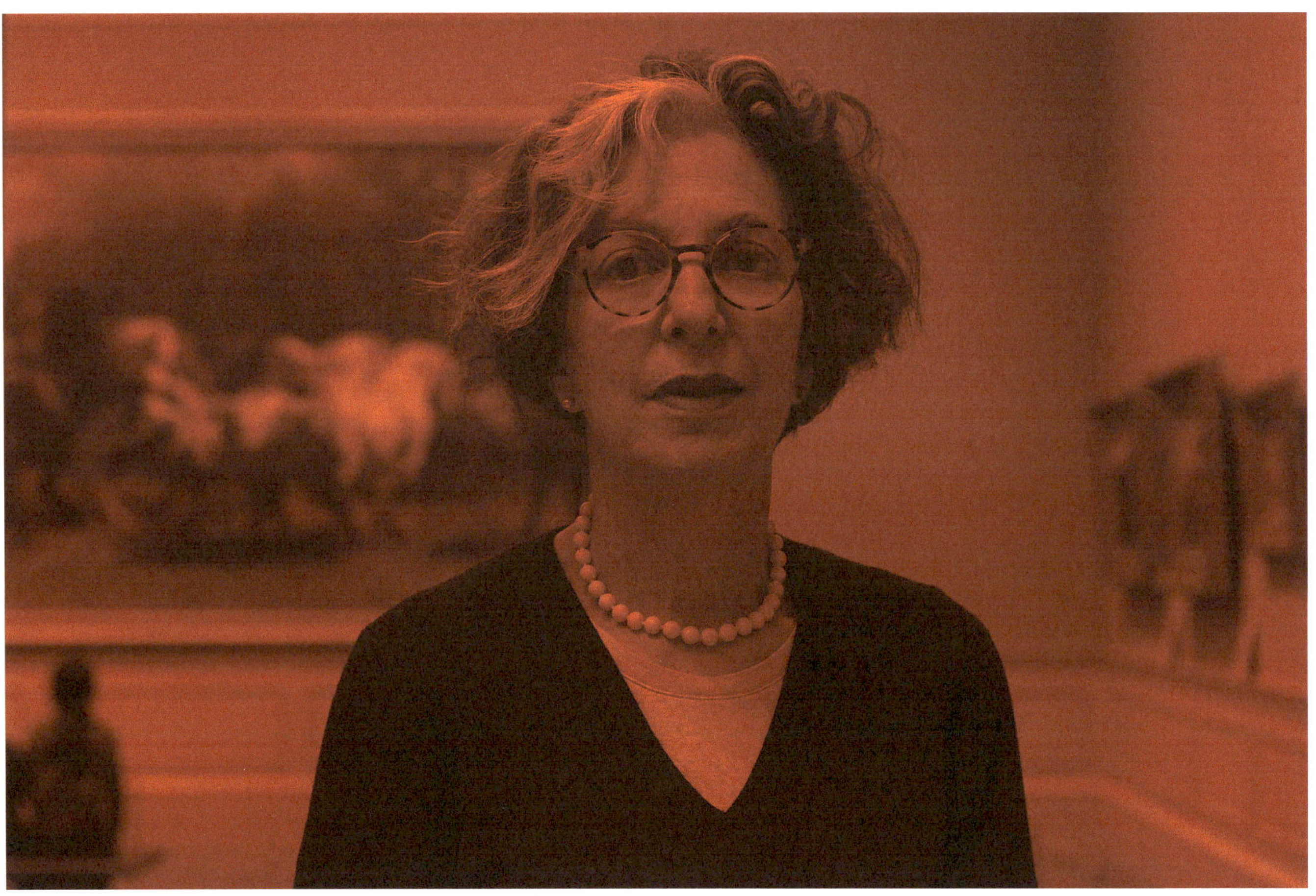

* 1951 in Los Angeles (CA), USA

is a visual artist who lives in New York. Her work spans mainly installation, sculpture, and photography and is marked by a conceptual approach. As an artist she studies a variety of subject matter such as design, interiors, asthetics, collecting, and display. She is specifically interested in questions of placement and constellations of objects, and how such relations visually generate narrative structures that underlay those spatial arrangements—implicit meanings can be traced and potentially decoded.[1]

Barbara Bloom studied in the augural class at the California Institute of the Arts, Valencia, CA, under John Baldessari and finished her BFA in 1972. Next to conceptualized arrangements and their relations,

in pieces such as *Mirror Mirror 7* (1989), *Hong Kong Four Colors* (1985), or *Vermeer Copy Copy* (2007) she also demonstrates her concern with the gaze and regimes of viewing. The usage of vestigial and referential elements like shadows, watermarks, fingerprints, tea stains, fragmented objects, or braille exhibits Bloom's ongoing interest in the nonpermanent, the absent, the invisible, or the fragile.[2] The installations *Barbara Bloom House* (2002) and *The French Diplomat's Office* (1997) illustrate an interest in simultaneous absence-presence.[3]

Bloom's work has been shown internationally. An early solo exhibition on her body of work, entitled *The Gaze*, was shown in 1985 at the Stedelijk Museum, Amsterdam.[4] Further solo exhibitions include *The Weather* at Galleria Raffaella Cortese,

Milan (2016), *Framing Wall* at the Modern Museum of Art, New York (2015) as well as *The Collections of Barbara Bloom* at Martin-Gropius-Bau, Berlin (2008).[5] She has taught at Columbia University, School of the Arts, Yale University, Graduate Department of Sculpture, the School of Visual Arts, New York, and Rijksakademie voor Beeldende Kunst, Amsterdam.[6]   LB

Barbara Bloom at the Metropolitan Museum of Art, New York (2015).

A SITUATION WHERE ART MIGHT HAPPEN

By Jacqueline Azarmi Eskandani

Which situations, events, or performances that took place at CalArts between 1970–78 can be reconstructed? How do these relate to the works that emerged from John Baldessari's situational teaching practice? Can Baldessari's teaching and learning methods be found in other artists who were also teachers at CalArts at the time? How does the creation of artworks relate to those teaching and learning methods?

The reception of Baldessari and his Post-Studio Class has, up to now, taken place primarily through the canonization of conceptual art, the concept of "artless art"[1] and its characterization concerning Baldessari's works. Under these conditions, Baldessari's situational, eventful, and performative teaching and learning methods are therefore often comparatively ignored. The focus, however, should not only lie on the interdependency of teaching and creating art in John Baldessari's Post-Studio class, but also on the other teachers and artists who worked at CalArts between 1970 and 1978. Such artists include Allan Kaprow, Alison Knowles, Nam June Paik, Michael Asher, and Simone Forti, as well as forgotten names such as the video artist Wolfgang Stoerchle. "A Situation Where Art Might Happen,"[2] therefore, means not only the situation in which it was possible for Baldessari to produce 'artless art,' but also refers to the general landscape at CalArts, through which it was possible to create art and experience its processes. John Baldessari's seminar structure was an essential part of the art-making process:

"Basically, I tried to give them sort of a brief history of contemporary art, so they could see that the things I was interested in didn't come out of the blue sky—that there was some continuity to it all. So a liberal use of slides and overhead projectors instead of books. And since I was on the road a lot in Europe and New York doing shows, I would bring back catalogs, magazines, and talk about the stuff I'd seen. These students had probably the quickest access to information of any art school in the U.S., I would wager. They didn't have to wait for it to come into the magazines. And plus the visiting artists. I would have at least one or two a week talking there. And field trips. But not necessarily art related, you know: going into the things that introduced them to culture in the broadest sense, like going to Forest Lawn, or the Hollywood Wax Museum, or what have you. And a lot of times just anything to get out of the studio. One of my tricks was that we'd have a map up on the wall, and somebody would just throw a dart at the map, and we would go there that day. [laughs] They could take their video cameras and still cameras, and do whatever they wanted in just staying out there. Try to do art around where we were."[3]

These field trips aimed to challenge the students by introducing them to random locations and using both the site and their equipment to create art. Photography and video cameras were used here to stage and document ephemeral or performative actions, gestures, or scenes.[4]

Jim Welling, a student of Baldessari, described his art project *Hair* in an interview. The idea and photographs for the work were taken during a routine field trip with the Post-Studio class in 1973:

"I remember I made this work *Hair* on a field trip John took with the Post-Studio class in 1973, six or eight of us. We went across the street from CalArts, at the time there was just a large open field there and we tramped around and made some work."[5]

At that time, Welling owned no camera, but instead borrowed one for the field trip and documented hair, including Baldessari's. A photo-series was created as a result, meant only as a "conceptual joke".[6]

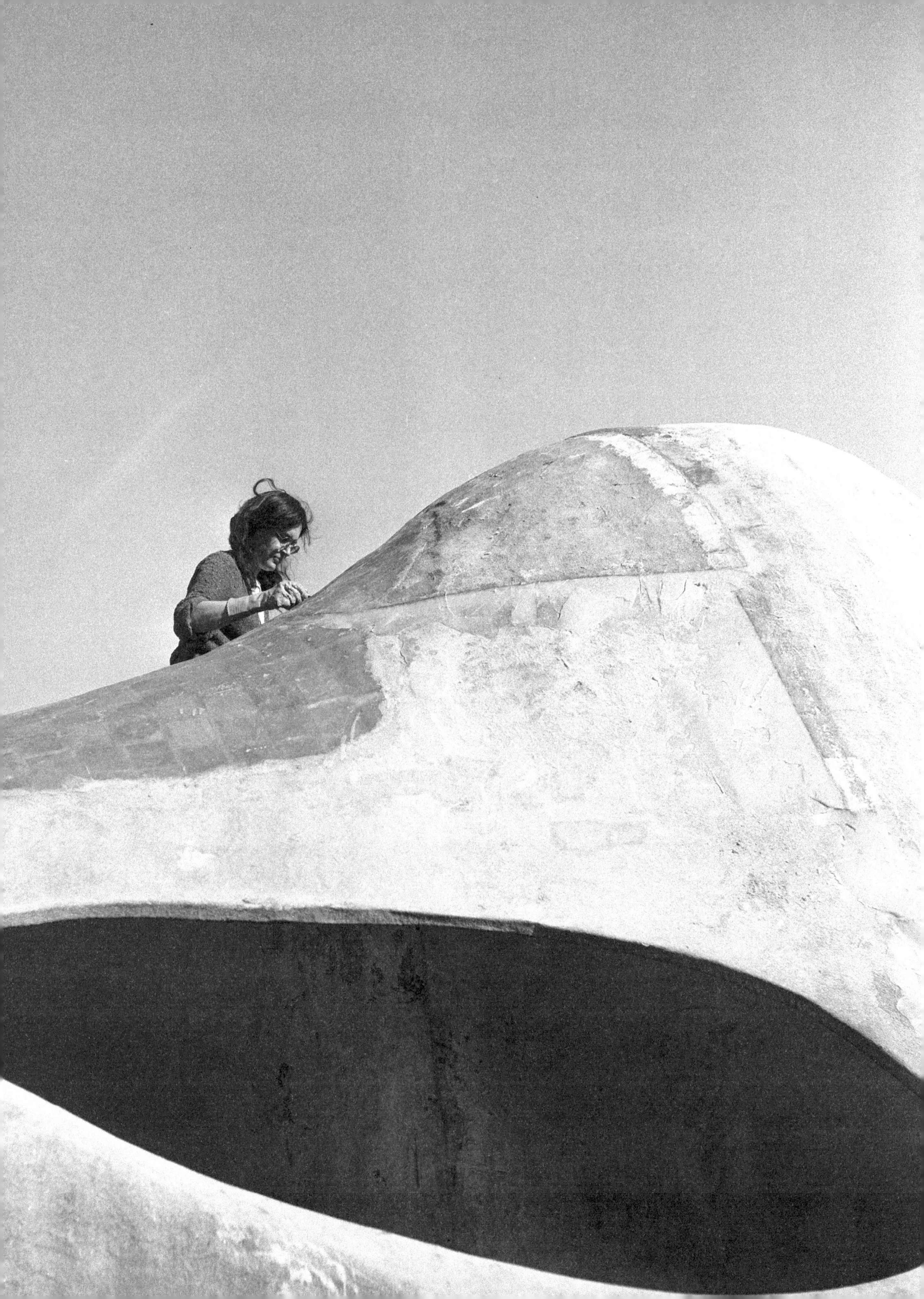

This example highlights the connection between art theory and art creation at CalArts and Baldessari's Post-Studio class. The field trips offered the students circumstances in which they could receive artistic inspiration in different settings. Artistic works, with situational moments as the starting point or reference, were also always created on these trips.

HAPPENINGS AT CALARTS

When CalArts revised its curriculum in 1970, the institute hired new faculty members, including Allan Kaprow. At CalArts, Kaprow organized, among many other things, happenings with his students as participants. *Entr'acte*, for example, from 1972, took place in one of the washrooms at CalArts, with the theme of hand washing as a ritual action. Images of these happenings are digitally available on the Getty Blog, including three photographs: hands with a washcloth, a hand under a faucet, handshaking, and Kaprow's notes for *Entr'acte*, written in ink on lined paper.[7]

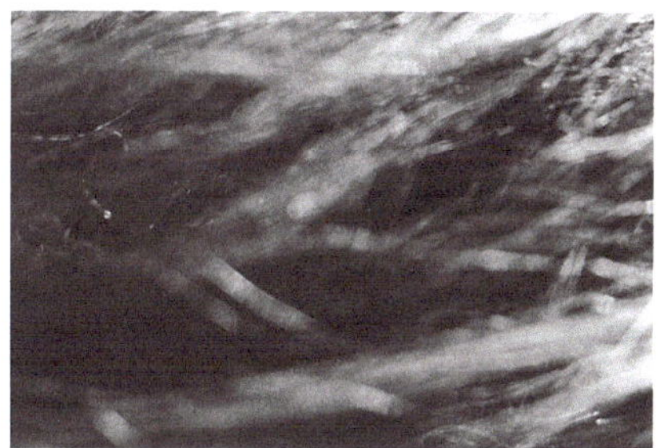

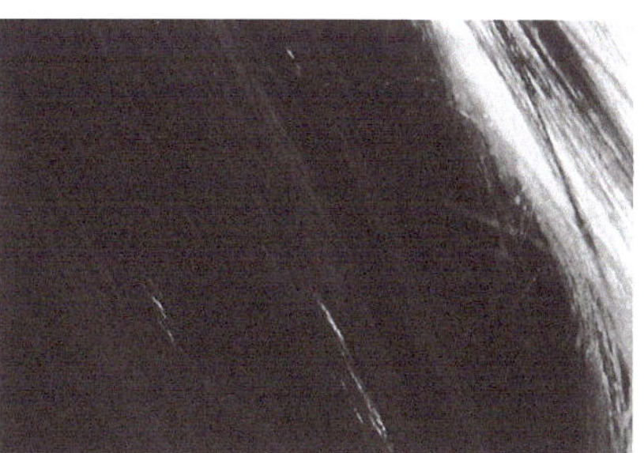

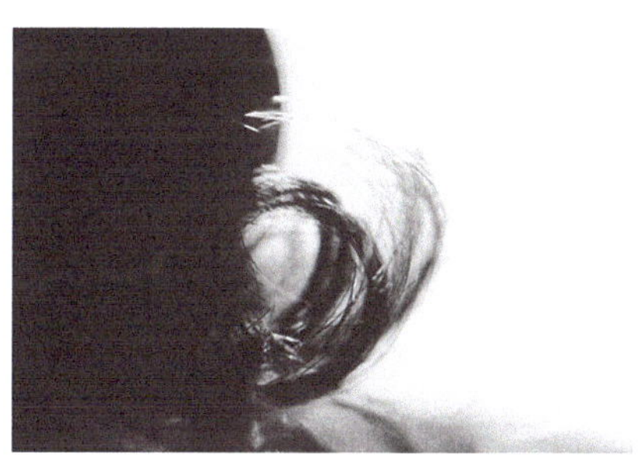

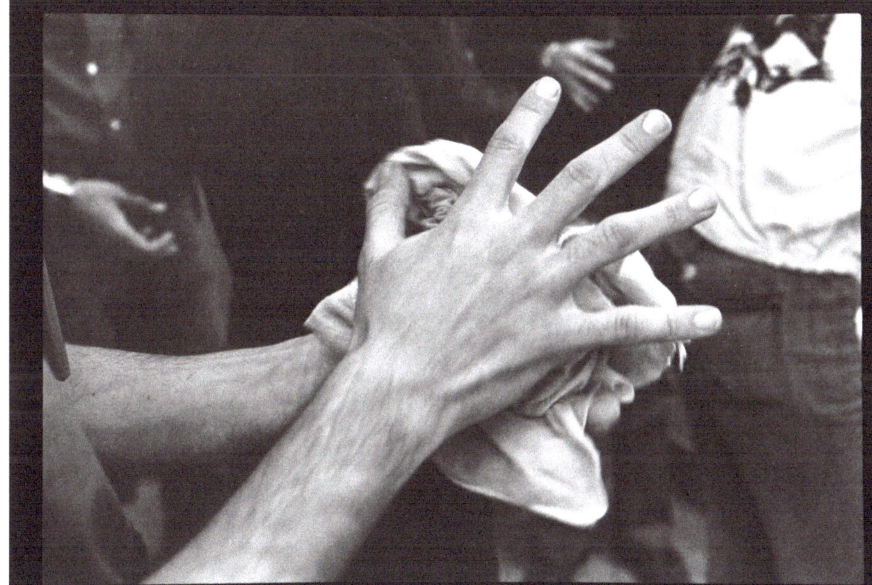

HOUSE OF DUST

Allan Kaprow was also the one who brought the artist Alison Knowles to CalArts in 1970; she agreed to a teaching position on the condition that her architectural sculpture *House of Dust* (1968), which was in New York at the time, be given a place on the CalArts campus:

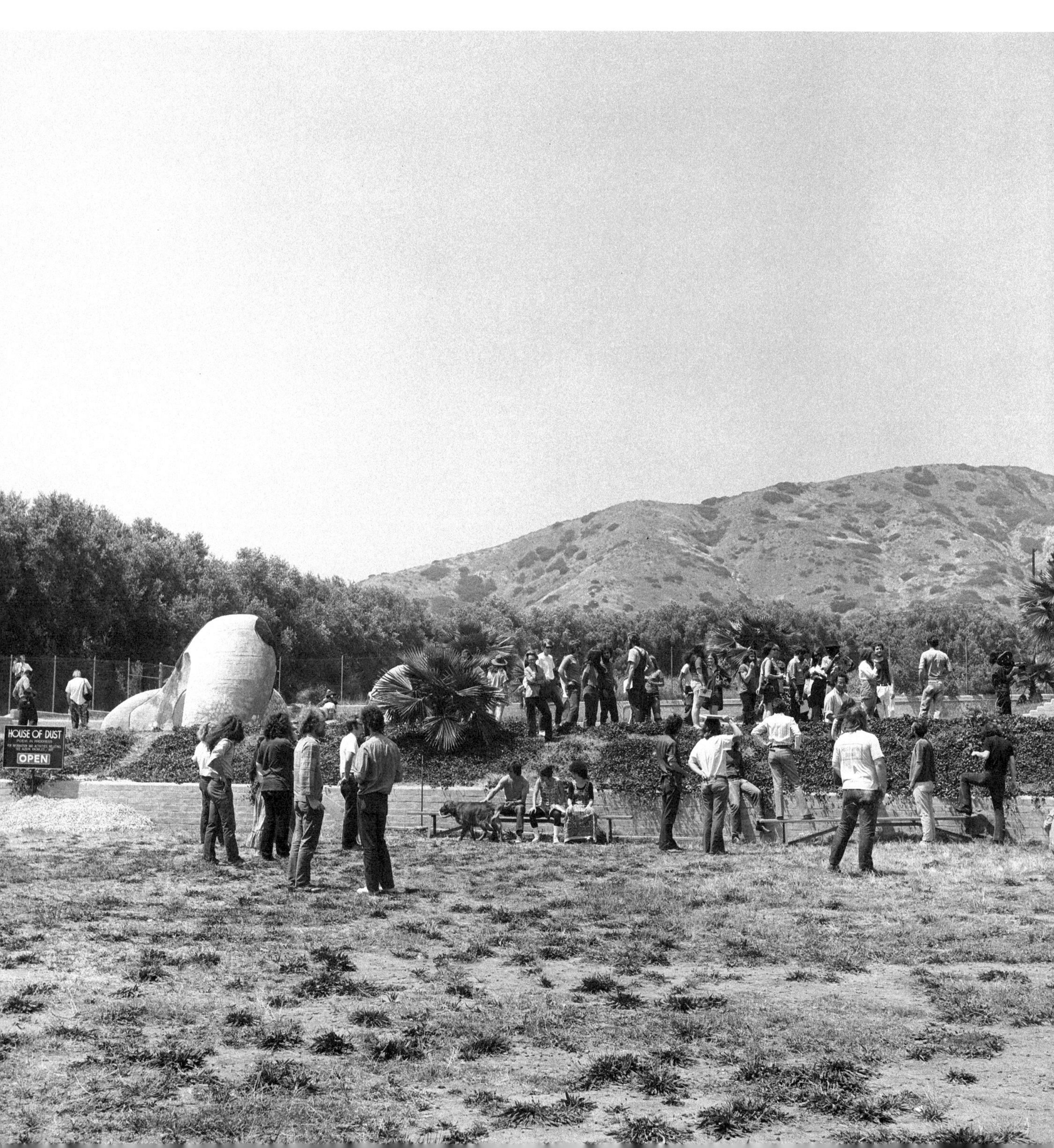

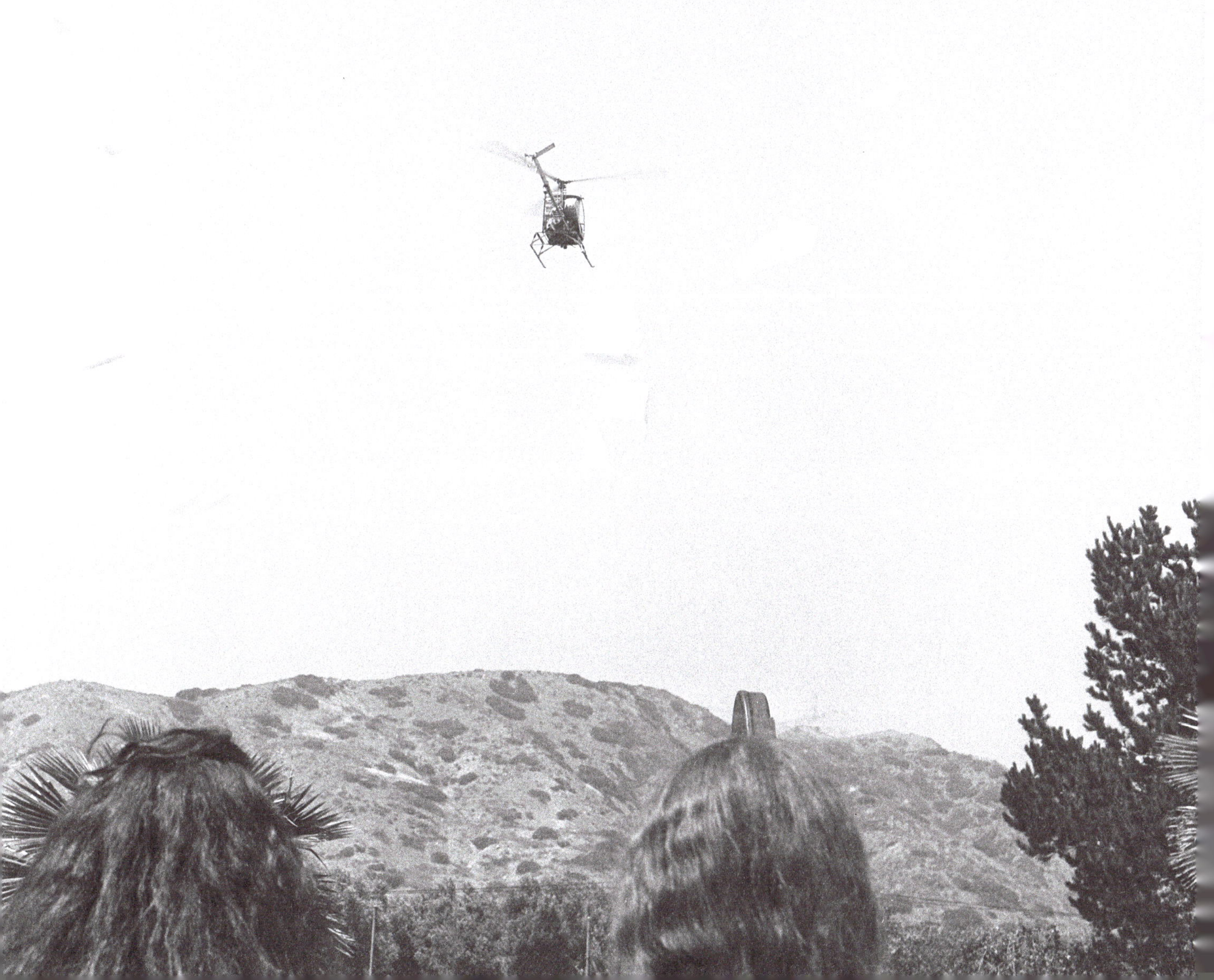

"I remember saying to Allan that I could come to CalArts only if they brought the *House of Dust*, too, and then there was sort of a long pause of a week because they had to fund the truck to bring it out from New York. But, as I said, it functioned very well not only next to the Villa Cabrini, where CalArts was temporarily, but also at CalArts itself. The small house was transported there from Villa Cabrini by helicopter."[8] —Alison Knowles

House of Dust was taken by truck to the temporary campus of the CalArts Institute at Villa Cabrini, a former Catholic girls' school in Burbank, and then later by helicopter to the permanent campus in the northern suburb of Valencia. The distinctive thing about *The House of Dust*, which was on the CalArts campus from 1970 to 1972, is the interweaving of art, technology, architecture, and teaching. The installation is based on the computer-generated poem of the same name, created three years earlier by Alison Knowles, James Tenney, and the Siemens 4004 computer system.

The photos published here do not show its transportation by helicopter, but the "poetry drop," in which a helicopter dropped the four-meter printouts of the computer-generated poem over the installation.

"Because of the access I had to the jet propulsion labs with Jim Tenney, I was able to get four feet of poetry generated from the computer. The folded paper had these very beautiful green lines. We've had the poetry drop reproduced in various situations, but it's never been as beautiful as what we dropped over *The House of Dust*. It was the old computer paper. Very fine, very lovely."[9] — Alison Knowles

The architectural-transferal installation at CalArts was an 'art space' for Knowles and her students. In addition to meetings and readings, performances, concerts, and screenings also took place—teaching and art practice went hand in hand:

"*The House of Dust* by Alison Knowles, as part of art in translation, explores Knowles's translations across processes of performance, drawing, writing, and architecture working with structures of language, computation, and building. Much of this is done through propositions and inhabitation. Physical interaction with books, maquettes, poetry writing, gatherings, and games run throughout the exhibition and related programs. The exhibition also presents contemporary artworks that draw on Knowles's thinking and processes, specifically working with translation of materials and languages."[10] — Hallie Scott

The House of Dust was thus subject to a constant process of art practice. A concrete example of this is the commissioning of the artist Max Neuhaus. From the beginning of the project, Alison Knowles commissioned the musician to create a kind of sound device in the smaller of the two houses. His sound installation is therefore directly related to the work of Knowles. The artist also repeatedly encouraged her students to deal with the architectural and conceptual premises of the artwork.[11]

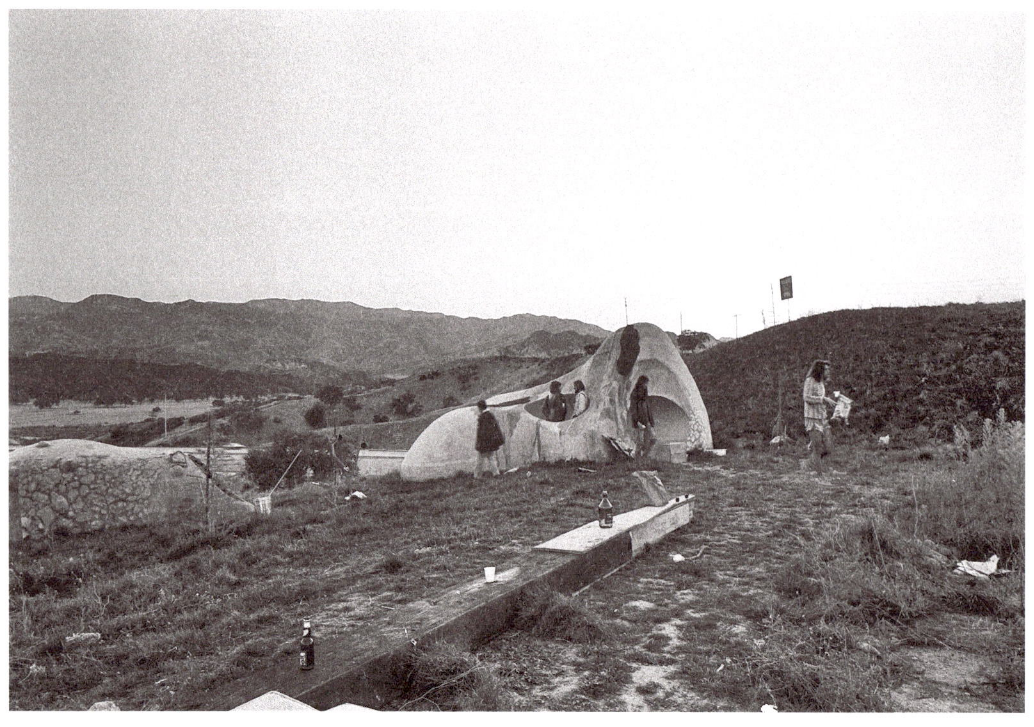

Previous page: Alison Knowles, poem drop over the *House of Dust* (1971), CalArts campus, Burbank (CA).
This page: Alison Knowles, *House of Dust*—Orientation Bonfire (1971), CalArts campus, Burbank (CA).

SITUATIONAL ACTIONS: WOLFGANG STOERCHLE AT CALARTS

At the request of Allan Kaprow, Wolfgang Stoerchle taught at CalArts between 1970 and 1972 as part of the Post-Studio program.[12] Stoerchle started out with performances and situational actions, which later also often became the focus of his video works. Stoerchle's estate can be found at the Getty Research Institute Los Angeles, which contains archive material of his last performance.

"Collectively, his video works show a complete dissection of the medium, isolating nearly every formal property of video and turning it towards often poignant efforts to capture and contain the body."[13] — Emmabeth Nanol

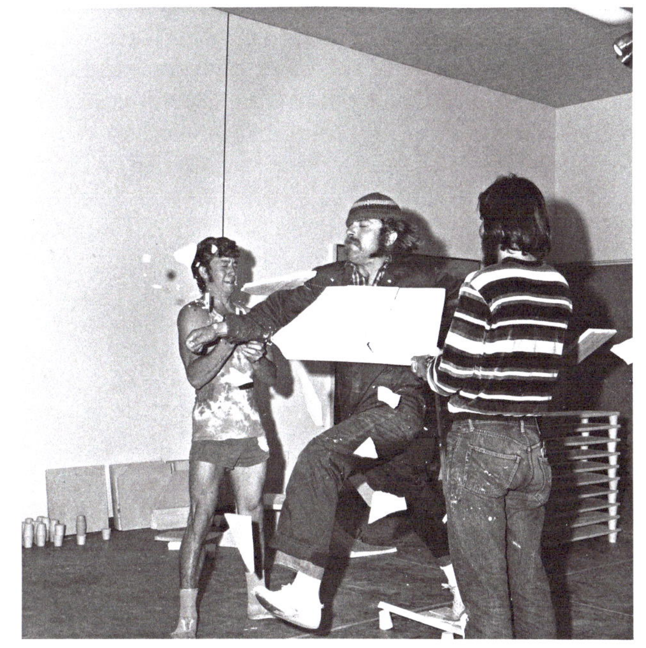

From top to bottom: Wolfgang Stoerchle, *Event Performance* (1970).
Wolfgang Stoerchle with piles of river rocks (1975). Photo by Carol Lingham.

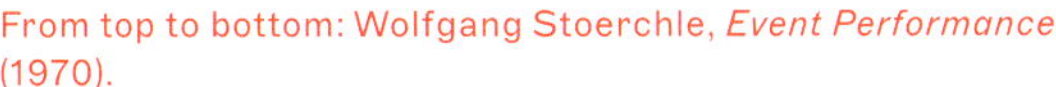

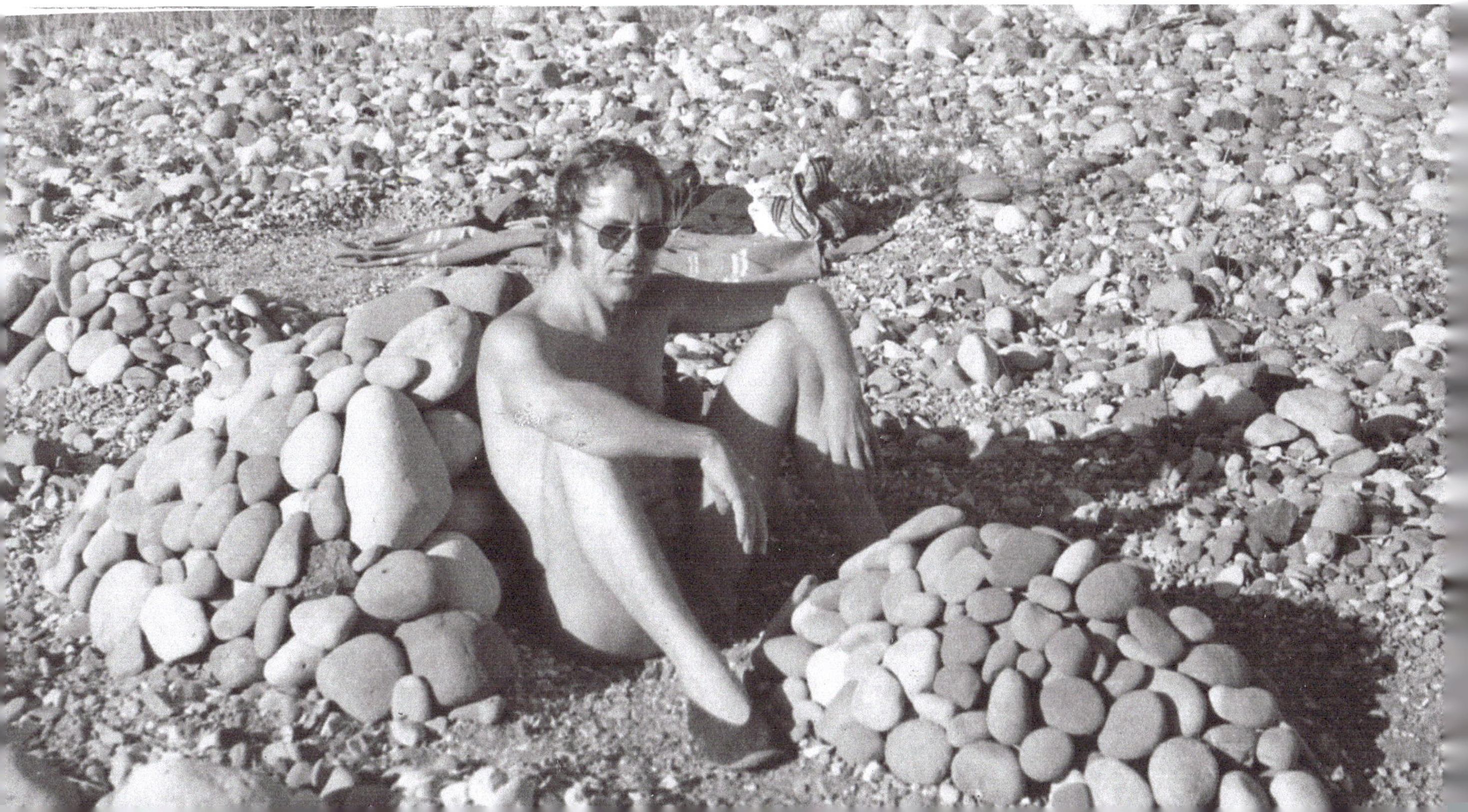

WOLFGANG STOERCHLE

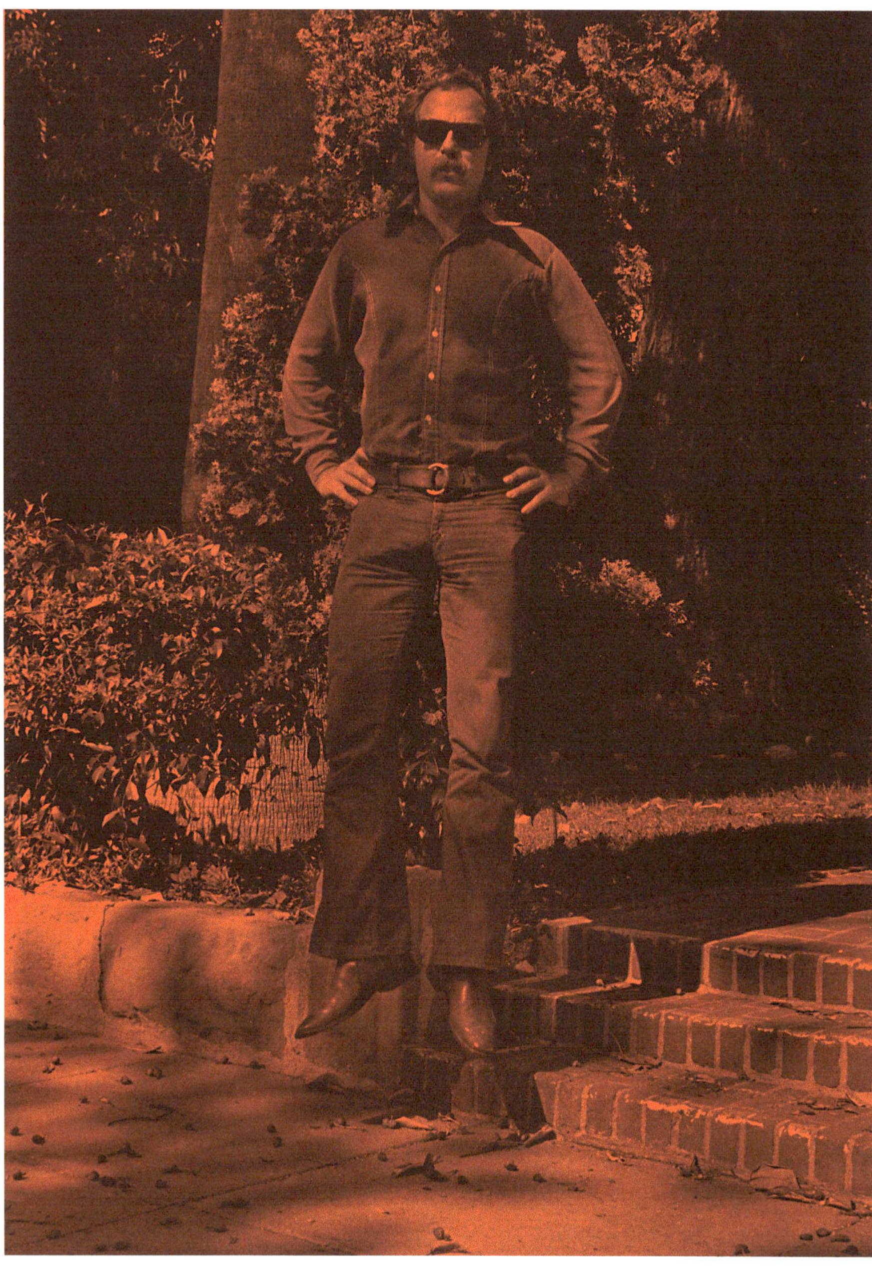

Wolfgang Stoerchle, Wolfgang Stoerchle hovering in mid-air (ca. 1970).

*in Germany, January 17, 1944
†March 14, 1976, New Mexico, USA

was a notable figure in the development of performance and video art in the early 1970s. In 1959, he emigrated with his family from Germany to Toronto, Canada. After a ten-month trip through the U.S. on horseback in 1962, he moved to L.A. until 1964. The following four years he studied painting at the University of Oklahoma before enrolling in the MFA program at the University of California, graduating in the same year. While there he started working with film, performance, and sound, and performed in a band with Daniel Lentz and Miles Varner under the name *California Time Machine*. In 1970, Allan Kaprow invited Stoerchle to join the faculty of the art department at CalArts. Gaining access to video there, he intensified his experiments with the filmic medium, using his own body as primary tool and material. His videos often document series of small actions and tasks mostly executed by the artist such as *Jumping in the Air, Running Upside Down*, and *Penis with Disney Characters* (1970–72).[1]

In 1973, Stoerchle moved to New York, where his rather abstract and conceptual approach shifted to "blunt depictions of sexuality and nudity."[2] In the last three years of his life, Stoerchle lived in Mexico City, L.A., and Santa Fe, producing mostly abstract pencil drawings and shrine-like, ephemeral sculptures. His last public performance took place on October 17, 1975, in John Baldessari's studio in L.A. Almost five months later the artist died in a car accident.[3]

His work was shown in a number of significant exhibitions in the early 1970s, such as *24 Young Artists* at LACMA, *Projects: Pier 18* at MoMA, and a two-person show with William Wegman at the Sidney Janis gallery (all 1971).[4]   JAE & VK

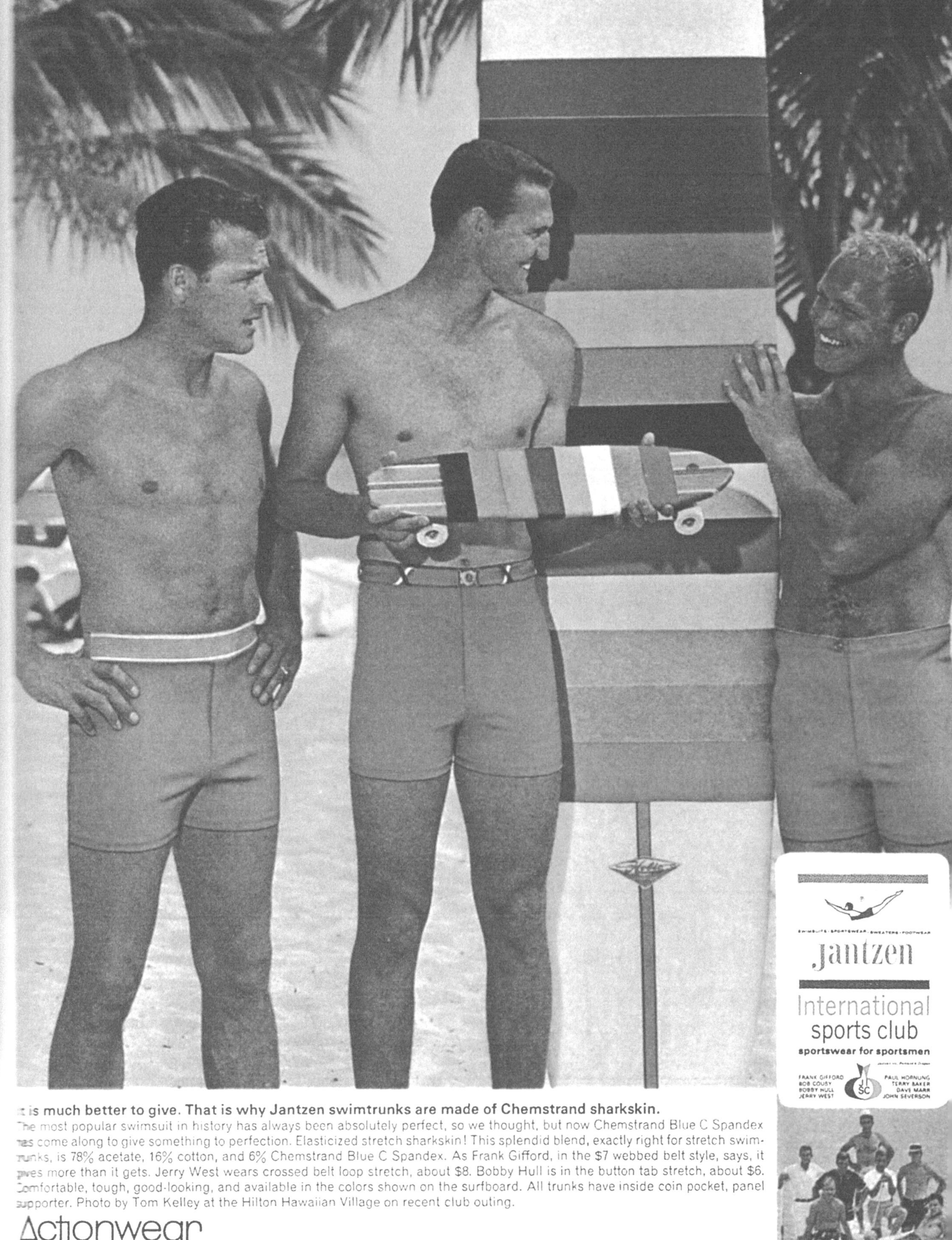

It is much better to give. That is why Jantzen swimtrunks are made of Chemstrand sharkskin.
The most popular swimsuit in history has always been absolutely perfect, so we thought, but now Chemstrand Blue C Spandex has come along to give something to perfection. Elasticized stretch sharkskin! This splendid blend, exactly right for stretch swimtrunks, is 78% acetate, 16% cotton, and 6% Chemstrand Blue C Spandex. As Frank Gifford, in the $7 webbed belt style, says, it gives more than it gets. Jerry West wears crossed belt loop stretch, about $8. Bobby Hull is in the button tab stretch, about $6. Comfortable, tough, good-looking, and available in the colors shown on the surfboard. All trunks have inside coin pocket, panel supporter. Photo by Tom Kelley at the Hilton Hawaiian Village on recent club outing.

Actionwear

MATT MULLICAN

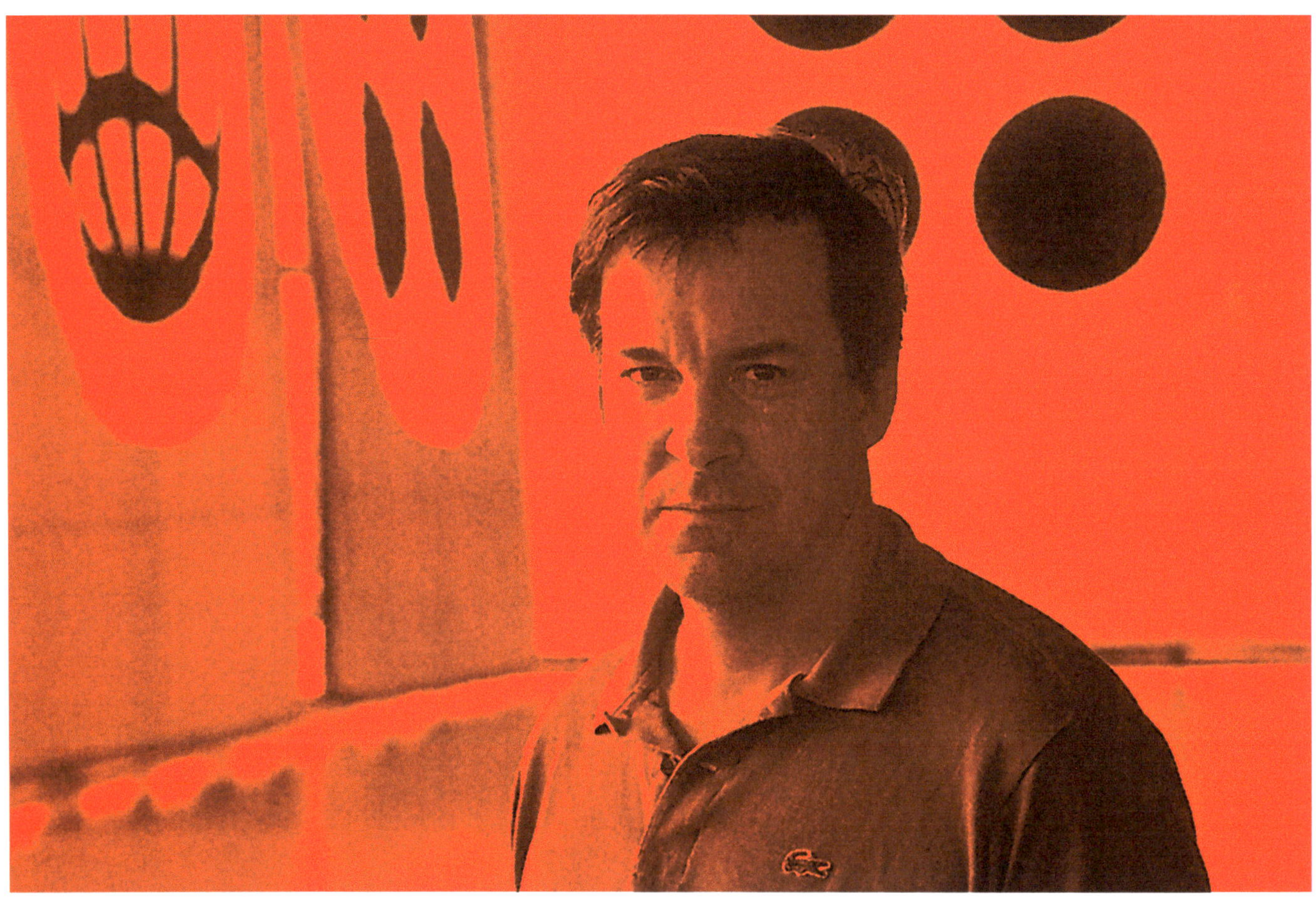

* September 18, 1951, Santa Monica (CA), USA

is an American-Venezuelan artist, who has worked as a lecturer in visual art at several schools and universities. His artistic practice spans a wide range of media such as painting, drawing, installation, graphic, illustration, collage, sculpture, video, and performance, and is characterized by an investigation into binarisms including subject-object, reality-fiction, or consciousness-unconsciousness.[1]

Matt Mullican studied at the California Institute of the Arts, Valencia. In 1974, he graduated with a BFA. He first received recognition as part of the Pictures Generation.[2] Starting in the late 1970s, he began experimenting with art under the condition of hypnosis. In that trance-like, liminal state of mind Mullican explored the subconscious world of what he calls 'that person'—his alter ego.[3] From there, he created art in two different states of being—as himself, the trained and conscious artist, and as 'that person', "an ageless and genderless being."[4] The art-making and mind-world of 'that person' is video-documented from a series of performances in *That Person's Workbook* (2007).[5] From the 1980s, furthermore, he started to develop a complex "model of cosmology,"[6] a specific semiotic system involving a concrete color-and-sign index,[7] based on an abstract formal language. He works with established pictograms, diagrams, photographs, or symbols and connects them with drafted ones, and translates and arranges them into his own cosmology.[8] The intention behind that systematic appropriation of the world could be described as an experiment to register the invisible as well as perceived reality.[9]

Mullican's work has been exhibited widely in the United States, as well as internationally at institutions such as Pirelli HangarBicocca, Milan (2018), The UCLA Hammer Museum, Los Angeles (2014), Haus der Kunst, Munich (2011, 2008), The Metropolitan Museum, New York (2009), Centre Georges Pompidou, Paris (2008), and art festivals like the Biennale Sao Paulo (2008) and documenta, Kassel (1997, 1992, 1982). LB

Matt Mullican, Neue Nationalgalerie (June 1995).
Photo by Christian Jungeblodt.

PLAYING WITH WORDS AND IMAGES

By Katharina Brandt

n 1970, John Baldessari made a radical decision: he burned most of his artworks. Known as *Cremation Project*, it initiated the new beginning of his artistic orientation—away from landscape painting and convention and toward postmodernism and conceptual art.

Conceptual art deals with the artistic heritage of modernity and postmodernism, bringing them together in a contextual relationship. Through the lens of postmodernism, the idea, context, and conditions of art are repeatedly questioned, without totally disregarding the traces of earlier art.[1]

The following year, he announced 'I will not make any more boring art'—a statement that also became the subject of his perhaps best-known conceptual performance.

The overall composition of the work is based on an idea; it plays with the relationship between the individual components of the work and the individual perception of the viewers. Baldessari's decision to ban boring art from his artistic repertoire is, at first glance, reflected in his direct and simple statement. At second glance, however, one sees the irony of creating such a visual statement, with its immensely pictorial quality. The work presents, in a conceptual form of a closed system of representation, the interplay between associative language and narrative image.[2]

I Will Not Make Any More Boring Art contains a reflexive statement that reflects on art and aesthetics, reorienting the concept of art itself. While Baldessari's sentence appears plausible as a statement, it becomes contradictory as soon as it is pulled into the work of art. The tedious repetition of the statement 'I will not make any more boring art' becomes, eventually, boring art.

Text and image in Baldessari's artwork are closely related to one another, even merging with each other. The statement becomes the overall composition. The work's performative act of punishment and seemingly endless and repetitive writing onto the gallery walls is also a performance of the boredom of art. At the same time, it refers to the traditional meaning of image and text in art. Baldessari doesn't

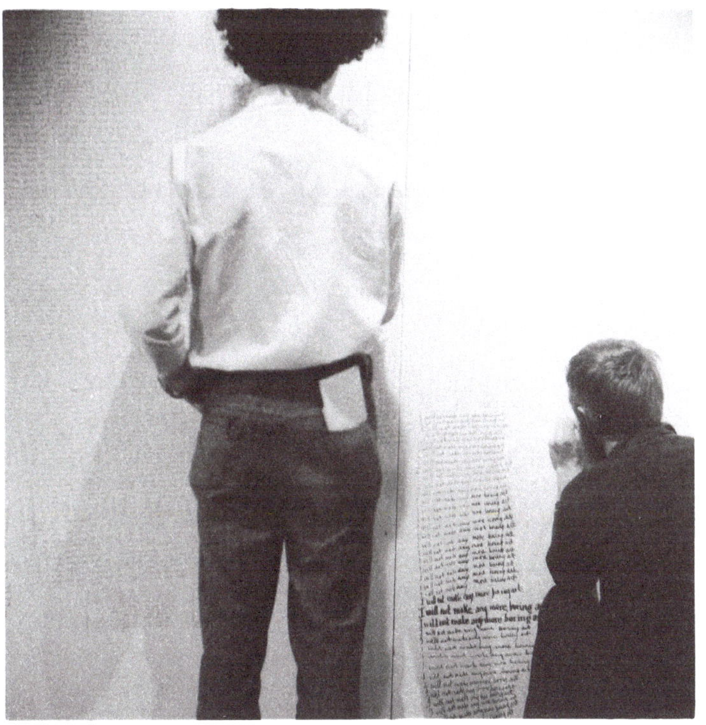

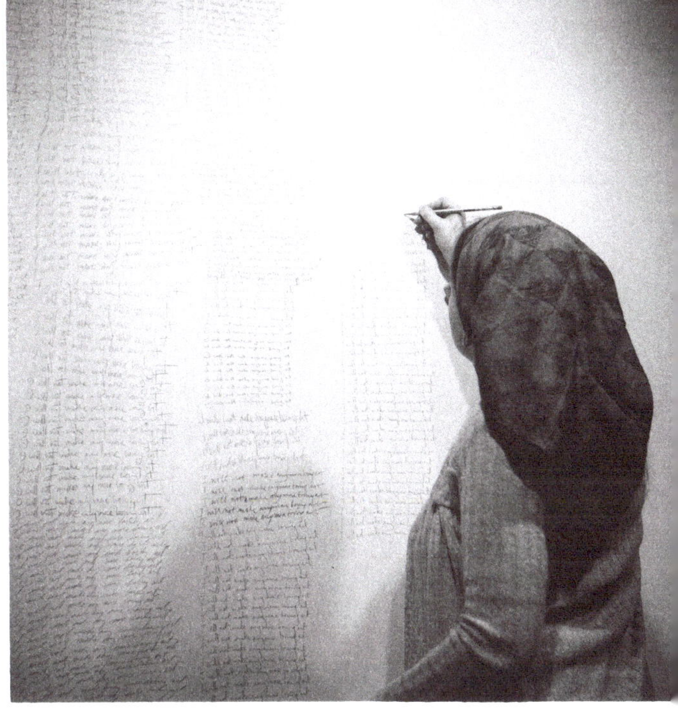

foreground the image, instead placing text at the center of his work. Text ultimately comes to define the image through perception, imagination, and meaning in the viewer's mind. This closed system of language and image is tautological, in which what is read and seen form a whole.[3]

Baldessari's work plays with the viewers' perceptions and preconceived expectations about the relationship between linguistic and pictorial signs. But Baldessari goes beyond puns, however, expanding semantic self-reference by letting the image reveal its supposed content and status through the text.

Baldessari breaks aesthetic norms in emblazoning his statement 'I will not make any more boring art' onto any brightly painted wall. With its unartistic, banal, and inconspicuous character, the work of art undermines art more generally. The work's pluralized authorship and its performativity further disturb art's conventions, as Baldessari did not act as the executor himself but let outsiders (in this case students) carry out the work. Moreover, Baldessari didn't sign the work with his name, suggesting a renouncement of authorship.[4] Instead he plays with the contradictions of aesthetic norms in the work of art, exploring the relation between text and image, statement and representation, in order to never again make boring art. The viewer cannot escape this ironic game of perception and expectation, but upon engaging with Baldessari's work the viewer is forced into an encounter with their own desire to satisfy their own urge for enlightenment, meaning, and definition.

Baldessari's intention is reflected equally in the thoughts and words of the viewer, who may begin to reflect on their own position within the work. *I Will Not Make Any More Boring Art* creates space for myriad interpretations, demonstrating the ways in which the interplay of language and image in art can become communication—at the same time evoking different responses among participants and viewers. In leaving the realization of the work to students (of Nova Scotia College of Art and Design), Baldessari also left space for interpretation. It was his only will, he said, "… to redeem themselves or whatever."[5]

John Baldessari, *I Will Not Make Any More Boring Art* (1971), graphic on wall (temporary installation).

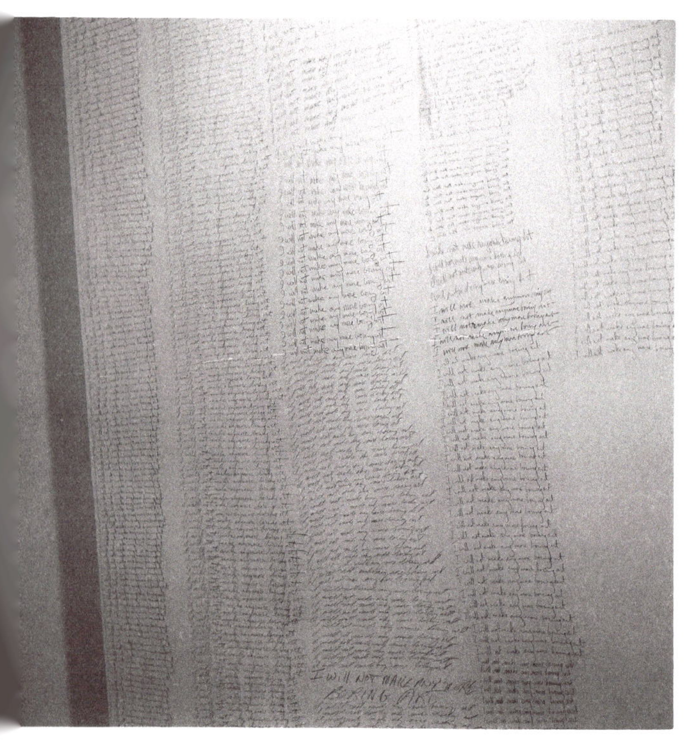
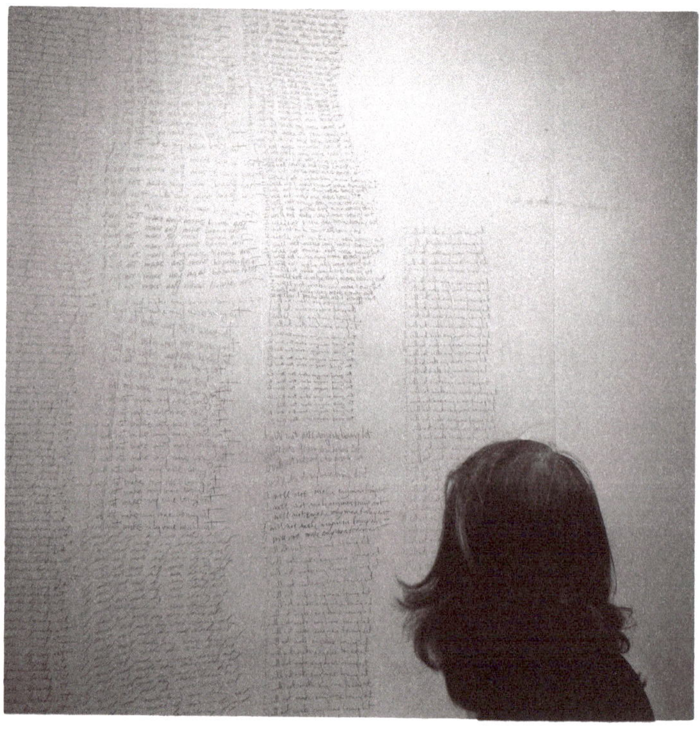

THE STATUS OF INSTRUCTIONAL LETTERS IN CONCEPTUAL ART

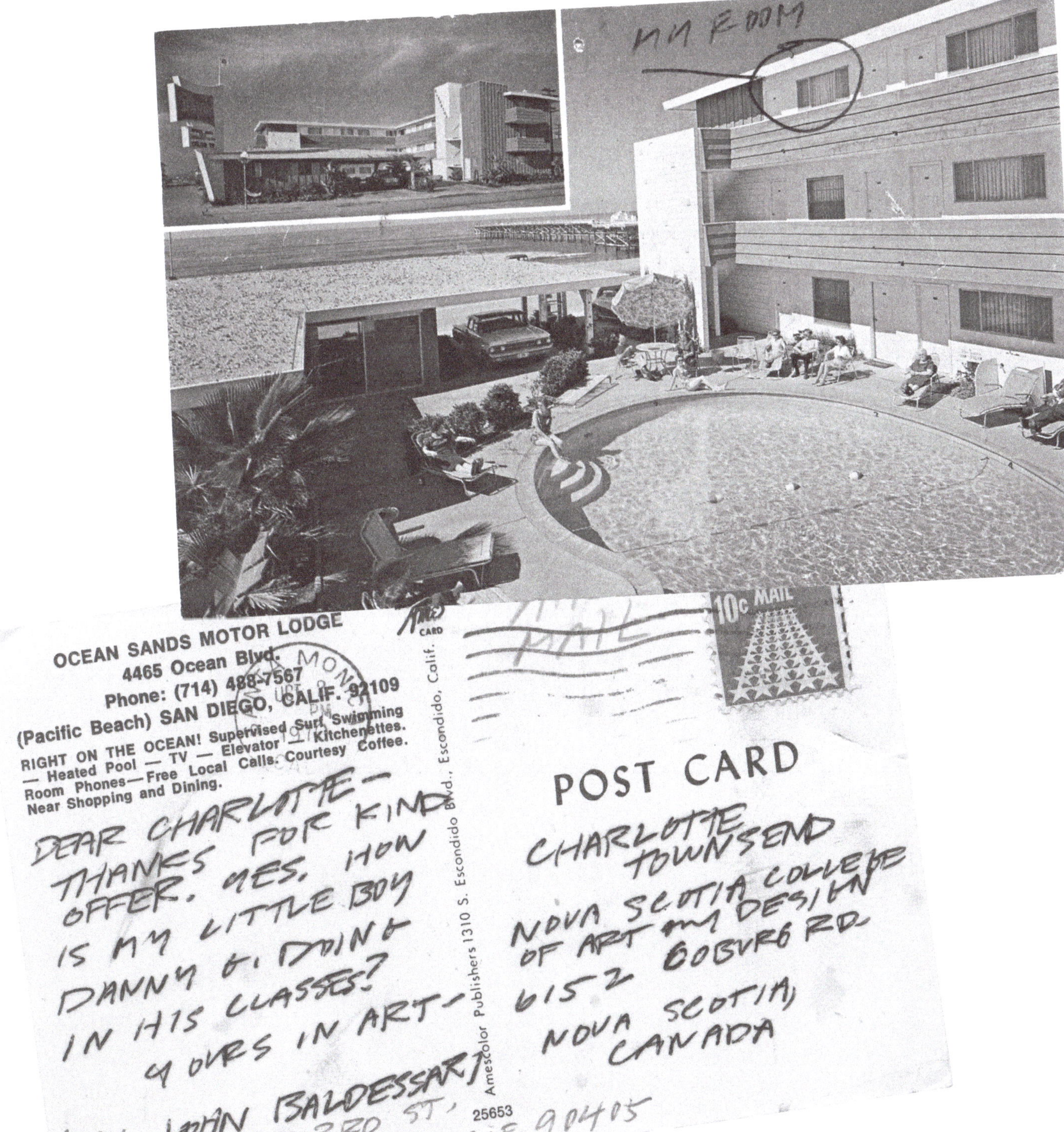

In 1970, the Nova Scotia College of Art and Design (NSCAD) asked John Baldessari to participate in an exhibition. In a letter to Charlotte Townsend-Gault (February 1, 1971), he provides instructions for his piece *I Will Not Make Any More Boring Art* for the mezzanine exhibition.

This letter, which was private correspondence between Baldessari and Townsend-Gault, is now part of NSCAD's Mezzanine Gallery Collection among other documents and correspondence from Baldessari, including a postcard sent by Baldessari to Townsend-Gault. The fact that the letter and other documental material of *I Will Not Make Any More Boring Art* have been added to the collection shows that it was given great importance and thus considered an integral part of the art piece.

This raises the question of the status of those documents, and more specifically of correspondence in art. The very existence of mail-art reveals this ambiguity. It is interesting to take a look at the project *I Got Up* from On Kawara, who sent 90 postcards to Baldessari from 1974 to 1975 saying only the sentence: 'I got up at' and the time that Kawara got up at in different cities.

However, there is a major difference between the letters in the collection of NSCAD and Kawara's mail-art: the former were not meant to be an art project, only the instructions for a piece of art.

It is interesting to see how, what was initially a document linked to the artistic process only, became part of the work of art itself. The documents are no longer a 'bonus.' On the one hand, they are vital for the understanding of *I Will Not Make Any Boring Art*, for instance, the way that the letter describes the work as a 'punishment piece.' Furthermore, the tone of the letter and the presentation is very typical of Baldessari's sense of humor and irony, and therefore is important for the interpretation of *I Will Not Make Any Boring Art*. We also gain information through the letter about the genesis of the artwork and how important the pragmatic aspect is: "I have no idea what your gallery looks like and I know you don't have much money for shows so that conditions my ideas." Therefore, those documents provide useful context for our reception of the piece. Baldessari's requests influence our perception of what is 'important' in this project. We understand, for example, that it did not really matter who wrote the lines but that it had to be the same sentence, handwritten and with correct spelling.

But on the other hand, the letter is more than simply a list of instructions for Townsend-Gault, nor is is merely information to the public. The question we could ask is: what makes the lines written on the walls more an artwork than those written in this letter? One could even think that the letter has more 'artistic value' than the sentences on the walls, because it is directly written by the hand of the artist. We could even state that, in the context of an exhibition, the letter becomes an artwork itself.

All of this has an influence on our perception of the piece: it raises questions about authorship, but also about the nature of the artwork itself: is the artwork the writing process, the sentences themselves, or the overall exhibition? The fact that Baldessari's letter is now part of their collection seems to indicate that the Nova Scotia College considers the artistic process to be on a par with the final result. LD

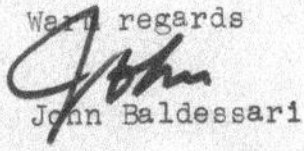

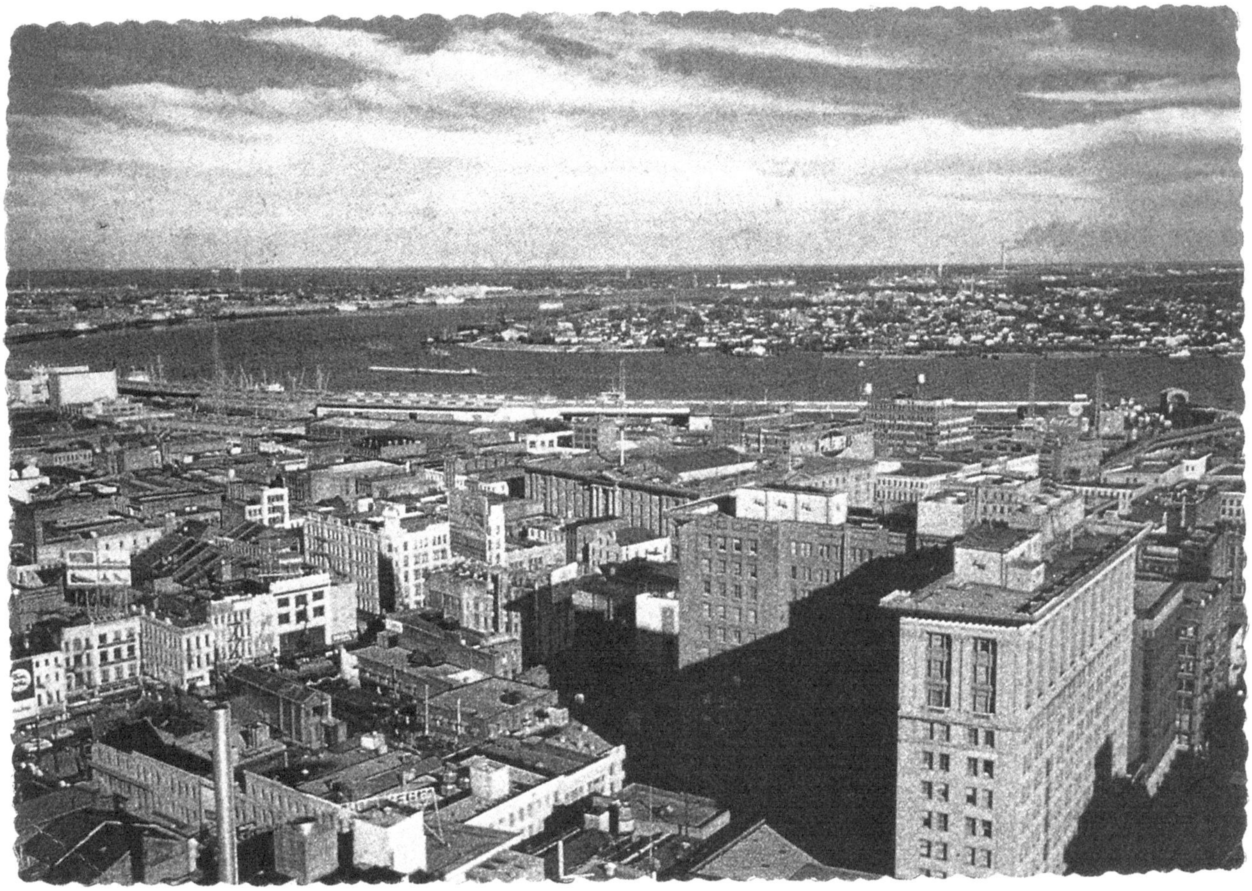

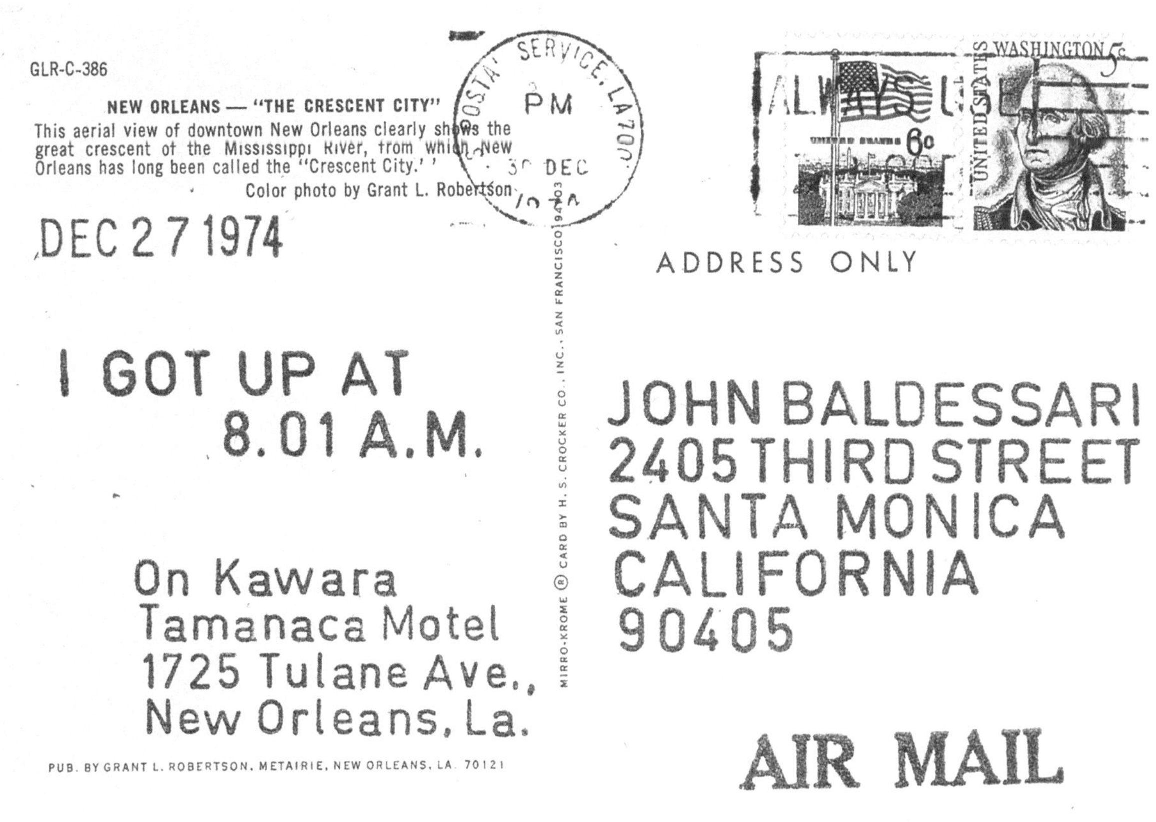

GLR-C-386

NEW ORLEANS — "THE CRESCENT CITY"
This aerial view of downtown New Orleans clearly shows the
great crescent of the Mississippi River, from which New
Orleans has long been called the "Crescent City."
Color photo by Grant L. Robertson

DEC 27 1974

I GOT UP AT
8.01 A.M.

On Kawara
Tamanaca Motel
1725 Tulane Ave.,
New Orleans, La.

PUB. BY GRANT L. ROBERTSON, METAIRIE, NEW ORLEANS, LA. 70121

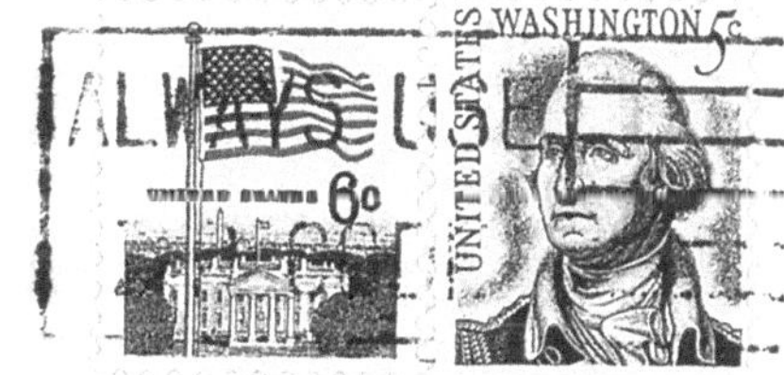

ADDRESS ONLY

JOHN BALDESSARI
2405 THIRD STREET
SANTA MONICA
CALIFORNIA
90405

AIR MAIL

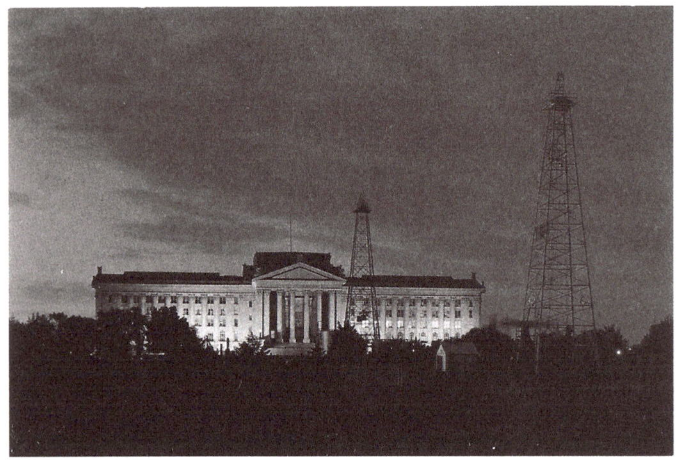

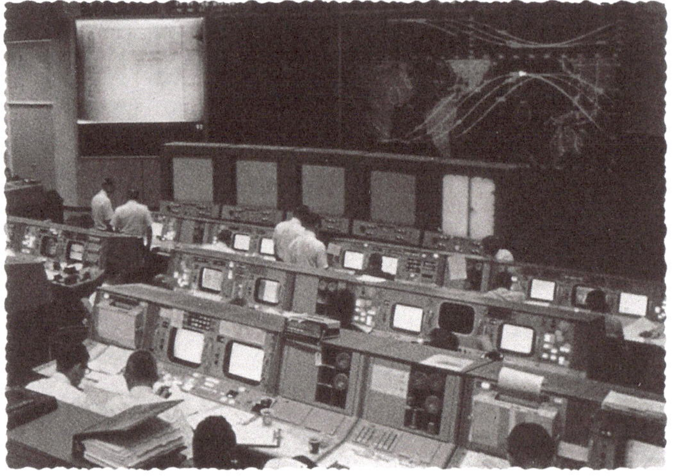

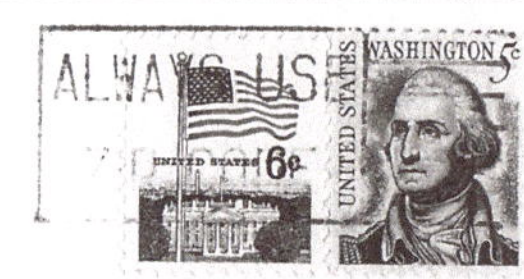
OKLAHOMA STATE CAPITOL
and Oil Derricks
JAN 4 1975
I GOT UP AT
8.12 A.M.
On Kawara
Holiday Inn
520 W. Main St.,
Oklahoma City, Okla.
This scene available in color slides.
Published by Bob Taylor Photography, Cordell, Oklahoma
Post Card
ALWAYS US
JOHN BALDESSARI
2405 THIRD STREET
SANTA MONICA
CALIFORNIA
90405
AIR MAIL

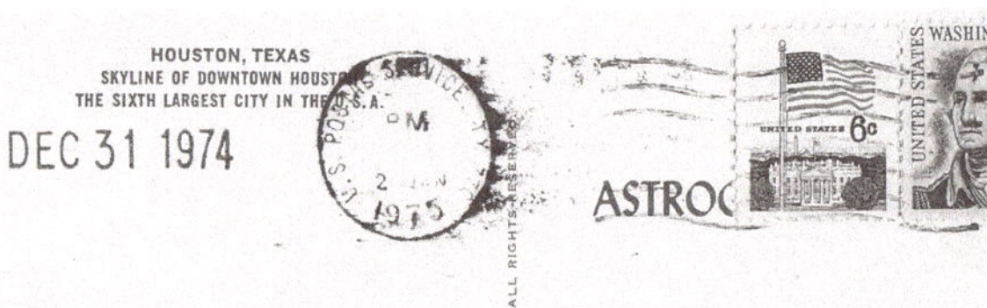
HOUSTON, TEXAS
SKYLINE OF DOWNTOWN HOUSTON
THE SIXTH LARGEST CITY IN THE U.S.A.
DEC 31 1974
I GOT UP AT
9.21 A.M.
On Kawara
Holiday Inn
2100 Memorial Dr.,
Houston, Texas
AC-100
ASTRO
ASTROCARD COMPANY, HOUSTON, TEXAS. ALL RIGHTS RESERVED.
JOHN BALDESSARI
2405 THIRD STREET
SANTA MONICA
CALIFORNIA
90405
AIR MAIL

JOHN BALDESSARI

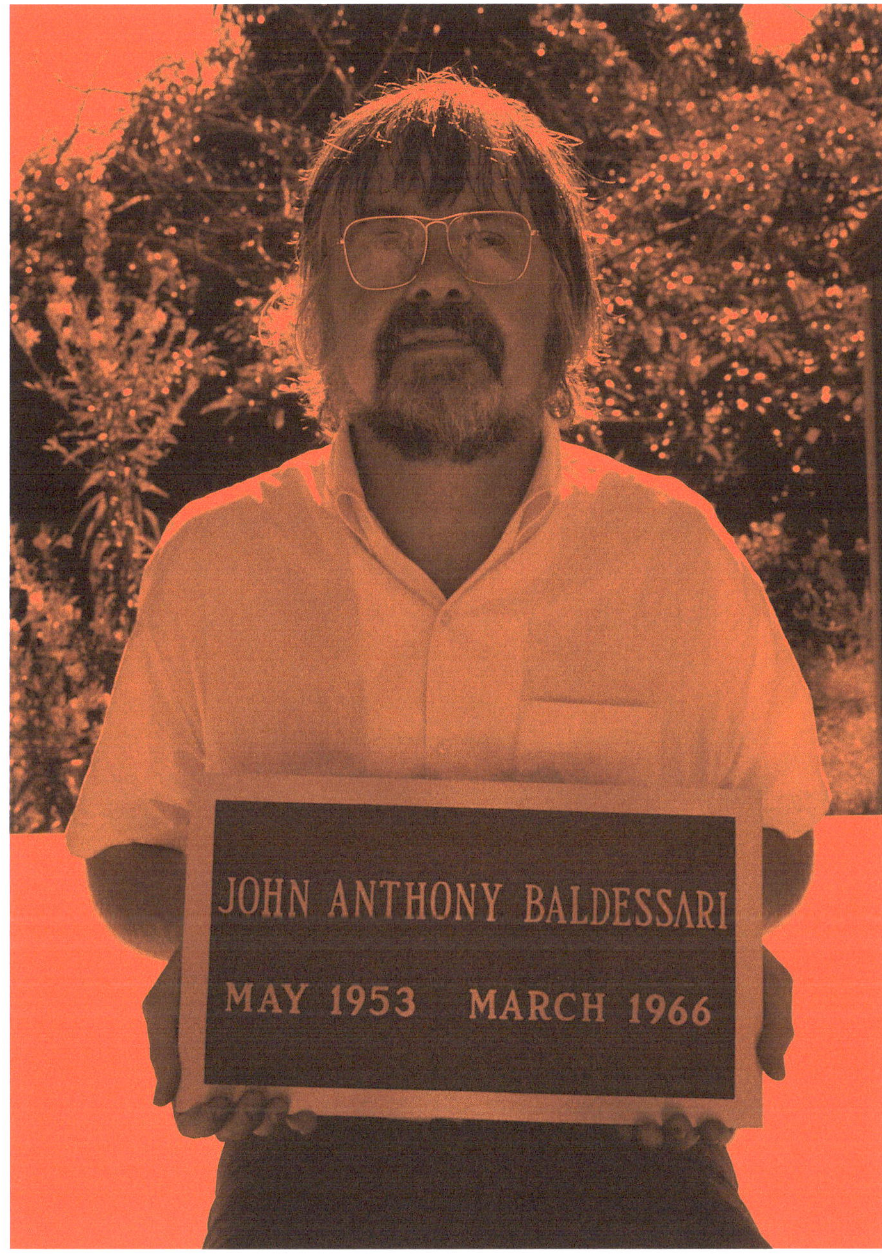

John Baldessari with bronze plaque from the
Cremation Project (1970).

*June 17, 1931, National City (CA),
USA

is an conceptual artist especially known for his appropriation of found images. He works with a variety of media, including painting, photography, printmaking, installation and sculpture, video, and performance.[1] Starting his career as a painter, he developed into a mixed-media multidisciplinary artist in the late 1960s/ 70s. His art practice is characterized by juxtaposition, appropriation of pictures, application of dots, and strategies of pointing.[2]

Baldessari taught at CalArts (1970–88) and influenced a whole generation of young artists in this time. His Post-Studio art classes were characterized by field trips, unconventional assignments, conceptual art practice, and medium-openness.[3] Characteristic works of that period were *I Will Not Make Any More Boring Art* (1971,) and the video performance *I Am Making Art* (1971), in which he video-documented himself while striking poses, each time repetitively proclaiming the phrase 'I am making art'.[4] *Wrong* (1967) is a key example of his use of juxtaposition of text and image, which displayed a new aesthetic potential.[5] After CalArts, he was a teacher at UCLA (1996– 2007).[6] Other notable visual works are *Everything is Purged* (1966–68), *Bloody Sundae* (1987), *Frames and Ribbon* (1988), and the *Hot & Cold* series (2018).

His work has been presented in international institutions, such as the Tate Modern, London, the Metropolitan Museum of Art, New York, and at Documenta 5 and 7, Kassel. His most recent exhibition is *John Baldessari, Hot and Cold* at Marian Goodman, NY (2019).[7] His work is held in collections at the MoMA, New York, the National Gallery of Art, Washington, D.C., and others.[8]   LB

THE SERIALITY OF REENACTMENTS:
I WILL NOT MAKE ANY MORE BORING ART

By Anna Sønderup

I will not make any more boring art.
I will not make any more boring art.
I will not make any more boring art.
I will not make any more boring art.
I will not make any more boring art.
I will not make any more boring art.
I will not make any more boring art.
I will not make any more boring art.
I will not make any more boring art.
I will not make any more boring art.
I will not make any more boring art.
I will not make any more boring art.
I will not make any more boring art.
I will not make any more boring art.
I will not make any more boring art.
I will not make any more boring art.

John Baldessari, *I Will Not Make Any More Boring Art* (1971).

n 2010, art students were invited to the Whitney Museum of American Art to reenact *I Will Not Make Any More Boring Art*, the conceptual work by American artist John Baldessari initially performed by students at the Nova Scotia College of Art and Design in 1971. Baldessari himself was absent from the performance, since he was unable to afford the trip. Instead, he wrote a letter with few instructions and requested the performance be videotaped. The instructions asked the students to repeatedly write the sentence 'I will not make any more boring art' directly onto the wall of the museum. The work prompted many questions regarding authorship and the role of the artist.[1]

The 2010 project at the Whitney Museum re-ignites these same questions, but also questions the role of repetition as reenactment. Reenactments are often associated with performance art of the 1970s, as a way of experiencing a new mode of embodiment in the here and now. However, Baldessari is no performance artist and even though his projects have performative elements, it is rarely the explicit focus.[2] This also pertains to *I Will Not Make Any More Boring Art*—while the process of students writing the same sentence repeatedly was certainly performative, it is not necessarily a performance piece. The performance art of the 1970s was often devised as a unique experience that would vanish immediately after it was performed. This contrasts with Baldessari's project, where uniqueness was replaced by the act of repetition. Baldessari wrote the sentence repeatedly, videotaped it, and had students repeat it once again. The work was not dictated by the here and now, but instead it worked as a process performed at different times and places. The form and the content of the work can easily be repeated because of the work's inherent seriality. Therefore, it is necessary to understand reenactments of Baldessari's work not as unique, once-in-a-lifetime experiences but rather as simple, serial repetitions.

In his dissertation, Ingo Maerker touches upon Baldessari's works and conceptual art in general. He offers some characteristics of conceptual art as a way of understanding and decoding this often complex field. One such characteristic is the serial and processual nature of many conceptual projects and art pieces. This refers to the open and uncompleted way a work is presented and perceived, as well as a series of repetitions of an 'original'.[3] Seriality is especially relevant in the case of reenactments, since the reenactment itself is part of a series of repetitions. Back in 1971, the work had a serial quality since the same sentence was repeated, albeit differently because of each student's handwriting. The reenactment built upon this seriality, thereby showing that the work is never ending.

The reenactment at the Whitney Museum held many similarities to the first performance in 1971. We see the same sentence repeated, again written by students. However, the repetition also highlights the differences between them.

At the reenactment at the Whitney Museum, there was an invitation to come see the art students perform their version of Baldessari's work.[4] This invitation highlights the performative act of writing the sentences, and thus places this writing at the center of the reenactment. The video documentation and photographs from the first performance by the Nova Scotian students are scarce. Instead, we often see photographs of Baldessari's handwritten text, which then becomes representational for the entire work. Therefore, the work from the Whitney Museum can be perceived as a reenactment with a difference, because of the way the archives of the previous project are represented. This can be seen, for example, on the MoMA Learning website, where we see only lithographs—there are no pictures of the students writing or working on the project.[5] Even though the first work had the same processual elements, we often focus on the lithographs of Baldessari's handwriting, which therefore makes it easier to ascribe the entire work to him alone.

Another Baldessari work from the same year was also subject for a reenactment, this time at the KW Institute for Contemporary Art in 2001. The project was part of a series called *A Little Bit of History Repeated* and consisted of reenactments of works by Vito Acconci, Yoko Ono, and Baldessari. Here a younger generation of artists reenacted Baldessari's work *I Am Making Art* based on video documentation. In the video, we see Baldessari performing different bodily movements while repeating the sentence 'I am making art'.[6] Once again, we see a strong element of repetition in the work itself, which prompts the question of what art can be and how it is produced. The performance is another example of processuality and seriality, showing that even the most mundane activities can produce art. As in *I Will Not Make Any More Boring Art*, the performance has an utterance at its center that is being repeated. The sentence remains the same throughout but each utterance is combined with a new movement that results in a series. At the same time, the art is produced throughout the video and thus the process of making art becomes the artwork itself. Unlike the reenactment at the Whitney Museum, the reenactment at the KW Institute for Contemporary Art was not documented, meaning it is more difficult to argue for processuality in this case.

However, what becomes apparent through these examples is how repetitions, no matter how mundane or simple they seem, will always deviate from the original based on the context of the

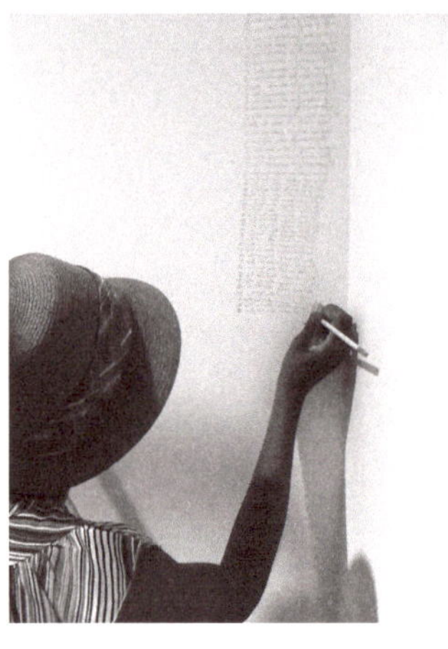
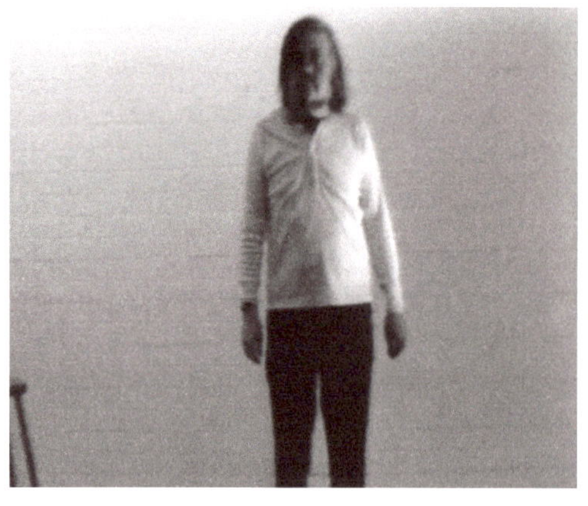
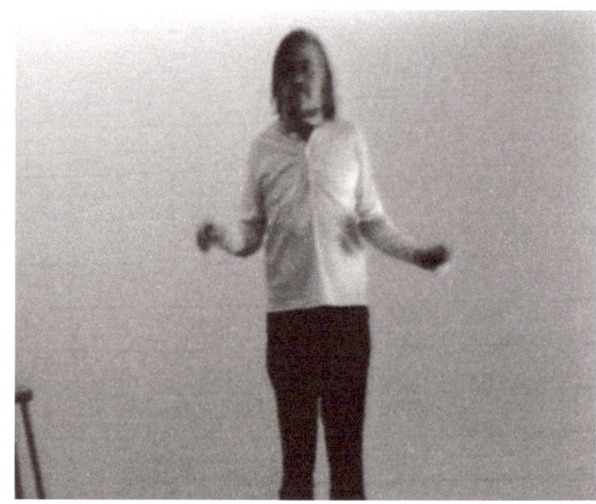
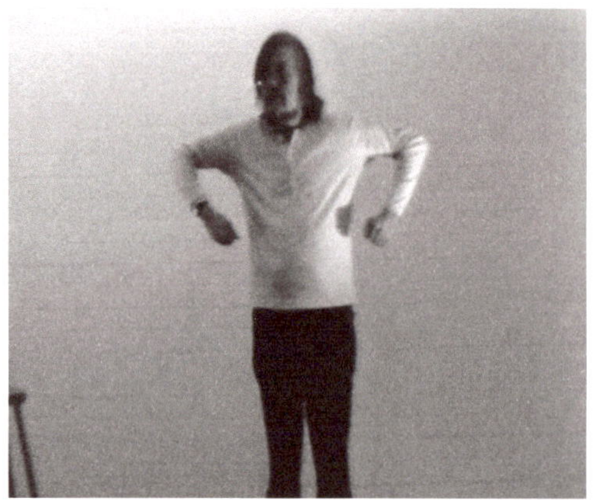
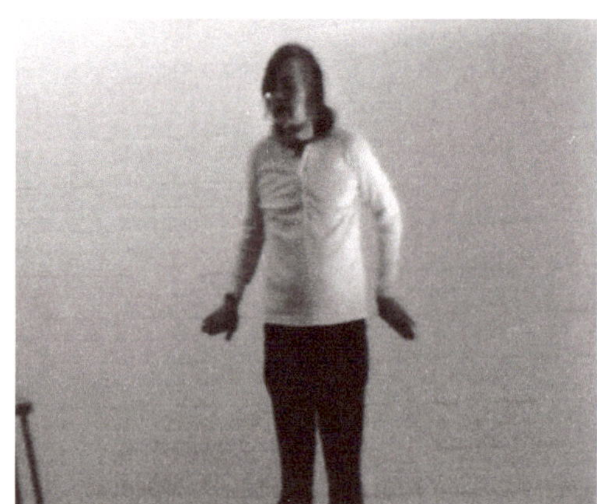
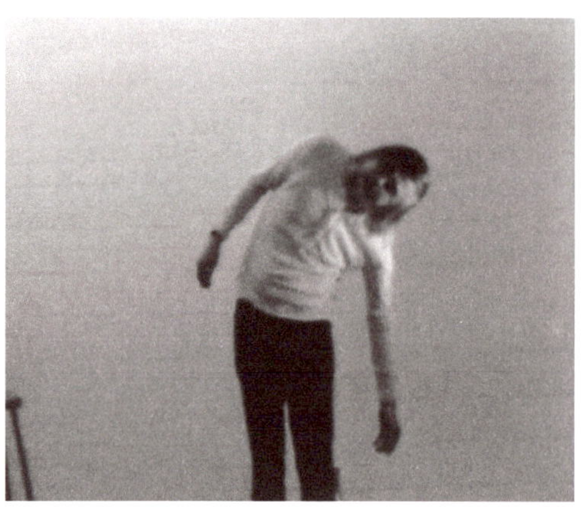
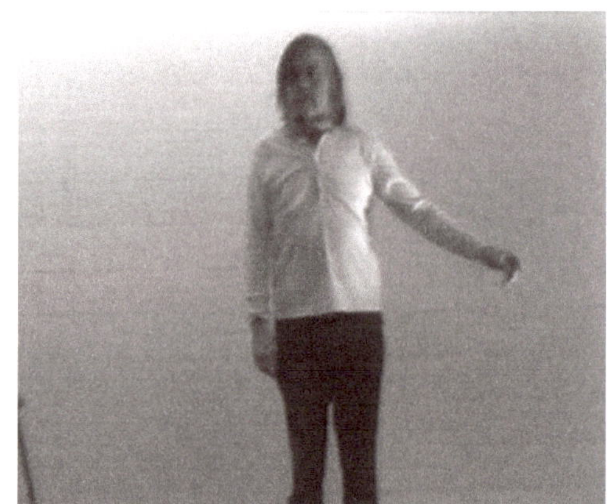

reenactments. The serial quality of Baldessari's works invites reenactment and repetition, and these reenactments reiterate the importance of his works and reactivate his ideas in the present.

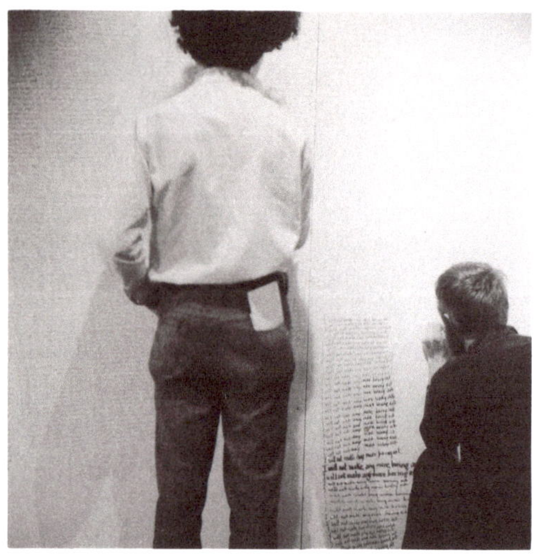

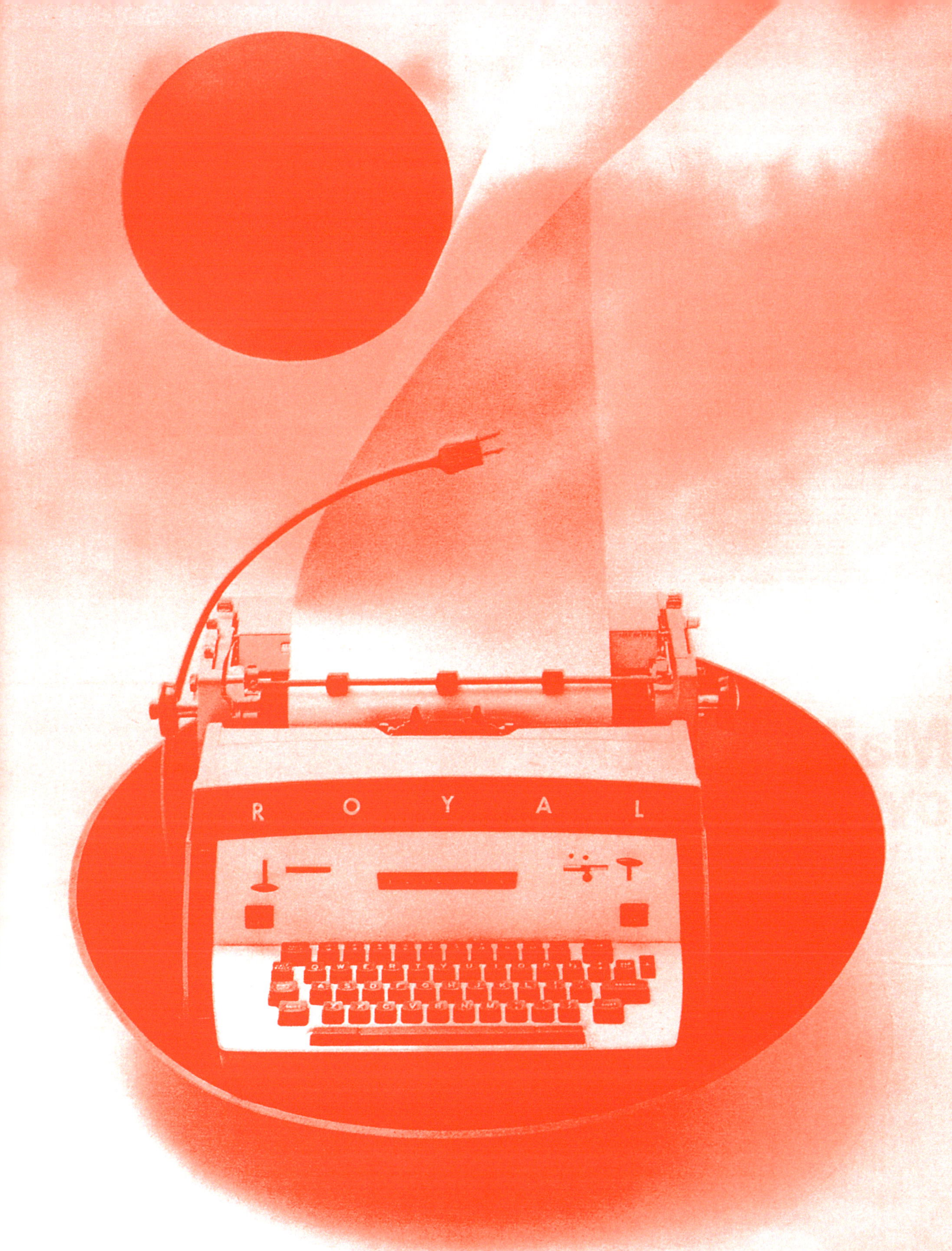

The new Royal Electric Typewriter is one of the <u>most</u> electric machines in business. You may be close to buying it. But before you make your decision, please do yourself, your secretary, and your company this service: see <u>all</u> the makes of electric typewriters. Check them for automation features, for touch, for printwork, for any other quality you wish. Only in this way can you really know the worth of the choice you will make.

JAMES WELLING

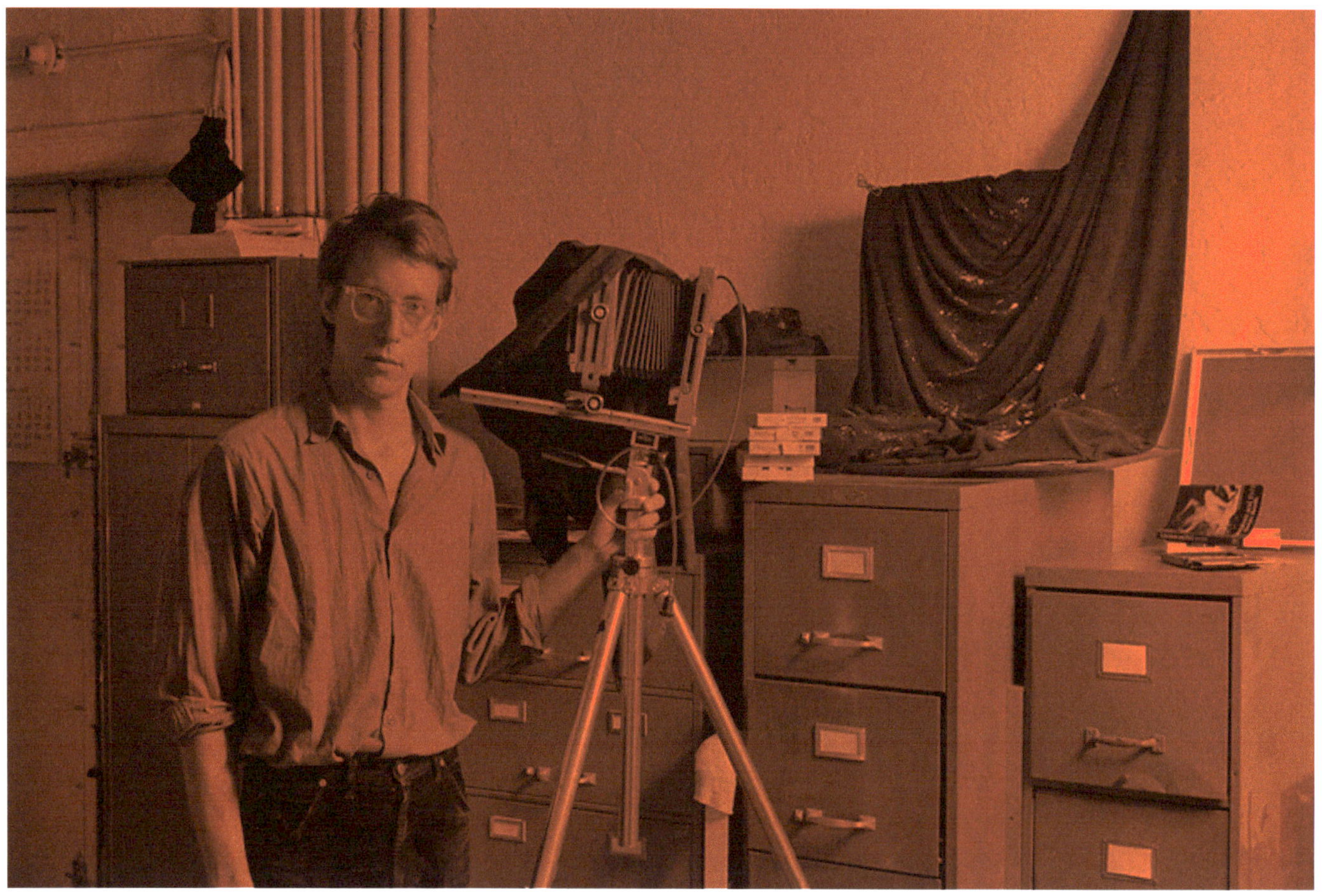

***1951, Hartford (CT), USA**

is an American photographer who has also worked with video, sculpture, and drawing.[1] Welling's body of work is diverse and difficult to summarize, but suggests an ongoing experimental approach.[2] Throughout his career, he experimented with different photography techniques from analog to digital—producing Polaroids, photograms, gelatin silver prints, and digital prints.[3] Welling can be considered "a post-conceptual artist,"[4] emerging through the influence of the California Institute of the Arts (CalArts) and early photographic experiences. His work is often marked by the renunciation of conventional concepts, established asthetical norms of photography, and he instead puts a spotlight on the medium's construction.[5]

James Welling studied at other universities before attending CalArts in 1971, where he received his MFA in 1974.[6] He was initially interested in painting and modern dance.[7] At CalArts he studied with John Baldessari and Wolfgang Stoerchle. He was Baldessari's teaching assistant from 1973–74. During this time, his work focus was on video before turning to photography.[8] His early photographic works include series like *Polaroid Photographs* (1975–76), *Los Angeles Architecture & Portraits* (1976–78), and *Diary / Landscape* (1977).[9] His art career began as part of the Pictures Generation next to artists such as Matt Mullican or Jack Goldstein.[10]

Welling's work covers a wide range of photographic styles, from a documentary, black and white aesthetic like the series *Railroad Photographs* (1987–94) to abstract photography such as the *Chemical* series (2013–16).[11] He often tries out different techniques to alter the outcome of photographic processes. Welling held different teaching positions, but most significant was probably the position as head of photography in the Department of Art at UCLA (1995–2016).[12] His work has been exhibited widely in North America, Europe, and Japan.[13]   LB

James Welling at his studio (ca. 1984).

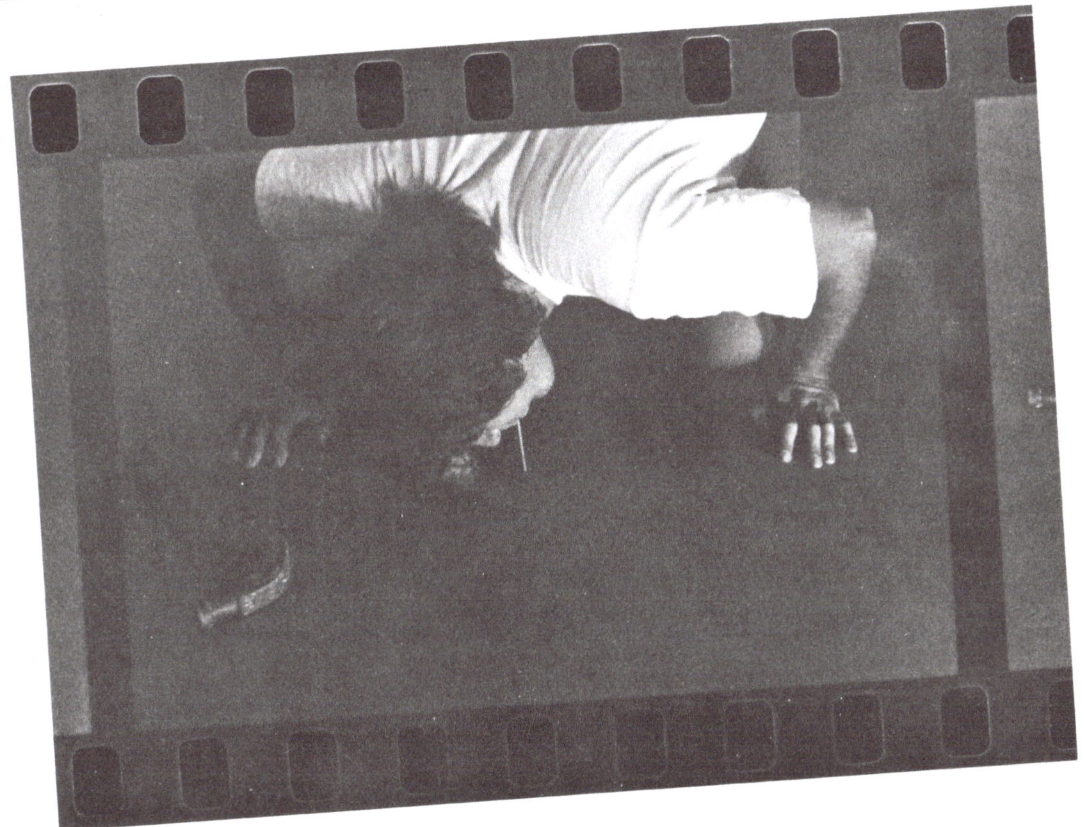

Performance piece: Sunday, November 19, 8-10 p.m.

JACK GOLDSTEIN

Films: November 21, 22, 24   1-3 p.m.

MIZUNO GALLERY
669 N. La Cienega Boulevard
659-3545

JACK GOLDSTEIN

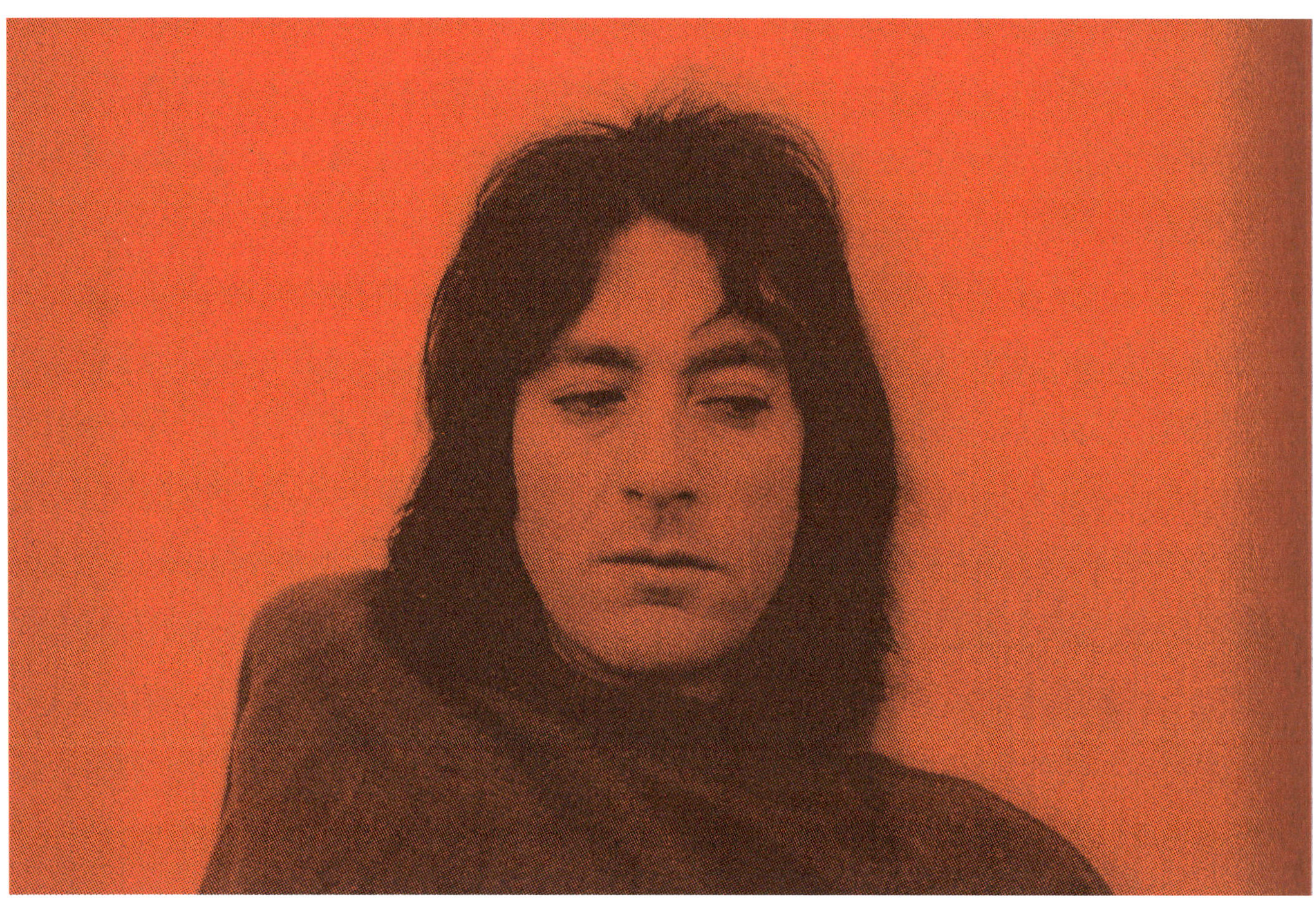

*September 27, 1945, Montreal, Canada
†March 4, 2003, San Bernadino (CA), USA

was a conceptual artist living in the U.S. who worked in performance art, video, sound recording, and painting. He is considered part of the Pictures Generation. His work was characterized by an an experimental practice, especially his video and sound work. Most of his subject matter for painting refers to phenomenons of science, technology, and nature. He intended to produce "the spectacular instant"—actual events that could not be captured with the human eye.[1] Photographic-based motives range from fireworks to thunder, lightening to radar—immaterial, ephemeral, or happening-like subjects.[2]

He first studied at Chouinard Art Institute and later at the California Institute of the Arts (1970–1972). Goldstein was a member of the first graduating class taught under John Baldessari and completed his MFA there.[3] As a graduate student, he was the teaching assistant of Wolfgang Stoerchle.[4] Early works include performances such as *The Artist's Studio* (1971), video projects like *The Jump* (1978), and experimental sound recordings like *Two Restling Cats* or *A Swim Against the Tide* (1976).[5] These unconventional audio recordings captured the sounds of the subject matter they are labeled after. In *The Six Minute Drown* (1977), the listener can hear the isolated painful sounds of a drowning man throughout the six-minute record. After studying in California he moved

to New York, where his work has been exhibited several times at Metro Pictures and John Weber Gallery.[6] He had solo exhibitions at Artists Space (1976), The Kitchen, and other galleries internationally.[7] During the 1980s art boom, he created paintings in a photorealistic style. Goldstein's work has been shown in the U.S., Canada, and European countries such as the UK, Italy, Germany, Netherlands, Austria, and France. More recently, he held a solo-exhibition at the Museum of Contemporary Art, L.A. (2012).[8]   LB

Jack Goldstein, East Tenth Street, New York (1978).

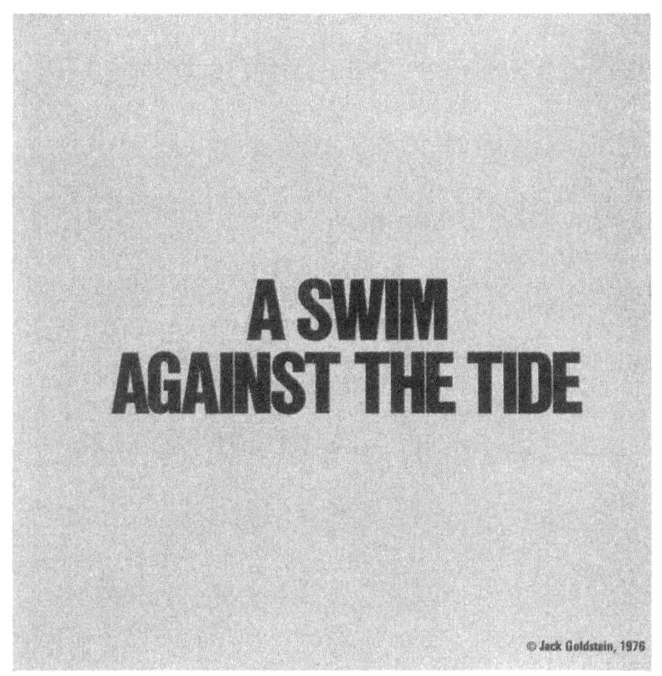

A SWIM
AGAINST THE TIDE
© Jack Goldstein, 1976

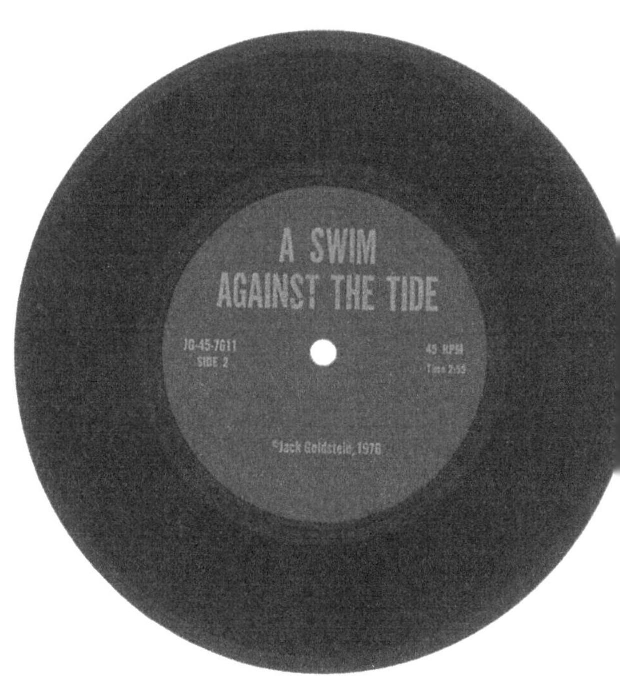

A SWIM
AGAINST THE TIDE
JG-45-7611
SIDE 2
45 RPM
Time 2:55
© Jack Goldstein, 1976

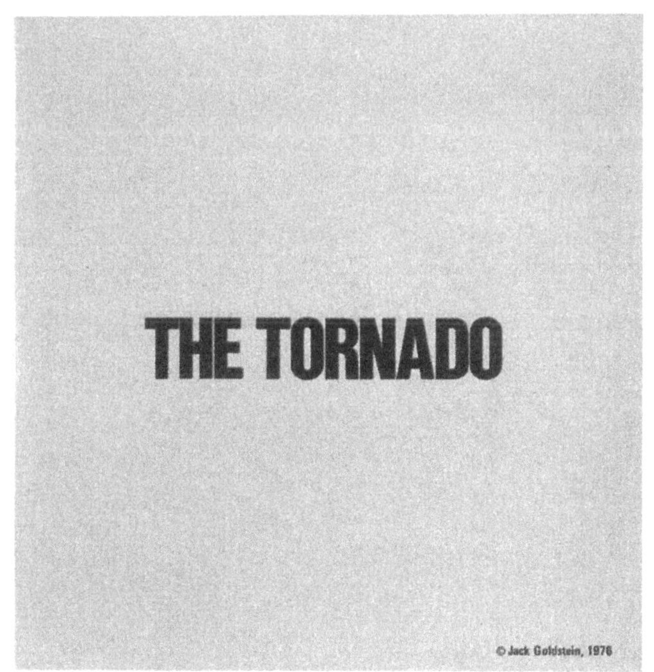

THE TORNADO
© Jack Goldstein, 1976

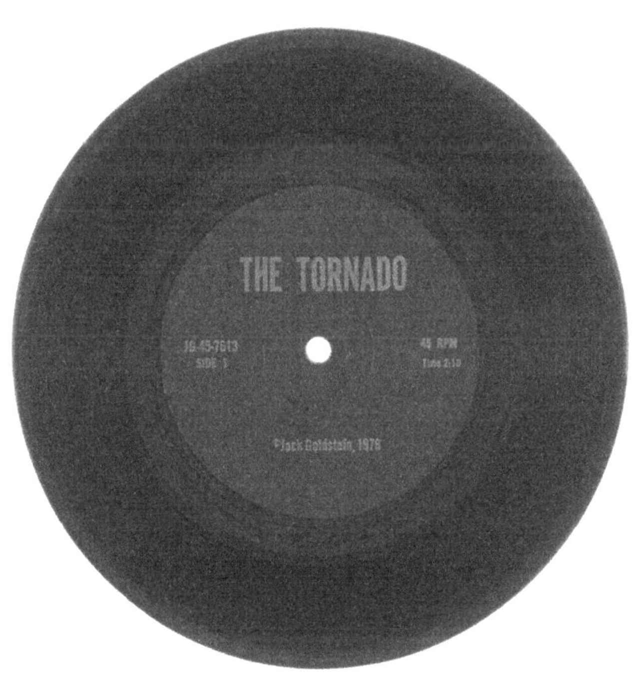

THE TORNADO
JG-45-7613
SIDE 1
45 RPM
Time 2:10
© Jack Goldstein, 1976

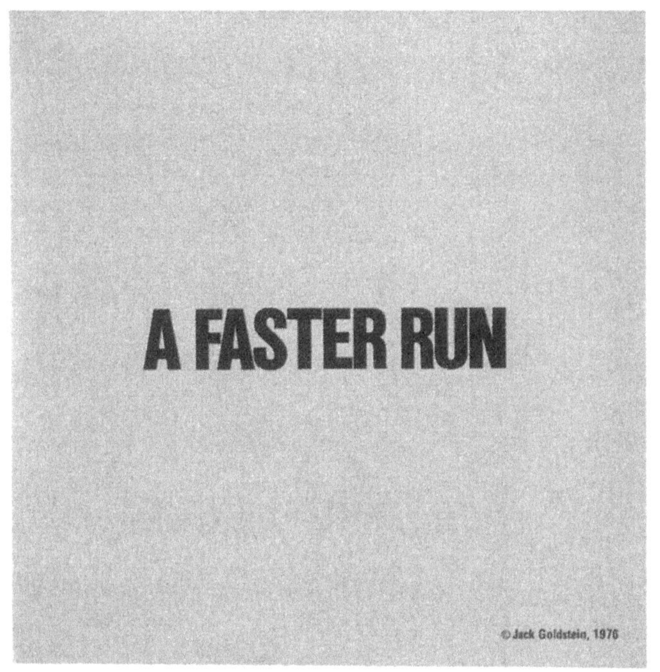

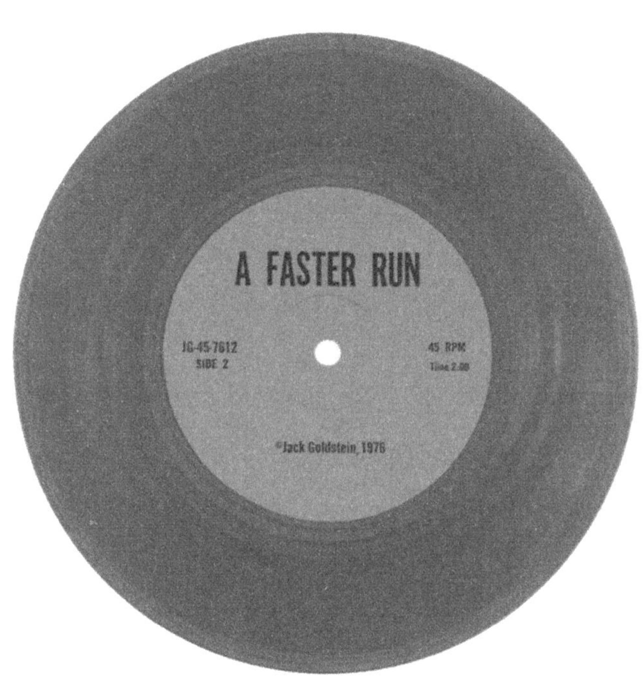

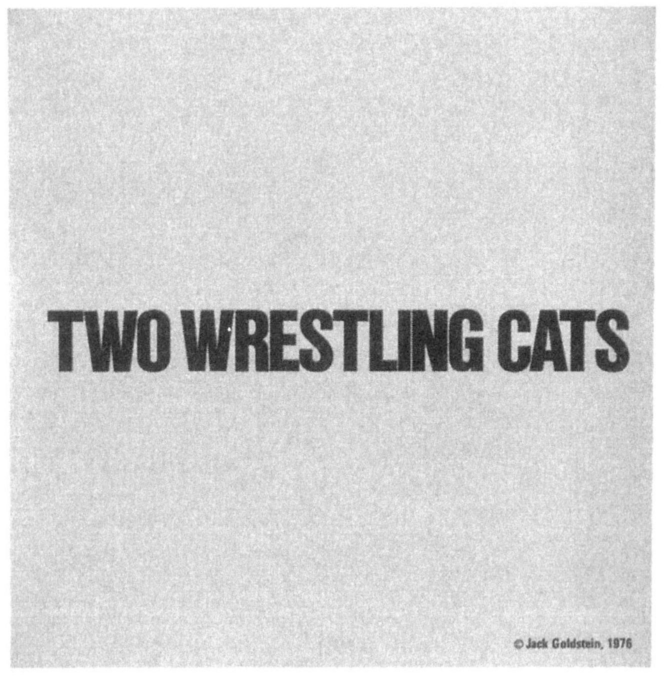

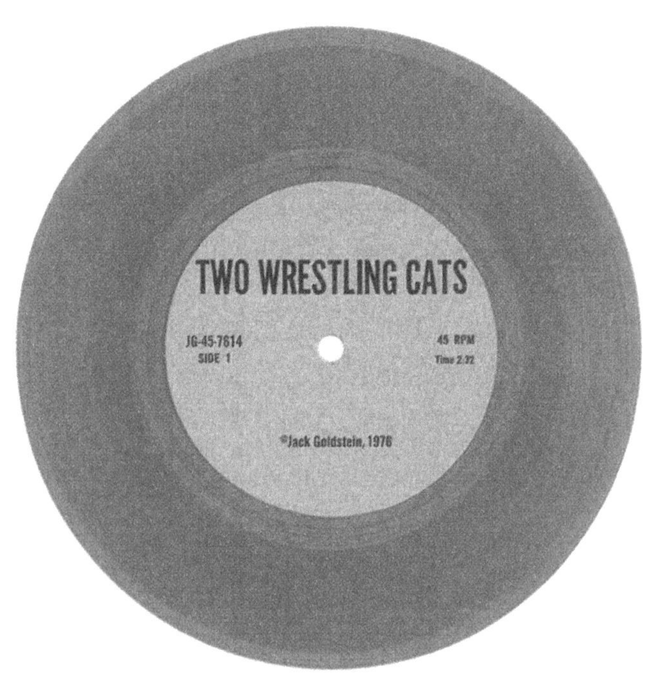

Jack Goldstein, *A Suite of Nine 7-Inch Records with Sound Effects* (detail) (1976).

HOW TO TEACH YOUR STUDENTS ABOUT CONCEPTUAL ART

1

First give them a general introduction to conceptual art:

"Beginning in the late 1960s, conceptual artists questioned long-held assumptions about what defined a work of art. In emphasizing ideas over visual forms, they gave language a central role in their work."[1]

Students will be introduced to two examples of conceptual art: Joseph Kosuth's *One and Three Chairs*, which consists of three parts, the photography of a chair, the photographed chair and the definition for 'chair' printed on a sheet of paper, and John Baldessari's *I Will Not Make Any More Boring Art*. Through discussion they will define and challenge the definition of these artworks and the art institutions in which these are shown. It starts with an introductory discussion. Students will be divided into groups of three, each student will be given a card with a word on it. The task is to draw what is written on the card for the other students to guess. One of the cards has a noun on it (for example, chair, cat), the other one a verb (e.g., run, eat), and the third one an idea or concept (e.g., freedom, community). Afterwards, the students should discuss which word was the easiest to represent and guess, and why.

2

Image-Based Discussion:
Show your students the image of *One and Three Chairs*. Ask them to define what they see and to consider the three elements of the work.

What is the difference between the different forms of 'chair?' Is one of the representations more accurate than the other?

3

Give your students some information on Kosuth:

"Kosuth, who said, 'art is making meaning,' emphasized ideas over the convention that art should reflect the artist's skill or be pleasing or beautiful in some way. Influenced by the artist Marcel Duchamp's readymades—everyday manufactured objects that Duchamp designated as art—Kosuth did not 'make' the chair but, rather, selected one to include in his installation. He had someone else photograph the chair in order to further remove artistic decision-making from the process."[2]

"Kosuth believed that the creative act should always be critical. Following the model established by Duchamp's readymades, he produced art that questioned supposedly 'unquestionable forms of authority of the culture.' Concerned that people accepted things to be works of art simply because they were exhibited at art museums, Kosuth made works that challenged the authority of art institutions to define objects as art."[3]

4

Ask your students if the work *One and Three Chairs* challenges art institutions. Show them the image of John Baldessari's *I Will Not Make Any More Boring Art*. Does it challenge definitions of art and the power of art institutions to define works as art? How does the fact that it is handwritten influence the perception of this work?

5

Give your students some information about Baldessari:

"Baldessari's art often examines how words as a form of communication are interpreted differently by different people because of their diverse experiences of life. He has stated, 'Everybody knows a different world, and only part of it. We communicate only by chance, as nobody knows the whole, only where overlapping takes place.'"[4]

Tell your students how this work was made by quoting Baldessari directly:

"*I Will Not Make Any More Boring Art* was my response to Nova Scotia College of Art and Design to do an exhibition there.... As there wasn't enough money for me to travel

6

Let your students discuss the following questions: how can Baldessari be considered the artist of *I Will Not Make Any More Boring Art*? How can Kosuth be considered the artist of *One and Three Chairs*? How are these works similar and what are the differences? How is language used in these works?

Tell your students about the early work of Baldessari and his *Cremation Project*. Does it change their perception of *I Will Not Make Any More Boring Art*?

Why is this teaching method presented by Oxford Art Online interesting? This process aims to teach students about conceptual art, not by offering a lot of information, but rather by challenging their thinking and leading them to a definition of conceptual art. The students have to reach this definition through games and discussion, the answer is not directly presented by the teacher. It is furthermore even questioned if there could be a 'right' answer. In some ways this process is similar to the teaching methods of John Baldessari himself.

To think about Baldessari and conceptual art is to think about the California Institute of Arts (CalArts) and art education as well. Baldessari, who taught the Post-Studio class at CalArts, was using many of the techniques that the progressive education movement introduced. His assignments challenged his students to find solutions to questions and problems. His way of treating his students not as his pupils but rather as fellow artists, and introducing them to other artists, who he invited as guest speakers in his classes, has parallels with progressive education.

Progressive education uses learning by doing as an important learning technique. It is a critique of normative education, which focuses on repetitive teaching methods and emphasizes gaining more knowledge through studying and taking tests.

Timothy Ridlen writes in his dissertation "The Research and Teaching of Art Despite Its Disappearance: Art in Academia, 1957–1977" about the question of art education. Can art be taught? Or is every academic attempt destined to fail, as art needs "freedom and transgression rather than prescribed methods and disciplined training?"[7] Ridlen also writes about Baldessari and his field trips. By throwing darts at a map, the decision is made where learning and art making are going to happen in his class, although, as Ridlen writes further, the decision is not really made by throwing darts but by "the constraints of map-making and the socially, historically, and institutionally determined boundaries of a place that is defined by social relations."[8]

Again, progressive education appears as an influential teaching method behind this:

Baldessari taught in schools and art institutions for years and incorporated ways of teaching art and the strategies of conceptual art into his work.[10]

The question of how art can be taught does not have a right answer. For there to be a right answer would confirm that art still functions within a set of rules that artists, critics, and institutions have agreed upon. Conceptual art disrupted this system and there is no way back.

As Baldessari stated: "There are no firm rules. If you find any, break them as soon as possible."[11]   AC

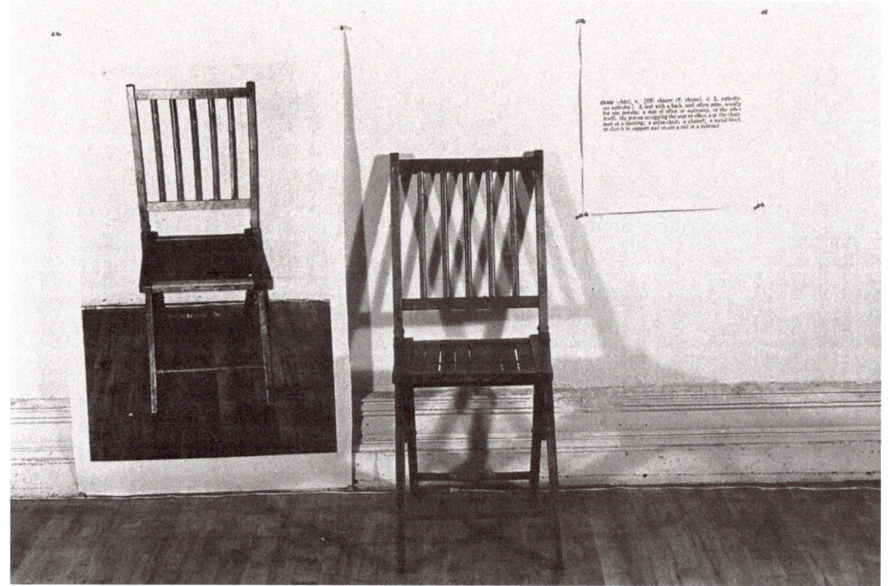

Joseph Kosuth, *One and Three Chairs* (1965).

make your move

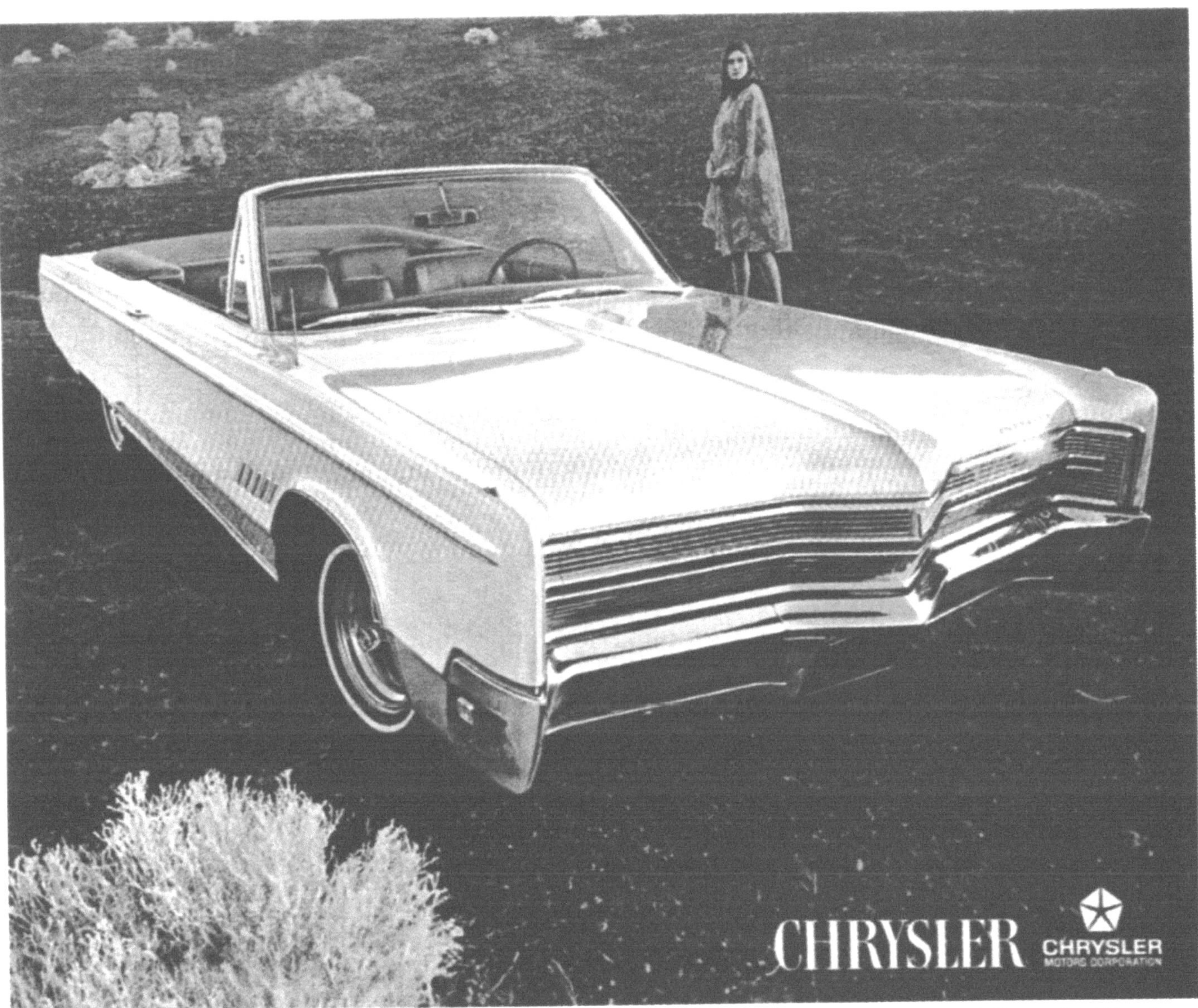

The next time you admire a Chrysler, make it your own.

Make it a 300. The sports-bred Chrysler that demands attention. And gets it.

New concealed headlights. 440 cubic inch V-8. Automatic transmission. Contoured bucket seats. All standard. Plus options like AM radio with stereo tape. Or AM/FM Stereo Multiplex Radio.

Chrysler caters to you. Quietly. Always with taste. Vinyls. Jacquard weave fabrics.

Optional leather upholstery.

Yet the 4 Newports are priced just a few dollars a month more than the most popular smaller cars, comparably equipped. And every Newport is full-size. We build no small Chryslers.

Newport to New Yorker. The '68 Chryslers are here. Make your move. Then sit back. And watch your friends watch.

MOVE UP TO CHRYSLER '68

DELEGATED PERFORMANCES

In her 2013 essay on John Baldessari's *I Will Not Make Any More Boring Art*, (1971) Ayun Halliday suggests a do-it-yourself course based on the artist's 13-minute video, in which he describes the pages of a notebook with the sentence 'I will not make any more boring art.'[1] In the article she proposes an example from the video that Baldessari later recorded: to write down the sentence "I will not make any more boring art" over the entire length of the video. Halliday suggests that the repeated writing of this sentence may change the careers, or even lives, of many participants of such a DIY course.

In a letter dated February 1, 1971, from John Baldessari to Charlotte Townsend-Gault, the instructions to the students are as follows:

"From ceiling to floor should be written by one or more people, one sentence under another the following statement—'I will not make any more boring art.'"[2]

At least one column of the sentence should be written before the opening of the exhibition. Every day the writing of the sentences should be continued, if possible over the whole period of the exhibition. It should be handwritten, clear and in correct spelling.

With this letter, Baldessari hands over the task entrusted to him as a teacher (to teach and create art with students) to the students. He gives an idea to the students to put into practice. This is how authorship is decoupled from the artist.

The instructions are given in such a way that the students have only limited creative freedom. They can choose the font size and shape and the type of writing instrument, because Baldessari does not make any specifications in this regard. They can also organize the division of the work themselves. But above all, they can choose whether they want to participate or not. When they participate, they do so as his deputies.

Whoever visited the exhibition may have watched students fill the walls of the exhibition rooms with the same sentence 'I will not make any more boring art' throughout the entire period of their stay. This is how the exhibition that emerged from Baldessari's instructions can be called a delegated performance.

Delegated performances are called performances in which the "presence of the artist, which was so important in body art in the 1970s, is outsourced to laymen."[3] According to Claire Bishop, the delegation turns performance into an "art form that relies on the continuous presence of committed performers."[4]

Based on instructions, delegated performances could be repeated in different contexts, which then led to their monetization in the early years of the 21st century. The shift work associated with the duration of the performances (here over the duration of the exhibition) refers to the assembly-line work of Fordism. The need for repetition and permanent presence makes delegated performances increasingly and clearly visible as a form of paid work.[5]

But with his delegated performance, Baldessari was ahead of his time and thus also ahead of today's discourse. What Bishop describes as a new and problematic phenomenon of the 1990s/2000s, Baldessari implemented ironically in his 1971 letter. He christened his idea a 'punishment piece' and used the appropriate choice of words from the 'punishment rhetoric.' Some students were needed as scapegoats, since unfortunately he could not be present to stand up for his self-imposed sins. In his ironic conviction strategy, he even refers to Jesus Christ, who also sacrificed himself for the sins of others. If

Charlotte Townsend-Gault could not convince volunteers to self-sacrificingly take Baldessari's sins on their shoulders, mercenaries would be needed to take over this task for a fee. Baldessari proposes $50.

Since the project was part of the art study, it was not a commercial project. The students also had the choice to participate, they were not bound by contract. If Townsend-Gault took the artist at his word, they could also participate for a fee. Which brings us back to the monetization of the delegated performance... CW

I WILL NOT MAKE ANY MORE BORING ART

TRAVELLING AND APPROPRIATION

The following contains a series of found quotations from Baldessari's *I Will Not Make Any More Boring Art* (1971) alongside pictoral commentary on his work.

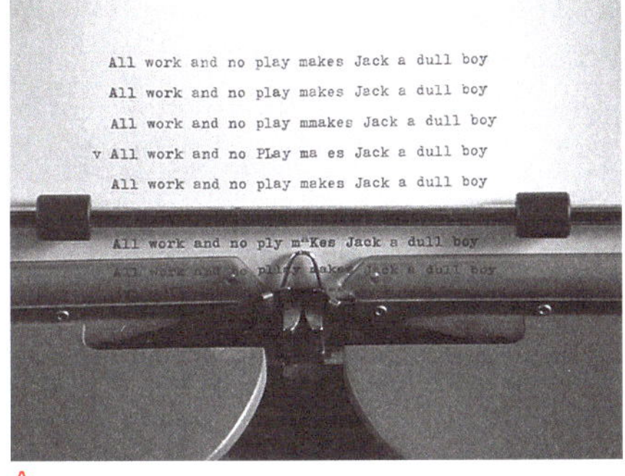

A

This is a picture from the movie *The Shining* (1980), directed by Stanley Kubrick. Kubrick seems to reference Baldessari's *I Will Not Make Any More Boring Art* with a similar sentence, which is concordant in its repetition.

The picture particularly seems to resemble Baldessari's *CalArts Post-Studio Art: Class Assignments (optional)* (1970).

45. Punishment. Write "I will not make any more art"
"I will not make any more boring art"
" I will make good art"
(or something similar)
1000 times
om wall.

B

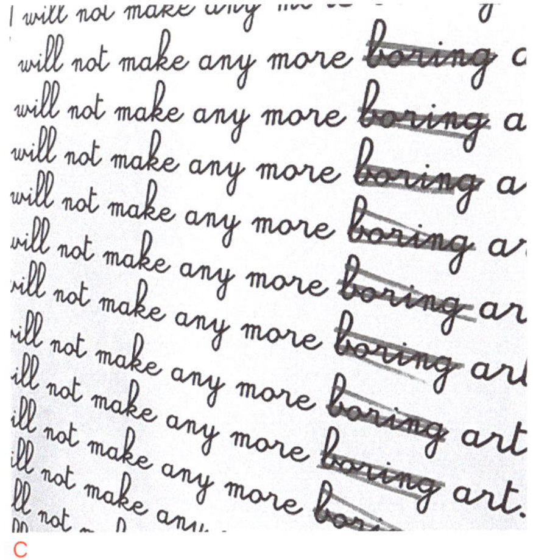

C

In this citation by Suso Fandino, 'boring' is deleted, resulting in the sentence 'I will not make any more art.' On the other hand, one could also interpret it in such a way that the art piece, by crossing out the word, appears 'less boring' and is thus 'interesting art.'

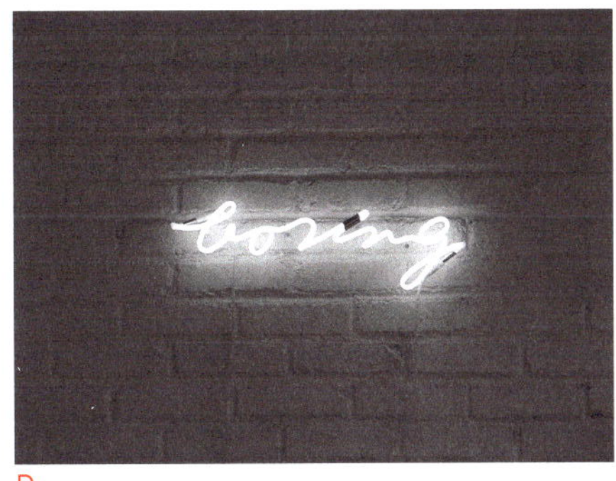

D

In contrast to the Suso Fandino's citation, Yann Serandour's reference from 2005 with the same name (*I Will Not Make Any More Boring Art*) contains only the word 'boring.' This time however, the other words are not crossed out, but instead neon text is used to highlight the word 'boring'. Here, too, as in the previous picture, one could consider it either 'boring' or 'interesting' because of its change.

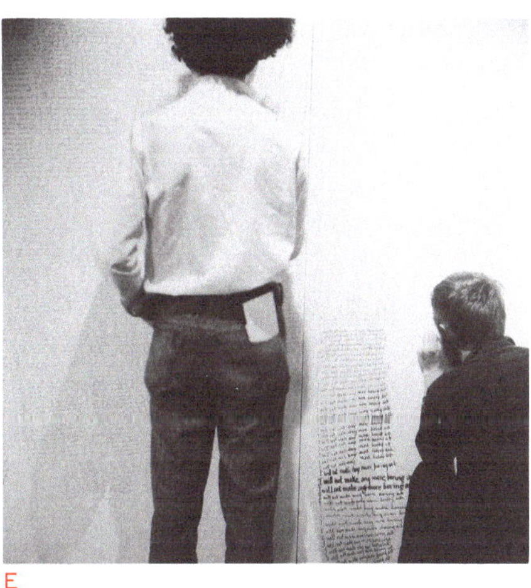

E

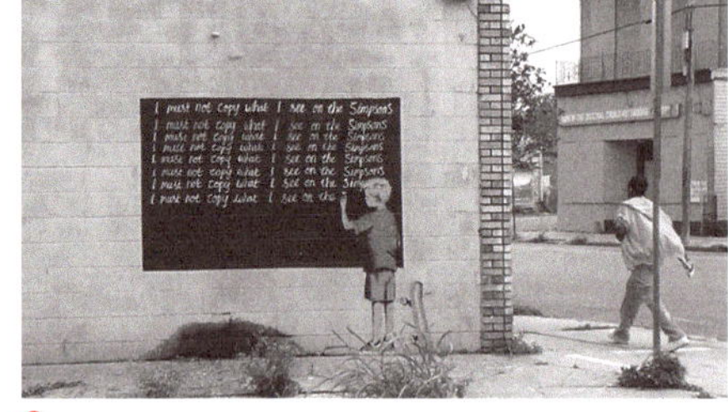

G

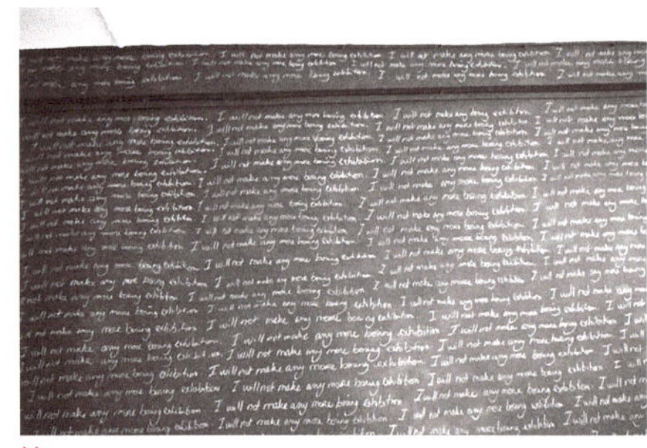

H

Baldessari's art is also often referenced within pop culture, for example in *The Simpsons*. First broadcast in 1989, the opening credits see Bart Simpson repeatedly inscribing 'I will not…' sentences onto the school's blackboard. This motif is also repeated every week, albeit with slight variety of 'crime'.

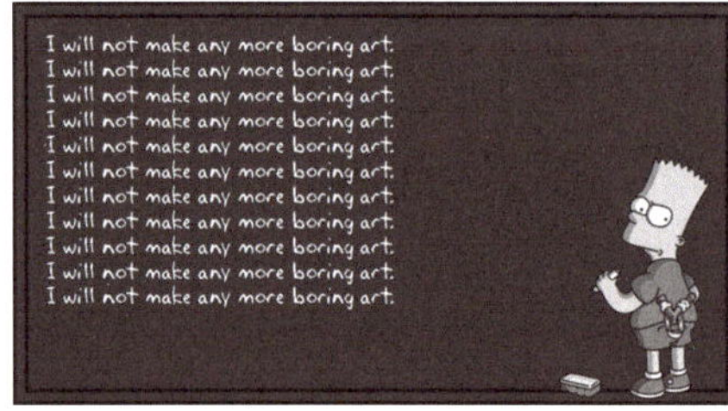

I

A QR code is used to generate this image, optional labels are possible.

Lines, as an example of punishment, demonstrate that repetition does not necessarily lead to a change in behavior, but rather, in Baldessari's sense of the sentence 'I will not make any more boring art,' creates exactly what is criticized: boring art.

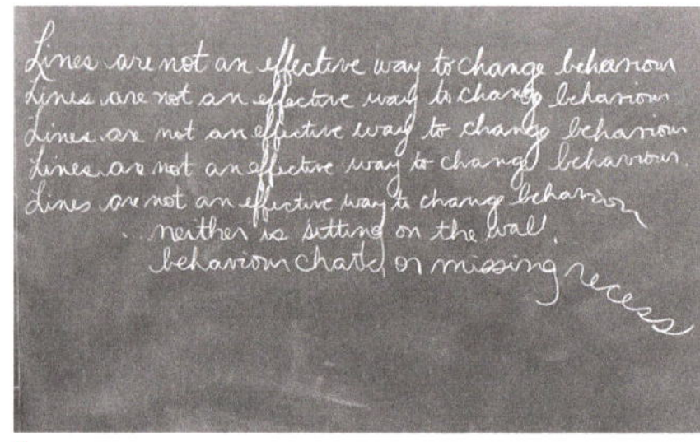

J

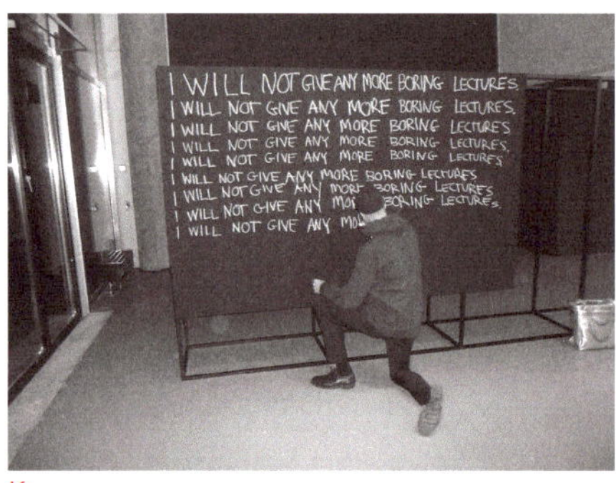

K

Kenneth Goldsmith also takes up Baldessari's art in his seminar "Uncreative Writing," changing his famous sentence to 'I will not make any more boring lectures.'

In his seminar he also deals with 'boring art' by teaching 'uncreative writing' through forms of appropriation, plagiarization, and replication.[1]

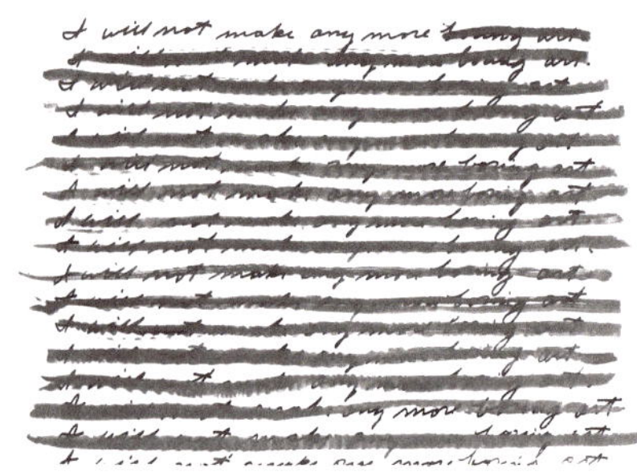

L

This example by Andrew Maize is very similar to the one in which 'boring' is crossed out, since here, too, deletion becomes an act of creation. However, the words that are left untouched—'I will not make any more'—have an exhausted meaning. Since Andrew Maize sees this as an

intervention,[2] in which the 'I' in the sentence refers to the original artist, Baldessari, one could also assume that Maize is also indirectly criticizing Baldessari's art, suggesting that he should not make any more art in general.

Generally, it can be said that the citations make use of parody, emergence, and appropriation. Parody is to distort the original,[3] emergence can be understood as the creation of something new from something old,[4] and appropriation as the copying of the original, which is intended to critically examine the original.[5]

Thus the examples all take up Baldessari's original idea and seem to create exactly what they want to avoid, namely something boring. The repetition of the sentence is particularly important here; as a single sentence, 'I will not make any more boring art' is a proclamation or decision. However, the effect is different when the phrase is repeated, since the act of repetition becomes increasingly boring with each iteration.

Not only does this seem ironic,[6] it even suggests a double bind.[7] The sentence's repetition leads its own negation. Neither the original nor the later references can easily be understood as ultimately boring or interesting art.

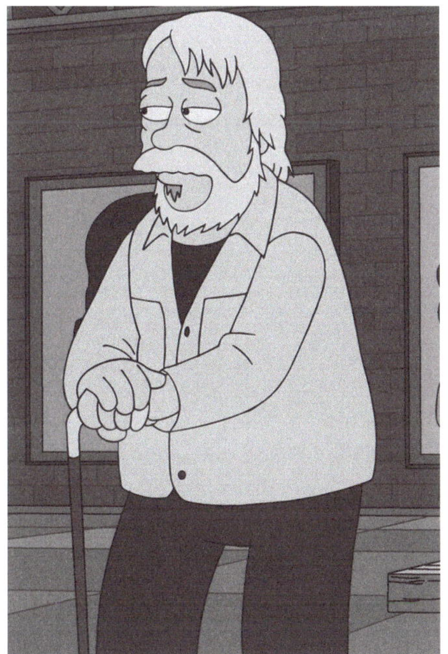

M

This is a portrait by John Baldessari from the 13th episode of the 29th season of the Simpsons: *Three Scenes Plus a Tag from a Marriage*. Thus Baldessari is not only referenced in Bart's punitive punishments in the opening credits, but also becomes a character himself.

In many museums you can find portraits of artists, but is their representation always necessary? This is a question especially pertinent in conceptual art, where authorship is not always clear.

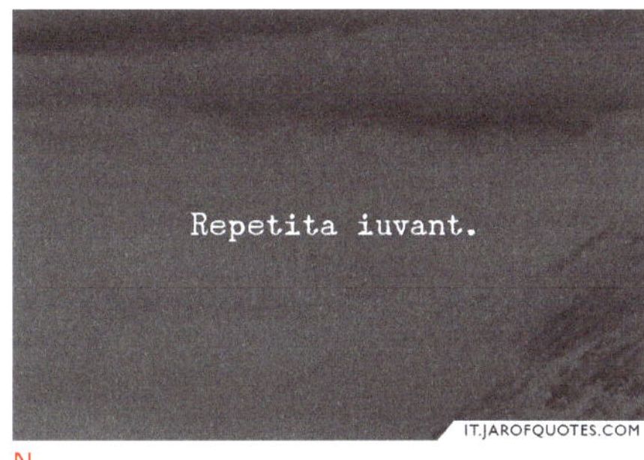

N

The Latin idiom *repetita iuvant*, or 'repeating helps', is still pertinent today. Especially in pop culture, repetition is often used as a rhetorical device. In contemporary meme culture, for instance, image repetition takes center stage. Thus one could infer that Baldessari in the 1970s used repetition not only as a punishment but also as a means of engaging with the language of advertising. His artwork *I Will Not Make Any More Boring Art* is a mixture of manifesto and advertising for his art.

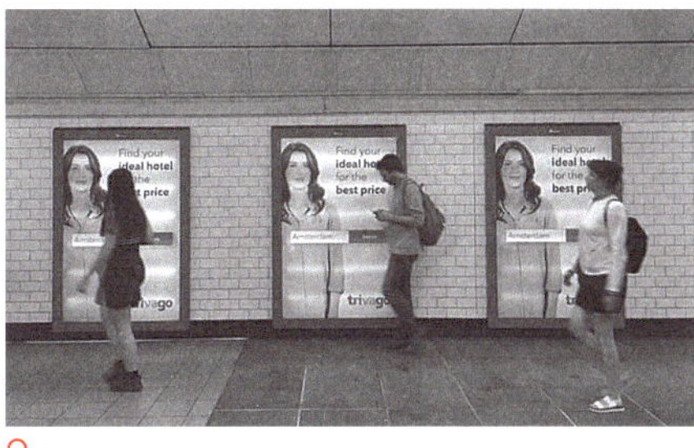

O

As this example makes clear, image repetition is commonplace in contemporary culture. This, like many other advertisements, becomes omnipresent not only in our environment, but also on our social media channels. However, how people are likely to use such cross-media

advertisements cannot always be predicted, as once in the public domain an advertisement may be appropriated and transformed. This is also the case with *I Will Not Make Any More Boring Art*, which was also appropriated and parodied by other artists.   VL & AR

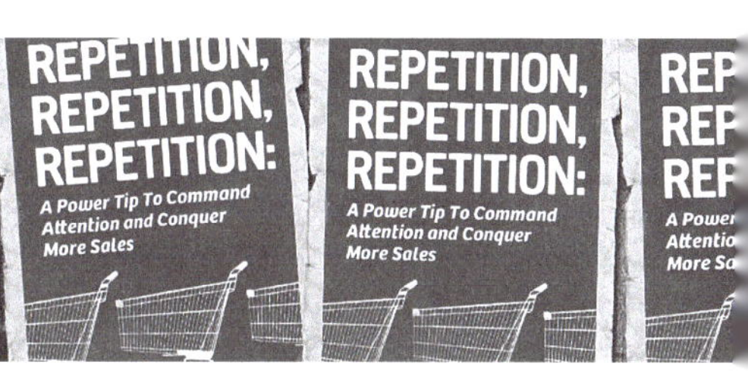

P

A   Stanley Kubrick, *The Shining* (1980).
B   John Baldessari, *CalArts Post-Studio Art: Class Assignments (optional)* (detail) (1970).
C   Suso Fandino, *I Will Not Make Any More Boring Art (n. d.)*.
D   Yann Serandour, *I Will Not Make Any More Boring Art* (2005).
E   John Baldessari, *I Will Not Make Any More Boring Art* (1971) graphic on wall (temporary installation).
F   Ara Shirinyan, *Resolution: I Promise to Write Better Poetry* (2005).
G   Banksy, *I Must Not Copy What I See on the Simpsons* (2008), New Orleans.
H   Camille Le Houezec, *I Will Not Make Any More Boring Exhibition* (2009).
I   Bart Simpson Chalkboard Wallpaper Generator, I will not make any more boring art.
J   Andrea Nair, *Lines Are Not An Effective Way to Change Your Children's Behaviour Pattern* (2016).
K   Kenneth Goldsmith, *John Baldessari Redo (Blackboard Intervention)* (2013), transmediale. Photo by Veronica Santos Ruiz.
L   Andrew Maize, *I Will Not Make Anymore (After John Baldessari)* (2012). Photo by Helen Teager.
M   John Baldessari in The Simpsons, "Scenes Plus a Tag from a Marriage," episode nr. 631.
N   Repetita iuvant, Jar of Quotes.
O   Trivago tube poster. Photo by Ed Cumming.
P   Repetition, Repetition, Repetition: A Power Tip to Command Attention and Conquer Sales.

PERFORMATIVE REPETITION IN CONCEPTUAL ART

"It's a nice space to just start thinking about my own work"[2]
— Murphy Chang

In 2010, the Whitney Museum of American Art commissioned a series entitled "Off the Wall: Part 1—Thirty Performative Actions" curated by Chrissie Iles, which set out to highlight actions using the body in live performance, on video, or in relation to space and time. The gallery space became the stage, focusing on the theatricality of a performance or action and how that initiates new thoughts or ideas based on the concept of the piece. One of the examples of these performative actions was to re-produce (or re-perform) John Baldessari's *I Will Not Make Any More Boring Art* (1971). This re-performance was the first of its kind since the 1971 original, in which students of Nova Scotia College of Art and Design (Nova Scotia) were asked to write out the phrase on Baldessari's behalf, who was unable to travel to Nova Scotia due to budgetary reasons. Originally, Baldessari wanted only volunteer art students to perform the piece, in order to emphasize the pedagogical aspect of the art (what happens when an artist writes the ironic phrase over and over again?) rather than viewing the action as a form of punishment (a monotonous, boring replication of words).

For the Whitney reenactment, 28 art students were invited to write on the museum walls on Wednesdays, Thursdays, and Fridays during normal museum hours, allowing the audience of museumgoers to view the repetitive act happening in the moment, as each student wrote the phrase continuously for hours on end. This action of repetition was a key element in defining the movement known today as conceptual art. Alone, the sentence is a mere banality; when put into the context of a specific place and time, however, in this case in the galleries of the Whitney Museum of American Art in New York City in 2010, the phrase suddenly levitates into another realm, becoming a performance piece: a young artist stands on a ladder, writing on the walls of the Whitney, the spectator stops and observes the action, and the phrase comes to life. What does the phrase mean in this context? How does this performative repetition influence or change the meaning? What developments occur for the artist through this act of repetition? What is the relationship that forms between spectator and artist?

Murphy Chang, a student in the Illustration Department at the Rhode Island School of Design was one of the students invited to participate in the re-performance. In talking about her experience, she showed much interest and curiosity in how she would respond and react to the long duration of repeating the same words:

"I just wanted to see how I would be by the end of the day and how the words would be."[1]

Furthermore, Chang used the rigid and structured rules set out by Baldessari to her advantage, by taking her time with the banal action and using the time to think about her own work. Baldessari's task has perhaps left an even bigger impact in 2010 than in the 1970s; in today's climate of rapid technological advancements, a time when society expects everything within an instant, forcing an artist to slow down and focus on one task for hours takes on even greater significance.

Through Baldessari's assignment, the student, or the writer, benefits from the repetitive action. Much like with schoolchildren, who had to write 'I will turn in my homework on time' monotonously as punishment, this action of repeating can help ascend the artist into another realm of thinking; the action becomes contemplation, one that can help produce thoughtful explanations of one's own work or actions. It forces an artist to think beyond the action of writing the phrase. The performance (or the idea) is the machine that propels the artist forth, and through this repetition can also help push the spectator forth. It engages the mind, creating an untold dialogue between spectator and illustrator: one of thought, attentiveness, and concentration.   CB

The Function of the Studio*

DANIEL BUREN

translated by THOMAS REPENSEK

Of all the frames, envelopes, and limits—usually not perceived and certainly never questioned—which enclose and constitute the work of art (picture frame, niche, pedestal, palace, church, gallery, museum, art history, economics, power, etc.), there is one rarely even mentioned today that remains of primary importance: *the artist's studio*. Less dispensable to the artist than either the gallery or the museum, it precedes both. Moreover, as we shall see, the museum and gallery on the one hand and the studio on the other are linked to form the foundation of the same edifice and the same system. To question one while leaving the other intact accomplishes nothing. Analysis of the art system must inevitably be carried on in terms of the studio as the *unique space* of production and the museum as the *unique space* of exposition. Both must be investigated as customs, the ossifying customs of art.

What is the function of the studio?

1. It is the place where the work originates.
2. It is generally a private place, an ivory tower perhaps.
3. It is a *stationary* place where *portable* objects are produced.

The importance of the studio should by now be apparent; it is the first frame, the first limit, upon which all subsequent frames/limits will depend. What does it look like, physically, architecturally? The studio is not just any hideaway, any room.[1] Two specific types may be distinguished:

1. The European type, modelled upon the Parisian studio of the turn of the century. This type is usually rather large and is characterized

* This essay, written in 1971 and published here for the first time, is one of three texts dealing with the art system. The others were "Function of the Museum," published first by the Museum of Modern Art, Oxford, and subsequently in *Artforum*, September 1973; and "Function of an Exhibition," *Studio International*, December 1973.

1. I am well aware that, at least at the beginnings of and sometimes throughout their careers, all artists must be content with squalid hovels or ridiculously tiny rooms; but I am describing the studio as an archetype. Artists who maintain ramshackle work spaces despite their drawbacks are obviously artists for whom the *idea* of possessing a studio is a necessity. Thus they often dream of possessing a studio very similar to the archetype described here.

DANIEL BUREN
The Function of the Studio
1971

OC

. influence of geography on works of art. To accomplish my study, I
.veled throughout southeastern France but also visited a large number
om the youngest to the oldest, from the obscure to the famous. My visi
.e the opportunity to view their work in the context of their studios. W
.ne about all their work was first its diversity, then its quality and
especially the sense of reality, that is, the "truth," that it possessed, w
artist and whatever his reputation. This "reality/truth" existed not on
of the artist and his work space but also in relation to the enviro
landscape.

It was when I later visited, one after the other, the exhibitions of
that my enthusiasm began to fade, and in some cases disappear, as if
had seen were not these, nor even produced by the same hands. Torr
context, their "environment," they had lost their meaning and died,
as forgeries. I did not immediately understand what had happened, n
co disillusioned. One thing was clear, however: deception. More
revisited certain artists, and each time the gap between studio and gall
finally making it impossible for me to continue my visits to either.
reasons were unclear, something had irrevocably come to an end fo

I later experienced the same disillusion with friends of my ow
whose work possessed a "reality/truth" that was clearly much clos
loss of the object, the idea that the context of the work corrupts the ir
work provokes, as if some energy essential to its existence escap
through the studio door, occupied all my thoughts. This sense that
of the work is lost somewhere between its place of production
consumption forced me to consider the problem and the significan
place. What I later came to realize was that it was the reality
"truth," its relationship to its creator and place of creation, that w
lost in this transfer. In the studio we generally find finished
progress, abandoned work, sketches—a collection of visible e
simultaneously that allows an understanding of process; it is th
work that is extinguished by the museum's desire to "install."
installation come to replace *exhibition*? In fact, isn't what is i
being established?

2. The only artist who has always seemed to me to exhibit
in his dealings with the museum system and its consequences, a
sought to oppose it by not permitting his works to be fixed
according to the whim of some departmental curator, is Consta
disposing of a large part of his work with the stipulation that it b
studio where it was produced, Brancusi thwarted any attempt to
frustrated speculative ventures, and afforded every visitor the sa
himself at the moment of creation. He is the only artist who, i
the relationship between the work and its place of production, c
work in the very place where it first saw light, thereby sh

*Constantin Brancusi. P
c. 1925.*

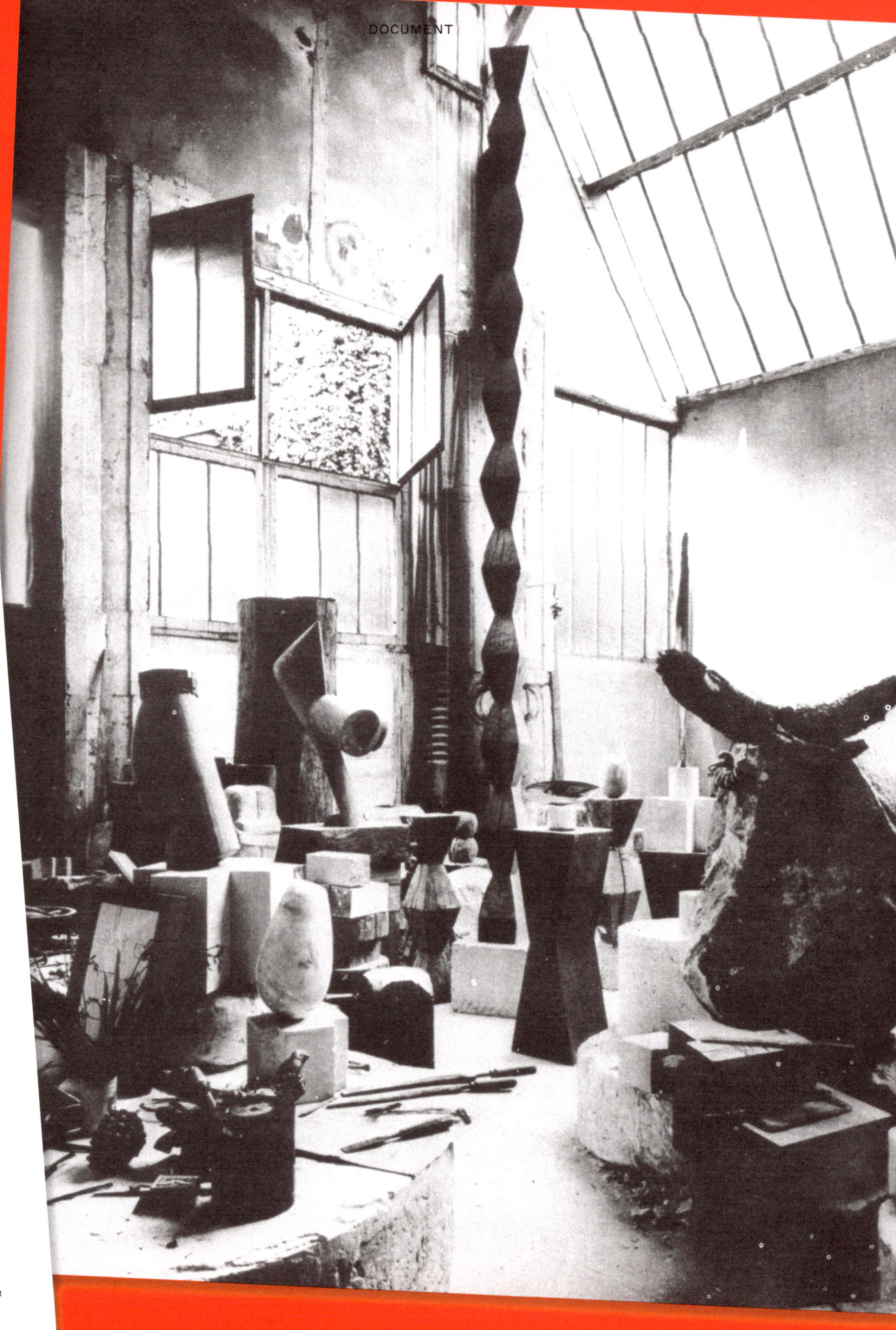

of his studio taken

APPROPRIATION ART

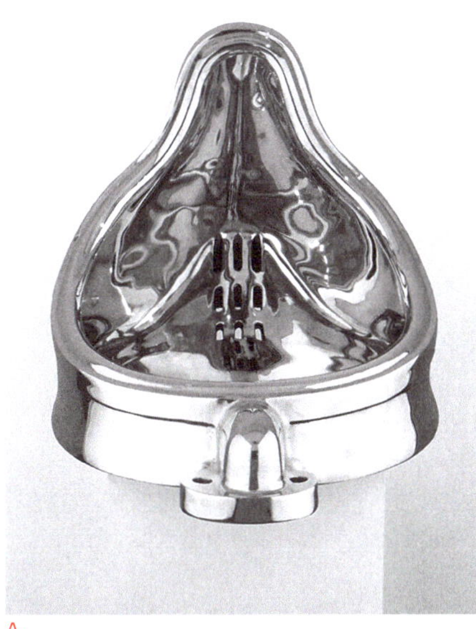

A

Appropriation art intentionally takes, borrows, and copies pre-existing objects and artworks in order to create an artwork which has no (financial) value. The original material should remain unaltered. Appropriation art questions conventional notions such as originality, authenticity, and authorship, themes that modernists held in high esteem. With this in mind, appropriation art remains the best example of doubtful authorship.[1]

This artistic strategy can be traced back to the history of the early 20th century. For instance, the Cubist collages and constructions of Pablo Picasso and Georges Braque often featured objects like newspaper cuttings, parts of musical instruments, music scores, tobacco boxes, and fabrics. These served not only as a representation of themselves but also submerged their reality in a new visual realm. From 1915, Marcel Duchamp began the work that led to the creation of his notorious ready-made sculpture, *Fountain* (1917)—a standard urinal, laid flat on its back, signed and titled. Later on other art movements like Surrealism and Pop Art developed this same method in their artworks by applying or using ordinary household objects. During the 1970s–80s appropriation was legitimized as a methodology, even fashionable, and therefore took on new significance. Numerous artists, later dubbed the Pictures Generation, invested new meanings in new contexts through incorporating this strategy in their work.

REACTING TO ABSTRACT ART AND SOCIAL ABSTRACTION

The postwar era's malaise and alienation led to the birth of abstraction. This was an abstraction that was, beyond formal concerns, related to the abstraction of society and its people. The increasing number of people living together, in the same house, yet apart in separate rooms was a notable example of this phenomenon, as this separation led to an avoidance of facial confrontation.

As a result, abstract art became a reflection of the reality of the abstract world. Throughout the 20th century many theorists diagnosed this, in particular Jean Baudrillard who argued that "abstraction" in the digital age "is no longer that of the map, the double, the mirror, or the concept. Simulation is no longer that of a territory, a referential being, or a substance. It is the generation by models of a real without origin or reality."[2] Therefore, over time artists tried to question the inevitability of an abstract world, as well as the impossibility of criticizing it, with the aim of reaching utopia. They sought an alternative, trying to go beyond the limits of convention regarding originality.

THE PICTURES GENERATION

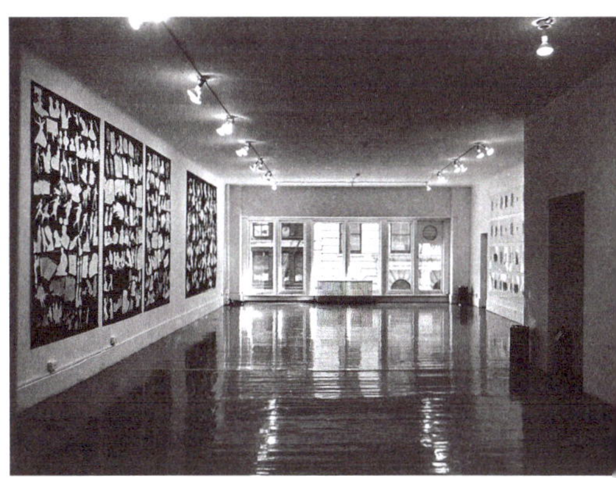

B

As mentioned before, the development of abstract art also engenders the genesis of appropriation art. It reaches its peak in the 1970s, with the rise of consumerism and the manipulation of the media. Therefore, some artists—who identified as the Pictures Generation—tried to extend the boundaries of these contexts.

Pictures was the title given to an exhibition curated by Douglas Crimp in 1977 at Artists Space in New York, following his famous essay published in *October* magazine that year. The show presented the work of five emerging artists—Troy Brauntuch, Jack Goldstein, Sherrie Levine, Robert Longo, and Philip Smith. In his accompanying exhibition text, Crimp suggested that the influence of photo-conceptualists such as John Baldessari is incontrovertible, who was arguing at that time that the younger artists were taking concepts like beauty and desire, latent anxiety, fetishism, and romanticism and bringing them to the fore; this created a new art that amplified the media-obsessed and post-Vietnam age and made use of quotation, excerption, framing, and staging.[3]

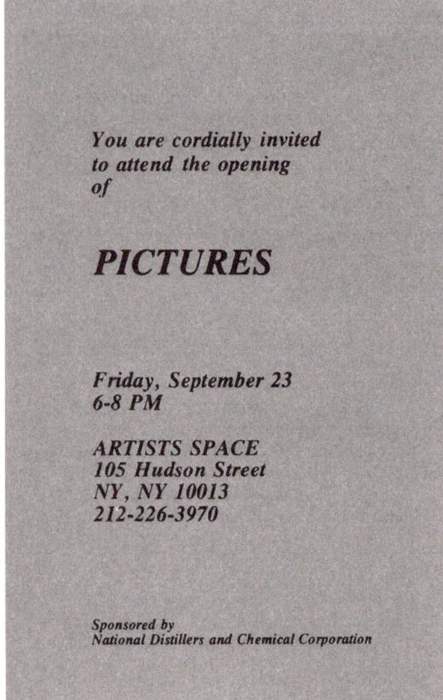

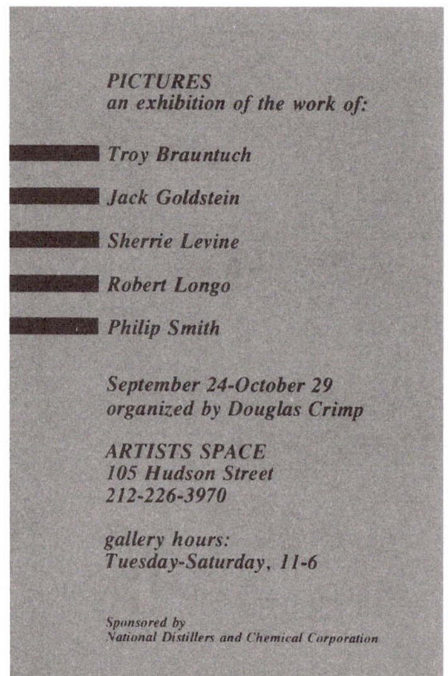

C

Cindy Sherman took photographs of
herself dressed as B-movie heroines;
Richard Prince deconstructed mass
consumerism with his pictures of
cowboys taken from adverts. "They
were the first kids to be raised with
television, fast food, and disposable
everything."[4]

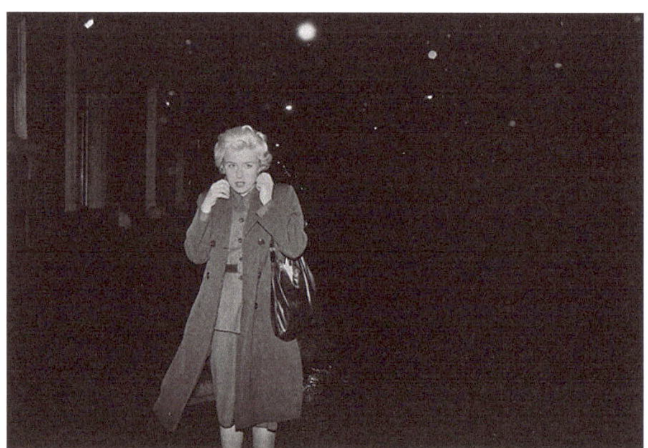

D

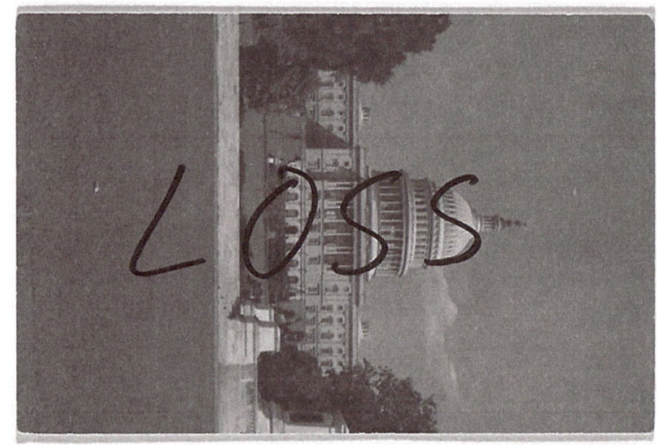

E

The Pictures Generation's relationship
to such materials at that time was
productively schizophrenic. While
they were first and foremost consum-
ers, at the same time they learned
to adopt a critical attitude toward such
a mechanism.

They worked in photography, film,
video, and performance, creating art
that used the same mechanisms of
seduction and desire that played upon
them. At that time, photography
was entirely separate from the art-
forms that were considered to be more
prestigious, so they used it not as
a material but the main idea behind
their approach.

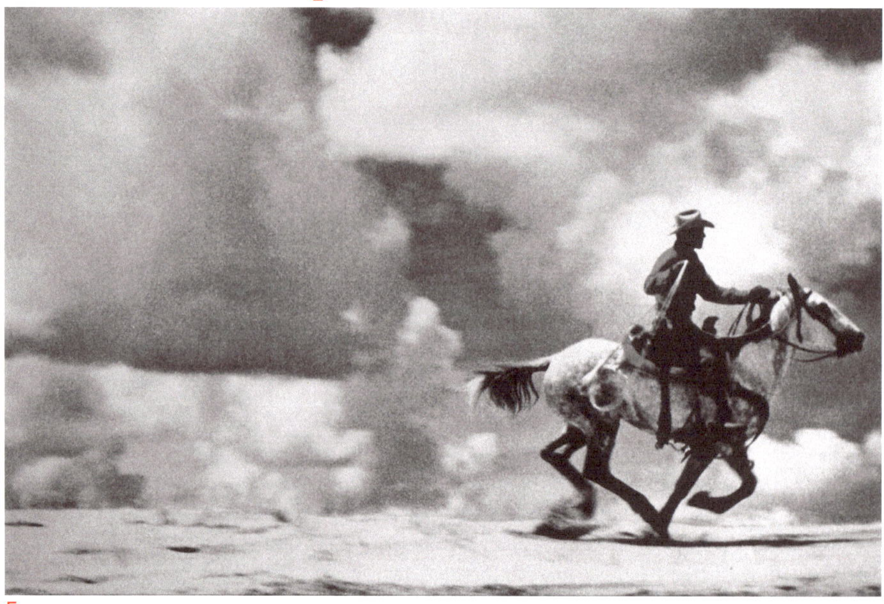

F

EAST AND WEST COAST

The Pictures Generation consisted of students from both the East and West Coasts. The first group belonged to students who studied at Buffalo Stage College in New York, and had professors like photographer Barbara Jo Revelle and encountered prominent artists like Sol LeWitt, Richard Serra, and Philip Glass to encourage them to experiment.

The Pictures Generation art movement included Robert Longo, Charles Clough, Cindy Sherman, Barbara Kruger, Richard Prince, Louise Lawler, and Laurie Simmons, who were working in New York City in the mid-1970s.[5]

The westerly group were those that had been taught by John Baldessari at CalArts in 1970. They graduated from his famous Post-Studio class, which gave them the opportunity to broaden their artistic practices through an access to multiple medias such as documentaries, films, photography, and advertisements. Among these artists one can name, among others, Barbara Bloom, James Welling, Jack Goldstein, and Matt Mullican.[6]

In 1977, it was Helene Winer, the director of the Pomona College Museum of Art in Claremont, California during 1970–1972 and Artist Space in New York from 1975 that tied these two coastal groups to each other, encouraging Douglas Crimp to curate the exhibition.[7]

AUTHORSHIP AND ORIGINALITY

These artists engaged with the idea of appropriation under the influence of postmodernism and new theories such as "The Death of the Author," an essay written by Roland Barthes in 1968.[8] The essay outlines the impossibility of originality and concentrates on interpretation rather than creation.

G

Therefore, this generation challenged conservative academic notions of authorship, originality, and plagiarism. Levine's work in particular prompted serious questions, not only about the role of an artist, but also about authenticity of art and the aura surrounding it, as carrying both commercial and cultural value. For example, in *After Walker Evans* (1981), Levine re-photographed a 1936 picture by Walker Evans of the wife of an Alabama sharecropper. Though it is hard to point to the difference between two pictures, from 1936 and 1981, it is necessary to mention that, instead of using Evans's negative, she took the photograph from a catalog reproduction of Evans' original image. In other words, Levine's reproduction of photographic reproductions challenges the medium of photography and any preconceived ideas about originality. We are also reminded of the words of Douglas Crimp, who wrote, "underneath each

picture, there is always another picture."[9]

GENDER, RACE AND IDENTITY

They magnified the manipulated imagery of self, and deconstructed gender, race, and the patriarchal narratives of popular media, advertisements, and art history. "In works by Kruger and Sherman, for example, deconstructed and appropriated images displayed the disparity between individual agency and expectations that stemmed from social construction of femininity."[10]

The aforementioned elusive relationship between art and authorship often led to lawsuits against appropriation artists. Since the establishment of copyright law in the United States in 1976, the determination of the intellectual owner became a case-by-case study. As Jessica Meiselman elucidates:

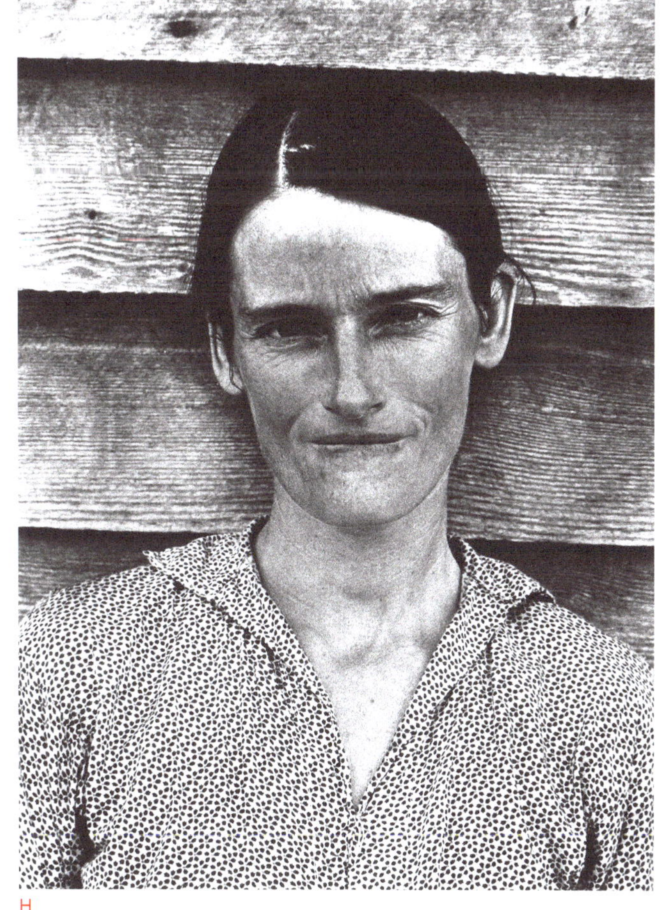

H

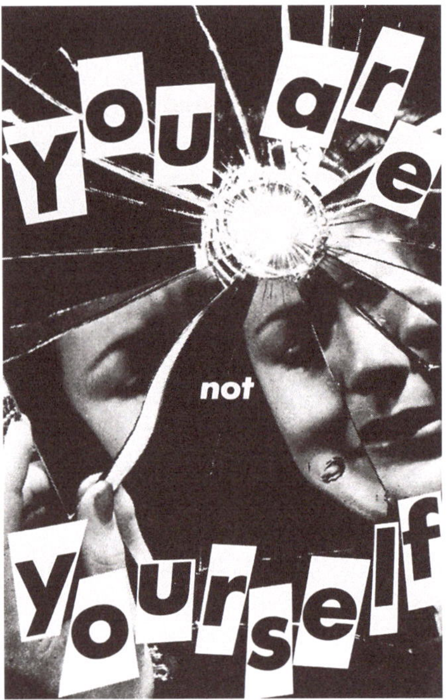

I

"To determine if fair use applies, the court will analyze four statutory factors: (1) the purpose and character of the use, including whether the use made of the underlying work is for a commercial purpose or for commentary; (2) the nature of the underlying copyrighted work, including whether it contains unprotectable elements; (3) the amount and substantiality of the original work used; and (4) the effect of the use on the market value of the original."[11]

One famous trial is that between Jeff Koons, an early appropriation artist, and the photographer Art Rogers. Inspired by Rogers's photograph of a couple holding puppies, Koons decided to make a sculpture with the same motif.

Koons lost the trial after arguing that his sculpture was an example of appropriation art and therefore did not contravene the law. The court dismissed his argument.[12]

Even though appropriation art and artists are often clearly defined, there is a interesting conspicuity regarding John Baldessari's work *I Will Not Make Any More Boring Art* in 1971. At that time Baldessari was teaching at the Novia Scotia College of Art and Design, but couldn't make it to the work's performance due to financial reasons. He suggested, instead, that his students write the sentence 'I will not make any more boring art' on the walls of the gallery. Surprisingly, the students covered the entirety of the gallery and even made a print. Baldessari decided to re-create this artwork, writing it himself while recording it. Here the question of authorship is clearly doubtful regarding the work's stages that led to the creation of this art piece. One could say that Baldessari actually steps into the role of an appropriation artist rather than the owner of the intellectual content. The original work is the assignment for his students. Consequently, the students are the rightful authors of the famous installation and the print. However, one might also argue that it was in fact the other way around. Baldessari first had the idea of covering the walls of the gallery, which makes the students appropriation artists. CG & NN

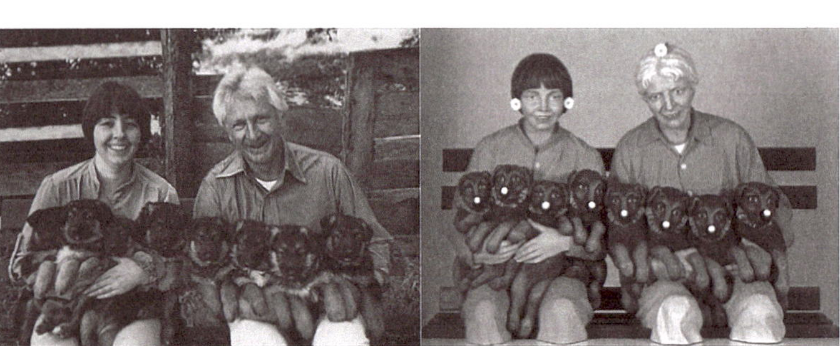

J

A   Sherrie Levine, *Fountain (Madonna)* (1991).

B   Installation view of *Pictures*, Artists Space, 1977. Photo by D. James Dee.

C   Invitation for *Pictures*, Artists Space (1977).

D   Cindy Sherman, *Untitled Film Still #54)* (1980).

E   Paul McMahon, *Untitled [Loss]* (1973–74).

F   Richard Prince, *Untitled (Cowboy)* (1989).

G   Matt Mullican, *Framed Section of an Angel's Wing* (1978).

H   Walker Evans, *Allie Mae Burroghs, Wife of a Sharecropper* (1936)

I   Barbara Kruger, *Untitled (You Are Not Yourself)* (1981).

J   Left: Art Rogers, *Puppies* (1985); right: Jeff Koons, *String of Puppies* (1988).

INTERVIEW WITH PHILIPP KAISER & CHRISTINA VÉGH

Christina Végh is the director of the Kestner Gesellschaft in Hanover. Together with Philipp Kaiser, formerly a museum curator and director and currently Chief Executive Director of Artists and Programs at Marian Goodman Galleries, she curated *Where Art Might Happen— The Early Years of CalArts*. The exhibition, running from August 30 to November 10, 2019, at the Kestner Gesellschaft and from March to May 2020 at Kunsthaus Graz, is the core of the collaborative research project *Tacit Knowledge. Post Studio / Feminism—CalArts (1970–77)*. The collaboration between the Kestner Gesellschaft, the Institute for Theater Studies, Freie Universität Berlin, and metaLAB (at) Harvard further provides the framework for this publication, as well as a conference with the same name at Schloss Herrenhausen in late October 2019. In this interview, Christina Végh and Philipp Kaiser discuss their curatorial concept, the challenges of an exhibition about an art school, the significance of the California Institute of the Arts (CalArts) for the art scene in Los Angeles in the 1970s and today, and transatlantic artistic exchange—especially with Germany.

VERENA KITTEL (VK)   Philipp and Christina, your idea to organize an exhibition about the early years of CalArts sparked the three-year research collaboration between the Kestner Gesellschaft, Hanover, the Freie Universität Berlin, and metaLAB (at) Harvard. Could you tell us a little bit more about your interest in CalArts and how the idea to make an exhibition about its founding years came up?

PHILIPP KAISER (PK)   Having lived and worked in southern California for several years, I've worked closely with a multigenerational group of artists who made CalArts the site of radical artistic pedagogy for which it is known, as well as younger artists who have been formed by that legacy. It became clear to me, especially following celebrations of other important art educational institutions like the Bauhaus and Black Mountain College, that the discourse was missing CalArts, arguably the most crucial component of this history for the late 20th century. Even more important, the artists who make up this show are conventionally understood within dominant critical frameworks such as feminist art, the Pictures Generation, conceptualism, and institutional critique, yet these very frameworks keep these artists and their practices far apart. CalArts demands we consider these key frameworks together; it was a school where all of these important innovations emerged together, and considering that simultaneity is a major motivation for the exhibition.

CHRISTINA VÉGH (CV)   I've always had a great interest in the art scene of the West Coast, especially after working more than once with John Baldessari and visiting Los Angeles on a regular basis. Baldessari's art is very much informed by his teaching, and I think it is safe to say that his teaching, in turn, is some other order of art. Many of his former students have emphasized the impact of his unique style of mentorship, a style that never imposed the conventional authority of a teacher. In the meantime, I have been working with various artists who were at CalArts, such as Rita McBride, Jorge Pardo, and Christopher Williams, to name a few. It is clear that the influence of the Post-Studio practice, how it was understood and taught at CalArts, cannot be overestimated. CalArts was the singular and first institution in which Post-Studio and feminist art practice came into being at the same time, with Fluxus artists in an important position somewhere in between. The Feminist Art Program (FAP), initiated by Judy Chicago and Miriam Schapiro, along with various artists tied to Fluxus such as Allan Kaprow or Alison Knowles, for instance, were instrumental in forming a mesh of different

artistic approaches, all of which tended to favor time-based practices, film, video, or performance. It was clear that we needed to open up the scope, and try to see more of the picture (all of it is impossible), in order to try to understand what made this school so particular and influential for generations of artists worldwide. There are still plenty of artists around who can tell us what is was like to attend or teach at CalArts in the early years; this was also an exciting prospect.

VK Could you further describe the basic curatorial concept for the show? What were the challenges you encountered during the process?

PK The exhibition looks at the school's trajectory over the full decade of the 1970s, beginning with its early years in Burbank before the new school's campus opened in Valencia in 1971. This birth is followed by the fast-paced development of its major lines of pedagogical experimentation—personified by many of its major teachers—including Allan Kaprow's and Alison Knowles's and Dick Higgins's Happenings and Fluxus-driven pedagogy, Baldessari's Post-Studio, and Judy Chicago's and Miriam Schapiro's FAP. The latter part of the exhibition considers the transformations of these foundations in the second half of the decade, as well as a selection of the first major generation of artists who studied at CalArts and emerged onto the L.A., New York, and European art scenes in the late 1970s and early 1980s. 'CalArts' of course means many things to many of its faculty, students, and observers. A major challenge for any exhibition like this one is how to appropriately circumscribe its wide-ranging history. We strove to bring together a range of voices—familiar, less familiar, and surprising—to capture the school's unique zeitgeist and legacy.

CV As Philipp has pointed out the concept, I'll speak more to the challenges. The challenges are manifold. They lie in the fact that there is never one but many stories in history, and that capturing aspects like teaching methods, a social mesh, or a historic momentum can naturally not be translated into a show easily. We chose to follow a conventional path, even though the school was everything but conventional. This allowed us to circle around the three major impulses—Fluxus, Post-Studio, and FAP—and include various artists 'in-between,' such as Suzanne Lacy or Stephan von Huene. We end the exhibition with artists of a somewhat

younger generation, making visible the ways in which the fundamental artistic approaches and forces transformed and ultimately merged in different, but fruitful, ways. A series of oral history interviews with various artists give voice to various aspects of school life. Finally, the exhibition also includes a selection of archival material, again trying to capture specific times and place. It is the nature of such a project that you can never include and speak with all artists of interest and the research is never truly complete. Much like *Century City* (Tate Modern 2001) by Okwui Enwezor, an exhibition in which cultural creativity was tackled through the relationships artists had been able to foster from 'their' metropolis, the show aims to highlight the connections between a specific place and time, artistic approaches and attitudes that were cultivated, and personal narratives. What made the place and the moment so special? How did it become so formative and influential?

VK In the late 1960s and early 1970s, other art schools in North America and Canada, like the Nova Scotia College of Art and Design or the University of California, Irvine, offered unconventional teaching and learning approaches, gathering outstanding artists of the period to serve as teachers like Larry Bell, Robert Irwin, David Hockney, and Frank Stella (at UC Irvine) or David Askevold, Gerald Ferguson, and Dan Graham (at Nova Scotia). Furthermore, UC Irvine taught students like Michael Asher, Chris Burden, Barbara T. Smith, and James Turrell. Chris Burden performed his seminal work *Shoot* (1971) while at Irvine, at the student-organized F Space Gallery. Why did you choose to make an exhibition on CalArts?

PK A distinguishing characteristic of CalArts in the 1970s was its outward orientation and model of open international exchange. Seemingly banal, though totally crucial, were John Baldessari's tactics in the classroom: he would assign for reading the period's key art publications, drive his students in his Volkswagen bus to exhibitions throughout southern California, and invite artists and thinkers from all over the world to campus. Unlike, for comparison, the Kunstakademie Düsseldorf, a contemporaneous and peer counterpart, which contained and still contains a 19th-century pedagogic model based on master and apprentice, CalArts incubated new ideas through its connection to networks large and small and the radical refusal of a traditional curriculum. CalArts represents

a major point of historical evolution—after schools like the Bauhaus and Black Mountain College—for how artists learn and mature, an important model for artist education amidst the late 20th century art world's increasing globalism and mediatization.

VK   Philipp, as former curator at MOCA and resident of Los Angeles, you know the Californian art scene quite well. What impact does CalArts have on L.A.'s artistic landscape today?

PK   The spheres of thought and practice that emerge in CalArts's early years remain salient organizing principles for thinking artistic practice in L.A. today. The enduring impact of CalArts is undeniable when you consider the ways successive generations of artists consistently look back at these early years. Consider, for example, artists like Andrea Bowers interrogating the FAP's history or Mario Garcia Torres's examination of Asher's Post-Studio. The continuous reinvention of the ideas at stake in CalArts's early years is another major reason we wanted to organize this exhibition now.

VK   Christina, how influential were the artistic and educational practices at CalArts in the early 1970s on the German art scene?

CV   There are various important links across the Atlantic. Consider the European reception of conceptual art. Its starting point can be seen in Europe in 1969, with *When Attitudes Become Form* in Bern and *Op Losse Schroeven* in Amsterdam, followed shortly after by documenta 5 (1972). Conceptualism (although not feminism) was first fully recognized in Europe; only later did it come to the States. The Konrad Fischer Galerie in Düsseldorf played a decisive role by inviting John Baldessari early on and introducing him to peers from here. Bernd and Hilla Becher were soon guest lecturers at CalArts, and Ulrike Rosenbach was later invited by Baldessari to teach. Long before digital access to information, John was not only known for bringing many guest lecturers from Europe to his class, but also leaflets and catalogs from European shows. The Fluxus artists, Nam June Paik or Emmett Williams for instance, also had close ties to the Rheinland. Transatlantic exchange was constant and bore various facets: artists from Los Angeles who decided to live in Europe (Barbara Bloom,

Christopher Williams), European artists who were at CalArts (Ulrike Rosenbach, Klaus vom Bruch). The artistic practices influenced each other more than the educational, I think. Only later, with artists such as Rita McBride or Christopher Williams becoming professors at the Kunstakademie Düsseldorf, was there a very direct impact or influence from CalArts's practice.

VK   What relevance does the exhibition *Where Art Might Happen—The Early Years of CalArts* have for your institution, the Kestner Gesellschaft, but also for a German audience in general?

CV   We all strive to understand how creativity, good ideas in whatever field, are fostered. Looking at the early years of CalArts helps us to see what it took to build a specific structure, to make situations possible, "where art might happen," to invoke Baldessari's key phrase. We are still able to meet artists who were involved in the school's early years. It is important to trace their views and approaches in this light, even though historic situations are not to be reproduced. The links between conceptualism and feminism have been discovered only recently. It is just astonishing that there was a place in which these two approaches were developed side-by-side, at exactly the same time. Anybody who visits a great survey show of younger artists nowadays understands the impact and relevance of that simultaneity for today. For a German public, one may see the influence not only on their own tradition in photography, taking off with Bernd and Hilla Becher, but also in conceptual approaches in painting, such as the Kapitalistischer Realismus (K. P. Brehmer, K. H. Hödicke, Sigmar Polke, Konrad Lueg, Wolf Vostell, Gerhard Richter). These works cannot be understood without the transatlantic exchange of ideas and approaches. At the Kestner Gesellschaft there have been shows by Christopher Williams or Rita McBride recently, while earlier there have been shows with John Baldessari, Eric Fischl, David Salle, Klaus vom Bruch, or Stephan von Huene. In a sense, our project shows how all of these artists come together! I am particularly happy to finally also introduce more of the women artists who have been neglected for too long. It is telling that, while we were preparing the show, artists such as Judy Chicago, Suzanne Lacy, Ulrike Rosenbach, and Mira Schor have held well-deserved larger shows and projects.

Arlington Heights Fruit Co.
GOLDEN ORANGE BRAND
FRUIT GROWN ON
ARLINGTON HEIGHTS,
RIVERSIDE COUNTY.
CALIFORNIA
FUCK OFF
Perry's PIZZA
PEPSI

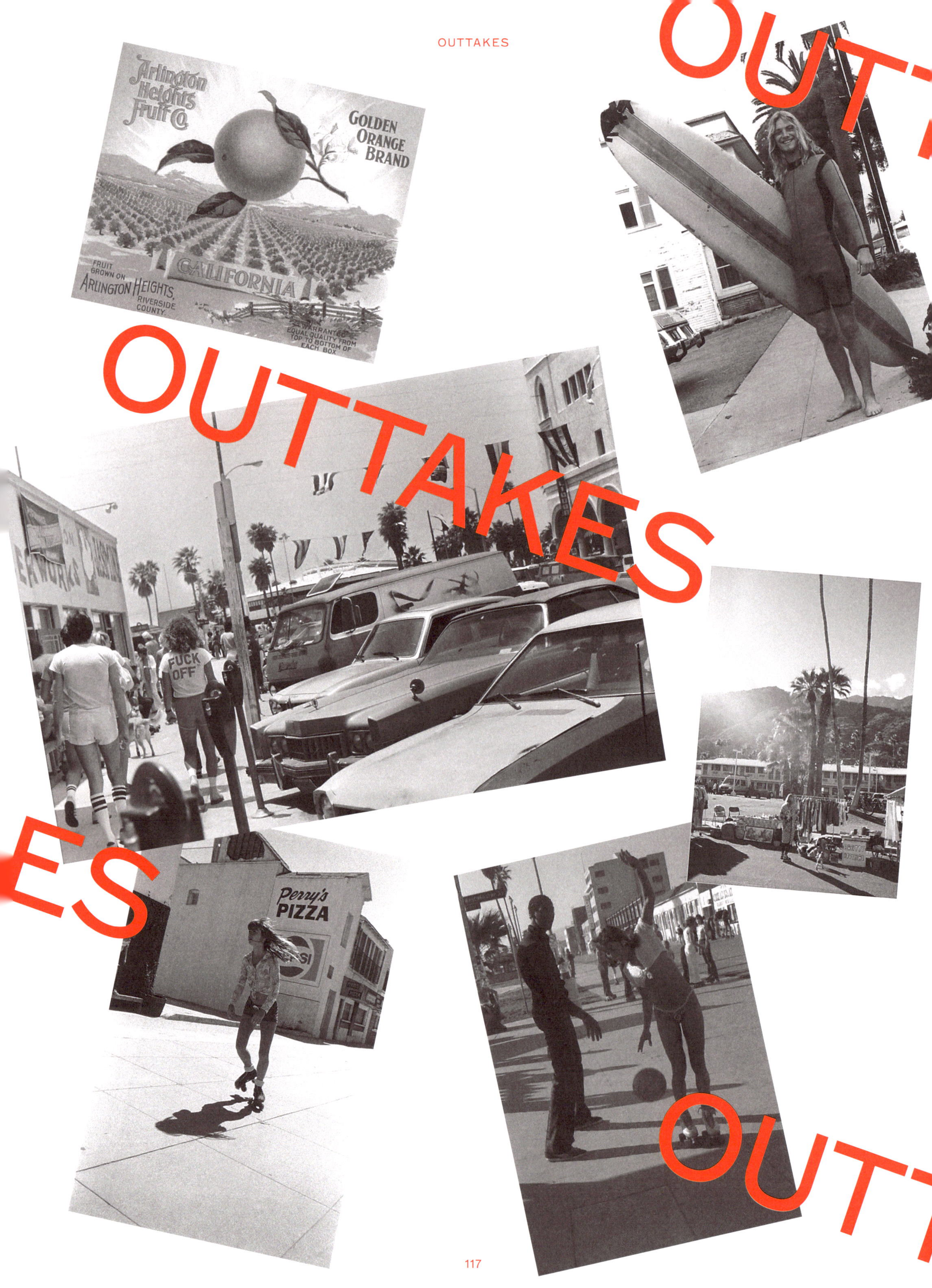

OUTTAKES

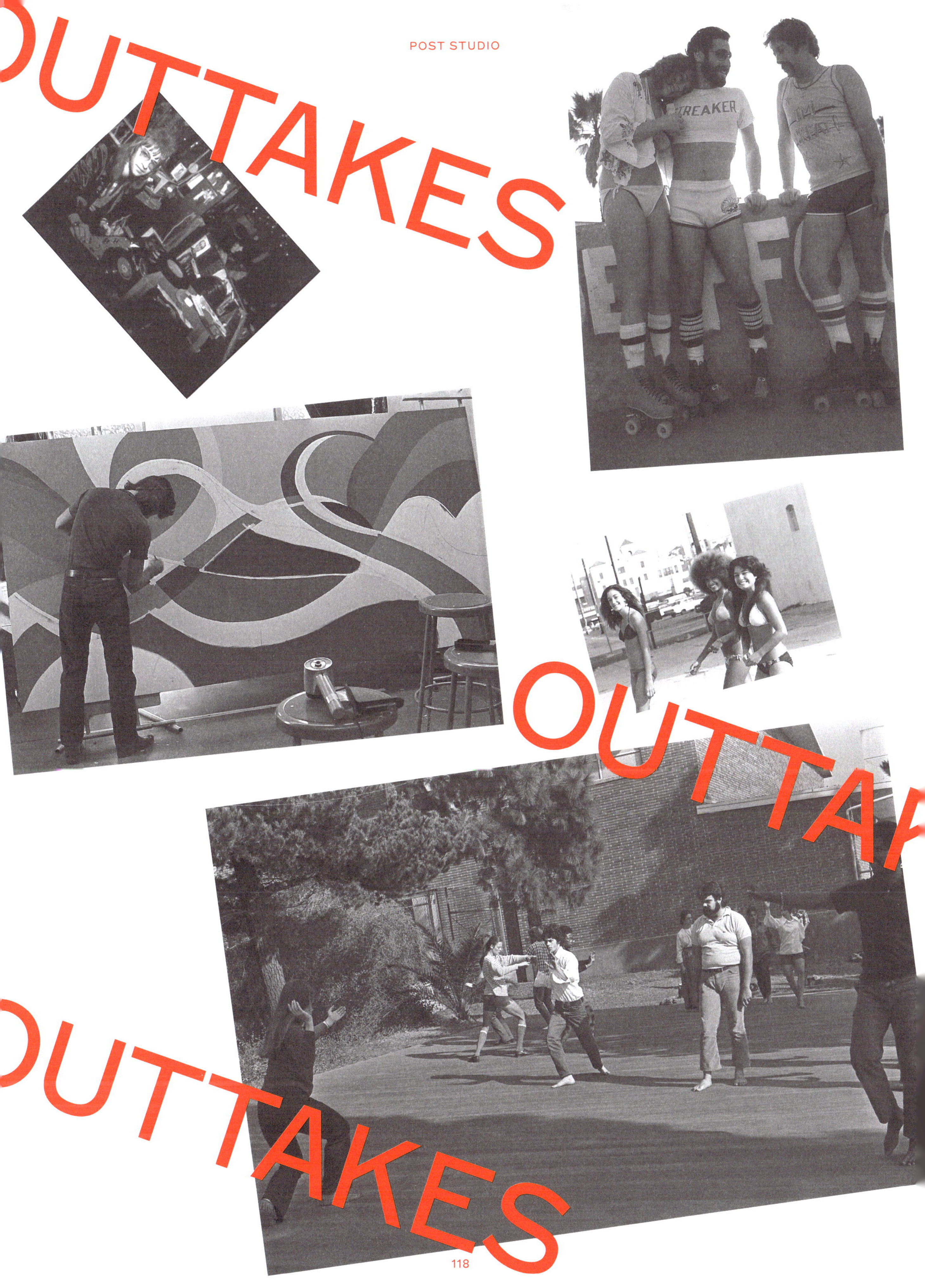

OUTTAKES
OUTTAKES
OUTTAP
OUTTAKES

NOTES

STATEMENTS

1   John Baldessari quoted in John Baldessari and Michael Craig-Martin, "School is Out: Rethinking Art Education Today," *Modern Painters* 19, no. 7 (September 2007), 76.

2   Hiro Kosaka, "Reflections by Hiro Kosaka," in *Jack Goldstein and the CalArts Mafia,* ed. Richard Hertz (Ojai: Minneola Press, 2003), 35.

3   James Real, "When You Wish Upon a School," *West*, (1972): 18, quoted in Janet Sarbanes, "A Community of Artists: Radical Pedagogy at CalArts, 1969–72," *East of Borneo,* June 5, 2014, accessed June 13, 2019, https://eastofborneo.org/articles/a-community-of-artists-radical-pedagogy-at-calarts-1969-72/.

4   John Baldessari, "Reflections by John Baldessari," in *Jack Goldstein and the CalArts Mafia,* ed. Richard Hertz (Ojai: Minneola Press, 2003), 61.

5   Mira Schor, "Authority and Learning," *M / E / A / N / I / N / G*, no. 8 (November 1990): 35.

6   Janet Sarbanes, "A Community of Artists: Radical Pedagogy at CalArts, 1969–72," *East of Borneo,* June 5, 2014, accessed June 13, 2019, https://eastofborneo.org/articles/a-community-of-artists-radical-pedagogy-at-calarts-1969-72/.

7   James Welling, "Reflections by James Welling," in Hertz, *Jack Goldstein,* 107.

8   David Salle quoted in Robert Storr, "Wise Guy," in *John Baldessari. Catalogue Raisonné: Volume 4: 1994–2004,* ed. Patrick Pardo and Robert Dean (New Haven: Yale University Press, 2017), 7.

9   Schor, "Authority and Learning," 34.

10 Jack Goldstein, "Early Days at CalArts," in Hertz, *Jack Goldstein,* 53.

11 Conceptual artist quoted in Judith E. Adler, *Artists in Offices. An Ethnography of an Academic Art Scene* (New Brunswick: Transaction Books, 1979), 124.

12 John Baldessari, "Reflections," in Hertz, *Jack Goldstein*, 66.

13 Jack Goldstein, "Chouinard and the Los Angeles Art Scene in the Late Sixties," in ibid., 23.

14 Baldessari, "Reflections," 60.

15 John Baldessari quoted in Baldessari and Craig-Martin, "School is Out," 77.

INTERVIEW WITH VERENA KITTEL & ANNETTE JAEL LEHMANN

1   Robin Mitchell quoted in Betty Ann Brown, "Feminist Art Education at the Los Angeles Woman's Building," in *Fromsite Tovision. The Woman's Building in Contemporary Culture,* ed. Sondra Hale and Terry Wolverton (Los Angeles: Otis College of Art and Design, 2011), 144.

2   See Michael Polanyi, *The Tacit Dimension* (Garden City, NY: Doubleday & Company, inc., 1966), accessed June 25, 2019, https://monoskop.org/images/1/11/Polanyi_Michael_The_Tacit_Dimension.pdf.

EDUCATION: IN AND OUT OF THE CLASSROOM | TD

1   Judith Adler, *Artists in Offices: An Ethnography of an Academic Art Scene* (New Brunswick: Transaction Books, 1979), 72.

2   See Robert Corrigan, *Inter-office Memorandum. Arts in Society* (1970), 92, accessed June 7, 2019, http://digicoll.library.wisc.edu/cgi-bin/Arts/Arts-idx?type=article&did=Arts.ArtsSocv07i3.i0028&id=Arts.ArtsSocv07i3&isize=M.

3   See Janet Sarbanes, "A Community of Artists: Radical Pedagogy at CalArts, 1969–72," *East of Borneo*, June 5, 2014, accessed June 13, 2019, https://eastofborneo.org/articles/a-community-of-artists-radical-pedagogy-at-calarts-1969-72/.

4   Adler, *Artists in Offices*, 102.

5   "CalArts Admissions Bulletin 1969–1970," quoted in ibid.

6   Sarbanes, "A Community of Artists."

7   "CalArts Admissions Bulletin 1969–1970."

8   Sarbanes, "A Community of Artists."

9   Course schedule bulletin quoted in ibid.

10 Ibid.

11 See Adler, *Artists in Offices*, 133.

12 See Sarbanes, "A Community of Artists."

13 Owen Smith, "Playing with Difference: Fluxus as a Worldview" (1992), quoted in Sarbanes, "A Community of Artists."

14 See Adler, *Artists in Offices*, 105.

15 Alison Knowles quoted in Janet Sarbanes, "A School Based on What Artists Wanted to Do: Alison Knowles on CalArts," *East of Borneo*, August 12, 2012, accessed June 7, 2019, https://eastofborneo.org/articles/a-school-based-on-what-artists-wanted-to-do-alison-knowles-on-calarts/.

16 Ibid.

17 See Arlene Raven, *Womanhouse. The Power of Feminist Art* (New York: Harry Abrams, 1994), 50.

18 John Baldessari, "Reflections by John Baldessari," in *Jack Goldstein and the CalArts Mafia*, ed. Richard Hertz (Ojai: Minneola Press, 2003), 60.

19 See ibid.

20 Quote from the audio feature *Disney's Dough Takes Flight* (1970), quoted in Sarbanes, "A Community of Artists."

21 Ibid.

22 Herbert Blau quoted in Adler, *Artists in Offices*, 72.

23 See Sarbanes, "A Community of Artists."

24 Impressions of this work and its artistic influences are shown in "Bringing Light into a Windowless Room," Capitain Petzel, accessed June 7, 2019, http://www.capitainpetzel.de/exhibitions/bringing-light-into-a-windowless-room/.

PAULO FREIRE, PEDAGOGY OF THE OPPRESSED (1970)

Paulo Freire, *Pedagogy of the Oppressed,* trans. Myra Bergman Ramos, with an introduction by Donaldo Macedo (New York: The Continuum International Publishing Group Ltd, 2005), accessed June 12, 2019, https://commons.princeton.edu/inclusivepedagogy/wp-content/uploads/sites/17/2016/07/freire_pedagogy_of_the_oppresed_ch2-3.pdf.

MOVEMENTS OF THE L. A. ART SCENE IN THE 1960s | TD

1   See Sven Behrisch, "Mami hat Dich Immer Mehr Geliebt," *Die Zeit,* no. 48 (October 6, 2011), accessed June 10, 2019, https://www.zeit.de/2011/41/Baldessari-Kunstgeschichte.

2   See ibid.

3   See Tim Ackermann, "Die Stunde der Westlichsten Welt," *Welt am Sonntag*, (September 25, 2011), accessed June 10, 2019, https://www.welt.de/print/wams/kultur/article13624258/Die-Stunde-der-westlichsten-Welt.html.

4   Bob McTavish quoted in "L.A.'s Finish Fetish," exhibition announcement of Franklin Parrasch Gallery (2003), accessed June 10, 2019, franklinparrasch.com/wp-content/uploads/2003/09/badb0e43.pdf.

5   John Baldessari quoted in Ackermann, "Die Stunde der Westlichsten Welt." Original quote: "Über die Kunstszene von L.A. hört man immer dieselben Klischees."

6   John Baldessari quoted in ibid. Original quote: "Finish Fetish. Light and Space. Ferus – dabei gibt es so viel mehr."

7   Ibid. Original quote: "'Es ist komisch,' meint John Baldessari, 'aber aus irgendeinem Grund muss ich ein bisschen wütend sein, damit ich arbeiten kann. Und L.A. macht mich etwas wütend. Die Stadt ist wirklich nicht schön. Und ich finde, die Leute sind nicht besonders schlau. Es gibt für mich also wenig Ablenkung in Los Angeles. Das Wetter ist gut. Ich kann hier wirklich gut arbeiten.'"

8   See Behrisch, "Mami."

9   John Baldessari quoted in ibid. Original quote: "weil auch kaum jemand eine Ahnung davon hatte."

10 See ibid.

11 See N. N., "Tief im Westen. Berlin präsentiert die kalifornische Kunstproduktion der Jahre zwischen 1950 und 1980," *Osnabrücker Zeitung*, n. p., March 22, 2012, accessed June 10, 2019, https://www.noz.de/deutschland-welt/kultur/artikel/192046/tief-im-westen#gallery&0&0&192046.

12 See Ackermann, "Die Stunde der Westlichsten Welt."

PETER PLAGENS, REVIEWS OF WEST COAST ART EXHIBITIONS

1   Peter Plagens, "Michael Asher: The Thing of It Is…," *Artforum* 10, no. 8 (April 1972): 72.

2   Peter Plagens, "Los Angeles: The Ecology of Evil," *Artforum* 11, no. 4 (December 1972) 67.

I WILL NOT MAKE ANY MORE BORING ART: PREHISTORY | PG

1   See Beth Harris and Steve Zucker, "John Baldessari. I Will Not Make Any More Boring Art," video produced by ibid., published by *Khan Academy* (April, 30, 2013), accessed June 11, 2019, https://www.khanacademy.org/humanities/global-culture/conceptual-performance/v/baldessari-i-will-not-make-any-more-boring-art.

2   John Baldessari quoted in Coosje van Bruggen, *John Baldessari* (New York: Rizzoli International Publications, 1990), 27.

3   See Jean-Pierre Krief, "John Baldessari," documentary serial *Contact*, no. 20 (2002) directed by ibid., produced and published by *arte france* and *ks visions*, accessed June 11, 2019, https://sales.arte.tv/fiche/JOHN_BALDESSARI.

4   See ibid.

5   See John Baldessari, "A Situation Where Art Might Happen: John Baldessari on CalArts," interview by Christopher Knight, Santa Monica (CA), April 4–5, 1992, East of Borneo, November 19, 2011, accessed June 23, 2019, https://eastofborneo.org/articles/a-situation-where-art-mighthappen-john-baldessari-on-calarts/.

6 John Baldessari quoted in Mark Cator, "John Heartfield, Robert Heinecken, John Baldessari," *Utterbooks* (30 July, 2018), accessed June 11, 2019, http://www.utterbooks.com/single-post/2018/08/03/John-Heartfield-Robert-Heinecken-John-Baldessari.

7 John Baldessari quoted in Hugh M. Davies and Andrea Hales, "Interview with John Baldessari" in *John Baldessari: National City,* ed. ibid. (San Diego: Museum of Contemporary Art, 1996), catalogue of an exhibition at Museum of Contemporary Art San Diego (March 9–June 19, 1996), 88.

THE SHIFT FROM RADICAL PEDAGOGY: CONCEPTUAL AND STRUCTURAL UPHEAVALS | TD

1 Herbert Blau in "Notes from Idyllwild Faculty Retreat, June 1971," quoted in Janet Sarbanes, "A Community of Artists. Radical Pedagogy at CalArts, 1969–72," June 5, 2014, *East of Borneo*, accessed June 24, 2019, https://eastofborneo.org/articles/a-community-of-artists-radical-pedagogy-at-calarts-1969-72/.

2 Ibid.

3 Other faculty members in "Notes from Idyllwild Faculty Retreat, June 1971," quoted in ibid.

4 See Sarbanes, "A Community of Artists."

5 Alan Rich, "They Used to Call it Mickey Mouse U, But Not These Days," Smithsonian Magazine (January 1983), quoted in ibid.

6 Robert Fitzpatrick in Herbert Gold, "Walt Disney Presents: *Adventures in Collegeland*!," quoted in ibid.

7 See Herbert Blau, "Fantasia and Simulacra: Subtext of a Syllabus for the Arts in America," in *The Dubious Spectacle: Extremities of Theater*, ed. ibid. (Minneapolis: University of Minnesota Press, 2002), 175.

JOHN BALDESSARI AND THE DISSOLUTION OF THE TEACHER-STUDENT RELATIONSHIP | LH

1 John Baldessari, "John Baldessari," interview by David Salle, June 2013, New York, *Interview Magazine,* October 9, 2013, accessed June 23, 2019, https://www.interviewmagazine.com/art/john-baldessari.

2 Cf. John Baldessari, *Teaching a Plant the Alphabet* (1972), open reel video excerpt, b&w, 00:30, accessed June 25, 2019, http://www.vdb.org/titles/teaching-plant-alphabet.

3 Robert W. Corrigan quoted in John Miller, "Mike Kelley (1954–2012). From My Institution to Yours. A Personal Remembrance," *Art Agenda Reviews*, February 6, 2012, accessed June 23, 2019, https://www.art-agenda.com/features/233339/mike-kelley-1954-2012.

4 John Baldessari, "Interview with John Baldessari," telephone interview by Henry Ward, November 2, 2012, Henry Ward website, accessed June 23, 2019, http://www.henryhward.com/interview-with-john-baldessari/.

5 Baldessari, interview, 2013.

6 John Baldessari, "A Situation Where Art Might Happen: John Baldessari on CalArts," interview by Christopher Knight, Santa Monica (CA), April 4–5, 1992, *East of Borneo,* November 19, 2011, accessed June 23, 2019, https://eastofborneo.org/articles/a-situation-where-art-might-happen-john-baldessari-on-calarts/.

7 Ibid.

8 Baldessari, interview, 2013.

9 David Salle quoted in ibid.

10 Baldessari, interview, 2011.

11 Ibid.

12 David Salle quoted in Baldessari, interview, 2013.

13 Baldessari, interview, 2011.

I THINK THAT'S THE CLOSEST YOU GET. JOHN BALDESSARI'S ASSIGNMENTS | JG

1 John Baldessari, "A Situation Where Art Might Happen: John Baldessari on CalArts," interview by Christopher Knight, Santa Monica (CA), April 4–5, 1992, *East of Borneo,* November 19, 2011, accessed June 23, 2019, https://eastofborneo.org/articles/a-situation-where-art-might-happen-john-baldessari-on-calarts/.

2 See Jacquelyn Ardam, "On Not Teaching Art: Baldessari, Pedagogy, and Conceptualism," *ASAP Journal* 3, no. 1 (January 2018): 152–154, 157, accessed June 24, 2019, https://muse.jhu.edu/article/686306/pdf.

3 Baldessari, interview, 2011.

4 Ibid.

5 Lexico powered by OXFORD, s.v. "assignment," accessed June 24, 2019, https://en.oxforddictionaries.com/definition/assignment.

6 Baldessari, interview, 2011.

7 See ibid.

8 Ibid.

9 James Welling quoted in: Amy Heibel, "Post Studio Art: Remembering John Baldessari's Famous CalArts Class," *Unframed,* July 6, 2010, accessed June 24, 2019, https://unframed.lacma.org/2010/07/06/post-studio-art-remembering-john-baldessari%25e2%2580%2599s-famous-cal-arts-class.

10 John Baldessari, "John Baldessari," interview by David Salle, June 2013, New York, *Interview Magazine,* October 9, 2013, accessed June 23, 2019, https://www.interviewmagazine.com/art/john-baldessari.

11 Baldessari, interview, 2011.

12 See John Baldessari, Letter to Charlotte Townsend-Gault, February 1, 1971, Mezzanine Gallery Collection, accessed June 24, 2019, https://nscad.cairnrepo.org/islandora/object/nscad%3A4873.

13 See Sidra Stich, "Conceptual Alchemy: A Conversation with John Baldessari," *American Art* 19, no 1 (Spring 2005): 80; Ardam, "On Not Teaching Art," 162, 165.

14 See Baldessari, interview, 2013.

MICHAEL POLANYI, THE TACIT DIMENSION

Michael Polanyi, *The Tacit Dimension* (Garden City, NY: Doubleday & Company, inc., 1966), accessed June 25, 2019, https://monoskop.org/images/1/11/Polanyi_Michael_The_Tacit_Dimension.pdf.

JOHN BALDESSARI, THROWING THREE BALLS IN THE AIR TO GET A STRAIGHT LINE AND OTHER WORKS FROM THE 1970s | FK

1 See images and description of this work in "LOT 82: John Baldessari Throwing Three Balls In The Air To Get A Straight Line (Twelve Works), 1973," Paddle 8, accessed June 11, 2019, https://paddle8.com/work/john-baldessari/144395-throwing-three-balls-in-the-air-to-get-a-straight-line-twelve-works.

2 See short biography of John Baldessari, "About the Photographer," Museum of Contemporary Photography at Columbia College Chicago, accessed June 11, 2019, http://www.mocp.org/detail.php?type=related&kv=3219&t=people.

3 Marie-Josée Jean quoted in "John Baldessari: 1970s Film and Video Work," exhibition at VOX—Centre de l'Image Contemporaine, Montréal, Canada, April 1, 2010–May 1, 2010, accessed June 11, 2019, http://www.centrevox.ca/en/exposition/john-baldessari-2/.

4 The proverb, which has existed since 1575, appeared for the first time in 1678 in John Ray's Proverb collection. The complete sentence was: "Haste makes waste, and waste makes want, and want makes strife between the goodman and his wife," see *The Free Dictonary by Farflex,* accessed June 11, 2019, https://www.theidioms.com/haste-makes-waste/.

5 See Charles Bensinger, "Chapter 12: The Video Portapak. How to Take it with You," in ibid., *The Video Guide* (New York: Scribner, 1981), 155–186.

6 Wulf Herzogenrath has written an overview text on the historical development of video art, see ibid.,"Videokunst und Videoskulptur in vier Jahrzehnten. Der Fernseher als Objekt," in *TV Kultur. Das Fernsehen in der Kunst seit 1879,* ed. ibid. et al (Amsterdam/Dresden: Philo & Philo Fine Arts, 1997), 110–115.

7 John Baldessari quoted in "Artists. John Baldessari," The Art Story. Modern Art Insight, accessed June 11, 2019, https://www.theartstory.org/artist-baldessari-john.htm.

8 John Baldessari quoted in MoCP, "Bio".

9 Cf. excerpt of John Baldessari, *The Meaning of Various Photographs to Ed Henderson—Part 1,* filmed 1973 by ibid., b&w, accessed June 11, 2019, http://www.vdb.org/titles/meaning-various-photographs-ed-henderson-1.

10 See ibid.

11 John Baldessari quoted in "The Meaning of Various News Photos to Ed Henderson, John Baldessari," Electronic Arts Intermix, accessed June 11, 2019, https://www.eai.org/titles/the-meaning-of-various-news-photos-to-ed-henderson.

12 See Craig Owens, "From the Archives: Telling Stories," *Art in America* (May 1, 1981), accessed June 11, 2019, https://www.artinamericamagazine.com/news-features/magazines/from-the-archives-telling-stories/.

13 Ibid.

14 See ibid.

UNREALIZED PROJECTS | PG

1 See 14 Rooms, exhibition curated by Klaus Biesenbach and Hans Ulrich Obrist at Art Basel (June 14, 2014–June 22, 2014), accessed June 12, 2019, https://waysofcurating.withgoogle.com/exhibition/11-rooms-exhibitions-manchester/media/5106770607341568.

2 "Baldessari Sings Lewitt," Online Archive Museum Moderner Kunst Stiftung Ludwig Wien, accessed June 12, 2019, https://www.mumok.at/de/baldessari-sings-lewitt.

3 See "Teaching a Plant the Alphabet," Werkleitz Gesellschaft, accessed June 12, 2019, http://werkleitz.de/teaching-a-plant-the-alphabet.

4 See "Throwing Four Balls in the Air to Get a Square. John Baldessari," *Thing of Wonder*, accessed June 12, 2019, http://www.thingofwonder.com/curiosities/john-baldessari/.

ALISON KNOWLES | JAE

1 Alison Knowles, "A School Based on What Artists Wanted to Do: Alison Knowles on CalArts," interview by Janet Sarbanes, *East of Borneo,* August 7, 2012, accessed June 13, 2012, https://eastofborneo.org/articles/a-school-based-on-what-artists-wanted-to-do-alison-knowles-on-calarts.

2 Ibid.

BARBARA BLOOM | LB

1 See "Barbara Bloom," biography, Galleria Raffaella Cortese, accessed June 14, 2019, https://raffaellacortese.com/artists/barbara-bloom/biography.html.

2 See ibid.

3 See ibid; "Barbara Bloom. The Weather," press release, Capitain Petzel, accessed June 14, 2019, http://www.capitainpetzel.de/exhibitions/the-weather/.

4 See "Barbara Bloom," Galleria Rafaelle Cortese.

5 See ibid.

6 See ibid.

A SITUATION WHERE ART MIGHT HAPPEN | JAE

1 John Baldessari quoted in Sidra Stich, "Conceptual Alchemy: A Conversation with John Baldessari," *American Art*, no. 19, issue 1 (Spring 2005): 61.

2 John Baldessari quoted in John Baldessari, "A Situation Where Art Might Happen: John Baldessari on CalArts," interview by Christopher Knight, Santa Monica (CA), April 4–5, 1992, *East of Borneo*, November 19, 2011, accessed June 23, 2019, https://eastofborneo.org/articles/a-situation-where-art-might-happen-john-baldessari-on-calarts/.

3 Ibid.

4 See Timothy Michael Ridlen, *The Research and Teaching of Art Despite Its Disappearance: Art in Academia 1957–1977*, dissertation at University of California, San Diego (2018), accessed June 13, 2019, https://cloudfront.escholarship.org/dist/prd/content/qt2fc1w4xm/qt2fc1w4xm.pdf?t=paxzgn.

5 James Welling quoted in Amy Heibel, "Post Studio Art: Remembering John Baldessari's Famous CalArts Class," (July 6, 2010), *Unframed*, accessed June 13, 2019, https://unframed.lacma.org/2010/07/06/post-studio-art-remembering-john-baldessari%25e2%2580%2599s-famous-cal-arts-class.

6 Ibid.

7 See documentary material of this performance at *Pacific Standard Time at the Getty Center*, accessed June 13, 2019, http://blogs.getty.edu/pacificstandardtime/explore-the-era/worksofart/entr'acte-happening-at-calarts/.

8 Alison Knowles quoted in Janet Sarbanes, "A School Based on What Artists Wanted to Do: Alison Knowles on CalArts," *East of Borneo* (August 7, 2012), accessed June 13, 2019, https://eastofborneo.org/articles/a-school-based-on-what-artists-wanted-to-do-alison-knowles-on-calarts.

9 Ibid.

10 Hallie Scott quoted in "The House of Pedagogy," in *The House of Dust*, James Gallery; CUNY, New York (September 8–October 29, 2016), accessed June 13, 2019, https://www.artbytranslation.org/publications/houseofdust2.

11 See Maud Jacquin and Sébastien Pluot, "Poetry in Translation," in Hannah B. Higgins, Benjamin H.D. Buchloh, Janet Sarbanes, Maud Jacquin, Sébastien Pluot, *The House of Dust by Alison Knowles*, in *Art by Translation* (n.d.), accessed June 13, 2019, https://www.artbytranslation.org/publications/houseofdust1.

12 See *California Video Artists and Histories*, ed. Glenn Phillips (Los Angeles: The Getty Research Institute, 2008), 5.

13 Emmabeth Nanol, "Finding Aid for the Wolfgang Stoerchle Papers, 1952–2007, Bulk 1968–1998," Online Archive of California, accessed June 13, 2019, http://www.oac.cdlib.org/findaid/ark:/13030/kt0v19r6d2/entire_text/.

WOLFGANG STOERCHLE | JAE & VK

1 See Emmabeth Nanol, "Finding Aid for the Wolfgang Stoerchle Papers, 1952–2007, bulk 1968–1998," Biographical/Historical Note, The Getty Research Institute, Special Collections, Online Archive of California, accessed June 24, 2019, https://oac.cdlib.org/findaid/ark:/13030/kt0v19r6d2/entire_text/.

2 "Wolfgang Stoerchle. Before You Can Pry Any Secrets From Me," press release, archive, OVERDUIN & CO, accessed June 24, 2019, http://www.overduinandco.com/archive/other/wolfgang_stoerchle/press_release.pdf.

3 See ibid.

MATT MULLICAN | LB

1 See "Matt Mullican," Biography, Widewalls, accessed June 13, 2019, https://www.widewalls.ch/artist/matt-mullican/.

2 Ibid.

3 See "Matt Mullican," Künstler, Georg Kargl, accessed June 13, 2019, https://www.georgkargl.com/de/kuenstler/matt-mullican.

4 Widewalls, "Matt Mullican."

5 See ibid.; "Matt Mullican. That Person's Workbook," Printed Matter Inc., accessed June 13, 2019, https://www.printedmatter.org/catalog/23148/.

6 Joshua Decter, "Matt Mullican," *Artforum International,* February 1993, article preview, Questia, accessed June 13, 2019, https://www.questia.com/read/1G1-14376689/matt-mullican.

7 See "Matt Mullican," Künstler/Künstlerin, art-in.de, accessed June 13, 2019, https://www.art-in.de/biografie.php?id=719.

8 See Georg Kargl, "Matt Mullican."

9 See Art-in, "Matt Mullican."

PLAYING WITH WORDS AND IMAGES | KB

1 See Ingo Maerker, "John Baldessaris Arbeiten aus den sechziger und siebziger Jahren als Modell einer kritischen Selbstbefragung der Kunst. Eine Untersuchung der Rolle der Conceptual Art für den Paradigmenwechsel zur Postmoderne" (PhD diss., Albert-Ludwigs-Universität Freiburg i.Br., 2006), 89–91, accessed June 19, 2019, https://freidok.uni-freiburg.de/data/6354.

2 See ibid, 98–90.

3 See ibid, 99–100.

4 See ibid, 101–102.

5 John Baldessari quoted in Calvin Tomkins, "No More Boring Art. John Baldessari's crusade," *The New Yorker*, October 11, 2010, accessed June 19, 2019, https://www.newyorker.com/magazine/2010/10/18/no-more-boring-art.

JOHN BALDESSARI | LB

1 See "John Baldessari," Artworks, artnet, accessed June 22, 2019, http://www.artnet.com/artists/john-baldessari/.

2 See ibid.; "Baldessari, John," Künstlerverzeichnis, Lempertz, accessed June 23, 2019, https://www.lempertz.com/de/kataloge/kuenstlerverzeichnis/detail/baldessari-john.html.

3 See ibid.; Amy Heibel, "Post Studio Art: Remembering John Baldessari's Famous CalArts Class," *Unframed*, July 6, 2010, accessed June 24, 2019, https://unframed.lacma.org/2010/07/06/post-studio-art-remembering-john-baldessari%25e2%2580%2599s-famous-cal-arts-class.

4 See John Baldessari, "I Am Making Art," YouTube, accessed June 23, 2019, https://www.youtube.com/watch?v=MOF3qhM6vIA&t=49s.

5 See "Wrong," Artworks, Wikiart, accessed June 22, 2019, https://www.wikiart.org/en/john-baldessari/wrong-1967.

6 See "Bio," John Baldessari website, acccessed June 24, 2019, http://www.baldessari.org/bio.

7 See "Exhibitions," John Baldessari website, accessed June 24, 2019, http://www.baldessari.org/exhibitions.

8 See "John Baldessari," artnet.

THE SERIALITY OF REENACTMENTS: I WILL NOT MAKE ANY MORE BORING ART | AS

1 See "I Will Not Make Any More Boring Art," MoMA Learning, accessed June 19, 2019, https://www.moma.org/learn/moma_learning/john-baldessari-i-will-not-make-any-more-boring-art-1971/.

2 See "I Am Making Art," Electronic Arts Intermix, accessed June 19, 2019, https://www.eai.org/titles/i-am-making-art.

3 See Ingo Maerker, "John Baldessaris Arbeiten aus den sechziger und siebziger Jahren als Modell einer kritischen Selbstbefragung der Kunst. Eine Untersuchung der Rolle der Conceptual Art für den Paradigmenwechsel zur Postmoderne" (PhD diss., Albert-Ludwigs-Universität Freiburg i.Br., 2006), 89–91, accessed June 19, 2019, https://freidok.uni-freiburg.de/data/6354.

4 See "The Writing Is On the Wall: John Baldessari's 'I Will Not Make Any More Boring Art,'" Education Blog, Whitney Museum of American Art, July 9, 2010, accessed June 19, 2019, https://whitney.org/Education/EducationBlog/JohnBaldessariIWillNotMakeAnyMoreBoringArt.

5 MoMA Learning, "I Will Not Make Any More Boring Art."

6 See "History Will Repeat Itself: Strategies of Re-enactment in Contemporary Art," event announcement, KW Institute for Contemporary Art, November 18, 2007–January 13, 2008, accessed June 19, 2019, https://www.kw-berlin.de/en/history-will-repeat-itself-strategies-of-re-enactment-in-contemporary-art/.

JAMES WELLING | LB

1 See "James Wellling", James Welling website, accessed June 13, 2019, http://jameswelling.net/biography; "James Welling," biography, artnet, accessed June 13, 2019, http://www.artnet.com/artists/james-welling/biography.

2   See ibid.; "James Welling," artists, David Zwirner, accessed June 23, 2019, https://www.davidzwirner.com/artists/james-welling/biography.
3   See "James Welling," artnet.
4   Steel Stillman quoted in James Welling, "In the Studio: James Welling," interview by Steel Stillman, *Art in America Magazine,* January 26, 2011, accessed June 13, 2019, https://www.artinamericamagazine.com/news-features/magazines/james-welling/.
5   See "James Welling," David Zwirner.
6   See ibid.
7   See "James Wellling," website.
8   See ibid.
9   See ibid.
10 See "James Welling," Artists, Guggenheim, accessed June 13, 2019, https://www.guggenheim.org/artwork/artist/james-welling.
11 See "James Wellling," website.
12 See ibid.
13 See "James Welling," David Zwirner.

JACK GOLDSTEIN | LB

1   Lorne Lanning, "Jack Goldstein, Glitch Artist?," interview by Michael Connor, May 21, 2013, *Rhizome,* accessed June 25, 2019, http://rhizome.org/editorial/2013/may/21/jack-goldstein-glitch-artist/; "Jack Goldstein," Rosenthal Fine Art website, accessed June 25, 2019, http://www.rosenthalfineart.com/jack-goldstein.
2   See "Biography," The Official Website for the Estate of Jack Goldstein, accessed June 25, 2019, http://www.jackgoldstein-artist.com/bio.htm; "Jack Goldstein," Biography, artnet, accessed on June 25, 2019, http://www.artnet.com/artists/jack-goldstein/biography.
3   See "Jack Goldstein," artnet.
4   See Jack Goldstein, "Chouinard and the Los Angeles Art Scene," in *Jack Goldstein and the CalArts Mafia,* ed. Richard Hertz (Ojai: Minneola Press, 2003), 31.
5   See "Jack Goldstein", Estate of Jack Goldstein.
6   See ibid.
7   See ibid.
8   See ibid.

HOW TO TEACH YOUR STUDENTS ABOUT CONCEPTUAL ART | AC

1   "Unit 8 Lesson 2: Language Art," Oxford Art Online, accessed June 25, 2019, https://www.oxfordartonline.com/page/unit-8-lesson-2/unit-8-lesson-2.
2   Ibid.
3   Ibid.
4   Ibid.
5   John Baldessari quoted in Coosje van Bruggen, *John Baldessari* (New York: Rizzoli, 1990), 11.
6   Nicole Rangel, "Progressive Education," in *The SAGE Encyclopedia of Classroom Management*, ed. W. George Scarlett (Thousand Oaks: Sage Publications, 2014), 2, accessed June 25, 2019, http://sk.sagepub.com/reference/the-sage-encyclopedia-of-classroom-management/i2526.xml.
7   Timothy Ridlen, "The Research and Teaching of Art Despite Its Disappearance. Art in Academia, 1957–1977" (PhD diss., University of California, 2018), 159.
8   Ibid., 166.
9   Rangel, "Progressive Education," 3.
10 See Ridlen, "The Research and Teaching of Art," 171.
11 John Baldessari in an advertisement by the Rolex Mentor and Protégé Art Initiative, April 2008, *Plaza Magazine,* quoted in Lee Plested, "Interview with Lee Plested from The Apartment," interview by Amarie Bergman, *Whitehot Magazine,* May 2008, accessed June 25, 2019, https://whitehotmagazine.com/articles/with-lee-plested-from-apartment/1280.

DELEGATED PERFORMANCES | CW

1   See Ayun Halliday, "John Baldessari's *I Will Not Make Any More Boring Art:* A 1971 Conceptual Art Piece/DIY Art Course," August 21, 2013, *Open Culture,* accessed June 25, 2019, http://www.openculture.com/2013/08/john-baldessaris-i-will-not-make-any-more-boring-art-a-1971-conceptual-art-piecediy-art-course.html.
2   John Baldessari, Letter to Charlotte Townsend-Gault, February 1, 1971, Mezzanine Gallery Collection, accessed June 25, 2019, https://nscad.cairnrepo.org/islandora/object/nscad%3A4873
3   Claire Bishop, "Black Box, White Cube, Public Space," *Out of Body* (Spring 2016): 2, accessed June 25, 2019, http://www.skulptur-projekte.de/skulptur-projekte-download/SP17-Out/Out_of_Body_DE.pdf. Original quote: "…Präsenz des Künstlers, die in der Body Art der 1970er Jahre noch so wichtig war, an Laien ausgesourct wird."
4   Ibid. Original quote: "… Kunstform, die auf die kontinuierliche Präsenz engagierter Darsteller setzt"
5   See ibid.

I WILL NOT MAKE ANY MORE BORING ART. TRAVELLING AND APPROPRIATION | VL & AR

1   See Molly Petrilla, "Wasting Time on the Internet," *The Pennsylvania Gazette,* November 25, 2014, accessed June 25, 2019, http://thepenngazette.com/wasting-time-on-the-internet/.
2   See "I will not make any more (after John Baldessari)," Projects, Andrew Maize website, accessed June 25, 2019, http://andrewmaize.ca/site/?page_id=52.
3   See *Lexikon,* s.v. "Parodie," accessed June 25, 2019, https://www.wissen.de/lexikon/parodie-literatur.
4   See *Großes Wörterbuch der Deutschen Sprache*, s.v. "Emergenz," accessed June 25, 2019, https://www.wissen.de/rechtschreibung/emergenz.
5   See *Lexikon,* s.v. "Appropriation Art," accessed June 25, 2019, https://www.wissen.de/lexikon/appropriation-art.
6   See *Wahrig Herkunftswörterbuch*, s.v. "Ironie," accessed June 25, 2019, https://www.wissen.de/wortherkunft/ironie.
7   See *Merriam-Webster,* s.v. "double bind," accessed June 25, 2019, https://www.merriam-webster.com/dictionary/double%20bind.

PERFORMATIVE REPETITION IN CONCEPTUAL ART | CB

1   Murphy Chang, "I Will Not Make Any More Boring Art: Spotlight on a Student Performer," interview by Whitney Museum of American Art, July 12, 2010, accessed June 25, 2019, https://whitney.org/Education/EducationBlog/SpotlightOnABaldessariStudentPerformer.
2   Ibid.

DANIEL BUREN, THE FUNCTION OF THE STUDIO

Daniel Buren, "The Function of the Studio," trans. Thomas Repensek, *October* 10 (Autumn 1979): 51–58, accessed June 25, 2019, http://www.kim-cohen.com/Assets/CourseAssets/Texts/Buren_Function%20of%20the%20Studio.pdf.

APPROPRIATION ART | CG & NN

1   See Mark Penner-Howell, "Appropriation Defined," Mark Penner-Howell Artwork, accessed June 25, 2019, http://www.markpennerhowell.com/?page_id=555.
2   Jean Baudrillard, "The Precession of Simulacra," in *Media and Cultural Studies. Key Works,* eds. Meenakshi Gig Durham and Douglas M. Kellner (Malden: Blackwell, 2016), 453.
3   See Douglas Crimp, *Pictures* (New York: Committee for the Visual Arts, Inc., 1977), catalog of an exhibition at Artists Space, New York, September 24–October 29, 1977, 8, accessed June 25, 2019, http://artistsspace.org/exhibitions/pictures.
4   Holland Cotter, "At the Met, Baby Boomers Leap Onstage," *The New York Times,* April 23, 2009, accessed June 25, 2019, http://assets-p.artcat.com/file_uploads/file_asset/asset/3fa3365addd4eb5d323734c8539c219f3aa3930a/bb295c212aa8404830b6fda22d8b5cd9.pdf.
5   See Linda Yablonsky, "Photo Play: The Story of the Pictures Generation," *Art in America,* July 31, 2017, accessed June 25, 2019, https://www.artinamericamagazine.com/news-features/magazines/photo-play/.
6   See ibid.
7   See The Editors of ARTnews, "Making 'Pictures'. A Short History of Douglas Crimp's Famous Show at Artists Space in 1977," *ARTnews,* October 14, 2016, accessed June 25, 2019, http://www.artnews.com/2016/10/14/making-pictures-a-short-history-of-douglas-crimps-famous-show-at-artists-space-in-1977/.
8   See "Pictures Generation," Art Terms, Arts & Artists, Tate, accessed June 25, 2019, https://www.tate.org.uk/art/art-terms/p/pictures-generation.
9   Douglas Crimp quoted in Jordana Moore Saggese, "The Pictures Generation," Khan Academy, accessed June 25, 2019, https://www.khanacademy.org/humanities/global-culture/identity-body/identity-body-united-states/a/the-pictures-generation.
10 "Beginnings of the Pictures Generation," Movements, *The Art Story*, accessed June 25, 2019, https://www.theartstory.org/movement-the-pictures-generation-history-and-concepts.htm.
11 Jessica Meiselman, "When Does an Artist's Appropriation Become Copyright Infringement?," *Artsy,* December 28, 2017, accessed June 25, 2019, https://www.artsy.net/article/artsy-editorial-artists-appropriation-theft.
12 See ibid.

IMAGE RIGHTS

All image references are listed in order of appearance and from left to right per page beginning from top left.

Cover: John Baldessari (b. 1931), *I Will Not Make Any More Boring Art* (1971). New York, Museum of Modern Art (MoMA). Lithograph, composition: 22 ⅜ × 29 ⁹⁄₁₆ in. (56.8 × 75.1 cm); sheet: 22 ⁷⁄₁₆ × 30 ⅛₆ in. (57 × 76.4 cm). John B. Turner Fund. Acc. n.: 1.1972. © 2019. Digital image, The Museum of Modern Art, New York / Scala, Florence.

4 Madeleine Schwinge, *The Psychedelic Chicks. Live on Sunset Strip* (2019).

16–21 EDUCATION: IN AND OUT OF THE CLASSROOM

16 Opening Day at Burbank (1970). California Institute of the Arts Photographic Materials Collection. Courtesy of California Institute of the Arts Archives.

– CalArts Idyllwild Retreat, Faculty Conference (1971). Courtesy of California Institute of the Arts Archives, in Catherine Wagley, "Experimental Impulse," Daily Serving, December 16, 2011, accessed July 12, 2019, https://www.dailyserving.com/2011/12/experimental-impulse/.

– Idyllwild Retreat (1971). California Institute of the Arts Photographic Materials Collection. Courtesy of California Institute of the Arts Archives.

17 Alison Knowles, *House of Dust* (1971). California Institute of the Arts Photographic Materials Collection. Courtesy of California Institute of the Arts Archives.

18 Grasstains Environmental Dance Concert (1981). California Institute of the Arts Photographic Materials Collection. Courtesy of California Institute of the Arts Archives.

– Cover of the *Womanhouse* catalog (1972), edited by Judy Chicago and Miriam Schapiro and designed by Sheila Levrant de Bretteville © Judy Chicago / Artists Rights Society (ARS), New York / VG Bild-Kunst, Bonn 2019. Photo courtesy of Through the Flower Archives.

20 Alison Knowles, *House of Dust–Orientation Bonfire* (1971). California Institute of the Arts Photographic Materials Collection. Courtesy of California Institute of the Arts Archives.

– Matt Mullican, *Bringing the Light into a Windowless Room and Burning a Leaf* (1972), performance views, CalArts, Valencia (CA), ten silver gelatine prints / baryte paper / modern prints, wooden frames with museum glass size of paper: each sheet 26,5 × 36,5 cm (10.4 × 14.4 in.), image size: each 21,2 × 31,4 cm (8.4 × 12.4 in.) © Matt Mullican. Courtesy Capitain Petzel, Berlin, in "Bringing Light into a Windowless Room," Exhibitions, Capitain Petzel, accessed July 29, 2019, http://www.capitainpetzel.de/exhibitions/bringing-light-into-a-windowless-room/.

21 CalArts unknown (ca. 1971–72). California Institute of the Arts Photographic Materials Collection. Courtesy of California Institute of the Arts Archives.

26–27 THE CALARTS STORY, WALT DISNEY PRODUCTIONS

The CalArts Story, starring Sebastian Cabot, Hollywood (CA), Walt Disney Productions, August 27, 1964, 17:48, accessed June 13, 2019, https://calarts.edu/about/institute/history.

29–31 MOVEMENTS OF THE L.A. ART SCENE IN THE 1960s

29 *Primary Atmospheres: Works from California 1960–1970*, installation view, January 8–February 6, 2010, David Zwirner, New York. Photo by Cathy Carver. Courtesy of David Zwirner, New York, in "Primary Atmospheres: Works from California 1960–1970," accessed July 12, 2019, https://www.davidzwirner.com/exhibitions/primary-atmospheres-works-california-1960-1970.

30 John McCracken, *Mykonos* (1965), lacquer, fiberglass, and plywood, 15 × 16 ½ × 7 in. (38.1 × 41.9 × 17.8 cm). Courtesy of the Orange County Museum of Art, in "John McCracken. Works from 1963–2011," David Zwirner website, accessed July 13, 2019, https://www.davidzwirner.com/exhibitions/works-1963-2011.

– De Wain Valentine, *Large Wall* (1968). Courtesy of the Norton Simon Museum, in Rachel Rivenc, Emma Richardson, Tom Learner, "The LA Look From Start to Finish: Materials, Processes and Conservation of Works by the Finish Fetish Artists," 3, accessed July 12, 2019, https://www.getty.edu/conservation/our_projects/science/art_LA/article_2011_icom_cc.pdf.

– Larry Bell in his studio, Venice Beach, California (1969). Photo by Malcolm Lubliner (American, b. 1933). Courtesy Malcolm Lubliner and Craig Krull Gallery, Santa Monica. Art © Larry Bell / VG Bild-Kunst, Bonn 2019, in Rebecca Peabody, ed., *Pacific Standard Time. Los Angeles Art, 1945–1980*, (Los Angeles: Getty Research Institute, 2011), catalog of an exhibition at J. Paul Getty Museum, Los Angeles, October 1, 2011–February 5, 2012, and Martin-Gropius-Bau, Berlin, March 15–June 10, 2012, 169.

– Helen Pashgian, *Untitled* (1968–69). Photo by Brian Forrest. Courtesy of Brian Forest and Helen Pashgian, in Rachel Rivenc, Emma Richardson, Tom Learner, "The LA Look From Start to Finish: Materials, Processes and Conservation of Works by the Finish Fetish Artists," 5, accessed July 12, 2019, https://www.getty.edu/conservation/our_projects/science/art_LA/article_2011_icom_cc.pdf.

– Robert Irwin, *Untitled* (1969). Anderson Collection at Stanford University © VG Bild-Kunst, Bonn 2019, in "Robert Irwin, Untitled, 1969," Anderson Collection at Stanford University, accessed July 12, 2019, https://anderson.stanford.edu/collection/untitled-by-robert-irwin/.

– John McCracken, *Untitled* (1972), in: "John McCracken, Untitled, 1972," Art Basel, accessed July 12, 2019, https://www.artbasel.com/catalog/artwork/56862/John-McCracken-Untitled.

– Robert Irwin, *Prism* (1971), acrylic, 143 ⁷⁄₁₀ × 5 ⁹⁄₁₉ × 5 ⁹⁄₁₀ × 5 ⁹⁄₁₀ in., 365 × 15 × 15 cm, installation view, *Plastic Show*, curated by De Wain Valentine, February 09—March 25, 2017, London, Grosvenor Hill. Anderson Collection at Stanford University © VG Bild-Kunst, Bonn 2019, in "Robert Irwin, *Prism,* 1971," *Artsy*, accessed July 12, 2019, https://www.artsy.net/artwork/robert-irwin-prism.

31 Artists outside the Ferrus Gallery in Los Angeles (1959). Clockwise from top: Billy Al Bengston, Irving Blum, Ed Moses, and John Altoon. Photo by William Claxton. Courtesy Demont Photo Management, LLC, in Rebecca Peabody, ed., *Pacific Standard Time. Los Angeles Art, 1945–1980,* (Los Angeles: Getty Research Institute, 2011), catalog of an exhibition at J. Paul Getty Museum, Los Angeles, October 1, 2011–February 5, 2012, and Martin-Gropius-Bau, Berlin, March 15–June 10, 2012, 126.

– Wallace Berman at Stone Brothers (1957). Photo by Charles Brittin (1928–2011). Getty Research Institute, Los Angeles (2005.M.11) © J. Paul Getty Trust.

35–40 I WILL NOT MAKE ANY MORE BORING ART: PREHISTORY

35 John Baldessari, *Wrong* (1966–68), photographic emulsion and acrylic on canvas, 59 × 45 in. (149.9 × 114.3 cm). Courtesy of John Baldessari.

36 John Baldessari, *Econ-O-Wash, 14th and Highland, National City Calif.* (1966–68), acrylic, photographic emulsion and acrylic on canvas, 59 × 45 in. (149.9 × 114.3 cm). Courtesy of John Baldessari.

37 Documentation of *Cremation Project* (1970). Courtesy of John Baldessari.

38–39 John Baldessari, *California Map Project, Part 1: California* (1969), eleven color photographs and one text on paper photos and text: 8 × 10 in. each. Courtesy of John Baldessari.

39 John Baldessari, *What is Painting* (1966–68), acrylic on canvas, 67 ¾ × 56 ¾ in. Courtesy of John Baldessari.

– John Baldessari, *Composing on a Canvas* (1966–68), acrylic on canvas, 113 ¾ × 96 in. Courtesy of John Baldessari.

– John Baldessari, *Painting and Drawing* (1966–68), acrylic on canvas, ½ × 56 in. Courtesy of John Baldessari.

40 John Baldessari, *Commissioned Painting: A Painting by Anita Storck* (1969), acrylic and oil on canvas, 59 ¼ × 45 ½ in. (150.5 × 115.57 cm). Courtesy of John Baldessari.

– John Baldessari, *Commissioned Painting: A Painting by Pat Perdue* (1969), acrylic and oil on canvas, 59 ¼ × 45 ½ in. (150.5 × 115.6 cm). Courtesy of John Baldessari.

– John Baldessari, *Commissioned Painting: A Painting by Jane Moore* (1969), acrylic and oil on canvas, 59 ¼ × 45 ½ in. (150.5 × 115.6 cm). Courtesy of John Baldessari.

– John Baldessari, *Commissioned Painting: A Painting by George Walker* (1969), acrylic and oil on canvas, 59 ¼ × 45 ½ in. (150.5 × 115.6 cm). Courtesy of John Baldessari.

– John Baldessari, *Commissioned Painting: A Painting by Elmire Bourke* (1969), acrylic and oil on canvas, 59 ¼ × 45 ½ in. (150.5 × 115.6 cm). Courtesy of John Baldessari.

– John Baldessari, *Commissioned Painting: A Painting by Dante Guido* (1969), acrylic and oil on canvas, 59 ¼ × 45 ½ in. (150.5 × 115.6 cm). Courtesy of John Baldessari.

CalArts Bulletin (1971–72). California Institute of the Arts Collection. Courtesy of California Institute of the Arts Archives.

Opening Day at Burbank (1970). California Institute of the Arts Photographic Materials Collection. Courtesy of California Institute of the Arts Archives.

46   John Baldessari, *Teaching a Plant the Alphabet* (1972), 18:40 min, b&w, sound. Courtesy of John Baldessari.
47   Robert Corrigan and students (ca. 1971–72). California Institute of the Arts Photographic Materials Collection. Courtesy of California Institute of the Arts Archives.
48–49 John Baldessari, *Police Drawing* (1971), conte crayon on paper, three b/w photographs and video, drawing 39 × 23 ¼ in., photos 7 ¼ × 10 ½ in. each. Courtesy of John Baldessari.
50   John Baldessari and students (1974). Photo by James Welling. Courtesy of John Baldessari.
51   John Baldessari, *Rolling: Tire* (1972), five b/w photographs and photocopy, photos: 16 × 24 in. each, text: 6 ¼ × 10 in. Courtesy of John Baldessari.

John Baldessari, *CalArts Post-Studio Art: Class Assignments (optional)* (1970), 8.5 × 11 in. each. Courtesy of John Baldessari.

64–65 John Baldessari, *Throwing Three Balls in the Air to Get a Straight Line (Best of Thirty-Six Attempts)* (1973), artist's book, 9 ¾ × 12 ⅞ in. Edizioni Giampaolo Prearo and Halleria Toselli, Milan. Edition of 2000. Courtesy of John Baldessari.
66   John Baldessari, *Heaven and Hell* (1988), lithograph with aquatint sheet: 47 ¼ × 31 ½ in. each image: left sheet: 40 ¹³⁄₁₆ × 24 ⅛ in. (103.7 × 61.3 cm) right sheet: 34 × 27 ⁹⁄₁₆ (86.4 × 70 cm). Publisher: Peter Blum Edition, New York. Edition of 45. Courtesy of John Baldessari.
–   John Baldessari, *Haste Makes Waste* (1973), four min, b&w, silent. Courtesy of John Baldessari.
67   John Baldessari, *Cremation Project* (1970), six color photographs, flat plaque (bronze), bronze urn in shape of book, mounted affidavit, extra box of ashes. Courtesy of John Baldessari.
68   John Baldessari, *The Meaning of Various News Photos to Ed Henderson* (1973), 15 min, b&w, sound. Courtesy of John Baldessari.

69   Andrea Mantegna, *The Lamentation Over the Dead Christ* (c.1490), tempera on canvas, 68 × 81 cm.
–   John Baldessari, *Baldessari Sings LeWitt* (1972), 12:38 min, b&w, sound. Courtesy of John Baldessari.
70   John Baldessari, *Throwing Four Balls in the Air to Get a Square (Best of Thirty-Six Tries)* (detail) (1972–73), eight color photographs, 9 ½ × 13 ¾ in. each. Courtesy of John Baldessari.

Alison Knowles, poem drop over the *House of Dust* (1971), CalArts campus, Burbank (CA). Knowles in front of *House of Dust* (1968). California Institute of the Arts Photographic Materials Collection. Courtesy of California Institute of the Arts Archives. The original photograph is entirely black and white.

Barbara Bloom at the Metropolitan Museum of Art, New York (2015), in "The Artist Project," The Met, accessed July 2, 2019, http://artistproject.metmuseum.org/5/barbara-bloom/. The original photograph is entirely in color.

74–75 Alison Knowles, *House of Dust* (1971), CalArts campus, Burbank (CA). Knowles sitting on the *House of Dust*. California Institute of the Arts Photographic Materials Collection. Courtesy of California Institute of the Arts Archives.
76   James Welling, *Hair* (1973), three gelatin silver prints, each print, 3 × 5 in., in "Early Work," James Welling website, accessed July 19, 2019, http://jameswelling.net/video-sculpture-and-photoworks-los-angeles/253.
–   Allan Kaprow (1927–2006), *Entr'Acte Happening* (1972), CalArts. Getty Research Institute, Los Angeles (980063).
77–78 Alison Knowles, poem drop over the *House of Dust* (1971), CalArts campus, Burbank (CA). California Institute of the Arts Photographic Materials Collection. Courtesy of California Institute of the Arts Archives.
79   Alison Knowles, *House of Dust—Orientation Bonfire* (1971), CalArts campus, Burbank (CA). California Institute of the Arts Photographic Materials Collection. Courtesy of California Institute of the Arts Archives.
80   Wolfgang Stoerchle (1944–76), *Event Performance* (1970). Getty Research Institute, Los Angeles (2009.M.16).
–   Wolfgang Stoerchle with piles of river rocks (1975). Photo by Carol Lingham. Wolfgang Stoerchle Papers. Getty Research Institute, Los Angeles (2009.M.16).

Wolfgang Stoerchle, Wolfgang Stoerchle hovering in mid-air (ca. 1970). Wolfgang Stoerchle papers © J. Paul Getty Trust. Getty Research Institute, Los Angeles (2009.M.16). The original photograph is entirely black and white.

Matt Mullican, Neue Nationalgalerie (June 1995). Photo by Christian Jungeblodt/SIGNUM, in "Matt Mullican in der Neuen Nationalgalerie," ed. Berliner Künstlerprogramm DAAD (Berlin: n.p., 1995), 61.

John Baldessari, *I Will Not Make Any More Boring Art* (1971), graphic on wall (temporary installation), dimensions variable. Courtesy of John Baldessari.

86   Postcard to Charlotte Townsend-Gault from John Baldessari (front) (October 8, 1970). Mezzanine Gallery Collection, Nova Scotia College of Art & Design Collection, accessed June 26, 2019, https://nscad.cairnrepo.org/islandora/object/nscad%3A4870#page/1/mode/1up.
–   Postcard to Charlotte Townsend-Gault from John Baldessari (back) (October 8, 1970). Mezzanine Gallery Collection, Nova Scotia College of Art & Design Collection, accessed June 26, 2019, https://nscad.cairnrepo.org/islandora/object/nscad%3A4872.
87   Letter to Charlotte Townsend-Gault from John Baldessari (February 1, 1971). Mezzanine Gallery Collection, Nova Scotia College of Art & Design Collection, accessed June 26, 2019, https://nscad.cairnrepo.org/islandora/object/nscad%3A4873.
88   On Kawara, *I Got Up* (December 27, 1974), typewritten on postcard, in *On Kawara. Horizontality/Verticality,* ed. Ulrich Wilmes (Köln: Walther König, 2000), catalog of an exhibition at Städtische Galerie im Lehnbachhaus und Kunstbau, Munich, October 21, 2000–January 14, 2001.
89   On Kawara, *I Got Up* (January 4, 1975), typewritten on postcard, in ibid.
–   On Kawara, *I Got Up* (December 31, 1974), typewritten on postcard, in ibid.

John Baldessari with bronze plaque from the *Cremation Project* (1970). Courtesy of John Baldessari. The original photograph is entirely black and white.

91   John Baldessari, *I Will Not Make Any More Boring Art* (1971). New York Museum of Modern Art (MoMa), lithograph, composition: 22 ⅜ × 29 ⁹⁄₁₆ in. (56.8 × 75.1 cm); sheet: 22 ⁷⁄₁₆ × 30 ¹⁄₁₆ in. (57 × 76.4 cm). Edition of 50. John B. Turner Fund. Acc. n.: 1.1972. Courtesy of John Baldessari. © 2019. Digital image, The Museum of Modern Art, New York/Scala, Florence.
93   Hawa Allen re-performs John Baldessari's *I Will Not Make Any More Boring Art* (2010). Photograph by Danielle Canter, in Sarah Meller, "The Writing Is On The Wall: John Baldessari's 'I Will Not Make Any More

Boring Art'," July 9, 2010, Education Blog, Whitney Museum of American Art website, accessed July 13, 2019, https://whitney.org/Education/EducationBlog/JohnBaldessariIWillNotMakeAnyMoreBoringArt.
– John Baldessari, *I Am Making Art* (1971), 18:40 min, b&w, sound. Courtesy of John Baldessari.
– John Baldessari, *I Will Not Make Any More Boring Art* (1971), graphic on wall (temporary installation), dimensions variable. Courtesy of John Baldessari.

95 JAMES WELLING

James Welling at his studio (ca. 1984), in "Films Around Photography," announcement, April 26, 2007, Hammer Museum, Los Angeles, accessed July 2, 2019, https://hammer.ucla.edu/programs-events/2007/04/films-around-photography/. The original photograph is entirely black and white.

96 JACK GOLDSTEIN, EXHIBITION ANNOUNCEMENT, MIZUNO GALLERY

Jack Goldstein, exhibition announcement, Mizuno Gallery (November 1972), offset lithograph © Jack Goldstein Estate. Getty Research Institute, Los Angeles (2010.M.84).

97–99 JACK GOLDSTEIN

97 Jack, East Tenth Street, New York (1978) © James Welling, in Richard Hertz, ed., *Jack Goldstein and the CalArts Mafia* (Ojai: Minneola Press, 2003), 176. The original photograph is entirely black and white.
98–99 Jack Goldstein (American, 194–2203), *A Suite of Nine 7-Inch Records with Sound Effects* (detail) (1976), vinyl records (45rpm, mono) and sleeves, framed: 34½ × 59½ × 4½ in. (87.6 × 151.1 × 11.4 cm) Shown here: "A Swim against the Tide," blue vinyl; "A Faster Run," orange vinyl; "The Tornado," purple vinyl; "Two Wrestling Cats" yellow vinyl. Courtesy Galerie Buchholz Cologne/Berlin and the Estate of Jack Goldstein, in Rebecca Peabody, ed., *Pacific Standard Time. Los Angeles Art, 1945–1980,* (Los Angeles: Getty Research Institute, 2011), catalog of an exhibition at J. Paul Getty Museum, Los Angeles, October 1, 2011–February 5, 2012, and Martin-Gropius-Bau, Berlin, March 15–June 10, 2012, 290.

100–101 HOW TO TEACH YOUR STUDENTS ABOUT CONCEPTUAL ART

101 Joseph Kosuth, *One and Three Chairs* (1965) © 2007 Joseph Kosuth/Artists Rights Society (ARS)/VG Bild-Kunst, Bonn 2019, in Joseph Kosuth, "The Making of Meaning. Selected Writings and Documentation of Investigations on Art Since 1965," (Stuttgart: Staatsgalerie Stuttgart, 1981), 186.

104–106 I WILL NOT MAKE ANY MORE BORING ART: TRAVELLING AND APPROPRIATION

104 Stanley Kubrick, *The Shining* (1980), accessed June 26, 2019, https://images.wired.it/wp-content/uploads/2014/11/1417102907_all_work.jpg /.

– Suso Fandino, *I Will Not Make Any More Boring Art* (n.d.), accessed June 26, 2019, http://susofandino.com/fandino/en/boring_art.
– John Baldessari, *CalArts Post-Studio Art: Class Assignments (optional)* (detail) (1970), 8.5 × 11 in. each. Courtesy of John Baldessari.
– Yann Serandour, *I Will Not Make Any More Boring Art* (2005), neon, 15 × 55 cm. Edition/3 (+ 1 A.P.), accessed June 26, 2019, http://www.luisadelantadovlc.com/en/yann-serandour-en/.
– John Baldessari, *I Will Not Make Any More Boring Art* (1971), graphic on wall (temporary installation), dimensions variable. Courtesy of John Baldessari.
– Ara Shirinyan, *Resolution: I Promise to Write Better Poetry* (2005), accessed June 26, 2019, http://www.ubu.com/contemp/shirinyan/shirinyan_2005_resolution.pdf.
105 Ara Shirinyan, *Resolution: I Promise to Write Better Poetry* (2005), accessed June 26, 2019, http://www.ubu.com/contemp/shirinyan/shirinyan_2005_resolution.pdf.
– Banksy, *I Must Not Copy What I See on the Simpsons* (2008), New Orleans, accessed June 26, 2019, https://www.reddit.com/r/pics/comments/6zbb3/i_must_not_copy_what_i_see_on_the_simpsons_pic/.
– Andrea Nair, *Lines Are Not An Effective Way to Change Your Children's Behaviour Pattern*, in Andrea Nair, "Does Your Child's Teacher Use Punishment? Here's What to Do…," October 04, 2016, accessed June 26, 2019, http://www.yummymummyclub.ca/blogs/andrea-nair-connect-four-parenting/20161003/does-your-childs-teacher-use-punishment-heres-what.
– Camille Le Houezec, *I Will Not Make Any More Boring Exhibition* (2009), performance, chalk on painted wall, 250 × 400 cm, accessed June 26, 2019, http://search.it.online.fr/covers/?p=608.
– Ara Shirinyan, *Resolution: I Promise to Write Better Poetry* (2005), accessed June 26, 2019, http://www.ubu.com/contemp/shirinyan/shirinyan_2005_resolution.pdf.
– Kenneth Goldsmith, *John Baldessari Redo (Blackboard Intervention)* (2013), transmediale. Photo by Veronica Santos Ruiz, accessed June 26, 2019, https://transmediale.de/content/john-baldessari-redo-by-kenneth-goldsmith-blackboard-intervention.
– Bart Simpson Chalkboard Wallpaper Generator, I will not make any more boring art, accessed June 26, 2019, http://www.addletters.com/pictures/bart-simpson-generator/6478350.htm#.XMcI5JMzaLI.
– Ara Shirinyan, *Resolution: I Promise to Write Better Poetry* (2005), accessed June 26, 2019, http://www.ubu.com/contemp/shirinyan/shirinyan_2005_resolution.pdf.
– Andrew Maize, *I Will Not Make Anymore (After John Baldessari)* (2012). Photo by Helen Teager, accessed June 26, 2019, http://andrewmaize.ca/site/?page_id=52.
106 Repetition, Repetition, Repetition: A Power Tip to Command Attention and Conquer Sales, accessed June 26, 2019, http://wordsmith.hk/wordwise-blog/2015/11/2/reading-is-believing-the-power-of-repeating-messages.
– Repetita iuvant, Jar of Quotes, accessed June 26, 2019, https://it.jarofquotes.com/s/repetita-iuvant-146995/.
– John Baldessari in The Simpsons, "Scenes Plus a Tag from a Marriage," episode no. 631, accessed June 26, 2019, https://simpsonswiki.com/wiki/John_Baldessari_(character).

– Trivago tube poster. Photo by Ed Cumming, in Sam Wolfson, "The Trivago Woman: 'People have an opinion, but don't know me from a bar of soap," *The Guardian,* December 19, 2017, accessed June 26, 2019, https://www.theguardian.com/lifeandstyle/2017/dec/19/trivago-girl-tv-adverts-gabrielle-miller-phenomenon.

110–113 APPROPRIATION ART

110 Sherrie Levine (b. 1947), *Fountain (Madonna)* (1991), cast bronze, 15 × 15½ × 25 in. (38.1 × 39.4 × 63.5 cm). Private collection. © Sherrie Levine; image courtesy Simon Lee Gallery, London, and Paula Cooper Gallery, New York, in "Sherrie Levine, *Fountain (After Marcel Duchamp),* 1991, and *Fountain (Buddha)*, 1996," Whitney Museum of American Art website, accessed July 13, 2019, https://www.whitney.org/WatchAndListen/760.
– Installation view of *Pictures*, Artists Space, September 24–October 29, 1977. Photo by D. James Dee © D. James Dee/Courtesy Artists Space New York.
111 Invitation for *Pictures,* Artists Space, September 24–October 29, 1977.
– Cindy Sherman (American, b. 1954), *Untitled Film Still (#54)* (1980), b/w photograph; 8 × 10 in. (20.3 × 25.4 cm). Private collection. Courtesy of the Artist and Metro Pictures, in "The Pictures Generation 1974–1984," The Met, accessed July 13, 2019, https://www.metmuseum.org/exhibitions/listings/2009/pictures-generation/photo-gallery.
– Paul McMahon (American, b. 1950), *Untitled [Loss]* (1973–74), ink on photomechanical reproduction; 3¼ × 5½ in. (8.3 × 14 cm). Collection of the artist, in ibid.
– Richard Prince (American, born Canal Zone (Panama), 1949), *Untitled (Cowboy)* (1989), chromogenic print, 50 × 70 in. (127 × 177.8 cm), frame: 61 × 87 in. (154.9 × 221 cm). Purchase, The Horace W. Goldsmith Foundation Gift, through Joyce and Robert Menschel, and Jennifer and Joseph Duke Gift, 2000, 2000.272 © Richard Prince, in Gary Indiana, "These '80s Artists Are More Important Than Ever," *New York Times,* February 13, 2017, accessed July 13, 2019, https://www.nytimes.com/2017/02/13/t-magazine/pictures-generation-new-york-artists-cindy-sherman-robert-longo.html.
112 Matt Mullican (American, b. 1951), *Framed Section of an Angel's Wing* (1978), ink on paper; 23⅝ × 29¾ in. (60 × 75.6 cm). Collection of Ann A. Wyatt, in "The Pictures Generation 1974–1984," The Met.
– Walker Evans (American, 1903–75), *Allie Mae Burroghs, Wife of a Sharecropper* (1936), in Thomas W. Southall, ed., *Of Time & Place: Walker Evans, William Christenberry* (Forth Worth [TX]: The Friends of Photography/Amon Carter Museum, 1990), catalog of an exhibition at Amon Carter Museum, April 27–June 24, 1990, 33.
113 Barbara Kruger (American, b. 1945), *Untitled (You Are Not Yourself)* (1981), gelatin silver print; 72 × 48 in. (182.9 × 121.9 cm). Private collection. Courtesy Skarstedt Fine Art, New York, in "The Pictures Generation 1974–1984," The Met.

– Left: Art Rogers, *Puppies* (1985). Right: Jeff Koons, *String of Puppies* (1988), polychrome on wood, in "Art Rogers vs. Jeff Coons," Copyright in Visual Arts, accessed July 13, 2019, https://cpyrightvisualarts.wordpress.com/2011/12/20/art-rogers-vs-jeff-koons/.

117–118 OUTTAKES

117 Arlington Heights Fruit Company, Golden Orange Brand, in "Riverside Blue Ribbon Groves Records," Riverside Public Library, accessed July 13, 2019, https://www.riversideca.gov/library/history_aids_blueribbon.asp.
– Byron, Venice Beach (1970s). Photo by David Scott, in JP, "1970s Vintage Venice Beach Shots. Epic Surf, Sun & Skate Radness," The Selvedge Yard, April 12, 2011, accessed July 13, 2019, https://selvedgeyard.com/2011/04/12/1970s-vintage-venice-beach-shots-epic-surf-sun-skate-radness/.
– Venice Beach CA (1970s), in Sizzle, accessed July 13, 2019, https://onsizzle.com/i/fuck-off-venice-beach-ca-back-in-1970-676881.
– Palm Springs (CA). Photo by Johannes Huwe, in Lianna Bruhlman, "Antiques Roadshow Meets Petrolheads in Palm Springs," Classic Driver, February 28, 2018, accessed July 13, 2019, https://www.classicdriver.com/en/article/classic-life/antiques-roadshow-meets-petrolheads-palm-springs.
– Becky in Hermosa Beach (late 1960s, 70s). Photo by Spot, in "Fast and Furious: California's First Rollergirls and Skate-boarders—In Pictures," *The Guardian,* December 10, 2014, accessed July 13, 2019, https://www.theguardian.com/artanddesign/gallery/2014/dec/10/california-first-rollergirls-and-skateboarders-in-pictures.
– Basketball and Rollerskating on Venice Beach (CA) (1979), in Super Seventies. The Original 1970s tumblr blog, accessed July 13, 2019, https://superseventies.tumblr.com/post/376473731738/fashion-shopping-education-college-books-home-garden-ant.
118 Rodney Bingenheimer at Rodney's English Disco (1972–75). Photo courtesy: Rodney Bingenheimer, in Alison Martino, "It's All Happening! Rodney Bingenheimer's Long Gone '70s–Era Disco Returns," *Los Angeles Magazine,* September 5, 2017, accessed July 13, 2019, https://www.lamag.com/citythinkblog/its-all-happening-rodney-bingenheimers-long-gone-70s-era-disco-returns/.
– Venice Beach Roller Skaters, in Flynn Matthews, "Venice Beach Roller Skaters: Drifting The Promenade Of LA's Chillest Neighborhood," FREEYORK, 2017, accessed July 13, 2019, https://freeyork.org/people/venice-beach-roller-skaters-drifting-promenade-las-chillest-neighborhood/.
– Burbank Campus Classes (1970). California Institute of the Arts Photographic Materials Collection. Courtesy of California Institute of the Arts Archives.
– Hermosa Beach, 1970s (?). Photo courtesy: Spot, in N. N., "A New Photography Book Points Its Curious Lens on the Punk and Beach Scene of 1970's Los Angeles," Golden State. Made in California, accessed July 13, 2019, https://goldenstate.is/new-photography-book-points-curious-lens-punk-beach-scene-1970s-los-angeles/.

– Burbank Campus Classes (1970). California Institute of the Arts Photographic Materials Collection. Courtesy of California Institute of the Arts Archives.

ADVERTISEMENTS

inside cover Ford, Futura (1978), in *All-American Ads 70s,* ed. Jim Heimann (Köln: TASCHEN, 2004), 139.
1 Volkswagen, Beatle (1962), in *All-American Ads 60s,* ed. Jim Heimann (Köln: TASCHEN, 2002), 199.
2 Western Electric (1968), in *All-American Ads 60s,* ed. Jim Heimann (Köln: TASCHEN, 2002), 513.
3 Pioneer Electronics (1975), in *All-American Ads 70s,* ed. Jim Heimann (Köln: TASCHEN, 2004), 213.
7 General Electric Televisions (1979), in *All-American Ads 70s*, ed. Jim Heimann (Köln TASCHEN 2004), 203.
12 Polaroid SX -70 Alpha 1 (1971), in *All-American Ads 70s*, ed. Jim Heimann (Köln: TASCHEN), 225.
22 Polaroid Sonar Camera (1978), in *All-American Ads 70s,* ed. Jim Heimann (Köln: TASCHEN, 2004), 224.
28 Polaroid MinuteMaker Camera (1977), in *All-American Ads 70s,* ed. Jim Heimann (Köln: TASCHEN, 2004), 225.
34 Coca Cola (1968), in *All-American Ads 60s,* ed. Jim Heimann (Köln: TASCHEN, 2002), 760.
62 Enka (1974), in *All-American Ads 70s,* ed. Jim Heimann (Köln: TASCHEN, 2004), 456.
71 Landlubber Clothes, 1971, in *All-American Ads 70s,* ed. Jim Heimann (Köln: TASCHEN, 2004), 456.
82 Jantzen Actionwear, Swimtrunks (1966), in *All-American Ads 60s,* ed. Jim Heimann (Köln: TASCHEN, 2002), 610.
94 Royal Electric, Typewriter (1961), in *All-American Ads 60s,* ed. Jim Heimann (Köln: TASCHEN, 2002), 291.
102 Chrysler (1968), in *All-American Ads 60s,* ed. Jim Heimann (Köln: TASCHEN, 2002), 251.
127 Guerlain Cologne (1974), in *All-American Ads 70s*, ed. Jim Heimann (Köln: TASCHEN, 2004), 428.

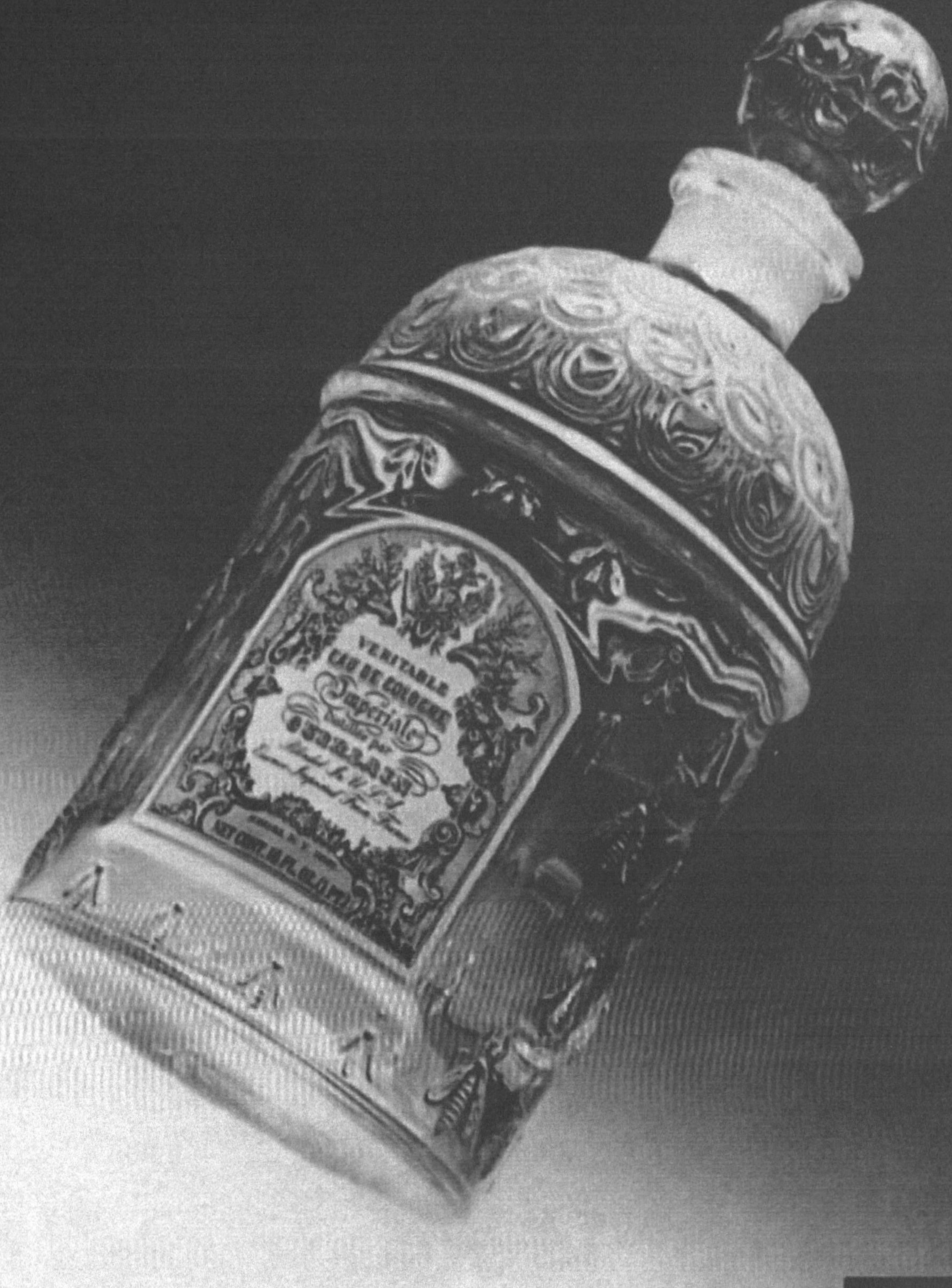

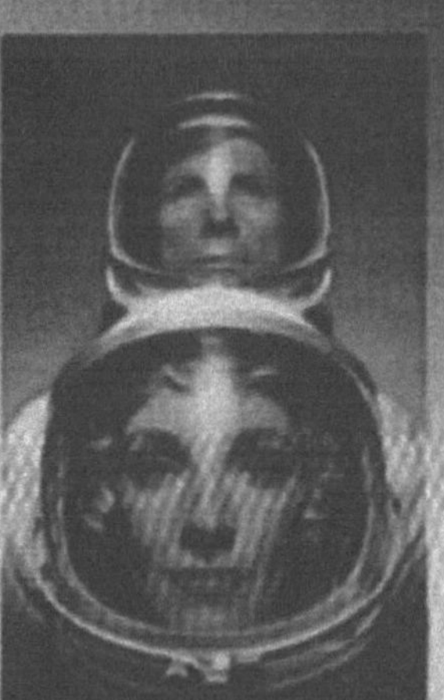

"I would like to create a cologne that will last as long as there are men and women."

PIERRE FRANÇOIS PASCAL GUERLAIN·1853

Tacit Knowledge. Post Studio—CalArts (1970–77) is published on the occasion of a research project by the same name between the Institute for Theater Studies, Freie Universität Berlin, the Kestner Gesellschaft, Hanover, and metaLAB (at) Harvard. It also coincides with the exhibition *Where Art Might Happen—The Early Years of CalArts*, running from August 30–November 10, 2019, at the Kestner Gesellschaft, Hanover, and curated by Christina Végh and Philipp Kaiser. This part of the book in the shape of a magazine deals with Post-Studio strategies developing at the California Institute of the Arts in the early 1970s, particularly practices that evolved around John Baldessari's legendary class, but also Fluxus and other performative activities at the art school.

Institut für Theaterwissenschaft
Freie Universität Berlin
Grunewaldstr. 35
12165 Berlin
Germany

First edition in 2019, printed in Germany
ISBN: 978-3-95905-341-9

All rights reserved, including the right of reproduction in whole or in part in any form.

With support by: Volkswagen Foundation, German Federal Cultural Foundation

Editor-in-Chief	Annette Jael Lehmann
Editor	Verena Kittel
Copy Editing	Verena Kittel, Siobhan Leddy, Marius Legowski
Authors	Kim Albrecht (KA), Lea Becker (LB), Katharina Brandt (KB), Christoph Buchegger (CB), Antonija Cvitic (AC), Teresa Depenau (TD), Léïla Douliba (LD), Jacqueline Azarmi Eskandani (JAE), Carla Gabriel (CG), Jennifer Gaschler (JG), Pauline Gründing (PG), Leonie Hahn (LH), Philipp Kaiser (PK), Verena Kittel (VK), Friederike Krause (FK), Vivien Lambert (VL), Annette Jael Lehmann (AJL), Nazanin Namdarfard (NN), Alice Rugai (AR), Jeffrey Schnapp (JS), Anna Sønderup (AS), Christina Végh (CV), and Carla Weingarten (CW)
Translation	Siobhan Leddy
Design	Studio Pandan – Ann Richter & Pia Christmann
Image Editing	Norbert Dietsche Perfektbild
Printing	Druckhaus Köthen GmbH & Co. KG
Fonts	New Century Schoolbook by Linotype, Gothic by Dinamo

Published by	Spector Books, Harkortstraße 10, 04107 Leipzig, www.spectorbooks.com

Distribution: Germany, Austria: GVA, gemeinsame Verlagsauslieferung Göttingen gmbH & Co.Kg, www.gva-verlage.de; Switzerland: AVA Verlagsauslieferung AG, www.ava.ch; France, Belgium: Interart Paris, www.interart.fr; UK: Central Books Ltd., www.centralbooks.com; USA, Canada, Central and South America, Africa, Asia: ARTBOOK | D.A.P., www.artbook.com; Australia, New Zealand: Perimeter Distribution, www.perimeterdistribution.com

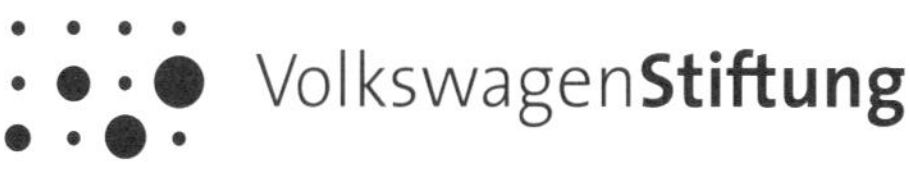
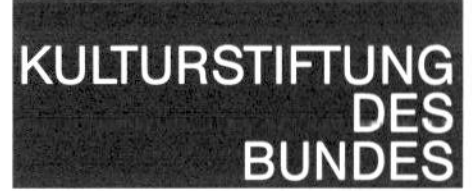
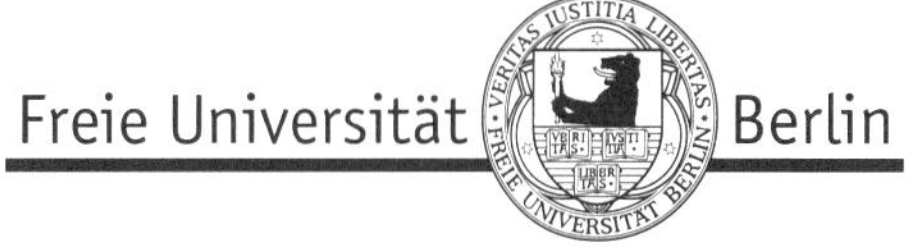
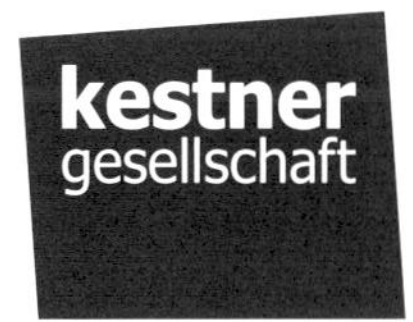
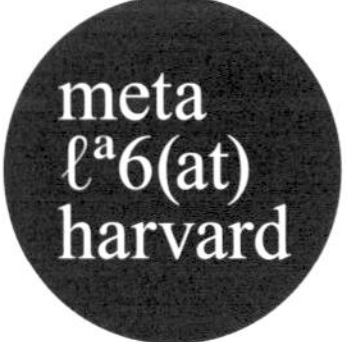

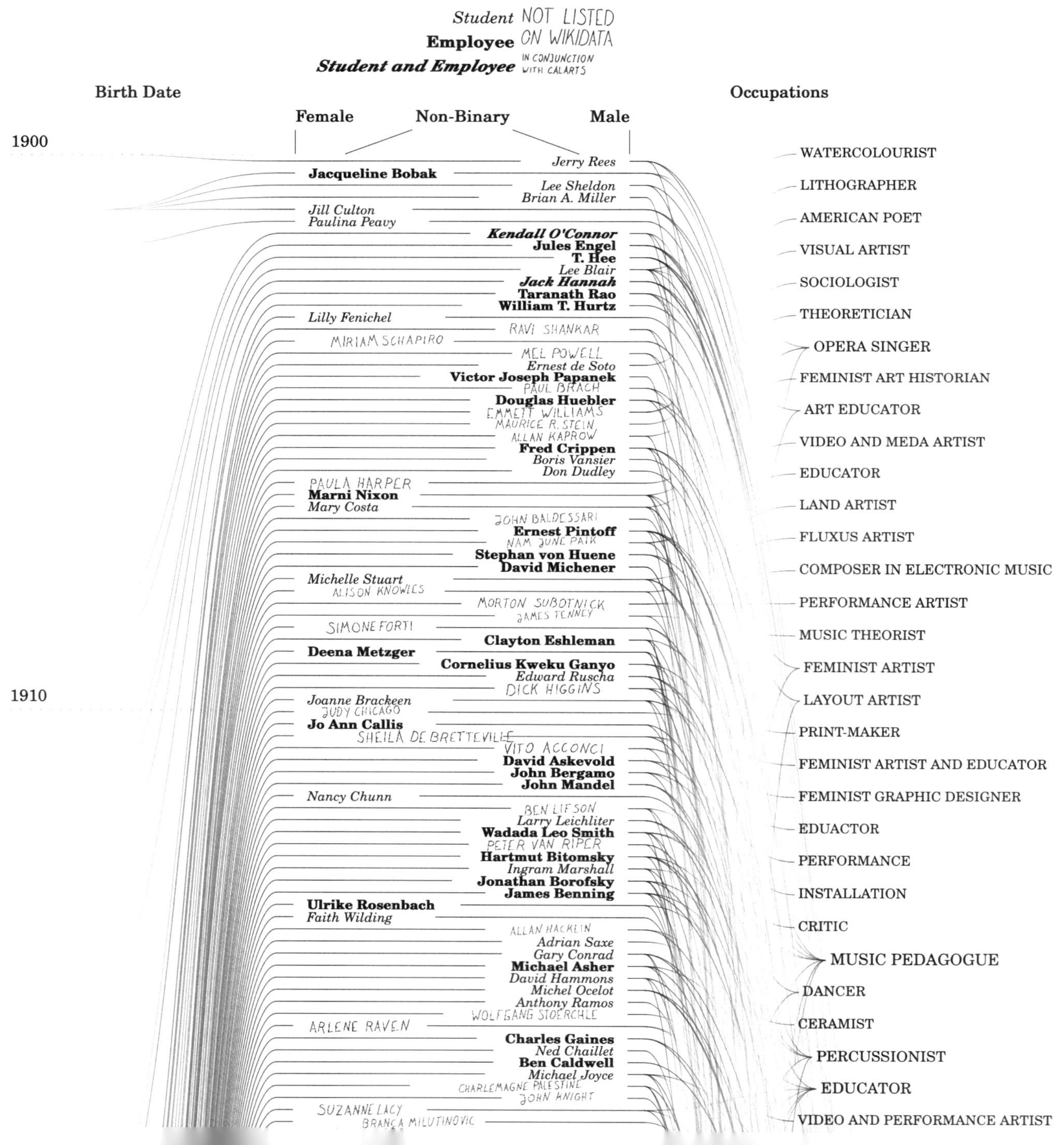

Occupations

Birth Date

1900

1910

Student NOT LISTED
Employee ON WIKIDATA
IN CONJUNCTION WITH CALARTS
Student and Employee

Female — Non-Binary — Male

Occupations:

WATERCOLOURIST
LITHOGRAPHER
AMERICAN POET
VISUAL ARTIST
SOCIOLOGIST
THEORETICIAN
OPERA SINGER
FEMINIST ART HISTORIAN
ART EDUCATOR
VIDEO AND MEDA ARTIST
EDUCATOR
LAND ARTIST
FLUXUS ARTIST
COMPOSER IN ELECTRONIC MUSIC
PERFORMANCE ARTIST
MUSIC THEORIST
FEMINIST ARTIST
LAYOUT ARTIST
PRINT-MAKER
FEMINIST ARTIST AND EDUCATOR
FEMINIST GRAPHIC DESIGNER
EDUACTOR
PERFORMANCE
INSTALLATION
CRITIC
MUSIC PEDAGOGUE
DANCER
CERAMIST
PERCUSSIONIST
EDUCATOR
VIDEO AND PERFORMANCE ARTIST

Names:

Jerry Rees
Lee Sheldon
Brian A. Miller
Kendall O'Connor
Jules Engel
T. Hee
Lee Blair
Jack Hannah
Taranath Rao
William T. Hurtz
RAVI SHANKAR
MEL POWELL
Ernest de Soto
Victor Joseph Papanek
PAUL BRACH
Douglas Huebler
EMMETT WILLIAMS
MAURICE R. STEIN
ALLAN KAPROW
Fred Crippen
Boris Vansier
Don Dudley
JOHN BALDESSARI
Ernest Pintoff
NAM JUNE PAIK
Stephan von Huene
David Michener
MORTON SUBOTNICK
JAMES TENNEY
Clayton Eshleman
Cornelius Kweku Ganyo
Edward Ruscha
DICK HIGGINS
VITO ACCONCI
David Askevold
John Bergamo
John Mandel
BEN LIFSON
Larry Leightliter
Wadada Leo Smith
PETER VAN RIPER
Hartmut Bitomsky
Ingram Marshall
Jonathan Borofsky
James Benning
ALLAN HACKLIN
Adrian Saxe
Gary Conrad
Michael Asher
David Hammons
Michel Ocelot
Anthony Ramos
WOLFGANG STOERCHLE
Charles Gaines
Ned Chaillet
Ben Caldwell
Michael Joyce
JOHN KNIGHT
CHARLEMAGNE PALESTINE

Jacqueline Bobak
Jill Culton
Paulina Peavy
Lilly Fenichel
MIRIAM SCHAPIRO
PAULA HARPER
Marni Nixon
Mary Costa
Michelle Stuart
ALISON KNOWLES
SIMONE FORTI
Deena Metzger
Joanne Brackeen
JUDY CHICAGO
Jo Ann Callis
SHEILA DE BRETTEVILLE
Nancy Chunn
Ulrike Rosenbach
Faith Wilding
ARLENE RAVEN
SUZANNE LACY
BRANCA MILUTINOVIC

CALARTS DATA PORTRAITURE

A project by Kim Albrecht and Jeffrey Schnapp, metaLAB (at) Harvard

How to paint a portrait of an institution? A portrait of its history, its growth, its development? A likeness of the legions of people who built and sustained it over the arc of its existence?

The task is daunting because portraiture works best not at the scale of 1000s of people or the scale of decade-after-decade, but instead at the scale of the face-to-face and the here-and-now. Portraiture is a selective art. Some individuals are over-represented; others go under-recognized; others still are omitted, erased from the historical record, irrespective of their relative significance or merit.

Founders are always likely to be counted among the often portrayed and the well-remembered. Such is the case with the man who first dreamed of a multidisciplinary community of the arts in Southern California designed to merge recent commercial art practices like animation with the fine arts of painting, music, and theater: Walt Disney. The inventor of Disneyland dreamed of a campus far from the hustle and bustle of Los Angeles: an institution analogous to the California Institute of Technology (Caltech) but exclusively dedicated to culture, creative practice, and the arts. When it opened its doors in the town of Valencia (Santa Clarita) in the fall of 1970, the California Institute of the Arts (CalArts) became North America's first degree-granting institution of higher learning specializing in the visual and performing arts.

The reality of the institution often proved less than irenic. The Board of Trustees, led by Walt's brother Roy, was decidedly conservative, while the CalArts faculty and students were not. The latter quickly succeeded in transforming the campus into a counterculture hotbed and a hub for the most exciting, if wild-eyed, West Coast art. Clashes erupted and led to the dismissal of Maurice Stein, the founding dean of the School of Critical Studies, driven out before the end of the second year for his embrace of radical causes and efforts to hire the Marxist philosopher Herbert Marcuse. Others would soon follow Stein down the path of dismissal.

We evoke such early events because they leave abundant traces in the opening section of the suite of visualizations that follow where Stein appears in the company of such early CalArts faculty as the musician Mel Powell (dean of the School of Music), Miriam Schapiro (co-founder of the Feminist Art Program), the concrete poet Emmett Williams, and artists like Allan Kaprow, Nam June Paik, and John Baldessari. As the timeline proceeds, our attempt to capture the life of CalArts from the time of its foundation to the present grapples with the realities of who makes it into (and who does not) the gallery of data portraiture known as Wikidata.

Wikidata is an open knowledge base that serves as the central repository for structured data derived from such projects as Wikipedia, Wiktionary, and Wikisource. It is from this public source that we have extracted the birthdates and professional identities of nearly 500 individuals whose life trajectories were shaped by their experience of CalArts, whether as students, faculty, or in some other capacity. The resulting timelines trace a genealogy of contemporary West Coast art in all the domains encompassed by the CalArts curriculum. Lesser known facets of institutional history, however, may find themselves occluded (like the key role played by Herbert Blau, the founding CalArts provost and dean of the School of Theater and Dance, who was fired not long after the departure of Stein). Most of all, they expose the overrepresentation of Hollywood stars—Ed Harris and David Hasselhoff feature prominently—and media figures—somewhat improbably, the Playboy Playmate Alexandra Tyler figures as the youngest member of the CalArts tribe—in the internet's highly selective memory banks.

In the foldout we present two visualizations of the same Wikidata collection. The first graphic is a list view of all Wikidata entries associated with CalArts. Each individual's gender, role within the university, and profession is mapped out and sequenced according to listed birthdates (whether accurate or not). On the verso of the foldout, an alternate timeline maps an individual's length of direct involvement in CalArts, along with their their principal mentors and influences. In both graphics, the incomplete Wikidata perspective is altered by means of entries written in by hand that add back into the historical record the names of artists listed in this publication but absent from Wikidata. The gesture underscores the comprehensiveness as well as the contingent and uncertain character of contemporary networked knowledge and memory structures.